Culture
and Values

reproduced on the cover and title page:
Antonio Canaletto (1697–1768). *The Lord Mayor's Procession, at Westminster Bridge, London, 1747.* Oil on canvas, 38 × 50″ (96.5 × 127 cm). Yale Center for British Art, Paul Mellon Collection, New Haven.

Holt, Rinehart and Winston
New York Chicago San Francisco Philadelphia Montreal Toronto
London Sydney Tokyo Mexico City Rio de Janiero Madrid

Culture and Values

A Survey of the Western Humanities

Lawrence Cunningham   John Reich

The Florida State University

ALTERNATE EDITION

Library of Congress Cataloging in Publication Data

Cunningham, Lawrence.
　Culture and values.

　Bibliography: p.
　Includes index.
　1. Civilization, Occidental.　2. Europe—Intellectual
life. I. Reich, John. II. Title.
CB245.C86　1985　　909′.09821　　84-12864

ISBN 0-03-063511-X

Publisher　Susan Katz
Editor　Karen Dubno
Special Projects Editor　Jeanette Ninas Johnson
Picture Editor　Joan Scafarello
Picture Research　Marion Geisinger
Permissions Editor　Nicolette C. Harlan
Production Manager　Pat Sarcuni
Art Director　Louis Scardino
Book and Cover Design　Caliber Design Planning

Composition and camera work　York Graphic Services
Color separations　The Lehigh Press, Inc.
Printing and binding　R. R. Donnelley & Sons Co.

CBS COLLEGE PUBLISHING
Holt, Rinehart and Winston
The Dryden Press
Saunders College Publishing

Photograph credits and acknowledgements　The authors and publisher wish to thank the custodians of the works of art for supplying photographs and granting permission to use them. Photographs have been obtained from sources noted in the captions, unless listed below.
A/AR: Alinari/Art Resource, New York
A/Ma: Alinari/Mansell, London.
AF: Alison Frantz, Princeton.
AFK: A.F. Kersting, London
AH: André Held, Ecublens
AM: Ann Münchow, Aachen
ARB: Art Reference Bureau, Pittsfield, Mass.
BM: British Museum, London
BN: Bibliothèque Nationale, Paris
BPK: Bildarchiv Preussicher Kulturbesitz, West Berlin
CAISSE: Caisse Nationale des Monuments Historiques et des Sites, Paris, © ARCH. PHOT., Paris/SPADEM/VAGA, New York, 1985.
FU: Fototeca Unione, Rome.
G/AR: Giraudon, Art Resource, New York
GAI: German Archaeological Institute
H: Hirmer, Munich
HH: Colorphoto Hans Hinz, Allschwill
HRV: H. Roger Violett, Paris
JR: Jean Roubier, Paris
LVM: Leonard Von Matt, Buochs
M: Marburg, Marburg/Lahn
MA/EA: Mikael Audrain/Editions Arthaud, Paris/fapc.
MAS: MAS, Barcelona
MPA: Reproduced through the courtesy of the Michigan-Princeton-Alexandria Expedition to Mount Sinai
NYPL: New York Public Library, Astor, Lenox and Tilden Foundations
OI: Oriental Institute of the University of Chicago
PR: Photo Researchers, New York
RMN: Service de Documentation Photographique de la Réunion des Musees Nationaux, Paris
S/AR: Scala/Art Resource
SG: Soprintendenza alle Gallerie, Florence
WS: Wim Swann, New York
　Color: Plate 1: HH. **Plate 2:** BPK. **Plate 3:** Dimitri Kessel, Paris. **Plate 4:** H. **Plate 6:** John Lewis Stage/Image Bank. **Plate 7:**

H. **Plate 8:** LVM. **Plate 9:** S/AR. **Plate 10:** WS. **Plate 11:** LVM. **Plate 12:** WS. **Plates 13, 14:** S/AR. **Plate 15:** G. Barone, Shostal. **Plates 16, 18, 19:** S/AR. **Plate 20:** G/AR. **Plate 22:** MAS. **Plate 25:** Lauros/G/AR. **Plate 26:** AFK. **Plate 27:** S/AR. **Plate 34:** Henry Groskinsky, LIFE Magazine © 1980, Time, Inc. **Plate 37:** Dimitri Kessel, Paris.
　Chapter 1　**2, 4, 5:** H. **7:** Photography by the Egyptian Expedition, The Metropolitan Museum of Art. **8:** George Holton/PR. **9.** Center and bottom, **10, 11, 12, 13, 14:**H **15:** G/AR. **19:** Robert E. Mates & Mary Donlon. **20:** AF. **21:** After S. Marinatos, *Kreta und das Mykenische Hellas,* Hirmer Verlag, München, 1959, fig. 4/NYPL. **22, 23, 24:** H. **25:** Painting and photo by Alton S. Tobey, Larchmont, New York.
　Chapter 2　**26, 27:** OI. **28, 29, 30:** Lee C. Ellenberger for The American Schools of Oriental Research, Philadelphia. **31:** Under the direction of Bernhard W. Anderson, this sketch was made by Charles S. Winters, assisted by Janet Michalson Clasper; photographed by James Stewart. **32:** OI. **33:** The Mansell Collection Limited, London. **34, 35:** A/AR. **36:** Consulate General of Israel in New York. **337:** Inger McCabe/PR. **38:** The Jewish Museum/AR. **40:** Rare Books and Manuscripts Division, NYPL **41:** A. Louis Goldman/PR.
　Chapter 3　**42:** S/AR. **43:** G/AR. **45, 46:** GAI, Athens. **47, 48, 49:** H. **50:** GAI, Athens. **52, 53:** H. **54:** A/AR. **55, 56:** H. **57:** Laboratories Photographiques Devos. **60:** H. **61:** GAI, Athens.
　Chapter 4　**63:** AF. **64:** A/AR. **65:** Rev. Raymond V. Schoder, SJ., Loyola University, Chicago. **68:** David Seymour/Magnum, New York. **69:** F. Kaufmann, Munich. **70:** Soprintendenza alle Antichita della Campania, Naples. **71:** H. **72:** Reconstruction drawing: From Helmut Berve and Gottfried Gruben, *Griechische Tempel und Heiligtumer,* Hirmer Verlag, München, 1964, fig. 10/NYPL. **73:** AF. **75:** Top-AF; Bottom-After Isobel Grinnell, *Greek Temples,* Metropolitan Museum of Art, 1943, p. 34/NYPL. **76, 77, 78, 79:** H. **80:** AF. **82:** Courtesy Professor Manolis Andronikos. **84:** A/AR. **85:** Barbara Malter-Musei Capitolini. **87, 88:** H. **89:** From Hermann Thiersch, *Pharos Antike Islam und Occident,* B.G. Teubner, Leipzig, 1909, opp. title page/ NYPL.
　Chapter 5　**94:** A/AR. **95:** GAI, Rome. **96:** A/AR. **97:** FU. **98:** A/AR. **99:** After H. Kähler, "Das Fortunaheiligtum von Palestrina Praeneste," in *Annales Universitatis Saraviensis,* Vol. VII, p. 198 Saarbrüken, 1958/NYPL. **100:** A/AR. **102:** A.C. Cooper,
(continued on page 492)

Preface

Our purpose in writing *Culture and Values* is quite simple: to create a readable and reliable textbook for undergraduate courses in the humanities that will satisfy the standards of professors and engage the interest of students. We attempt to describe, as enthusiastically and accurately as we are able, the crucial landmarks in the Western cultural tradition. We hope that the excellence of these works and the genius of their creators will inspire the minds and hearts of students as they inspired our own when we first encountered them.

Our aim has been to set out the very finest that human genius has produced in our culture so that we can learn from—and perhaps improve upon—those achievements. A study of the humanities can give us some criteria to confront our present situation from the vantage point of historical perspective. We are a notoriously non-historical-minded people. That is a perilous condition. It was a wise person who said that those who marry today's fads soon find themselves widowed.

It is one thing to propose a book of this sort and another thing to write it. At the outset, we made some very basic decisions, decisions which would give the book its shape and tone. First of all, this book is organized chronologically rather than thematically. We provide some context with a chapter on the Near East and then describe our cultural roots in ancient Israel, Greece, and Rome. Subsequent chapters lead to the Renaissance period through a discussion of Byzantine, Carolingian, and medieval culture. From its beginnings in Italy we follow the Renaissance from Florence and Rome to the North and its encounters with the Reformation and the flowering of the Baroque. The neoclassical and revolutionary-romantic cultures of the eighteenth and nineteenth centuries are discussed. The final two chapters sketch our humanistic culture "between the Wars" and in the period after 1945.

We feel little need to justify this chronological arrangement. Students are always enriched when they gain historical perspective. We think it important to tell our story as an unfolding one with references back to the past and pointers to the future. This chronological framework is enhanced by illustrated cultural chronologies at the head of each chapter so

that, at a glance, the student may see what is occurring in the time period under discussion. We hope that the maps will also help in this regard.

A second decision was made to integrate the various arts as closely as we could in each chapter. We tried to avoid a "salad bar" approach to culture in order to demonstrate how the various arts do intersect. In the chapter on the High Middle Ages, to cite one particular example, our focus was not on the separate disciplines of architecture, sculpture, and theology, but on how these were brought to bear on the construction of the Gothic cathedral.

Our third decision was to be selective in what we discussed. Any survey of this kind runs the risk of becoming a catalogue of names or an encyclopedia of mere data. We have attempted to single out those persons and artistic monuments that illumine their own age and have proved pertinent for our own. One of the joys of studying the humanities is to meet something (or someone) from the past that leaps across the centuries to become very much ours.

In deciding what to include we had both an easy time (one *must* speak of the Parthenon; one *must* deal with J. S. Bach) and a difficult time; once the clear works of genius were selected we then had to decide what to leave out. Any user of the text would probably come up with a different list. We are comforted by the knowledge that instructors can fill in what we have left out.

This single-volume edition of *Culture and Values,* unlike the two-volume edition, does not include literary extracts. It does retain, however, the discussion of literature as an integral part of the unfolding of the humanistic tradition. We have also included copious black and white illustrations as well as color plates. Each chapter has study questions, which might prove useful either for class discussion or term papers. Important technical terms (in italics) are defined in a glossary. A brief annotated bibliography of secondary sources and a short discography conclude the text.

A final word. We have described our method in writing this book and acknowledged our limitations. We know where some of our shortcomings are, and our readers may soon find others. Our consolation is that we regard this book only as an aid for the instructors, not as their replacement. We trust that they will qualify where we generalize and fill in where we have been silent.

In addition to all those colleagues who helped us to develop the original edition of *Culture and Values* the following colleagues provided helpful criticism of the several drafts of this *Alternate Edition*: C. Stephen Byrum, Chattanooga State Technical Community College, Tennessee; Charles M. Carroll, St. Petersburg Community College, Florida; Thomas J. Cleman, Northern Arizona University, Flagstaff; William R. Cook, State University of New York at Geneseo; Julian E. Farris, Florida Junior College at Jacksonville; Arthur Juncker, Galvin College, California; Deborah E. Patterson, Edison Community College, Ft. Myers, Florida; Katherine Wyly, Hillsborough Community College, Florida. We thank all of these people for their fine work.

We appreciate the dedication of the staff at Holt, Rinehart and Winston who worked on this project.

Our thanks go especially to Marion Geisinger, Jeanette Ninas Johnson, Pat Sarcuni, Joan Scafarello, and Louis Scardino. We are particularly grateful to Karen Dubno, who was, at the same time, tough editor, constant supporter, mother confessor, and unfailing friend.

In the course of this project we received aid and encouragement from any number of people. We would like to thank Professor Leon Golden, Director of the Florida State University Humanities Program. Our tolerant spouses, Cecilia Cunningham and Barbara Reich, both trained art historians, provided us with much help. Dianne Weinstein typed the manuscript with speed and accuracy. To them, and all those who gave us informal criticism, help, and encouragement we owe a debt of gratitude.

L.C.
J.R.

Contents

5

THE ROMAN LEGACY   105

6

THE WORLD OF BYZANTIUM   131

7

THE AGE OF CHARLEMAGNE   157

8

THE HIGH MIDDLE AGES: THE SEARCH FOR SYNTHESIS   179

9

THE 14TH CENTURY: A TIME OF TRANSITION 201

10

THE EARLY RENAISSANCE 223

11

THE HIGH RENAISSANCE IN ITALY 249

12

THE RENAISSANCE IN THE NORTH 267

Maps

INTRODUCTION

This book has an ambitious aim. It surveys the major cultural achievements of Western civilization from ancient Greece and Israel to the present day. At the outset, we feel we should set forth our basic philosophy, our orientation, and our hopes; we owe this statement both to the instructor and, even more, to the student.

In the first place, we emphasize that this book is a *survey* of the humanities. Many of the persons, objects, and ideas that are discussed here in a few pages or paragraphs have been the subjects of lengthy books and numerous monographs. Also, much that is of great cultural interest is not mentioned at all here. Still, we do believe that what we have chosen to treat is representative of the highest achievement of Western culture.

We hope that this book will not be considered as the last word. Indeed, we think of it very much as the first word; we rely on both the accumulated wisdom of the instructor and the curiosity of the student to fill in what we have omitted and expand what we have only touched on. We fervently hope that users of this book will extend their explorations far beyond its contents. We are only fingers pointing the way, as the Zen monks put it. Learning is open-ended—it can last for a lifetime; it need not end at the end of a "quarter" or a "semester." Those who go beyond the scope of this book are setting forth on this life-long process.

Second, we have been unabashedly élitist in our focus on the high culture of the Western tradition. We share a passionate conviction that the very best of our human achievement in the past is of far more than archaeological or antiquarian interest. We view a "masterpiece" not as something of rare value but as a human work that exemplifies the best of a past historical moment and at the same time as an inspiration for the present. Accordingly, we have taken pains to emphasize both the revolutionary and the historical character of the cultural achievements described. For example, the cubism of Picasso and Braque at the beginning of this century was revolutionary in the history of art, but its revolutionary character is intelligible only against a historical background. In tracing back the ancestry of cubism to the artists of the preceding generation, like Paul Cézanne, we are inevitably led much farther into the past—back to the birth of modern concepts of art at the Renaissance.

Just as looking back can throw light on contemporary developments, so earlier achievements can throw light on our own lives. Thus we still read the plays of William Shakespeare, partly to gauge the achievements of the age of Elizabeth I in England but primarily because we feel that contemporary readers and writers can learn much about the use of language, the meaning of the human condition, and the possibility of beauty from his writings.

To obtain this perspective on our accumulated artistic experience, we have had to draw on a wide range of disciplines. We have used techniques developed by art historians, literary critics, and musicologists. Nonetheless, we have described this book as a survey of the humanities. What does the term *humanities* mean?

The humanities, like love and hate, are easier to discuss than to define. By the humanities we mean the art, music, and literature of our common culture and the main ideas that underpin these achievements and at the same time give subsequent coherence to them. The humanities as an area of study fall somewhere between aesthetics and intellectual history without quite being either.

The tense but creative relationship between aesthetics and the history of ideas might serve as a starting point in defining the humanities as an area of academic study. Neither aesthetic objects nor ideas exist in a vacuum. They influence, and are influenced by, politics, economics, social institutions, religion, war, and a host of other external factors. We have noted such large cultural contexts in this book while trying not to let them take over our discussion. No one factor—neither economics nor religion nor politics nor even "art for art's sake"—explains our cultural achievement. Nevertheless, such movements must receive recognition. In recognizing them we have tried to remain impartial. As no intellectual approach to the study of culture is value-free, however, we trust that our values (and biases) are relatively apparent for assessment.

We hope that students will learn certain specific things from their encounter with this book and the material it contains.

First, most obviously, we hope that students will learn something about our common cultural tradition set in some kind of historical context. Our aim is to provide a degree of cultural literacy. It is important to know that Shakespeare lived before Milton and that Columbus sailed to the Americas during the palmy days of the Italian Renaissance. Henry Ford to the contrary, history is not bunk. Our first aim, then, is to give a sense of our common tradition. It is only through knowledge of the unfolding of our story (which is what history is) that we gain understanding of the fact that we share a common past and move to a common destiny.

Second, we hope that students will learn to listen, look, and ponder. If there is any advantage in the limited selection that can be included in this work it is that the student need cope with only a manageable amount. We hope that we have provided enough information so that students can understand some of the art, music, and literature but not so much as to overwhelm them and discourage them from raising questions, reflecting on our (or their) observations, and making informed judgments. To listen, look, and ponder is to cultivate a critical sense.

Finally, we believe students will be personally and socially enriched by their encounter with the Western cultural tradition. We do not wish to make grandiose claims for the study of the humanities. We do not propose that a study of the humanities will solve our urban problems, save our souls, give us peace of mind, or increase the gross national product. But we are sure that a certain openness to the humanities teaches us to love language, to be sensitive to ideas, and to open our eyes and ears to beauty. Furthermore, an acquaintance with the best often makes us impatient with the shoddy, angry at the ugly, and intolerant of the vulgar. That, by any standard, is a good start for fully human living. The humanities, after all, reflect that which is truly human.

The humanities are not a luxury for the few. While the humanities may be taken for granted in a free and prosperous society, they must never be underestimated. It is a dreary but instructive truth that every authoritarian regime, whether of the Right or the Left, rigidly controls its artists and ruthlessly suppresses those who do not conform to the dictates of official ideology. Those who regard the humanities as peripheral to "real" life should meditate on that fact. Our own concert halls, publishing houses, art galleries, and universities are enhanced by artists and writers who have fled, or been expelled from, their homelands for wishing to express what they see as truth through the medium of words, music, film, dance, or the plastic arts.

In a certain sense the greatest achievements of the cultural tradition have a revolutionary tinge to them. Modern art is now so much a part of our common experience that we cannot imagine the howls of outrage and derision that greeted the work of the Impressionists in the last century, just as the present generation cannot believe that not too many decades ago people had to smuggle copies of James Joyce's *Ulysses* past customs officers. Great works of art have often been seen as subversive. They are, in that they undermine our old way of seeing, hearing, thinking, and reacting. The great tradition of the humanities is a tradition of revolution. When we understand these revolutionary moments of the past and when we are alert for them today we realize how diverse and how limitless are the riches of the human spirit.

PREHISTORY

2,000,000 B.C. ———————————

c. 100,000 First ritual
burying of dead

c. 30,000–25,000 *Venus of
Willendorf;* worship of female
creative power

c. 15,000–10,000 Cave art at
Lascaux and Altamira

Hunting predominates

Stone weapons

8000 ———————————

PALEOLITHIC PERIOD (OLD STONE AGE)

Domestication of animals;
cultivation of food

Villages formed

First wars

c. 5000 Pottery invented

First large-scale
architecture; bronze tools

NEOLITHIC PERIOD (LATE STONE AGE)

3000 ———————————

Most dates are approximate

EGYPT

8000 B.C. ———————————

NEOLITHIC PERIOD

3200–2700 PREDYNASTIC PERIOD

c. 3100 Development of hieroglyphic writing

3000

2700–2250 OLD KINGDOM: development of
mummification ritual; art reflects confidence and certainty

c. 2650 Imhotep constructs first pyramid for King Zoser
at Saqqara

2650–2514 Great Pyramids
and Sphinx built at Giza

c. 2470 *Seated Scribe,* from Saqqara

2250–1990 FIRST INTERMEDIATE PERIOD

1990–1790 MIDDLE KINGDOM: art reflects new
uncertainty

c. 1878–1841 Reign of Sesostris III; Portrait: *Sesostris III*

1790–1570 SECOND INTERMEDIATE PERIOD

1570–1185 NEW KINGDOM

1379–1362 Reign of Amenhotep IV (Akhenaton);
religious and political reform; worship of single god
Aton; capital moved from Thebes to Tel el-Amarna;
naturalism in art

c. 1370 Portrait: *Nefertiti;* Akhenaton,
"Hymn to Aton"

1361–1352 Reign of Tutankhamen;
return to conservatism

1298–1232 Reign of Ramses II;
colossal buildings constructed at
Luxor, Karnak, Abu Simbel

1185–500 LATE PERIOD: Egypt's
power declines; artists revert to
Old Kingdom styles

BRONZE AGE

1000 ———————————

IRON AGE (1000 B.C. –)

671–663 Assyrian occupation of Egypt

600 ———————————

1

The Beginnings of Civilization

c. 6000 Introduction of new agricultural techniques from the East

3500–2350 SUMERIAN PERIOD: development of pictographic writing; construction of first ziggurats; cult of mother goddess

c. 3000 *Lady of Warka*

2800–2000 Early Minoan Period on Crete; growth of Cycladic culture

c. 2700 Reign of Gilgamesh

c. 2500 Cycladic idol

c. 2600–2400 *Ram in a Thicket,* from Royal Cemetery at Ur

2000–1600 Middle Minoan Period on Crete; construction of palace complexes; development of linear writing

2350–2150 AKKADIAN PERIOD: rule of Sargon and descendants; ended by invasion of Gutians from Iran

2330–2320 *Head of Akkadian king,* probably Sargon

c. 2300 *Stele of Naram-Sin*

2150–1900 NEO-SUMERIAN PERIOD

c. 1700 Knossos Palace destroyed by earthquake and rebuilt on grander scale; *Wasp Pendant,* from Mallia

2100–2000 Construction of ziggurat at Ur

1600–1400 Late Minoan Period on Crete

c. 2100 Gudea, governor of Lagash

c. 1600 First Mycenaean palace constructed; Royal Grave Circle at Mycenae

c. 2000 Earliest version of *The Epic of Gilgamesh*

c. 1600 *Snake Goddess,* from Knossos

1900–1600 BABYLONIAN PERIOD

1792–1750 *The Law Code of Hammurabi*

c. 1550 Gold death mask, from Mycenae

c. 1760 *Stele of Hammurabi*

1500 Frescoes from House Delta, Thera

1400 Fall of Knossos and decline of Minoan civilization

1400–1200 Mycenaean empire flourishes

1250 Mycenaean war against Troy

1600–1150 KASSITE PERIOD

100 Final collapse of Mycenaean power

1150–612 ASSYRIAN PERIOD

1100–1000 DARK AGE

883–859 Reign of Assurnasirpal II; palace at Nimrud

1000–750 HEROIC AGE

c. 900–700 Evolution of Homeric epics *Iliad* and *Odyssey*

668–626 Reign of Assurbanipal; palace at Nineveh

750–600 AGE OF COLONIZATION

612 Fall of Nineveh

The Western Cultural Tradition

The Western cultural tradition began almost three thousand years ago with the Greeks. This tradition spread from the Mediterranean basin throughout all of Europe and, in due course, to the New World. From age to age and place to place, though the tradition has taken on new forms and faced new problems, a basic unity has always linked the many diverse stages in its development. It is this unity that justifies us in thinking of our cultural tradition as a continuous one.

The unity is twofold: intellectual and historical. From the time of the Greeks, artists, writers, and thinkers in the Western tradition have all shared many of the same intellectual concerns. One of the principal areas they have explored is the relationship of individual human beings to the world around them and, in particular, to each other. Their approach has been recognizably different from that of other cultures. For example, the concept of romantic love, although by no means unique to the Western tradition, has played a stronger part in it than in other cultural traditions. Another example of a recurring theme in Western thought has been the importance of social justice—though all too often practice has not lived up to the ideal.

Most striking of all in the West has been the continuing attempt to discover a purpose for existence and to relate that purpose to the universal fact of death. With the rise of Christianity, the two great streams of Western thought, the classical and the Judeo-Christian, merged to provide new and complex answers to these questions—answers that often have in turn raised new, equally complex questions.

As we move now into a world where Western culture no longer dominates but takes its place among equals, it becomes increasingly clear that the problems that challenged the earlier shapers of our tradition are no nearer solutions. We may have little chance of solving them ourselves, but there is some comfort in at least identifying them and seeing how others have tried to deal with them.

The purpose for existence—a central problem—has been questioned in all cultures throughout history. In the Western cultural tradition, however, there has been a continuous attempt to come to grips with it by approaching it intellectually. Such an approach is certainly not to be considered superior. In fact, Western culture has paid a price for its obsessive drive to understand. It is notably deficient in faith. It tends always to search for rational solutions to problems, ignoring the very real possibilities offered by instinctive solutions. But, for better or worse, Western culture has produced this continuous tradition of intellectual inquiry of which we are the heirs.

Tradition depends on history—the sense of historical continuity that is the other part of the basic unity in Western culture. The Western cultural tradition has evolved through a continual building on the past. Some achievements and events of the past have been deliberately imitated; others have been deliberately disregarded. But whether the reaction to past events has been positive or negative, the Western tradition has always been firmly aware of their existence. This sense of history is not, of course, unique to our tradition. All cultures have their own history. But our history is in a real sense ours. Greek philosophers like Aristotle or Renaissance artists like Michelangelo have permanently changed the way we think and see; Confucius or Chinese artists have not. Only in the last hundred years or so has contact with non-Western cultures enriched our own.

Our art and civilization did not begin in Greece. Long before the Greeks other peoples had already constructed societies and created works of art. In fact, the basic advances that made possible the growth of Western civilization were first achieved by the earlier civilizations of the ancient Middle East.

These ancient peoples were the first who systematically produced food, mined and processed metals, organized themselves into cities, and devised legal and moral codes of behavior, together with systems of government and religion. In all these areas they had a profound influence on later peoples. At the same time they produced a major artistic tradition which, quite apart from its high intrinsic interest, was to have a number of effects on the development of Western art.

To discover the origins of Western civilization, therefore, we must look at cultures that at first seem remote in both time and place. Yet these peoples produced the achievements described in this chapter—achievements that form the background to the history of our own culture.

The Earliest People and Their Art

Even the earliest civilizations appeared relatively late in human history, at the beginning of the period known as the Neolithic or Late Stone Age (c. 8000 B.C.). The process of human evolution is long and confusing, and many aspects of it remain uncertain. Our first ancestors probably appeared between a million and half a million years ago, in the Paleolithic period or Old Stone Age. For most of the succeeding millennia, people were dominated by the physical forces of geography and climate, able to keep themselves alive only by a persistent search for food and shelter. Those who chose the wrong places or the wrong methods did not survive, while others were preserved by their instincts or good fortune.

Primitive conditions hardly encouraged the growth of civilization, yet there is some evidence of a kind of intellectual development. Archaeological evidence has shown that about one hundred thousand years ago the ancestors of *Homo sapiens* belonging to the type known as Neanderthal people were the first to bury their dead carefully and place funerary offerings in the graves—the earliest indication of the existence of religious beliefs.

Toward the end of the Paleolithic period, around 15,000 B.C., there was a major breakthrough. The human desire for self-expression resulted in the invention of visual art. The cave paintings of Lascaux and Altamira and statuettes like the *Venus of Willendorf* are among the earliest products of the human creative urge. Although the art of this remote age would be valuable for its historical significance alone, many of the paintings and statues can stand as masterpieces in their own right. The lines are concentrated but immensely expressive. In some cases artists used the surface on which they were painting to create an added sense of realism—a bulge on a cave wall suggested the hump of a bull [Plate 1, page 21]. The combination of naturalistic observation and abstraction can only be described as sophisticated. It is not at all surprising that since their discovery in our own century the paintings have served as a powerful inspiration to modern eyes.

The choice of subjects tells us something about the world view of Paleolithic people. The earliest cave paintings show animals and hunting, not surprising as these played a vital part in providing food and clothing. More significant, perhaps, is the fact that all the oldest known statuettes of human figures represent women, who are shown with their sexual characteristics emphasized or enlarged [1]. The Paleolithic world perhaps saw woman's practical role—the source of birth and life—as symbolic of a more profound feminine life force that underlay the masculine world of the hunt. Worship of female creative power was also to play an important part in the religion of the ancient Middle East and of Bronze Age Greece. Even though the Greeks of a later period emphasized other aspects of human power, reverence for a mother goddess or Earth Mother was to live on.

The Neolithic period (c. 8000 B.C.) represents in all aspects a major break with the past. After a million years of hunting, ways to domesticate animals and cultivate food were discovered. People began to gather together in villages where they could lead a

1 *Venus of Willendorf.* Lower Austria, c. 30,000–25,000 B.C. Limestone, height 4⅜″ (11 cm). Natural History Museum, Vienna. This tiny statuette is one of a series of female figurines from the Upper Paleolithic period that are known as Venus figures. The statuette, which has no facial features, is evidently a fertility symbol.

settled existence. The development of improved farming techniques made it possible for a community to accumulate stores of grain and thereby become less dependent for their survival on a good harvest each year. But these stores provided a motive for raids by neighboring communities. Thus war, for the first time in human history, became profitable. Other more constructive changes followed at a rapid pace. Pottery was invented around 5000 B.C. and not long afterward metal began to replace stone as the principal material for tools and weapons. The first metal used was copper, but it was soon discovered that an alloy of copper and tin would produce a much stronger metal, bronze. The use of bronze became widespread, giving its name to the Bronze Age, which lasted from around 3000 B.C. to the introduction of iron around 1000 B.C.

At the beginning of the Bronze Age, large-scale architecture began to appear. The fortified settlements that had been established in Egypt and Mesopotamia now were able to develop those aspects of existence which entitle them to be called the first true civilizations.

Egypt and Mesopotamia have much in common. Their climates are similar, and both are dominated by great rivers, Egypt by the Nile and Mesopotamia by the Tigris and Euphrates (see map below). Yet each was to develop its own distinct culture and make its own contribution to the history of civilization.

Ancient Egypt

One major determinant in the development of ancient Egyptian culture was geography. In total area, ancient Egypt was only a little larger than the State of Maryland. At the delta of the Nile was Lower Egypt, broad and flat, within easy reach of neighboring parts of the Mediterranean. Upper Egypt, more isolated from foreign contacts, consisted of a long narrow strip of fertile soil, hemmed in by high cliffs and desert, running on either side of the Nile for most of its 1250 miles (2000 kilometers). Since rainfall was very sparse along the Nile, agriculture depended on the yearly flooding of the river.

The immensely long span of Egyptian history was divided into 31 dynasties by an Egyptian priest,

Manetho, who wrote a *History of Egypt* in Greek around 280 B.C. Modern scholars still follow his system, putting the dynasties into four groups and calling the period that preceded them the Predynastic. The four main divisions, with their approximate dates, are: the Old Kingdom, c. 2700 B.C., the Middle Kingdom, c. 1990 B.C., the New Kingdom, c. 1570 B.C., and the Late Period, c. 1185 B.C. until Egypt was absorbed into the Persian empire around 500 B.C. The periods were separated from one another by intermediate times of disturbances and confusion.

In spite of its long history, the most striking feature of Egyptian culture is its unity and consistency. Nothing is in stronger contrast to the process of dynamic change initiated by the Greeks and still characteristic of our own culture than the relative absence of change of Egyptian art, religion, language, and political structure over thousands of years. Naturally, even the Egyptians were subject to outside influences, and events at home and abroad affected their world view. It is possible to trace a mood of increasing pessimism from the vital, life-affirming spirit of the Old Kingdom to the New Kingdom vision of death as an escape from the grim realities of life. Nevertheless, the Egyptians maintained a strong re-

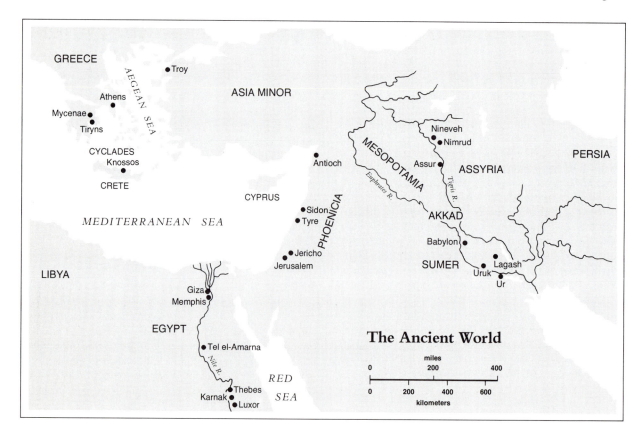

The Ancient World

sistance to change. Their art, in particular, remained conservative and rooted in the past.

In a land where regional independence already existed in the natural separation of Upper from Lower Egypt, national unity was maintained by a strong central government firmly controlled by a single ruler, the pharaoh. He was regarded as a living god, the equal of any other deity. He had absolute power, although the execution of his orders depended on a large official bureaucracy whose influence tended to increase in time.

Beneath the pharaoh were the priests, who saw as their responsibility the preservation of traditional religious beliefs. One of the most fundamental of these was the concept of divine kingship involving the pharaoh himself, a concept that reflected the Egyptian view of creation. The first great god of Egyptian religion, the Sun god Aton-Ra, had created the world by imposing order on the primeval chaos of the universe; in the same way, the pharaoh ordered and controlled the visible world.

The most striking aspect of Egyptian religious thought, however, is its obsession with immortality and the possibilities of life after death. All Egyptians, not only the ruling class, were offered the hope of survival in the next world as a reward for a good life, a survival that was thought of in literal, physical terms. Elaborate funeral rituals began to develop at which the dead would be judged and passed as worthy to move on to the next life. The god who presided over these ceremonies was Osiris [2]. The worship of Osiris, his wife Isis, and their son, the falcon god Horus, which came in time to symbolize a sense of spiritual afterlife, as opposed to simple material survival, represented the mystical side of Egyptian religion.

At the same time the Egyptians worshiped a host of other deities, subdeities, and nature spirits, whose names were often confused and sometimes interchangeable. These deities, responsible for all aspects of existence, inspired mythology and ritual that affected the daily life of every Egyptian. The deities included Hathor, the goddess of beauty and love, often represented as a cow; Bes, the god of war; and Hapi, the god of the Nile. A number of animals, like the jackal and the cat, also had special sacred significance.

Traditional Egyptian religion involved, then, a bewildering confusion of deities whose rights and privileges were jealously guarded by their priests. One of the ways to worship them was to give them visible form in works of art—a principal function of Egyptian artists. Egyptian art as a whole, in fact, like every aspect of Egyptian life, was conditioned by religion. In addition to producing images of deities,

2 Painted relief from the funerary temple of Sethos I at Abydos. c. 1300 B.C. Sethos in the guise of the god Osiris, standing at left, is conversing with Thoth, the ibis-headed god of writing.

artists were required to provide temples and shrines where they could be worshiped. Even the buildings that commemorated the names and deeds of real people served religious purposes. Thus the same central authority that controlled religion affected the development of the arts. The pharaoh's court laid down the standards applied throughout Egypt. Individual artists had little opportunity to exercise their own ingenuity by deviating from them.

The Old and Middle Kingdoms

The huge scale of many Egyptian works of art is at least in part the result of the easy availability of stone, the most frequently used material from the early Old Kingdom to the Late Period. In the Third Dynasty, the architect Imhotep used stone to construct the earliest pyramid as a tomb for his master, the pharaoh Zoser. This began the tradition of building massive funerary monuments that would serve to guarantee immortality for their occupants. At the same time, the practice of mummification developed. The body

3 Sphinx at Giza. c. 2540–2514 B.C. Limestone; length 240′ (73.2 m), height 65′ (19.83 m). The lion's body symbolizes immortality. The pharaohs were often buried in lion skins. About 500 yards (457 meters) away is the Pyramid of Chefren.

was embalmed to preserve its physical form, since Egyptian religious belief held that preservation of the body was necessary for the survival of the soul. Imhotep himself, who is, incidentally, the first architect known to history, was in later ages regarded as the epitome of wisdom and was deified.

The great age of the pyramid came in the Fourth Dynasty with the construction of the three colossal pyramids at Giza for the pharaohs Cheops, Chefren, and Mycerinus [3]. In size and abstract simplicity, these pyramids show Egyptian skill in design and engineering on a massive scale—a scale made possible only by slave labor. The pyramids and almost all other Egyptian works of art perpetuate the memories of members of the upper classes, but their life style would not have been possible without slaves. There were also many poor Egyptians who were farmers. We still know little about the farmers and slaves.

The construction of the pyramids was an elaborate and complex affair. Stone quarried on the spot formed the core of each structure, but the fine limestone blocks used for facing came from across the Nile. These were quarried in the dry season; then when the floods came they were ferried across the river, cut into shape, and dragged into place. At the center of each pyramid was a chamber in which was placed the mummified body of the pharaoh, sur-

rounded by the treasures that were to follow him into the next life. These massive constructions the pharaohs planned as their resting places for eternity and as monuments that would perpetuate their names. Their success was partial. Four and a half thousand years later, their names are remembered—their pyramids, still dominating the flat landscape, symbolize the enduring character of ancient Egypt. As shelters for their occupants and their treasures, however, the pyramids were vulnerable. The very size of the pyramids drew attention to the riches hidden within them, and robbers were quick to tunnel through and plunder them, sometimes only shortly after the burial chamber had been sealed.

Chefren, who commissioned the second of the three pyramids at Giza, was also responsible for perhaps the most famous of all Egyptian images, the colossal Sphinx [3], a guardian for his tomb. The aloof tranquility of the human face, perhaps a portrait of the pharaoh, set on a lion's body made an especially strong impression fifteen hundred years later on the Classical Greeks, who saw it as a divine symbol of the mysterious and enigmatic. Greek art makes frequent use of the sphinx as a motif, and it also appears in Greek mythology, most typically in the story of how Oedipus solved its riddle and thereby saved the Greek city of Thebes from disaster.

4 *Chefren*. Giza, c. 2560 B.C. Dark green diorite, height 5′ (1.52 m). Egyptian Museum, Cairo.

5 *Sesostris III*. c. 1878–1841 B.C. Black granite, height 4′10½″ (1.5 m). Egyptian Museum, Cairo.

The appearance of Chefren himself is preserved for us in a number of statues that are typical of Old Kingdom art [4]. The sculptor's approach to anatomy and drapery is realistic, and details are shown with great precision. But the features of the pharaoh are idealized; it is a portrait not of an individual but of the concept of divine power, power symbolized by the falcon god Horus perched behind the pharaoh's head. The calmness, even indifference, of the expression is particularly striking.

The art of the Old Kingdom reflects a mood of confidence and certainty that was brought to an abrupt end around 2200 B.C. by a period of violent disturbance. Divisions between the regions began to strengthen the power of local governors. By the time of the Middle Kingdom, it was no longer possible for pharaoh, priests, or nobles to face the future with complete trust in divine providence. Middle Kingdom art reflects this new uncertainty in two ways.

On the one hand, the Old Kingdom came to represent a kind of Golden Age; artists tried to recapture its lofty serenity in their own works. At the same time, the more troubled spirit of the new period is reflected in the massive weight and somber expressions of some of the official portraits. The furrowed brow and grim look of Sesostris III convey the impression that to be a Middle Kingdom pharaoh was hardly a very relaxing occupation [5].

The New Kingdom

In spite of increasing contacts with foreign cultures, New Kingdom artists continued basically to work within age-old traditions. In the Eighteenth Dynasty, however, there was a remarkable change. The pharaoh Amenhotep IV, who ruled from 1379 to 1362 B.C., single-handedly attempted a total reform of Egyptian religious and political life. He replaced the numberless deities of traditional religion with a single one, the sun god Aton, and changed his own name to Akhenaton, or "the servant of Aton." In order to make these revolutionary changes more effective and to escape from the influence of the priests at the royal court of Thebes, he moved the capital to a new location, known today as Tel el-Amarna.

Here a new kind of art developed. The weight and idealism of the traditional style gave way to a new lightness and naturalism. For the first time, physical characteristics are depicted in detail, and scenes are relaxed and even humorous. A stone relief showing the royal couple and three of their children sitting quietly under the rays of the sun disc is an astonishing departure from the dignified style of the preceding thousand years [6]. Queen Nefertiti herself is the subject of perhaps the most famous of all Egyptian portraits [Plate 2, page 21], a sculpture that shows none of the exaggeration to which Amarna art is sometimes prone, but a grace and elegance very different from earlier official portraits.

All these artistic changes were, of course, the result of Akhenaton's sweeping and revolutionary religious reforms. These reforms did not last long. Akhenaton's belief in a single god who ruled the universe was threatening to the priests, who had a vested interest in preserving the old polytheistic traditions. Not surprisingly, Akhenaton's successors branded him a heretic and fanatic and cut his name out of all the monuments that survived him.

The reaction against Akhenaton's religious reforms and the Amarna style was almost immediate. His successor, Tutankhamen, however, is remembered not for leading the reaction, nor indeed for any event in his short life. He owes his fame to the treasures found intact in his unrobbed tomb. These sumptuous gold objects, enriched with ivory and precious stones, still show something of the liveliness of Amarna art, but a return to conservatism is beginning; in fact by the Nineteenth and Twentieth Dynasties Akhenaton had been completely forgotten.

In any case, it is not so much for what they reveal about the trends in art that the treasures of Tutankhamen are significant. The discovery of the tomb is important for a different reason. Our knowledge of the cultures of the ancient world is constantly being revised by the discoveries of archaeologists; many of these finds are minor, but some are major and spectacular. When major finds are made, such as the tomb of Tutankhamen, the process of uncovering the past sometimes becomes as exciting and significant as what is discovered. The long search conducted by Howard Carter in the Valley of the Kings, which culminated in the opening of the inner chamber of the sealed tomb of Tutankhamen on February 17, 1923, and the discovery of the intact sarcophagus of the king, has become part of history [7].

The excavations of Knossos and Mycenae, discussed later in this chapter, and the discovery of Pompeii (Chapter 5) are also major turning points in the growth of our knowledge of the past. But sensational finds like these are exceptions. Understanding the cultural achievements of past civilizations involves a slow and painstaking series of minor discoveries, each of which adds to the knowledge that thus must be constantly revised and reinterpreted.

By the end of the New Kingdom the taste for monumental building had returned. The temples constructed during the reign of Ramses II (1298–1232 B.C.) at Luxor, Karnak, and Abu Simbel are probably the most colossal of all Egyptian buildings [8].

below: 6 *Akhenaton, Nefertiti, and Three of Their Children.* Amarna, c. 1370–1350 B.C. Limestone relief, height 17″ (43 cm). Egyptian Museum, State Museums, West Berlin. The naturalism of this relief, verging on sentimentality, is typical of late Amarna art.

opposite above: 7 The first view of the treasures of Tutankhamen: this is what Howard Carter saw when he opened the doorway of the antechamber of the tomb of Tutankhamen on November 26, 1922. The objects include three gilt couches in the form of animals and, at the right in back, the pharaoh's golden throne. The tomb itself was opened three months later.

opposite below: 8 Temple of Ramses II at Abu Simbel, c. 1257 B.C. Height of statues about 60′ (18.3 m). These four huge statues, erected in commemoration of Ramses' military victories, are all of the pharaoh himself. Between and near the feet are small statues of Ramses' mother, wife, and children. Below are statues of the pharaoh as the god Osiris and the falcon god Horus, to whom the temple was dedicated. (This photograph shows the temple in its original site. In 1968 the whole temple was moved to higher ground to save it from submersion in the new Aswan Dam reservoir.)

Within a century, however, internal dissensions and foreign events had produced a sharp decline in Egypt's power. Throughout the Late Period, artists reverted again to the styles of earlier periods. Tombs were once again constructed in the shape of pyramids, as they had been in the Old Kingdom, and sculptors tried to recapture the realism and sense of volume of Old and Middle Kingdom art. Even direct contacts with the Assyrians, Persians, and Greeks—during the period between the Assyrian occupation of 671–633 B.C. and Alexander's conquest of Egypt in 331 B.C.—produced little effect on late Egyptian art. To the end of their history, the Egyptians remained faithful to their three-thousand-year-old tra-

9 *Top:* Picture writing: Copy of a limestone tablet from Kish. c. 3200 B.C. Ashmolean Museum, Oxford; original in Baghdad Museum. *Center:* Hieroglyphics: detail of a pillar of a festival building of Sesostris I, Karnak. c. 1940 B.C. Egyptian Museum, Cairo. *Bottom:* Cuneiform: detail of the *Stele of Hammurabi* (see figure **15**). c. 1760 B.C. The limestone tablet is the oldest known example of picture writing. Among the signs are several representing parts of the human body, including a head, hand, and foot. This writing system later developed into cuneiform. The Egyptians, however, continued to use hieroglyphics throughout their history.

dition. Probably no other culture in human history has ever demonstrated so strong a conservatism and determination to preserve its separate traditions.

The Cultures of Mesopotamia

The unity so characteristic of ancient Egyptian culture has no parallel in the history of ancient Mesopotamia. A succession of different races, each with its own language, religion, and customs, produced a wide variety of achievements. This makes it far more difficult to generalize about Mesopotamian culture than about ancient Egyptian. The picture is further complicated by the presence of a series of related peoples on the periphery of the Mesopotamian territory. The Hittites, the Syrians, and the peoples of early Iran all had periods of prosperity and artistic greatness, although in general they were overshadowed by the more powerful nations of Mesopotamia and Egypt. A description of their achievements would be beyond the scope of this book.

Sumer

The history of Mesopotamia can be divided into two major periods, the Sumerian (c. 3500–2350 B.C.) and the Semitic (c. 2350–612 B.C., when Nineveh fell). The earliest Sumerian communities were agricultural settlements on the land between the Tigris and Euphrates rivers. Unlike Upper Egypt, the land here is flat, and so dikes and canals were needed to prevent flooding during the rainy season and to provide water during the rest of the year. When the early settlers found that they had to undertake these large-scale construction projects in order to improve their agriculture, they began to merge their small villages to form towns.

By far the most important event of this stage in the development of Sumerian culture was the invention of the first system of writing. It consisted of a series of simplified picture signs that represented the objects they showed and, in addition, related ideas. Thus a leg could mean either a leg itself or the concept of walking. The signs were drawn on soft clay tablets that were then baked hard. The Egyptian hieroglyphic system of writing, which was probably derived from this method, retained throughout its history the use of recognizable pictures. The Sumerians, however, evolved their pictorial signs into a series of wedge-shaped marks that were pressed in clay with a split reed. The system was known as cuneiform [9]. The ability to write made it possible to trade and to administer on a wider scale, and with the increasing

economic strength this more highly organized society brought, a number of powerful cities began to develop.

The central focus of life in these larger communities was the temple, the dwelling place of the particular god who watched over the town. Religion, in fact, played a central part in all aspects of Sumerian culture. The gods themselves were manifest in natural phenomena, sky and earth, sun and moon, lightning and storm. The chief religious holidays were closely linked to the passage of the seasons. The most important event of the year was the New Year, the crucial moment when the blazing heat of the previous summer and the cold of winter gave way to the possibility of a fertile spring. The fertility of the earth was symbolized by the Great Mother and the sterility of the winter by the death of her partner, Tammuz. Each year his disappearance was mourned at the beginning of the New Year festival. But when his resurrection was celebrated at the end of the festival, hope for the year to come was expressed by the renewal of the sacred marriage of god and goddess.

As in the Paleolithic period, the importance of female creative power is reflected in Sumerian art. Among its finest achievements is the so-called *Lady of Warka* [10], a female head from the city of Uruk (now

10 *Lady of Warka*. Uruk, c. 3000 B.C. White marble, height 7⅞" (20 cm). Iraq Museum, Baghdad. Originally, the hair was probably gold leaf and the eyes and eyebrows were colored inlays.

called Warka). It is not certain whether the head is of a divine or mortal figure. The face shows an altogether exceptional nobility and sensitivity.

The governing power in cities like Uruk was in the hands of the priests, who controlled and administered both religious and economic affairs. The ruler himself served as the representative on earth of the god of the city, but, unlike the pharaoh, was never thought of as divine and never became the center of a cult. His purpose was to watch over his people's interests by building better temples and digging more canals, rather than acquiring personal wealth or power. Over the centuries rulers began to detach themselves increasingly from the control of the priests, but the immense prestige of the temples assured the religious leaders a lasting power.

The Epic of Gilgamesh

The most famous of all Sumerian rulers was Gilgamesh, who ruled at Uruk around 2700 B.C. Around his name grew up a series of legends that developed into one of the first great masterpieces of poetic expression. *The Epic of Gilgamesh* begins with the adventures of Gilgamesh and his warrior friend Enkidu. Gilgamesh himself is courted by the queen of heaven, the goddess Ishtar. He rejects her advances and later kills a bull sent against him as a punishment. In revenge, the gods kill Enkidu; his death marks the turning point of the poem's mood. With the awareness of death's reality even for the bravest, Gilgamesh now sets out to seek the meaning of life. Toward the end of his journey he meets Utnapishtim, the only person to whom the gods have given everlasting life; from him Gilgamesh seeks the secrets of immortality. Utnapishtim, in the course of their conversation, tells him the story of the flood as it was known in Babylonia. By the end of the epic, Gilgamesh fails to achieve immortality and returns home to die.

Originally composed in Sumerian c. 2000 B.C., the epic was eventually written down on clay tablets in their own languages by Babylonians, Hittites, and others. The epic was widely known. The story of the flood, recorded in tablet eleven, bears a striking resemblance to that of the biblical story in *Genesis,* except for the tone. The God of the Hebrews acts out of moral disapproval, while the divinities in the epic were disturbed in their sleep by noisy mortals.

The Epic of Gilgamesh is a profoundly pessimistic work. Unlike the ancient Egyptians, the Mesopotamians saw life as a continual struggle whose only alternative was the bleak darkness of death. The dying Egyptian—if he were righteous—could expect a happy existence in the next life, but for the Mesopotamian there was only the bleak prospect of eternal gloom.

The story of Gilgamesh rises to a universal level in the section that describes the last stages of his journey. Then the epic touches on universal questions: Is all human achievement futile in the face of death? Is there a purpose in human existence? If so, how can it be discovered? The quest of Gilgamesh is the basic human search. The remote Sumerian king is the remote ancestor of a type who appears time and again in the humanistic tradition. The choice of the journey as a symbol of the spiritual and intellectual quest will be used again with brilliance in the later tradition. Odysseus in Homer's *Iliad* (pages 54–59), Aeneas in Vergil's *Aeneid* (pages 116–119), and Dante in *The Divine Comedy* (pages 196–199) are three different examples of the traveler as symbol of search.

Only at the end of Gilgamesh's journey do we sense that the purpose of the journey may have been

11 Head of a king (Sargon?), from Ninevah. Akkadian, c. 2330 B.C. Bronze, height 14¼″ (37 cm). Iraq Museum, Baghdad. Originally, the eyes were probably precious stones.

the journey itself and that what was important was to have asked the questions. Weary as he was on his return he was wiser than when he left, and in leaving us an account of his experiences, "engraved on a stone," he communicates them to us, a powerful and moving illustration of the power of the written word.

Akkadian and Babylonian Culture

In the years from 2350 to 2150 B.C. the whole of Mesopotamia fell under the control of the Semitic king Sargon and his descendants. The art of this Akkadian period (named for Sargon's capital city, Akkad) shows a continuation of the trends of the Sumerian age, although total submission to the gods is replaced by a more positive attitude to human achievement. A bronze head from Nineveh [11], perhaps a portrait of Sargon himself, expresses a pride and self-confidence

that recur in other works of the period like the famous *Stele of Naram-Sin* (*stele*: sculpted stone slab), showing a later Akkadian king standing on the bodies of his enemies [12].

When Akkadian rule was brought to an abrupt and violent end by the invasion of the Gutians from Iran, the cities of Mesopotamia reverted to earlier ways. As in the early Sumerian period, the chief buildings constructed were large brick platforms with superimposed terraces, known as *ziggurats*. These clearly had religious significance; the one built

12 *Stele of Naram-Sin,* from Susa, Iran. Akkadian, c. 2300 B.C. Red sandstone, height 6'6" (2 m). Louvre, Paris. The king, wearing a horned crown, stands beneath symbols of the gods. The diagonal composition is well suited to the triangular shape of the stele.

at Ur around 2100 B.C. [13] had huge staircases that led to a shrine at the top. The same return to traditional beliefs is illustrated by the religious inscriptions on the bases of the many surviving statues of Gudea, the governor of the city of Lagash around 2100 B.C., as well as by his humble attitude [14].

By around 1800 B.C., Mesopotamia had once again been unified, this time under the Babylonians.

Their most famous king, Hammurabi, was the author of a law code that was one of the earliest attempts to achieve social justice by legislation—a major development in the growth of civilization. The laws were carved on a stele, with Hammurabi himself shown at the top in the presence of the sun god Shamash [15]. Many of the law code's provisions deal with the relationship between husbands, wives,

13 Ziggurat at Ur. Neo-Sumerian, c. 2100–2000 B.C. Mudbrick faced with baked brick laid in bitumen. The drawing shows the probable original appearance. The photograph shows the zuggurat now, partially restored. The Akkadian word ziggurat means "pinnacle" or "mountain top"—a place where the gods were thought to reveal themselves. These plains dwellers made artificial mountains surmounted by shrines.

and other family members. They often show a surprisingly enlightened attitude toward equal rights in the 18th century B.C.—almost four thousand years ago, as the following extracts show:

from THE LAW CODE OF HAMMURABI

131. If a man accuse his wife and she have not been taken in lying with another man, she shall take an oath in the name of god and she shall return to her house.

136. If a man desert his city and run away, and afterward his wife enter into another house, if that man return and seize his wife, because he hated his city and fled, the wife of the fugitive shall not return to her husband.

138. If a man put away his wife who has not borne him children, he shall give her money to the amount of her marriage settlement and he shall make good to her the dowry which she brought from her father's house and then he may put her away.

below: 14 *Gudea.* c. 2100 B.C. Diorite, height 41″ (105 cm). Louvre, Paris. Gudea is shown in an attitude of devotion, hands tightly clasped, as he stands before the gods.

right: 15 *Stele of Hammurabi.* c. 1760 B.C. Basalt, height 7′3¾″ (2.25 m). Louvre, Paris. The sun god is dictating the law to the king, who is listening reverently. They are shown on a mountain, indicated by the irregular ridges beneath the god's feet. Below is *The Law Code of Hammurabi,* carved in cuneiform.

142. If a woman hate her husband and say, "Thou shalt not have me," her past shall be inquired into for any deficiency of hers; and if she have been careful and be without past sin and her husband have been going out and greatly belittling her, that woman has no blame. She shall take her dowry and go to her father's house.

145. If a man take a wife and she do not present him with children, and he set his face to take a concubine, that man may take a concubine and bring her into his house. That concubine shall not take precedence of his wife.

162. If a man take a wife and she bear him children and that woman die, her father may not lay claim to her dowry. Her dowry belongs to her children.

The Assyrians

By 1550 B.C., Babylon had been taken over by the Kassites, a formerly nomadic people who had occupied Babylonia and settled there, but they too were to fall in turn under the domination of the Assyrians, who evolved the last great culture of ancient Mesopotamia. The peak of Assyrian power was between 1000 and 612 B.C.—the time when Greek civilization was developing, as described in Chapter 3. But Assyrian achievements are the culmination of the culture of ancient Mesopotamia.

A huge palace constructed at Nimrud during the reign of Assurnasirpal II (883–859 B.C.) was decorated with an elaborately carved series of relief slabs. The subjects are often religious, but a number of slabs that show the king on hunting expeditions have a vigor and freedom that are unusual in Mesopotamian art. The palaces of later Assyrian kings were decorated with similar reliefs. At Nineveh the palace of Assurbanipal (668–626 B.C.) was filled with scenes of war appropriate to an age of increasing turmoil. The representations of dead and dying soldiers on the battlefields are generally conventional, if highly elaborate. But again the hunting scenes are different— they show a genuine and moving identification with the suffering animals [16].

With the fall of Nineveh in 612 B.C. Assyrian domination ended. The Assyrian empire fell into the hands of two nomadic tribes, first the Medes and then the Persians; the great age of Mesopotamia was over. Lacking the unifying elements provided in Egypt by the pharaoh and a national religion, the peoples of Mesopotamia perhaps never equaled Egyptian achievements in the arts. However, they formed ordered societies within independent city-states that anticipated the city-states of the Greeks. They also evolved a comparatively enlightened view of human relationships, as shown by *The Law Code of Hammurabi.*

Aegean Culture in the Bronze Age

Neither the Egyptians of the Old Kingdom nor the Sumerians seem to have shown any interest in their contemporaries living to the west of them, and with

16 Detail, relief from the Palace of Assurbanipal at Nineveh, 668–626 B.C. Gypsum slab carved in low relief, height 19″ (50 cm). British Museum, London (reproduced by courtesy of the Trustees). Wild asses are being hunted by mastiffs. The mare below turns in her flight to look back for her foal.

above: **Plate 1** Hall of Bulls, left wall, Lascaux (Dordogne), France. c. 15,000–10,000 B.C. Paintings like these were not intended to be decorations, since they are not in the inhabited parts of the caves but in the dark inner recesses. They probably had magical significance for their creators, who may have believed that gaining control of an animal in a painting would help to defeat it in the hunt.

left: **Plate 2** *Queen Nefertiti*. Tel el-Amarna. c. 13/0 B.C. Painted limestone, height 20″ (51 cm). State Museums, West Berlin. Though the portrait is not exaggerated, it is idealized.

Plate 3 Room with landscape frescoes, House Delta, Thera. Minoan, c. 1500 B.C. National Archaeological Museum, Athens. A springtime scene—bright flowers and soaring birds—covers three sides of a small room.

good reason. In Greece and the islands of the Aegean Sea, though the arrival of immigrants from further east in the early Neolithic period (c. 6000 B.C.) had brought new agricultural techniques, in general, life continued there for the next three thousand years almost completely untouched by the rise of organized cultures elsewhere.

Yet, beginning in the early Bronze Age, there developed in the area around the Aegean Sea a level of civilization as brilliant and sophisticated as any other in the ancient world. Then around 1100 B.C., after almost two thousand years of existence, this civilization disappeared as dramatically as it had arisen. The rediscovery in the 20th century of these peoples, the Minoans of Crete and the Mycenaeans of mainland Greece, is perhaps the most splendid achievement in the history of archaeology in the Mediterranean—an achievement that has opened up vast new perspectives in the study of the later Greeks.

What connection is there between later Greek culture and the magnificent achievements of the Bronze Age? Did much of later Greek religion, thought, and art have its origins in this earlier period, even though the Greeks themselves seemed to know nothing about it? Or was the culture of the Minoans and Mycenaeans an isolated phenomenon, destroyed utterly near the end of the Bronze Age, lost until it was found again in our own time? The Aegean culture is important not only for the possible light it throws on later times. Its existence also shows that the ancient world could reach beyond the monumentality and earnestness of the Egyptians and Mesopotamians, that it could attain a way of life that valued grace, beauty, and comfort—a life that could truly be called civilized.

Cycladic Art

During most of the Bronze Age the major centers of Aegean culture were on Crete or the mainland, but in the early phase there were settlements on a group of islands of the central Aegean, the Cyclades. Little is known about these Cycladic people. They used bronze tools. They also produced pottery which, though less finely made than that produced elsewhere in the Aegean at the time, sometimes shows remarkable imagination and even humor [17]. The chief claim to fame of Cycladic art—a considerable one— lies in the marble statues, or idols, that were produced in large quantities and in many cases buried with the dead. The statues range in height from a few inches to almost lifesize; the average is about a foot (30.5 centimeters) high. Most of the figures are female; the most common type shows a naked woman standing or, more probably, lying, with her arms folded and head tilted back [18]. The face is indicated

17 Cycladic vase in the shape of a hedge hog drinking from a bowl. Syros, c. 2500–2200 B.C. Painted clay, height 4¼″ (11 cm). National Archaeological Musuem, Athens.

18 Cycladic idol. c. 2500 B.C. Marble, height 19¾″ (50 cm). British Museum, London.

19 Amedeo Modigliani.
Jeanne Hébuturne with Yellow Sweater. 1919.
Oil on canvas, 39⅜ × 25½″ (100 × 65 cm).
Solomon R. Guggenheim Museum, New York.

only by a central ridge for the nose. The simplicity of the form and the fine working of the marble—marble of superb quality—often produce an effect of great beauty.

The purpose of the Cycladic idols remains uncertain. The fact that most of them have been found in graves suggests that they had a religious function in the funeral ritual. The overwhelming preponderance of female figures seems to indicate that they were in some way connected with the cult of the mother goddess, which was common in Mesopotamia and which dominated Aegean Bronze Age religion. Whether the figures actually represent goddesses remains uncertain. In any case, the abstract elegance of the statues has a special appeal for modern eyes. A number of contemporary artists have been influenced by them, most notably the Italian painter Amedeo Modigliani (1884–1920) [19]. Even in the Bronze Age they seem to have been popular—they were exported to Crete and mainland Greece.

We now know that the period of the production of the Cycladic idols was one of increasing development on Crete. Yet for the classical Greeks of the 5th century B.C. Crete was chiefly famous as the home of the legendary King Minos, who ruled at Knossos. Here, according to the myths, was a Labyrinth that housed the Minotaur, a monstrous creature, half man and half bull, the product of the union of Minos' wife Pasiphae with a bull. Minos exacted a regular tribute from Athens of seven boys and seven girls, who were sent to be devoured by the Minotaur. According to the myths, after this had been going on for some time, the Athenian hero Theseus volunteered to stop the grisly tribute. He went to Knossos with the new group of intended victims and, with the help of the king's daughter Ariadne, who had fallen in love with him, killed the Minotaur in his lair in the middle of the Labyrinth. He then escaped with Ariadne and the Athenian boys and girls. Theseus later somewhat heartlessly abandoned Ariadne on the island of Naxos, but the god Dionysus discovered her there and comforted her. The story had many more details, and other myths describe other events. The important point is that the later Greeks had a mythological picture of Knossos as a prosperous and thriving community ruled by a powerful and ruthless king from his palace. Nor was Knossos the only center mentioned in Greek stories of Crete. In the *Odyssey* Homer even refers to "Crete of a hundred cities."

But these were legends. By the time of Classical Greece no evidence whatever for the existence of the Palace of Minos or the other cities could be seen. It is not surprising that the Greeks themselves showed no inclination to try to find any hidden traces. Archaeology, after all, is a relatively modern pursuit, and there is little indication of any serious enthusiasm in Classical antiquity for the material remains of the past. Later ages continued to accept the Greeks' own judgment. For many centuries the story of Minos and the Labyrinth was thought to be a good tale with no foundation in fact.

The Excavation of Knossos

By the end of the 19th century, however, things had changed. Heinrich Schliemann had proved that the stories of the war against Troy and the Mycenaeans who had waged it were far from mere legends (see page 28). Was it possible that the mythical palace of King Minos at Knossos also really existed?

In 1894 the English archaeologist Arthur Evans first went to Crete to see if he could discover something of its history in the Bronze Age. At Knossos he found evidence of ancient remains, some of them already uncovered by amateur enthusiasts. He returned in 1899 and again in 1900, this time with a permit to excavate. On March 23, 1900, serious work began at Knossos, and within days it became apparent that the finds represented a civilization even older than that of the Mycenaeans. The quantity was staggering: pottery, frescoes, inscribed tablets, and, on April 13, a room with elaborate paintings and a raised seat with high back—the throne room of King Minos. Evans' discoveries at Knossos (and finds later made elsewhere on Crete by other archaeologists) did much to confirm legendary accounts of Cretan prosperity and power. But these discoveries did far more than merely give a true historical background to the myth of the Minotaur.

Evans had in fact found an entire civilization, which he called Minoan after the legendary king. Evans himself is said to have once remarked modestly: "Any success as an archaeologist I owe to two things: very short sight, so I look at everything closely, and being slow on the uptake, so I never leap to conclusions." Actually, the magnitude of his achievement cannot be exaggerated. All study of the Minoans has been strongly influenced by his initial classification of the finds, especially the pottery. He divided the history of the Bronze Age in Crete into three main periods, Early Minoan, Middle Minoan, and Late Minoan, and further subdivided each of these into three. The precise dates of each period can be disputed, but all the excavations of the years following Evans have confirmed his initial description of the main sequence of events.

20 Throne Room, Palace of Minos at Knossos. The room was reconstructed about 1450 B.C., shortly before the final destruction of the palace. The frescoes around the throne show sacred flowers and griffins—mythological beasts with lion bodies and bird heads.

Life and Art in the Minoan Palaces

The Early Minoan period was one of increasing growth. Small towns began to appear in the south and east of Crete, and the first contacts were established with Egypt and Mesopotamia. Around 2000 B.C., however, came the first major development in Minoan civilization, marking the beginning of the Middle Minoan period. The earlier scattered towns were abandoned, and large urban centers evolved. These centers were generally called palaces, although their function was far more than just to provide homes for ruling families.

The best known of these centers is Knossos (other important ones have been excavated at Phaistos, Mallia, and Zakro). The main palace building, which was constructed around an open rectangular courtyard, contained rooms for banquets, public receptions, religious ceremonies, and administrative work. In addition, there were living quarters for the royal family and working areas for slaves and craftsmen [20, 21]. Around the palace were the private houses of the aristocrats and chief religious leaders. The technical sophistication of these great centers was remarkable. There were elaborate drainage systems, and the palaces were designed and constructed to remain cool in summer and be heated easily in winter.

Middle Minoan art shows great liveliness and color. The brilliantly painted pottery, superb jewelry such as the famous *Wasp Pendant* from Mallia [22], and the many exquisitely carved seal stones all attest to the Minoans' love of beauty and artistic skill. Unlike their contemporaries in Egypt and Mesopotamia, the Minoans showed little interest in monumental art. Their greatest works are on a small, even miniature, scale. At the same time, they invented a

theatral area

main north
entrance

(destroyed)

main
east
entrance

west
court

central
court

1

2

3

5

4

7

6 6

N

royal living
apartments

main west
entrance

main south entrance

0   50   100 ft
0   10   20   30 m

1 Throne Room
2 Main staircase to second floor
3 Temple Repositories
4 Pillar crypt
5 Corridor of the
  West Magazines
6 Hall of the Double Axes
  (main reception room)
7 Grand Staircase to
  royal living quarters

21 Plan of the Palace of Minos at Knossos. c. 1600–1400 B.C. Each Cretan palace had a central court oriented north-south, state apartments to the west, and royal living apartments to the east.

22 *Wasp Pendant,* from Mallia. c. 1700 B.C. Gold, width 1⅞″ (5 cm). Archaeological Museum, Heraklion. This enlarged view shows the exquisite craftsmanship, using the techniques of granulation and wire-working. Two wasps (or perhaps hornets) are curved around a honeycomb.

AEGEAN CULTURE IN THE BRONZE AGE **27**

writing system of hieroglyphic signs that was used in the archives of the palace for administrative purposes.

Toward the end of the Middle Minoan period (c. 1700 B.C.) the palaces were destroyed, probably by an earthquake, and then rebuilt on an even grander scale. There was further rebuilding about a century later, perhaps because of another earthquake. These palaces of the Late Minoan period represent the high point of Minoan culture. The wall paintings of this period are among the greatest treasures of all. Their spontaneity and freedom create a mood very different from Egyptian and Mesopotamian art, and they show a love of nature expressed with brilliant colors and vivid observation. Most of the best examples of these later paintings are from Knossos, but some particularly enchanting scenes have been found in the recent excavation of a Minoan colony on the island of Thera [Plate 3, page 22].

Although the rulers of the palaces seem to have been male, the central figure of Minoan religion was a mother goddess who was connected with fertility. She seems to have taken on different forms, or rather the function of female divinity was divided among several separate deities. Sometimes when she is shown flanked by animals, the Mistress of the Beasts, she seems to be the ancestor of the Greek goddess Artemis. Other depictions show goddesses of vegetation. The most famous of all Minoan figurines is the so-called *Snake Goddess* [23].

Throughout the last great age of the palaces, the influence of Minoan artistic styles began to spread to the mainland. But Minoan political and military power was on the wane, and Knossos seems to have been invaded and occupied by mainlanders around 1450 B.C. Shortly afterwards, both at Knossos and elsewhere, there is evidence of widespread destruction. By 1400 B.C., Minoan culture had come to an abrupt end. The causes are mysterious and have been much argued; we shall probably never know exactly what happened. The eruption of a volcano on Thera a century earlier, about 1500 B.C., may have played some part in changing the balance of power in the Aegean. In any case, there is no doubt that throughout the last period of the palaces a new power was growing, the Mycenaeans. These people may well have played a part in the destruction of Knossos.

Schliemann and the Discovery of Mycenae

The Mycenaeans, the people of mainland Greece in the Bronze Age, are named after the largest of their settlements, Mycenae. Most of the Mycenaean centers were in the southern part of Greece known as the Peloponnesus, although there were also some settlements farther north, of which the two most important were Athens and Thebes. Like the Minoans, the Mycenaeans were familiar from Greek myths long before their material remains were excavated. They were famous in legend mainly for launching an expedition against Troy, across the Aegean Sea. The Trojan War (c. 1250 B.C.) and its aftermath provided the material for many later Greek works, most notably the *Iliad* and the *Odyssey,* the two great epic poems of Homer, but for a long time it was believed that the war and even the very existence of Troy were myths.

Heinrich Schliemann dedicated his life and work to proving that the legends were founded on reality.

23 *Snake Goddess,* from the Temple Repository at Knossos. c. 1600 B.C. Faience, height 11½" (30 cm). Archaeological Museum, Heraklion. The bare breasts are typical for Minoan court ladies, but the apron indicates a religious function. The figure probably represents a priestess serving the goddess, not the goddess herself.

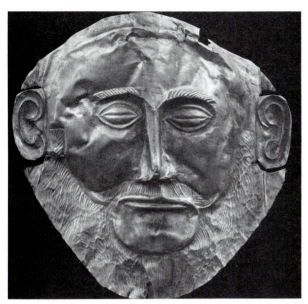

24 "Mask of Agamemnon," from Shaft Grave V, Mycenae. c. 1550 B.C. Beaten gold, height 10⅛″ (26 cm). National Archaeological Museum, Athens. This death mask is actually a portrait of a Mycenaean ruler of three centuries earlier than Agamemnon.

Schliemann, who was born in Germany in 1822, was introduced to the Homeric poems as a child by his father and was overwhelmed by their incomparable vividness. He became determined to discover Homer's Troy and prove the poet right. Excavation has always been expensive, and Schliemann therefore decided to make his fortune in business, retire early, and devote his profits to the pursuit of his goal. By 1863, this remarkable man had accumulated a considerable amount of money from trading in, among other things, tea and was ready to devote himself to this second career. After a period of study and travel, in 1870 he finally began excavations on the site where he had decided the remains of Homer's Troy lay buried beneath the Roman city of Ilium. By 1873 he had found not only walls and the gate of the city but quantities of gold, silver, and bronze objects.

Inspired by the success of his Trojan campaign, Schliemann moved on to the second part of his task: to discover the Mycenaeans who had made war on Troy. In 1876 he began to excavate within the walls of Mycenae itself, and there he almost immediately came upon the Royal Grave Circle with its stupendous quantities of gold treasures [24]. Homer had described Mycenae as "rich in gold," and Schliemann was always convinced that the royal family whose graves he had unearthed was that of Agamemnon, leader of the Mycenaean expedition against Troy. We

now know that the finds date to an even earlier period, and later excavations both at Mycenae and at other mainland sites have provided a much more exact picture of Mycenaean history. This does not diminish Schliemann's achievement. However unscientific his methods, he had proved the existence of a civilization in Bronze Age Greece that surpassed in splendor even the legends; he had opened a new era in the study of the past.

Mycenaean Art and Architecture

Like the Minoans, the Mycenaeans centered their life around great palace complexes. In Mycenae itself, the palace probably was first built around 1600 B.C., and the graves found by Schliemann date to shortly thereafter. Until the fall of Knossos in 1400 B.C., the Mycenaeans were strongly under the influence of Minoan culture, but with the end of Minoan power they became the natural leaders in the Aegean area. From 1400 to 1200 B.C., Mycenaean traders traveled throughout the Mediterranean, from Egypt and the Near East as far west as Italy. The Mycenaean empire grew in power and prosperity. Toward the end of this period, around 1250 B.C., the successful expedition was launched against Troy, perhaps for reasons of trade rivalry. A short time later, around 1200 B.C., the Mycenaean empire itself fell, its major centers destroyed and most of them abandoned. Invasion by enemies, internal strife, and natural causes have all been suggested, but the fall of the Mycenaeans still remains mysterious.

Their collapse is made even more incomprehensible by the massive fortifications that protected most of the palaces. At Mycenae itself, the walls are 15 feet (4.6 meters) thick and probably were 50 feet (15.3 meters) high. As in the case of other Mycenaean centers, the actual location was chosen for its defensibility [25]. The somber character of these fortress-palaces is reflected in the general tone of Mycenaean civilization. Unlike the relaxed culture of the Minoans, Mycenaean culture as reflected in its art was preoccupied with death and war. It is no coincidence that many of the richest finds came from tombs. Like the Minoans, the Mycenaeans decorated their palaces with frescoes, although the Mycenaean paintings are more solemn and dignified than their Minoan counterparts.

The disaster of 1200 B.C. brought a violent end to the Mycenaeans' political and economic domination of the Mediterranean, but their culture lingered on for another hundred years. A few of the palaces were inhabited again, and some Mycenaeans fled eastwards, where they settled on the islands of Rhodes

25 Reconstruction of the Citadel of Mycenae as it would have looked around 1300 B.C. The very thick walls are visible. The palace has a commanding position at the summit.

and Cyprus. By 1100 B.C., however, renewed violence had extinguished the last traces of Bronze Age culture in Greece. A century later, after a period which our lack of information forces us to call the Dark Age, the story of Western culture truly begins with the dawning of the Iron Age.

Before leaving the rich achievements of the Bronze Age world, both in Greece and farther afield, it is worth asking how much survived to be handed down to our own civilization. For the Greeks themselves, the Iron Age brought a new beginning in most material respects. At the same time, however, there are links with the earlier era in less tangible areas. In particular, although Greek religion never placed as strong an emphasis on worship of the mother goddess as the Bronze Age did, she remained a potent force in traditional beliefs. Behind the official reverence for Zeus, father of the gods and mortals, there lay a profound respect for goddesses like Hera, patroness of the family, Artemis, Mistress of the Beasts and goddess of childbirth, and Demeter, the goddess of fertility and agriculture. The continued worship of these goddesses, which was to last under different guises for centuries, represents a reverence for female creative power which is one of the oldest legacies from the period before our culture began—we saw it as far back as the Paleolithic period—and perhaps one of the most significant.

As for Egypt and Mesopotamia, much of their impact on later culture was secondhand. In the course of their growth and development, the Greeks were brought into contact with the later Egypt and Mesopotamia of their own times, and Greek art and architecture were decisively influenced by them. Although the Greeks retained their artistic independence, the style they developed under the inspiration of eastern models has conditioned the entire history of Western art. The cultures of ancient Egypt and the Middle East had very little direct influence on the formation of our civilization, partly because Greek culture had a vitality that was by this time lacking in the older peoples and at least partly because of historical accident. Egypt and Assyria, powerful though they were, fell to the Persians, while Greece managed not only to survive but even to inflict an ignominious defeat on its Persian invaders.

Yet even if ancient Egypt and Mesopotamia lie outside the mainstream of our cultural tradition, they continue to exert a powerful influence on the Western imagination, as the Tutankhamen exhibitions and their accompanying "Tut mania" showed in the 1970s. In part their fascination lies in their exoticism and in the excitement of their rediscovery in our own day. The pharaoh who can curse his excavator from beyond the grave is certainly a dramatic, if fictional, representative of his age. At the same time, the artistic achievements of those distant times need no historical justification. Created in a world very remote from our own, they serve as a reminder of the innate human urge to give expression to the eternal problems of existence.

Questions for Further Discussion

1. All the civilizations described in this chapter eventually declined and collapsed. Did they share certain characteristics which made them unlikely to survive? Are any of these present in our own world?
2. Our picture of the past is inevitably conditioned by the nature of the evidence that has survived, and in the case of ancient Egypt and Mesopotamia most of it casts light only on the lives of the upper classes. Why is this, and what kind of discoveries would need to be made for us to reconstruct the lives of the average Egyptian or Sumerian?
3. It is often said that the art of the Egyptians was strongly influenced by their natural environment. The rectangles formed by the line of the flat desert meeting the vertical cliffs at its edge have been compared to the cubic forms that Egyptian sculptors preferred, and the sense of being enclosed which the landscape produces perhaps finds a parallel in the burial chambers of the pyramids and other tombs. Does it seem probable that the natural landscape exerted a strong influence on artists? Is there any evidence of this in the art of today?
4. The worship of the mother goddess played an important part in the religious life of many early peoples. Why did it disappear? Are there any traces of its survival in later times?
5. The excavations at Knossos, Mycenae, and Troy proved that stories which were thought to be only legends had a strong factual basis. What aspects of the myths have been confirmed by archaeological discoveries? Are there other examples of apparently mythical events that have subsequently been found to be true?

		GENERAL EVENTS	LITERATURE & PHILOSOPHY	ART

3000 B.C.

BRONZE AGE

Before 1260 B.C.

1800–1600 Age of the Hebrew Patriarchs: Abraham, Isaac, Jacob

1600 Israelite tribes in Egypt

1280 Exodus of Israelites from Egypt under leadership of Moses

1260

Period of the Judges

1260 Israelites begin to penetrate land of Canaan

1040

1040–1000 Reign of Saul, first king of Israel

1000

Age of the Monarchy

1000–961 Reign of King David

961–922 Reign of Solomon; use of iron-tipped plow and iron war chariots; height of ancient Israel's cultural power: achievements form basis of Judaic, Christian, and Islamic religions

c. 1000 Formation of the Scriptures in written form

c. 950 Book of Psalms

10th–9th cent. Book of Kings

c. 961–c. 922 Hiram of Tyre constructs bronze "sea" in courtyard of Solomon's Temple

922

Age of the Two Kingdoms

922 Civil war after death of Solomon; split of Northern Kingdom (Israel) and Southern Kingdom (Judah); classical prophetic period begins

721 Northern Kingdom destroyed by Assyria

8th–6th cent. Old Testament books of Isaiah, Jeremiah, and Ezekiel

Depiction of divinity in art prohibited in Jewish religion

734 Oxen from bronze "sea" given to King of Assyria by King Achaz

587

Age of Exile, Return, and Occupations

587 Southern Kingdom defeated; Jews driven into captivity in Babylonia

539 Cyrus the Persian permits Jews to return to Jerusalem

516 Dedication of Second Temple in Jerusalem

332 Conquest of Jerusalem by Alexander the Great

after 5th cent. Book of Job

63

63 Conquest of Jerusalem by Romans under Pompey

37 B.C.–A.D. 4 Reign of Herod the Great under Roman tutelage

c. 6 B.C. Birth of Jesus

B.C.
A.D.

Roman Period

c. A.D. 30 Death of Jesus; beginnings of Christianity in Palestine

45–49 First missionary journeys of Saint Paul

66–70 Jewish rebellions against Romans

c. 70 Titus destroys Jerusalem and razes the Temple; Jews sent into exile

c. A.D. 70 "Sermon on the Mount" in Gospel of Saint Matthew, New Testament

c. A.D. 81 Reliefs from Arch of Titus, Rome, commemorate Roman victory in Jerusalem

IRON AGE (1000–)

324 A.D.

Dates before the 10th cent. B.C. are approximate and remain controversial

2

Jerusalem and the Biblical Tradition

c. 961–c. 922 Building of Temple of Solomon; city of Megiddo rebuilt by Solomon

Music often accompanied the Psalms; musical instruments in use: drums, reed instruments, lyre, harp, horns

587 Solomon's Temple destroyed by Babylonians

c. 536–515 Second Temple of Solomon constructed

19 Herod the Great begins rebuilding Third Temple of Solomon

A.D. 70 Herod's Temple destroyed by the armies of Titus under Emperor Vespasian

c. 81 Arch of Titus, Rome, commemorates victory of Roman army in Jerusalem

Solomon as King and Hero

Nearly a thousand years after his death, the magnificence of Solomon was so proverbial among the Jewish people that Jesus could allude to it and expect that the audience would immediately recognize the point of his comparison: "Consider the lilies of the field, how they grow; they neither toil nor spin; yet I tell you, even Solomon in all his glory was not arrayed like one of these" (Matthew 6:28–29). The reign of Solomon the King (from about 961 to 922 B.C.) marked the high point of Israelite power and achievement, as well as a turning point in the history of Israel. The Israelites had come out of Egypt (the Exodus) some three centuries before, about 1280 B.C., and, after their wanderings in the Sinai, penetrated and slowly conquered the land of Palestine. An essentially tribal people became a monarchy in the time of Saul (c. 1040–1000 B.C.), who was succeeded by the great King David. Solomon ascended the throne after the death of David, his father. He was to be the last king of the United Kingdom, since civil war split the country after his death.

When Solomon became king of Israel in 961 B.C., the times were auspicious for a brilliant reign. The traditional "superpowers," neighboring Egypt and Assyria, were relatively weak; their internal problems dampened their taste for external conquest. To consolidate his position, Solomon entered into alliance with the always potentially dangerous Egyptians by marrying the daughter of the pharaoh.

Solomon was a decisive ruler who took advantage of this tranquil period both to consolidate and extend his power. He expanded foreign trade and equipped his armies with iron war chariots (a relatively new innovation of the times); he also was a renowned trader of horses used for farming and war. It was probably during Solomon's reign that the iron-tipped plow came into general agricultural use, thus increasing food output. Solomon reorganized Israel's administrative districts to make the country more responsive to the demands of the royal administration in Jerusalem, which he kept as his capital, following David's decision. Archaeological excavations in this century have revealed the far-ranging projects of Solomon outside Jerusalem. The fortified city of Megiddo (I Kings 10:26) had elaborate stables that testify to the use of the war chariot and the horse [26, 27]. Excavations at the Red Sea port city of Ezion-geber (conducted in 1940 by the American scholar Nelson Glueck) revealed a huge smelting operation for refining copper, a metal that was of the utmost importance for Solomon's other projects.

In addition to his economic and administrative ability, Solomon is remembered in the biblical tradition as a man of wisdom; indeed, the "wisdom of Solomon" has not only become proverbial in our language but has long been a revered subject for the artists of subsequent centuries. The Bible attributes Solomon's wisdom to a gift from God.

The Bible also contains anecdotes that emphasize the wisdom of Solomon and his immense wealth such as the visit of the Queen of Sheba (modern Yemen) to the court of Solomon (I Kings 10:1–13). The opulent character of the biblical description and the romantic nature of the theme have inspired any number of artists to try and capture its lushness on canvas.

Had Solomon only presided wisely over a wealthy and successful kingdom we would pay little attention to him. The history of humanity is studded with such monarchs. Solomon remains important, in both culture and religion, because he centered the Israelite cult of God at Jerusalem and built the first magnificent temple there.

Solomon's Temple as Monument and Myth

Solomon's Temple was not merely an architectural or artistic triumph; it marked a symbolic moment in the history of Western values, a moment that has had immense ramifications for both our history and our cultural consciousness down to the present time.

Chapters 5 through 9 of the First Book of Kings describe the building of the Temple of Solomon in Jerusalem. None of that Temple is now extant, so we must reconstruct its main outlines from the information in the Bible and what little evidence we have from the archaeological remains of pagan temple-building in Israel.

A temple, unlike a church or a synagogue, was not designed primarily for the worshiper. A temple housed a divinity. That distinction is important, since it determines, to a large extent, why temple architecture is so different from church architecture. At the very core of the temple was a space that was the dwelling place of the god. In another space, the priests ministered to the needs of the god and conducted the rites that honored the presence of the divinity. The worshipers generally held their services and offered their prayers outside the temple proper in a courtyard. They might go into the temple to "visit" the god in prayer or homage, but that is not where they usually worshiped.

The temple was the "sacred space" of the god; indeed, our word "profane" etymologically means "outside the sacred place." The ancients had a clear

26 Megiddo. c. 950 B.C. This aerial view was taken in 1932 by a balloon-carried camera from a height of 820′ (250 m). It is one of the first photographs of an archaeological site taken from a balloon. (Photography from tethered balloons is essential in such archaeological work because airplanes cannot fly low enough to record details and helicopters vibrate, raise dust, and ruffle water surfaces over submerged sites. Sophisticated radio-controlled cameras and infrared and color films are now used.)

27 Excavated stables at Megiddo. This ancient city was rebuilt by Solomon. Archaeological work has uncovered fortified gates, palaces, and these stables from his time. It is thought that 450 to 480 horses were stabled here. Stone mangers can be seen at center.

28 Reconstruction drawing of the altar of Solomon's Temple. The three levels may have symbolized a mountain. The altar is similar in style to Babylonian temple towers, ziggurats (see figure **13**, page 18).

29 Reconstruction drawing of the "sea" outside Solomon's Temple. The Bible also mentions ten mobile bronze layers—large basins used for carrying water. The symbolism of this great bowl is not clear, but some scholars think it may have represented the primordial sea of chaos overcome by God at the time of the creation (see page 43).

distinction in mind between sacred and profane space. The difference becomes clear if we compare the functions of the temple and the synagogue. Synagogues (from the Greek meaning "to gather together") were developed by the Jews outside the land of Israel in a much later period as places for prayer, study, and assembly (indeed, Yiddish-speaking Jews call the synagogue a *shul*—a school or a place of study). The temple, by contrast, was the house of God; it was in the temple that the *Shekinah* (The Presence) uniquely dwelt.

In a vast courtyard in front of Solomon's Temple was a great bronze altar for burnt offerings [28]. The altar was about 15 feet (4.6 meters) high and 30 feet (9.2 meters) square at its base. Next to this huge altar

was perhaps the most spectacular object commissioned by Solomon for his Temple: the large bronze bowl known as the "sea."

This great "sea" was a huge bowl about 7 ½ feet (2.29 meters) high and 15 feet (4.6 meters) in diameter [29]. It rested on twelve bronze oxen who, in groups of three, indicated the four cardinal points of the compass. Cast in bronze, it was "the thickness of a handbreadth; its rim was made like that of a cup, shaped like the calyx of a lily" (I Kings 7:26). Archaeologists have estimated its weight at about 25 tons (22.7 metric tons). The design and execution of the bronze "sea" were done by Hiram of Tyre, an artisan brought to Jerusalem by Solomon. No piece of this great "sea" has survived. The oxen were given as tribute to the King of Assyria by King Achaz in 734 B.C., while the bowl itself was broken up and carried off as spoils of war when the Babylonians herded the Jews into exile in 587 B.C.

Two huge bronze pillars flanked the entrance of the temple [30]. About 18 feet (5.5 meters) high, they were called *Jakin* (it shall stand) and *Boaz* (in strength), presumably from the first words of inscriptions carved on them. The temple vestibule measured about 15 feet (4.6 meters) by 30 feet (9.2 meters). Great wooden doors leading to the temple itself were carved with palms, flowers, and cherubim, which were winged beasts that symbolized guardianship of sacred places.

The first room of the temple proper was the *Hekal,* the Holy Place, about 45 feet (13.7 meters) high, 60 feet (18.3 meters) long, and 30 feet (9.2 meters) wide. Light entered through windows at the top of the walls, which were paneled in cedarwood (the famous cedars of Lebanon) richly carved in floral motifs. This main room contained sacred furnishings appropriate for the cult of God. There were ten large lampstands, five on each side of the hall. To one side was an inlaid table for the priestly offerings of bread (the "shewbread" of the Bible), and at the far end of the room, directly in front of a small set of steps, was a cedarwood altar covered with gold for the offering of incense. The room as a whole—with its rich odors of incense and cedarwood, its filtered light and flickering lamplight, its soft burnished gold furnishings—was designed to give a sense of the sacredness of the place befitting the presence of God [31].

30 Reconstruction drawing of Solomon's Temple. The significance of the two bronze pillars is uncertain, but some scholars suggest that they may have represented the twin pillars of fire and smoke that guided the Israelites during their wanderings in the desert after the Exodus.

31 Reconstruction cutaway drawing of Solomon's Temple. Used with permission from Bernhard W. Anderson, *Understanding the Old Testament* (3rd ed., 1975). The Temple had a court with gates for public worshipers and another court that connected with Solomon's palace next to the Temple.

37

32 Cherubim guarding a citadel gate, Khorsabad, Iraq. Assyrian, c. 725 B.C. Winged animals with human faces are often found in the art of the Canaanites, Hittites, Mesopotamians, Assyrians, and Egyptians. For scale, note the man standing at right.

Steps directly in front of the incense altar led to the most sacred spot of the Temple; the Holy of Holies. This windowless cubicle, 30 feet (9.2 meters) square, contained the ancient Ark of the Covenant, which the Jews had carried during their sojourn in the wilderness as a sign of God's presence among them. The Ark rested on the floor flanked by two great carved cherubim made from olivewood covered with gold. The cherubim took up nearly all the space in the Holy of Holies, since each wing was about 7 ½ feet (2.29 meters) long. Cherubim, common in the art of the time, were variously shown with human or animal faces. They were guardians not only of sacred places but even of cities [32].

The Temple of Solomon, though it was the crowning achievement of his reign, was also a costly one—economically, socially, and politically. The forced levies of workers who were either sent to Lebanon to quarry the stone (the Book of Kings mentions about thirty thousand workers involved in this project alone) or who labored on the construction site in Jerusalem demoralized the nation. Solomon spent such vast sums on this and other building projects that he was forced to cede whole villages to his creditors. These huge expenditures, of both manpower and money, split the nation after his death, and a civil war between north and south followed.

Furthermore, Solomon's activities endangered the purity of the Israelite religion. When he built the Temple, Solomon had to import artists and materials from the lands to the north. He also imported, inevitably, ideas. To a greater or lesser degree, the cult of God at the Temple thus became set in the context of Canaanite and Phoenician symbolism. Some scholars have argued that several of the Temple appurtenances, including the great "sea" and the bronze altar in the courtyard, echoed pagan symbolic motifs. The Bible itself says that in his old age Solomon was led astray and away from God, influenced by some of his foreign wives. Solomon, then, symbolized both the highest cultural achievement of Israel and the dangers prestige and cosmopolitanism could bring to it. In the centuries after Solomon, the prophets would fiercely warn against these dangers.

The civil war after Solomon's death eventually led to the establishment of the Kingdom of Israel in the north and the Kingdom of Judah (with the capital at Jerusalem) in the south. This weakened political and social situation invited outside intervention. The Kingdom of Assyria invaded and eventually destroyed the Kingdom of Israel in 721 B.C. [33]. The Kingdom of Judah, along with the holy city of Jerusalem, lasted until 587 B.C., when Jerusalem was destroyed by the Babylonians and the Jews were herded into exile.

The Jews were permitted to return to their homeland by the Persians who had conquered Babylonia. The returnees began to rebuild the Temple of Solomon sometime after 537 B.C.; it was dedicated in 515 B.C. For the next four centuries the restored Temple was in use despite repeated invasions and occupations of the country.

In 19 B.C., Herod the Great decided to rebuild the Temple again in a project that was to be lengthy. It was Herod's Temple that Jesus knew and to which the Gospels make constant reference. In fact, this Temple, one of the focal points of the Gospel narratives, assumes a deeply symbolic significance in the New Testament.

In A.D. 70, only six years after the final completion of Herod's Temple, the armies of the Emperor Vespasian, led by his son Titus, marched into Jerusalem, destroyed the city, burned down the Temple, and dispersed its inhabitants. The triumphal Arch of Titus near the Colosseum in Rome—which visitors can still see—has sculptured reliefs showing Roman

33 Attack on a walled city. Assyrian. c. 700 B.C. Gypsum bas-relief, 3'7" (1.09 m) square. British Museum, London (reproduced by courtesy of the Trustees). Note the armored archers and the covered battering ram. At upper left are naked prisoners impaled on stakes to frighten those in the city. Near them a city dweller on a turret pleads for mercy.

soldiers marching off with the booty of victory [34]. On one relief soldiers are shown carrying away the massive seven-branch candelabrum, the *menorah* [35]. The modern state of Israel uses a stylized version of the menorah for its official seal [36].

The Temple was never rebuilt, but it was never forgotten. To this day, pious Jews pray at the Western Wall of Herod's Temple—the Wailing Wall—the only part of the Temple left standing [37]. Observant Jews remember the destruction of the Temple in other ways in their religious life. Homes and synagogues maintain a *mizrah,* usually a plaque or framed print, to show the direction toward which the faithful should pray—toward Jerusalem and its Temple [38]. The destruction of Jerusalem and the Temple are recalled in other ways. The Jewish liturgical year

below: 34 *The Triumph of Titus,* from Arch of Titus, Rome, c. A.D. 81. Passageway relief.
The relief, now marred by the ravages of time, is one of those that commemorated Titus' triumphal return to Rome after the destruction of Jerusalem. (The whole arch is shown in figure **111,** page 123).

bottom: 35 *The Spoils of Jerusalem,* from Arch of Titus, Rome. c. A.D. 81. Passageway relief.
The menorah is prominent in the scene.

below: 36 Official emblem of the state of Israel. The menorah is modeled after the one on the Arch of Titus. The Hebrew word is "Israel."

bottom: 37 The Wailing Wall in Jerusalem. Observant Jews pray at this wall daily and leave petitions and prayers written on papers that they push into the crevices of the wall.

right: 38 *Mizrah*. Safed, Palestine, 1887. Lithograph on paper, 29½ × 21½″ (75 × 55 cm). Jewish Museum, New York (gift of Harry G. Friedman). The Hebrew word *mizrah* (the East) is at the top, crowned between two lions. Below is a menorah, symbol of the Temple. The lower part is a stylized representation of the Temple.

includes a day of fasting and prayer, the feast of *Tishah b'Av;* appropriately, the scriptural readings are taken from the Lamentations of the prophet Jeremiah. Jewish tradition advises observant Jews to leave a bit of their home unfinished, such as an unplastered section of wall, also in memory of Jerusalem and its Temple. Each year, at the Passover meal, Jews pray that the Passover next year will be in Jerusalem.

The destruction of Jerusalem and the Temple by the Romans had a profound impact on the later development of Judaism. Judaism did not have a geographical center after A.D. 70. The synagogue, not the Temple, became the focal point of Jewish worship. The priesthood went into decline, and the rabbis (teachers) became central to Jewish life. Jewish religious energies, under the leadership of the rabbis, became centered around the study of the biblical writings and the oral tradition that grew up around them. It was the rabbis who maintained Jewish culture and preserved the Hebrew language as a living language. They jealously guarded the integrity of the sacred text of the Bible and systematized the daily and festival liturgy, thus preventing Judaism from becoming regionalized. They also interpreted the meaning of the Law in terms of new needs and new cultural challenges. This devotion to the traditions of Israel kept Judaism alive during centuries of segregation, persecution, and dispersal. The memory of the Temple became a powerful symbol for maintaining a people as a people during their long period of exile.

The God of the Bible

When the Roman soldiers first broke into the Temple in Jerusalem, they were surprised to find that the Holy of Holies contained no cult figure. A thousand years earlier, in Solomon's Temple, the room contained only the Ark of the Covenant guarded by the cherubim. The Ark was destroyed during the Babylonian siege of Jerusalem; there is no mention of it in the historical books of the Bible after the period of the Babylonian exile. The Holy of Holies was, in fact, an empty room. The Israelites were unique among the ancient peoples of the world in maintaining a strict monotheism and a divinely sanctioned prohibition against the depiction of divinity in any art form: "You shall have no other gods before me. You shall not make yourself a graven image, or any likeness of anything that is in heaven above, or that is in the earth beneath, or that is in the water under the earth; you shall not bow down to them or serve them; for I the Lord your God am a jealous God" (Exodus 20:3–5).

The prohibition against the making of images in the Jewish religion was a clear indication of how different culturally the Jews were from their neighbors. This prohibition was a very effective way of saying that the God of Israel was different from any other god, that he was one God. God was, in fact, unknowable except as he revealed himself. Even in those revelations, he is well hidden. This was not a speculative form of monotheism. The Israelites had not come to the idea of a single God on the basis of metaphysical reason. In fact, they had no Hebrew word for philosophy. Their belief in one God was experiential. That is, their faith was certain because God had done "mighty things" for them. The reality of the one God was to be found, not in philosophy, but in history.

Who was this God? What were his characteristics? How did the Israelite concept of divinity eventually become the starting point for the great theologies of the Western religions of Judaism, Christianity, and Islam?

The Bible recognizes that the Temple is a pale attempt to represent God's presence among the people of Israel. God is beyond the confines and precincts of the Temple. That might seem like a commonplace to us (we are, after all, heirs of this tradition), but many ancient peoples believed their temples contained the exclusive presence of the divinity—the presence that guaranteed the health and well-being of the political and social order. God's presence for the ancient Israelites was far beyond the confines of a particular people or a physical structure. The second point to note is that God is passionately involved in the history of the people of Israel. He led them out of Egypt; he chose them as a special people and entered into a covenant with them; he guided them into the Promised Land.

The prayer of Solomon in I Kings 8:22–61, for instance, contains two concepts that might seem at first to be paradoxical or even contradictory: God is above all human affairs and somewhat removed from the reality of the world; in other words, God is transcendent. God is, at the same time, intimately involved with the history and the destiny of his people; indeed, as some prophets would later insist, God is concerned with the destiny of all people while maintaining a special relationship with Israel.

The relationship of God to the world and its relationship to him is further clarified by one of the most familiar passages from the Bible—the creation story that opens the Book of Genesis.

When one reads the accounts of creation in the opening chapters of the Book of Genesis a number of things become clear. First, God creates the world effortlessly by simply speaking his word over the chaos of the earth. In the creation accounts of the peoples neighboring Israel, the world is created only after a fierce battle between the gods and the forces of chaos. In the famous Babylonian creation myth, the *Enuma Elish,* Marduk defeats the goddess Ti'amat and from her dismembered carcass creates the earth and the heavens. Humanity is created by mixing the blood of another semidivinity with the clay of the earth.

Second, there is a distance between God and His creation. God existed before the creation; he was not born out of the chaos before creation, as in many Middle Eastern creation myths. Nor is any part of the creation divine. This account of creation in the Bible is careful to describe the sun and the moon as mere creations of the power of God. There is a hidden polemic in this statement, since the *Enuma Elish* depicted the heavenly bodies as images of various divinities. In the Genesis account, only God is divine. The universe of the Bible is not a divine universe; it is a created universe that comes from the power of the Divine.

Finally, God pronounces the world to be good. The Bible sees the world as neither evil nor divine. In that sense the biblical view of the world is radically different from the Hindu or Buddhist view of the material world as illusion (*maya*) to be penetrated. Nor is it the world view of many primal religions like that of the American Indian, which sees the world as divine or animated by divinity. Finally, the world view of the Bible must be distinguished from those that consider the created physical world as essentially evil.

Some scholars have suggested that one of the reasons why technology and science have been so successful in the Western world is that we are cultural heirs to a biblical tradition that has never mystified the world by considering it divine or by avoiding it as illusory. More recent writers considering ecological problems have also pointed out that the biblical view of the world has made it easier for the West to think of nature only in terms of domination and exploitation.

The Psalms

Another fruitful source in the Bible for our understanding of the image of God is "Israel's Prayer Book"—the Book of Psalms. The psalms are in our common culture not only because they are part of the

Bible but also because so much of their language has entered our heritage in our hymns, our prayer books, and our music. The psalms have provided much of our common terminology used to describe God: our refuge (Psalm 7); our strength (Psalm 18); a shepherd (Psalm 23); our light and salvation (Psalm 27); our shelter (Psalm 46); our judge (Psalm 82).

The 150 psalms in the Bible are Hebrew poems composed, for the most part, to be sung at religious services, and many were probably used in the Temple services in Solomon's time. This ancient Hebrew poetry has a rather distinctive style, characterized by *parallelism.* Parallelism means that a thought expressed in a line (or series of lines) is reexpressed in the following lines in different words. *Antithetical parallelism* means that an idea expressed in a line is contrasted in a following line with the statement of an opposite idea. The first psalm in the Book of Psalms illustrates both types of parallelism quite graphically:

> Blessed is the man
>   who walks not in the counsel of the wicked,
> nor stands in the way of sinners,
>   nor sits in the seat of scoffers.
>
> But his delight is in the law of the Lord,
>   and on his law he meditates day and night.
>
> He is like a tree
>   planted by the streams of water,
> that yields its fruit in its season,
>   and its leaf does not wither.
> In all that he does, he prospers.
>
> The wicked are not so,
>   but are like chaff which the wind drives away.
>
> Therefore the wicked will not stand in the judgment,
>   nor sinners in the congregation of the righteous.
>
> For the Lord knows the way of the righteous,
>   but the way of the wicked will perish.
>
> (Psalm 1)

The first verse of the psalm contrasts the good and wicked man; verses 2 and 3 spell out what the good man is like by antithetical parallelism. Verse 4 provides another contrast with the evil man; verse 5 (by the use of parallelism) states that the evil man will not stand, while verse 6 contrasts the fate of both the good and the evil person.

Many of the psalms were sung to musical accompaniment. We have no accurate knowledge about the musical notation of the ancient Near East. Indeed, even the musical instruments mentioned in the Bible are only imperfectly understood by comparing biblical descriptions with contemporary illustrations from neighboring cultures such as that of Egypt [39]. The Bible mentions drums, reed instruments, stringed instruments such as the lyre and harp, and horns of various kinds. In the Book of Psalms there are some tantalizing, but fragmentary, notations in the text about musical usage. Some psalms (for example, 4, 6, 54, 55) are to be accompanied by strings, Psalm 5 by the flute, and Psalm 8 "with the harp of Gath." Other psalms have notations that seem to indicate that they were to be sung to a certain melody (for example, 57, 58, 59), but those melodies are lost to us. The word *selah* at the head of a number of psalms may have indicated a musical mode, but its meaning is total conjecture. A large number of the psalms seem to have been used for specific purposes in the public worship of Israel: mourning, thanksgiving, praise of God, and so on.

It is generally recognized that many of the psalms were used for ritual purposes, especially in the Tem-

ple worship at Jerusalem. Many of the psalms express a deep awareness of the individual person ("The Lord is my Shepherd") or a single cry for mercy and aid ("My God, my God, why have you forsaken me?"), but there is strong evidence that many were written to be sung congregationally or antiphonally by a congregation. Some psalms are structurally antiphonal in that they repeat a single phrase after each verse, a phrase the congregation repeated in response to a leader who sang the verses. Psalm 136 is a good example of this kind of liturgical psalm.

39 The Blind Harper of Leiden, detail from the tomb of Patenemheb. Saqqara, c. 1340–1330 B.C. Limestone bas-relief, height 11½" (29 cm). Rijksmuseum van Oudheden, Leiden, Netherlands. The instrument may be similar to the harp mentioned in the Book of Psalms.

O give thanks, to the Lord, for he is good,
  for his steadfast love endures forever.
O give thanks to the God of gods,
  for his steadfast love endures forever.
O give thanks to the Lord of Lords,
  for his steadfast loves endures forever.

to him who alone does great wonders,
  for his steadfast love endures forever.
to him who by understanding made the heavens,
  for his steadfast love endures forever.
to him who spreads out the earth upon the waters,
  for his steadfast love endures forever.
to him who made the great lights,
  for his steadfast love endures forever.
the sun to rule over the day,
  for his steadfast love endures forever.
the moon and the stars to rule over the night,
  for his steadfast love endures forever.

(From Psalm 136)

The Book of Psalms has continued to be the hymnbook and prayer book of both Judaism and Christianity. Psalms make up a large part of the daily worship of devout Jews. The weekly singing of the entire Book of Psalms is at the heart of Christian monastic worship. The many beautiful illustrated psalters that have been preserved from the Middle Ages testify to the central importance of the psalms in Christianity. During the Reformation the psalms were considered the chief source of formal prayer for the church. The first book printed in the English colonies in North America was the *Bay Psalm Book* [40]. To this day, even outside the church, the psalms continue to inspire; for example, there are Igor Stravinsky's *Symphony of Psalms* of 1930 (based on the Latin Vulgate version of the psalms) and Leonard Bernstein's *Chichester Psalms* of 1965 (based on the Hebrew text of the psalms).

The Book of Job

However close God is to his people, he is ultimately beyond human comprehension. The mysteriousness of God's relationship to humanity is described with poetic intensity in the Book of Job. The Book of Job (written probably after the 5th century B.C.) is the only example of dialogue genre in Hebrew literature. The prologue of the book, which sets the stage for the dialogue itself, describes Job, a pious and holy man, reduced from great wealth to abject poverty and from health to leprosy so that God can test Job's faith to quiet the jibes of a skeptic Satan. Job refuses either to curse God or deny his faith in him.

The great bulk of the book records the speeches of the friends of Job as they come to "comfort" him in his affliction. To each of their explanations of his state of dejection and misery Job answers with contrary evidence to refute them. The crux of this argument is in the form of a dilemma: suffering is visited on the impious as a punishment from God, but, since

40 Title page of the *Bay Psalm Book.* Cambridge, Massachusetts, 1640. Rare Books and Manuscripts Division, New York Public Library. Note that the title page describes an introductory essay that insists on the "lawfullnes" and "necessity" of singing the psalms in church worship.

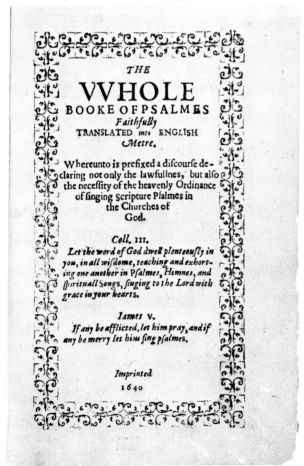

Job is just, why does he suffer? His friends maintain that he must be guilty before God and they advise Job to confess this fact. Job vehemently insists on his innocence before God. Since the Hebrew religion had no clear idea of heaven, it was not possible for Job to argue that he would be rewarded in the next life. Indeed, the whole power of the book comes precisely from the fact that there is only this life and "fairness" would seem to demand that the just should flourish. In chapters 32–37, a rather bumptious young man, Elihu, approaches Job to expound the educative and moral values of suffering. Job, however, will have none of it.

At the end of the book, God enters the dialogue "out of the whirlwind." In the hand of a lesser artist God would then have solved Job's theological problem, but, as the British writer G. K. Chesterton once said, the enigmas of God are even darker than the enigmas of Job. Rather than answer Job's questions about his sufferings, God puts a further question to him: How can you plumb the mystery of human suffering when you cannot even begin to grasp the very fact of existence? Strangely enough, the skepticism of God comforts Job more than the rationalizations of his friends. God's challenge does not answer Job's questions; it merely gives Job a way of living with them. Job is to see life not as a problem to be solved but a mystery to be lived.

The Book of Job, as difficult and, in some ways, as atypical a book as one can find in the Bible, has been a favorite for modern interpretations. Archibald MacLeish even rewrote it as a stage play in 1958 under the title of *J.B.* Job is a very "existentialist" work. It poses God as a "problem." (How can a just God afflict a good person?) It depicts human beings as urgent searchers after the meaning of existence. (The proverbial "patience of Job" is wide of the mark; Job was outraged at his situation and wanted it changed as quickly as possible.) Finally, the Book of Job takes on the most persistent problem of philosophy and theology: Why is there evil in the world? Beyond that, the Book of Job contains some of the most powerful poetry in the Hebrew Bible. The concluding chapters (Job 38–42), in which God speaks to Job of the wonders of creation and receives Job's repentance for questioning his intent, are unparalleled in their strength and majesty.

The Prophets: God and History

The word "prophet" derives from the Greek *prophetes,* one who speaks for another. That etymological meaning is as good a definition of the biblical prophet as one could hope for: the prophet is one who speaks for God. We normally think of the prophet as one who foretells the future or reveals secret knowledge. Though the biblical prophets did speak of an ideal future age, this was not their primary task or their function in Israelite religion. The Hebrew concept of the prophet was a unique contribution to the history of religion. The prophet was not a seer or an oracle or a diviner but a spokesman for God. This prophetic understanding of religion was to have a profound and lasting influence on the subsequent development of Western religion and culture.

Prophets were not a hereditary religious caste of functionaries as were the priests who received their office by virtue of their birth into the tribe of Levi. Nor were the prophets ordained or commissioned for their task by some religious hierarchy. Prophets felt themselves called by God in unique and mysterious ways. Furthermore, they had no special training for their tasks and, in some cases, were reluctant to undertake the duty of prophetism. The Bible records highly sacred and awe-inspiring language to describe the prophetic call, as Isaiah 6 and the opening chapters of Jeremiah and Ezechiel so vividly demonstrate.

All these prophets lived after the division of the monarchy following the death of Solomon. In the period before and during the united monarchy, prophetism seems to have had more of an ecstatic character—prophets spoke in trances or to the accompaniment of music. The prophets tended to belong to schools or guilds and were more likely to be attached, though unofficially, to shrines or royal households. In the period of classical prophetism—from the 8th century B.C. on—the office of the prophet developed some unique and distinctive characteristics.

For one thing, the prophets persistently emphasized ethical monotheism together with some tension with (and, indeed, opposition to) the official religion of the priestly worship of the temple and the shrines. The classical prophets tended to think more in universal terms and less in exclusive, nationalistic terms. The classical prophets all affirmed the ancient covenant that God had made with the people of Israel ("I will be your God, you shall be my people"), but they had a clearer sense that the God of Israel was destined to be the God of all people: "And you will say in that day: 'Give thanks to the Lord, call upon his name; make known his deeds among the nations, proclaim that his name is exalted. Sing praises to the Lord, for he has done gloriously; let this be known in all the earth. Shout, and sing for joy, O inhabitant of Zion, for great in your midst is the Holy One of Israel'" (Isaiah 12:4–6).

Finally, the prophets were passionate preachers of social justice. They felt called directly by God; they were commanded to preach. Some prophets were reluctant to take up the task given them. Most of the prophetic utterances began with the stylized phrase "Thus says the Lord" or "This is the word of the Lord." Precisely because they mediated God's word they felt no social or political restraint on the content of their message. They were called to reprove, correct, and bring back an errant people who were not faithful to the Israelite covenant with God. For that reason they saw in the foreign oppression of their own people a moral evil that affronted the majesty of God's prior intervention on behalf of the people of Israel. Their language could at times be stinging and unyielding as a reading of a prophet like Amos so clearly shows.

Hate evil, and love good,
    and establish justice in the gate;
it may be that the Lord, the God of hosts,
    will be gracious to the remnant of Joseph.

Therefore thus says the Lord, the God of hosts, the
        Lord:
"In all the squares there shall be wailing;
    and in all the streets they shall say, 'Alas! alas!'
They shall call the farmers to mourning
    and to wailing those who are skilled in lamentation,
and in all vineyards there shall be wailing,
    for I will pass through the midst of you," says the
        Lord.

Woe to you who desire the day of the Lord!
    Why would you have the day of the Lord?
It is darkness, and not light;
    as if a man fled from a lion,
    and a bear met him;
or went into the house and leaned with his hand
        against the wall,
    and a serpent bit him.
Is not the day of the Lord darkness, and not light,
    and gloom with no brightness in it?

"I hate, I despise your feasts,
    and I take no delight in your solemn assemblies.
Even though you offer me your burnt offerings and
        cereal offerings,
    I will not accept them,
and the peace offerings of your fatted beasts
    I will not look upon.
Take away from me the noise of your songs;
    to the melody of your harps I will not listen.
But let justice roll down like waters,
    and righteousness like an everflowing stream."
                                                (Amos 5:14–24)

Needless to say, the prophets were not popular with the ruling elite of Israel. Centuries after the age of the classical prophets Jesus would say: "O Jerusalem, Jerusalem, killing the prophets and stoning those who are sent to you!" (Matthew 23:37), echoing the long-held tradition of Israel that the ancient prophets had all died violent deaths because of the severity of their reforming message.

The prophetic message was characterized by its tone of moral censure, its constant threat of divine displeasure, and its call for conversion to the obligations of its religious heritage. The prophetic role of direct mediator of God's word and will to an errant people is a hallmark of Jewish religiousness. One cannot understand the picture of Jesus in the New Testament without reference to it. The tension between Jesus' scrupulous observance of Jewish law and temple ritual and his fierce denunciations of the Jewish rulers is understandable only in light of the prophetic tradition of Israel. When Jesus drove the money-changers from the temple he quoted from both the prophets Isaiah and Jeremiah about the sanctity of God's house and the turning of it into a den of thieves. Perhaps nowhere in the New Testament is the prophetic sense of social justice, ethical religion, and a passion for religious purity so clear as in the famous Sermon on the Mount in the fifth chapter of the Gospel of Matthew.

The later history of Western culture gives ample evidence that the style of prophetic religion has persisted through the ages. It usually appears as a protest "in the name of God" against the vested religious or social powers of the day. When an institution becomes encrusted with privilege or complacency, a prophetic figure may come along to denounce and reform that institution in the name of God and the imperatives of God's justice. Martin Luther's protest against the immobility and decadence of the medieval church may be seen as a prophetic movement, as may the earlier attempts of Saint Francis of Assisi to preach poverty to a materialistic religious culture.

One person of our own era who understood and adopted the prophetic style of religious protest was Martin Luther King, Jr. When King was in jail in Birmingham, Alabama, as a result of his struggle for the civil rights of black Americans, he wrote a letter to white religious leaders of the city who had accused him of stirring up divisive violence in the city. King's famous letter consciously referred to the prophetic right of the biblical preacher to refuse injustice and to denounce evils. Note the appeal to the prophets in the third paragraph of his "Letter from Birmingham Jail":

April 16, 1963

My Dear Fellow Clergymen:
    While confined here in the Birmingham city jail, I came across your recent statement calling my present activities "unwise and untimely." Seldom do I pause to answer criticism of my work and ideas. If I sought to answer all the criticisms that cross my desk, my secretaries would have little time for anything other than such correspondence in the course of the day, and I would have no time for constructive work. But since I feel that you are men of genuine good will and that your criticisms are sincerely set forth, I want to try to answer your statement in what I hope will be patient and reasonable terms.

    I think I should indicate why I am here in Birmingham, since you have been influenced by the view which argues against "outsiders coming in." I have the honor of serving as president of the Southern Christian Leadership Conference, an organization operating in every southern state, with headquarters in Atlanta, Georgia. We have some eighty-five affiliated organizations across the South, and one of them is the Alabama Christian Movement for Human Rights. Frequently we share staff, educational and financial resources with our affiliates. Several months ago the affiliate here in Birmingham asked us to be on call to engage in a nonviolent direct-action program if such were deemed necessary. We readily consented, and when the hour came we lived up to our promise. So I, along with several members of my staff, am here because I was invited here. I am here because I have organizational ties here.

    But more basically, I am in Birmingham because injustice is here. Just as the prophets of the eighth century B.C. left their villages and carried their "thus saith the Lord" far beyond the boundaries of their home towns, and just as the Apostle Paul left his village of Tarsus and carried the gospel of Jesus Christ to the far corners of the Greco-Roman world, so am I compelled to carry the gospel of freedom beyond my own home town. Like Paul, I must constantly respond to the Macedonian call for aid.

    Moreover, I am cognizant of the interrelatedness of all communities and states. I cannot sit idly by in Atlanta and not be concerned about what happens in Birmingham. Injustice anywhere is a threat to justice everywhere. We are caught in an inescapable network of mutuality, tied in a single garment of destiny. Whatever affects one directly, affects all indirectly. Never again can we afford to live with the narrow, provincial "outside agitator" idea. Anyone who lives inside the United States can never be considered an outsider anywhere within its bounds.

King's beliefs and his public life had many of the characteristics of the prophetic style. He preached that civil rights come from God; he, like many of the prophets, symbolized his message by dramatic action. As the prophets of old walked naked through a town or shattered pots to show the future of the land of Israel, so King led boycotts, sit-ins, and parades.

King also shared another characteristic with some classical prophets: he died a violent death because of his beliefs.

The Cultural Significance of the Biblical Period

In some ways Solomon is a lesser figure in the biblical tradition than some of the other Hebrew heroes. He was not the father of his people that the patriarch Abraham was. He pales against the mighty figure of the lawgiver Moses. His *persona* is neither as complex nor as attractive as that of his father, King David. He certainly lacked the moral rigor and religious intensity of Jeremiah or Isaiah. Nonetheless, Solomon is a pivotal figure in the history of Israel. In a sense, he stands as a complex symbol of Israel's contribution to later Western culture.

Solomon's reign was the high-water mark of ancient Israel's cultural power. Before his time there was an ascending line of development from tribal origins to a powerful and opulent monarchy. After his time there was a descending line of civil disorder, division, conquest, and subservience. He reshaped the city of Jerusalem, giving it a symbolic character that persists to this day. By building the first great Temple in Jerusalem, he institutionalized the considerable strengths of biblical religion. It was because of the increased power and pressure of the Temple cult that the ancient stories and tales about the patriarchs, the Exodus, and the penetration of the land of Palestine began to be shaped into a literary whole.

Most scholars believe that it was during the period of David and Solomon that the scattered, and largely oral, tradition of Israel began to be remolded into a literary tradition. In short, the Bible, as we know it today, first began to take its present form during the times of Solomon. If the Temple was a great historical achievement, the creative energies unleashed by it resulted in one of Israel's most permanent gifts to our culture: the Bible.

It was the formalism, the richness, and the expensive complexity of the temple cult that the prophets devoted much of their energies to attacking. They did not reject the worship of the Temple (Isaiah, after all, was called while praying in the Temple), but they demanded that it be purified and brought into line with the ethical obligations of the ancient Hebrew covenant. In other words, classical prophetism can only be understood against the background of the priestly religion of the Temple and its later development. A millennium after Solomon, in the stories of Jesus preserved in the New Testament, we can still detect the strong dialectical tension between Temple and prophetism. The public life of Jesus is intelligible only against the long historical tradition of both Temple and prophetic traditions.

As we have already noted, Solomon's reign also bore within it the seeds of social decline and the destruction of the united kingdom. The invasions of the Northern and Southern Kingdoms, the periods of exile and return, the building and rebuilding of the Temple—all contributed to the mighty sense of nostalgia that the people of Israel felt (and still feel) for Jerusalem and its ancient Temple. With the destruction of the Second Temple in A.D. 70, Jerusalem became, not a home for the Jews, but the object of their dreams. "Next year in Jerusalem" they prayed each year during centuries of exile. Nobody can understand the volatile situation in the Middle East without understanding the long Jewish memory of the glory of Jerusalem and its Temple and the hope for their restoration.

Finally, Solomon's achievements made Jerusalem the center of Israel's religion. Jerusalem and its Temple marked the stable point of ancient Israel's life and culture. It is from that center that the great tradition of monotheistic religion in the West springs. Judaism, Christianity, and Islam are all religions of the Book. They all look back to Abraham as to a common father. Islam was born in the deserts of Arabia, but the Prophet ended his days in Jerusalem. Christianity was born in the streets and around the sacred precincts of Jerusalem itself. The modern visitor to Jerusalem sees that quickly and clearly. In the old city of Jerusalem, surrounded by the Crusader walls of the Middle Ages, in ten minutes one can walk to major shrines of the three great faiths of the West: the Church of the Holy Sepulchre, the Western Wall of Herod's Temple, and, on what was once the Temple mount, the Dome of the Rock, a magnificent mosque that marks the spot where tradition has it the Prophet Mohammed ascended to heaven [41]. The swirling crowd of Hasidic Jews, Franciscan friars, veiled Moslem women, pilgrims, Orthodox monks, pious rabbis, and caftaned mullahs tells more about the lasting significance of Jerusalem than words can convey.

By the standards of the great cultures against which we must study the history of Israel—the cultures of Egypt, Assyria, Babylonia, and Persia—the achievement of Solomon for "all his glory" was not impressive. His building program would have been unthinkable without the aid and technology of his neighbors to the North, the Phoenicians. Nor did his reign sustain itself for very long. At the level of human culture, Israel in general and Solomon in particular made no lasting contribution to the great monuments of civilization if one excepts the Bible, which began to take shape during Solomon's time. "If one excepts the Bible . . ." That is a monumentally important "if." The contribution of Israel was precisely in that collection of writings that we call the Bible and the ideas that those writings contain.

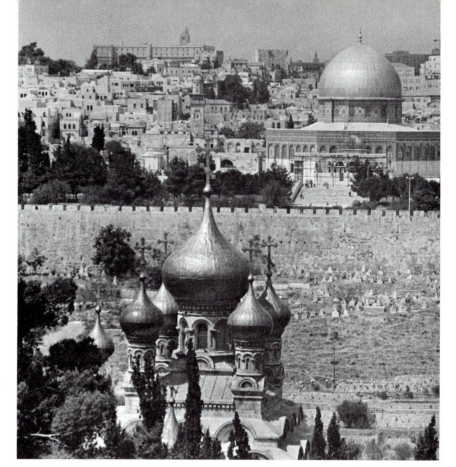

41 Jerusalem. The Moslem Dome of the Rock is in the background, with the old city to the left of and behind it. Below the wall is a Jewish cemetery in the Kidron Valley. In the foreground is the Russian Orthodox Church of Saint Mary Magdalene. This view graphically shows the presence of the three major Western faiths in Jerusalem.

This chapter on Jerusalem precedes the two chapters that deal with the far more advanced civilization of Greece. In Greece we find the origins of our politics, philosophy, science, and literary culture. Yet when these two cultures began to merge, much later in history, indeed when Solomon was already a proverbial figure, the tradition of Israel was a determinative factor in the shaping of the ideals and values of the West. The God of this rather insignificant people, cradled in the none-too-loving embrace of hostile civilizations, energized the art and architecture of the Western world and was the fount for the two great religions of the West. The theological culture of Israel provided the ethical ideal of a tradition that is now nearly three thousand years old.

Questions for Further Discussion

1. Solomon's Temple was designed as a space for the God of Israel to inhabit. Churches and synagogues are built as spaces for worshipers. In what basic way do you think architects modify their buildings to reflect these two different attitudes? Since Greek temples were also dwelling places for gods and goddesses, are they functionally close to a temple like that of Solomon?

2. Throughout the Psalms (and other books of the Bible) God is given many titles like "king," "shepherd," "Father," etc. What do these titles say about the nature of Hebrew culture? Do feminist critics of Hebrew religion have a case when they argue that divine imagery in the Bible is too unremittingly masculine?

3. The Book of Job raises the question of the meaning of suffering. Do you accept the notion that suffering is ultimately a mystery about which we can say little, or would you prefer to make a statement about your own understanding of evil in the world? If you were to recast the Job story into modern terms, where would you set the story? Who would make up your cast of characters?

4. The prophets, through fierce language and symbolic action, called down God's judgment on an erring world. Can you imagine a contemporary prophet? How would he or she act out a prophetic message for our age? What do you suspect would be the subject of divine denunciation today?

5. Read through one of the gospels in the New Testament. Note the significant references to the psalms, the Temple, the general teachings of the Hebrew scriptures. To what degree does Jesus conform to the idea of the Hebrew prophet?

6. Find out more about modern Jerusalem as the city of the three great monotheistic faiths—Judaism, Christianity, and Islam. How do religious concerns affect the politics of the city?

	GENERAL EVENTS	LITERATURE & PHILOSOPHY	ART

BRONZE AGE

3000 B.C.

Mycenaean Period

c. 1184 Fall of Troy

1100

Dark Age

1100 Collapse of Mycenaean Empire

1000

1000 Development of Iron Age culture at Athens

Heroic Age

900–700 Greeks begin colonizing in East and Italy

c. 900–700 Evolution of Homeric epics *Iliad* and *Odyssey*

1000–900 Protogeometric pottery decoration: bold circular shapes similar to Mycenaean motifs

776 First Olympic Games

c. 775 First Greek colony in Italy founded at Pithekoussai

8th cent. Hesiod, *Works and Days* and *Theogony*

900–700 Geometric pottery decoration: linear designs of zigzags, triangles, diamonds, meanders

750

750–600 Greeks found colonies throughout Mediterranean, from Egypt to Black Sea

c. 700 Greeks adapt Phoenician alphabet for their own language

8th cent. Geometric pottery incorporates stylized human figure in painted design; Dipylon amphora

c. 650 Large freestanding sculpture evolves

IRON AGE (1000 B.C. –)

Age of Colonization

late 7th cent. Orientalizing styles in vase painting; Corinthian aryballos

c. 600 *New York Kouros*; Athenians develop narrative style in black-figure vase painting; increased naturalism in Greek art

600

c. 590 Solon reforms Athenian constitution

early 6th cent. Sappho, *Poems*

c. 550 *Calf-Bearer*
c. 540 *Peplos Kore*
c. 530 *Anavysos Kouros*
c. 525 Exekias, *Suicide of Ajax*, amphora

Archaic Period

546 Rule of Pisistratus begins growth of Athenian power; Persian Empire expands to take over Greek colonies in Asia Minor

6th cent. Development of Presocratic schools of philosophy: Materialists, Pythagoreans, Dualists, Atomists

late 6th cent. Playwriting competition begins

510 Restoration of democracy at Athens

after 525 First official version of Homeric epics written

late 6th cent. Red-figure style of vase painting introduced; *Euphronios Vase*, krater

490 Start of the Persian Wars; forces of King Darius defeated at Marathon

c. 490 *Critian Boy*; turning point between Archaic and Classical periods

480

Classical Period

480 Xerxes leads a second expedition against Greece; wins battle of Thermopylae and sacks Athens; Greeks defeat Persians decisively at Salamis

479 Greek victories at Plataea and Mycale end Persian Wars

c. 440 Herodotus begins *History of the Persian Wars*

323

Many dates are approximate

3

Early Greece

Early music primarily vocal with instrumental accompaniment; use of flute and simple lyre popular

7th cent. Development of aulos, used to accompany songs

c. 600 Form of Doric temple fully established, derived from early wooden structures; Temple of Hera at Olympia

c. 675 Terpander of Lesbos popularizes cithara

c. 550 Basilica at Paestum

c. 540 Temple of Apollo at Corinth

c. 500 Temple of Aphaia, Aegina

586 Sacadas of Argos composes first known purely instrumental work for performance on aulos at Pythian Games in Delphi

c. 550 Pythagoras discovers numerical relationship of music harmonies and our modern musical scale

5th cent. First widespread use of Ionic order

late 5th cent. Earliest surviving fragment of Greek music

One of the major turning points of history is the period around 1000 B.C., the change from the Bronze Age to the Iron Age throughout the Mediterranean area. In the following centuries a culture developed in a small corner of southeastern Europe, Greece, which was to form the foundation of Western civilization. By the 5th century B.C., this culture had produced one of the greatest eras of human achievement.

In certain basic ways, of course, there was some continuity between the Bronze Age and the Iron Age. For example, Athens, which in the 5th century B.C. became the intellectual center of Classical Greece, had been a Mycenaean city long before the Iron Age began. In most significant respects, however, the Iron Age Greeks had to discover for themselves almost all the cultural skills associated with civilization—the visual arts, architecture, literature, philosophy, even the art of writing. The Mycenaeans had known how to write and build and create art. However, their abrupt and violent end around 1100

42 *Zeus (Poseidon?).* c. 465 B.C. Bronze, height 6'10" (2.08 m). National Archaeological Museum, Athens. Whether this striding god is Zeus or Poseidon, god of the sea, the combination of majestic dignity and physical strength reflects the Greeks' view of their gods as superior beings with definitely human attributes. This statue, which was found in the sea off Cape Artemisium, comes from the end of the period of this chapter; it may have been intended to commemorate the Greek victory over the Persians.

B.C. was followed by a century of disturbance and confusion that cut off the Bronze Age from the new world of the Iron Age. To follow the first attempts of these Iron Age people to develop an artistic style, organize their societies, and question the nature of the universe is to witness the birth of Western culture.

The history of early Greece falls naturally into three periods, each marked by its own distinctive artistic achievement. During the first three hundred years or so of the Iron Age, development was slow and the Greeks had only limited contact with other Mediterranean peoples. During this period the first great works of literature were created—the epic poems known as the *Iliad* and the *Odyssey*. Because these works treat heroic themes, the early Iron Age in Greece is sometimes known as the Heroic Age.

By the beginning of the 8th century B.C. Greek travelers and merchants had already begun to explore the lands to the east and west. In the next 150 years (c. 750–600 B.C.), called the Age of Colonization, many new ideas and artistic styles were brought to Greece. These foreign influences were finally absorbed in the third era of early Greece known as the Archaic period (c. 600–480 B.C.). This period, the culmination of the first five hundred years of Greek history, paved the way for the Classical period, discussed in Chapter 4. The Greeks' relationship to the world around them took a decisive turn at the very end of the Archaic period with their victory over the Persians in the wars that lasted from 490 to 479 B.C. The events of the Persian Wars thus end this chapter.

The Heroic Age

During the Mycenaean period most of Greece had been united under a single influence. When the Mycenaeans fell, however, Greece split up into a series of independent regions that corresponded to the geographically separated areas created by the mountain ranges and high hills that crisscross the terrain. Within each of these geographically discrete areas there developed an urban center that controlled the surrounding countryside. Thus Athens became the dominating force in the geographical region known as Attica; Thebes controlled Boeotia; Sparta controlled Laconia, and so on (see map, page 54). A central urban community of this kind was called by the Greeks of a later period a *polis*, a term generally translated as "city-state."

The polis served as focal point for all political, religious, social, and artistic activities within its region. Its citizens felt toward their own individual city a loyalty that was far stronger than any generalized sense of community with their fellow Greeks over the mountains. Each of the leading cities developed its own artistic style, which led to fierce competition and in time bitter and destructive rivalries. The polis was, therefore, both the glory and the ruin of Greek civilization, producing on the one hand an unequaled concentration of intellectual and cultural development, on the other a tendency to internal squabbling at the least provocation.

The fragmentation of social and cultural life had a marked effect on the development of Greek mythology and religion. Religion played an important part in Greek life, as Greek art and literature demonstrate, but it was very different in nature from the other religions that influenced our culture, Judaism and Christianity. For one thing, Greek mythology offers no central body of information or teaching corresponding to the Old or New Testaments. Often there are varying versions of the same basic story; even when these versions do not actually contradict one another, they often are difficult to reconcile. For another thing, the very characters of the Greek gods and goddesses often seem confused and self-contradictory. For example, Zeus, President of the Immortals and Father of gods and humans, generally represented the concept of an objective moral code to which both gods and mortals were expected to conform; Zeus imposed justice and supervised the punishment of wrongdoers [42]. Yet this same majestic ruler was also involved in many love affairs and seductions, in the course of which his behavior was often undignified and even comical. How could the Greeks have believed in a champion of morality whose own moral standards were so lax?

The answer lies in the fact that Greek myth and religion of later times consist of a mass of folk tales, primitive customs, and traditional rituals that grew up during the Heroic Age and were never developed into a single unified system. Individual cities had their own mythological traditions, some of them going back to the Bronze Age, others gradually developing under the influence of neighboring peoples. Poets and artists felt free to choose the versions that appealed to their own tastes or helped them to express their ideas. Later Greeks, it is true, tried to organize all these conflicting beliefs into something resembling order. Father Zeus ruled from Mount Olympus, where he was surrounded by the other principal Olympian deities. His wife Hera was the goddess of marriage and the protectress of the family. His daughter Athena symbolized intelligence and understanding. Aphrodite was the goddess of love, Ares, her lover, the god of war, and so on. But the range and variety of the Greek imagination defied

Ancient Greece

this kind of categorization. The Greeks loved a good story, and so tales that did not fit the ordered scheme continued to circulate.

These contradictions were, of course, perfectly apparent to the Greeks themselves, but they used their religion to illuminate their own lives, rather than to give them divine guidance. One of the clearest examples is the contrast that Greek poets drew between the powers of Apollo and Dionysus, two of the most influential of their gods. Apollo represented logic and order, the power of the mind; Dionysus was the god of the emotions, whose influence, if excessive, could lead to violence and disorder. By worshiping both these forces, the Greeks were acknowledging their obvious dual existence in human nature and trying to strike a prudent balance between them.

The Greek deities served many purposes, therefore, but these purposes were very different from those of the other Western religions. No Greek god, not even Zeus, represents supreme good. At the other end of the moral scale, there is no Greek figure of supreme evil corresponding to the Christian concept of Satan. The Greeks turned to their deities for explanations of both natural phenomena and psychological characteristics they recognized in themselves. At the same time they used their deities as yet another

way of enhancing the glory of their individual city-states, as in the case of the cult of Athena at Athens. Problems of human morality required human, rather than divine, solutions. The Greeks turned to art and literature, rather than prayer, as a means of trying to discover them.

The Earliest Greek Literature: Homer and His World

At the beginning of Greek history stand two epic poems which even the quarrelsome Greeks themselves saw as national, indeed universal, in their significance. The *Iliad* and the *Odyssey* have, from the time of the Greeks, been held in the highest esteem. Homer, their accepted author, is generally regarded as not only the first figure in the Western literary tradition but also one of the greatest. Yet even though Homer's genius is beyond doubt, little else about him is clear. In fact, the many problems and theories connected with the Homeric epics and their creator are generally summed up under the label, "the Homeric Question."

The ancient Greeks themselves were not sure who had composed the *Iliad* and the *Odyssey,* when and where the author had lived, or even if one person was left: **Plate 4** *Peplos Kore*. c. 540 B.C. Marble, height 4′ (1.21 m). Acropolis Museum, Athens. The statue is identified by the woolen peplos or mantle the woman is wearing over her dress. The missing left arm was extended. The Greeks painted important parts of their stone statues; traces of paint show here.

above: **Plate 5** Euphronios, painter; Euxitheos, potter. Red-figure calyx krater. c. 515 B.C. Terra cotta; height of vase 18″ (46 cm), diameter 21¾″ (55 cm). Metropolitan Museum of Art, New York (bequest of Joseph H. Durkee, gift of Darius Ogden Mills, and gift of C. Ruxton Love, by exchange, 1972). This masterpiece of red-figure vase painting, generally known as the *Euphronios Vase*, shows the moment when Sarpedon falls in battle during the Trojan War. As his body stiffens in agony, his wounds streaming blood, the twin gods Death (on the right) and Sleep come to his aid. The god Hermes, who leads the souls of the dead to Hades, stands sympathetically behind.

Plate 6 Basilica at Paestum. c. 550 B.C. This temple to Hera is one of the earliest surviving Greek temples. The bulging columns and spreading capitals are typical of Doric architecture in the Archaic period. (Visible through the columns and above the entablature are columns and part of the pediment of a second temple of Hera beyond, built a century later.)

responsible for both of them. In general, tradition ascribed the epics to a blind poet called Homer; almost every city worthy of the name claimed to be his birthplace. Theories about when he had lived ranged from the time of the Trojan War, around 1250 B.C., to 500 years later.

The problem of who Homer was, and even whether he existed at all, continues to vex scholars to this day. In any case most experts would probably now agree that the creation of the *Iliad* and the *Odyssey* was a highly complex affair. Each of the epics basically consists of a number of shorter folk ballads or "lays" that were combined, gradually evolving over a century or more into the works as we now know them. The first crystallization of these popular tales had probably occurred by around 800 B.C., but the poems were still not in their final form. The first written official version of each epic was probably not made before the late 6th century B.C. The edition of the poems that we now have was made by a scholar working at Alexandria in the 2nd century B.C.

Where, then, in this long development must we place Homer? He may perhaps have been the man who first began to combine the separate lays into a single whole; or perhaps he was the man who sometime after 800 B.C. imposed an artistic unity on the mass of remembered folk tales he had inherited. The differences between the *Iliad* and the *Odyssey* have suggested to a number of commentators that a different "Homer" may have been responsible for the crea-

43 Siren Painter. *Odysseus and the Sirens,* detail of red-figure vase. c. 475 B.C. Terra cotta, height of vase 13⅞″ (35 cm). British Museum, London (reproduced by courtesy of the Trustees). Odysseus is tied to the mast of his ship, at his own order, so he can resist the call of the Sirens' song. He has ordered his men to put wax in their ears.

tion or development of each work, but here we are in the realm of speculation. Perhaps after all it would be best to follow the ancient Greeks themselves, contenting ourselves with the belief that at some stage in the evolution of the poems, they were filtered through the imagination of the first great genius of the Western literary tradition, without being too specific about which stage it was.

Although the two poems are clearly the result of a single tradition, they are very different in spirit. The *Iliad* is somber, taut, direct. The concentration of its theme makes it easier to understand, and certainly easier to explain, than the more digressive and light-hearted *Odyssey*. But the *Odyssey* is certainly not a lesser work; if anything, its range and breadth of humanity are even greater, and its design is more elaborate.

The principal theme of the *Odyssey* is the return home of the Greek hero Odysseus from the war against Troy. Odysseus' journey, which takes ten years, is filled with adventures involving one-eyed giants, monsters of various kinds, a seductive enchantress, a romantic young girl, a floating island, a trip to the underworld, and many other fairy-tale elements [43]. Into this main narrative is woven a description of the wanderings of Odysseus' son, Telemachus, who, searching for his missing father, visits many of the other Greek leaders who have returned safely from Troy.

In the last half of the poem Odysseus finally returns home in disguise. Without revealing his identity to his ever-faithful wife Penelope, he kills the suitors who have been pestering her for ten years to declare her husband dead and remarry [44]. Homer keeps us waiting almost to the very end for the grand recognition scene between husband and wife. All ends happily, with Penelope, Odysseus, and his aged father Laertes peacefully reunited.

The action of the *Iliad* takes place before that of the *Odyssey*, during the final year of the Greeks' siege of Troy, or Ilium. Its subject is only indirectly concerned with the Trojan War, however, and the poem ends before the episode of the wooden horse and the fall of the city. Its principal theme is stated in the opening lines of Book I, which establish the tragic mood of the work. Here the poet invokes the goddess of poetic inspiration: "Sing, goddess, of the anger of Peleus' son Achilles, which disastrously inflicted countless sufferings on the Greeks, sending the strong souls of many heroes to Hades and leaving their bodies to be devoured by dogs and all birds. . . ."

The subject of the *Iliad*, then, is the anger of Achilles and its consequences. Its message is a direct one: We must be prepared to answer for the results of our own actions and realize that when we act wrongly we

44 Pintoricchio. *Scenes from the Odyssey.* c. 1500. Fresco transferred to canvas, 4′1½″ × 4′11¾″ (1.26 × 1.52 m). National Gallery, London. Telemachus, ignoring Penelope's suitors, is returning to his mother after a journey in search of his father. Penelope is seated at her loom. She has told the eager suitors that she will choose one of them when she finishes weaving a shroud, but each night she unravels the day's work. The ship seen through the window is of the artist's time, not at all like the Greek ship on the vase in figure **43**.

will cause suffering both for ourselves and, perhaps more importantly, for those we love. Although the setting of the *Iliad* is heroic, even mythic, the theme of human responsibility is universal.

The story of Achilles' disastrous mistake is told in a basically simple and direct narrative. It begins with a quarrel between Agamemnon, commander-in-chief of the Greek forces, and Achilles, his powerful ally, who resents Agamemnon's overbearing assertion of authority. After a public argument, Achilles decides to punish Agamemnon by withdrawing his military support and retiring to his tent, in the hope that without his aid the Greeks will be unable to defeat the Trojans. In the battles that follow he is proved correct; the Trojans inflict a series of defeats on the Greeks, killing many of their leading warriors.

Agamemnon eventually (Book IX) admits that he behaved too high-handedly and offers Achilles, through intermediaries, not only a handsome apology but a generous financial inducement to return to the fighting and save the Greek cause. Achilles, however, rejects this attempt to make amends and stubbornly nurses his anger as the fighting resumes and Greek casualties mount. Then his dearest friend Patroclus is killed by the Trojan leader Hector, son of their king (Book XVI). Only then does Achilles return to battle, his former anger against Agamemnon now turned against the Trojans in general and Hector in particular.

After killing Hector in single combat (Book XXII), Achilles maltreats Hector's corpse in order to relieve his own sense of guilt at having permitted

Patroclus' death. Finally Priam, the old king of Troy, steals into the Greek camp by night to beg for the return of his son's body (Book XXIV). In this encounter with Priam, Achilles at last recognizes and accepts the tragic nature of life and the inevitability of death. His anger melts and he hands over the body of his dead enemy. The *Iliad* ends with the funeral rites of Hector, "tamer of horses."

As is clear even from this brief summary, there is a direct relationship between human actions and their consequences. The gods appear in the *Iliad* and frequently play a part in the action, but at no time can divine intervention save Achilles from paying the price for his unreasonable anger. Furthermore, Achilles' crime is committed not against a divine code of ethics but against human standards of behavior. All his companions, including Patroclus, realize that he is behaving unreasonably.

From its earliest beginnings, therefore, the Greek tradition of morality is in strong contrast to the Judeo-Christian tradition. At the center of the Homeric universe is not God but human beings, who are at least partly in control of their own destiny. If they cannot choose the time when they die, they can at least choose how they live. The standards by which human life will be judged are those established by one's fellow humans. In the *Iliad* the gods serve as divine "umpires." They watch the action and comment on it and at times enforce the rules, but they do not effect the course of history. Humans do not always, however, fully realize the consequences of their behavior. In fact, they often prefer to believe that things happen "according to the will of the gods" rather than because of their own actions. Yet the gods themselves claim no such power. In a remarkable passage at the beginning of Book I of the *Odyssey* we see the world for a moment through the eyes of Zeus as he sits at dinner on Mount Olympus: "How foolish men are! How unjustly they blame the gods! It is their lot to suffer, but because of their own folly they bring upon themselves sufferings over and above what is fated for them. And then they blame the gods." These are hardly words we can imagine coming from the God of the Old Testament.

It is worth examining the Homeric world view at some length, because the *Iliad* and the *Odyssey* formed the basis of education and culture throughout the Greek and Roman world; children learned the two poems by heart at school. Ideas changed and developed, but reverence for Homer remained constant. Nor was this reverence limited to the ancient world. In the *Divine Comedy* (*Inferno, IV*), Dante describes Homer as the greatest of all poets. In Raphael's *Parnassus* fresco in the Vatican, he occupies a prominent position to the left of Apollo. The Ho-

meric epics have never ceased to inspire artists, musicians, and writers. One of the most important novels of the 20th century, for example, is James Joyce's *Ulysses* (Odysseus' Latin name).

The Visual Arts

Our impressions of the first three hundred years of Greek art (1000–700 B.C.) are based largely on painted pottery, hardly a major art form even in later times, for little else has survived. Of architecture there is almost no trace. Although small bronze and ivory statuettes and relief plaques were being made from the 9th century B.C. on, the earliest surviving large stone sculptures date to the mid-7th century B.C.

Painted vases, therefore, are our major source of information about artistic developments. It comes as something of a surprise to find that Homer's contemporaries decorated their pots with abstract geometric designs, with no attempt at the qualities most typical of their literature, vividness and realism. This style has given its name to the two subdivisions of the period, the Protogeometric (1000–900 B.C.) and the Geometric (900–700 B.C.).

For the first hundred years, artists decorated their vases with simple, bold designs consisting mainly of concentric circles and semicircles [45]. In some ways

45 Protogeometric amphora. c. 950 B.C. Height 21 ¾" (56 cm). Kerameikos Museum, Athens. The circles and semicircles typical of this style were drawn with a compass.

this period represents a transition from the end of the Mycenaean age, but the memory of Mycenaean motifs soon gave way to a new style. If Protogeometric pottery seems a long way from Greek art of later centuries, it does show qualities of clarity and order that reappear later, although in a very different context.

In the Geometric pottery of the following two centuries (900–700 B.C.) the use of abstract design continued, but the emphasis changed. Circles and semicircles were replaced by linear designs, zigzags, triangles, diamonds, and above all the *meander* (a maze pattern). The size of the pots increased and their shape became increasingly distorted to accommodate more and more bands of geometric design [46].

There is something strangely obsessive about many of these vessels—a sense of artists searching for a subject, meanwhile working out over and over the implications of mathematical formulas. Once again we seem a long way from the achievements of later Greek artists, with their emphasis on realism. Yet precise mathematical relationships lie behind the design of much of the greatest Greek art. The Geometric period is best thought of not as a temporary aberration, a wrong track that was abandoned, but as an expression of the obsession with order and balance so characteristic of Greek culture in general.

By the 8th century B.C., artists had begun to find their way toward the principal subject of later Greek art, the human form. Thus human and animal figures begin to appear among the meanders and zigzags. This is a moment so important in the history of Western art that we should not take it for granted. We have been so conditioned by the art of the ancient Greeks that from the late Geometric period until our own time Western art has been primarily concerned with the depiction of human beings. Landscapes are a popular subject, it is true, and in our own century art has become abstract again. Yet most paintings and sculptures deal with the human form, treated in a more or less realistic way.

This realism may seem so obvious as to be hardly worth stating, but it must be remembered that the art of peoples who were not influenced by the Greeks is very different. Islamic art, for example, deals almost exclusively in abstract design. Indian sculptors depicted their gods and heroes in human form, but they certainly did not treat them realistically. The Hindu god Shiva, for example, is often shown with many arms. It is a tribute to the Greeks' overwhelming influence on our culture that, from the Roman period to the 20th century, artists have accepted the Greeks' decision to make the realistic treatment of the human form the central focus of art, whether the forms were

46 Geometric pitcher. c. 800 B.C. Height 31¼″ (80 cm). National Archaeological Museum, Athens. The bands of decoration cover the entire surface. The lid has a handle in the form of a miniature pitcher, and it too is covered with geometric designs.

those of mortal people or divine gods and goddesses.

The Greeks themselves did not achieve this naturalism overnight. The first depictions of human beings, which appear on Geometric vases shortly after 800 B.C., are highly stylized. They are painted in silhouette, and a single figure often combines front and side views, the head and legs being shown in profile while the upper half of the body is seen from the front. Clearly these are abstractions of men and women, rather than literal depictions, although the artists do sometimes try to distinguish between the

The Age of Colonization

Throughout the period of Homer and Geometric art, individual city-states were ruled by small groups of aristocrats who concentrated wealth and power in their own hands. Presumably, it is their graves that were marked with great amphoras like the *Dipylon* vase. By the 8th century B.C., however, two developments had occurred. First, two centuries of peace had allowed the individual city-states to become quite prosperous. Second, the continuing rule of a small hereditary aristocracy left a growing urban population increasingly frustrated. Both increasing wealth and the problem of overpopulation produced a single result, colonization.

Throughout the 8th and 7th centuries, enterprising Greeks went abroad either to make their fortunes or to increase them. To the west, Italy and Sicily were colonized and Greek cities established there. Some of these, like Syracuse in Sicily or Sybaris in southern Italy, became even richer and more powerful than the mother cities from which the colonizers had come. Unfortunately, if inevitably, the settlers took with them not only the culture of their *polis* but their intercity rivalries, often with disastrous results. To the south and east, cities were also established in Egypt and on the Black Sea.

The most significant wave of colonization was that which moved eastward to the coast of Asia Minor, in some cases back to territory that had been inhabited by the Mycenaeans centuries earlier. From here the colonizers established trade contacts with peoples in the ancient Near East. Within Greece itself the effect on art and life of this expansion to the east was immense. After almost three hundred years of cultural isolation, in a land cut off from its neighbors by mountains and sea, the Greeks were brought face to face with the immensely rich and sophisticated cultures of the ancient Near East. Oriental ideas and artistic styles were seen by the colonizers and carried home by the traders. A growing quantity of eastern artifacts, ivories, jewelry, and metalwork was sent back to the mother cities and even to the Greek cities of Italy. So great was the impact of Near Eastern art on the Greeks from the late 8th century to around 600 B.C., that this period and its style are generally known by the name *Orientalizing*.

Vase Painting at Corinth and Athens

Different Greek cities reacted to Oriental influences in different ways, although all reacted strongly. In particular, the growing hostility between the two

47 *Dipylon Amphora.* c. 750 B.C. Height 4'11" (1.24 m). National Archaeological Museum, Athens. This immense vase originally was a grave marker. The main band, between the handles, shows the lying-in-state of the dead man on whose grave the vase stood; on both sides of the bier are mourners tearing their hair in grief. Note the two bands of animals, deer and running goats, in the upper part of the vase.

sexes by adding small projections below the armpits to represent female breasts.

A number of the vases decorated with stick figures of this kind are of immense size. One of them, the *Dipylon Amphora,* is almost 5 feet (1.24 meters) tall [47]. These vases were set up over tombs to serve as grave markers; they had holes in their bases so that offerings poured into them could seep down to the dead below. The scenes on them frequently show the funeral ceremony. Others show processions of warriors, both on foot and in chariots.

richest city-states, Athens and Corinth, which two centuries later led to the Peloponnesian War and the fall of Athens, seems already symbolized in the strong differences between their Orientalizing pottery. The Corinthian artists developed a miniature style that made use of a wide variety of eastern motifs—sphinxes, winged human figures, floral designs—all of them arranged in bands covering almost the entire surface of the vase. Individual figures were depicted in the so-called *black-figure technique*. They were first painted in silhouette, in black, and details were then etched in by scratching lines with a fine point. White, yellow, and purple were often used to highlight details, producing a bold and striking effect. After the monotony of Geometric pottery the variety of subject and range of color come as a welcome change.

The small size of the pots made them ideal for export. Corinthian vases have in fact been discovered not only throughout Greece but in Italy, Egypt, and the Near East. Clearly, any self-respecting woman of the 7th century B.C. wanted an elegant little Corinthian flask [48] for her perfume, oil, or make-up. The vases are well made, the figures lively, and the style instantly recognizable as Corinthian—an important factor for commercial success. Corinth's notable political and economic strength throughout the 7th and early 6th centuries B.C. was, in fact, built on the sale of these little pots and their contents.

In Athens, potters were slower to throw off the effects of the Geometric period and less able to develop an all-purpose style like the Corinthian. The vases remain large and the attempts to depict humans and animals, using a combination of the black-figure technique and freehand drawing, are often clumsy. The achievements of the later Athenian art are nonetheless clearly foreshadowed in the vitality of the figures and the constant desire of the artists to illustrate events from mythology [49] or daily life, rather than simply to decorate a surface in the Corinthian manner.

By 600 B.C. the narrative style had become established at Athens, and the full-scale use of the black-figure technique permitted the designer greater artistic control. As Athens began to take over an increasing share of the market for painted vases and their contents, Corinth's position inevitably declined, and

48 Aryballos. Middle Corinthian, c. 625 B.C. State Museums, West Berlin. This little flask held perfumed oil. The black-figure technique and the very Eastern-looking panther are characteristic of the Orientalizing style. Also characteristic are the flowerlike decorations, which are blobs of paint scored with lines. The musculature and features of the panther are also the result of scoring.

49 *The Blinding of Polyphemus*, detail of proto-Attic amphora. c. 650 B.C. Height of frieze 17″ (43 cm). Museum, Eleusis. The technique is crude, but the artist shows imagination and even humor in depicting an episode from the *Odyssey*. At the center is Odysseus himself, guiding a sharpened, heated pole into the single eye of Polyphemus, the Cyclops, seated drunkenly at the right—note the wine cup in his hand.

the trade rivalry that later had devastating results began to develop.

The Beginnings of Greek Sculpture

The influence of Near Eastern and Egyptian models on Greek sculpture is more consistent and easier to trace than on pottery. The first Greek settlers in Egypt were given land around the mid-7th century B.C. by the Egyptian pharaoh Psammetichos I. It is surely no coincidence that the earliest Greek stone sculptures, which date from about the same period, markedly resemble Egyptian cult statues, and were placed in similarly grandiose temples. (The earliest surviving temple, that of Hera at Olympia, dates at least in part to this period.) These stone figures consist of a small number of types repeated over and over. The most popular were the standing female, or *kore,* clad in drapery [50], and the standing male, or *kouros,* always shown nude [51]. This nudity already

50 *Kore* from Delos, dedicated by Nikandre. c. 650 B.C. Marble. National Archaeological Museum, Athens. Unlike the *kouros,* the figure is completely clothed, though both have the same rigid stance, arms by sides, and wiglike hair.

51 *Kouros.* c. 615 B.C. Marble, height 6'1½" (1.87 m). Metropolitan Museum of Art, New York (Fletcher Fund, 1932).

marks a break with the Egyptian tradition in which figures wore loincloths and foreshadows the heroic male nudity of Classical Greek art. The stance of the *kouros* figures, however, was firmly based on Egyptian models. One foot (usually the left) is forward, the arms are by the sides, and the hands are clenched. The elaborate wiglike hair is also Egyptian in inspiration.

By 600 B.C., only a few years after the first appearance of these statues, Greek art had reached a critical stage. After the slow and cautious progress of the Geometric period, the entire character of painting and sculpture had changed within the century following 700 B.C. Greek artists had abandoned abstract design for increasing realism. At this point in their development the Greek spirit of independence and inquiry asserted itself. Instead of following their eastern counterparts and repeating the same models and conventions for centuries, Greek painters and sculptors allowed their curiosity to lead them in a new direction, one that changed the history of art. The early stone figures and painted silhouettes had represented human beings, but only in a schematic, stylized form. Beginning in the Archaic period artists used their work to try to answer such questions as: What do human beings really look like? How do perspective and foreshortening work? What in fact is the true nature of appearance? For the first time in history they began to reproduce the human form in a way true to nature rather than merely echoing the achievements of their predecessors.

The Archaic Period

It is tempting to see the works of art and literature of the Archaic period (600–480 B.C.) as steps on the road that leads to the artistic and intellectual achievement in the Classical Age of the 5th and 4th centuries B.C. rather than to appreciate them for their own qualities. This would be to underestimate seriously the vitality of one of the most creative periods in the development of our culture. In some ways, in fact, the spirit of adventure, of striving toward new forms and new ideas, makes the Archaic achievement more exciting, if less perfected, than that of the Classical period. It is better to travel hopefully than to arrive, as Robert Louis Stevenson put it.

The change in Archaic art is, of course, a reflection of similar social changes. The hereditary aristocrats were being replaced as rulers by a new class of rich merchant traders who had made their fortunes in the economic expansion and who won power by playing on the discontent of the oppressed lower classes. These new rulers were called "tyrants"—although the word had none of the unfavorable sense that it now has. Many of them, in fact, were patrons of the arts. The most famous of them all was Pisistratus, who ruled Athens from 546–528 B.C. Clearly, revolutions like those that brought him and his fellow tyrants to power were likely to produce revolutionary changes in the arts.

Sculpture and Painting

In sculpture there was an astounding progress from the formalized *kouroi* of the early Archaic period, with their flat planes and rigid stances, to the fully rounded figures of the late 6th century, toward the end of the period. Statues like the *Anavysos Kouros* [52] show a careful study of the human anatomy. The conventions remain the same, but the statues have a new life and vigor.

Although most of the male figures are shown in the traditional stance, there are a few important exceptions. The finest is perhaps the famous *Calf-Bearer* [53] from the Athenian Acropolis (the central hill). The essential unity between man and beast is conveyed simply but with great feeling by the diagonals formed by the man's hands and the calf's legs and by the alignment of the two heads.

The finest female figures of the period also come from the Acropolis. The Persians broke them when they sacked Athens in 480 B.C., and then the Athenians buried them when they returned to their city the next year after defeating the Persians. Rediscovered by modern excavators, the figures are among the most impressive of Archaic masterpieces. They show a gradual but sure development from the earliest *korai* to the richness and variety of the work of the late 6th century, with its emphasis on elaborate drapery and delicate details [Plate 4, page 55].

In addition to these freestanding figures, two other kinds of sculpture now appeared: large-scale statues made to decorate temples and carved stone slabs. In both cases sculptors used the technique of *relief* carving: figures do not stand freely, visible from all angles, but are carved into a block of stone, part of which is left as background. In *high relief* the figures project from the background so much as to seem almost three-dimensional. In *low relief* the carving preserves the flat surface of the stone. Although the technique is generally used for stone, it can also be applied to metalwork. Temple sculpture, or as it is often called, architectural sculpture, was frequently in high relief, as in the depiction of the decapitation

52 *Kouros* from Anavysos. c. 530 B.C. Marble, height 6′4″ (1.93 m). National Archaeological Museum, Athens. Note the realism of the muscles and the new sense of power. According to an inscription on the base, this was the funerary monument to a young man, Kroisos, who had died heroically in battle.

53 *Calf-Bearer.* c. 550 B.C. Marble, height 5′5″ (1.65 m). Acropolis Museum, Athens. The archaic smile is softened in this figure. Realism appears in the displacement of the man's hair by the animal's legs and in the amazingly lifelike expression of the calf.

54 Metope showing the decapitation of Medusa.
Selinus, c. 540 B.C. Archaeological Museum, Palermo.
Medusa was a gorgon whose look turned anyone to stone.
Perseus is cutting off Medusa's head with the encouragement of
Athena, who stands at left. The gorgon's son Pegasus, the
winged horse, leaps up at her side. Medusa is shown in the
conventional pose indicating rapid motion.

of Medusa from Selinus [54]. Individual carved stone
slabs are generally in low relief. Most that have survived were used as grave markers. The workmanship
is often of a remarkable subtlety, as on the grave
stele, or gravestone, of Aristion [55].

The range of Archaic sculpture is great, and the
best pieces communicate something of the excitement of their makers in solving new problems. Almost all of them, however, have in common one feature that often disturbs the modern viewer—the
famous "archaic smile." This facial expression,
which to our eyes may seem more like a grimace, has
been explained in a number of ways. Some believe
that it is merely the result of technical inexperience
on the part of the sculptors. Others see it as a reflection of the Archaic Greeks' sense of certainty and
optimism in facing a world that they seemed increasingly able to control. Whatever its cause, by the end
of the 6th century B.C., and with the increasing threat
posed by the Persians, the archaic smile had begun to
fade. It was replaced by the more somber expression
of works like the *Critian Boy* [56]. This statue marks a
literal "turning point" between the late Archaic
world and the early Classical period. For the first

55 Aristokles. *Stele of Aristion*. c. 510 B.C. Height without base
8′ (2.44 m). National Archaeological Museum, Athens. The
leather jacket contrasts with the soft folds of the undershirt.

57 Exekias. *The Suicide of Ajax*. c. 525 B.C. Black-figure vase, height 21¼″ (54 cm). Musée des Beaux-Arts, Boulogne. Ajax buries his sword in the ground so that he can throw himself onto it. The pathos of the warrior's last moments is emphasized by the empty space around him, the weeping tree, and his now useless shield and helmet.

56 *Critian Boy*. c. 490 B.C. Marble, height 34″ (86 cm). Acropolis Museum, Athens. The archaic smile has been superseded by a more natural expression.

time in ancient art the figure is no longer looking or walking straight ahead. The head and the upper part of the body turn slightly; as they do so, the weight shifts from one leg to the other and the hips move. Having solved the problem of representing a standing figure in a realistic way, the sculptor has tackled a new and even more complex problem—showing a figure in motion. The consequences of this accomplishment were explored to the full in the Classical period.

By the mid-6th century B.C. the art of vase painting had also made great progress. Works like those of Exekias, perhaps the greatest of black-figure painters, combine superb draftsmanship and immense power of expression [57]. For so restricted a medium, vase painting shows a surprising range. If Exekias' style is serious, somber, sometimes even grim, the style of his contemporary the Amasis painter is relaxed, humorous, and charming.

The end of the 6th century B.C. marks a major development in vase painting with the introduction of the new *red-figure style*. Instead of painting the figures in black silhouette against the red clay of the vase and then etching out the details, the artist paints the background black and leaves the figures in the red color of the clay. Details are now filled in with the brush, allowing much greater variation in fineness or thickness of line. The increased subtlety made possible by this style was used to develop new techniques of foreshortening, perspective, and three-dimensionality.

Although some artists continued to produce black-figure works, by the end of the Archaic period around 525 B.C. almost all had turned to the new style. The last Archaic vase painters are among the greatest red-figure artists. Works like the *Euphronios Vase* [Plate 5, page 55], have a solidity and monumentality that altogether transcend the usual limitations of the medium.

Architecture:
The Doric and Ionic Orders

In architecture, the Archaic period was marked by the construction of a number of major temples in the Doric style or order. This order seems to have been firmly established by 600 B.C., though none of the earlier examples of the evolving style have survived. Important Doric temples include the Temple of Hera at Olympia, the Temple of Apollo at Corinth, and the earliest of the three Doric temples at Paestum, often called the Basilica (meeting hall), though it is now known to have been dedicated to the goddess Hera [Plate 6, page 56]. The Ionic style of temple architecture, which was widely used in Classical Greece, did not become fully established until later. In the Archaic period, Ionic buildings were constructed at such sites as Samos and Ephesus, but most Ionic temples date to the 5th century B.C. and later. For the sake of convenience both the Doric and Ionic orders [58] are described here.

The Doric order is the simpler and the grander of the two. Some of its characteristics seem directly derived from construction methods used in earlier wooden buildings, and its dignity is perhaps in part related to the length of its history. Doric columns have no base but rise directly from the floor of a building. They taper toward the top and have twenty flutes, or vertical grooves. The *capital,* which forms the head of each column, consists of two sections, a spreading convex disc (the *echinus*) and, above, a square block (the *abacus*). The upper part of the temple, or *entablature,* is divided into three sections. The lowest, the *architrave,* is a plain band of rectangular blocks, above which is the *frieze,* consisting of alternating *triglyphs* and *metopes*. The triglyphs are divided by grooves into three vertical bands. The metope panels are sometimes plain, sometimes decorated with sculpture or painting. The building is crowned by a *cornice,* or projecting upper part, consisting of a horizontal section and two slanting sections meeting at a peak. The long extended triangle thus formed is the *pediment,* often filled with sculptural decoration.

In contrast, the Ionic order is more graceful and

58 The Doric and Ionic orders.

more elaborate in architectural details. Ionic columns rise from a tiered base and have 24 flutes. These flutes do not meet at a sharp angle as Doric flutes do but are separated by narrow vertical bands. The capitals consist of a pair of spirals, or *volutes*. The architrave is not flat as in the Doric order but composed of three projecting bands. In place of the Doric triglyphs and metopes is a continuous band often decorated with a running frieze of sculpture.

The differences between the two orders produced different effects. The Doric order suggested simple dignity; the absence of decorative detail drew attention to the weight and massiveness of the Doric temple itself. Ionic temples, on the other hand, conveyed a sense of lightness and delicacy by means of ornate decorations and fanciful carving. The surface of an Ionic temple is as important as its structural design.

Literature: Lyric Poetry

Our knowledge of literary developments between the time of Homer and the Archaic period is very limited. An exception is Hesiod, who probably lived shortly before 700 B.C. He is the author of a poetic account of the origins of the world called the *Theogony* and a rather more down-to-earth work, the *Works and Days,* which mainly concerned the disadvantages in being a poor, oppressed (and depressed) farmer in Boeotia, where the climate is "severe in winter, stuffy in summer, good at no time of year." In the Archaic period, however, the same burst of creative energy that revolutionized the visual arts produced a wave of new poets. The medium they chose was lyric verse.

The emergence of lyric poetry was, like developments in the other arts, a sign of the times. The heroic verse of Homer was intended for the ruling class of an aristocratic society, who had the leisure and the inclination to hear of the great and not so great deeds of great men and who were interested in the problems of mighty leaders like Agamemnon and Achilles. Lyric poetry is concerned above all else with the poet's own feelings, emotions, and opinions. The poets of the 6th century B.C. do not hesitate to tell us what they themselves feel about life, death, love, drinking too much wine, or anything else that crosses their minds. Heroes and the glories of battle are no longer the ideal.

Above all other Greek lyric poets, Sappho has captured the hearts and minds of the following ages. She is the first woman to leave a literary record that reflects her own personal experiences. Her poems have survived only in fragmentary form, and the details of her life remain confused and much disputed. We must be grateful, then, for what we have and not try to overinterpret it.

Sappho was born around 612 B.C. on the island of Lesbos, where she spent most of her life. She seems to have been able to combine the roles of wife and mother with those of poet and teacher; within her own lifetime she was widely respected for her works and surrounded by a group of younger women who presumably came to Lesbos to finish their education, in much the same way that Americans used to go to Paris for a final cultural polish.

The affection between Sappho and her pupils was deep and sincere and is constantly reflected in her poems. The nature of this affection has been debated for centuries. The plain fact is that apart from her poetry we know almost nothing about Sappho herself. Even her appearance is debatable; she is described by one ancient authority as "beautiful day" and by another as short, dark, and ugly. Her fellow poet Alcaeus calls her "violet-haired, pure, and honey-smiling." Thus those who read Sappho must decide for themselves what the passion of the poems expresses, for passionate they certainly are.

Perhaps Sappho's greatest quality lies in her ability to probe the depths of her own responses and by describing them to understand them. Just as contemporary sculptors and painters sought to understand the workings of their own bodies by depicting them, so

Sappho revealed both to herself and to us the workings of her emotions.

The First Philosophers: The Presocratics

The century that saw the expression of the intimate self-revelations of lyric poetry was marked by the development of rational philosophy, which challenged the traditional religious ideas of Homer and Hesiod and scoffed at gods who took human form. If horses and cows had hands and could draw, they would draw gods looking like horses and cows, wrote Xenophanes of Colophon in the second half of the 6th century B.C. Other thinkers began to debate the nature of the universe and try to account for the diversity of the natural world with as few as possible fundamental principles.

There developed a wide variety of schools of thought originated by philosophers generally described by the somewhat confusing label *Presocratics*. The label is accurate in that they all lived and died before the time of Socrates (469–399 B.C.), who, together with his pupil Plato (c. 427–347 B.C.), is the greatest name in Greek philosophy. On the other hand, these 6th-century philosophers had little in common except the time when they lived. Thus it is important to remember that the term "Presocratic" does not describe any single philosophical system.

The earliest school to develop was that of the *Materialists,* who sought to explain all phenomena in terms of one or more elements. Thales of Miletus (c. 585 B.C.), for example, thought that water underlay the changing world of nature. Later, Empedocles of Acragas (c. 495 B.C.) introduced four elements—fire, earth, air, water. The various combinations (through love) and separations (through strife and war) of these elements in a cyclical pattern explained how creatures as well as nations were born, grew, decayed, and died. Anaxagoras of Clazomenae (c. 500 B.C.) postulated an infinite number of small particles, which, however small they might be, always contained not only a dominant substance (for example, bone or water) but also stray bits of other substances in lesser quantities. Unity in nature, he claimed, came from the force of Reason.

The Presocratic philosopher who had the greatest influence on later times was Pythagoras of Samos (c. 550 B.C.). He left his home city for political reasons and settled in southern Italy, where he founded a school of his own. He required his followers to lead pure and devout lives, uniting together to uphold morals and chastity, as well as order and harmony, for the common good. These apparently noble principles did nothing to win him favor from the people among whom he had settled; according to one account he and three hundred of his followers were killed.

It is difficult to know which of the principles of *Pythagoreanism* can be directly attributed to Pythagoras himself and which were added later by his disciples. His chief religious doctrines seem to have been belief in the transmigration of souls and the kinship of all living things, teachings that led to the development of a religious cult that bore his name. In science, his chief contribution was in mathematics. He discovered the numerical relationship of musical harmonies. Our modern musical scale, consisting of an *octave* (a span of eight tones) divided into its constituent parts, derives ultimately from his researches. Inspired by this discovery, Pythagoras went on to claim that mathematical relationships represented the underlying principle of the universe and of morality, the so-called "harmony of the spheres." He is chiefly remembered today for a much less cosmic discovery, the geometrical theorem that bears his name.

In contrast to Pythagoras' belief in universal harmony, the *Dualists* claimed that there existed two separate universes, the world around us, subject to constant change, and another ideal world, perfect and unchanging, which could only be realized through the intellect. The chief proponent of this school was Heraclitus of Ephesus (c. 500 B.C.), who summed up the unpredictable, and therefore unknowable, quality of Nature in the well-known saying, "It is not possible to step twice into the same river." But if the world were too changeable to be known directly, knowledge of the Reason by which the world works was still open to the philosopher. Similarly, Parmedides of Elea (c. 510 B.C.) went so far as to claim that all change, motion, and what we commonly call nature were but a sham and delusion, whereas true reality was all perfect, unchanging, and spherical in shape. His younger pupil, Zeno (c. 490 B.C.), presented a number of difficult paradoxes in support of their doctrines. These paradoxes were later discussed by Plato and Aristotle.

The last and perhaps the greatest school of Presocratic philosophy was that of the *Atomists,* led by Leucippus and Democritus (c. 460 B.C.), who believed that the ultimate, unchangeable reality consisted of atoms (small "indivisible" particles not obvious to the naked eye) and the void (nothingness). Atomism survived into Roman times in the later philosophy of Epicureanism (see pages 113–114) and into the 19th century in the early Atomic Theory of John Dalton. Even in our own times, the great physicist Werner Heisenberg (1901–1976), who astonished the world of science with his discoveries in quantum mechanics, derived his initial inspiration from the Greek Atomists.

Music and Dance in Early Greece

In comparison with art and literature, the history of Greek music is highly problematic. The very small quantity of evidence is as confusing as it is helpful. Although the frequent references to musical performance make it clear that music played a vital role in all aspects of Greek life, less than a dozen fragments of actual Greek music have survived; the earliest of these dates from the late 5th century B.C. Unfortunately, the problem of understanding the system of notation makes authentic performance of these fragments impossible.

Our inability to re-create even the music we have is particularly frustrating because from the earliest times music was renowned for its emotional and spiritual power. For the Greeks music was of divine origin; the gods themselves had invented musical instruments: Hermes or Apollo the lyre, Athena the flute, and so on. Many of the earliest myths told of the powerful effect of music. Orpheus could move trees and rocks and tame wild beasts by his song; the lyre playing of Amphion brought stones to life. Nor was music-making reserved for professional performers or women, as so often in later centuries. When, in Book IX of the *Iliad,* Agamemnon's ambassadors arrive at the tent of Achilles they find the great hero playing a lyre, "clear-sounding, splendid and carefully wrought," and entertaining himself by singing "of men's fame." How one would like to have heard that song.

The first figure in music about whose existence we can be relatively certain was Terpander, who came from the island Lesbos. Around 675 B.C. he used the *kithara,* an elaborate seven-string lyre, to accompany vocal music on ceremonial occasions. The simple lyre, relatively small and easy to hold, had a sounding box made of a whole tortoise shell and sides formed of goat horns or curved pieces of wood. On the other hand, the kithara had a much larger sounding box made of wood, metal, or even ivory and broad, hollow sides, to give greater resonance to the sound. The player had to stand while performing on it; the instrument had straps to support it, leaving the player's hands free [59].

Another musical instrument developed about this time was the *aulos,* a double-reed instrument similar to the modern oboe [60], which had first been brought into Greece, according to the traditional account, by Olympus, a figure who seems mainly legendary. Like the kithara and lyre, the aulos was generally used to accompany songs.

The little evidence we have suggests that early Greek music was primarily vocal—the instruments

59 Berlin Painter. Detail of red-figure amphora. Nola, c. 490 B.C. Terra cotta, height of vase 16⅜″ (42 cm). Metropolitan Museum of Art, New York (Fletcher Fund, 1956). This vase gives a good idea of the Greeks' enthusiasm for music in general and the cithara in particular. The young musician is singing to his own accompaniment.

60 Karneia Painter. Detail of red-figure krater. Ceglie del Campo, c. 410 B.C. Terra cotta. Museo Nazionale, Taranto. A young woman plays the aulos for the god Dionysus. The flowing lines of the dress accentuate her figure. The necklace and bracelets are in low relief.

were used mainly to accompany the singers. The breakthrough into purely instrumental music seems to have come at the beginning of the Archaic period. We know that in 586 B.C. Sacadas of Argos composed a work to be played on the aulos for the Pythian Games at Delphi—a piece that remained well known and popular for centuries. Also, its character confirms the Greek love of narrative, for it described in music Apollo's fight with the dragon that the Pythian Games commemorated. The information is tantalizing indeed, since this first piece of "program music," the remote ancestor of Richard Strauss' *Till*

Eulenspiegel and *Don Quixote,* must have been highly effective for its appeal to have lasted so long.

We know little more of the music of the Archaic period than these odd facts. The lyrics of some of the songs have survived, including some of the choral odes performed in honor of various gods. Apollo and his sister Artemis were thanked for delivery from misfortune by the singing of a *paean,* or solemn invocation to the gods, while the *dithyramb,* or choral hymn to Dionysus, was sung in his honor at public ceremonies. Certainly it is clear that the roles of poet and musician were closely linked. Although we asso-

61 Geometric bowl showing dancing. c. 740 B.C.
Diameter 6¼" (16 cm). National Archaeological Museum, Athens.
The dancers include both women and men, three playing lyres.

ciate poets like Anacreon and Sappho with their
verses, they were equally well known to their contemporaries as musicians. The combination of words
and music is also intimately bound up with the origins of drama (this is a very complex and controversial topic, still not fully understood).

Also closely tied to music was dance, which also
played its part in the development of drama. We
know both more and less about the early stages of
Greek dance than we do about music. On the one
hand, we have from as early as the late Geometric
period actual depictions of dances in progress [61],
whereas the sound of music of the same period is
entirely lost to us. On the other hand, in the Classical
period the function of dance remained religious and
social, whereas a vast literature on music theory developed, with philosophical implications that became
explicit in the writings of Plato and Aristotle;
through this literature some information on early
music has been preserved.

What we do know about dancing and individual
dances suggests that here, as in music and visual arts,
telling a story was important. One famous dance was
called the *geranos,* from the word for "crane." The
dancers apparently made movements reminiscent of
the bird, but the steps of the dance had a more specific meaning. According to tradition, it was first
performed by Theseus outside the Labyrinth with the
boys and girls he had saved by killing the Minotaur
(see pages 25–26). The intricate patterns of the dance
were supposed to represent the Labyrinth itself. Having accomplished two dangerous feats—killing the
Minotaur and finding his way out of the Labyrinth—

Theseus still stayed around long enough to lead a
complicated performance. Dancing was obviously of
great importance to the Greeks.

The Persian Wars

At the beginning of the 5th century B.C. the Greeks
had to face the greatest challenge in their history.
Their success in meeting the challenge precipitated a
decisive break with the world of Archaic culture. In
499 B.C. the Greek cities of Asia Minor, with Athenian support, rebelled against their Persian rulers.
The Persian king, Darius, succeeded in checking this
revolt; he then resolved to lead a punitive expedition
against the mainland Greek cities that had sent help to
the eastern cities [62]. In 490 B.C. he took a massive
army to Greece; to everyone's surprise, the army was
defeated by the Athenians at the Battle of Marathon.
After Darius' death in 486 B.C., his son Xerxes
launched an even more grandiose expedition in 480
B.C. Xerxes defeated the Spartans at Thermophylae
and then attacked and sacked Athens itself. While the
city was falling, the Athenians took to their ships,
obeying an oracle which enjoined them to "trust to
their wooden walls." Eventually, they inflicted a
crushing defeat on the Persian navy at nearby Salamis. In 479 B.C., after being conquered on land and

62 Darius Painter. Darius in council before his expedition
against Greece, detail of a krater. c. 335 B.C.
Museo Archeologico Nazionale, Naples. Above the king Greece,
symbolized by the figure of a woman, is being entrusted to the
protection of the gods. Below, soldiers are collecting booty
for a war chest.

sea, at Plataea and Mycale, the Persians returned home, completely beaten.

The great historian Herodotus (484–420 B.C.) has left us, in the nine books of his *History of the Persian Wars,* a detailed account of the closing years of the Archaic Period. He also, however, has two other claims on our attention. He is the first writer in the Western tradition to devote himself to historical writing rather than epic or lyric poetry, a fact that has earned him the title "Father of History." At the same time he is one of the greatest storytellers, always sustaining the reader's interest, in both the main line of his narrative and the frequent and entertaining digressions. One of these digressions, the tale of Rhampsinitus and the thief, has been described as the first detective story in Western literature.

Herodotus was not a scientific historian in our terms—he had definite weaknesses. He never really understood the finer points of military strategy. He almost always interpreted events in terms of personalities, showing little interest in underlying political or economic causes. His strengths, however, were many. Although his subject involved conflict between Greeks and foreigners, he remained remarkably impartial and free from national prejudice. His natural curiosity about the world around him and about his fellow human beings was buttressed by acute powers of observation. Above all, he recorded as much information as possible, even when versions conflicted. He also tried to provide a reasonable evaluation of the reliability of his sources, so that later readers could form their own opinions.

Herodotus' analysis of the Greek victory was based on a serious philosophical, indeed theological, belief—that the Persians were defeated because they were morally in the wrong. Their moral fault was *hubris,* excessive ambition; thus the Greeks' victory was at the same time a triumph of right over might and a demonstration that the gods themselves would guarantee the triumph of justice.

Modern readers, however, less influenced by Herodotus' religious beliefs, will be more inclined to draw a political message from the Persian defeat. The Greeks triumphed at least partly because for once they had managed to unite in the face of a common enemy. Their victories inaugurated the greatest period in Greek history, the Classical Age.

Questions for Further Discussion

1. Although the Homeric epics primarily reflect a man's world, they also give much information on the role of women in early Greek society—so much that in the 19th century Samuel Butler even suggested that the *Odyssey* might have been written by a woman. What actual evidence is there in the *Iliad* and the *Odyssey* about the position of women in Homer's time?

2. Many of the most elaborate works of art of the Geometric period are concerned with funeral ceremonies. To what extent does the culture of our own day make use of art in a funerary context? Does it reflect on the general attitude of our own time to life and death?

3. Examine some of the paradoxes of Zeno. Try to identify their fallacies.

4. The period of colonization was one of the most productive and formative in Greek history. How did Greek colonization differ from the colonization by England, France, and other European nations in the 17th, 18th, and 19th centuries? How did the differences affect its results?

5. Sappho's friends and students formed an exclusively female group bound together by intellectual and emotional ties. Later ages have sometimes had difficulty in understanding and interpreting the nature of this group; thus the name of Sappho's birthplace, Lesbos, has acquired its modern overtones. Where else, either in the past or present, can we find a comparable group that might help to throw light on Sappho's world?

6. Although defeated by Xerxes, the Spartans emerge as the heroes of the Battle of Thermopylae, yet in general their reputation in the Greek world was not so favorable. What were the chief characteristics of life in Sparta, and why have the words "spartan" and "laconic" come to have their present meaning?

	GENERAL EVENTS	LITERATURE & PHILOSOPHY	ART
500 B.C.			
			c. 490 *Critian Boy;* turning point between Archaic and Classical Periods
480	478 Formation of Delian League; beginning of Athenian empire		480–323 First naturalistic sculpture and painting appear
	461 Pericles comes to prominence at Athens		c. 460 Sculptures at Temple of Zeus, Olympia
	454 Treasury of Delian League moved to Athens	458 Aeschylus, *Oresteia* trilogy wins first prize in drama festival of Dionysus	
450			

CLASSICAL PERIOD

Golden Age

	443–430 Pericles in full control of Athens		c. 450 Myron, *Discus Thrower*
	432 Peloponnesian War begins		
	429 Pericles dies of plague that devastates Athens	c. 429 Sophocles, *Oedipus the King*	
	421 Peace of Nicias	c. 421 Euripides, *The Suppliant Women*	c. 440 Polyclitus, *Doryphorus,* treatise *The Canon*
	413 Renewed outbreak of Peloponnesian War	c. 420–c. 399 Thucydides, *History of Peloponnesian War*	432 Phidias completes Parthenon sculptures
		414 Aristophanes, *The Birds*	late 5th cent. Funerary relief sculpture and white-ground vase painting; lekythos, *Warrior Seated at His Tomb*
		411 Aristophanes, *Lysistrata*	
404			

Late Classical Period

	404 Fall of Athens and victory of Sparta		
	404–403 Rule of Thirty Tyrants	399 Trial and execution of Socrates	
	387 King's Peace signed	before 387 Plato, *Republic*	c. 350 Scopas, *Pothos*
	371–362 Ascendancy of Thebes	387 Plato founds Academy	
	359–336 Philip II, king of Macedon	c. 385 Xenophon chronicles teachings of Socrates	c. 350 Frescoes, Royal Cemetery at Vergina
	338 Macedonians defeat Greeks at Battle of Chaeronea	c. 347–c. 399 Aristotle, *Politics, Metaphysics*	c. 340 Praxiteles, *Hermes with Infant Dionysus*
	336–323 Alexander the Great, king of Macedon		
	331 City of Alexandria founded	335 Aristotle founds Lyceum	c. 325 Lysippus, *Apoxymenos*
323			

HELLENISTIC PERIOD

	323–281 Wars of Alexander's successors		323–146 Development of realistic portraiture
	262 Pergamum becomes independent kingdom		
	197–156 Eumenes II, king of Pergamum		
	146 Romans sack Corinth; Greece becomes Roman province		c. 150 *Laocoön;* mosaic, House of Masks, Delos
146			

Classical Greece and Its Aftermath

470–456 Libon of Elis, Temple of Zeus at Olympia

c. 500–425 Music serves as accompaniment in dramatic performances

449 Pericles commissions work on Acropolis

447–438 Ictinus and Callicrates, Parthenon

437–432 Mnesicles, Propylaea

c. 427–424 Callicrates, Temple of Athena Nike

421–406 Erechtheum

c. 400 Music dominates dramatic performances

4th cent. Instrumental music becomes popular

356 Temple of Artemis at Ephesus destroyed by fire and rebuilt

c. 350 Theater at Epidaurus

323–146 *Tholos* and other new building forms appear

279 Lighthouse at Alexandria

c. 180–160 Menocrates of Rhodes, Pergamum Altar

late 2nd cent. Earliest surviving Greek music

75

The victories in the Persian Wars produced a new spirit of optimism and unity in Greece. Divine forces, it appeared, had guaranteed the triumph of right over wrong. There seemed to be no limit to the possibilities of human development. The achievements of the Classical period, which lasted from 479 B.C. to the death of Alexander the Great in 323 B.C., do much to justify the Greeks' proud self-confidence. They certainly represent a level of civilization that has rarely, if ever, been reached since—a level that has been a continuing inspiration to our culture.

Classical civilization reached its high point in Athens during the last half of the 5th century B.C., a time of unparalleled richness in artistic and intellectual achievement that is often called the Golden Age of Greece. To some extent, the importance of the great figures who dominated this period lies in the fact that they were the first in their fields. There are, in fact, few areas of human thought in which the 5th century Greeks were not pioneers. In subjects as diverse as drama and historiography, town planning and medicine, painting and sculpture, mathematics and government, they laid the foundations of later achievements. Even more astonishing, often they were not merely the first in their fields but also among the greatest of all time. Greek tragedies, for example, are still read and performed today because they give experiences that are as intense emotionally and intellectually as anything in the Western dramatic tradition.

In the Late Classical period, from 404 to 323 B.C., artists and writers continued to explore ideas and styles first outlined in the century before, though in different ways. Greek cultural life was no longer dominated by Athens; a single center no longer governed artistic developments. This 4th-century period was therefore one of greater variety, with individual artists following their own personal visions. The greatest of all Late Classical contributions to our cultural tradition was in the field of philosophy. The works of Plato and Aristotle became the basis of Western thought for the next two thousand years.

Even after the death of Alexander the Great in 323 B.C. and the end of the Classical Age, the Hellenistic period that followed was characterized by an artistic vitality that ultimately drew its inspiration from Classical achievements. Only when Greece was conquered by the Romans in the late 2nd century B.C. did Greek culture cease to have an independent existence.

Although the Roman conquest of Greece ended the glories of the Classical Age, in a way it also perpetuated them by contributing to the melding of Greek culture into the Western humanistic tradition. It was not the Greeks themselves but their conquerors who spread Greek ideas throughout the ancient world—and thus down in time to our own day. These conquerors were first the Macedonians and then, above all, the Romans, possessors of practical skills that they used to construct a world sufficiently at peace for ideas to have a place in it. The Greeks did not live in such a world; we must always remember that the Athenians of the Golden Age existed not in an environment of calm contemplation but in an environment of tension and violence. Their tragic in-

63 The Acropolis, Athens, from the northwest. The Parthenon, temple to Athena, is at the highest point. Below it spreads the monumental gateway, the Propylaea. Far left is the Erechtheum.

ability to put into practice their own noble ideals and live in peace with other Greeks—the darker side of their genius—proved fatal to their independence; it led to war with the rest of Greece in 431 B.C. and to the fall of Athens in 404 B.C. In this context, the Greek search for order takes on an added significance.

It was the belief that a search for reason and order could succeed that gave a unifying ideal to the immense and varied output of the Classical Age. The central principle of this Classical Ideal was that existence can be ordered and controlled, that human ability can triumph over the apparent chaos of the natural world and create a balanced society. In order to achieve this balance, individual human beings should try to stay within what seem to be reasonable limits, for those who do not are guilty of hubris, excessive pride—the same hubris of which the Persian leader Xerxes was guilty and for which he paid the price (see page 72). The aim of life should be a perfect equilibrium: everything in due proportion and nothing in excess. "Nothing too much" was one of the most famous Greek proverbs.

The emphasis that the Classical Greeks placed on order affected their spiritual attitudes. Individuals can achieve order, they believed, by understanding why people act as they do and, above all, by understanding the motives for their *own* actions. Thus confidence in the power of both human reason and human self-knowledge was as important as belief in the gods. The greatest of all Greek temples of the Classical Age, the Parthenon, which crowned the Athenian Acropolis [63], was planned not so much to glorify the goddess Athena as to glorify Athens and thus human achievement. Even in their darkest days the Classical Greeks never lost sight of the magnitude of human capability and, perhaps even more important, human potential—a vision that has returned over the centuries to inspire later generations and has certainly not lost its relevance in our own times.

Athens in the 5th Century B.C.

The political and cultural center of Greece during the first half of the Classical period was Athens. Here, by the end of the Persian Wars in 479 B.C., the Athenians had emerged as the most powerful people in the Greek world. For one thing, their role in the defeat of the Persians had been a decisive one. For another, their democratic system of government, first established in the late 6th century B.C., was proving to be both effective and stable. It was under Athenian leadership that in the years following the wars a defensive

organization of Greek city-states was formed to guard against any future attack from outside. The money collected from the participating members was kept in a treasury on the island of Delos, sacred to Apollo and politically neutral. This organization became known as the Delian League.

Within a short time a number of other important city-states, including Thebes, Sparta, and Athens' old trade rival Corinth, began to suspect that the League was serving not so much to protect all of Greece as to strengthen Athenian power. They believed the Athenians were turning an association of free and independent states into an empire of subject peoples. Their suspicions were confirmed when in 454 B.C. the funds of the League were transferred from Delos to Athens and some of the money was used to pay for Athenian building projects, including the Parthenon. The spirit of Greek unity was starting to dissolve; the Greek world was beginning to divide into two opposing sides: on the one hand Athens and her allies (the cities that remained in the League) and, on the other, the rest of Greece. Conflict was inevitable. The Spartans were finally persuaded to lead an alliance against Athens to check her "imperialistic designs." This war, called the Peloponnesian War after the homeland of the Spartans and their supporters, began in 431 B.C. and was dragged on until 404 B.C.

Our understanding of the Peloponnesian War and its significance owes much to the account by the great historian Thucydides, who himself lived through its calamitous events. Born around 460 B.C., Thucydides played an active part in Athenian politics in the years before the war. In 424 B.C. he was elected general and put in charge of defending the city of Amphipolis in northern Greece. When the city fell to Spartan troops, Thucydides was condemned in his absence and sentenced to exile. He did not return to Athens until 404 B.C.

Thucydides intended his *History of the Peloponnesian War* to describe the entire course of the war in 404 B.C., but he died before completing it; the narrative breaks off at the end of 411 B.C. The work is extremely valuable for its detailed description of events, for although its author was an Athenian he managed to be both accurate and impartial. At the same time, however, Thucydides tried to write more than simply an account of a local war. The *History* was an attempt to analyze human motives and reactions so that future generations would understand how and why the conflict occurred and, in turn, understand themselves. The work was not meant to entertain by providing digressions and anecdotes but to search out the truth and use it to demonstrate universal principles of human behavior. This emphasis on reason makes Thucydides' work typical of the Classical period.

The hero of Thucydides' account of the years immediately preceding the war is Pericles, the leader whose name symbolizes the achievements of the Athenian Golden Age [64]. An aristocrat by birth, Pericles began his political career in the aftermath of the transfer of the Delian League's funds to Athens. By 443 B.C. he had unofficially assumed the leadership of the Athenian democracy, although he continued democratically to run for reelection every year. Under his guidance the few remaining years of peace were devoted to making visible the glory of Athens by constructing on the Acropolis the majestic buildings that still, though in ruins, evoke the grandeur of Periclean Athens.

Had Pericles continued to lead Athens during the war itself, the final outcome might have been differ-

64 Kresilas. *Pericles*. Roman copy after original of c. 440 B.C. Marble. Vatican Museum, Rome. Pericles is wearing a helmet, pushed up over his forehead, because his official rank while leader of Athens was that of general.

ent, but in 430 B.C. the city was ravaged by disease, perhaps bubonic plague, and in 429 B.C. Pericles died. No successor could be found who was capable of winning the respect and support of the majority of his fellow citizens. The war continued indecisively until 421 B.C., when an uneasy peace was signed. Shortly thereafter the Athenians made an ill-advised attempt to replenish their treasury by organizing an unprovoked attack on the wealthy Greek cities of Sicily. The expedition proved a total disaster; thousands of Athenians were killed or taken prisoner. When the war began again in 411 B.C. the Athenian forces were fatally weakened. The end came in 404 B.C. After a siege that left many people dying in the streets, Athens surrendered unconditionally to the Spartans and their allies.

The Drama Festivals of Dionysus

The tumultuous years of the 5th century B.C., passing from the spirit of euphoria that followed the ending of the Persian Wars to the mood of doubt and self-questioning of 404 B.C., may seem unlikely to have produced the kind of intellectual concentration characteristic of Classical Greek drama. Yet it was, in fact, in the plays written specifically for performance in the theater of Dionysus at Athens in these years that Classical literature reached its most elevated heights. The tragedies of the three great masters, Aeschylus, Sophocles, and Euripides, not only illustrate the development of contemporary thought but also contain some of the most memorable scenes in the history of the theater.

Tragic drama was not itself an invention of the 5th century B.C. It had evolved over the preceding century from choral hymns sung in honor of the god Dionysus, and the religious character of its origins was still present in its fully developed form. The plays that have survived from the Classical period at Athens were all written for performance at one of the two annual festivals sacred to Dionysus before an audience consisting of the entire population of the city. To go to the theater was to take part in a religious ritual; the theaters themselves were regarded as sacred ground [65].

Each of the authors of the works given each year normally submitted four plays to be performed consecutively on a single day—three tragedies, or a "trilogy," and a more light-hearted play called a *satyr* play (a satyr was a mythological figure: a man with an animal's ears and tail). The "trilogies" often narrated parts of a single story, although often the three plays were based on different stories with a common theme. At the end of each festival the plays were judged and a prize awarded to the winning author.

65 Polyclitus. Theater, Epidaurus. c. 350 B.C. Diameter 373′ (113.69 m), orchestra 66′ (20.12 m) across.

The dramas were religious not only in time and place but also in nature. The plots, generally drawn from mythology, often dealt with the relationship between the human and the divine. To achieve an appropriate seriousness, the style of performance was lofty and dignified. The actors, who in a sense served as priests of Dionysus, wore masks, elaborate costumes, and raised shoes.

The chorus, whose sacred dithyrambic hymn had been the original starting point in the development of tragedy, retained an important function throughout the 5th century B.C. In some plays, generally the earlier ones, the chorus forms a group centrally involved in the action, as in Aeschylus' *Suppliants* and *Eumenides*. More often, as in Sophocles' *Oedipus the King* or *Antigone,* the chorus represents the point of view of the spectator, rather than that of the characters participating directly in the events on stage; in these plays the chorus reduces to more human terms the intense emotions of the principals and comments on them. Even in the time of Euripides, when dramatic confrontation became more important than extended poetic or philosophical expression, the chorus still retained one important function, that of punctuating the action and dividing it into separate episodes by singing lyric odes whose subject was sometimes only indirectly related to the action of the play.

These aspects of Classical tragedy are a reminder that the surviving texts of the plays represent only a small part of the total experience of the original performances. The words—or at least some of them—have survived; but the music to which the words were sung and which accompanied much of the action, the elaborate choreography to which the chorus moved, indeed the whole grandiose spectacle performed out-of-doors in theaters located in sites of extreme natural beauty before an audience of thousands—all of this can only be recaptured in the imagination. It is perhaps relevant to remember that when, almost two thousand years later, around A.D. 1600, a small group of Florentine intellectuals decided to revive the art of Classical drama, they succeeded instead in inventing opera. Similarly, in the 19th century the German composer Richard Wagner was inspired by Greek tragedy to devise his concept of a *Gesamtkunstwerk* (literally, "total work of art"), a work of art that combined all the arts into one; he illustrated this concept by writing his dramatic operas.

66 Dokimasia Painter. *The Murder of Agamemnon,* detail of red-figure krater. Attic, c. 470–465 B.C. Terra cotta. Museum of Fine Arts, Boston (William Francis Warden Fund). Aegisthus strikes the blow in this version of the story, with Clytemnestra standing behind him grasping an axe. Agamemnon, killed as he was about to take a bath, is wearing only a light robe.

The Athenian Tragic Dramatists

Even if some elements of the surviving Greek dramas are lost, we do have the words. And the differing world views of the authors of these words vividly illustrate the changing fate of 5th-century B.C. Athens. The earliest of the playwrights, Aeschylus (525–456 B.C.), died before the lofty aspirations of the early years of the Classical period could be shaken by contemporary events. His work shows a deep awareness of human weakness and the dangers of power (he had himself fought at the Battle of Marathon in 490 B.C.), but he retains an enduring belief that in the end right will triumph. In Aeschylus' plays the process of learning what is right is painful: One must suffer to learn one's errors; yet the process is inevitable, controlled by a divine force of justice personified under the name of Zeus.

The essential optimism of Aeschylus' philosophy must be kept in mind because the actual course of the events he describes is often violent and bloody. Perhaps his most impressive plays are the three that form the *Oresteia* trilogy. This trilogy, the only complete one that has survived, won first prize in the festival of 458 B.C. at Athens. The subject of the trilogy is nothing less than the growth of civilization, represented by the gradual transition from a primitive law of "vendetta" and blood for blood to the rational society of civilized human beings.

The first of the three plays, *Agamemnon,* presents the first of these systems in operation. King Agamemnon returns to his homeland, Argos, after leading the Greeks to victory at Troy. Ten years earlier, on the way to Troy, he had been forced to choose either to abandon the campaign because of unfavorable tides or to obtain an easy passage by sacrificing his daughter Iphigenia. (The situation may seem contrived, but it clearly symbolizes a conflict between public and personal responsibilities.) After considerable hesitation and self-doubt he had chosen to sacrifice his daughter. On his return home at the end of the Trojan War, he pays the price for her death by being murdered by his wife Clytemnestra [66]. Her ostensible motive is vengeance for Iphigenia's death, but an equally powerful, if less noble, one is her desire to replace Agamemnon both as husband and king by her lover Aegisthus. Thus Aeschylus shows us that even the "law of the jungle" is not always as simple as it may seem, while at the same time the punishment of one crime creates in its turn another crime to be punished. If Agamemnon's murder of his daughter merits vengeance, then so does Clytemnestra's murder of her husband. Violence breeds violence.

The second play, *The Libation Bearers,* shows us the effects of the operation of this principle on Agamemnon and Clytemnestra's son, Orestes. After spending years in exile Orestes returns to Argos to avenge his father's death by killing his mother. Although a further murder can accomplish nothing except the transfer of blood guilt to Orestes himself, the primitive law of "vendetta" requires him to act. With the encouragement of his sister Electra, he kills Clytemnestra. His punishment follows immediately. He is driven mad by the Furies, the implacable goddesses of vengeance, who hound him from his home.

The Furies themselves give their name to the third play, in which they are tactfully called *The Eumenides,* or "the kindly ones." In his resolution of

67 Scene from the Oedipus story. c. 1475. Manuscript illumination, Biblioteca Nazionale Marciana, Venice. The tragedy of Oedipus remained a favorite story long after Sophocles' time. In the 1st century A.D. the Roman philosopher Seneca wrote a play called *Oedipus,* and this miniature showing Jocasta's death and Oedipus' self-blinding comes from a 15th-century edition of it.

68 A modern performance of *Oedipus the King* in the ancient theater at Delphi. 1951. The columns in the background are the ruins of the Temple of Apollo.

the tragedy of Orestes and his family, Aeschylus makes it clear that violence can only be brought to an end by the power of reason and persuasion. After a period of tormented wandering, Orestes comes finally to Athens where he stands trial for the murder of his mother before a jury of Athenians, presided over by Athena herself. The Furies insist on his condemnation on the principle of blood for blood, but Orestes is defended by Apollo, the god of reason, and finally acquitted by his fellow human beings. Thus the long series of murders is brought to an end, and the apparently inevitable violence and despair of the earlier plays is finally dispelled by the power of persuasion and human reason, which—admittedly with the help of Athena and Apollo—have managed to bring civilization and order out of primeval chaos.

In spite of all of the horror of the earlier plays, therefore, the *Oresteia* ends on a positive note. Aeschylus affirms his belief that progress can be achieved by reason and order. This gradual progression from darkness to light is handled throughout the three plays with unfailing skill. Aeschylus matches the grandeur of his conception with majestic language. His rugged style makes him sometimes difficult to understand, but all the verbal effects are used to dramatic purpose. The piling up of images and complexity of expression produce an emotional tension that has never been surpassed.

The life of Sophocles (496–406 B.C.) spanned both the glories and the disasters of the 5th century B.C. Of the three great tragic poets, Sophocles was the most

prosperous and successful; he was a personal friend of Pericles. He is said to have written 123 plays, but only seven have survived, all of them from the end of his career. They all express a much less positive vision of life than that of Aeschylus. His philosophy is not easy to extract from his work, since he is more concerned with exploring and developing the individual characters in his dramas than with expounding a point of view; in general, he seems to combine an awareness of the tragic consequences of individual mistakes with a belief in the collective ability and dignity of the human race.

Paradoxically, however, the choice between good and evil is never clear or easy and is sometimes impossible. More than any of his contemporaries, Sophocles emphasizes how much lies outside our own control, in the hands of destiny or the gods. His insistence that we respect and revere the forces that we cannot see or understand makes him the most traditionally religious of the tragedians. These ambiguities appear in his best-known play, *Oedipus the King,* which has stood ever since Classical times as a symbol of Greek tragic drama [67]. A century after it was first performed around 429 B.C., Aristotle used it as his model when, in the *Poetics,* he discussed the nature of tragedy. Its unities of time, place, and action, the inexorable drive of the story with its inevitable yet profoundly tragic conclusion, the beauty of its poetry—all these have made *Oedipus the King* a true classic, in all senses. Its impact has lasted down to our own times [68]; it had a notable effect on the ideas of Sigmund Freud. Yet in spite of the universal admiration which the play has excited, its message is far from clear.

The story concerns Oedipus, doomed even before his birth to kill his father and marry his mother, his attempts to avoid fate, and his final discovery that he has failed. If the play seems, in part, to be saying that we cannot avoid our destiny, it leaves unanswered the question of whether we deserve that destiny or not. Certainly Oedipus does not choose deliberately to kill his father and marry his mother, even though unknowingly everything he does leads to this end. Then why does he deserve to suffer for his actions?

One of the traditional answers to this question can be found in Aristotle's analysis of tragedy in the *Poetics*. Referring particularly to *Oedipus*, Aristotle makes the point that the downfall of a tragic figure is generally the result of a tragic flaw (the Greek word is *hamartia*) in his character. Thus Oedipus' pride and stubbornness in insisting on discovering who he is and the anger he shows in the process bring about the final disastrous revelation. In this way the flaws, or weaknesses, in his character overcome his good points and destroy him.

As a description of Oedipus' behavior, this explanation is convincing enough, but it fails to provide a satisfactory account of the original causes of his condition. Perhaps the message of the play is, in fact, that there are some aspects of existence beyond our understanding, aspects that operate by principles outside our range of experience. If this is so, and many literary critics would deny it, Sophocles seems to be describing the final helplessness of humanity in the face of forces that we cannot control and warning against too great a belief in self-reliance.

The significance for the Athenians themselves of Oedipus' fall from greatness emerges in full force in the work of Euripides (c. 484–406 B.C.). Although only a little younger than Sophocles, Euripides expresses all the weariness and disillusion of the wartorn years at the end of the 5th century B.C. Of all the tragedians he is perhaps the closest to our own time, with his concern for realism and his determination to expose social, political, and religious injustices.

Although Euripides admits the existence of irrational forces in the universe that can be personified in the form of gods and goddesses, he certainly does not regard them as worthy of respect and worship. This skepticism won him the charge of impiety. His plays show characters frequently pushed to the limits of endurance; their reactions show a new concern for psychological truth. In particular, Euripides exhibits a profound sympathy and understanding for the problems of women who live in a society dominated by men. Characters like Medea and Phaedra challenge many of the basic premises of contemporary Athenian society.

Euripides' deepest hatred is reserved for war and its senseless misery. Like the other dramatists he draws the subject matter of his plays from traditional myths, but the lines delivered by the actors must have sounded in their hearer's ears with a terrible relevance. *The Suppliant Women* was probably written in 421 B.C., when ten years of indecisive fighting had produced nothing but an uneasy truce. Its subject is the recovery by Theseus, ruler of Athens, of the bodies of seven chiefs killed fighting at Thebes in order to return them to their families for burial. He yields to their mothers—the women of the title—who beg him to recover the bodies. The audience would have little need to be reminded of the grief of wives and mothers or of the kind of political processes that produced years of futile fighting.

If Aeschylus' belief in human progress is more noble, Euripides is certainly more realistic. Although unpopular in his own time, he later became the most widely read of the three tragedians. As a result, more of his plays have been preserved (nineteen in all), plays with a wide range of emotional expression. They extend from romantic comedies like *Helen* and *Iphigenia in Taurus* to the profoundly disturbing *Bacchae,* his last completed play, in which Euripides the rationalist explores the inadequacy of reason as the sole approach to life. In this acknowledgement of the power of emotion to overwhelm the order and balance so typical of the Classical ideal, he is most clearly speaking for his time.

Aristophanes and Greek Comedy

Euripides was not, of course, the only Athenian to realize the futility of war. The plays of Aristophanes (c. 450–385 B.C.), the greatest comic poet of 5th-century B.C. Athens, deal with the same theme. His work combines political satire with a strong vein of fantasy.

In *The Birds,* produced in 414 B.C., two Athenians decide to leave their city and find a better place to live. They join forces with the birds and build a new city in mid-air called Cloudcuckooland. But the city cuts off contact between gods and humans by blocking the path of the steam rising from sacrifices. The gods are forced to come to terms with the new city and Zeus hands over his sceptor of authority to the birds.

This is simple escapism, but *Lysistrata,* written a few years later, in 411 B.C., deals with the problem of how to prevent war in a more practical fashion. In the course of the play the main protagonist, Lysistrata, persuades her fellow women of Athens to refuse to make love with their husbands until peace is made. At the same time her followers seize the Acropolis. The men, teased and frustrated, finally give in and envoys are summoned from Sparta. The play ends with the Athenians and Spartans dancing together for joy at the new peace.

The Visual Arts

Like the writers and thinkers of their time, artists of the mid-5th century B.C. were concerned with ideas of balance and order. Very early Classical works like the *Critian Boy* [see 3.16] showed a new interest in realism, and the sculptors who came later began to explore the exciting possibilities of representing the human body in motion.

Among the most famous 5th-century sculptors working at Athens was Myron. Although none of his sculptures has survived, there are a number of later copies of one of his most famous pieces, the *Discus Thrower* [69]. The original, which was made around 450 B.C., is typical of its age in combining realistic treatment of an action with an idealized portrayal of the athlete himself.

69   Myron. *Discobolos (Discus Thrower)*. Roman copy after bronze original of c. 450 B.C. Marble, lifesize. National Museum, Rome.

While striving for naturalism, artists like Myron tried also to create a new standard of human beauty by controlling the human form according to principles of proportion, symmetry, and balance. Around 440 B.C., one of the greatest of Classical sculptors, Polyclitus of Argos, devised a mathematical formula for representing the perfect male body, an ideal canon of proportion, and wrote a book about it. The idea behind *The Canon* was that ideal beauty consisted of a precise relationship between the various parts of the body. Polyclitus' book must have set

70 Polyclitus. *Doryphoros (Spear Bearer)*. Roman copy after bronze original of c. 450 B.C. Marble, lifesize. Archaeological Museum, Naples.

71 Grave stele of Crito and Timarista. c. 420 B.C. Marble. Museum, Rhodes.

forth the details of his system of proportion. To illustrate his theory, he also produced a bronze statue of a young man holding a spear, the *Doryphoros*. Both book and original statue are lost; only later copies of the *Doryphoros* survive [70].

We do not know, therefore, exactly what Polyclitus' system was. Nevertheless, we have some indication in the writings of a later philosopher, Chrysippus (c. 280–207 B.C.), who wrote that "beauty consists of the proportion of the parts; of finger to finger; of all the fingers to the palm and the wrist; of those to the forearm; of the forearm to the upper arm; and of all these parts to one another, as set forth in *The Canon* of Polyclitus." Even if the exact relationships are lost, what was important about Polyclitus' ideal—and what made it so characteristic of the Classical vision as a whole—was that it depended on precisely ordered and balanced interrelationships of the various parts of the human body. Furthermore, the ideal beauty this created was not produced by nature, but by the power of the human intellect.

In the late 5th century B.C., sculpture and vase painting were characterized by a growing concern with the individual rather than a generalized ideal. Artists began to depict the emotional responses of ordinary people to life and death instead of approaching these responses indirectly through the use of myths. Thus, death and mourning became increasingly common subjects.

Among the most touching works to survive from the period are a number of oil flasks used for funerary offerings [Plate 7, page 89]. They are painted with mourning or graveside scenes, on a white rather than red background. The figures are depicted with quiet and calm dignity but with considerable feeling. This personal rather than public response to death is found also on the gravemarkers, of the very end of the 5th century B.C., which show a grief that is perhaps resigned but still intense [71].

Architecture

In architecture, as in sculpture, designers were concerned with proportion and the interrelationship of the various parts that constitute a complete structure. Nowhere is this more apparent than in the Temple of Zeus at Olympia [72], the first great artistic achievement of the years following the Persian Wars, begun in 470 B.C. and finished by 456 B.C. By the time of its completion it was also the largest Doric temple in mainland Greece. The architect of this temple, Libon of Elis, clearly intended it to illustrate the new Classical preoccupation with proportion. The distance from the center of one column to the center of the next was the unit of measurement for the whole temple. Thus the height of each column is equal to two units, and the combined length of a triglyph and a metope equals half a unit.

The theme of order, implicit in the architecture of the temple, became explicit in the sculpture that dec-

72 Reconstruction drawing of east façade, Temple of Zeus, Olympia. c. 470–456 B.C. The pediment shows Zeus between two contestants prior to a chariot race.

orated it. At the center of the west pediment, standing calmly amidst a fight raging between Lapiths and Centaurs, was the figure of Apollo, the god of reason, exerting his authority by a single confident gesture [73].

Like the works of Aeschylus, the sculptures from Olympia express a conviction that justice will triumph and that the gods will enforce it. The art of the second half of the 5th century B.C., however, is more concerned with human achievement than divine will. Pericles' building program for the Acropolis, or citadel of Athens, represents the supreme expression in visual terms of Classical ideals [74].

This greatest of all Classical artistic achievements has a special grandeur and poignancy. The splendor of its conception and execution has survived the vicissitudes of time; the great temple to Athena, the Parthenon, remains to this day an incomparable sym-

73 Apollo intervenes in the battle between the Lapiths and Centaurs, from the west pediment of the Temple of Zeus, Olympia. c. 470–456 B.C. Museum, Olympia.

74 Model reconstruction of the Acropolis. Royal Ontario Museum, Toronto. Most of the smaller buildings no longer exist, leaving an unobstructed view of the Parthenon that was not possible in ancient times.

75 Ictinus and Callicrates. The Parthenon, Athens.
447–432 B.C. Height of columns 34′ (10.36 m).
At right is a plan of the temple.

bol of the Golden Age of Greece. Yet it was built during years of growing division and hostility in the Greek world—the last sculpture was barely in place before the outbreak of the Peloponnesian War in 431 B.C. Pericles died in 429 B.C., but fighting and building both dragged on. The Erechtheum, the final temple to be completed, was not finished until 406 B.C., two years before the end of the war and the fall of Athens. Pericles had intended the whole program to perpetuate the memory of Athens' glorious achievements, but instead it is a reminder of the gulf between Classical high ideals and the realities of political existence in 5th century B.C. Greece.

Even the funding of the Parthenon symbolizes this gap, since it was paid for at least in part from the treasury of the Delian League (see page 77). The transfer of the League's funds to Athens in 454 B.C. clearly indicated Pericles' imperialist intentions, as did the use to which he put them. It is ironic that the supreme monument of Periclean Athens was built

with money originally intended for a pan-Hellenic League. It is even more ironic that Athens' further highhanded behavior created a spirit of ill feeling and distrust throughout the Greek world that led inevitably to the outbreak of the Peloponnesian War—a war that effectively destroyed the Athenian glory the Parthenon had been intended to symbolize.

The great outcrop of rock that forms the Acropolis was an obvious choice by Pericles for the Parthenon and the other buildings planned with it. The site, which towers above the rest of the city, had served as a center for Athenian life from Mycenaean times, when a fortress was built on it. Throughout the Archaic period a series of temples had been constructed there, the last of them destroyed by the Persians in 480 B.C.

Work on the Acropolis was begun in 449 B.C. under the direction of Phidias, the greatest sculptor of his day and a personal friend of Pericles. The Parthenon [75] was the first building to be constructed;

its architects were Ictinus and Callicrates (the name of the temple comes from the Greek *parthenos,* or virgin, that is, the goddess Athena). It was built between 447 and 438 B.C.; its sculptural decoration was complete by 432 B.C. Even larger than the Temple of Zeus at Olympia, the building combines the Doric order of its columns (seventeen on the sides and eight on the ends) with some Ionic features, including a continuous running frieze inside the outer colonnade, at the top of the temple wall and inner colonnades. The design incorporates a number of refinements intended to prevent any sense of monotony or heaviness and gives to the building an air of richness and grace. Like earlier Doric columns, those of the Parthenon are thickest at the point one-third from the base and then taper to the top, a device called *entasis.* In addition, all the columns tilt slightly toward each other (it has been calculated that they would all meet if extended upward for 2 miles, or 3.2 kilometers). The columns at the corners are thicker and closer together than the others and the entablature leans outwards. The flat floor is not really flat at all but convex. All these refinements are, of course, extremely subtle and barely visible to the naked eye. The perfection of their execution, requiring incredible precision of mathematical calculation, is the highest possible tribute to the Classical search for order.

The sculptural decoration of the Parthenon occupied three parts of the building and made use of three different techniques of carving. The figures in the pediments are freestanding; the frieze is carved in low relief; the metopes are in high relief (see page 91). The Ionic frieze, 520 feet (158.6 meters) long, is carved in low relief; it depicts a procession that took place every four years on the occasion of the Great Panathenaic Festival. It shows Athenians walking and riding to the Acropolis in a ceremony during which an ancient wooden statue of Athena was presented with a new robe. The variety of movement, gesture, and rhythm achieved in the relatively limited technique of low relief makes the frieze among the greatest treasures of Greek art [76]. At the beginning of the 19th century, most of the frieze, together with other Parthenon sculptures, was removed from the building by the British Ambassador to Constantinople, Lord Elgin; these are now in the British Museum. (All the sculptures from the Parthenon that are in the British Museum are generally known as the Elgin Marbles.)

Equally impressive are the surviving figures from the east and west pediments, which are freestanding. They show, respectively, the birth of Athena and her contest with Poseidon, god of the sea, to decide which of them should be patron deity of the city.

76 Equestrian group, detail of Parthenon frieze (north face). c. 442–432 B.C. Pentelic marble, height 41⅜" (106 cm). British Museum, London (reproduced by courtesy of the Trustees). The composition is elaborate but clear. The riders, with their calm, typically Classical expressions, are shown in various positions: note especially the last figure on the right.

right: Plate 7 Reed Painter. *Warrior Seated at His Tomb*. Late 5th century B.C. White-ground lekythos, height 18⅞″ (48 cm). National Archaeological Museum, Athens. A youth is at one side. On the other side is a young woman who holds the warrior's shield and helmet.

below: Plate 8 Wall painting from the Tomb of Hunting and Fishing, Tarquinia. c. 520 B.C. Fresco. Men, fish, and birds are all rendered naturalistically, with acute observation. Note the bird perched on the waves to the left of the diving fish and the hunter at right.

Plate 9 Wall paintings from the Villa of the Mysteries, Pompeii. c. 60 B.C. Frescoes. Probably no ancient work of art has been more argued about than these paintings. They seem to relate to the cult of the Greek god Dionysus and the importance of the cult for girls approaching marriage, but many of the details are difficult to interpret. There is no argument, however, about the high quality of the paintings.

77 *Three Goddesses,* from Parthenon east pediment. c. 438–432 B.C. Marble, over lifesize. British Museum, London (reproduced by courtesy of the Trustees). The robes show the sculptor's technical virtuosity in carving drapery.

They are badly damaged; even so, statues like the group of three goddesses [77], from the east pediment, show a combination of idealism and naturalism that has never been surpassed. The anatomy of the figures and the drapery, which in some cases covers them, are both treated realistically, even in places where the details of the workmanship would have been barely visible to the spectator below. The realism is combined, however, with a characteristically Classical preoccupation with proportion and balance; the result is sculptures that achieve an almost perfect blend of the two elements of the Classical style: ideal beauty represented in realistic terms.

In contrast to the frieze, the technique employed on the metopes is high relief, so high, in fact, that some of the figures seem almost completely detached from their background. These metopes, which illustrate a number of mythological battles, represent a lower level of achievement, although some are more successful than others at reconciling scenes of violence and Classical idealism. The most impressive ones show episodes from the battle between Lapiths and Centaurs [78], the same story we saw on the west pediment at Olympia.

The monumental entrance to the Acropolis, the Propylaea [79], was begun in 437 B.C. and finished on the eve of the outbreak of war, although probably only by a modification of the architect Mnesicles' original plan. An unusual feature of its design is that

78 *Lapith and Centaur,* metope from Parthenon (south face). c. 448–442 B.C. Pentelic marble, height 4'4¼" (1.34 m). British Museum, London (reproduced by courtesy of the Trustees). The assailed Lapith has dropped to one knee.

ATHENS IN THE 5TH CENTURY B.C. **91**

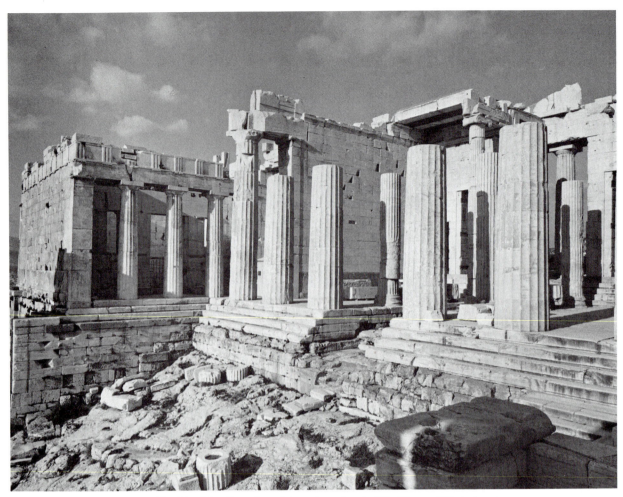

79 Mnesicles. Propylaea, Athens (west front). 437–431 B.C. This is the view from the Temple of Athena Nike. Note the contrast between the simple Doric columns of the façade and the Ionic columns that line the center passageway.

both Doric and Ionic columns are used, the Doric ones visible from the front and the back and the Ionic ones lining the passageway through the outer porch.

The other major building on the Acropolis is the Erechtheum, an Ionic temple of complex design, which was begun in 421 B.C. but not completed until 406 B.C. The chief technical problem facing the architect, whose identity is unknown, was the uneven ground level of the site. The problem was solved by creating a building with entrances on different levels. The nature of the building itself produced other design problems. The Erechtheum had to commemorate a whole series of elaborate religious events and honor a number of different deities. One of its four chambers housed the ancient wooden statue of Athena that was at the center of the Great Panathenaic Festival shown on the Parthenon frieze. Else-

where in the temple were altars to Poseidon and Erechtheus, an early Athenian king; to the legendary Athenian hero Butes; and to Hephaistos, the god of the forge. Furthermore, the design had to incorporate the marks in the ground made by Poseidon's trident during the competition with Athena, as shown on the west pediment of the Parthenon, and the site of the grave of another early, and probably legendary, Athenian king, Cecrops. The result of all this was a building whose complex plan is still not fully understood. In fact, the exact identification of the inner chambers remains in doubt.

The decoration of the temple is both elaborate and delicate, almost fragile. Its most well-known feature is the South Porch, where the roof rests not on columns but on the famous *caryatids,* statues of young women [80]. These graceful figures, who stand

80 *Porch of the Maidens,* Erechtheum, Athens. 421–406 B.C. Height of caryatids 7'9" (2.36 m).

gravely upright with one knee slightly bent as if to sustain the weight of the roof, represent the most complete attempt until then to conceal the structural functions of a column behind its form.

In many respects innovations such as these make the Erechtheum as representative of the mood of the late 5th century B.C. as the confident Parthenon is of the mood of a generation earlier. The apparent lack of a coherent overall plan and the blurring of traditional distinctions between architecture and sculpture, structure and decoration, seem to question traditional architectural values in a way that parallels the doubts of Euripides and his contemporaries.

The Late Classical Period

With the end of the Peloponnesian War in 404 B.C. and the fall of Athenian democracy, both art and political life were to be affected by an atmosphere of considerable confusion. Though Athens had been removed as the dominating force in Greece, there was no successor among her rivals. The vacuum was not filled until the mid-4th century with the appearance on the scene of Philip of Macedon. Earlier, a disastrous series of skirmishes between Sparta, Thebes, Athens, Corinth, and Argos had been temporarily suspended by the intervention of the Great King of the Persians himself, and the so-called King's Peace was signed in 387 B.C. But after a brief respite, the Thebans decisively defeated the Spartan forces at

Leuctra in 371 B.C. and remained for a few years the dominating force in Greek political life.

With the accession of Philip in Macedon in 359 B.C., however, the balance of power in Greece began to change. The hitherto backward northern kingdom of Macedon began to exert a new unifying influence, despite opposition in Thebes and in Athens, where the great Athenian orator Demosthenes led the resistance. In 338 B.C., at the Battle of Chaeronea (see map, page 54), Philip defeated Athenian and Theban forces and unified all the cities of Greece, with the exception of Sparta, in an alliance known as the League of Corinth.

Even before his assassination in 336 B.C., Philip had developed schemes for enlarging his empire by attacking Persia. His son and successor, Alexander, carried them out. He spent the ten years from 333 B.C. until his own death in 323 B.C. in an amazing series of campaigns across Asia, destroying the Persian Empire and reaching as far as India. The effects of the breakup of this new Macedonian Empire after the death of Alexander were to be felt throughout the Hellenistic period that followed.

The Philosophies of Socrates and Plato

The intellectual and cultural spirit of the new century was foreshadowed in its very first year in an event at Athens. In 399 B.C. the philosopher Socrates was charged with impiety and corruption of the young, found guilty, and executed. Yet the ideas that Socrates represented—concern with the fate of the individual and the questioning of traditional values—could not be killed so easily. They had already begun to spread at the end of the 5th century B.C. and came to dominate the culture of the 4th century B.C.

Socrates is one of the most important figures in Greek history. He is also one of the most difficult to understand clearly. Much of the philosophy of the Greeks and of later ages and cultures has been inspired by his life and teachings. Yet Socrates himself wrote nothing; most of what we know of him comes from the works of his disciple, Plato. Socrates was born around 469 B.C., the son of a sculptor and a midwife; in later life he claimed to have followed his mother's profession in being a "midwife to ideas." He seems first to have been interested in natural science, but he soon turned to the problems of human behavior and morality. Unlike the sophists, the professional philosophers of the day, he never took money for teaching, nor did he ever found a school. Instead he went around Athens, to both public places like the markets and the gymnasia and private gatherings, talking and arguing, testing traditional ideas by subjecting them to a barrage of questions—as he put it, "following the argument wherever it led." Socrates gradually gained a circle of enthusiastic followers, drawn mainly from the young. At the same time he acquired many enemies, disturbed by both his challenge to established morality and the uncompromising persistence with which he interrogated those who upheld it. Socrates was no respecter of the pride or dignity of others, and his search for the truth inevitably exposed the ignorance of his opponents.

Among Socrates' supporters were a number who had taken part in an unpopular and tyrannical political coup at Athens immediately following the Peloponnesian War. The rule of the so-called Thirty Tyrants lasted only from 404 to 403 B.C.; it ended with the death or expulsion of its leading figures. The return of democracy gave Socrates' enemies a chance to take advantage of the hostility felt toward those who had "collaborated" with the tyrants; thus in 399 B.C. he was put on trial.

It seems probable that to some degree the trial was intended for show and that those who voted for the death sentence never seriously thought it would be carried out. Socrates was urged by his friends to escape from prison, and the authorities themselves offered him every opportunity to do so. However, the strength of his own morality and his reverence for the laws of his city prohibited him from doing so. After a final discussion with his friends he was put to death by the administration of a draught of hemlock.

Many of Socrates' disciples tried to preserve his memory by writing accounts of his life and teachings. The works of only two have survived. One of these is the Greek historian Xenophon, whose *Apology, Symposium,* and *Memorabilia* are interesting, if superficial. The other is Plato, who, together with his pupil Aristotle, stands at the forefront of the whole intellectual tradition of Western civilization.

The dialogues of Plato claim to record the teachings of Socrates. Indeed, in almost all of them Socrates himself appears, arguing with his opponents and presenting his own ideas. How much of Plato's picture of Socrates is historical truth and how much is Plato's invention, however, is debatable. The Socratic problem has been almost as much discussed as the identity of Homer. In general, modern opinion supports the view that in the early dialogues Plato tried to preserve something of his master's views and methods, while in the later ones he used Socrates as the spokesman for his own ideas.

There can certainly be no doubt that Plato was deeply impressed by Socrates' life and death. Born in 428 B.C., he was drawn by other members of his aristocratic family into the Socratic circle. Plato was present at the trial of Socrates, whose speech in his own defense Plato records in the *Apology,* one of three works that describe Socrates' last days. In the *Crito,* set in prison, Socrates explains why he refuses to escape. The *Phaedo* gives an account of his last day spent discussing with his friends the immortality of the soul and his death.

After Socrates' death, Plato left Athens, horrified at the society that had sanctioned the execution, and spent a number of years traveling. He returned in 387 B.C. and founded the Academy, the first permanent institution in Western civilization devoted to education and research, and thus the forerunner of all our universities. Its curriculum concentrated on mathematics, law, and political theory. Its purpose was to produce experts for the service of the state. Some twenty years later, in 368 B.C., Plato was invited to Sicily to put his political theories into practice by turning Syracuse into a model kingdom and its young ruler, Dionysius II, into a philosopher king. Predictably, the attempt was a dismal failure, and by 366 B.C. he was back in Athens. Apart from a second visit to Syracuse in 362 B.C., equally unsuccessful, he seems to have spent the rest of his life in Athens, teaching and writing. He died there in 347 B.C.

Much of Plato's writing deals with political theory and the construction of an ideal society. The belief in an ideal is, in fact, characteristic of most of his work. It is most clearly expressed in his Theory of Forms, according to which in a higher dimension of existence there are perfect Forms of which all the phenomena we perceive in the world around us represent

81 Rembrandt. *Aristotle with a Bust of Homer.* 1653. Oil on canvas, 4'8½" × 4'5¼" (1.44 × 1.37 m). Metropolitan Museum of Art, New York (purchased with special funds and gifts of friends of the Museum, 1961). In this painting the great Dutch painter brings together the first and the last great names in the Greek intellectual tradition.

pale reflections. There can be no doubt that Plato's vision of an ideal society is far too authoritarian for most tastes, involving among other restrictions the careful breeding of children, the censorship of music and poetry, and the abolition of private property. In fairness to Plato, however, it must be remembered that his works are intended not as a set of instructions to be followed literally but as a challenge to think seriously about how our lives should be organized. Furthermore, the disadvantages of democratic government had become all too clear during the last years of the 5th century B.C. If Plato's attempt to redress the balance seems to veer excessively in the other direction, it may in part have been inspired by the continuing chaos of 4th century Greek politics.

Aristotle's Lyceum

Plato's most gifted pupil, Aristotle (384–322 B.C.), continued to develop his master's doctrines, at first wholeheartedly and later critically, for at least twenty years. In 335 B.C., Aristotle founded a school in competition with Plato's Academy, the Lyceum, severing fundamental ties with Plato from then on. Aristotle in effect introduced a rival philosophy—one that has attracted thinking minds ever since [81]. Indeed, in the 19th century the English poet Samuel Taylor Coleridge was to comment, with much truth, that one was born either a "Platonist" or an "Aristotelian."

The Lyceum seems to have been organized with typically Aristotelian efficiency. In the morning Aristotle himself lectured to the full-time students, many of whom came from other parts of Greece to attend his courses and work on the projects he was directing. In the afternoon the students pursued their research in the library, museum, and map collection attached to the Lyceum, while Aristotle gave more general lectures to the public. His custom of strolling along the Lyceum's circular walkways, immersed in profound contemplation or discourse, gained his school the name *Peripatetic,* or the "walking" school.

As a philosopher Aristotle was the greatest systematizer. He wrote on every topic of serious study of the time. Many of his classifications have remained valid to this day, although some of the disciplines, such as psychology and physics, have severed their ties with philosophy and have become important sciences in their own right.

The most complex of Aristotle's works is probably the *Metaphysics,* in which he deals with his chief dispute with Plato, which concerned the Theory of Forms. Plato had postulated a higher dimension of existence for the Ideal Forms and thereby created a split between the apparent reality that we perceive and the genuine reality that we can only know by philosophical contemplation. Moreover, knowledge of these forms depended on a theory of "remembering" them from previous existences. Aristotle, on the other hand, claimed that the forms were actually present in the objects we see around us, thereby eliminating the split between the two realities.

Elsewhere in the *Metaphysics* Aristotle discusses the nature of God, whom he describes as "thought thinking of itself" and "the Unmoved Mover." The nature of the physical universe ruled over by this supreme being is further explored in the *Physics,* which is concerned with the elements that compose the universe and the laws by which they operate.

Other important works by Aristotle include the *Rhetoric,* which prescribes the ideal model of oratory, and the *Poetics,* which does the same for poetry and includes the famous definition of tragedy mentioned earlier (see page 82). Briefly, Aristotle's formula for tragedy is as follows: the tragic hero, who must be noble, through some undetected "tragic flaw" in character meets with a bad end involving the reversal of fortune and sometimes death. The audience, through various emotional and intellectual relations with this tragic figure, undergoes a "cleansing" or "purgation" of the soul, called *catharsis.* Critics of this analysis sometimes complain that Aristotle was trying to read his own very subjective formulas into the Greek tragedies of the time. This is not entirely just, since Aristotle was probably writing for future tragedians, prescribing what ought to be rather than what was.

Aristotle's influence on later ages was vast, although not continuous. Philip of Macedon employed him to tutor young Alexander, but the effect on the young conqueror was probably minimal. Thereafter his works were lost and not recovered until the 1st century B.C., when they were used by the Roman statesman and thinker Cicero (106–43 B.C.). During the Middle Ages, they were translated into Latin and Arabic and became a philosophical basis for Christian theology. Saint Thomas Aquinas' synthesis of Aristotelian philosophy and Christian doctrine still remains the official philosophical position of the Catholic Church.

In philosophy, theology, and scientific and intellectual thought as a whole, many of the distinctions first applied by Aristotle were rediscovered in the early Renaissance and are still valid today. Indeed, no survey such as this can begin to do justice to one described by Dante as "the master of those who know." In the more than two thousand years since his death only Leonardo da Vinci has come near to equaling his creative range.

Music and the Visual Arts

Both Plato and Aristotle found a place for music in their ideal states; their comments on it provide some information on the status of Greek music in the late Classical period. Throughout the 5th century B.C., music had played an important part in dramatic performances but had been generally subordinated to the poetry. By the end of the Peloponnesian War, however, the musical aspect of tragedy had begun to predominate. It is interesting to note that Euripides was criticized by his contemporaries for the lack of form and symmetry and the overemotionalism of his music, not of his verse. With its release from the function of mere accompaniment, instrumental music became especially popular in the 4th century B.C.

The actual sound of Greek music and the principles according to which it was composed are not easy to reconstruct or understand. The numerical relationship of notes to one another established by Pythagoras (see page 69) was used to divide the basic unit of an octave (series of eight notes) into smaller intervals named after their positions in relation to the lowest note in the octave. The interval known as a *fourth,* for example, represents the space between the lowest note and the fourth note up the octave. The intervals were then combined to form a series of scales, or *modes.* Each was given a name and was associated with a particular emotional range. Thus the Dorian mode was serious and warlike, the Phrygian exciting and emotional, and the Mixolydian plaintive and pathetic. It was on the basis of the kind of music likely to be written in a particular mode that Plato permitted some modes in his ideal state and prohibited others.

The unit with which Greek music was constructed was the *tetrachord,* a group of four notes of which the two outer ones are a perfect fourth apart and the inner ones variably spaced. The combination of two tetrachords formed a mode. The Dorian mode, for example, consisted of the following two tetrachords:

The Lydian mode was composed of two different tetrachords:

The origin of the modes and their relationship to one another is uncertain; it was disputed even in ancient times. The situation has not been made easier by the fact that medieval church music adopted the same system of mathematical construction and even some of the same names, but applied them to different modes. Nor do we know much more about Greek concepts of rhythm and harmony. It is probably safest to conclude that although we can form some idea of the importance the Classical Greeks themselves ascribed to music and even understand some of its philosophical implications, we are a long way from being able to re-create its actual sound.

Our knowledge of the visual arts in the 4th century B.C. is similarly incomplete. Greek fresco paint-ing of the period has been entirely lost, though recent discoveries in northern Greece at the Royal Cemetery of Vergina suggest that some of it may yet be found again [82]. In sculpture, fortunately, Roman copies of lost original statues enable us to form a fairly good estimate of the main developments. It is clear that Plato's interest in the fate of the individual soul finds its parallel in the sculptural treatment of the human form. Facial expressions become more human, often characterized by a mood of dreamy tenderness. Technical skill in depicting drapery and the anatomy beneath are put to the service of a new virtuosity. The three sculptors who dominated the art of the 4th century B.C. are Praxiteles, Scopas, and Lysippus.

The influence of Praxiteles on his contemporaries was immense. His particular brand of gentle melancholy is well illustrated by the *Hermes* at Olympia [83] that is generally attributed to him. Equally im-

below: 82 *Pluto Seizing Persephone,* detail of wall painting from Royal Tomb I, Vergina. Mid-4th century B.C. This unique example of Late Classical monumental painting was discovered by the Greek archaeologist Manolis Andronikos in 1977. It shows a remarkable fluency and freedom of technique.

right: 83 Praxiteles. *Hermes with the Infant Dionysus.* c. 340 B.C. Marble, height 7′1″ (2.16 m). Museum, Olympia. Hermes' missing right arm held a bunch of grapes just out of the baby's reach.

portant is his famous statue of Aphrodite nude [84], of which some fifty copies have survived. This represents the discovery of the female body as an object of beauty in itself; it was also one of the first attempts in Western art to introduce the element of sensuality into the portrayal of the female form.

The art of Scopas was more dramatic, with an emphasis on emotion and intensity. Roman copies of his statue of *Pothos,* or Desire [85], allow comparison of this yearning figure with Praxiteles' more relaxed *Hermes.*

The impact of Lysippus was as much on succeeding periods as on his own time. One of his chief claims to fame was as the official portraitist of Alexander the Great. Lysippus' very individual characteristics—a new, more attenuated system of proportion, greater concern for realism, and the large scale of many of his works—had a profound effect later on Hellenistic art [86].

In architecture, as in the arts generally, the Late Classical period was one of innovation. The great sanctuaries at Olympia and Delphi were expanded

left: 84 Praxiteles. *Aphrodite of Cyrene.* Roman copy of c. 100 B.C. Marble, height 5' (1.52 m). National Museum, Rome. This copy was found by chance in the Roman baths at Cyrene, North Africa. The statue is also called *Venus Anadyomene,* the Roman name for Aphrodite and a Greek word meaning "rising up from the sea," often used in referring to Aphrodite because she was supposed to have arisen from the sea at her birth. The porpoise is a reminder of the goddess' oceanic associations.

below: 85 Scopas. *Pothos.* Roman copy after original of c. 350 B.C. Marble. Palazzo dei Conservatori, Rome.

and new building forms were invented, including the *tholos,* or circular building [87]. The most grandiose work of the century was probably the Temple of Artemis at Ephesus, destroyed by fire in 356 B.C. and rebuilt on the same massive scale as before.

Although the Greeks of the 4th century B.C. lacked the certainty and self-confidence of their predecessors, their culture shows no lack of ideas or inspiration. Furthermore, even before Alexander's death the Macedonian Empire had spread Greek culture throughout the Mediterranean world. If Athens itself

86 Lysippus. *Apoxyomenos (The Scraper).* Roman copy after bronze original of c. 330 B.C. Marble, height 6'9" (2.06 m). Vatican Museums, Rome. The young athlete is cleaning off sweat and dirt with a tool called a strigil.

87 Theodoros of Phokaia. Tholos of the Sanctuary of Athena Pronaia, Delphi. c. 390 B.C. Marble and Limestone; diameter of cella 28'2⅝" (8.6 m), present height 27'2½" (8.29 m). This is one of the first circular designs in Greek architecture. Originally, twenty Doric columns encircled the temple and ten Corinthian columns were set against the wall of the cella within.

had lost any real political or commercial importance, the ideas of its great innovators began to affect an ever-growing number of people.

When Alexander died in the summer of 323 B.C., the division of his empire into separate independent kingdoms spread Greek culture even more widely. The kingdoms of the Seleucids in Syria and the Ptolemies in Egypt are the true successors to Periclean Athens. Even as far away as India sculptors and town planners were influenced by ideas developed by Athenians of the 5th and 4th centuries B.C.

In due course, the cultural achievement of Classical Greece was absorbed and reborn in Rome, as Chapter 5 will show. Meanwhile, in the period known as the Hellenistic Age, which lasted from the death of Alexander to the Roman conquest of Greece in 146 B.C., that achievement took a new turn.

The Hellenistic Period

The inability of Alexander's generals to agree on a single successor after his death made the division of the Macedonian Empire inevitable. The four most important kingdoms that split off, Syria (the kingdom of the Seleucids), Egypt, Pergamum, and Macedonia itself (see map below), were soon at loggerheads and remained so until they were finally conquered by Rome. Each of them, however, in its own way continued the spread of Greek culture, as the name of the period implies (it is derived from the verb "to Hellenize," or to spread Greek influence).

The greatest of all centers of Greek learning was in the Egyptian city of Alexandria, where Ptolemy, Alexander's former personal staff officer and bodyguard, planned a large institute for scholarship known as the Temple of the Muses, or the Museum. The Library at the Museum contained everything of importance ever written in Greek, up to seven hundred thousand separate works, according to contemporary authorities. Its destruction by fire when Julius Caesar besieged the city in 47 B.C. must surely be one of the greatest intellectual disasters in the history of Western culture.

In Asia Minor and farther east in Syria the Hellenistic rulers of the new kingdoms fostered Greek art and literature as one means of holding foreign influences at bay. Libraries were built at Pergamum and the Syrian capital of Antioch, and philosophers from Greece were encouraged to visit the new centers of learning and lecture there. In this way Greek ideas not only retained their hold but began to make an impression on more remote peoples even farther east. The first Buddhist monumental sculpture, which is called Gandharan after the Indian province of Gandhara where it developed, made use of Greek styles and techniques. There is even a classic Buddhist religious work called *The Questions of King Milinda* in which a local Greek ruler, probably called Menandros, is described exchanging ideas with a Buddhist sage, ending with the ruler's conversion to Buddhism—one example of the failure of Greek ideas to convince.

Yet, however much literature and philosophy could do to maintain the importance of Greek culture, it was primarily to the visual arts that Hellenistic rulers turned. In doing so they inaugurated the last great period of Greek art.

The most powerful influence on the period immediately following Alexander's death was the memory

88 *Alexander the Great*. Pergamum, c. 160 B.C. Marble. Archaeological Museum, Istanbul. Note the emotional quality of the eyes and mouth, emphasized by the set of the head.

The artists responsible for these innovations created their works for a new kind of patron. Most of the great works of the Classical period had been produced for the state, with the result that the principal themes and inspirations were religious and political. With the distintegration of the Macedonian Empire and the establishment of prosperous kingdoms at Pergamum, Antioch, and elsewhere, there developed a group of powerful rulers and wealthy businessmen who commissioned works either to provide lavish decoration for their cities or to adorn their private palaces and villas. The artist was no longer responsible to humanity and to the gods, but to whoever paid for the work. As a result, the artist was encouraged to develop new techniques and surpass the achievements of rivals.

At the same time, the change in the artist's social role produced a change in the function of the work. Whereas in the Classical period architects had devoted themselves to the construction of temples and religious sanctuaries, the Hellenistic age is notable for its marketplaces and theaters, as well as for scientific and technical buildings like the Tower of the Winds at Athens and the Lighthouse at Alexandria [89].

Among the rich cities of Hellenistic Asia, none was richer than Pergamum, ruled by a dynasty of kings known as the Attalids. Pergamum was founded in the early 3rd century B.C. and reached the

of his life. The daring and immensity of his conquests, his own heroic personality, the new world that he had sought to create—all these produced a spirit of adventure and experiment. Artists of the Hellenistic period sought not so much to equal or surpass their Classical predecessors in the familiar forms as to discover new subjects and invent new techniques. The development of realistic portraiture dates to this period [88], as does the construction of buildings like the Lighthouse at Alexandria [89], in its day the tallest tower ever built and one of the Seven Wonders of the World.

The all-pervading spirit of the Classical Age had been order. Now artists began to discover the delights of freedom. Classical art was calm and restrained, but Hellenistic art was emotional and expressive. Classical artists sought clarity and balance even in showing scenes of violence, but Hellenistic artists allowed themselves to depict riotous confusion involving strong contrasts of light and shade and the appearance of perpetual motion. It is not surprising that the term *baroque,* originally used to describe the extravagant European art of the 17th century A.D., is often applied to the art of the Hellenistic period.

89 Reconstruction of the Lighthouse on Pharos, north of Alexandria harbor, 279 B.C. Original height 440′ (134.2 m). The beam of light from the lantern at top was intensified by a system of reflectors. The name of the island, Pharos, became, and still is, another word for lighthouse or beacon.

above: **90** Reconstruction model of Upper City, Pergamum. State Museums, East Berlin. The steeply sloping theater is at left; the altar to Zeus is in the center foreground.

right: **91** *Athena Slaying Giant,* detail of Altar to Zeus frieze, Pergamum. c. 180 B.C. Marble, height 7′6″ (2.29 m). State Museums, East Berlin. Athena is grasping the giant Alcyoneus by the hair to lift him off the ground, source of his strength. His mother Ge, the earth goddess, looks on despairingly from below.

high point of its greatness in the reign of Eumenes II (197–159 B.C.). The layout of the chief buildings in the city represents a rejection of the Classical concepts of order and balance. Unlike the Periclean buildings on the Athenian Acropolis, the buildings in Pergamum were placed independently of one another with a new and theatrical use of space. The theater itself, set on a steep slope, seemed to be falling dramatically down the hillside [90].

The chief religious shrine of Pergamum was the immense altar to Zeus erected by Eumenes II around 180 B.C. to commemorate the victories of his father, Attalus I, over the Gauls. Its base is decorated with a colossal frieze depicting the battle of the gods and giants. The triumphant figure of Zeus presumably stands as a symbol for the victorious king of Pergamum. The drama and violence of the battle find perfect expression in the tangled, writhing bodies, which leap out of the frieze in high relief, and in the intensity of the gestures and facial expressions [91]. The immense emotional impact of the scenes may prevent us from appreciating the remarkable skill of the artists, some of whom were brought from Athens to work on the project. However, the movement of the figures is very far from random and the surface of the stone has been carefully worked to reproduce the texture of hair, skin, fabric, metal, and so on.

The Altar of Zeus represents the most complete illustration of the principles and practice of Hellenistic art. It is, of course, a work on a grand, even grandiose, scale, intended to impress a wide public. But many of its characteristics occur in freestanding pieces of sculpture like the *Laocoön* [92]. This famous work shows the Trojan priest Laocoön, punished by the gods for his attempt to warn his people against bringing into their city the wooden horse left by the Greeks. To silence the priest, Apollo sends two sea serpents to strangle him and his sons. The large piece is superbly composed, with the three figures bound together by the sinuous curves of the serpents; each of them turns in a different direction under the agony of the creatures' coils.

By the end of the Hellenistic period both artists and public seemed a little weary of so much richness and elaboration and returned to some of the principles of Classical art. At the same time the gradual conquest of the Hellenistic kingdoms by Rome and their absorption into the Roman Empire produced a new synthesis in which the achievements of Classical and Hellenistic Greece fused with the native Italian culture and passed on to later ages.

92 Agesander, Athenodorus, and Polydorus of Rhodes. *Laocoön Group*. c. 150 B.C. Marble, height 8' (2.44 m). Vatican Museums, Rome. This statue was uncovered in 1506 in the ruins of Nero's Golden House. Note the similarity between Laocoön's head and the head of the giant Alcyoneus on the Pergamum frieze. The sons were made relatively small probably to indicate that, though they were grown men, they were sons.

Questions for Further Discussion

1. Ever since the 4th century B.C., thinking human beings have categorized themselves—and others—as either "Platonists" or "Aristotelians." What are the chief distinctions between the two? Do they still have any validity in our own time?
2. On a very few occasions in the history of our culture a single city has, for a short time, produced a large number of great artists, writers, and thinkers—Athens in the 5th century B.C., for example, and Florence in the Renaissance. What kind of conditions made this possible?

Could they be reproduced artificially, and, if so, should they be?
3. Greek mythology, and the dramas based on it, covers a wide range of human experience, but not all of it. What are some of the aspects of life that apparently did *not* interest the Greeks?
4. Thucydides wrote his *History of the Peloponnesian War* in the belief that people could learn from the mistakes of the past and thereby live better lives. If he was wrong—and events seem to show him so—what other justification is there for writing and reading history?
5. From the very beginning, Greek sculptors were accustomed to carve their male figures nude, and by the 4th century B.C. were also producing nude female figures. What does the Greek obsession with the naked body suggest about their world view? How does it compare with our own?
6. The Greek word for Greece is *Hellas* and for its people *Hellenes*. Why do we use the word, "Greece," and what does it tell us about the transmission of Greek culture?

| | **GENERAL EVENTS** | **LITERATURE & PHILOSOPHY** |

753 B.C. ─────────────────────────────────────

753 B.C. Founding of Rome (traditional date)

c. 700 Development of Etruscan culture

509 ─────────────────────────────────────

509 Expulsion of Etruscan kings and foundation of Roman Republic

c. 390 Sack of Rome by Gauls

264–241 First Punic War: Roman conquest of Sicily, Sardinia, Corsica

218–201 Second Punic War: Roman conquest of Spain

146 Destruction of Carthage: Africa becomes Roman province. Sack of Corinth: Greece becomes Roman province

c. 200–160 B.C. Ennius, *Annales,* epic poem; Plautus, *Mostellaria,* Roman comedy; Terence, Roman comedies

2d cent. Epicureanism and Stoicism imported to Rome

133 ─────────────────────────────────────

90–88 Social War

82–81 Sulla dictator at Rome

60 First Triumvirate: Pompey, Caesar, Crassus

58–56 Caesar conquers Gaul

48 Battle of Pharsalus: war of Caesar and Pompey ends in death of Pompey. Caesar meets Cleopatra in Egypt

46–44 Caesar rules Rome as dictator until assassinated

43 Second Triumvirate: Antony, Lepidus, Octavian

c. 65–43 Lucretius, *On the Nature of Things,* Epicurean poem; Cicero, orations and philosophical essays; Catullus, lyric poems; Caesar, *Commentaries,* on Gallic wars

31 ─────────────────────────────────────

31 Battle of Actium won by Octavian

30 Death of Antony and Cleopatra

27–14 Octavian under name of Augustus rules as first Roman emperor

c. 27 B.C.–A.D. 14 Horace, *Odes* and *Ars Poetica;* Vergil, *Aeneid, Georgics, Eclogues;* Ovid, *Metamorphoses,* mythological tales; Livy, *Annals of the Roman People*

B.C. ─────────────────────────────────────
A.D.

c. 6 Birth of Jesus; crucified c. A.D. 30

A.D. 14–68 Julio-Claudian emperors: Tiberius, Caligula, Claudius, Nero

69–96 Flavian emperors: Vespasian, Titus, Domitian

70 Capture of Jerusalem by Titus; destruction of Solomon's Temple

79 Destruction of Pompeii and Herculaneum

96–138 Adoptive emperors: Nerva, Trajan, Hadrian, et al.

138–192 Antonine emperors: Antoninus Pius, Marcus Aurelius, et al.

c. A.D. 100–150 Tacitus, *History;* Juvenal, *Satires;* Pliny the Younger, *Letters;* Suetonius, *Lives of the Caesars;* Epictetus, *Enchiridion,* on Stoicism

c. 166–179 Marcus Aurelius, *Meditations,* on Stoicism

180 ─────────────────────────────────────

193–235 Severan emperors: Septimius Severus, Caracalla, et al.

212 Edict of Caracalla

284 ─────────────────────────────────────

284–305 Reign of Diocletian; return of civil order

301 Edict of Diocletian, fixing wages and prices

305 Constantius and Galerius rule as joint emperors

307–337 Reign of Constantine; sole emperor after 324

330 Founding of Constantinople

409–455 Vandals and Visigoths invade Italy, Spain, Gaul, Africa

476 Romulus Augustulus forced to abdicate as last Western Roman emperor

476 A.D. ─────────────────────────────────────

ROMAN REPUBLIC

ROMAN EMPIRE

Conquest of Italy and Mediterranean

Political Crisis at Rome

Stability

Disintegration

Reconstruction and Decline

ART   ARCHITECTURE   MUSIC

c. 650–500 B.C.
Influence of Greek and
Orientalizing styles
on Etruscan art

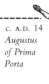

late 6th cent.
Etruscan
Apollo,
from Veii

c. 616–509 B.C.
Etruscans drain
marshes, build temples,
construct roads

Extension of Greek
trumpet into Roman
tuba, used in games,
processions, battles

c. 2d cent. B.C. Greek
music becomes popular
at Rome

1st cent. Discovery
of concrete

1st cent. Realistic
portraiture; *Portrait
of Cicero*

c. 82 Sulla commissions
Sanctuary of Fortuna
Primagenia,
Praeneste

c. 30 B.C.–A.D. 30
Villa of Mysteries
frescoes, Pompeii

c. 20 *View of a Garden,*
fresco from Augustus'
villa, Prima Porta

13–9 *Ara Pacis*

Use of arch,
vault, dome,
principles of stress/
counterstress

c. A.D. 14
*Augustus
of Prima
Porta*

1st cent. A.D. Pont du
Gard, Nîmes; atrium-
style houses at Pompeii

c. 126 Pantheon,
Rome

Decline of realism

300–305 Diocletian's
palace, Split

306–315 Basilica of
Constantine, Rome

324–330 Colossal head
from Basilica of
Constantine, Rome

5

The Roman Legacy

The Importance of Rome

The contribution of Rome to the development of Western civilization is tremendous. In fields like language, law, politics, religion, and art Roman culture continues to affect our lives. The road network of modern Europe is based on one planned and built by the Romans some two thousand years ago; the alphabet we use is the Roman alphabet; and the division of the year into twelve months of unequal length is a modified form of the calendar introduced by Julius Caesar in 45 B.C. Even after the fall of the Roman Empire the city of Rome stood for centuries as the symbol of civilization itself; later empires deliberately shaped themselves on the Roman model.

The enormous impact of Rome on our culture is partly due to the industrious and determined character of the Romans themselves, who very early in their history saw themselves as the divinely appointed rulers of the world. In the course of fulfilling their mission they spread Roman culture from the north of England to Africa, from Spain to India (see map). This Romanization of the entire known world permitted the spread of ideas the Romans had drawn from other peoples. It was through the Romans that Greek art and literature were handed down into the Western tradition, and not from the Greeks themselves. The rapid spread of Christianity in the 4th century A.D. was a result of the decision of the Roman emperors to adopt it as the official religion of the Roman Empire. In these and in other respects, the legacy Rome was to pass on to Western civilization had been inherited from its predecessors.

The Romans themselves were surprisingly modest about their own cultural achievements, in fact, believing that their strengths lay in good government and military prowess rather than in artistic and intellectual attainments. It was their view that Rome should get on with the job of ruling the world and leave luxuries like sculpture and astronomy to others.

93 Gladiatorial contest with orchestra of hydraulic organ, trumpet, and horn players. Mosaic from villa near Zliten, North Africa, c. A.D. 70. Museum of Antiquities, Tripoli.

It is easy but unfair to accept the Romans' estimate of themselves as uncreative without questioning it. True, in some fields the Roman contribution was not very impressive. What little we know about Roman music, for example, suggests that its loss is hardly a serious one. It was intended mainly for performance at religious events like weddings and funerals, and as a background for social occasions. Musicians were often brought into aristocratic homes to provide after-dinner entertainment at a party, and individual performers, frequently women, would play before small groups in a domestic setting. Small bands of traveling musicians, playing on pipes and such percussion instruments as cymbals and tambourines, provided background music for the acrobats and jugglers who performed in public squares and during gladiatorial contests [93].

Nonetheless, for the Romans music certainly had none of the intellectual and philosophical significance it bore for the Greeks, and when Roman writers mention musical performances it is often to complain about the noise. The only serious development in Roman music was the extension of the Greek trumpet into a longer and louder bronze instrument known as the *tuba*, which was used on public occasions like games and processions and in battle, when an especially powerful type some 4 feet (1.2 meters) long gave the signals for attack and retreat. The sound was not pleasant.

In general, Roman music-lovers contented themselves with Greek music played on Greek instruments. Although serious music began to grow in popularity with the spread of Greek culture, it always remained an aristocratic rather than popular taste.

The emperor Nero's love of music, coupled with his insistence on giving public concerts on the lyre, may even have hastened his downfall.

In areas other than music, the Roman achievement is considerable. There is no doubt that Roman art and literature rarely show the originality of their Greek predecessors, but originality is not the only artistic virtue, nor is its absence always a defect. The Roman genius, in fact, lay precisely in absorbing and assimilating influences from outside and going on to create from them something typically Roman. The lyric poetry of 1st-century B.C. writers like Catullus was inspired by the works of Sappho, Alcaeus, and other Greek poets of the 6th century B.C., but nothing could be more Roman in spirit than Catullus' poems. In architecture, the Romans achieved a style that is one of the most impressive of all our legacies from the ancient world.

It is useful to emphasize the very real value of Roman art and literature because there has been a tendency since the 19th century to exalt the Greek cultural achievement at the expense of the Roman. All agree on the superior quality of Roman roads, sewers, and acqueducts; Roman sculpture or drama has in general been less highly rated, mainly because of comparisons with that of the Greeks. Any study of Roman culture inevitably involves examining the influences that went to make it up, and it is necessary always to remember the Roman ability to absorb and combine outside ideas and create something fresh from them.

Rome's history was a long one, beginning with the foundation of the city in the 8th century B.C. As the empire grew, Roman civilization developed along with it, assimilating the cultures of the peoples who fell under Roman domination. But long before the Romans conquered Greece or anywhere else, they were themselves conquered by the Etruscans, and the story of Rome's rise to power truly begins with the impact on Roman life made by Etruscan rule there.

The Etruscans and Their Art

The late 8th century B.C. was a time of great activity in Italy. The Greeks had reached the south coast and the island of Sicily. In the valley of the river Tiber, farmers and herdsmen of a group of tribes known as the Latins (origin of the name of the language spoken by the Romans throughout their history) were establishing small village settlements, one of which was to become the future imperial city of Rome. The most flourishing area at the time, however, was to the north of Rome, where in central Italy a new culture—the Etruscan—was appearing.

The Etruscans are among the most intriguing of ancient peoples, and ever since early Roman times scholars have argued about who they were, where they came from, and what language they spoke. Even today, in spite of the discoveries of modern archaeologists, we still know little about the origins of the Etruscans and their language has still not been deciphered. By 700 B.C. they had established them-

selves in the part of Italy named for them, Tuscany; but it is not clear whether they arrived from abroad or whether their culture was merely a more developed form of an earlier Italian one. The ancient Greeks and Romans believed that the Etruscans had come to Italy from the East, perhaps from Lydia, an ancient kingdom in Asia Minor. Indeed, many aspects of their life and much of their art have pronounced Eastern characteristics. In other ways, however, the Etruscans have much in common with their predecessors in central Italy. Even so, no other culture related to the Etruscans' has ever been found. Whatever their origins, they were to have a major effect upon Italian life, and on the growth of Rome and its culture in particular [94].

From the very beginning of their history the Etruscans showed an outstanding sophistication and technological ability. The sumptuous gold treasures buried in their tombs are evidence both of their material prosperity and of their superb craftsmanship. The commercial contacts of the Etruscans extended over most of the western Mediterranean, and in Italy itself Etruscan cities like Cerveteri and Tarquinia developed rich artistic traditions. Much Etruscan art shows the presence of Greek ideas. The Etruscans, like the Greeks, were strongly affected by Orientalizing influences. Nonetheless, Etruscan art has its own special character, a kind of elemental force almost primitive in spirit, although the craftsmanship and techniques are highly sophisticated. Unlike the

94 *Capitoline She-Wolf.* Etruscan, late 6th or early 5th century B.C. Bronze, length 4′4″ (1.32 m). Capitoline Museum, Rome. Although this statue or one very like it became the mascot of Rome, it was probably made by an Etruscan craftsman. The twins Romulus and Remus, legendary founders of the city, were added during the Renaissance.

Greeks, the Etruscans were less interested in intellectual problems of proportion or understanding how the human body works than in producing an immediate impact upon the viewer. The famous statue of Apollo found in 1916 at Veii [95] is unquestionably related to Greek models, but the tension of the god's pose and the sinister quality of his smile produce an effect of great power in a typically Etruscan way. Other Etruscan art is more relaxed, showing a love of nature rarely found in Greek art. The wonderful paintings in the Tomb of Hunting and Fishing at Tarquinia (Plate 8, page 89) convey a marvelous sense of light and air, the hazy blue background evoking all the sensations of sea and spray.

This immensely gifted people was bound to exert a strong influence on the development of civilization in Italy; Etruscan occupation of Rome from 616 to 510 B.C. marks a turning point in Roman history. According to later tradition, the city of Rome had been founded in 753 B.C. and was ruled in its earliest days by kings (in actual fact Rome was probably not much more than a small country town for most of this period). The later Romans' own grandiose picture of the early regal days of their city was intended to glamorize its origins, but only with the arrival of the Etruscans did anything like an urban center begin to develop. Etruscan engineers drained a large marshy area, previously uninhabitable, which became the community's center, the future Roman Forum. They built temples and shrines and constructed roads. Under Etruscan instruction new crafts developed and guilds were established, including those of the bronze workers, goldsmiths, and carpenters. Among other innovations the Etruscans introduced a number of things we are accustomed to think of as typically Roman, including public games like chariot racing and even the toga, the most characteristic form of Roman dress.

Most important, however, was the fact that under Etruscan domination the Romans found themselves for the first time in contact with the larger world. Instead of being simple villagers living in a small community governed by tribal chiefs they became part of a large cultural unit with links throughout Italy and abroad. Within a hundred years Rome had truly learned the lessons of Etruscan technology and culture, had driven out the Etruscans, and had begun her unrelenting climb to power.

The rise of Rome signaled the decline of the Etruscans throughout Italy. In the centuries following their expulsion from Rome in 510 B.C., their cities were conquered and their territory taken over by the Romans. In the 1st century B.C. they automatically received the right of Roman citizenship and became

95 *Apollo of Veii.* Etruscan, late 6th or early 5th century B.C. Terra cotta, height 5'10" (1.78 m). Museo Nazionale di Villa Giulia, Rome.

absorbed into the Roman empire. The gradual collapse of their world is mirrored in later Etruscan art. The wall paintings in the tombs become increasingly gloomy, suggesting that for an Etruscan of the 4th or 3rd century B.C. the misfortunes of this life were followed by the tortures of the next in an underworld ruled by demons and monsters. The old couple from

Volterra whose anxious faces are so vividly depicted on the lid of their sarcophagus [96] give us some idea of the troubled spirit of the final days of Etruscan culture.

Republican Rome

The end of Etruscan rule brought a change in the system of Roman government. Instead of choosing a new king, Rome constituted itself a republic, governed by the people somewhat along the lines of the Greek city-states, although less democratically. Two chief magistrates or consuls were elected for a one-year term by all the male citizens, but the principal assembly, the Senate, drew most of its members from Roman aristocratic families. From the very beginning, therefore, power was concentrated in the hands of the upper class, the patricians, although the lower class (the plebeians) was permitted to form its own assembly. The leaders elected by the plebeian assembly, the tribunes, represented the plebeians' interests and protected them against state officials who treated them unjustly. The meeting place for both the Senate and the assemblies of the people was the *forum,* the large open space at the foot of the Palatine and Capitoline hills that had been drained and made habitable by the Etruscans [97].

From the founding of the Roman Republic to its bloody end in the civil wars following the murder of Julius Caesar in 44 B.C., its history was dominated by agitation for political equality. Yet, the first major confrontation, the conflict between patricians and plebeians, never seriously endangered political stability in Rome or military campaigns abroad. Both sides showed a flexibility and spirit of compromise that produced a gradual growth in plebeian power while avoiding any split disastrous enough to interrupt Rome's growing domination of the Italian peninsula. The final plebeian victory came in 287 B.C. with the passage of the Hortensian Law, which made the decisions of the plebeian assembly binding on the entire Senate and Roman people. By then most of Italy had already fallen under Roman control.

Increasing power brought increasing problems. In the 3rd and 2nd centuries B.C. Rome began to build its empire abroad. By the 1st century B.C. the whole Hellenistic world had been conquered. From Spain to the Middle East stretched a vast territory consisting of subject provinces, protectorates, and nominally free kingdoms, all of which depended on Roman good will and Roman administrative efficiency.

Unfortunately, the Romans had been too busy in acquiring their empire to think very hard about how to rule it; the results were frequently chaotic. Provincial administration was incompetent and often corrupt. The long series of wars had hardened the Roman character, leading to insensitivity and, frequently, brutality in the treatment of conquered peoples. This situation was not helped by increasing political instability at home. The old balance of power struck between the patricians and plebeians was being increasingly disturbed by the rise of a middle class, many of whom were plebeians who had made their fortunes in the wars. Against this background were fought bitter struggles that eventually caused the collapse of the Republic.

By the 1st century B.C. it was apparent that the political system that had been devised for a thriving

96 Lid of a funerary urn showing the dead couple whose ashes it contains. Etruscan, 1st century B.C. Terra cotta, length 18½" (47 cm). Museo Guarnacci, Volterra.

97 Aerial view of the Roman forum—center of the political, economic, and religious life of the Roman world—as it appears today.

but small city five hundred years earlier was hopelessly inadequate for a vast empire. Discontent among Rome's Italian allies led to open revolt. Although the Romans were victorious in the Social War of 90–88 B.C. the cost in lives and economic stability was tremendous. The ineffectiveness of the Senate and the frustration of the Roman people led to a series of struggles among the leading statesmen for supreme power. The Roman general Sulla ruled as dictator for a brief and violent period beginning in 82 B.C., but suddenly resigned three years later, in 79 B.C. There followed a long-drawn-out series of political skirmishes between Pompey, the self-appointed defender of the Senate, and Julius Caesar, culminating in Caesar's withdrawal to Gaul and subsequent return to Rome in 49 B.C. After a short but bitter conflict Caesar defeated Pompey in 48 B.C. at the Battle of Pharsalus and returned to Rome as dictator, only to be assassinated himself in 44 B.C. The civil wars that followed brought the Republic to its unlamented end.

The years of almost uninterrupted violence had a profound effect upon the Roman character, and the relief felt when a new era dawned under the first emperor, Augustus, can only be fully appreciated in this light. Yet the figures who dominated the events of the late Republic—or were dominated by them— are among the most fascinating in Roman history. Julius Caesar (100–44 B.C.) is perhaps the most famous Roman of them all. Brilliant politician, skilled general, expert administrator and organizer, he was also able to write the history of his own military campaigns in his *Commentaries,* in a simple but gripping style. In the four years during which he ruled Rome he did much to repair the damage of the previous decades. His assassination on March 15, 44 B.C., at the hands of a band of devoted republicans served only to prolong Rome's agony for another thirteen years—as well as providing Shakespeare with the plot for one of his best-known plays.

Among the most lasting achievements of Julius Caesar's dictatorship and of Roman culture in general was the creation of a single unified code of civil law, the *Ius Civile*. The science of law is one of the few original creations of Roman literature. The earliest legal code of the Republic was the so-called Law of the Twelve Tables of 451–450 B.C. By the time of Caesar, however, most of this law had become either irrelevant or out of date and had been replaced by a mass of later legislation, much of it contradictory and confusing. Caesar's *Ius Civile,* produced with the help of the most eminent legal experts of the day, served as the model for later times. The most complete collection of Roman law was, in fact, made during Byzantine times by the Byzantine emperor Justinian I (A.D. 527–565).

Perhaps the most endearing figure of the late Republic was Marcus Tillius Cicero (106–43 B.C.), who first made his reputation as a lawyer. He is certainly the figure of this period about whom we know the most, for he took part in a number of important legal cases and embarked on a political career. In 63 B.C., he served as consul. A few years later, the severity with which he had put down a plot against the government during his consulship earned him a short period in exile as the result of the scheming of a rival political faction. He returned in triumph, however, and in the struggle between Pompey and Caesar supported Pompey, although Caesar seems to have forgiven him.

We can derive an incomparably vivid picture of Cicero and his world from the many letters he wrote that have survived. Almost nine hundred were published, most of them after his death. If they often reveal Cicero's weaknesses—his vanity, his inability to make a decision, his stubbornness—they confirm his humanity and sensitivity. For his contemporaries and for later ages his chief fame was nevertheless as an orator. Although the cases and causes that prompted his speeches have ceased to have any but historical interest, the power of a Ciceronian oration can still thrill the responsive reader, especially when it is read aloud.

Literary Developments

The Romans put most of their energy into political and military affairs, leaving little time for art or literature. By the 3rd century B.C., when most of the Mediterranean was under their control and they could afford to relax, they were overwhelmed intellectually and artistically by the Greeks. Conquest of the Hellenistic kingdoms of the East and of Greece itself brought the Romans into contact with Hellenistic Greek culture (see pages 100–103). Thus, from the 3rd century B.C. most Roman works of art followed Greek models in form and content. Roman plays were based on Greek originals, Roman temples imitated Greek buildings, and Roman sculpture and painting depicted episodes from Greek mythology.

Greek influence extends to the works of Ennius (239–169 B.C.), known to later Romans as the father of Roman poetry. Almost all of his works are lost, but from later accounts Ennius' tragedies appear to have been adapted from Greek models. His major work was the *Annals,* an epic chronicle of the history of Rome, in which for the first time a Greek metrical scheme was used to write Latin verse.

The two comic playwrights Plautus (c. 254–184 B.C.) and Terence (c. 195–159 B.C.) are the first Roman writers whose works have survived in quantity. Their plays are adaptations of Greek comedies. Plautus, the more boisterous of the two, is fond of comic songs and farcical intrigues. Terence's style is more refined and his characters show greater realism. It says something about the taste of the Roman public that Plautus was by far the more successful. In later times, however, Terence's sophisticated style was much admired. His plays were studied and imitated both during the Middle Ages and in more recent times. Both authors were fond of extremely elaborate plots involving mistaken identities, identical twins, and general confusion, with everything sorted out in the last scene.

In general, however, when educated Romans of the late Republic stopped to think about something other than politics it was likely to be love. Roman lyric poetry, often on a romantic theme, is one of the most rewarding genres of Latin literature. The first great Roman lyric poet, Catullus (c. 80–54 B.C.), is one of the best-loved of all Roman authors. Instead of philosophical or historical themes, he returned to a traditional subject from Sappho's time—personal experience—and charted the course of his own love affair with a girl whom he calls Lesbia. Among his works are 25 short poems describing the course of his relationship that range from the ecstasy of its early stages to the disillusionment and despair of the final breakup. The clarity of his style is the perfect counterpart to the direct expression of his emotions.

These poems, personal though they are, are not simply an outpouring of feelings. Catullus makes his own experiences universal. However trivial one man's unhappy love affair may seem in the context of the grim world of the late Republic, Lesbia's inconstancy has achieved a timelessness unequaled by many more serious events.

Art and Architecture

In the visual arts as in literature, the late Republic shows the translation of Greek styles into new Roman forms. The political scene was dominated by individuals like Cicero and Caesar; their individualism was captured in portrait busts that were both realistic and psychologically revealing. To some extent these realistic portraits are based on such Etruscan models as the heads of the old couple on the Volterra sarcophagus [see 96] rather than on Hellenistic portraits, which idealized their subjects. However, the subtlety and understanding shown in portraits like those of Cicero and Caesar represent a typically Roman combination and amplification of others' styles. In many respects, indeed, Roman portraiture represents Roman art at its most creative and sensitive. It certainly opened up new expressive possibilities, as artists discovered how to use physical appearance to convey something about character. Many of the best Roman portraits serve as revealing psychological documents, expressing, for example, Cicero's self-satisfaction as well as his humanity [98]. Realistic details like the lines at the corners of the eyes and mouth, the hollows in the cheeks, or the set of the lips are used to express both outer appearance and ethical question. In consequence most of the great Roman philosophical writers devoted their energies to expounding Greek philosophy to a Roman audience. The two principal schools of philosophy to make an impact at Rome, *Epicureanism* and *Stoicism,* were both imported from Greece.

Epicureanism never really gained many followers, in spite of the efforts of the poet Lucretius (99–55 B.C.), who expounded its doctrines to a Roman audience in his brilliant poem *On the Nature of Things (De Rerum natura)*. A remarkable synthesis of poetry and philosophy, this work alone is probably responsible for whatever admiration the Romans could muster for a system of thought so different from their own traditional virtues of simplicity and seriousness. According to Epicurus (341–271 B.C.), the founder of the school, the correct goal and principle of human

98 *Bust of Cicero.* Roman, 1st century B.C. Uffizi, Florence. This portrait of one of the leading figures of the late Republic suggests the ability of Roman sculptors of the period to capture both likeness and character. Cicero is portrayed as thoughtful and preoccupied.

inner character. The new skill, as it developed, could of course be put to propaganda use, and statesmen and politicians soon learned that they could project their chosen self-image through their portraits.

The powerful political figures of the period also used the medium of architecture to express their authority. The huge sanctuary constructed by Sulla at Praeneste (modern Palestrina) around 82 B.C. [99] has all the qualities of symmetry and grandeur we associate with later Roman imperial architecture, although it took its inspiration from massive Hellenistic building programs such as that at Pergamum. Caesar himself had a large area in the center of Rome cleared for the construction of a forum, or public meeting place, to be named after him. In time it was dwarfed by later monumental fora, but it had initiated the construction of public buildings for personal display and glory.

Roman Philosophy

The Romans produced little in the way of original philosophical writing. Their practical nature made them suspicious of professional philosophers and unable to appreciate the rather subtle delights involved in arguing both sides of a complex moral or

99 Plan of the Sanctuary of Fortuna Primigenia, Praeneste (Palestrina). This vast complex, constructed by Sulla after his destruction of the city in 82 B.C., is a series of six immense terraces crowned by a semicircular structure in front of which stood an altar.

actions is pleasure. Although Epicureanism stresses moderation and prudence in the pursuit of pleasure, the Romans insisted on thinking of the philosophy as a typically Greek enthusiasm for self-indulgence and debauchery.

Lucretius tried to correct this impression by emphasizing the profoundly intellectual and rational aspects of Epicureanism. Its principal teaching was that the gods, if they exist, play no part in human affairs or in the phenomena of nature; as a result we can live our lives free from superstitious fear of the unknown and the threat of divine retribution. The Epicurean theory of matter explains the universe in purely physical terms. It describes the universe as made up of two elements: small particles of matter, or atoms, and empty space. The atoms are completely solid, possessing the qualities of size, shape, and mass, and can be neither split nor destroyed. Their joining together to form complex structures is entirely caused by their random swerving in space, without interference from the gods. As a result, human life can be lived in complete freedom; we can face the challenges of existence and even natural disasters like earthquakes or plagues with complete serenity, since their occurrence is random and outside our control. According to Epicurus, at death the atoms that make up our body separate, and neither body, mind, nor soul survives. Since no part of us is in any way immortal, we should have no fear of death, which offers no threat of punishment in a future world but brings only the complete ending of any sensation.

Epicureanism's rejection of a divine force in the world and its campaign against superstition probably appealed to the Romans as little as its claim that the best life was one of pleasure and calm composure. The hardheaded practical moralizing of the Roman mentality found far more appeal in the other school of philosophy imported into Rome from Greece, Stoicism. The Stoics taught that the world was governed by Reason and that Divine Providence watched over the virtuous, never allowing them to suffer evil. The key to becoming virtuous lay in willing or desiring only that which was under one's own control. Thus riches, power, or even physical health—all subject to the whims of Fortune—were excluded as objects of desire. For the Stoic all that counted was that which was subject to the individual's will.

Although Stoicism had already won a following at Rome by the 1st century B.C. and was discussed by Cicero in his philosophical writings, its chief literary exponents came slightly later. Seneca (8 B.C.–A.D. 65) wrote a number of essays on Stoic morality. He had an opportunity, and the necessity, to practice the moral fortitude about which he wrote when his former pupil, the emperor Nero, ordered him to commit suicide, since the taking of one's own life was fully sanctioned by Stoic philosophers. Perhaps the most impressive of all Stoic writers is Epictetus (c. A.D. 50–134), a former slave who established a school of philosophy in Rome and then in Greece. In his *Encheiridion* (*Handbook*) he recommends an absolute trust in Divine Providence to be maintained through every misfortune. For Epictetus the philosopher represented the spokesman of Providence itself "taking the human race for his children."

Epictetus' teachings exerted a profound influence on the last great Stoic, the emperor Marcus Aurelius (A.D. 121–180), who was constantly plagued with the difficulty of being a Stoic and an emperor at the same time. Delicate in health, sentimental, inclined to be disillusioned by the weaknesses of others, Marcus Aurelius struggled hard to maintain the balance between his public duty and his personal convictions. While on military duty he composed his *Meditations,* which are less a philosophical treatise than an account of his own attempt to live the life of a Stoic. As many of his observations make clear, this was no easy task: "Tell yourself every morning 'Today I shall meet the officious, the ungrateful, the bullying, the treacherous, the envious, the selfish. All of them behave like this because they do not know the difference between good and bad.'"

Yet, even though Stoicism continued to attract a number of Roman intellectuals, the great majority of Romans remained immune to the appeal of the philosophical life. Both in the 1st century B.C. and later, the very superstition both Stoicism and Epicureanism sought to combat remained deeply ingrained in the Roman character. Festivals in honor of traditional deities were celebrated until long after the advent of Christianity. Rituals that tried to read the future by the traditional examination of animals' entrails and other time-honored methods continued to be popular. If the Romans had paused more often to meditate on the nature of existence, they would probably have had less time to civilize the world.

The Age of Augustus

With the assassination of Julius Caesar a brief respite from civil war was followed by further turmoil [100]. Caesar's lieutenant, Mark Antony, led the campaign to avenge his death and punish the conspirators. He was joined in this by Caesar's young great-nephew, Octavius, who had been named by Caesar as his heir and had recently arrived in Rome from the provinces. It soon became apparent that Antony and

Octavius (or Octavian, to use the name he now took) were unlikely to coexist very happily. After the final defeat of the conspirators in 42 B.C. a temporary peace was obtained by putting Octavian in charge of the western provinces and sending Antony to the East. A final confrontation could not be long delayed, and Antony's fatal involvement with Cleopatra alienated much of his support at Rome. The end came in 31 B.C., at the Battle of Actium. The forces of Antony, reinforced by those of Cleopatra, were routed, and the couple committed suicide. Octavian was left as sole ruler of the Roman world, a world that was now in ruins. His victory marked the end of the Roman Republic.

When Octavian took supreme control after the Battle of Actium, Rome had been continuously involved both in civil and external wars for much of a century. The political and cultural institutions of Roman life were beyond repair, the economy was wrecked, and large areas of Italy were in complete turmoil. By the time of Octavian's death in A.D. 14, Rome had achieved a peace and prosperity unequaled in its history before or after. The art and literature created during his rule represents the peak of the Roman cultural achievement. To the Romans of his own time it seemed that a new Golden Age had dawned, and for centuries afterward his memory was revered. As the first Roman emperor, Octavian inaugurated the second great period in Roman history— the Empire, which lasted technically from 27 B.C.,

when he assumed the title Augustus, until A.D. 476, when the last Roman emperor was overthrown. In many ways, however, the period began with the Battle of Actium and continued in the subsequent Western and Byzantine empires.

Augustus' cultural achievement was stupendous, but it could only have been accomplished in a world at peace. Perhaps Augustus' greatest achievement, then, was to restore calm and dignity to Roman life. Once again the Romans were inspired with a sense of destiny and purpose, and the results are visible in their art.

Augustan Literature: Vergil

Augustus himself played an active part in supporting and encouraging the writers and artists of his day; many of their works echo the chief themes of Augustan politics—the return of peace, the importance of the land and agriculture, the putting aside of ostentation and luxury in favor of a simple life, and above all the belief in Rome's destiny as world ruler. Many of the greatest works of Roman sculpture commemorate Augustus and his deeds; Horace and Vergil sing his praises in their poems. It is sometimes said that much of this art was propaganda, organized by the emperor to present the most favorable picture possible of his reign. Even the greatest works of the time do relate in some way or other to the Augustan world view, and it is difficult to imagine a poet

100 Sacrificial scene from the frieze of Domitius Ahenobarbus, originally on the Temple of Neptune, Rome. 1st century B.C. Louvre, Paris. The sacrifice possibly commemorates a victory in the civil war that followed Julius Caesar's assassination. Mars, god of war, stands to the left of an altar toward which a huge bull is being led for sacrifice.

101 View of a garden, from the villa of Augustus at Prima Porta. c. 20 B.C. Fresco, detail, Museo Nazionale Romano, Rome. The peaceful scene, with its abundance of fruit and flowers, reflects the interest in country life expressed in Vergil's *Eclogues* and *Georgics*.

whose philosophy differed radically from that of the emperor being able to give voice to it. But we have no reason to doubt the sincerity of the gratitude felt toward Augustus or the strength of what seems to have been an almost universal feeling that at last a new era had dawned. In any case, from the time of Augustus art at Rome became in large measure official. Most of Roman architecture and sculpture of the period was public, commissioned by the state, and served state purposes.

The greater the artist, the more complex was the response to the Augustan vision. The greatest of all Roman poets, Publius Vergilius Maro (70–19 B.C.), devoted the last ten years of his life to the composition of an epic poem intended to honor Rome, and, by implication, Augustus. The result was the *Aeneid*, one of the great poems of the world, not completely finished at the poet's death. For much of the Middle Ages, Vergil himself was held in the highest reverence. A succession of great poets has regarded him as their master—Dante, Tasso, Milton, among others. Probably no work of literature in the entire tradition of Western culture has been more loved and revered than the *Aeneid*—described by T. S. Eliot as *the classic* of Western society—yet its significance is complex and by no means universally agreed upon.

The *Aeneid* was not Vergil's first poem. The earliest authentic works that have survived are ten short pastoral poems known as the *Eclogues* or sometimes

the *Bucolics,* which deal with the joys and sorrows of the country and the shepherds and herdsmen who live there. Vergil himself was the son of a farmer; his deep love of the land emerges also in his next work, the four books of the *Georgics* (29 B.C.). Their most obvious purpose is to serve as a practical guide to farming, and they offer helpful advice on such subjects as cattle breeding and beekeeping as well as a deep conviction that the strength of Italy lies in its agricultural richness. In a great passage in the second book of the *Georgics* Vergil hails the "ancient earth, great mother of crops and men." He does not disguise the hardships of the farmer's life, the poverty, hard work, and frequent disappointments, but still feels that only life in the country brings true peace and contentment [101].

The spirit of the *Georgics* clearly matched Augustus' plans for an agricultural revival. Indeed, it was probably the emperor himself who commissioned Vergil to write an epic poem that would be to Roman literature what the *Iliad* and *Odyssey* were for Greek: a national epic. The task was immense. Vergil had to find a subject that would do appropriate honor to Rome and its past as well as commemorate the achievements of Augustus. The *Aeneid* is not a perfect poem (on his deathbed Vergil ordered his friends to destroy it), but in some ways it surpasses even the high expectations Augustus must have had for it. Vergil succeeded in providing Rome with its national epic and stands as a worthy successor to Homer. At the same time, he created a profoundly moving study of the nature of human destiny and personal responsibility.

The *Aeneid* is divided into twelve books. Its hero is a Trojan prince, Aeneas, who flees from the ruins of burning Troy and sails west to Italy to found a new city, the predecessor of Rome. Vergil's choice was significant: Aeneas' Trojan birth establishes connections with the world of Homer; his arrival in Italy involves the origins of Rome; and the theme of a fresh beginning born, as it were, out of the ashes of the past corresponds perfectly to the Augustan mood of revival. We first meet Aeneas and his followers in the middle of his journey from Troy to Italy, caught in a storm that casts them up on the coast of North Africa. They make their way to the city of Carthage, where they are given shelter by the Carthaginian ruler, Queen Dido. At a dinner in his honor Aeneas describes the fall of Troy (Book II) and his wanderings from Troy to Carthage (Book III), in the course of which his father Anchises had died.

In Book IV, perhaps the best known, the action resumes where it had broken off at the end of Book I. The tragic love that develops between Dido and Aeneas tempts Aeneas to stay in Carthage and thereby abandon his mission to found a new home in Italy. But a divine messenger is sent to remind Aeneas of his responsibilities. He leaves after an agonizing encounter with Dido, and the distraught queen kills herself [102].

Book V brings the Trojans to Italy. In Book VI, Aeneas journeys to the underworld to hear from the spirit of his father the destiny of Rome. This tremendous episode provides the turning point of the poem. Before it we see Aeneas, and he sees himself, as a man prone to human weaknesses and subject to human feelings. After Anchises' revelations, Aeneas' humanity is replaced by a sense of mission and the weary, suffering Trojan exile becomes transformed into a "man of destiny."

In Books VII and VIII, the Trojans arrive at the river Tiber and Aeneas visits the future site of Rome while the Italian peoples prepare to resist the Trojan invaders. The last four books describe in detail the war between the Trojans and the Latins, in the course of which there are losses on both sides. The *Aeneid* ends with the death of the great Italian warrior Turnus and the final victory of Aeneas.

It is tempting to see Aeneas as the archetype of Augustus; certainly Vergil must have intended for us to draw some parallels. Other historical analogies can also be found: Dido and Cleopatra, for example, have much in common. The *Aeneid* is, however, far more than an allegorical retelling of the events leading up to the foundation of the empire. Put briefly, Aeneas undertakes a responsibility for which initially he has no real enthusiasm and which costs him and others considerable suffering. It would have been much easier for him to have stayed in Carthage, or settled somewhere else along his way, rather than push forward under difficult circumstances into a foreign land where he and his followers were not welcome.

Once he has accepted his mission, however, he fulfills it conscientiously and in the process learns to sublimate his own personal desires to a common good. If this is indeed a portrait of Augustus, it repre-

102 Joshua Reynolds. *The Death of Dido.* 1781. Oil on canvas, 4'8" × 7'10" (1.42 × 2.39 m). Buckingham Palace. By gracious permission of Her Majesty the Queen. Copyright reserved.

103 Aeneas sacrificing, from the *Ara Pacis*, Rome. 13–9 B.C. Marble.
Aeneas is depicted in the manner of a Classical Greek god;
the landscape and elaborate relief detail are typical of late Hellenistic art.

104 *Ara Pacis* of Augustus, Rome. 13–9 B.C. Marble, 36 × 33′ (11 × 10 m). The central doorway, through which the altar itself is just visible, is flanked by the reliefs showing Romulus and Remus and Aeneas. On the right-hand side is the procession led by Augustus. The altar originally stood on the ancient Via Flaminia. Fragments were discovered in the 16th century; the remaining pieces were located in 1937 and 1938 and the structure was reconstructed near the mausoleum of Augustus.

sents a much more complex view of his character than we might expect. And Vergil goes further. If greatness can only be acquired by sacrificing human individuals, is it worth the price? Is the future glory of Rome a sufficient excuse for the cruel and unmanly treatment of Dido? Readers will provide their own answers. Vergil's might have been that the sacrifices were probably worth it, but barely. Much, of course, depends on individual views on the nature and purpose of existence, and for Vergil there is no doubt that life is essentially tragic. The prevailing mood of the poem is one of melancholy regret for the sadness of human lives and the inevitability of human suffering.

Augustan Sculpture

Many of the characteristics of Vergil's poetry can also be found in contemporary sculpture. In a relief from one of the most important works of the period, the *Ara Pacis* (Altar of Peace), Aeneas himself performs a

105 *Augustus of Prima Porta.* c. A.D. 14. Marble, height 6'8" (2.03 m). Vatican Museums, Rome.

sacrifice on his arrival in Italy in front of a small shrine that contains two sacred images brought from Troy [103]. More significantly, the *Ara Pacis* depicts the abundance of nature that could flourish again in the peace of the Augustan age. The altar, begun on Augustus' return to Rome in 13 B.C. after a visit to the provinces, was dedicated on January 30, 9 B.C., at a ceremony that is shown in the surrounding reliefs [104]. The procession making its way to the sacrifice is divided into two parts. On the south side Augustus leads the way, accompanied by priests and followed by the members of his family; the north side shows senators and other dignitaries. The lower part of the walls is decorated with a rich band of fruit and floral motifs, luxuriantly intertwined, amid which swans are placed. The actual entrance to the altar is flanked by two reliefs—on the right, the one showing Aeneas, and on the left, Romulus and Remus.

The *Ara Pacis* is perhaps the single most comprehensive statement of how Augustus wanted his contemporaries—and future generations—to see his reign. The altar is dedicated neither to Jupiter or Mars nor to Augustus himself but to the spirit of Peace. Augustus is shown as the first among equals rather than supreme ruler; although he leads the procession, he is marked by no special richness of dress. The presence of Augustus' family indicates that he intends his successor to be drawn from among them, and that they have a special role to play in public affairs. The reliefs of Aeneas and of Romulus and Remus relate the entire ceremony to Rome's glorious past. Further reliefs at the back showing the Earth Mother and the goddess of war emphasize the abundance of the land and the need for vigilance. The rich vegetation of the lower band is a constant reminder of the rewards of agriculture, rewards that can be enjoyed once more in the peace to which the whole altar is dedicated.

Amazingly enough, this detailed political and social message is expressed without pretentiousness and with superb workmanship. The style is deliberately and self-consciously "classical," based on works like the Parthenon frieze. To depict the New Golden Age of Augustus, his artists have chosen the artistic language of the Golden Age of Athens, although with a Roman accent. The figures in the procession, for instance, are portrayed far more realistically than those in the sculpture of 5th-century-B.C. Athens.

The elaborate message illustrated by the *Ara Pacis* can also be seen in the best-preserved statue of the emperor himself, the *Augustus of Prima Porta,* so called after the spot where an imperial villa containing the statue was excavated [105]. The statue probably dates from about the time of the emperor's death; the face is in the full vigor of life, calm and deter-

106 Aerial view of the excavated portion of Pompeii as it appears today. The long, open rectangular space in the lower center is the forum. The total area is 166 acres (67.23 hectares). Although excavations at Pompeii have been in progress for more than two hundred years, some two-fifths of the city is still buried.

107 Cast of a woman trapped in volcanic pumice during the eruption of Mount Vesuvius at Pompeii, A.D. 79. Museo Nazionale, Naples.

mined. The stance is one of quiet authority. The ornately carved breastplate recalls one of the chief events of Augustus' reign. In 20 B.C. he defeated the Parthians, an eastern tribe, and recaptured from them the Roman standards that had been lost in battle in 53 B.C. On that former occasion Rome had suffered one of the greatest military defeats in its history, and Augustus' victory played an important part in restoring national pride. The breastplate shows a bearded Parthian handing back the eagle-crowned standard to a Roman soldier. The cupid on a dolphin at Augustus' feet serves two purposes. The symbol of the goddess Venus, it connects Augustus and his family with Aeneas (whose mother was Venus) and thereby with the origins of Rome. At the same time it looks to the future by representing Augustus' grandson Gaius, who was born the year of the victory over the Parthians and was at one time considered a possible successor to his grandfather.

The choice of his successor was the one problem that Augustus never managed to solve to his own satisfaction. The death of other candidates forced him to fall back reluctantly on his unpopular stepson Tiberius—a problem that was to recur throughout the long history of the empire, since no really effective mechanism was ever devised for guaranteeing a peaceful transfer of power. (As early as the reign of Claudius [A.D. 41–54], the right to choose a new emperor was seized by the army.) In every other respect the Augustan age was one of high attainment. In the visual arts, Augustan artists set the styles that dominated succeeding generations, while writers like the poets Vergil, Horace, Ovid, and Propertius, and the historian Livy established a Golden Age of Latin literature.

Curiously enough, perhaps the only person to have any real doubts about the Augustan achievement may have been Augustus himself. The Roman

108 Carbonized dates, walnuts, sunflower seeds, and bread from Pompeii, August 24, A.D. 79. Museo Nazionale, Naples.

writer and gossip Suetonius (A.D. c. 69–c. 160) tells us that as the emperor lay dying he ordered a slave to bring a mirror so that he could comb his hair. He looked at himself, then turned to some friends standing by and asked, "Tell me, have I played my part in the comedy of life well enough?"

Life in the Roman Empire

The Evidence of Pompeii

The 1st and 2nd centuries A.D. are probably the best-documented times in the whole of classical antiquity. From the many literary sources and the wealth of art and architecture that has survived, it is possible to reconstruct a detailed picture of life in imperial Rome. Even more complete is our knowledge of a prosperous but unimportant little town some 150 miles (240 kilometers) south of Rome that owes its worldwide fame to the circumstances of its destruction [106]. On August 24 in the year A.D. 79, the volcano Vesuvius above the Gulf of Naples erupted and a number of small towns were buried, the nearer ones under flowing lava and those some distance away under pumice and ash. By far the most famous is Pompeii, situated some 10 miles (16 kilometers) southeast of the erupting peak. Excavation first began there more than two hundred years ago. The finds preserved by the volcanic debris give us a rich and vivid impression of the way of life in a provincial town of the early empire—from the temples in which the Pompeians worshiped and the baths in which they cleaned themselves to their food on the fatal day [107, 108].

With a few exceptions, like the frescoes in the Villa of the Mysteries [Plate 9, page 90], the works of art unearthed at Pompeii are not masterpieces. Their importance lies precisely in the fact that they show us how the ordinary Pompeian lived, worked, and played [109]. The general picture is very impressive. Cool, comfortable houses were decorated with charming frescoes and mosaics and included quiet gardens, remote from the noise of busy streets and watered by fountains. The household silver and other domestic ornaments found in the ruins of houses were often of very high quality. Although the population of Pompeii was only twenty thousand, there were no fewer than three sets of public baths, a thea-

109 Peristyle of the House of the Silver Wedding, Pompeii. 1st century A.D. The open plan of substantial houses such as this helped keep the interior cool in summer; the adjoining rooms were closed off by folding doors in winter.

ter, a concert hall, an amphitheater large enough to seat the entire population, and a more-than-adequate number of brothels. The forum was closed to traffic, and the major public buildings ranged around it include a splendid basilica or large hall that served as both stock exchange and law courts. Life must have been extremely comfortable at Pompeii, even though it was far from the most prosperous of the towns buried by Vesuvius. Although only a small part of Herculaneum has been excavated, some mansions found there far surpass the houses of Pompeii. In the last few years work has begun at Oplontis, where a superbly decorated villa has already come to light.

Apart from its historic importance, the excavation of Pompeii in the 18th and 19th centuries had a profound effect on contemporary writers and artists. Johann Wolfgang von Goethe visited the site in 1787 and wrote of the buried city that "of all the disasters there have been in this world, few have provided so much delight to posterity." Johann Winckelmann (1717–1768), sometimes called the father of archaeol-ogy, used material from the excavations in his *History of Ancient Art*. Artists like Ingres, David, and Canova were influenced by Pompeian paintings and sculptures; on a more popular level a style of Wedgwood china was based on Pompeian motifs. Countless poets and novelists of the 19th century either set episodes in the excavations at Pompeii or tried to imagine what life there was like in Roman times.

The Architectural Grandeur of Imperial Rome

All the charm and comfort of Pompeii pale before the grandeur of imperial Rome itself, where both public buildings and private houses were constructed in numbers and on a scale that still remains impressive [110]. The Roman achievement in both architecture and engineering had a lasting effect on the development of later architectural styles. In particular their use of the arch, probably borrowed from the Etruscans, was widely imitated, and pseudo-Roman tri-

110 Model of ancient Rome as it was in about A.D. 320. Museo della Civiltà, Rome. In the right center is the emperor's palace on the Palatine Hill, with the Colosseum above and the mammoth Basilica of Constantine at the upper left.

umphal arches have sprung up in such unlikely places as the Champs Élysées in Paris and Washington Square in New York. The original triumphal arches commemorated military victories [111]; each was a permanent version of the temporary wooden arch erected to celebrate the return to the capital of a victorious general.

Equally important was the use of internal arches and vaults [112] to provide roofs for structures of increasing size and complexity. Greek and Republican Roman temples had been relatively small, partly because of the difficulties involved in roofing a large space without supports. With the invention of concrete in the 1st century B.C. and growing understanding of the principles of stress and counterstress, Roman architects were able to experiment with elaborate new forms, many of which—like the barrel vault and the dome—were to pass into the Western architectural tradition.

The Greeks had rarely built arches, but the Etruscans used them as early as the 5th century B.C., and the Romans may well have borrowed the arch form from them. From the 2nd century B.C. on, stone arches were regularly used for bridges and aqueducts. Vaults of small size were often used for domestic buildings, and by the time of Augustus architects had begun to construct larger-scale barrel vaults, semicylindrical in shape, two or more of which could intersect to roof a large area. The dome, which is really a hemispherical vault, became increasingly popular with the building of the vast public baths of imperial Rome. Using both bricks and concrete, architects could combine vaults, barrel vaults, and domes to construct very elaborate buildings capable of holding thousands of people at a time. The inside and outside surfaces of the buildings were then covered with a marble facing to conceal the elaborate internal support structures.

Much of the work of these architects was destroyed during the barbarian invasions of the 5th and 6th centuries A.D. and more was wrecked in the Renaissance by builders looking for bricks or marble.

111 Arch of Titus, Rome. A.D. 81.
Height 47′4″ (14.43 m).
This structure commemorates the Roman capture of Jerusalem in A.D. 70.

112 *Top:* Simple arch composed of wedge-shaped blocks (or *voussoirs*) and *keystone;* the curve of the arch rises from the *springers* on either side. *Center:* Tunnel or barrel vault composed of a series of arches. *Bottom:* Dome composed of a series of arches intersecting each other around a central axis.

But by great good fortune one of the most superb of all imperial structures has been preserved almost intact. The Pantheon [113] was built around 126, during the reign of Hadrian (117–138) to a design by the emperor himself. An austere and majestic exterior portico is supported on granite columns with Corinthian capitals [114]. It leads into the central rotunda, an astonishing construction approximately 142 feet (43.3 meters) high and wide in which a huge concrete dome rests on a wall interrupted by a series of niches. The building's only light source is a huge *oculus* (eye) at the top of the dome, an opening 30 feet (9.2 meters) across. The proportions of the building are very carefully calculated and contribute to its air of balance. The height of the dome from the ground, for example, is exactly equal to its width.

The Pantheon was dwarfed by the huge complex of buildings that made up the imperial fora. Completed by the beginning of the 2nd century A.D., they formed a vast architectural design unsurpassed in antiquity and barely equaled since [115]. Elsewhere in the city baths, theaters, temples, race tracks, and libraries catered to the needs and fancies of a huge urban population. In many of these buildings architects continued to experiment with new techniques

above: 113 Pantheon, Rome. c. A.D. 126. Height of portico 59' (17.98 m).

left: 114 Corinthian capital. This elaborate bell-shape design, decorated with acanthus leaves, first became commonly used in Hellenistic times. It was especially popular with Roman architects, who in general preferred it to both the Doric and Ionic styles.

124 THE ROMAN LEGACY

of construction, and architectural principles developed in Rome were applied throughout the Roman Empire. From Spain to the Middle East theaters, amphitheaters, and other public structures were erected according to the same basic designs, leaving a permanent record of construction methods for later generations.

Urban life on such a scale required a constant supply of one of the basic human necessities, water. Their system of aqueducts is one of the most impressive of the Romans' engineering achievements. A vast network of pipes brought millions of gallons of water a day into Rome, distributing it to public fountains and baths and to the private villas of the wealthy. At the same time a system of covered street drains was built, eliminating the open drains that had been usual before Roman times. These open drains were to return during the medieval period, when many of the Roman engineering skills were gone.

With the passage of time, most of the aqueducts that supplied ancient Rome have been demolished or have collapsed. Elsewhere in the Roman Empire, however, examples have survived that give some idea of Roman engineering skill. The famous Pont du Gard [116], which can still be seen in southern

115 Plan of the imperial fora, Rome. Unlike the Republican forum, which served as a public meeting place, these huge complexes were constructed as monuments to the emperors who commissioned them.

116 Pont du Gard, near Nîmes in southern France. Late 1st century B.C. Length 902′ (274.93 m), height 161′ (49.07 m). Note the careful positioning of the three rows of arches along the top of which ran the water channel. The whole aqueduct was 25 miles (40 kilometers) long. This section carried the water over the river Gard.

117 Reconstruction drawing of the garden façade of the Insula dei Dipinti, an apartment block in Ostia, the seaport of ancient Rome.

France, was probably first constructed during the reign of Augustus. It carried the aqueduct that supplied the Roman city of Nîmes with water—a hundred gallons (387.5 liters) a day for each inhabitant—and was made of uncemented stone. The largest blocks weigh 2 tons (1.8 metric tons).

Even with the provision of such facilities, imperial Rome suffered from overcrowding. The average Roman lived in an apartment block, of which there were some 45,000. Most of these have long since disappeared, although their appearance can be reconstructed from examples excavated at Ostia, Rome's port [117]. The height of the apartment blocks was controlled by law to prevent the construction of unsafe buildings, but it was not unheard of for a building to collapse and fire was a constant danger. No doubt the grandeur of the public buildings in Rome was intended at least in part to distract the poorer Romans from thoughts of their humble private residences.

The End of the Roman Empire

Few historical subjects have been as much discussed as the fall of the Roman Empire. It is not even possible to agree on when it fell, let alone why. The traditional date, A.D. 476, marks the deposition of the last Roman emperor, Romulus Augustulus. By that time, however, the political unity of the empire had already disintegrated. Perhaps the beginning of the end was A.D. 330, when the emperor Constantine moved the capital from Rome to a new city on the Bosporus, Constantinople, although in another sense the move represented a new development as much as a conclusion. It might even be possible to argue that Constantine's successors in the East, the Byzantine emperors, were the successors of Augustus and that there is a continuous tradition from the beginning of the empire in 31 B.C. to the fall of Constantinople in A.D. 1453.

Fascinating though the question is, in a sense it is theoretical rather than practical. The Roman Empire did not fall overnight. Many of the causes for its long decline are obvious though not always easy to order in importance. One important factor was the growing power and changing character of the army. The larger it became, the more necessary it was to recruit troops from the more distant provinces—Germans, Illyrians, and others, the very people the army was supposed to be holding in check. Most of these soldiers had never been anywhere near Rome. They felt no loyalty to the empire, no reason to defend Roman interests. A succession of emperors had to buy their support by raising their pay and promising gifts of lands. At the same time, the army came to play an increasingly prominent part in the choice of a new emperor, and, since the army itself was largely non-Roman, so were many of the emperors chosen. Emperors of the 3rd and 4th centuries included Africans, Thracians, a Syrian, and an Arab, men unlikely to feel any strong reason to place the interests of Rome over those of themselves and their men.

Throughout this late period the empire was increasingly threatened from outside. To the west, barbarian tribes like the Huns, the Goths, and the Alemanni began to penetrate farther and farther into its defenses and even to sack Rome itself. Meanwhile, in the East, Roman armies were continually involved in resisting the growing power of the Persians. In many parts of the empire it became clear that Rome could provide no help against invaders, and some of the provinces set themselves up as independent states with their own armies.

Problems like these inevitably had a devastating effect on the economy. Taxes increased and the value of money declined. The constant threat of invasion or civil war made trade impossible. What funds there were went for the support of the army, and the general standard of living suffered a steady decline. The eastern provinces, the old Hellenistic kingdoms, suffered rather less than the rest of the empire, since they were protected in part by the wealth accumulated over the centuries and by their long tradition of civilization. As a result, Italy sank to the level of a prov-ince rather than remaining the center of the imperial administration.

Total collapse was prevented by the efforts of two emperors: Diocletian, who ruled from A.D. 284 to 305, and Constantine, who ruled from 306 to 337. Both men were masterly organizers who realized that the only way to save the empire was to impose the most stringent controls on every aspect of life—social, administrative, and economic. In 301 the Edict of Diocletian was passed, establishing fixed maximums for the sale of goods and for wages. A vast bureaucracy was set up to collect taxes and administer the provinces. The emperor himself became once again the focal point of the empire, but to protect himself from the dangers of coups and assassinations, he never appeared in public. As a result, an elaborate court with complex rituals developed, and the emperor's claim to semidivine status invested him with a new religious authority.

Late Roman Art and Architecture

Even if the emperor did not show himself to his subjects, he could impress them in other ways, and the reigns of Diocletian and Constantine marked the last great age of Roman architecture. The immense Basilica of Constantine [118], with its central nave rising to a height of 100 feet (30.5 meters), is now in ruins,

118 Basilica of Constantine, the last great imperial building in Rome. Begun in A.D. 306 by Maxentius, it was finished by Constantine after 315. Only the northern side is still standing; the central nave and south aisle collapsed during antiquity.

119 Head of the colossal statue of Constantine that stood in the Basilica of Constantine, Rome. A.D. 324–330. Marble, height 8′6″ (2.59 m). Palazzo dei Conservatori, Rome. The massive and majestic simplicity of this portrait is very different from the detailed observation of earlier, much smaller Roman portraits like that of Cicero (figure **98**), illustrating the new belief in the emperor as God's regent on earth.

but in its day this assembly hall must have been a powerful reminder of the emperor's authority. It also contained a 30-foot (9.2 meter) statue of the emperor himself [119]. The palace Diocletian had built for him at Split, on the Adriatic coast, is constructed on the plan of a military camp, with enormous central avenues dividing it into four quarters [120]. The decoration makes use of Eastern motifs, and the whole design is far from the classical style of earlier times.

In sculpture, too, classical forms and styles were increasingly abandoned. Realistic portraiture and naturalistic drapery were neglected, and sculptors no longer tried to express depth or reality in their relief carving. The lack of perspective and precision in their work foreshadows the art of the early Middle Ages [121]. The general abandonment of classical ideas these artistic changes indicate went along with a waning of interest in Stoicism and Epicureanism and a new enthusiasm for Eastern religious cults. Traditional Roman religion had always been organized by the state, and from the time of the late Republic some Romans had sought a more personal religious satisfaction in the worship of Eastern deities. During the last stages of the empire strong cults developed around the Phygian goddess Cybele, the Egyptian Isis, and the sun god Mithras.

The appearance and eventual triumph of Christianity is outside the scope of this account, but its emergence as the official religion of the empire played a final and decisive part in bringing to an end the classical era. Pagan art, pagan literature, and pagan culture as a whole represented forces and ideals Christianity strongly rejected, and the art of the early Christians is fundamentally different in its inspiration. Yet even the fathers of the early Church, implacable opponents of paganism, could not fail to be moved by the end of so great a cultural tradition.

The memory of Rome's greatness lived on through the succeeding ages of turmoil and achievement and the classical spirit survived, to be reborn triumphantly in the Renaissance.

Questions for Further Discussion

1. Art and literature were never at the center of Roman life, but always took second place to more practical affairs. What effects did this have on the development of Roman culture, and to what extent were the Romans justified in seeing the arts as a distraction from the real world?
2. In what ways have the Roman political and legal systems influenced Western systems of government, in particular that of the United States? How and why were the Romans chosen as models?
3. What kind of evidence do we have for the origins of the

120 Reconstruction model of the Palace of Diocletian at Split, Yugoslavia. A.D. 300–305. Museo della Civiltà Romana, Rome. Note the octagonal dome of the emperor's mausoleum.

121 *Constantine Receiving Homage from the Senate,* frieze on the Arch of Constantine, Rome. A.D. 315. Marble, 3'4″ × 17'6″ (1.02 × 5.33 m). On both sides of the emperor (seated in the center) his officials distribute money to the crowds below. The simplified style, in which most of the puppetlike figures are shown frontally, foreshadows Byzantine and medieval art and is certainly very different from the style of earlier reliefs (figures **103, 104**).

Etruscans, and what conclusions does it suggest? Is there any chance that the mysteries of Etruscan origins and the Etruscan language will ever be fully understood?

4. How sympathetic a hero is Aeneas, and how does our opinion of his character influence our interpretation of the *Aeneid?*

5. What are the chief problems presented by the frescoes in the Villa of the Mysteries at Pompeii, and what are some of the solutions scholars have proposed? What light do the frescoes throw on the role of women and marriage in Roman times?

6. It is sometimes said that late imperial Rome and America in the late 20th century share many of the same weaknesses, including an indifference to the arts, an inability to adapt traditional values to changing times, and the lack of a satisfactory relationship between the individual and society as a whole. How far are these charges justified, and what (if anything) can be learned from the Roman example?

		GENERAL EVENTS	LITERATURE & PHILOSOPHY	ART
64 A.D.				
EARLY CHRISTIAN ERA	Period of Persecution	250 Persecution of Christians under Decius 286 Diocletion divides Roman Empire into East and West parts ruled by himself and Maximian 305 Abdication of Diocletian and Maximian; Constantius and Galerius rule as joint emperors 307–327 Reign of Constantine	c. 67 Apostle Paul, bearer of Christian message throughout Mediterranean, martyred at Rome	
313				
	Period of Recognition	313 Edict of Milan, giving Christians freedom of religion 324 Constantine convenes Council of Nicaea 330 Constantine dedicates new capital of Roman Empire on site of Byzantium, naming it Constantinople 337 Constantine is baptized a Christian on his deathbed 383 Ostrogoths accept Christianity	c. 350 *Codex Sinaiticus,* earliest extant Greek codex of New Testament c. 374–404 Saint John Chrysostom active as writer and preacher c. 386 Saint Jerome translates Bible into Latin	c. 390 Obelisk of Theodosius erected in Hippodrome at Constantinople
395				
BYZANTINE ERA	Growth of Empire	395 Division of Roman Empire begun by Diocletian becomes total separation 4th–5th cent. Decline of Western Roman Empire 410 Visigoths sack Rome 455 Vandals sack Rome 476 Romulus Augustulus forced to abdicate as last Western Roman emperor; Ostrogoths rule Italy 493–526 Theodoric the Ostrogoth reigns in Italy 527–565 Reign of Justinian as Eastern Roman emperor in Constantinople 532 Nika revolt; civil disorders in Constantinople c. 533 Justinian codifies Roman Law 540 Belisarius conquers Ostrogoths in Italy for Justinian; Ravenna comes under Byzantine rule	397 Augustine of Hippo, *The Confessions* 413–426 Augustine of Hippo, *The City of God* c. 522–524 Boethius, *The Consolation of Philosophy,* allegorical treatise; translation of Aristotle's writings 524 Execution of Boethius by Theodoric the Ostrogoth c. 562 Procopius, *History of the Wars, The Buildings, Secret History*	c. 415 Theodosius II moves gilded horses and chariot from Rome to Hippodrome c. 425 Mosaics at Mausoleum of Galla Placidia, Ravenna c. 450 Dome mosaic in Orthodox Baptistery, Ravenna 6th cent. Art tied to theological doctrine and liturgical practice of Orthodox Church c. 547 Ivory throne of Archbishop Maximian, given by Justinian for San Vitale c. 550 Mosaics at Sant' Apollinare Nuovo and San Vitale, Ravenna; *Metamorphosis of Christ,* apse mosaic from Katholikon, Monastery of Saint Catherine, Mount Sinai
565				
	Territorial Decline	730–843 Iconoclastic Controversy: ban on religious imagery 800 Pope Leo III crowns first Western Roman emperor (Charlemagne) at Rome since 5th cent.		730–843 Ban on religious imagery; most earlier pictographic art destroyed
900				
	Second Growth	988–989 Russians accept Christianity 1054 Eastern and Western Church formally split		Renewal of icon tradition
1100				
	Final Decline	1204 Crusaders sack Constantinople on way to Holy Land 1453 Constantinople falls to Ottoman Turks, ending Byzantine Empire; Church of Hagia Sophia becomes a mosque		12th cent. Mosaics at Palermo, Sicily c. 1410 Rublev active as painter of icons in Moscow
1453				

6

The World of Byzantium

c. 324 Constantine has stadium in Constantinople enlarged to form Hippodrome

c. 326 Holy Sepulchre, Jerusalem

c. 333 Old Saint Peter's Basilica, Vatican

Use of basilica plan and central plan with dome

after 350 Beginnings of Byzantine music, based probably on Syriac and Hebrew music

386 Saint Ambrose of Milan begins use of vernacular hymns in church

c. 450 Mausoleum of Galla Placidia, Neonian and Arian Baptisteries, Ravenna

c. 493–526 Sant' Apollinare Nuovo, Ravenna

c. 526–547 San Vitale, Ravenna

526 Theodoric's Tomb, Ravenna

527 Hagia Eirene, Constantinople, begun

532–537 Anthemius of Tralles and Isidore of Miletus rebuild Hagia Sophia, Constantinople, combining basilica plan and central plan with dome

549 Sant' Apollinare in Classe

c. 550 Stephanos, Monastery of Saint Catherine, Mount Sinai

590–602 Gregorian Chant established at Rome during papacy of Gregory the Great

7th cent. Golden Age of Byzantine hymnody

1063 Saint Mark's, Venice, begun

11th cent. Codification of Greek liturgy; musical modifications decline

c. 1166 Church of the Intercession of the Virgin, near Vladimir, Russia; "onion dome" adapted from central dome

The Rise of Christianity and Decline of Rome

The Message of Paul

The greatest missionary of the religion of Jesus was the Apostle Paul. After his conversion to Christianity, Paul traveled to the major cities of the Mediterranean—called by the Romans *mare nostrum* (our sea)—from about A.D. 49 until A.D. 60. Paul's message was that Jesus was the anointed (the Greek word *christ* and the Hebrew word *messiah* both mean "anointed one") savior of the world. This strange new idea from the little-regarded backwater of Jerusalem took hold in both Jewish and Gentile circles in various cities of the empire, including Rome itself.

There are many reasons for the widespread success of Christianity in the 1st-century A.D. Roman world.

The Roman Empire was at peace; there was a common language in it; the roads were relatively safe and the Mediterranean was free of marauding pirates. The widespread interest in various Oriental philosophies and religions testified to a hunger for religious experience and a passive dissatisfaction with the emotional content of official Roman religion. Christianity also appealed to all segments of society from the massive slave population of Rome to the intellectuals. And, unlike Mithraism (an Oriental religion popular with the military), it permitted female members.

Roman authorities were relatively tolerant of most religious ideas, but Christianity's insistence that only the God of the Christians could be worshiped seemed to them a subversive and dangerous idea. Such preaching struck at the heart of the Roman notion of *pietas*—the virtue by which children were bound to their parents by love and obedience, by which the parents in turn were bound to the state, and by which

122 *Christ Teaching among the Apostles.* c. A.D. 300. Wall painting. 1'3" × 4'3" (.38 × 1.3 m). Cemetery of Domitilla, Rome. Note the young beardless Christ in this early representation (compare figure **139**).

above left: **123** Old Saint Peter's Basilica. Rome. c. A.D. 333. Length of grand axis 835′ (254.5 m), width of transcript 295′ (86.87 m). Reconstruction study by Kenneth J. Conant.

above right: **124** Plan of old Saint Peter's Basilica.

right: **125** Church of the Holy Sepulchre, Jerusalem, as it appeared in about A.D. 345. Reconstruction drawing by Kenneth J. Conant. Note that the basilica church has given way to a domed building.

the state was bound to the gods of Rome. To deny those gods was to subvert the social "glue" that held the empire together. As a consequence of this distrust, Roman emperors from Nero in the 1st century to Diocletian in the late 3rd century intermittently persecuted Christians and outlawed the Christian religion. At times the persecutions were empire-wide and bloodily oppressive (as, for example, the persecution of Decius in A.D. 250), while at other periods the persecutions were localized and sporadic.

The spread of Christianity nevertheless continued. At the beginning of the 4th century (and after a fierce but ineffectual persecution in 303 under the Emperor Diocletian) the Emperor Constantine issued an edict of toleration (the Edict of Milan, A.D. 313) for the Christians. By the middle of the 4th century Christianity was the state religion of the empire [122].

Constantine became formally a Christian only on his deathbed, but his interest in the religion had been manifest and generous. He drew Christianity closer to the state and provided it the freedom to expend some of the energies that had been suppressed during the times of the persecutions.

Two of the most famous churches in Christendom are associated with the reign of the Emperor Constantine. The present Saint Peter's Basilica in the Vatican rests on the remains of a basilica dedicated in 326. We do not have a fully articulated plan of that church, but its main outlines are clear. The faithful would enter into a courtyard called an *atrium* around which was a colonnaded arcade and from there through a vestibule into the church proper. The basilica, modeled after secular counterparts in Rome, featured a long central *nave* (from Latin, meaning "ship") with two parallel side aisles. The nave was intersected at one end by a *transept,* the roof of which was pitched with wooden trusses and supported by the outer walls and the columned interiors. High up on the walls above the arches and below the roof was the so-called *clerestory,* windows that provided most of the interior illumination. This basilica-type church [123, 124] became a model from which much of later church architecture evolved.

The other famous church built in the Constantinian period is the church of the Holy Sepulchre in Jerusalem [125]. This church was also built in the basilica style, its atrium in front of the basilica hall, but with a significant addition. Behind the basilica was a domed structure that covered—it was believed—the rocky place where the body of Christ had been buried for three days. The domelike structure was utilized in Christian architecture as an adaptation of existing domed structures in pagan Rome, most notably the Pantheon and some of the vast baths.

The period between Saint Paul and Constantine saw the Roman Empire slip from undisputed mastery of the known world to a tottering and endangered realm. Economic problems and threats from the barbarians at the borders of the empire threatened the stability of the far-flung outreaches of Roman control, and the 4th and 5th centuries saw the gradual but inexorable decline of the empire in the West. The last Roman emperor in the West died at Ravenna in 476, by which time imperial power had already shifted to Byzantium in the East (see map below).

Augustine of Hippo

The greatest writer of the Christian Latin West, Augustine of Hippo, was a witness to this decline. Born in 354 in North Africa (then part of the Roman provinces), Augustine received a thorough classical education in Africa and in Rome. He was converted to Christianity in Milan and soon afterward returned to his native country, where he was named bishop of Hippo in 390. When the Visigoths sacked Rome in 410, the pagan world was aghast and many blamed the rise of Christianity for this event. Partially as a response to this charge, Augustine wrote *The City of God* as an attempt to show that history had a direc-

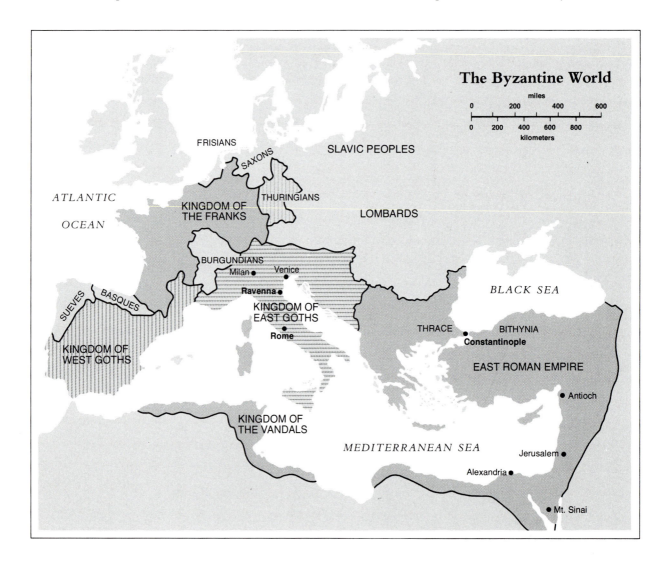

tion willed by God and that "in the end" all would be made right as the city of man gave way to the city of God. This work, packed with reflections on scripture, philosophy, and pagan wisdom, is often cited as one of the most influential philosophies of history written in the Western world.

Indeed, it is difficult to overestimate the intellectual impact of Augustine of Hippo on the subsequent cultural history of the West. His influence within Christianity is without parallel. Until Thomas Aquinas in the 13th century, all Christian theologians started from explicitly Augustinian premises. Even Thomas did not shake off his debt to Augustine, although he replaced Augustine's strong Platonic orientation with a more empirical Aristotelian one. Augustine emphasized the absolute majesty of God, the immutability of God's will, and the flawed state of the human condition (notions derived from Saint Paul). These tenets received a powerful reformulation in the Protestant Reformation by Martin Luther (who as a Catholic friar had lived under the rule of Saint Augustine) and by John Calvin, a profound student of Augustine's theological writings.

Augustine also made a notable impact beyond theology. *The City of God,* begun about 412, was an attempt to formulate a coherent and all-embracing philosophy of history, the first such attempt in the West. For Augustine, history moves on a straight line in a direction from its origin in God until it ends, again in God, at the consummation of history in the Last Judgment. Augustine rejected the older notion that history repeats itself endlessly in cycles. His reading of the Bible convinced him that humanity had an origin, played out its story, and would terminate. The city of man would be judged and the city of God would be saved. Subsequent philosophers of history have secularized this view but, with very few exceptions (Vico, a 17th-century Italian philosopher, was one), have maintained the outlines of Augustine's framework to some extent. "A bright future," "An atomic wasteland of the future," and "Classless society" are all statements about the end of history, all statements that echo, however dimly, the world view of Augustine.

Augustine also invented the genre of self-reflective writing in the West. "I would know myself that I might know Thee," Augustine writes of God in *The Confessions.* Before Augustine's time, memoirs related a life in terms of social, political, or military affairs (as Caesar's *Gallic Wars* did), but Augustine's intimate self-scrutiny of the significance of life was new in Western culture. There would not be another work like *The Confessions* until Petrarch, an indefatigable student of Augustine, wrote his *Letter to Posterity* in the mid-14th century. The Renaissance writers,

an extremely self-conscious generation, were devoted students of Augustine's stately Latin prose; even the great later autobiographies of our inherited culture—those of Gibbon, Mill, Newman—are literary and spiritual descendants of Augustine's.

Augustine's *The Confessions* is a compelling analysis of his spiritual and intellectual development from his youth until the time of his conversion to Christianity and readiness to return to his native Africa. The title must be understood in a triple sense—a confession of sin, an act of faith in God, and a confession of praise—so it is appropriate that Augustine wrote his book as a prayer to God.

Although strongly autobiographical, *The Confessions* is actually a long meditation by Augustine on the hidden grace of God as his life is shaped toward its appointed end. Augustine "confesses" to God (and the reader) how his early drive for fame as a teacher of rhetoric, his flirtation with the Manichean sect with its belief in two gods of evil and good, his liaison with a woman that resulted in the birth of a son, and his restless movement from North Africa to Rome and Milan were all part of a seamless web of circumstance that made up an individual life. Interspersed in the narrative line of his early life are Augustine's reflections on the most basic philosophical and theological questions of the day, always linked to his own experience. Augustine meditates on the "strange phenomenon" of the mind's inability completely to rule the will. And this is no mere exercise in speculation: Augustine is concerned about his own unruly will and its tendency toward evil, and about his inability to lead a sexually chaste life. Augustine always moves from general principle to a specific application in his own life and experience.

If *The Confessions* can be said to be the beginning of autobiography, beyond that historic importance it is classic and singular in its balance of immense learning, searching speculation, and intense self-scrutiny. It is a work concerned first of all with meaning at the deepest philosophical level, and its full power is evident only to the reader who will take the time to enter Augustine's line of argument.

The Ascendancy of Byzantium

The Emperor Constantine dedicated a Greek trading town on the Bosporus as his eastern capital in May 330, changing its name from Byzantium to Constantinople (the city of Constantine). It contained a mix of pagan, Christian, and Greek elements. Constantine built churches and monasteries as well as the obligatory palaces, fora, markets, and civic monuments, although only a few foundations and other archaeological remains have survived.

Constantine's choice of Byzantium for what he intended as the "New Rome" proved felicitous. Rome itself was reduced to a shadow of its former glory by the 5th century. Among the other major possibilities, Alexandria in Egypt had long been suffering an economic decline in this period and Antioch was eventually devastated by an earthquake in 525.

Constantinople had some obvious geographic advantages for a major city: it straddled the most prominent land route between Asia and Europe. It also had a deep-water port with natural shelter. It guarded the passage between the Mediterranean and the Black Sea. The surrounding countryside was rich in woodlands and natural springs of drinkable water. The neighboring areas of Europe (Thrace) and Asia (Bithynia) were rich in agricultural lands, providing the city a ready food supply.

Justinian and Theodora

Justinian became emperor in Constantinople in 527. He fully intended to restore the empire to a state of grandeur. In this he was aided by his beautiful and ruthless wife Theodora. A former dancer and prostitute whose ascent to the royal purple "cannot be applauded as the triumph of feminine virtue," as the 18th-century English historian Edward Gibbon observed rather starchily, Theodora was a tough-minded and capable woman who added strength and resolve to the grandiose ideas of the emperor. She was Justinian's equal, and perhaps more.

The reign of Justinian and Theodora was impressive, if profligate, by any standard. The emperor encouraged Persian monks residing in China to bring back silkworms for the introduction of the silk industry into the West. Because the silk industry of China was a fiercely guarded monopoly, the monks accomplished this rather dangerous mission by smuggling silkworm eggs out of the country in hollow tubes, and within a decade the silk industry in the Western world rivaled that of China.

Justinian also revised and codified Roman Law, a gigantic undertaking of scholarship and research. Roman law had evolved over a thousand-year period, and by Justinian's time was a vast jumble of disorganized and often contradictory decisions, decrees, statutes, opinions, and legal codes. Under the aegis of the emperor, a legal scholar named Tribonian produced order out of this chaos. First a *Code* that summarized all imperial decrees from the time of Hadrian (in the 2nd century) to the time of Justinian was published. The *Code* was followed by the *Pandects* (digest), which synthesized a vast quantity of

legal opinion and scholarship from the past. Finally came the *Institutes,* a legal collection broken down into four categories by which the laws concerning persons, things, actions, and personal wrongs (in other words, criminal law) were set forth. The body of this legal revision became the basis for the law courts of the empire and, in later centuries, the basis for the use of Roman law in the West.

Justinian and Theodora were fiercely partisan Christians who took a keen interest in theology and ecclesiastical governance. Justinian's fanatical devotion prompted him to shut down the last surviving Platonic academy in the world on the grounds that its paganism was inimical to the true religion. His own personal life—despite evidences of cruelty and capriciousness—was austere and abstemious, influenced by the presence of so many monks in the city of Constantinople. His generosity to the church was great, with his largess shown most clearly in openhanded patronage of church-building. Hagia Sophia, his most famous project, has become legendary for the beauty and opulence of its decoration.

Hagia Sophia: Monument and Symbol

Hagia Sophia (Greek for "Holy Wisdom") was the principal church of Constantinople. It had been destroyed twice, once by fire and—during Justinian's reign—during the terrible civil disorders of the Nika revolt in 532 that devastated most of the European side of the city. Soon afterward Justinian decided to rebuild the church using the plans of two architects, Anthemius of Tralles and Isidore of Miletus. Work began in 532 and the new edifice was solemnly dedicated five years later in the presence of Justinian and Theodora.

The church of Hagia Sophia was a stunning architectural achievement that combined the longitudinal shape of the Roman basilica with a domed central plan. Two centuries earlier Constantine had used both the dome and basilica shapes in the church of the Holy Sepulchre in Jerusalem, as we have seen, but he had not joined them into a unity. In still earlier domed buildings in the Roman world such as the Pantheon and Santa Costanza, the dome rested on a circular drum. This gave the dome solidity but limited its height and expansiveness. Anthemius and Isidore solved this problem by the use of *pendentives* [126], triangular masonry devices that carried the weight of the dome on massive piers rather than straight down to the drum. In the church of Hagia Sophia the central dome was abutted by two half-domes so that a person looking down at the building from above might see a nave in the form of an oval instead of a quadrangle [127].

left: 126 Dome construction:
1. pendentive; 2. drum; 3. cupola; 4. lantern.

below: 127 Anthemius of Tralles and Isidore of Miletus. Hagia Sophia. Constantinople (Istanbul). 532–537, 553–563. Exterior view from the southeast. The towers, of Turkish inspiration, are of later date.

The church—184 feet (55.2 meters) high, 41 feet (12.3 meters) higher than the Pantheon—retained a hint of the old basilica style as a result of the columned side aisles and the gallery for female worshipers in the triforium space above the arches of the aisles, but the overwhelming visual impression came from the massive dome. Since the pendentives reduced the weight of the dome, the area between drum and dome could be pierced by forty windows that made the dome seem to hang in space. Light streamed into the church from the windows and refracted off the rich mosaics and colored marbles that covered the interior [Plate 10, page 139].

Light, in fact, was a key theoretical element behind the entire conception of Hagia Sophia. Light is the symbol of divine wisdom in the philosophy of both Plato and the New Testament. A common metaphor in pagan and biblical wisdom had the sun and its rays represent the eternity of God and his illumination of mortals. The suffusion of light was an element in the Hagia Sophia that went far beyond the functional need to illuminate the interior of the church. Light refracting in the church created a spiritual ambiance analogous to that of heaven, where the faithful would be bathed in the actual light of God.

The sequence of the various parts of the worship

service at Constantinople—the *liturgy*—was developed from the efforts of Saint John Chrysostom (345–407), patriarch of the city in the century before Justinian. The official liturgy of Byzantine Christianity is still the Divine Liturgy of Saint John Chrysostom, modified and added to over the centuries. In that liturgy, the worshiping community visualized itself as standing in the forecourt of heaven when it worshiped in the church. Amid the swirling incense, the glittering light, and the stately chants of the clergy and people comes a sense of participation with the household of heaven standing before God. A fragment from the liturgy—added during the reign of Justinian's successor Justin II (565–578)—underscores the point dramatically. Note the characteristic cry of *Wisdom!* and the description of the congregation as mystically present in heaven:

PRIEST Wisdom! That ever being guarded by Thy power, we may give glory to thee, Father, Son, and Holy Spirit, now and forevermore.
CONGREGATION Amen. Let us here who represent the mystic Cherubim in singing the thrice holy hymn to the life-giving Trinity now lay aside every earthly care so that we may welcome the King of the universe who comes escorted by invisible armies of angels. Alleluia. Alleluia. Alleluia.

Hagia Sophia was enriched by subsequent emperors, and after repairs were made to the dome in 989 new mosaics were added to the church. After the fall of Constantinople in 1453 the Turks turned the church into a mosque; the mosaics were whitewashed or plastered over since the Koran prohibits the use of images. When the mosque was converted to a museum by the modern Turkish state, some of the mosaics were uncovered, and we can get some sense of the splendor of the original interior.

Other monuments bear the mark of Justinian's creative efforts. His church of the Holy Apostles, built on the site of an earlier church of the same name destroyed by an earthquake, did not survive the fall of the city in 1453 but did serve as a model for the church of Saint Mark in Venice. Near the church of the Hagia Sophia is the church of Hagia Eirene (Holy Peace), now a mosque, whose architecture also shows the combination of basilica and dome. The church, dedicated to the martyr saints Sergius and Bacchus and begun in 527, was a preliminary study for the later Hagia Sophia. In all, Justinian built more than 25 churches and convents in Constantinople. His program of secular architecture included an impressive water-conduit system that still exists.

The Games at Byzantium

Part of Rome's legacy to Byzantium was a taste for spectator sports. The ancient Greeks had preferred individual participation in athletics, and the status of victorious athletes was high. The Romans held chariot races and gladiatorial combat on a massive scale before a vast public. The charioteers and fighters were generally slaves or criminals, however, since no respectable Roman citizen would compete in public. Prizes were very large; a successful gladiator or charioteer could easily amass a fortune and become the idol of a rabid clique. The enthusiasm of the public was further stimulated by the division of the charioteers into four teams—the Reds, Whites, Blues, and Greens—each supported by its partisans.

In Byzantium, the gladiatorial and animal combats so popular in Rome were suppressed. It was hardly in accordance with Christian principles to watch men or men and animals tear each other to pieces for the entertainment of others. To this extent at least, the Byzantine games in the time of Justinian were a notable improvement over their predecessors. Chariot races, staged in the racetrack of Byzantium, the Hippodrome, before tremendous crowds, nevertheless soon came to dominate Byzantine life in ways that may seem strange to us today. Enthusiasm for one's own team and contempt for the supporters of a rival one is not unknown today among spectators at sports events and can sometimes lead to violent demonstrations and fighting. But the Byzantine crowds combined sport and religion in a way that illustrates vividly and disturbingly the obsession of the Byzantine populace with theological argument. By A.D. 500 the number of teams had been reduced from four to two, the Blues and the Greens, each upholding and racing in support of a different doctrine. The Greens fought for Monophysitism (the belief that Christ had only one, divine nature) while the Blues upheld the dual nature of Christ—both human and divine.

It is scarcely credible now that a debate of such subtlety and complexity, worthy of the attention of the most sophisticated theologian, should have become associated with chariot racers and their supporters. Nevertheless, the partisanship reached a level of popular frenzy which thankfully remains unequaled since. Every inhabitant of Byzantium became an adherent of one team or the other and followed its fortunes both in the Hippodrome and elsewhere. Supporters adopted styles of dress by which they could easily be recognized: some of the Blues, for example, shaved their heads in the front and let their hair grow long at the back in imitation of the barbarian Huns.

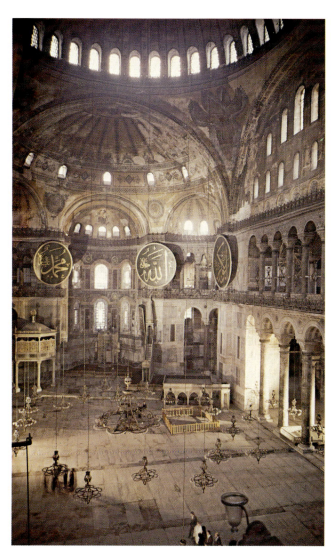

left: **Plate 10** Anthemius of Tralles and Isidore of Miletus. Hagia Sophia, Constantinople (Istanbul). 532–537, 553–563. This view of the interior, looking toward the apse, shows how the windows between drum and dome give an impression of floating lightness that continues down, reinforced by the other windows, to the floor.

below: **Plate 11** Empress Theodora, detail of wall mosaic, San Vitale, Ravenna. c. 547. This is a detail of figure **145,** page 150.

Plate 12 *Notre Dame de Belle Verrière,* Chartres Cathedral. Early 13th century. The heavy vertical and horizontal lines are iron bars for reinforcement. The thinner lines are the leading. Note the painting on the glass in such features as the eyes, nose, and mouth of the Virgin. This window is an excellent example of the famous red-colored glass of the Chartres workshop.

By the time of Justinian the Blues had acquired the support of the emperor himself, although Theodora was rumored to follow her father's allegiance to the Greens. The Hippodrome, decorated with art treasures from Greece, Rome, and Egypt, now became the center of political life in Byzantium. Enlargement of an earlier stadium had been one of Constantine's first projects after the move of the capital to Byzantium in 324, and the Hippodrome in Justinian's time not only accommodated most of the population of the city but also included stables and living quarters for the charioteers. Emperor and empress had their own private boxes [128] that could be entered directly from the palace and resembled small houses, with private and public rooms, more than mere viewing stands. The center of the stadium was called the *spina;* around it lay the racing track, which consisted of a bed of stone covered with sand. The spina was adorned with statues of famous charioteers and masterpieces by such famous artists of the past as Phidias. Above the emperor's box was a chariot drawn by four gilt horses made of an alloy of copper, silver, and gold, thought to have been the work of the great 4th-century-B.C. sculptor Lysippus [129]. It had been taken to Rome by Nero and was moved to Byzantium in the early 5th century A.D. by Theodosius II. During the Fourth Crusade, in 1204, the horses made another journey when they were taken by the Venetians to decorate the entrance porch of the church of Saint Mark, although even this did

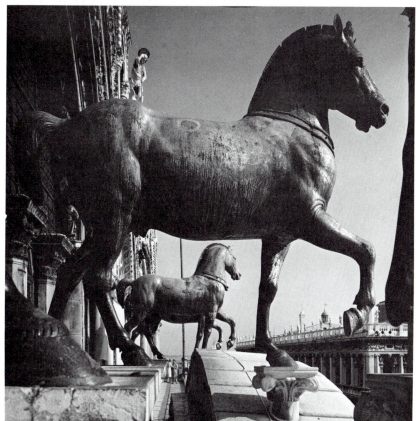

above left: 128 Detail of relief from the Obelisk of Theodosius, which once stood in the spina of the Hippodrome of Constantinople. c. A.D. 390. The relief shows the emperor in the royal box, surrounded by his family, holding a wreathed crown for a winning charioteer.

left: 129 Four horses of Greek origin. 1st century A.D. Gilt bronze, life size. Basilica of Saint Mark, Venice. These gilt horses once stood over the emperor's box in the Hippodrome at Constantinople.

141

not end their wanderings. At the end of the 18th century they were removed by Napoleon and taken to Paris, only to return after Napoleon's defeat in 1815 yet again to Venice, where they are still to be seen.

The Hippodrome and the factions associated with it were the cause of a particularly violent riot in January 532 known as the Nika Revolt after the password *Nika* (Conquer) used by some of the rioters. A vivid account has been preserved in the writings of the great Byzantine historian Procopius, who himself served on the staff of Belisarius, the foremost of Justinian's generals. Procopius was born at Caesarea in Palestine around 500 and accompanied Belisarius on his travels in Persia, Africa, and Italy. Procopius' task was to write an official history of the campaigns. This *History of the Wars* reflects his official status and with *The Buildings,* which describes the chief architectural achievements of Justinian's reign, paints a generally favorable portrait of both Justinian and Theodora. His other surviving work, the *Secret History,* was not intended for publication in his lifetime. It retraces the events covered in the *History of the Wars,* this time in the form of a virulent and sustained attack on the emperor and his wife. The antecedents and character of Theodora are described in scurrilous detail, while Justinian is blamed for every kind of disaster from bankruptcy to earthquakes.

Ravenna

For all the beautiful remains that we may see in modern Istanbul—especially the impressive Hagia Sophia—it is still Ravenna that provides us the more complete archaeological and monumental picture of the period of Justinian and of the Byzantine world. Ravenna is a rather small, not particularly attractive city on the northeast Adriatic coast of Italy. In 402 the Roman emperor Honorius made Ravenna the capital of the western empire because of the hazardous conditions in Rome. In 476 the Ostrogoth king Odoacer conquered Ravenna, bringing to an end the line of Roman emperors in the West. From then until 540 the Ostrogoths ruled Ravenna until they were defeated by Belisarius, commander-in-chief of Justinian's army.

Boethius

In this twilight period between the death of the last Roman emperor and the arrival of Justinian's troops an important figure who bridged the gap between classical paganism and Christianity lived and died. Anicius Manlius Severinus Boethius was a highly educated Roman who entered the service of the Goth king Theodoric in 522. Imprisoned for reasons that are not clear, Boethius wrote a treatise called *The Consolation of Philosophy* while awaiting execution. Cast as a dialogue between Lady Philosophy and the author on the philosophical and religious basis for human freedom, the work blends the spirit of the Book of Job with Roman stoicism. Attempting to console him for his sad state of disgrace and imprisonment, Lady Philosophy demands that the author avoid self-pity, that he face his troubles with serenity and hope. Insisting that a provident God overcomes all evil, Philosophy insists that blind fate has no control over humanity. She explains that human freedom exists along with an all-knowing God and that good will triumph. Although Christian themes permeate the work, there is no explicit mention of Christian doctrine. What one does sense is the recasting of Roman thought into Christian patterns. In a way, *The Consolation of Philosophy* is one of the last works of the late Roman period. It reflects the elegance of Roman expression, the burgeoning hope of Christianity, and the terrible sadness that must have afflicted any sensitive Roman in this period.

The Consolation of Philosophy was one of the most widely read and influential works of the Middle Ages (Chaucer made an English translation of it from an already-existing French version). Its message of hope and faith was liberally quoted by every major medieval thinker from Thomas Aquinas to Dante Alighieri.

Boethius sets out a basic problem and provides an answer that would become normative Christian thought for subsequent centuries. In *The Consolation* Boethius asks how one can reconcile human freedom with the notion of an all-knowing God. To put it another way: If God knows what we do before we do it, how can we be said to be free agents who must accept responsibility for personal acts? The answer, Boethius insists through Lady Philosophy, is to look at the problem from the point of view of God, not from the human vantage point. God lives in eternity. Eternity does not mean a "long time" with a past and a future. Eternity means "no time": God lives in an eternal moment that for Him is a "now." In that sense God doesn't "foresee" the future. There is no future for God. God sees everything in one simple moment that is only past, present, and future from the human point of view. Boethius says that God does not exercise *praevidentia* (seeing things before they happen) but *providence* (seeing all things in the simultaneity of their happening). Thus God, in a single eternal, ineffable moment, grasps all activity, which for us is a long sequence of events. More specifically, in that moment, God sees our choices, the events that follow from them, and the ultimate consequences of those choices.

The consolation of Boethius, as Lady Philosophy explains it, rests in the fact that people do act with freedom, that they are not in the hands of an indifferent fate, and that the ultimate meaning of life rests with the all-seeing presence of a Person, not a blind force. Lady Philosophy sums up her discussion with Boethius by offering him this "consolation." It is her assurance that his life, even while awaiting execution in a prison cell, was not the product of a blind fate or an uncaring force in the universe.

The language of Boethius, with its discussion of time, eternity, free will, and the nature of God, echoes the great philosophical tradition of Plato and Aristotle (Boethius had translated the latter's works) as well as the stoicism of Cicero and the theological reflections of Augustine. It is a fitting end to the intellectual tradition of the late Roman Empire in the West.

Art and Architecture

Ravenna is a repository of monuments that reflect its late-Roman, barbarian Gothic, and Byzantine history. The mausoleum (burial chapel) of Galla Placidia (who reigned as regent from 430 to 450) was built at the end of the Roman period of Ravenna's history [130]. Once thought to be the tomb of the empress (hence its name), it is more likely a votive chapel to Saint Lawrence originally attached to the nearby church of the Holy Cross. The huge sarcophagi in the building are probably medieval. This small chapel in the shape of a cross, very plain on the outside, shows the architectural tendency to combine the basilica-style nave with the structure of a dome (it even uses a modified pendentive form) used later in monumental structures like Hagia Sophia.

The importance of Galla Placidia rests in the complete and breathtakingly beautiful mosaics that decorate the walls and ceiling. The north niche, just above

130 The so-called Mausoleum of Galla Placidia, Ravenna. Early 5th century. The building has sunk more than a meter—about 4 feet—into the marshy soil, thus making the building seem rather smaller than it must originally have appeared.

131 *The Good Shepherd,* from the Mausoleum of Galla Placidia, Ravenna. 5th century. Mosaic. The "Persian-rug" motif can be seen in the vaulting above the lunette mosaic.

the entrance, has a *lunette* (a small arched space) mosaic depicting Christ as the Good Shepherd [131]. Clothed in royal purple and with a gold staff in his hand, the figure of Christ has a courtly, almost languid elegance that refines the more rustic depictions of the Good Shepherd theme in earlier Roman Christian art. The vaulting of both the *apse* (the altar end of the church) and the dome is covered with a deep blue mosaic interspersed with stylized sunbursts and stars in gold. This "Persian-rug" motif symbolized the heavens, the dwelling place of God. Since the *tesserae,* the small cubes that make up the mosaic, are not set fully flush in the wall, the surfaces of the mosaic are irregular. These surfaces thus refract and break up the light in the chapel, especially from flickering lamps and candles. (The translucent alabaster windows now in the chapel were installed in the 20th century.)

Opposite the lunette of the Good Shepherd is another lunette that depicts the deacon martyr of the Roman Church, Saint Lawrence, who stands next to the gridiron that was the instrument of his death. Beyond the gridiron is an open cabinet containing codices of the four gospels [132]. The spaces above these mosaics are filled with figures of the apostles. Between these are symbols of the search for religious understanding—deer, doves, fountains. In the arches, more spectacular and often overlooked are the abstract interlocking designs with their brightness and *trompe l'œil* (trick-the-eye) quality.

The two baptisteries of Ravenna represent a major

132 *The Martyrdom of Saint Lawrence,* from the Mausoleum of Galla Placidia, Ravenna. 5th century. Mosaic. The window above is one of the modern alabaster ones. According to tradition, Saint Lawrence was roasted to death on a gridiron. He was one of the most revered saints in early Christianity.

144 THE WORLD OF BYZANTIUM

133 Ceiling mosaic of the Orthodox Baptistery, Ravenna. Mid-5th century. The original mosaic work begins with the arched floral motifs above the present windows; the stucco motifs and columns between the windows are of much later date.

religious division of the time between the Orthodox Christians, who accepted the divinity of Christ, and the Arian Christians, who did not. The Neonian Baptistery, built by Orthodox Christians in the early 5th century next to the ancient cathedral of the city, is octagonal—as were most baptisteries, because of their derivation from Roman bath houses. The ceiling mosaic, directly over the baptismal pool, is particularly striking. The lower register of the mosaic, above the windows, shows floral designs based on common Roman decorative motifs. Just above are a circle of empty thrones interspersed with altars with biblical codices open on them [133]. In the band above are the apostles, who seem to be walking in a stately procession around the circle of the dome. In the central disc is a mosaic of the baptism of Christ by John the Baptist in the Jordan River. The spirit of the river is depicted as Neptune.

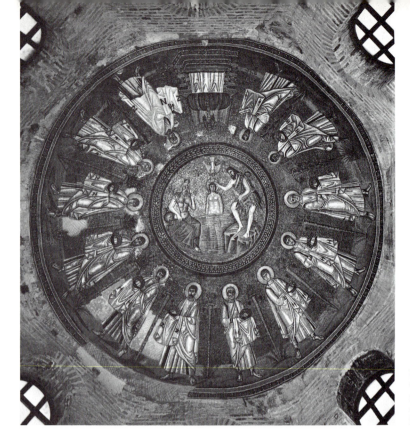

The mosaic ensemble in the ceiling was designed to reflect the beliefs of the participants in the ceremonies below. The circling apostles reminded the candidates for baptism that the church was founded on the apostles; the convert's baptism was a promise that one day they would dwell with the apostles in heaven. Finally, the codices on the altars taught of the sources of their belief, while the empty thrones promised the new Christians a place in the heavenly Jerusalem. The art, then, was not merely decorative but, in the words of a modern Orthodox thinker, "theology in color."

The Arian Baptistery, built by the Goths toward the end of the 5th century, is much more severely decorated. Again the traditional scene of Christ's baptism is in the central disc of the ceiling mosaic. Here the figure of the River Jordan has lobsterlike claws sprouting from his head—a curiously pagan marine touch [134]. The twelve apostles in the lower register are divided into two groups, one led by Peter and the other by Paul. These two groups converge at a throne bearing a jeweled cross (the crucifix with the body of Christ on the cross is very uncommon in this period) that represents in a single symbol the passion and the resurrection of Christ.

Theodoric, the emperor of the Goths who had executed Boethius and reigned from 493 to 526, was buried in a massive mausoleum that may still be seen

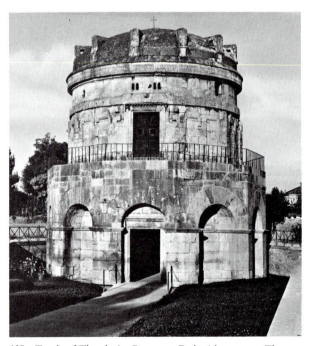

135 Tomb of Theodoric, Ravenna. Early 6th century. The cap of the mausoleum is a great stone about 36′ (11 m) in diameter and 10′ (3 m) high. Inside is a huge porphyry coffin, now pillaged, that contained the king's body. Theodoric maintained peace in Italy during his reign.

136 South-wall mosaic, Sant' Apollinare Nuovo, Ravenna. Early 6th century. The procession of male saints is in the lower register, with prophets and apostles between the windows and scenes from the Gospels in the upper register. Details are shown in figure **138**.

137 North-wall mosaic, Sant' Apollinare Nuovo, Ravenna. The procession of female saints is in the lower register, with scenes from the life of Christ in the upper register. Details are shown in figures **139** and **140**.

on the outskirts of Ravenna [135]. The most famous extant monument of Theodoric's reign aside from his mausoleum is the church of Sant' Apollinare Nuovo, originally called the Church of the Redeemer, the palace church of Theodoric. This church is constructed in the severe basilica style: a wide nave with two side aisles partitioned off from the nave by double columns of marble. The apse decorations have been destroyed, but the walls of the basilica, richly ornamented with mosaics, can be seen. The mosaics, however, are of two different dates and reflect in one building both the Roman and Byzantine styles of art. On each side of the aisles, in the spaces just above the aisle arches, are processions of male and female saints, each procession facing toward the apse and main altar [136, 137]. They move to an enthroned

top: 138 Mosaic of Theodoric's palace (palatium), detail of south-wall mosaic, Sant' Apollinare Nuovo, Ravenna. The curtains replaced the earlier figures in the mosaic.

above: 139 Jesus calling the first apostles, Peter and Andrew, detail of north-wall upper-register mosaic, Sant' Apollinare Nuovo, Ravenna. Note the youthful beardless Jesus and the Roman togas (compare figure **122**).

Christ on one side and toward a Madonna and Child on the other. These mosaics were added to the church when the building passed from the Goths into Byzantine hands in the reign of Justinian. The depiction of Theodoric's palace [138], in fact, still shows evidence of Orthodox censorship. In the arched spaces one can still see traces of halos of now-excised Arian saints (or perhaps members of Theodoric's court). On several columns of the mosaic can be seen the hands of figures that have now been replaced by decorative twisted draperies. The next register above has a line of prophetic figures. At the level of the clerestory windows are scenes from the New Testament—the miracles of Christ on one side [139] and scenes from his passion on the other. These mosaics

are very different in style from the procession of sainted martyrs on the lower level. The gospel sequence is more Roman in inspiration, more severe and simple. Certain themes of earlier Roman Christian iconography are evident. The procession of saints, most likely erected by artists from a Constantinople studio, is much more lush, reverent, and static in tone. The Orientalizing element is especially noteworthy in the depiction of the Three Magi (with their Phrygian caps) who offer gifts to the Christ Child [140].

The church of San Vitale most clearly testifies to the presence of Justinian in Ravenna [141]. Dedicated by Bishop Maximian in 547, it had been begun by Bishop Ecclesius in 526, the year Justinian came to

140 The Magi bearing gifts, detail of north-wall mosaic, Sant' Apollinare Nuovo, Ravenna. Christian legend had already given these figures the names that can be seen at the top of the mosaic; Balthasar, Melchior, and Caspar. Saint Apollinaris was a 2nd-century Phrygian bishop who defended the Christian faith in an address to the Roman emperor Marcus Aurelius.

left: **141** San Vitale, Ravenna. c. 530–548. Aerial view. This complex building was to be the inspiration for Charlemagne's church at Aachen (see pages 160–161).

above: **142** Sant' Apollinare in Classe, Ravenna. c. 549. Aerial view. The tower is an early-medieval addition.

the throne, while the Goths still ruled Ravenna. The church is octagonal, with only the barest hint of basilica length. How different it is may be seen by comparing it with Sant' Apollinare in Classe (the ancient seaport of Ravenna), built at roughly the same time [142]. The octagon has another octagon within it. This interior octagon, supported by columned arches and containing a second-story women's gallery, is the structural basis for the dome. The dome is supported on the octagonal walls by small vaults called *squinches* that cut across the angles of each part of the octagon.

The most arresting characteristic of San Vitale, apart from its intricate and not fully understood architectural design, is its stunning program of mosaics. In the apse is a great mosaic of Christ the Pantocrator, the one who sustains all things in his hands [143]. Christ is portrayed as a beardless young man, clothed in royal purple. He holds in his left hand a book with seven seals (a reference to the book of Revelation) and offers the crown of martyrdom to Saint Vitalis with his right. Flanked by the two archangels, Christ is offered a model of the church by the bishop, Ecclesius, who laid its foundations. Above

the figures are symbolic representations of the four rivers of paradise.

Mosaics to the left and right of the apse mosaic represent the royal couple as regents of Christ on earth. On the left wall of the sanctuary is a mosaic

143 Christ enthroned, with Saint Vitalis and Bishop Ecclesius, ceiling mosaic, San Vitale, Ravenna. c. 530.

144 Emperor Justinian and courtiers, wall mosaic, San Vitale, Ravenna. c. 547.

145 Empress Theodora and retinue, wall mosaic, San Vitale, Ravenna. c. 547.

depicting Justinian and his attendants [144]. It is not merely accidental nor an exercise of simple piety that the soldiers carry a shield with *chi* and *rho* (the first Greek letters in the name of Christ) or that there are twelve attendants or that the figure of the emperor divides clergy and laity. The emperor considered himself the regent of Christ, an attitude summed up in the *iconographic,* or symbolic, program: Justinian represents Christ on earth and his power balances both church and state. The only figure identified in the mosaic is Bishop (later Archbishop) Maximian flanked by his clergy, who include a deacon with a jeweled gospel and a subdeacon with a chained incense pot.

Opposite the emperor's retinue, the Empress Theodora and her attendants look across at the imperial group [145; Plate 11, page 139]. Theodora holds a chalice to complement the bread basket (paten) held by the emperor. At the hem of Theodora's gown is a small scene of the Magi bringing gifts to the Christ Child. Scholars disagree whether the two mosaics represent the royal couple bringing the eucharistic gifts for the celebration of the liturgy or the donation of the sacred vessels for the church. It was a custom for the rulers to give such gifts to the more important churches of their realm. The fact that the empress seems to be leaving her palace (two male functionaries of the court are ushering her out) makes the latter interpretation the more probable one. The women at Theodora's left are striking; those to the extreme left are stereotyped, but the two closest to the empress appear more individualized, leading some art historians to suggest that they are idealized portraits of two of Theodora's closest friends: the wife and daughter of the conqueror of Ravenna, Belisarius.

The royal generosity extended not only to the

capitals typical of the Byzantine style, its elaborate mosaic portraits of saints and prophets, its lunette mosaics of Old Testament prefigurations of the Eucharist, and monumental mosaic scenes, is a living testimony to the rich fusion of imperial, Christian, and Middle Eastern cultural impulses. San Vitale is a microcosm of the sociopolitical vision of Byzantium fused with the religious world view of early Christianity.

Saint Catherine's Monastery at Mount Sinai

Justinian is remembered not only in Constantinople and Ravenna but also in the Near East, where he founded a monastery that is still in use some fifteen hundred years later—a living link back to the Byzantine world.

In her *Peregrinatio,* that wonderfully tireless traveler of the 4th century, Etheria, describes a visit to the forbidding desert of the Sinai to pray at the site where God appeared to Moses in a burning bush (that, Etheria assures us, "is still alive to this day and throws out shoots") and to climb the mountain where the Law was given to Moses. She says that there was a church at the spot of the burning bush with some hermits living nearby to tend it and see to the needs of pilgrim visitors. More than a century later, the Emperor Justinian built a monastery fortress at the foot of Mount Sinai and some pilgrimage chapels on the slopes of the mountain [147]. An Arabic inscription over one of the gates tells the story:

> The pious king Justinian, of the Greek Church, in the expectation of divine assistance and in the hope of divine promises, built the monastery of Mount Sinai and the Church of the Colloquoy [a church over the spot where Moses spoke to God in the burning bush] to his eternal memory and that of his wife, Theodora, so that all the earth and all its inhabitants should become the heritage of God; for the Lord is the best of masters. The building was finished in the thirtieth year of his reign and he gave the monastery a superior named Dukhas. This took place in the 6021st year after Adam, the 527th year [by the calendar] of the era of Christ the Savior.

Because of the number of factors—most important its extreme isolation and the very dry weather—the monastery is an immense repository of ancient Byzantine art and culture. It preserves, as well as the oldest icons in Christianity, some of Justinian's architecture. The monastery is also famous as the site of the rediscovery of the earliest Greek codex of the

146 Bishop's throne (cathedra) of Maximian. c. 546–556. Ivory panels on wood frame; height 4'11" (1.5 m), width 1'11⅝" (.6 m). Archepiscopal Museum, Ravenna.

building and decoration of the church of San Vitale. An ivory throne, now preserved in the episcopal museum of Ravenna, was a gift of the emperor to Bishop Maximian, the ecclesiastical ruler of Ravenna when San Vitale was dedicated [146]. A close stylistic analysis of the carving on the throne has led scholars to see the work of at least four different artists on the panels, all probably from Constantinople. The front of the throne bears portraits of John the Baptist and the four Evangelists, while the back has scenes from the New Testament with sides showing episodes from the Old Testament of the life of Joseph. The purely decorative elements of trailing vines and animals show the style of a different hand, probably Syrian. The bishop's throne (*cathedra* in Latin; a cathedral is a church where a bishop presides) bears a small monogram: *Maximian, Bishop.*

The entire ensemble of San Vitale, with its pierced

147 The fortress monastery of Saint Catherine in the Sinai Desert. 6th century. The church from Justinian's time is in the lower center of the walled enclosure, flanked on the right by a bell tower.

torial art remains from the period before the 8th century. Sinai survived the purges of the "image-breakers" (iconoclasts) that engulfed the rest of the Byzantine world because of its extreme isolation. At Sinai, a range of icons that date from Justinian's time to the modern period can be seen. In a real sense, the icons of the monastery of Saint Catherine show the entire evolution of icon painting.

The Greek word *icon* means image. In the Byzantine Christian tradition, *icon* refers to a painting of a religious figure or a religious scene that is used in the public worship (the liturgy) of the church. Icons are not primarily decorative and they are didactic only in a secondary sense: for the Orthodox Christian faithful the icon is a window into the world of the sacred. Just as Jesus Christ was in the flesh but imaged God in eternity, so the icon is a "thing," but it permits a glimpse into the timeless world of religious mystery. One stands before the icon and speaks through its image to the reality beyond it. This explains why the

148 *Christ Pantocrator*. c. 500–550. Encaustic on wood panel, 32¾ × 17¾" (84 × 46 cm). Monastery of Saint Catherine, Mount Sinai.

New Testament hitherto found. Called the *Codex Sinaiticus,* it was discovered in the monastery by the German scholar Konstantin von Tischendorf in the 19th century. The codex—from the middle of the 4th century—was given by the monks to the Tsar of Russia. In 1933 the Soviet Government sold it for £100,000 to the British Museum, where it remains today, a precious document.

The monastery is surrounded by heavy, fortified walls, the main part of which date from before Justinian's time. Within those walls are some modern buildings, including a fireproof structure that houses the monastery's library and icon collections. The monastic church, the Katholikon, dates from the time of Justinian, as recently discovered inscriptions carved into the wooden trusses in the ceiling of the church prove. Even the name of the architect—Stephanos—was uncovered. This church thus is unique: signed 6th-century ecclesiastical architecture.

One of the more spectacular holdings of the monastery is its vast collections of religious icons. Because of the iconoclastic controversies of the 8th and 9th centuries in the Byzantine Empire almost no picfigures in an icon are usually portrayed full-front with no shadow or sense of three-dimensionality. The figures "speak" directly and frontally to the viewer against a hieratic background of gold.

This iconic style becomes clear by an examination of an icon of Christ that may well have been sent to his new monastery by Justinian himself [148]. The icon is done by the *encaustic* method of painting (a technique common in the Roman world for funerary portraits): painting with molten wax that has been colored by pigments. Christ, looking directly at the viewer, is robed in royal purple; in his left hand he holds a jeweled codex and with his right hand he blesses the viewer.

This icon is an example from a large number found at Sinai that can be dated from before the 10th century. The later icons of the same monastery have not yet been published, but the entire corpus represents a continuous tradition of Byzantine art and piety. Mount Sinai is unique in its great tradition of historical continuity. Despite the rise of Islam, the harshness of the atmosphere, the vicissitudes of history, and the changing culture of the modern world, the monastery fortress at Sinai is living testimony to a style of life and a religiosity with an unbroken history to the time of Justinian's building program.

The Persistence
of Byzantine Culture

It is simplistic to describe Byzantine art as unchanging—it underwent regional, intellectual, social, and iconographic changes—but a person who visits a modern Greek or Russian Orthodox church is struck more by the similarities than by the dissimilarities with the art of early medieval Constantinople. Furthermore, the immediately recognizable Byzantine style can be found in the history of art in areas as geographically diverse as Sicily in southern Italy and the far-eastern reaches of Russia. What explains this basic persistence of style and outlook?

First of all, until it fell to the Turks in 1453, Constantinople exerted an extraordinary cultural influence over the rest of the Eastern Christian world. Russian emissaries sent to Constantinople in the late 10th century to inquire about religion brought back to Russia both favorable reports about Byzantine Christianity and a taste for the Byzantine style of religious art. It was the impact of services in Hagia Sophia that most impressed the delegates of Prince Vladimir, the first Christian ruler in Russia. Although art in Christian Russia was to develop its own

regional variations, it was still closely tied to the art of Constantinople; Russian "onion-dome" churches, for example, are native adaptations of the central-dome churches of Byzantium.

Russia, in fact, accepted Christianity about 150 years after the ban on icons was lifted in Constantinople in 843. By this time the second "golden age" of Byzantine art was well under way. By the 11th century Byzantine artists were not only working in Russia but had also established schools of icon painting in such centers as Kiev. By the end of the century these schools had passed into the hands of Russian monks, but their stylistic roots remained the artistic ideas of Byzantium. Even after the Mongol invasions of Russia in 1240, Russian religious art continued to have close ties to the Greek world, although less with Constantinople than with the monastic centers of Mount Athos and Salonica in Greece.

Byzantine influence was also very strong in Italy. We have already seen the influence of Justinian's court on Ravenna. Although northern Italy fell to Lombard rule in the 8th century, Byzantine influence continued in the south of Italy for the next five hundred years. During the iconoclastic controversy in the East many Greek artisans went into exile in Italy, where their work is still to be seen. Even while the Kingdom of Sicily was under Norman rule in the 12th century, Byzantine artisans were still active—as the great mosaics of Monreale, Cefalù, and Palermo testify. In northern Italy, especially in Venice, the trade routes to the East and the effects of the Crusades permitted a strong presence of Byzantine art, as the mosaics of the church of Saint Mark's (as well as Byzantine art looted when the Crusaders entered Constantinople in 1204) and the cathedral on the nearby island of Torcello attest. We shall see in later chapters the impact of this artistic presence on panel painting in Italy. Until the revolutionary changes by Cimabue and Giotto at the end of the 13th century, the pervasive influence of this style was so great that Italian painting up to that time is often characterized as Italo-Byzantine.

There is another reason that Byzantine aesthetics seem so changeless over the centuries. From the time of Justinian (and even more so after controversies of the 8th and 9th centuries) Byzantine art was intimately tied to the theology and liturgical practices of the Orthodox church. The use of icons, for example, is not merely a pious practice but a deep-rooted part of the faith. Each year the Orthodox church celebrated a feast commemorating the triumph of the Icon party called the Feast of the Triumph of Orthodoxy.

Art, then, is tied to theological doctrine and liturgical practice. Because of the innate conservatism of the theological tradition, innovation either in theology or in art was discouraged. The ideal of the artist was not to try something new but to infuse his work with a spirit of deep spirituality and unwavering reverence. This art, while extremely conservative, was never stagnant. The artists strove for fidelity to the past as their aesthetic criterion. As art historian André Grabar has noted: "Their role can be compared to that of musical performers in our day, who do not feel that their importance is diminished by the fact that they limit their talent to the interpretation of other people's work, since each interpretation contains original nuances."

This attitude of theological conservatism and aesthetic stability helps explain why, for example, the art of icon painting is considered a holy occupation in the Eastern Orthodox church. Today, when a new Orthodox church is built the congregation may commission from a monk or icon painter the necessary icons for the interior of the church. The expeditions of scholars who went to Saint Catherine's monastery to study the treasures there recall the sadness they felt at the funeral of a monk, Father Demetrios, in 1958. The last icon painter in the monastery, he marked the end of a tradition that stretched back nearly fifteen hundred years.

Travelers to Mount Athos in Greece can visit (with some difficulty) the small monastic communities (sketes) on the south of the peninsula, where monastic icon painters still work at their art. In our century there has been a renaissance of the appreciation of this style of painting. In Greece there has been a modern attempt to purge icon painting of Western influences (especially those of the Renaissance and the Baroque periods) in order to recover a more authentic link with the great Byzantine tradition of the past. Even in the Soviet Union, which for decades was indifferent to its religious heritage, there has been a surge of interest in the treasures of past religious art. This has resulted in careful conservation of the icons in Russia, exhibits of the art in the museums of Russia and abroad, and an intense scholarly study of this heritage.

Byzantine culture was not confined to artistic concerns. We have already seen that Justinian made an important contribution to legal studies. Constantinople also had a literary, philosophical, and theological culture. Although Justinian closed the pagan academies, later Byzantine emperors encouraged humanistic and theological studies. While the links between Constantinople and the West were strained over the centuries, those links did remain. At first a good deal of Greek learning came into the West (after having been lost in the early Middle Ages) through the agency of Arabic sources. The philosophical writings of Aristotle became available to Westerners in the late 12th and early 13th centuries in the form of Latin translations of Arabic translations of the Greek: Aristotle came to the University of Paris from the Moslem centers of learning in Spain and northern Africa. Not until the 15th century did Greek become a widely known language in the West; Petrarch and Boccaccio in the 14th century had a difficult time finding anyone to teach them the language. By the 15th century this had changed. One factor contributing to the Renaissance love for the classics was the presence of Greek-speaking scholars from Constantinople in Italy.

The importance of this reinfusion of Greek culture can be seen easily enough by looking at the great libraries of 15th-century Italy. Of the nearly four thousand books in the Vatican library listed in a catalogue of 1484, a thousand were in Greek, most of them from Constantinople. The core of the great library of Saint Mark's in Venice was Cardinal Bessarion's collection of Greek books, brought from the East when he went to the Council of Ferrara-Florence to discuss the union of the Greek and Latin churches in 1438. Bessarion brought with him, in addition to his books, a noted Platonic scholar, Genistos Plethon, who lectured on Platonic philosophy for the delighted Florentines. This event prompted Cosimo de' Medici to subsidize the collection, translation, and study of Plato's philosophy under the direction of Marsilio Ficino. Ficino's Platonic Academy, supported by Medici money, became a rallying point for the study of philosophical ideas.

The fall of Constantinople to the Turks in 1453 brought a flood of émigré Greek scholars to the West, in particular to Italy. The presence of these scholars enhanced the already considerable interest in Greek studies. Greek refugee scholars soon held chairs at the various studia (schools) of the leading Italian cities. These scholars taught language, edited texts, wrote commentaries, and fostered an interest not only in Greek pagan learning but also in the literature of the Greek Fathers of the Church. By the end of the 15th century the famous Aldine press in Venice was publishing a whole series of Greek classics to meet the great demand for such works. This new source of learning and scholarship spread rapidly throughout Western Europe so that by the early 16th century the study of Greek was an ordinary but central part of both humanistic and theological education.

The cultural world view of Justinian's Constantinople is preserved directly in the conservative traditionalism of Orthodox religious art [148] and indirectly by Constantinople's gift of Greek learning to Europe during the Renaissance. The great social and political power of the Byzantine Empire ended in the 15th century although it had been in decline since the end of the 12th century. Only the great monuments remain to remind us of a splendid and opulent culture now gone but once active and vigorous for nearly a thousand years.

Questions for Further Discussion

1. Augustine's *Confessions* is an intensely introspective work. Augustine tends to scrutinize himself in the light of his religious belief. A modern writer might be more psychological in self-scrutiny. How would a psychologically oriented person look at the life and problems of Augustine, especially with respect to his preoccupation with evil?

2. Certain buildings have become landmarks in the history of Western culture. Hagia Sophia is one of these. Compare the use of space in the Parthenon, Pantheon, Solomon's Temple, and Hagia Sophia.

3. Although mosaics and paintings are very similar (colored pictures on flat surfaces bound by defined planes), they are also very different as visual experiences. Compare a painting depicting a scene similar to that of one of the mosaics in this chapter with the mosaic and list the differences you see.

4. Think about the account of the riots in Constantinople by the historian Procopius. Does that event have anything in common with incidents in our own urban experience? Can large-scale organized sports be a catalyst for social upheaval, and why?

5. The icon had a sacred use. Do we normally "use" art for a sacred (or even a secular) purpose, or do we now only "enjoy" art? Explain.

| | | GENERAL EVENTS | LITERATURE & PHILOSOPHY | ART |

EARLY MIDDLE AGES

650

Rise of the Franks

714–741 Charles Martel, grandfather of Charlemagne, reigns as first ruler of Frankish kingdom

732 Charles Martel defeats Moslems at Battle of Poitiers

741–768 Reign of Pepin the Short, father of Charlemagne

735 Death of Venerable Bede, author of *Ecclesiastical History of the English People* and other religious writings

8th–9th cent. Irish *Book of Kells*

768

Carolingian Period

768 Charlemagne ascends Frankish throne

772–778 Charlemagne's military campaigns against Moslem Emirates

778 Battle of Roncesvalles

c. 790 Charlemagne settles his court at Aachen (Aix-la-Chapelle)

800 Charlemagne crowned Holy Roman emperor at Rome by Pope Leo III

814 Death of Charlemagne

910 Founding of monastery at Cluny

987–996 Reign of Hugh Capet in France ends Carolingian line of succession

after 780 Carolingian minuscule form of lettering developed

781 Charlemagne opens palace school, importing such scholars as Theodulf of Orléans and Alcuin of York

785 Alcuin, *Sacramentary*

after 814 Carolingian monasteries adopt *Rule* of Saint Benedict of Nursia (480–547?)

821 Einhard, *Vita Caroli (Life of Charlemagne)*

Illuminated manuscripts and carved ivories prevalent

c. 775 *Centula Evangeliary* and *Dagulf Psalter*

800–810 *Gospel Book of Charlemagne*

early 9th cent. *Crucifixion Ivory*, done at palace school of Charlemagne

c. 820–830 *Utrecht Psalter*

1000

Romanesque Period

11th cent. Pilgrimages become very popular

1066 Norman invasion of England by William the Conqueror

1096–1099 First Crusade; capture of Jerusalem by Christians

c. 1098 *Song of Roland*, *chanson de geste* inspired by Battle of Roncesvalles, written down after 300 yrs. of oral tradition

12th cent. Development of liturgical drama

c. 1125 Saint Bernard of Clairvaux denounces extravagances of Romanesque decoration

1100–1125 Sculptures at Abbey Church of Saint-Pierre, Moissac

1120–1132 Sculptures at Abbey Church of La Madeleine, Vézelay

c. 1140 Portal sculptures at Priory Church, Saint-Gilles-du-Gard

1140

GOTHIC PERIOD

1165 Charlemagne canonized at Cathedral of Aachen

1187 Sultan Saladin conquers Jerusalem

1202–1204 Fourth Crusade; sack of Constantinople by crusaders

1270 Eighth Crusade

1291 Fall of Acre, last Christian stronghold in Holy Land

14th–15th cent. Play cycles performed outside the church; *Everyman* (15th cent.), morality play

c. 1165 Reliquary of Charlemagne and candelabra commissioned for Aachen cathedral by Frederick Barbarossa for canonization of Charlemagne

1400

The Age of Charlemagne

Monastic complexes become important centers in rural life

c. 795 Palace and chapel of Charlemagne at Aachen

c. 800 Monasteries become centers for encouragement of sacred music; theoretical study of music at Charlemagne's palace school

9th cent. Use of semi-dramatic trope in liturgical music; *Quem Quaeritis* trope introduced into Easter Mass

c. 810 Gregorian plain chant *(cantus planus)* obligatory in Charlemagne's churches

c. 820 Plan for Abbey of Saint Gall, the "ideal" monastery

822 Earliest documented church organ

Use of massive walls and piers, rounded arches, and minimal windows

11th–12th cent. Gregorian chant codified

c. 1071–1112 Pilgrimage church at Santiago de Compostela, Spain

c. 1080–1130 Church of Saint Sernin, Toulouse, pilgrimage center

1088–1130 Great Third Church at Cluny

1096–1120 Abbey Church of La Madeleine, Vézelay

Charlemagne as Ruler and Diplomat

Charles the Great (742?–814)—known to subsequent history as Charlemagne—was crowned emperor of the Roman Empire in Saint Peter's Basilica in Rome on Christmas Day A.D. 800 by Pope Leo III, in the first imperial coronation in the West since the late 6th century. The papal coronation was rebellion in the eyes of the Byzantine court, and the emperor in Constantinople considered Charlemagne a usurper, but this act marked the revival of the Roman Empire in the West.

Leo III had compelling reasons to be grateful to Charlemagne. Driven from Rome by a conspiracy and riot in 799, he had taken refuge at Charlemagne's court and was restored to the holy see by the king's Frankish troops. Charlemagne had also created a buffer zone between the Christian West and the Moslems of Spain by his many conquests in southern France. He had destroyed the Longobard kingdom of northern Italy, which had been a consistent threat to the independence of papal rule in the center of Italy. His bloodily persistent wars against the Saxons of northern Germany had reduced the threat of these barbarian warriors and made possible their eventual Christianization. His coastal defenses on the northern shores offered some protection against the incursions of the dreaded Vikings, who made regular coastal raids from their fjord strongholds in Scandinavia (see map opposite).

Charlemagne was not only a conqueror; he was also an able administrator of lands brought under his subjugation. He modified and adapted the classic Roman administrative machinery to fit the needs of his own kingdom. Charlemagne's rule was essentially feudal—structured in a hierarchical fashion, with lesser rulers bound by acts of fealty to higher ones. Lesser rulers were generally large landowners who derived their right to own and rule their land from their tie to the emperor. Charlemagne also maintained a number of vassal dependents at his court who acted as counselors at home and as legates to execute and oversee the imperial will abroad. From his palace the emperor regularly issued legal decrees modeled on the old imperial Roman decrees [149]. These decrees were detailed sets of instructions that touched on a wide variety of secular and religious issues. Those that have survived give us some sense of what life was like in the very early medieval period. The legates of the emperor carried the decrees to the various regions of the empire and reported back on their acceptance and implementation. This burgeoning bureaucratic system required a class of civil servants with a reasonable level of literacy, an important factor in the cultivation of letters that was so much a part of the so-called Carolingian Renaissance.

The popular view of the early Middle Ages—often referred to as the Dark Ages—is of a period of isolated and ignorant peoples with little contact outside the confines of their own immediate surroundings, and at times that was indeed the general condition of life. Nonetheless, it is important to note that in the late 8th and early 9th centuries Charlemagne not only ruled over an immense kingdom (all of modern-day France, Germany, the Low Countries, and Italy as far south as Calabria) but also had extensive diplomatic contact outside that kingdom. Charlemagne maintained regular, if somewhat testy, diplomatic relations with the emperor in Constantinople (at one point he tried to negotiate a marriage between himself and the Byzantine empress Irene in order to consolidate the two empires). Envoys from Constantinople were regularly received in his palace at Aachen, and Charlemagne learned Greek well enough to understand the envoys speaking their own tongue.

Charlemagne's relationship with the rulers of Islamic kingdoms is interesting. Islam had spread all along the southern Mediterranean coast in the preceding century. Arabs were in complete command of all the Middle East, North Africa, and most of the

149 Charlemagne's seal. 9th century. Archives Nationales, Paris. This seal—a Roman gem with the head of an emperor or a philosopher—would have been impressed on molten wax to certify documents. The inscription reads *Christ, protect Charles, the King of the Franks.*

The Carolingian World

Iberian peninsula. Charlemagne's grandfather Charles Martel (Charles the Hammer) had defeated the Moslems decisively at the battle of Poitiers in 732, thus halting an Islamic challenge from Spain to the rest of Europe. Charlemagne himself had fought the Moslems of the Córdoba caliphate on the Franco-Spanish borders; the battle of Roncesvalles (778) was the historical basis for the later epic poem the *Song of Roland*.

Despite his warlike relationship with Moslems in the West, Charlemagne had close diplomatic ties with the great Harun al-Rashid, the caliph of Baghdad. In 787 Charlemagne sent an embassy to the caliph to beg protection for the holy places of the Christians in Moslem-held Palestine. The caliph (of *Thousand and One Nights* fame) received the Frankish legates and their gifts (mainly bolts of the much-prized Frisian cloth) with welcome and sent an elephant back to the emperor as a gesture of friendship. This gift actually arrived at Aachen and lived there for a few years before succumbing to the harsh winter climate. Charlemagne's negotiations were successful. From a pair of Palestinian monks he received the keys to the church of the Holy Sepulchre and other major Christian shrines, an important symbolic act that made the emperor the official guardian of the holiest shrines in Christendom.

Charlemagne's reign was also conspicuous for its economic developments. He stabilized the currency system of his kingdom. The silver *denier* struck at the royal mint in Frankfurt after 804 became the standard coin of the time; its presence in archaeological finds from Russia to England testifies to its widespread use and the faith traders had in it.

Trade and commerce were vigorous. Charlemagne welcomed Jewish immigration into his kingdom to provide a merchant class for commerce. There were annual trade fairs at Saint Denis near Paris, at which English merchants could buy foodstuffs, honey, and wine from the Carolingian estates. A similar fair was held each year at Pavia, an important town of the old Lombard kingdom of northern Italy. Port cities such as Marseilles provided mercantile contracts with the Moslems of Spain and North Africa. Jewish merchants operated as middlemen in France for markets throughout the Near East. The chief of Charlemagne's mission to Harun al-Rashid's court was a Jew named Isaac who had the linguistic ability and geographic background to make the trip to Baghdad and back—with an elephant—at a time when travel was a risky enterprise. Rivers such as the Rhine and the Moselle were utilized as important trade routes. One of the most sought-after articles from the Frankish kingdom was the iron broadsword produced from forges in and around the city of Cologne and sold to Arabs in the Middle East through

Jewish merchants at the port cities. Vivid testimony to their value can be read in the repeated embargoes (imposed under penalty of death) decreed by Charlemagne against their export to the land of the Vikings, who put them too often to effective use against their Frankish manufacturers in coastal raids on North Sea towns and trading posts.

Charlemagne's Palace at Aachen

Beyond his immediate commercial, military, and political goals, Charlemagne had an overwhelming desire to model his kingdom on that of ancient Rome. His coronation in Rome symbolized the fusion of the ancient imperial ideal with the notion of Christian destiny. Its was not accidental that Charlemagne's favorite book—he had it read to him frequently at meals—was Augustine's *The City of God.*

One highly visible way of making this ideal concrete was to build a capital.

At Aachen (in French it is called Aix-la-Chapelle) Charlemagne built his palace and royal chapel [150]. Except for the chapel (incorporated into the present cathedral), all the buildings of Charlemagne's palace have been destroyed and the Aachen city hall (itself built in the 14th century) covers the palace site. The palace itself was a long one-story building; its main room was the large royal hall, which measured roughly 140 by 60 feet (42.7 by 18.3 meters). So richly decorated that even the fastidious and sophisticated Byzantine legates were favorably impressed, the room had as its focal point at the western end the emperor's throne. In front of the palace was an open courtyard around which were outbuildings and apartments for the imperial retinue. Around the year 800 the courtyard held a great bronze statue of Theodoric, once king of the Ravenna Ostrogoths, that Charlemagne had brought back from Ravenna to adorn his palace.

150 Model reconstruction of Charlemagne's palace at Aachen. Römisch-Germanisches Zentralmuseum, Mainz. The royal hall with its long connecting gallery is in the foreground. The royal chapel is the octagonal building in the left background.

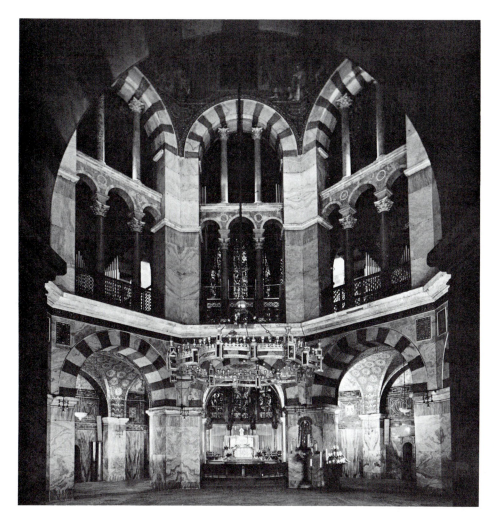

151 Interior of chapel of Charlemagne, Aachen. This view is eastward toward the emperor's tribune (second story center) from the side of the double altars. The mosaics above and the band of inscriptions at the lower level are modern.

The royal hall was joined to Charlemagne's chapel by a long wooden gallery. This royal chapel was probably built around 795. With sixteen exterior walls, the chapel was a central-plan church based on an octagon [151], its model undoubtedly the church of San Vitale in Ravenna, which Charlemagne had visited and admired. The octagon formed the main nave of the church, which was surrounded by *cloisters;* the building itself was two-storied. At the eastern end of the chapel was an altar dedicated to the Savior, with a chapel dedicated to the Virgin directly below it. The central space was crowned with an octagonal cupola, the lower part of which was pierced by windows, the main source of light in the church. The outside of the church was plain and severe; the inside was richly ornamented with marbles brought to Aachen from Ravenna and Rome. The interior of the cupola was decorated with a rich mosaic depicting Christ and the twenty-four elders of the Apocalypse (now destroyed; the present mosaics in the

chapel are modern copies) while the other planes of the interior were covered with frescoes (now also destroyed). The railing of the upper gallery was made from bronze screens that are still in place, wrought in geometrical forms.

The chapel included two objects that emphasized its royal status: the most important relic of the kingdom, Saint Martin of Tours' cape, and a throne. Charlemagne's throne was on the second floor, opposite the chapel of the Savior. From this vantage point the emperor could observe the liturgical services being conducted in the Savior chapel and at the same time view the Virgin chapel with its rich collection of relics.

Charlemagne's throne, with its curved back and armrests, was mounted by six stone steps. This arrangement was obviously taken from King Solomon's throne as described in the Bible (I Kings 10:18–19). Charlemagne was to be thought of as the "new Solomon" who, like his ancient prototype, was an ambitious builder, a sagacious lawgiver, and the symbol of national unity. That this analogy was not an idle fancy is proved by a letter from Alcuin, Charlemagne's friend and tutor, to the emperor in anticipation of his return to Aachen: "May I soon be allowed to come with palms, accompanied with children singing psalms, to meet your triumphant glory, and to see once more your beloved face in the Jerusalem of our most dear fatherland, wherein is the temple set up to God by this most wise Solomon."

Learning in the Time of Charlemagne

At Aachen Charlemagne opened his famous "palace school," an institution that was a prime factor in initiating what has been called the Carolingian Renaissance. Literacy in Western Europe before the time of Charlemagne was rather spotty; it existed, but hardly thrived, in certain monastic centers that kept alive the old tradition of humanistic learning taken from ancient Rome. Original scholarship was rare, although monastic copyists did keep alive the tradition of literacy conservation. Charlemagne himself could not write.

The scholars and teachers Charlemagne brought to Aachen provide some clues as to the various locales in which early medieval learning had survived. Peter of Pisa and Paul the Deacon (from Lombardy) came to teach grammar and rhetoric at his school since they had had contact with the surviving liberal arts curriculum in Italy. Theodulf of Orleans was a theologian and poet. He had studied in the surviving Christian kingdom of Spain and was an heir to the encyclopedic tradition of Isadore of Seville and his followers. Finally and most importantly, Charlemagne brought an Anglo-Saxon, Alcuin of York, to Aachen after meeting him in Italy in 781. Alcuin had been trained in the English intellectual tradition of the Venerable Bede (died 735), the most prominent intellectual of his day, a monk who had welded together the study of humane letters and biblical scholarship. These scholar-teachers were hired by Charlemagne for several purposes.

First, Charlemagne wished to establish a system of education for the young of his kingdom. The primary purpose of these schools was to develop literacy; Alcuin of York developed a curriculum for them. He insisted that humane learning should consist of those studies which developed logic and science. It was from this distinction that later medieval pedagogues developed the two courses of studies for

all schooling prior to the university: the *trivium* (grammar, rhetoric, and dialectic) and the *quadrivium* (arithmetic, geometry, music, and astronomy). These subjects remained at the heart of the school curriculum from the medieval period until modern times. (The now much-neglected "classical education" has its roots in this basic plan of learning.)

Few books were available and writing was done on slates or waxed tablets since parchment was expensive. In grammar, some of the texts of the Latin Grammarian Priscian might be studied and then applied to passages from Latin prose writers. In rhetoric, the work of Cicero was studied, or Quintilian's *Institutio Oratoria* if available. For dialectics, some of the work of Aristotle might be read in the Latin translation of Boethius. In arithmetic, multiplication and division was learned and perhaps there was some practice on the *abacus* since the Latin numerals were clumsy to compute with pen and paper. Arithmetic also included some practice in chronology as students were taught to compute the variable dates of Easter. They would finish with a study of the allegorical meaning of numbers. Geometry was based on the study of Euclid. Astronomy was derived from the Roman writer Pliny, with some attention to Bede's work. Music was the theoretical study of scale, proportion, the harmony of the universe, and the "music of the spheres." Music at this period was distinguished from *cantus,* which was the practical knowledge of chants and hymns for church use. In general, all study was based largely on the rote mastery of texts.

Beyond the foundation of schools, Charlemagne needed scholars to reform existing texts and to halt their terrible corruption, especially those used in church worship. Literary revival was closely connected with liturgical revival. Part of Charlemagne's educational reform envisioned people who would read aloud and sing in church from decent, reliable texts. Literacy was conceived of as a necessary prelude for intelligible worship.

It was mainly Alcuin of York who worked at the task of revising the liturgical books. Alcuin published a book of extracts of Old and New Testament passages in Latin for public reading during Mass. He sent for books from Rome in order to publish a sacramentary, the book of prayers and rites for the administration of the sacraments of the church. Alcuin's *Sacramentary* was made obligatory for the churches of the Frankish kingdom in 785. Charlemagne made the Roman chant (called *Gregorian* after Pope Gregory the Great, who was said to have initiated such chants in the end of the 6th century) obligatory in all the churches of his realm. Alcuin also attempted to correct scribal errors in the Vulgate Bible (the Latin version of Saint Jerome) by a comparative reading of manuscripts, a gigantic task he never completed.

Beyond the practical need for literacy there was a further aim of education in this period. It was generally believed that all learning would lead to a better grasp of revealed truth—the Bible. The study of profane letters (by and large the literature of Rome) was a necessary first step toward the full study of the Bible. The study of grammar would set out the rules of writing, while dialectics would help distinguish true from false propositions. Models for such study were sought in the works of Cicero, Statius, Ovid, Lucan, and Vergil. These principles of correct writing and argumentation could then be applied to the study of the Bible in order to get closer to its truth. The pursuit of analysis, definition, and verbal clarity are the roots from which the scholastic form of philosophy would spring in the High Middle Ages. Scholasticism, which dominated European intellectual life until the eve of the Renaissance, had its first beginnings in the educational methodology established by Alcuin and his companions.

152 The four Evangelists and their symbols, from the *Gospel Book of Charlemagne*. Palace school of Charlemagne. Aachen, early 9th century. Manuscript illumination. Cathedral Treasury, Aachen.

These educational enterprises were not centered exclusively at the palace school at Aachen. Under Charlemagne's direction Alcuin developed a system of schools throughout the Frankish Empire, schools centered in both monasteries and towns. Attempts were also made to attach them to parish churches in the rural areas. The monastic school at Metz became a center for singing and liturgical study; schools at Lyons, Orleans, Mainz, Tours, and Laon had centers for teaching children rudimentary literary skills and offered some opportunity for further study in the liberal arts and the study of scripture. The establishment of these schools was accomplished by a steady stream of decrees and capitularies emanating from the Aachen palace. A circular letter, written most likely by Alcuin, called *On the Cultivation of Learning*, encouraged monks to study the Bible and to teach the young to do the same. A decree of 798 insisted that prelates and country clergy alike start schools for children.

This program of renewal in educational matters was an ideal set forth at a time when education was at a low ebb in Europe. Charlemagne tried to reverse the trend and in so doing encouraged real hope for an educated class in his time. His efforts were not entirely successful; many of his reforms came to naught in the generations after him when Europe slipped back into violence and ignorance.

The Visual Arts

Given Charlemagne's preoccupation with literary culture, it should not be surprising that a great deal of artistic effort should have been expended on the production and illumination of manuscripts. Carolingian manuscripts were made of parchment (treated animal skins, mainly from cows and sheep) since papyrus was unavailable and the technical process of making paper was not known at this period. For very fine books the parchment was dyed purple and the letters were painted on with silver and gold pigments.

While a good deal of decoration of Carolingian manuscripts shows the influence of Irish models, the illustrations often show other influences. This is strikingly apparent in the illustrations of the *Gospel Book of Charlemagne* (800–810), where it is clear that the artists were conscious of the Roman style [152]. The page showing the four evangelists with their symbolic emblems is strikingly classical: the four evangelists are toga-clad like ancient Roman consuls. There is some evidence that the artists attempted some experiment in three-dimensionality. The wooded background in the receding part of the upper two illustrations tends to bring the evangelists forward and thus diminish the flatness we associate both with Byzantine and Celtic illustrations.

The *Utrecht Psalter* (so called because its present home is the University of Utrecht in Holland) has been called the masterpiece of the Carolingian Renaissance. Executed at Reims sometime around 820 to 840, it contains the whole psalter with wonderfully free and playful pen drawings around the text of the psalms. The figures are free from any hieratic stiffness; they are mobile and show a nervous energy. The illustration for Psalm 148, for example, has a scene at the bottom of the page showing various figures "praising God with horn and cymbals" [153]. There are two other interesting aspects of the same illustration. One is that the figures are in the act of praising Christ, who stands at the apex of the illustration with the symbols of his resurrection (the stafflike cross in his hand). Although the psalms speak of the praise of God, for the medieval Christian the "hidden" or true meaning of the scriptures was that they

154 *Crucifixion.* Palace school of Charlemagne. Early 9th century. Ivory, 9⅞ × 6⅛″ (25 × 16 cm). Treasury, cathedral of Saint Just, Narbonne. Such ivories were used as book covers for evangeliaries and other illustrated works.

153 Page from the *Utrecht Psalter.* Hautvillers (near Reims), c. 820–840. Pen and ink on vellum, 12⅞ × 10″ (33 × 26 cm). University Library, Utrecht. This page is typical of the fast, nervous style of the unknown illustrator who did similar symbolic drawings for the whole of the psalter.

speak in a prefigurative way of Christ. Thus the psalmist who praises God is a "shadow" of the church that praises Christ. A second thing to note in this illustration is the bottom-center scene of an organ with two men working the bellows to supply the air.

The style of the *Utrecht Psalter* has much in common with early Christian illustration. The lavish purple-and-silver manuscripts show a conscious imitation of Byzantine taste. We have also noted the influence of Celtic illustration. Carolingian manuscript art thus had a certain international flavor, and the various styles and borrowings give ample testimony to the cosmopolitan character of Charlemagne's culture. This universality diminished in the next century; not until the period of the so-called International Style in the 14th century would such a broad eclecticism again be seen in Europe.

One other art form that developed from the Carolingian love for the book is ivory carving. This technique was not unique to Charlemagne's time; it was known in the ancient world and highly valued in Byzantium, as noted in the discussion of Maximian's throne at Ravenna in Chapter 6. The ivories that have survived from Charlemagne's time were used for book covers. One beautiful example of the ivory carver's art is a crucifixion panel made at the palace workshop at Aachen sometime in the early 9th century [154]. Note the crowded scenes that surround the crucifixion event. Reading clockwise from the bottom left, one sees the Last Supper, the betrayal in the garden, and, at the top, a soldier piercing Jesus' side. As a balance at the top right another soldier offers Jesus a wine-soaked sponge on a lance. Below that scene is one of the women at the tomb and, at the bottom, of the incredulity of Thomas. Framing these scenes above are the ascension of Christ on the left and the Pentecost on the right, the two scenes separated by a stylized sun and moon. The entire ivory is framed with geometric and abstract floral designs. The composition indicates that the carver had seen some examples of early Christian carving, while the beardless Christ and the flow of the drapery indicate familiarity with Byzantine art.

One surviving Carolingian manuscript that allows us to see both illumination and ivory work is the *Dagulf Psalter,* made as a gift for Pope Hadrian I, who reigned from 772 to 795. The psalms are not illustrated like the ones in the *Utrecht Psalter;* instead, the illustrator begins a tradition that will be fairly normal for psalters in the future: he enlarges and illuminates the initial letter of the first, 51st, and 101st psalms. The *B* of the first word of Psalm 1, *Beatus vir qui* (Blessed is the man who), is enlarged and decorated in the swelling style of Celtic illumination; the same patterns are echoed on the page margin [155].

The ivory covers of the psalter have been preserved and are now in the Louvre [156]. Rather than the usual crowded scenes of most of these covers, the ivories from the *Dagulf Psalter* are composed of two scenes on each of the panels; the scenes make references to both the psalter and the papal connection. The panel on the left shows David and his court; below, David is shown singing one of his psalms to the accompaniment of his lyre. The right panel depicts Saint Jerome receiving a letter from Pope Damasus instructing him to correct the psalter; the scene below depicts Jerome in the act of working on the psalter while a grateful clergy looks on.

One other advance in manuscript production during the Carolingian period was in the area of fine handwriting or, as it is more technically known, calligraphy. Handwriting before the Carolingian period was cluttered, unformed, and cramped. It was very hard to read because of its erratic flourishes and its lack of symmetry. After 780 scribes in Carolingian scriptoria began to develop a precise and rounded form of lettering that became known as the Carolingian *minuscule,* as opposed to the *majuscule* or capital letter. This form of lettering was so crisp and legible that it soon became a standard form of manuscript writing. Even in the 15th century, the Florentine humanists preferred the minuscule calligraphy for their manuscripts. When printing became popular in the early 16th century, printers soon designed type fonts to conform to Carolingian minuscule. It overcame Gothic type in popularity and is the ancestor of modern standard lettering systems.

155 Beginning of Psalm 1, from the *Dagulf Psalter*. Late 8th century. Manuscript illumination, 7½ × 4⅝" (19 × 12 cm). Austrian National Library, Vienna.

156 Cover panels for the *Dagulf Psalter*. Late 8th century. Ivory, 6⅜ × 3⅛″ (17 × 8 cm). Louvre, Paris.

Beyond the sheer energy required to produce a book was a further difference between their culture and ours. We are a people who accept ideas only after testing and reflection. We do not accept the past as authority. The early medieval person was far more respectful of the wisdom of the past. Books represented authority, especially the Bible. Holy Scripture not only represented a plan of salvation; it was the authoritative word about the nature of reality and the structure of human existence. It was a commonplace in the medieval world that God had written "two books": the book of nature and the book of the Scriptures. Each had inexhaustible reserves of wisdom. In reproducing the book of Scripture there was a natural impulse to try to imitate the beauty of the book of nature, since in the creation of beauty one was imitating the creative genius of God.

Benedictine Monasticism

Monasticism—from the Greek *monos* (alone)—was an integal part of Christianity from the 3rd century on. Monasticism came into the West from the great Eastern tradition of asceticism (self-denial) and eremitism (the solitary life). Its development in the West was very complex, and we cannot speak of any one form of monasticism as predominant before the time of Charlemagne.

Celtic monasticism in Ireland was characterized both by austere living and by a rather lively intellectual tradition. Monasticism in Italy was far more simple and rude. Some of the monasteries on the continent were lax, and Europe was full of wandering monks. No rule of life predominated in the 6th and 7th centuries. Monastic life styles varied not only from country to country but also from monastery to monastery.

The Rule of Saint Benedict

One strain of European monasticism derived from a rule of life written in Italy by Benedict of Nursia (480–547?) in the early 6th century. Although it borrows from early monastic rules and was applied only to a small proportion of monasteries for a century after its publication, the Rule of Saint Benedict eventually became the Magna Carta of monasticism in the West. Charlemagne had Alcuin of York bring the Rule to his kingdom and impose it on the monasteries of the Frankish kingdom to reform them and impose on them some sense of regular observance. In fact, the earliest copy of the Rule of Saint Benedict we possess today (a 9th-century manuscript preserved in the monastery of Saint Gall) is a copy of a copy Charlemagne had made in 814 from Saint Benedict's autograph copy preserved at the abbey of Monte Cassino in Italy (now lost).

The Rule of Saint Benedict consists of a prologue and 73 chapters (some only a few sentences long), which set out the ideal of monastic life. Monks (the brethren) are to live a family life in community under the direction of a freely elected father (the abbot) for the purpose of being schooled in religious perfection. They are to possess nothing of their own (poverty); they are to live in one monastery and not wander (stability); their life is to be one of obedience to the abbot; and they are to remain unmarried (chastity). Their daily life is to be a balance of common prayer, work, and study. Their prayer life centered around duly appointed hours of liturgical praise of God that were to mark the intervals of the day. This prayer, called the "Divine Office," consisted of the public recitation of psalms, hymns, and prayers with readings from the Holy Scriptures. The offices were interspersed throughout the day and were central to the monks' life. The periods of public liturgical prayer themselves set off the times for reading, study, and the manual labor that was done for the good of the community and its sustenance. The life style of Benedictine monasticism can be summed up in its motto: "pray and work."

The daily life of the monk was determined by sunrise and sunset (as it was for most people in those days). Here is a typical day—called the *horarium*—in an early medieval monastery. The italicized words designate the names for the liturgical hours of the day:

Horarium Monasticum

2:00 A.M.	Rise
2:10–3:30	*Nocturns* (later called *Matins*; the longest office of the day)
3:30–5:00	Private reading and study
5:00–5:45	*Lauds* (the second office; also called "morning prayer")
5:45–8:15	Private reading and *Prime* (the first of the short offices of the day); at times, there was communal Mass at this time and, in some places, a light breakfast, depending on the season
8:15–2:30	Work punctuated by short offices of *Tierce, Sext,* and *None* (literally the third, sixth, and ninth hours)
2:30–3:15	Dinner
3:15–4:15	Reading and private religious exercises
4:15–4:45	*Vespers*—break—*Compline* (night prayers)
5:15–6:00	To bed for the night

This daily regimen changed on feast days (less work and more prayer) and during the summer (earlier rising, work later in the day when the sun was down a bit, more food, and so on). While the schedule now seems harsh, it would not have surprised a person of the time. Benedict would have found it absurd for people to sleep while the sun is shining and then stay up under the glare of artificial light. When we look at the horarium closely we see a day in which prayer and reading get four hours each, while there are about six hours of work. The rest of the day was devoted to personal chores, eating, and the like.

The triumph of the Benedictine monastic style of life (the early Middle Ages has been called the Benedictine centuries by some historians) is to be found in its sensible balance between the extreme asceticism of Eastern monastic practices and the unstructured life of Western monasticism before the Benedictine reforms. There was an even balance of prayer, manual labor, and intellectual life.

The Carolingian Monastery

In the period between Saint Benedict and Charlemagne the Benedictine monastery underwent a complex evolution. Originally the monasteries were made up of small communities with fewer than fifteen members who led a life of prayer and work in a rather simple setting. With the decline of city life and the disorders brought on by the repeated invasions of

1 church	4 refectory	7 abbot's house	10 workshop	13 gardens
2 cloister	5 kitchen	8 school	11 barns and stables	14 poultry houses
3 dormitory	6 scriptorium	9 guest house	12 infirmary-novitiate	15 cemetery-orchard

157 Plan for an ideal monastery. c. 820. Reconstruction interpretation developed by Walter Horn and Ernest Born from the manuscript in the library of the former monastery of Saint Gall. The original plan, 3'8" (112 cm) across, was drawn to scale on vellum. It shows a monastery on a site 480 × 640' (146 × 195 m), which was to house some 120 monks and 170 serfs. The plan was intended to be a guide for future monasteries, and so it was for centuries, greatly influencing monastery design.

the barbarians after the 5th century, the monastery became increasingly a center of life for rural populations. Monasteries not only kept learning alive and worship intact but were also called on to become a shelter for the traveler, a rudimentary hospital for the sick, a place of refuge in time of invasion, a granary for the farmer, a center of law for both religious and civil courts, and a place that could provide agricultural services such as milling and brewing.

This expansion of services, making the monastery into what has been called a "miniature civic center," inevitably changed the physical character of the monastery compound itself. By Charlemagne's time the monastery was an intricate complex of buildings suitable for the many tasks it was called on to perform. One vivid example of the complexity of the

Carolingian monastery can be gained by a study of a plan for an ideal monastery developed about 820 at the Benedictine abbey of Saint Gall in present-day Switzerland [157].

In the Saint Gall plan the monastic church dominated the area. Set off with its two round towers, it was a basilica-style church with numerous entrances for the use of the monks. To the south of the church was a rectangular garden space surrounded by a covered walkway (the *cloister*) from which radiated the monk's dormitory, dining hall (*refectory*), and kitchens. To the north of the church were a copying room (*scriptorium*), a separate house for the abbot, a school for youths and young novices, and a guest house. To the extreme south of the church were ranged workshops, barns, and other utilitarian outbuildings. To the east beyond the church were an infirmary and separate house for aspirant monks (the *novitiate*), gardens, poultry houses, and the community cemetery.

The Romanesque Style

The plan of Saint Gall was never realized in stone, but the Benedictines did participate in ambitious architectural works after the Carolingian period. In the 11th century, after a long period of desolation and warfare, Europe began to stir with new life. Pilgrimages became very popular as travel became safe. Pilgrimage routes—in particular to sites in Spain, England, and Italy—crisscrossed Europe. Crusades were mounted to free the holy places of the Middle East from the Moslems so that pilgrims could journey in peace to the most desired goal of the pilgrim: Jerusalem. In this period monks built and maintained pilgrimage churches and hostels on the major routes of the pilgrims.

The building style of this period (roughly from 1000 to 1200) is called Romanesque because the architecture was larger and more "Roman"-looking than the work done in the earlier medieval centuries. The two most striking characteristics of this architecture were the use of heavy stone arches and generous exterior decoration, mainly sculpture. The Romanesque style had two obvious advantages. One was that the use of heavy stone and masonry walls permitted larger and more spacious interiors. Secondly, the heavy walls could support stone arches (mainly the Roman barrel arch), at least in France and Spain, which in turn permitted fireproof stone and masonry roofs. Long experience had shown that basilica-style churches, with their wooden trusses and wooden roofs, were notoriously susceptible to destruction by fire.

Romanesque architecture sprouted all over Europe, and while it showed great regional variation its main lines are clear enough. The Benedictine pilgrimage church of Saint Sernin in Toulouse was designed to accommodate the large number of pilgrims as they made their way to the famous shrine of Santiago de Compostela in Spain. A glimpse at the floor plan [158] and the interior [159] shows clearly that

| 0 | 50 | 100 feet |
| 0 | 10 | 20 | 30 meters |

1 nave   5 transept
2 choir   6 aisles
3 ambulatory   7 apse
4 chapels   8 narthex

left: 158 Floor plan of the church of Saint Sernin, Toulouse. Notice the ample aisles for easy passage of groups of pilgrims around the entire church. The radiating chapels around the ambulatory permitted many services to be held simultaneously.

below: 159 Interior of the church of Saint Sernin, Toulouse. c. 1080–1120. The massive vaulting of the roof of the nave is called barrel vaulting or tunnel vaulting. Its heavy stonework required thick supporting walls. The galleries with their own vaults helped support these cut-stone vaults over the nave.

above: 160 Jamb of the central portal, Saint Gilles du Gard, France. c. 1140. Notice the echoes of classical Roman influence in the columns, capitals, and low-relief carving of parts of this jamb.

above right: 161 *Demon of Luxury,* nave capital sculpture, abbey church of La Madeleine, Vézelay. c. 1130. This figure is not untypical of the extravagant imagination reflected in Romanesque sculpture.

right: 162 The prophet Jeremiah, trumeau of south portal, Saint Pierre, Moissac. Early 12th century. Notice the sinuous curve of his figure as the prophet inclines toward the church while he holds his prophetic scroll. The lions reflect the influence of the Islamic art of southern Spain.

the generous interior space was articulated in such a manner that large numbers of persons besides the monastic community could move freely through the building. For example, the floor plan allows for an aisle parallel to the nave to go completely around the church. In that fashion the monastic choir, which extended out into the nave, was circumvented by the faithful—who could make a complete circle of the church without disturbing the monks.

Exterior church decoration was almost unknown in the Carolingian period, but during the Romanesque period there was a veritable explosion of exterior sculpture. The lack of interior light (precluded by the thick solid walls needed for the roof vaulting) drove the artist outside, in a sense. A favorite area of decoration was the *portal* or doorway, since the crowds would pass through the doors to enter the church and receive edifying instruction in the proc-

163 Pentecost scene, tympanum, abbey church of La Madeleine, Vézelay. c. 1120–1132.

ess. The artist might decorate a door jamb [160], a capital [161], or the central supporting post of a portal, the *trumeau* [162].

The fullest iconographic program of the Romanesque sculptor can usually be found in the half moon-shaped space called the *tympanum* over the portal; Romanesque churches in France offer many splendid examples of this elaborated art. The sculptural program over the inner west door of the Benedictine abbey church of Sainte Madeleine at Vézelay is representative of the elaborated art in stone [163].

The Vézelay tympanum depicts Christ, ascending into heaven, giving his church the mission to preach the gospel to the entire world. Christ, in the center almond-shape called the *mandorla*, sends the power of the Holy Spirit into the apostles who cluster on either side and just below with copies of the gospel in their hands. Below the apostles the lintel stone depicts the peoples of the world, including fanciful races known to the sculptor only through the legendary travel books and encyclopedias that circulated in Europe. The theme of the exotic peoples to be healed by the gospel is repeated in the eight arching compartments above the central scene, which depict strange peoples, lepers, cripples, and others who need to hear the gospel. The outer arches, or *archivolts,* depict the signs of the Zodiac and the symbolic seasons of the year, a reminder that the gospel depicted in the central scene is to be preached "in season and out"; these symbolic medallions are interspersed with mythical and fantastic beasts. The outer archivolts are purely decorative, derived perhaps from Islamic sources known to the artists through the Moslem architecture of Spain.

Romanesque style was a European phenomenon— its variant forms in Italy, Germany, and England give ample testimony—and a summing-up of much of European culture between the end of the Carolingian period and the rise of city life and the Gothic style in the late 12th century. The roots of the Romanesque were in the Benedictine tradition of service, scholarship, and solidity. Churches like Vézelay also manifest the period's concern with travel, expansion, and the attendant knowledge that comes from such mobility. When reaction came against the more extravagant forms of Romanesque decoration it came from Bernard of Clairvaux (1090–1153), who was primarily a monastic reformer. Bernard was horrified by the fantastic nature of Romanesque sculpture since he felt so many "and so marvelous are the varieties of diverse shapes that we are more tempted to read in the marbles than in the Book and to spend our whole day wondering at these things rather than meditating on the Law of God." Even Bernard's strictures testify to the close relationship between the Benedictines and the Romanesque (especially the French Romanesque), which is another reason the period after Charlemagne and before the primacy of the city can be called simply the Benedictine Age.

Monasticism and Gregorian Chant

The main occupation of the monk was the *Opus Dei* (work of God)—the liturgical common prayer of the monasteric horarium; life centered around the monastic church where the monks gathered seven times a day for prayer. The centrality of the liturgy also explains why copying, correcting, and illuminating manuscripts was such an important part of monastic life. Texts were needed for religious services as well as for spiritual reading. The monks were encouraged to study the scriptures as a lifelong occupation. For the monk this study was *lectio divina* (divine reading) and was central to his development as a monk. This monastic imperative encouraged the study of the Bible and such ancillary disciplines (grammar, criticism, and the like) as necessary for the study of Scripture. From the 7th century on, monastic scriptoria were busily engaged in copying a wealth of material, both sacred and profane.

The monasteries were also centers for the development of sacred music. We have already seen that Charlemagne was interested in church music. His biographer Einhard tells us that the emperor "made careful reforms in the way in which the psalms were chanted and the lessons read. He was himself an expert at both of these exercises but he never read the lesson in public and he would sing only with the rest of the congregation and then in a low voice." Charlemagne's keen interest in music explains why certain monasteries of his reign—notably those at Metz and Trier—became centers for church music.

Charlemagne brought monks from Rome to stabilize and reform church music in his kingdom as part of his overall plan of liturgical renovation. In the earlier period of Christianity's growth quite diverse traditions of ecclesiastical music developed in various parts of the West. Roman music represented one tradition—later called *Gregorian* chant after Pope Greg-

ory the Great (540–604), who was erroneously believed to have codified the music in the late 6th century. Milan had its own musical tradition, known as *Ambrosian* music—in honor of Saint Ambrose, who had been a noted hymn writer, as Saint Augustine attests in the *Confessions*. There was a peculiar regional style of music in Spain known as *Mozarabic* chant, while the Franks also had their own peculiar style of chant. All of these styles derive from earlier models of music which have their roots in Hebrew, Greco-Roman, and Byzantine styles. Lack of documentation permits only an educated reconstruction of this early music and its original development.

Gregorian chant as we know it today was not codified until the 11th and 12th centuries, so it is rather difficult to reconstruct precisely the music of Charlemagne's court. It was probably a mixture of Roman and Frankish styles of singing. It was *monophonic*—that is, one or many voices sang a single melodic line—and more often than not lacked musical accompaniment in the monastic churches. Most scholars believe that the majority of the music consisted of simple chants for the recitation of the psalms at the Divine Office; more elaborate forms were used for the hymns of the Office and the Mass chants. The music was simply called *cantus planus*, plainsong or plainchant.

In its more elementary form the chant consisted of a single note for each syllable of a word. The basic symbols used to notate Gregorian chant were called *neums*. Using the Gregorian notational system with its four-line staff and the opening line of Psalm 109, *Dixit Dominus Domino Meo, sede a dextris meis* (The Lord said to my Lord: sit on my right hand), a line of syllabic chant would look like this:

1. Di-xit Dóminus Dómino mé- o : * Séde a déxtris mé- is.

Even in the earliest form of chants, a cadence was created by emphasizing the final word of a phrase with the addition of one or two extra notes, as above. Later, more notes were added to the final words or syllables for elaboration and variation. For example:

1. Di-xit Dóminus Dómino mé- o : *Séde a *déxtris* mé- is.

or : mé- is.   or : mé- is.   or : mé- is.   or : mé- is.

or : mé- is.   or : mé- is.   or : mé- is.   or : mé- is.

The simplicity of syllabic chant should not be regarded as useful only for the monotonous chanting of psalm verses. Very simple yet hauntingly melodic Gregorian compositions still exist that do not use elaborate cadences while relying on simple syllabic notes. A fine example is the Gregorian melody for the Lord's Prayer, reproduced here in modern notation. No rests are indicated in the musical text; the singer should simply breathe on a skipped note (it is presumed that not all would skip the same note) so that the music flows without pause. Ordinarily, these chants would be sung *a capella* (without musical accompaniment).

Gregorian Chant

Our Fa-ther, who art in heav-en, hal-lowed be thy name; thy king-dom come; thy will be done on earth as it is in heav-en. Give us this day our dai-ly bread; and for-give us our tres-pass-es as we for-give those who tres-pass a-gainst us; and lead us not in-to temp-ta-tion, but de-liv-er us from e-vil.

Certain phrases, especially words of acclamation (like *Alleluia*) or the word at the end of a line, were elaborated beyond the few notes provided in syllabic chant. This extensive elaboration of a final syllable (or any syllable) by a chain of intricate notes was called a *melisma*. An example of melismatic chant may be noted in the elaboration of the final *ia* of the Easter *Alleluia* sung at the Easter Mass:

Lle-lú- ia. * *ij.*

V. Pás-cha nós-trum immo-lá-

tus est * Chrí- stus.

Liturgical Music and the Rise of Drama

The Liturgical Trope

One development connected with melismatic chant which evolved in the Carolingian period was the *trope*. Since books were scarce, monks memorized a great deal of liturgical chant. As an aid to memorization and, also, to provide some variety in the chant, words would be added to the long melismas. These words, tropes, would be verbal elaborations of the content of the text. Thus, for example, if there was a melismatic *Kyrie Eleison* (the Greek "Lord, have mercy on us" retained in the Latin Mass) with an elaboration of notes for the syllable *rie* of *Kyrie,* it became customary to add words such as *sanctus* (holy), *dominus* (lord), and the like, which were sung to the tune of the melisma. The use of tropes grew rapidly and became standard in liturgical music until they were removed from the liturgy at the time of the Counter-Reformation in the 16th century.

Scholars have pointed to the interpolation of tropes into liturgical music as the origin of drama in the Western world. There had been drama in the classical and Byzantine worlds, of course, but drama in Europe developed from the liturgy of the medieval church after it largely had been lost (or suppressed) in the very early Middle Ages.

A 9th-century manuscript (preserved at the monastery of Saint Gall) preserves an early trope that was added to the music of the Easter entrance hymn (the *Introit*) for Mass. It is in the form of a short dialogue and seems to have been sung by either two different singers or two choirs. It is called the *Quem Quæritis* trope from its opening lines:

THE *QUEM QUÆRITIS* TROPE

De Resurrectione Domini	Of the Lord's Resurrection
Int[errogatio]: *Quem quæritis in sepulchro, {o} Christicolæ?*	Question [of the angels]: *Whom seek ye in the sepulchre, O followers of Christ?*
R[esponsio]: *Jesum Nazarenum crucifixum, o cœlicolæ.*	Answer [of the Marys]: *Jesus of Nazareth, which was crucified, O celestial ones.*
[Angeli:] *Non est hic; surrexit, sicut prædixerat.*	[The angels:] *He is not here; he is risen, just as he foretold.*

Very shortly after the introduction of this trope into the Easter Mass the short interrogation began to be acted out, not at Mass but at the end of *Matins,* the night office of Easter. The dialogue was not greatly enlarged but the directions for its singing were elaborated into a short play. By the 11th and 12th centuries the dialogue was elaborated beyond the words of scripture and more personages were added. By the 12th century the stories became more elaborate.

It was but a step to remove these plays from the church proper and begin to perform them out-of-doors. By the 14th century there were sizable cycles of these plays performed at various times of the year, some of which told most of the major stories of the Bible from Adam to the Last Judgment. The repertory also began to expand to show lives of the saints and allegorical plays such as *Everyman* to illustrate the struggle of virtue and vice.

Everyman is a 15th-century play that may well be a translation from an earlier Dutch play. The subject is no longer a redoing of a biblical theme. Now we have rather personified abstractions representing a theme dear to the medieval heart: the struggle for the soul. The unprepared reader of *Everyman* will note the heavy-handed allegorizing and moralizing (complete with a "Doctor" who makes a final appearance to point up the moral of the play) with some sense of estrangement, but with a closer reading, students will also note the stark dignity of the play, the earnestness with which it is constructed, and the economy of its structure. Written in rather spare rhyming couplets, *Everyman* is a good example of the transitional play that forms a link between the earlier liturgical drama and the more secular drama that was to come at the end of the English medieval period.

The plot of *Everyman* is simplicity itself; it is quickly summarized by the messenger who opens the play. Everyman must face God in final judgment after death. None of the aids and friends of this life will support Everyman, as the speeches of the allegorical figures of Fellowship and others make clear. The strengths for Everyman come from the aiding virtues of Confession, Good Deeds, and Knowledge. The story, however, is not the central core of this play; the themes that run through the entire play are what should engage our attention. First is the common medieval notion of life itself as a pilgrimage, a notion that comes up again and again. It is embedded not only in the medieval penchant for pilgrimage but the use of that term (as one sees, for example, in Chaucer) as a metaphor. Second, the notion of the inevitability of death as the defining action of human life is omnipresent in medieval culture. *Everyman* has an extremely intense *memento mori* ("Keep death before your eyes!") motif. Finally, medieval theology puts great emphasis on the will of the human being in the attainment of salvation. It is not faith (this virtue is presumed) that will save Everyman; his or her willingness to learn (Knowledge), act (Good Deeds), and convert (Confession) will make the difference between salvation and damnation.

The Messenger says that *Everyman* is "By figure a moral play." It is meant not merely to instruct on the content of religion (as does a mystery play) but to instruct for the purposes of moral conversion. The earlier mystery plays usually point out a moral at the end of the performance. The morality uses its resources to moralize throughout the play.

The one lingering element from the liturgy one still sees in a play like *Everyman* is its pageant quality: the dramatic force of the presentation is enhanced by the solemn wearing of gowns, the stately pace of the speeches, and the seriousness of the message. The play depends less on props and place. Morality plays did not evolve directly out of liturgical drama (they may owe something to the study of earlier plays based on the classics studied in schools) but the liturgical overtones are not totally absent.

The Legend of Charlemagne: *Song of Roland*

Charlemagne's kingdom did not long survive intact after the death of the emperor. By the 10th century, the Frankish kingdom was fractured and Europe reduced to a state worthy of the name "Dark Ages." Anarchy, famine, ignorance, war, and factionalism were constants in 10th-century Europe; Charlemagne's era was looked back to as a long-vanished Golden Age. By the 12th century Charlemagne's reputation was such that he was canonized (in Aachen on December 29, 1165) by the Emperor Frederick Barbarossa. Charlemagne's cult was immensely popular throughout France—especially at the royal abbey of Saint Denis in Paris, which made many claims of earlier links with the legendary emperor.

A 15th-century oil painting in Aachen depicts an idealized Charlemagne as saint, wearing the crown of the Holy Roman Emperor and carrying a model of the church he had built at Aachen. Frederick Barbarossa commemorated the canonization by commis-

164 Reliquary of Charlemagne. Bust of Charlemagne after 1349, crown before 1349. Cathedral Treasury. Aachen.

sioning a great wrought-bronze candelabrum to hang in the Aachen cathedral. He also ordered a gold reliquary (now in the Louvre in Paris) to house the bones of one of his saintly predecessor's arms [164]; another reliquary in the form of a portrait bust that contains fragments of Charlemagne's skull is in the cathedral treasury at Aachen.

The memory of Charlemagne and his epoch was kept more vividly alive, however, in cycles of epic poems and in tales and memoirs developed, em-broidered, and disseminated by poets and singers throughout Europe from shortly after Charlemagne's time until the late Middle Ages. These are the famous *chansons de geste* (songs of deeds) or, as some were called, *chansons d'histoire* (songs of history): Of these songs, the oldest extant—as well as the best and most famous—is the *Song of Roland*.

The *Song of Roland* was written sometime late in the 11th century, but behind it lay some three hundred years of oral tradition and earlier poems celebrating a battle between Charlemagne's army and a Moslem force at the Spanish border. Charlemagne did indeed campaign against the emirate of Spain in 777 and 778, without conclusive result. In August 778 Charlemagne's rear guard was ambushed by the Basques while making its way through the Pyrenees after the invasion of Spain. The real extent of that battle (later placed, on not too much evidence, at the town of Roncesvalles) is unclear. Some experts maintain that it was a minor skirmish, remembered in the area in local legends later told and retold (and considerably embroidered in the process) by monks of the monasteries and sanctuaries on the pilgrimage routes to the great shrine of Saint James at Santiago de Compostela in Spain. Other historians insist that the battle was a horrendous bloodbath for the army of Charlemagne and that the tale was carried back to the Frankish cities; the legend was transformed as it was repeated by the descendants of the few survivors.

In any event, by the 11th century the tale was widely known in Europe. Excerpts from the *Song of Roland* were sung to inspire the Norman army before the Battle of Hastings in 1066, and in 1096 Pope Urban II cited it in an appeal to French patriotism when he attempted to raise armies for a crusade to free the Holy Land. Medieval translations of the poem into German, Norse, and Italo-French attest to its widespread popularity outside the French-speaking area.

The *Song of Roland* is an epic poem; its unknown writer or writers had little interest in historical accuracy or geographic niceties. Its subject matter is the glory of the military campaign, the chivalric nature of the true knight, the constant possibility of human deviousness, the clash of good and evil. The poem, although set in the 8th century, reflects the military values and chivalric code of the 11th century.

The story is simple: Moslems attack the retreating rear portion of Charlemagne's army (through an act of betrayal) while it is under the command of Roland, a favorite nephew of the emperor. Roland's army is defeated, but not before he sounds his ivory horn to alert the emperor to the peril. The emperor in turn raises a huge army from throughout Christendom while the Moslems also raise a great force. An epic battle follows; Charlemagne, with divine aid, is victorious.

The *Song of Roland* is some four thousand lines long; it is divided into stanzas, and each line contains ten syllables. It is impossible to reproduce the rhyme in English, since each stanza ends with an assonance, so the poem is best read in blank-verse translation—although that loses the recitative quality of the original.

This poem was meant to be heard, not read. It was recited by wandering minstrels—*jongleurs*—to largely illiterate audiences. This fact explains the verse style, the immediacy of the adjectives describing the characters and the situations, and the somewhat repetitive language. The still-unexplained AOI at the end of many stanzas may have something to do with the expected reaction of the *jongleur* as he uttered that particular sound to give emphasis to a stanza. (Some sense of the immediacy of the original may be gained by a reader today who declaims some of these stanzas with gesture and appropriate pauses.)

Certain details of the poem merit particular attention. A portion of the poem recounts Charlemagne's arrival on the scene and his victory over the Saracens who are beleaguering the forces commanded by Roland. Most striking is the mixture of military and religious ideals, not an uncommon motif in the medieval period. This mixture is reflected not only in the imagery and in the plot (Charlemagne's prayer keeps the sun from setting in order to allow time for victory, an echo of the biblical siege of Jericho by Joshua) but also in the bellicose Archbishop Turpin. Christian valor is contrasted with Saracen wickedness and treachery; the anti-Moslem bias of the poem is clear. The Moslem Saracens are pagans and idolaters—an odd way to describe the rigidly monotheistic followers of Islam. The *Song of Roland,* like much of the epic tradition from which it springs, is nevertheless devoted to the martial virtues of courage and strength, the comradeship of the battlefield, and the power of great men as well as the venality of evil ones.

The *Song of Roland* was immensely popular in its own time. It spawned a number of other compositions like the *Pseudo Turpin* and the *Song of Aspremont* in order to continue the story or elaborate portions of it. At a much later time in Italy the story was redone in the telling of the exploits of Orlando (Roland). To this day, children in Sicily visit the traditional puppet shows in which the exploits of brave Roland and his mates are acted out with great clatter and verve. Spectators at those shows witness stories that go back to the beginnings of the medieval period.

Questions for Further Discussion

1. It has often been said that monasticism was a form of counterculture in that it set forth an alternate form of life and community. Do you see similarities (and differences) between monastic communal life and some modern experiments in communal living and/or alternative life styles?

2. We have noted that drama in the early medieval period derived from the liturgy of the church. We also know that Greek tragedy had its roots in the worship of the fertility god Dionysus. Speculate on the reasons that drama should spring forth from corporate religious worship.

3. In the post-Vietnam period it is hard to think of a work of literature that would praise military and chivalrous values with the same enthusiasm as the *Song of Roland*. What kind of values and virtues have you noted as being singled out by contemporary writers or filmmakers when dealing with modern war?

4. What continuities and discontinuities do you see as you compare the aims and methods of Carolingian education with our own?

5. Speculate on the vastly different attitude the Carolingians showed toward books and ours to our own book culture today. List reasons that explain this difference.

	GENERAL EVENTS	LITERATURE & PHILOSOPHY	ART

768 ——

1000

987 Paris made center of
feudal kingdom of Hugh Capet

11th cent. Capetian kings consolidate
power and expand French kingdom

1096–1099 First Crusade; capture of
Jerusalem by Christians

12th cent. Golden Age of
University of Paris under
Saint Thomas Aquinas and
other scholastic masters

12th cent. *Notre Dame de Belle Verrière,*
stained glass window at Chartres

1113 Abelard begins teaching
in Paris; meets Heloise

1121 Abelard, *Sic et Non;*
birth of Scholasticism

1140 ——

1141 Saint Bernard of Clairvaux
leads condemnation of
Abelard at Council of Sens

c. 1150 Universities of
Paris and Bologna founded

c. 1163 Oxford University founded

after 1150 Recovery of
lost texts by Aristotle and
others via Arabic translations

c. 1145–1170 Tympanum of right door,
Royal Portal, Chartres

1180 Philip Augustus assumes
throne of France;
promotes Paris as capital

c. 1190 Maimonides,
Guide for the Perplexed

1194 ——

1202–1204 Fourth Crusade; crusaders
sack Constantinople on way to Holy Land

13th cent. Era of secular
poems; Goliardic verse

c. 1200 Charlemagne window at Chartres

c. 1209 Cambridge University founded

1215 Magna Carta, limiting powers of
king, signed in England

c. 1215 *Christ Blessing,* trumeau,
south porch, Chartres

c. 1220 Growth begins of mendicant friars:
Franciscans, Dominicans

c. 1215–c. 1250 Guild windows at
Chartres

1258 Robert de Sorbon founds Paris
hospice for scholars, forerunner of
Sorbonne

1270 Eighth Crusade; death of
Saint Louis of France

c. 1267–1273 Aquinas,
Summa Theologica

c. 1271–1293 Marco Polo travels
to China and India

1291 Fall of Acre, last Christian
stronghold in Holy Land

1300 Dante exiled
from Florence

c. 1303–1321 Dante,
Divine Comedy

1348–1367 Universities based on Paris
model founded in Prague, Vienna, Cracow, Pecs

c. 1385–1400 Chaucer,
The Canterbury Tales

1400 ——

Side labels: EARLY MIDDLE AGES · HIGH MIDDLE AGES · Romanesque Period · Early Gothic Period · Mature Gothic Period

The High Middle Ages: The Search for Synthesis

10th cent. Organum develops

11th cent. Guido of Arezzo invents musical notation used today

c. 1130 Halt of construction at Great Third Abbey Church of Cluny

12th cent. Notre Dame School of Paris is center of music study and composition

1140 Abbot Suger begins rebuilding Abbey Church of Saint Denis; Gothic style evolves: use of pointed arch, flying buttress, window tracery

12th–13th cent. French troubadours and trouvères flourish

c. 1163–1250 Cathedral of Notre Dame, Paris

1160 Léonin of Paris, *Magnus Liber Organi*

c. 1180 Philip Augustus commissions Louvre as royal residence and treasury

1181 Pérotin "the Great," director of Notre Dame School of Paris

1194 Chartres cathedral destroyed by fire; rebuilding begins 1195 (ends 1260)

13th cent. German minnesingers flourish

1220–1269 Cathedral of Amiens

c. 1250 Polyphonic motets are principal form of composition

c. 1235 Honnecourt, notebook

1243–1248 Sainte Chapelle, Paris

1247–1568 Cathedral of Beauvais; cathedral of Strasbourg

1399–1439 Spire of Strasbourg cathedral erected

The Significance of Paris

In Roman times Paris was a provincial outpost in the backwaters of the Roman Empire, mainly a crossroads for the Roman systems of transportation. With the decline of the empire, Paris fell into an obscurity saved from total oblivion in the early Middle Ages by the presence of churches and monasteries (every other social institution had gone into deep decline). Even in the age of Charlemagne, Rome or Aachen, not Paris, was the focal point of cultural and commercial interest. At the end of the brutal 10th century a feudal lord, Hugh Capet, began to consolidate his power into something like a monarchy and the fortunes of Paris began to improve. In 987 Hugh made Paris the center of his kingdom. The Capetian line of kings of the 11th century consolidated their power and added to their kingdom.

This political expansion naturally aided the growth and importance of Paris. By the 12th century, and certainly during the reign of Philip Augustus (who assumed the throne in 1180), the king was truly the king of France and Paris was a royal city, and in the subsequent century the kings of France would be the greatest monarchs of the time. Philip Augustus began building the Louvre, now a celebrated museum, as his royal residence and the place for the royal treasury. Additions by Charles V in the 14th century made the Louvre a totally self-sufficient royal city within a city.

From about 1150 to 1300 Paris could well claim to be the center of Western civilization. Beyond its position as a royal seat, it was a strong mercantile center. Its annual trade fair was famous. In addition, Paris gave birth to Gothic architecture, the philosophical and theological traditions known as scholasticism, and the educational community that in time became known as the university. These three creations have their own distinct history but they sprang from a common intellectual impulse: the desire to articulate all knowledge in a systematic manner.

The culture of the Middle Ages derives from the twin sources of all Western high culture: the humane learning inherited from the culture of Greece and Rome and the accepted faith of the West, which has its origin in the world view of the Judeo-Christian scriptures and religious world view.

The flowering of a distinct expression of culture in and around medieval Paris was made possible by a large number of factors. There was a renewed interest in learning, fueled largely by the discovery of hitherto lost texts from the classical world—especially the writings of Aristotle—which came to the West via the Moslem world. The often ill-fated crusades begun in the 11th century to recover the Holy Land and the increasing vogue for pilgrimages created a certain cosmopolitanism that, in turn, weakened the static feudal society. Religious reforms initiated by new religious orders like that of the Cistercians in the 12th century and the begging friars in the 13th breathed new life into the church.

Beyond these more generalized currents one can also point to individuals of genius who were crucial in the humanistic renaissance of the time. The University of Paris is inextricably linked with the name of Peter Abelard just as scholasticism is associated with the name of Thomas Aquinas. The Gothic style, unlike most art movements, can be pinpointed to a specific time at a particular place and with a single individual. Gothic architecture began near Paris at the Abbey of Saint Denis in the first half of the 12th century under the sponsorship of the head of the abbey, the Abbot Suger (1080–1151).

The Gothic Style

Suger's Building Program for Saint Denis

The Benedictine Abbey of Saint Denis over which Abbot Suger presided from 1122 until his death nearly 29 years later was the focal point for French patriotism. The abbey church—built in the Carolingian times—housed the relics of Saint Denis, a 5th-century martyr who had evangelized the area of Paris before his martyrdom. The crypts of the church served as burial places for Frankish kings and nobles from before the reign of Charlemagne, although it lacked the tomb of Charlemagne himself. One concrete link between the Abbey of Saint Denis and Charlemagne came through a series of literary works. The fictitious *Pèlerinage de Charlemagne* claimed that the relics of the Passion housed at the abbey had been brought there by Charlemagne himself when he returned from a pilgrimage-crusade to the Holy Land. Another work, the *Pseudo-Turpin,* has Charlemagne returning to the Abbey of Saint Denis after his Spanish campaign and proclaiming all France to be under the protection and tutelage of the saint. These two legends were widely believed in the Middle Ages; there is fair evidence that Suger himself accepted their authenticity. The main themes of the legends—pilgrimage, crusades, and the mythical presence of Charlemagne—created a story about the abbey that made it a major Christian shrine as well as one worthy of the royal city of Paris.

Pilgrims and visitors came to Paris to visit Saint Denis either because of the fame of the abbey's relics or because of the annual *Lendit,* the trade fair held near the precincts of the abbey. Accordingly, in 1124 Suger decided to build a new church to accommodate those who flocked to the popular pilgrimage center. This rebuilding program took the better part of fifteen years and never saw completion. Suger mentions as models two sacred buildings that by his time already had archetypal significance for Christianity. He wanted his church to be as lavish and brilliant as Hagia Sophia in Constantinople, which he knew only by reputation, and as loyal to the will of God as the Temple of Solomon as it was described in the Bible.

The first phase of Suger's project was basically a demolition and repair job; he had to tear down the more deteriorated parts of the old church and replace them. He reconstructed the western facade of the church and added two towers. In order better to handle the pilgrimage crowds and the increasingly elaborate processions called for in the medieval liturgy, the entrance was given three portals. The *narthex,* the

part of the church one enters first, before the nave, was rebuilt and the old nave was to be extended by about 40 feet (12.2 meters). About 1140 Suger abruptly stopped work on the narthex to commence work at the opposite end, the *choir,* the area of the church where the monks sang the Office. By his own reckoning, he spent three years and three months at this new construction. The finished choir made a revolutionary change in architecture in the West.

Suger's choir was surrounded by a double *ambulatory,* an aisle around the apse and behind the high altar. The outer ambulatory had nine radiating chapels to accommodate the increasing number of monks who were priests and thus said Mass on a daily basis. Two tall windows pierced the walls of each chapel so that there was little external masonry wall in relation to the amount of space covered by windows. The chapels were shallow enough to permit the light from the windows to fall on the inner ambulatory [165].

165 Plan of the abbey church of Saint Denis, built about 1140, and photograph of the ambulatory. The Abbot Suger was responsible for those parts of the existing church shaded black in the plan; the piers around the high altar were rebuilt after Suger's time. Note how use of the ribbed vault and the pointed arch in the ambulatory gave scope for the play of light from the lancet windows. Spans of differing widths could be brought easily to the same height.

1 choir	3 chapel
2 ambulatory	4 narthex

Although Suger's nave was never completed there is some evidence that it would have had characteristics similar to that of the choir: crossed rib vaults with an abundance of stained-glass windows to permit the flooding of light into the church. We can get some idea of what that nave might have looked like by looking at churches directly inspired by Saint Denis: the cathedrals of Senlis and Noyons [166] (their bishops were both at the consecration of Saint Denis in 1144), begun respectively in 1153 and 1157, as well as the cathedral of Notre Dame in Paris, the first stone of which was laid in 1163. This quick emulation of the style of Saint Denis blossomed by the end of the century into a veritable explosion of cathedral-building in the cities and towns radiating out from Paris, the so-called Île-de-France. The Gothic impulse so touched other countries as well that by the end of the 13th century there were fine examples of Gothic architecture in England, Germany, and Italy.

The term *Gothic* merits a word of explanation. It was used first in the 17th century as a pejorative term meaning "barbarous" or "rude" to distinguish buildings that did not follow the classical models of Greece and Rome, a use still current in the mid-18th century. It was only as a result of the reappraisal of the medieval period in the last century that the word lost its negative meaning.

It is tempting to say that the common characteristic of these cathedrals was the desire for verticality. We tend to identify the Gothic style with the pointed arch, pinnacles and columns, and increasingly higher walls buttressed from the outside by flying arches to accommodate the weight of a pitched roof and the sheer size of the ascending walls [167]. It is a truism

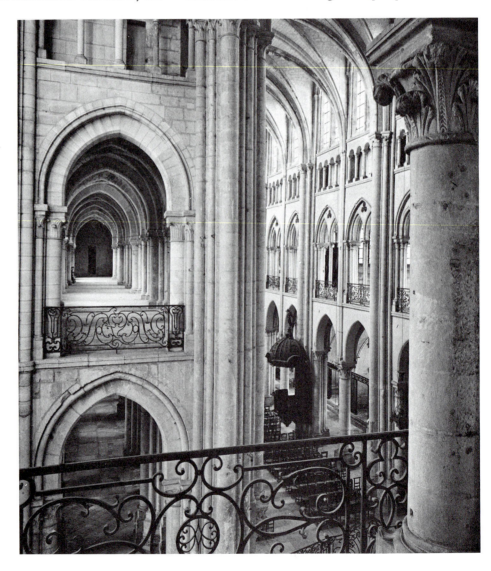

166 Interior of Noyons Cathedral. The nave was finished between 1285 and 1330. This is a fine example of the older style of Gothic architecture. The walls have four stories instead of the later three: the nave arcade at floor level, the tribune gallery, a triforium, and the clerestory with its windows. The somewhat thick arches of the triforium galleries give way in later Gothic churches to a much more pointed appearance.

1 nave arcade 3 clerestory 5 buttress 7 pitched roof 9 pointed arch
2 triforium 4 vault 6 flying buttress 8 pinnacle 10 gargoyle

167 Transverse half sectional drawing of a typical Gothic church (cathedral of Notre Dame, Paris). The height is about 140' (42.7 m). Note the tiny figure of a person for scale.

that the medieval builders seem to engage in contests to build higher and higher almost as a matter of civic pride: Chartres (begun in 1194) reached a height of 122 feet (37.2 meters); almost as a response the builders of Amiens (begun 1220) stretched that height to 140 feet (42.7 meters), while Beauvais (begun 1247) pushed verticality almost to the limit with a height of 157 feet (47.9 meters) from the cathedral pavement to the roof arch; indeed, Beauvais had a serious collapse of the roof when the building was barely completed.

That verticality typified Gothic architecture is indisputable, yet Romanesque architects only a generation before Suger had attempted the same verticality, as is evident in such churches as the proposed third abbey church of Cluny or the pilgrimage church at Santiago de Compostela in Spain. What prevented the Romanesque architect from attaining greater verticality was not lack of desire but insufficient technical means. The pointed arch was known in Romanesque architecture but not fully understood. It distributed weight more thoroughly in a downward direction and lessened the need for the massive interior piers of the typical Romanesque church. The size of the piers was further reduced by using buttresses outside the building to prop the interior piers and absorb some of the downward thrust. Furthermore,

the downward thrust of the exterior buttresses themselves could be increased by the addition of heavy decorative devices such as spires.

The net result of these technical innovations was to lessen the thickness, weight, and mass of the walls of the Gothic cathedral. This reduction provided an opportunity for greater height with less bulk to absorb the weight of the vaulted roof. Such a reduction made the walls more available as framing devices for the windows that are so characteristic of the period. It has been said, perhaps with some exaggeration, that walls in Gothic cathedrals were replaced by masonry scaffolding for windows [168]. In any case, the basic characteristic of Gothic architecture is not verticality but luminosity. The Gothic may be described as transparent—diaphanous—architecture.

The Mysticism of Light

Abbot Suger wrote two short booklets about his stewardship of the abbey and his ideas about the building and decorating program he initiated for the abbey church—extremely important sources for our understanding of the thought that stood behind the actual work of the builder and artist. Underlying Suger's description of the abbey's art treasures and architectural improvements was a theory or (perhaps, better) a theology of beauty. Suger was heavily indebted to his reading of certain mystical treatises written by Dionysius the Areopagite (whom Suger and many of his contemporaries assumed was the Saint Denis for whom the abbey was named), a 5th-century Syrian monk whose works on mystical theology were strongly influenced by neo-Platonic philosophers as well as by Christian doctrine. In the doctrine of the Pseudo-Dionysius (as later generations have called him), every created thing partakes, however imperfectly, of the essence of God. There is an ascending hierarchy of existence that ranges from inert mineral matter to the purity of light, which is God. The Pseudo-Dionysius described all of creation under the category of light: every created thing is a small light that illumines the mind a bit. Ultimately, as light becomes more pure (as one ascends the hierarchy) one gets closer to pure light, which is God.

The high point of this light mysticism is expressed in the stained-glass window. Suger himself believed that when he finished his nave with its glass windows (never completed in fact) to complement his already finished choir he would have a total structure that would make a single statement: "Bright is that which is brightly coupled with the bright, and bright is the noble edifice which is pervaded by the new light [*lux nova*]." The *lux nova* is an allusion to the biblical description of God as the God of light. Suger did not invent stained glass but he fully exploited its possibilities both by encouraging an architecture that could put it to its most advantageous employment and at the same time providing a theory to justify and enhance its use.

No discussion of light and glass in this period can overlook the famous windows of the cathedral of Chartres, a small but important commercial town just south of Paris. When the cathedral was rebuilt after a disastrous fire in 1194 (which destroyed everything except the west facade of the church), the new building gave wide scope to the glazier's art.

When the walls were rebuilt more than 173 windows were installed covering an area of about 2000 square yards (1672 square meters) of surface. It is important to note that, except for some fine details like facial contours, the glass is not painted. The glaziers produced the colors (the blues and reds of Chartres are famous and the tones were never again reproduced exactly) by adding metallic salts to molten glass. Individual pieces were fitted together like a jigsaw puzzle and fixed by leading the pieces together. Individual pieces were rarely larger than 8 feet (2.4 meters) square, but 30-foot (9.2 meter) sections could be bonded together safely in the leading process. The sections were set into stone frames (mullions) and reinforced in place by the use of iron retaining rods. Windows as large as 60 feet (18.3 meters) high could be created in this fashion.

It would be useful at this point to compare the aesthetics of the stained-glass window to the mosaics discussed in Chapter 6. There was a strong element

168 Interior of the upper chapel of La Sainte Chapelle, Paris. 1243–1248. Built to house major relics of Christ's Passion, this is a perfect example of Gothic luminosity. It has been restored heavily, but the overall effect is not unlike that of the original. Sainte Chapelle uniquely illustrates the skeletal nature of Gothic buildings.

169 Scenes from the life of the Virgin Mary, tympanum of the right door of the royal portal, west facade, Chartres Cathedral. Done between 1145 and 1170, the central panel shows the Virgin and Child as an almost mirror image of the Belle Verriere (see Plate 12). The arch over the Virgin has adoring angels, while the outer arch (archivolt) has symbolic representations of the Seven Liberal Arts with their ancient masters. At the lower left, for example, is Aristotle dipping his pen in ink with the female figure of Dialectic above him. Under the figure of the Virgin are panels showing scenes of the early life of Christ, beginning in the lower left corner with the Annunciation followed by the Visitation, and so on.

of light mysticism in the art of Byzantine mosaic decoration, derived from some of the same sources later utilized by Abbot Suger: neo-Platonism and the allegorical reading of the Bible. The actual perception of light in the two art forms, however, was radically different. The mosaic refracted light off an opaque surface. The "sacred" aura of the light in a Byzantine church comes from the oddly mysterious breaking up of light as it strikes the irregular surface of the mosaic tesserae. The stained-glass window was the medium through which the light was seen directly, even if it was subtly muted into diverse colors and combinations of colors.

You can only "read" the meaning of the window by looking at it from the inside with an exterior light source—the sun—illuminating it. It was a more perfectly Platonic analogy of God's relationship to the world and its creatures. The viewer sees an object (the illustrated window) but "through it" is conscious of a distant unseen source (the sun—God) that illumines it and gives it its intelligibility. (*Read* is not a rhetorical verb in this context. It was a commonplace of the period to refer to the stained-glass windows as the "Bible of the Poor" since the illiterate could "read" the biblical stories in their illustrated form in the cathedral.)

A close examination of one window at Chartres will illustrate the complexity of this idea. The *Notre Dame de Belle Verrière* (Our Lady of the Beautiful Window) [Plate 12, page 140], one of the most famous works in the cathedral, is a 12th-century work saved from the rubble of the fire of 1194 and reinstalled in the south choir. The window, with its characteristic pointed arch frame, depicts the Virgin enthroned with the Christ Child surrounded by worshiping angels bearing candles and censers. Directly above her is the dove that represents the Holy Spirit and at the very top a stylized church building representing the cathedral built in her honor.

To the simple viewer the window honored the Virgin, to whom one prayed in time of need and to whom the church was dedicated. The person of some theological sophistication would further recognize the particular scene of the Virgin enthroned as the symbol of Mary as the Seat of Wisdom, a very ancient motif in religious art. The window also has a conceptual link with the exterior sculptural program. In the tympanum of the portal is an enthroned Madonna and Christ Child with two censer-bearing angels. This scene is surrounded by sculptured arches, called *archivolts,* in which there is a symbolic representation of the Seven Liberal Arts [169], which

170 Grotesques and a gargoyle waterspout on a tower terrace of the cathedral of Notre Dame, Paris.

apt and deepened metaphor to be seen in the *Belle Verrière* of Chartres.

That kind of interpretation can be applied profitably to many aspects of Gothic art and architecture. Builders and theologians worked closely while a cathedral was under construction. The church authorities felt it a primary duty not only to build a place suitable for divine worship but also to utilize every opportunity to teach and edify the participating worshiper. The famous Gothic gargoyles [170] are a good example of this blend of functionality and didacticism. These carved beasts served the practical purpose of funneling rainwater off the roofs while, in their extended and jutting positions on the roofs and buttresses, signifying that evil flees the sacred precincts of the church. At a far more ambitious level, the whole decorative scheme of a cathedral was an attempt to tell an integrated story about the history of salvation, a story alluded to in both profane and divine learning. The modern visitor may be overwhelmed by what appears a chaotic jumble of sculptures depicting biblical scenes, allegorical figures, symbols of the labors of the month, signs of the Zodiac, representatives of pagan learning, and panoramic views of Last Judgments; for the medieval viewer the variegated scenes represented a patterned whole. The decoration of the cathedral was, as it were, the common vocabulary of sermons, folk wisdom, and school learning fleshed out in stone.

The Many Meanings of the Gothic Cathedral

Some theological and philosophical background is crucial for an appreciation of the significance of the Gothic cathedral, but it is a serious oversimplification to view the cathedral only in the light of its intellectual milieu. The cathedral was, after all, the preeminent building in the episcopal towns of the Île-de-France, as a view of any of the towns shows. The cathedral overwhelms the town either by crowning a hilly site, as at Laon, or rising up above the town plain, as at Amiens. The cathedrals were *town* buildings (Saint Denis, a monastic church, is a conspicuous exception) and one might well inquire into their functional place in the life of the town. It is simplistic to think that their presence in the town reflected a credulous faith on the part of the populace or the egomania of the civil and religious builders. In fact, the cathedral served vital social and economic functions in medieval society.

A modern analogy illustrates the social function of architecture and building. Many small towns in America, especially those in rural areas of the South and the Northeast, center their civic and commercial

together constitute a shorthand version of the window.

The Blessed Virgin depicted as the Seat of Wisdom would be an especially attractive motif for the town of Chartres. The cathedral school was a flourishing center of literary and philosophical studies, studies which emphasized that human learning became wisdom only when it led to the source of wisdom, God. The fact that Mary was depicted here in glass would also call to mind an oft-repeated *exemplum* (moral example) used in medieval preaching and theology: Christ was born of a virgin. He passed through her body as light passes through a window, completely intact without changing the glass. The Christ/light—Mary/glass analogy is an life around a town square. The courthouse symbolically emanates social control (justice), social structures (births, weddings, and deaths are registered there), power (the sheriff, commissioners or aldermen, and the mayor are housed there), and—to a degree—culture, with its adjacent park and military or civic monuments to the founders and war dead. The better stores, the "uptown" churches, and the other appurtenances of respectability—banks, lawyers' and physicians' offices—cluster about the square. (The urbanization and suburbanization of American has steadily destroyed this basic symmetry, replacing it with a far more diffuse city or suburban pattern where the concept of "center" is less easy to identify.) The cathedral square of the typical European or Latin American town is the ancestor of the courthouse square. The difference is that the medieval cathedral exercised a degree of social control and integration more comprehensive than that of the courthouse.

The cathedral and its power were a serious force that shaped both individual and social life in the town. The individual was baptized in, made a communicant of, married in, and buried from, the cathedral. Schooling was obtained from the cathedral school and social services (hospitals, poor relief, orphanages, and so on) directed by the decisions of the cathedral staff (the *chapter*). The daily and yearly round of life was regulated by the horarium of the cathedral. People rose and ate and went to bed in rhythm with the tolling of the cathedral bell just as they worked or played in line with the feast days of the liturgical calendar of the church year. Citizens could sue and be sued in the church courts, and those same courts dispensed justice on a par with the civil courts; the scenes of the Last Judgment over the central portals of medieval cathedrals referred to more than divine justice.

Far more significant than the social interaction of town and cathedral was the economic impact of the cathedral on the town. The building of a cathedral was an extremely expensive enterprise. When the people of Chartres decided to rebuild their cathedral in 1194 the bishop pledged all of the diocesan revenues for three years (three to five million dollars!) simply to initiate the project [171]. It should be re-

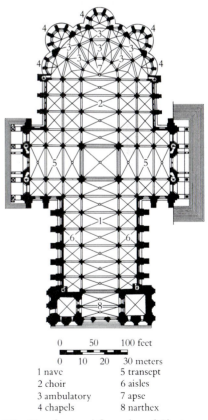

0   50   100 feet

0   10   20   30 meters

1 nave   5 transept
2 choir   6 aisles
3 ambulatory   7 apse
4 chapels   8 narthex

171 West front and floor plan of Chartres Cathedral. 1194–1240. Chartres is almost an archetype in plan of the Gothic cathedral.

THE GOTHIC STYLE **187**

membered that a town like Chartres was very small in the late 12th century, with no more than ten to fifteen thousand residents in the town itself. Some economic historians have attempted to show that the combination of civic pride and religious enthusiasm that motivated the town to build a cathedral was economically ruinous in the long run. The majority of scholars, however, insist that it was precisely economic gain that was the significant factor in construction. This was surely the case with Chartres.

From the late 9th century Chartres had been a major pilgrimage site. The cathedral possessed a relic of the Virgin (the tunic she wore when Jesus was born) given by Charles the Bald, the great-grandson of Charlemagne, in 876. Relics were very popular throughout the Middle Ages and this particular one was specially important to the pilgrims of the time. The relic had not been destroyed by the fire of 1194, a sure sign in the eyes of the populace that the Virgin wished the church rebuilt. Furthermore, the four great feasts of the Blessed Virgin in the liturgical year (the Purification of Mary on February 2, the Annunciation on March 25, the Assumption on August 15, and the Nativity of the Virgin on September 8) were celebrated in Chartres in conjunction with large trade fairs that drew merchants and customers from all over Europe.

These fairs were held in the shadow of the cathedral and their conduct was protected by legislation issued by the cathedral chapter. Regulations from the chapter, for example, stated that the prized textiles of the area were to be sold near the north portal while the purveyors of fuel, vegetables, fruit, and wine were to be located by the south portal. There were also sellers of images, medals, and other religious objects (forerunners of the modern souvenir) to the pilgrims who came both for the fair and for reasons of devotion. The church, then, was as much a magnet for outsiders as it was a symbol for the townspeople.

The patrons who donated the windows of Chartres Cathedral also give some indication of the economics of the place. It was only natural that some of the large windows—like a rose window—would be the gift of a royal family or that a tall, pointed *lancet* window like those in the choir would be given by the nobility or the higher clergy. A large number of the windows, however, were donated by the members of the various craft and commercial guilds in the town; their "signature frames" can be found at the bottoms of the windows. The fact that the five large windows in honor of the Virgin in the *chevet,* the east end of the cathedral, were donated by merchants—principally the bakers, butchers, and vintners—indicates the significant power of the guilds [172].

The guild, a fraternal society of craftsmen or merchants, was a cross between a modern-day union and a fraternal organization like the Elks or the Knights of Columbus. Members of the guilds put themselves under the patronage of a saint, promised to perform certain charitable works, and acted as a mutual-aid society. Many of the economic guilds appear to have developed out of earlier, more purely religious confraternities. One had to belong to a guild to work at any level beyond day labor. The guild accepted and instructed apprentices; certified master craftsmen; regulated prices, wages, working conditions; and maintained funds for the care of older members and the burial of their dead. The guilds were a crucial part of town life and would remain so well into the modern period. And, as we shall see, the university developed from the guild idea in the 12th century.

The motivation for the building of a medieval cathedral, then, came from theological vision, religious devotion, civic pride, and socioeconomic interest. The actual construction depended on a large number of people. The cathedral chapter decided to construct a building, raised the money, and hired the master-builder-architect. He in turn was responsible for hiring the various master craftsmen, designing the building, and creating the decorative scheme from ideas generated and approved by the theologians or church officials of the chapter. A great workshop was set up near the proposed site, with each master (mason, stonecutter, glazier) hiring his crew, obtaining his material, and setting up work quarters. Manual and occasional labor was recruited from the local population, but the construction crews were usually migratory groups who traveled from job to job.

172 Vintners, detail of stained-glass window, Chartres Cathedral. c. 1215. This panel, in a larger window donated by the vintners' guild, shows a carter taking casks to market.

The names of a number of master builders, including the builder of Chartres, have been lost, but others have survived in funerary inscriptions, commemorative plaques, and building records. Notes intended for students of buildings written by Villard de Honnecourt (about 1235), an architect from northern France, preserved in a unique copy at the Bibliothèque Nationale in Paris, provide us a rare glimpse into the skills of a medieval cathedral builder. Villard says in his book that he could teach a willing apprentice a wide range of skills ranging from carpentry and masonry to the more demanding skills of practical geometry [173] and plan drafting. The notebook also has random sketches and ideas jotted down for his own personal use; they include religious figures to serve as models for stonecarvers; animals and buildings that caught his eye; a perpetual-motion machine (which didn't work); the first example of clockworks in the West; and a self-operating saw for cutting huge timbers for buttressing and roofing, among others. He visited Rheims and made sketches of the cathedral. He tells of traveling as far as Hungary to get work. While not as complete and wide-ranging as the Renaissance notebooks of Leonardo da Vinci (with which they have often been compared), Villard's notebook reveals a highly skilled, persistently inquisitive, and very inventive man.

A look through Villard's notebook forcefully reminds us that because our tendency is to emphasize the religious and social significance of a cathedral (as that is what first strikes us about it), we easily overlook the basic fact that a cathedral is a stunning technological achievement. A prime example of the technological virtuosity of such buildings is the elegant spire of Strasbourg Cathedral. Finished in 1439, the spire is 466 feet (142.1 meters) high from pavement to tip—as high as a forty-story building. This stone structure remained the tallest in Europe until the mid-1960s, when the London Post Office Tower was completed.

Gothic cathedrals were possible only because a very precise knowledge of mathematics, geometry, architectural technology, and other practical sciences was increasingly available and refined for specific ends—a development that brought with it certain inevitable "spinoffs" in the areas of scientific knowledge. Just as, in our age, the space shots "spun off" advances in metallurgy, medicine, and so on, the building of so many cathedrals in a short time brought new solutions and new materials.

The Gothic cathedral is an almost perfect artifact for the study of the humanistic enterprise since it may be approached from so many angles and at so many levels. It was first an architectural and technological achievement. Its ensemble of walls, windows, sculpture, and decoration demonstrated a peculiar way of combining human knowledge and religious faith that provides a basic aesthetic experience to the viewer. It had a fundamental economic and social significance for the community in which it was located. Finally, it was, for those who entered it in faith, a transcenden-

173 Villard de Honnecourt. Page on "practical geometry," from his *Album. c.* 1275. Pen and ink. Bibliothèque Nationale, Paris. *Top row:* Measuring the diameter of a partly visible column; finding the middle of a circle; cutting the mold of an arch; arching a vault with an outer covering; making an apse with twelve windows; cutting the springing stone of an arch. *Second row:* Bringing together two stones; cutting a voussoir for a round building; cutting an oblique voussoir. *Third row:* Bridging a stream with timbers; laying out a cloister; measuring the width of a river without crossing it; measuring the width of a distant window. *Fourth row:* Placing the cornerstones of a cloister without plumb line or level; dividing a stone into square halves; shaping the screw of a press; making two vessels of different capacities. *Bottom row:* Cutting a regular voussoir.

174 Christ in the act of blessing, figure from trumeau of main portal, Chartres Cathedral. c. 1215. This statue symbolically blesses every pilgrim who enters the doors of the church (the "gates of heaven").

visit a real monument and, at the same time, hoped to find rest and salvation through the act [174]. It is no wonder Abbot Suger should have called Saint Denis the "Gate of Heaven": that is exactly what it was meant to be.

Music: The School of Notre Dame

It should not be surprising that in an age of artistic and architectural development such as the Gothic the rather austere music of the early church should also undergo development and change. From the time Charlemagne introduced Gregorian chant into the church life of the Frankish kingdom there had been further developments of that musical form. In the 11th century, Guido of Arezzo had worked out a system of musical notation that provided the basis for the development of the musical notation used today. Church musicians from the 10th century on also experimented with a single melodic line of plainchant by adding parallel voices at different musical intervals above the line of chant. This first step toward *polyphony,* a musical term for "many voices," is called *organum.* Outside the church, the knightly classes also composed and performed secular music. Some of the melodies of the *troubadours* and *trouvères* have survived, giving us an idea of secular music in the 12th and 13th centuries. The German *minnesingers* (*minne* means "love") of the 13th century utilized traditional church modes and melodies to create both secular and sacred songs.

The school of Notre Dame in Paris was the center of systematic musical study and composition in the 12th century. Léonin's *Magnus Liber Organi* (about 1160) is an important source for our knowledge of music in the period of the Gothic cathedral. Léonin's book was a collection of organum compositions for use during the liturgical services throughout the church year. Léonin's work was carried on by the other great composer of the century, Pérotin, who assumed the directorship of the music school of Notre Dame sometime around 1181.

In Pérotin's music, the Notre Dame organum utilized the basic melodic line of the traditional chant (the *cantus firmus*) while a second melodic line (the *duplum*), a third (*triplum*), and in some cases a fourth (*quadruplum*) voice was added above the melody. These added lines mirrored the rhythmic flow of the cantus firmus. It was soon learned, however, that pleasing and intricate compositions could be created by having the duplum and triplum move in opposition to the cantus firmus. This *counterpoint* (from *contrapunctum,* against the note) meant, at its most basic

tal religious experience of passing from the profane to the sacred world. Henry Adams, in his wonderfully eccentric book *Mont-Saint-Michel and Chartres,* says that only a person coming to Chartres as a pilgrim could understand the building. The pilgrim is a central metaphor for the period whether one speaks of the actual pilgrim on the road to Santiago de Compostela or Canterbury or life itself as a pilgrimage toward God. Pilgrims to Chartres or the other cathedrals were pilgrims in both senses: they traveled to level, that a descending series of notes in the cantus firmus would have an ascending series of notes in the melodic lines above it.

One development in the Gothic period deriving from the polyphony of organum was the *motet*. The motet usually had three voices (in some cases, four). The tenor—from the Latin *tenere* (to hold), another term for cantus firmus—maintained the traditional line, usually derived from an older ecclesiastical chant. Since some of the manuscripts from the period show no words for this tenor position, it has been thought that for many motets the tenor line was the musical accompaniment (perhaps the organ, then an instrument of increasing popularity). Above the tenor were two voices who sang interweaving melodies. In the early 13th century, these melodies were invariably in Latin and were exclusively religious in content. In the late 13th century it was not uncommon to sing the duplum in Latin and the triplum in French. Indeed, the two upper voices could be singing quite distinct songs: a hymn in Latin with a love lyric in French with a tenor voice (or instrument) maintaining an elaborated melody based on the melismas of Gregorian chant.

This increasingly sophisticated music, built on a monastic basis but with a new freedom of its own, is indicative of many of the intellectual currents of the period. It is a technically complex music rooted in the distant past but open to new and somewhat daring innovation, a blend of the traditional and the vernacular—all held together in an intellectually complicated balance of competing elements. Gothic music was an aural expression of the dynamism inherent in the medieval Gothic cathedral.

Scholasticism

The Rise of the Universities

A number of our contemporary institutions have roots in the Middle Ages. Trial by jury is one, constitutional monarchy another. By far the best-known and most widely diffused cultural institution that dates from the Middle Ages, however, is the university. In fact, some of the most prestigious centers of European learning today stand where they were founded eight hundred years ago: Oxford and Cambridge in England; the University of Paris in France; the University of Bologna in Italy. There is also a remarkable continuity between the organization and purposes of the medieval university and our own, except that we have coeducation. The medieval student would be puzzled, to be sure, by the idea of football games, coeducation, degrees in business or

agriculture, and well-manicured campuses, were he to visit a modern American university. He would find himself at home with the idea of a liberal arts curriculum, the degrees from the baccalaureate through the master's to the doctorate, and the high cost of textbooks. At a less serious level, he would be well acquainted with drinking parties, fraternities, and friction between town and gown (the phrase itself has a medieval ring). The literature that has come down to us from the period is full of complaints about poor housing, high rents, terrible food, and lack of jobs after graduation. Letters from the Middle Ages between students and parents have an almost uncanny contemporaneity about them.

European universities developed in the late 12th and early 13th centuries along with the emergence of city life. In the earlier medieval period schools were most often associated with the monasteries, which were perforce situated in rural areas. As cities grew in importance, schools also developed at urban monasteries or, increasingly, under the aegis of bishops whose cathedrals were in the towns. The episcopal or cathedral school was a direct offshoot of the increasing importance of towns and the increasing power of bishops, the spiritual leaders of town life. In Italy, where town life had been relatively strong throughout the early Middle Ages and where feudalism never took hold, there was also a tradition of schools controlled by the laity. The center of medical studies in Salerno and the law faculty of Bologna had been in secular hands since the 10th century.

A number of factors help to explain the rapid rise of formal education institutions in the 12th century. First, the increasing complexity of urban life created a demand for an educated class who could join the ranks of administrators and bureaucrats. Urban schools were not simply interested in providing basic literacy. They were designed to produce an educated class who could give support to the socioeconomic structures of society. Those who completed the arts curriculum of a 12th-century cathedral school (like the one at Chartres) could find ready employment in either the civil or the ecclesiastical bureaucracy as lawyers, clerks, or administrators.

There were also intellectual and cultural reasons for the rise of the universities. In the period from 1150 to 1250 came a wholesale discovery and publication of texts from the ancient world. Principal among these were lost books by Aristotle that came to the West through Moslem sources in Spain. Aristotle's writings covered a vast range of subjects ranging from meteorology and physics to logic and philosophy. Furthermore, with a closer relationship between Christian and Arabic scholars, a large amount of scientific and mathematical material was coming into

Europe [175]. There was also a renaissance of legal studies centered primarily at Bologna, the one intellectual center that could nearly rival Paris. Finally, there was a new tool being refined by such scholars as Peter Abelard and Peter Lombard: dialectics. Theologians and philosophers began to apply the principles of logic to the study of philosophy and theology. Abelard's book *Sic et Non* (1121) put together conflicting opinions concerning theological matters with contradictory passages from the Bible and the Church Fathers and then attempted to mediate and reconcile the apparent divergences. This method was later refined and stylized into the method which was to become *scholasticism,* so called because it was the philosophical method of the schools, the communities of scholars at the nascent universities.

The most famous and representative university to emerge in the Middle Ages was the University of Paris. The eminence of Paris rested mainly on the fame of the teachers who came there to teach. At this state of educational development, the teacher really was the school. Students in the 12th century flocked from all over Europe to frequent the lectures of teachers like William the Champeaux (1070–1121) and, later, his formal student and vehement critic, Peter Abelard (1079–1142). Besides these famous individual teachers Paris also had some established centers of learning that enjoyed a vast reputation. There was a cathedral school attached to the cathedral of Notre Dame, a theological center associated with the canons of the church of Saint Victor, and a school

175 A university lecture, detail from compendium of Aristotle's *Nichomachean Ethics*. German, 14th century. Manuscript illumination. State Museums, West Berlin. Note the professor in his chair (*cathedra*) expounding a text. Even today, in certain English universities the lower ranks of professors are called readers.

of arts maintained at the ancient monastery of Sainte Geneviève.

Although it is difficult to assign precise dates, it is safe to say that the university at Paris developed in the final quarter of the 12th and early part of the 13th centuries. Its development began with the masters (*magistri,* teachers) of the city forming a corporation after the manner of the guilds. At this time the word *universitas* simply meant a guild or corporation. The masters formed the *universitas* in Paris in order to exercise some "quality control" over the teaching profession and the students entrusted to their care. At Bologna the reverse was true. The students formed the *universitas* in order to hire the teachers with the best qualifications and according to the most advantageous financial terms.

The *universitas* soon acquired a certain status in law with a corporate right to borrow money, to sue (and be sued), and to issue official documents. As a legal body it could issue stipulations for the conduct of both masters and students. When a student finished the course of studies and passed his examinations the *universitas* would grant him a teaching certificate that enabled him to enter the ranks of the masters: he was a master of arts (our modern degree has its origin in that designation). After graduation a student could go on to specialized training in law, theology, or medicine. The completion of this specialized training entitled one to be called *doctor* (from the Latin *doctus* [learned]) in his particular field. The modern notion that a professional person (doctor, lawyer, and the like) should be university-trained is an idea derived directly from the usages of the medieval university.

Since the Carolingian period—indeed, earlier—the core of education was the arts curriculum. In the last 12th century in Paris the arts began to be looked on as a prelude to the study of theology. This inevitably caused a degree of tension between the arts faculty and the theology masters. This tension resulted in 1210 in a split, with the masters and students of arts moving their faculty to the Left Bank of the Seine, where they settled in the area intersected by the rue du Fouarre (Straw Street—so named because the students sat on straw during lectures). That part of the Left Bank has traditionally been a student haunt. The Latin Quarter name reminds us of the old language that was once the only tongue used at the university.

By the end of the 12th century Paris was the intellectual center of Europe. Students came from all over Europe to study there. We do not have reliable statistics about their number, but an estimate of five to eight thousand students would not be far from the mark for the early 13th century. The students were organized into *nationes* by their place of national origin. By 1294 there were four recognized *nationes* in Paris: the French, the Picard, the Norman, and the Anglo-German. Student support came from families, pious benefactors, church stipends, or civic grants to underwrite an education. Certain generous patrons provided funds for hospices for scholars, the most famous of which was that underwritten by Robert de Sorbon in 1258 for graduate students in theology; his hospice was the forerunner of the Sorbonne in Paris.

By our standards student life in the 13th century was harsh. Food and lodging were primitive, heating scarce, artificial lighting nonexistent, and income sporadic. The daily schedule was rigorous, made more so by the shortage of books and writing material. An "ideal" student's day, as sketched out in a late medieval pamphlet for student use, now seems rather grim:

A Student's Day at the University of Paris

4:00 A.M.	Rise
5:00–6:00	Arts lectures
6:00	Mass and breakfast
8:00–10:00	Lectures
11:00–12:00	Disputations before the noon meal
1:00–3:00	"Repetitions"—study of morning lectures with tutors
3:00–5:00	Cursory lectures (generalized lectures on special topics) or disputations
6:00	Supper
7:00–9:00	Study and repetitions; bed at 9:00 P.M.

The masters' lectures consisted of detailed commentaries on certain books the master intended to cover in a given term. Since books were expensive, emphasis was put on note-taking and copying so that the student might build up his own collection of books. Examinations were oral, before a panel of masters. Students were also expected to participate in formal debates (called disputations) as part of their training.

Geoffrey Chaucer provides us an unforgettable, albeit idealized, portrait of the medieval student (the clerk or cleric—many of the students were members of the minor clerical orders of the church) in his Prologue to the *Canterbury Tales*:

> A clerk from Oxford was with us also,
> Who'd turned to getting knowledge, long ago.
> As meagre was his horse as is a rake,
> Nor he himself too fat, I'll undertake,
> But he looked hollow and went soberly.
> Right threadbare was his overcoat; for he
> Had got him yet no churchly benefice,
> Nor was so worldly as to gain office.
> For he would rather have at his bed's head
> Some twenty books, all bound in black and red,
> Of Aristotle and his philosophy
> Than rich robes, fiddle, or gay psaltery.

> Yet, and for all he was philosopher,
> He had but little gold within his coffer;
> But all that he might borrow from a friend
> On books and learning he would swiftly spend,
> And then he'd pray right busily for the souls
> Of those who gave him wherewithal for
>   schools.
> Of study took he utmost care and heed.
> Not one word spoke he more than was his
>   need;
> And that was said in fullest reverence
> And short and quick and full of high good
>   sense.
> Pregnant of moral virtue was his speech;
> And gladly would he learn and gladly teach.

Chaucer's portrait of the lean, pious, poor, zealous student was highly idealized to create a type. We get probably a far more realistic picture of what students were actually doing and thinking about from the considerable amount of popular poetry that comes from the student culture of the medieval period. This poetry depicts a student life we are all familiar with: a poetry of wine, women, song, sharp satires at the expense of pompous professors or poor accommodations, and the occasional episodes of cruelty that most individuals are capable of only when they are banded into groups.

The student subculture had also invented a mythical Saint Golias, who was the patron saint of wandering scholars. Verses (called Goliardic verse) were written in honor of the "saint." The poems that have come down to use are a far cry from the sober commentaries on Aristotle's *Metaphysics* that we usually associate with the medieval scholar.

One of the more interesting collections of these medieval lyrics was discovered in a Bavarian monastery in the early 19th century. The songs in this collection were written in Latin, Old French, and German and seem to date from the late 12th and the 13th centuries. Their subject range was wide but, given the nature of such songs, predictable. There were drinking songs, laments over the loss of love or the trials of fate, hymns in honor of nature, salutes to the end of winter and the coming of the spring, and cheerfully obscene songs of exuberant sexuality. The lyrics reveal a shift of emotions ranging from the happiness of love to the despair of disappointment just as the allusions range from classical learning to medieval piety. One famous song, for example, praises the beautiful powerful virgin in language that echoes the piety of the church. The last line reveals, however, that the poem salutes not Mary but generous Venus.

In 1935 and 1936 the German composer Carl Orff set a number of these poems to music under the title *Carmina Burana*. His brilliantly lively blending of heavy percussion, snatches of ecclesiastical chant, strong choral voices, and vibrant rhythms have made this work a modern concert favorite. The listener gets a good sense of the vibrancy of these medieval lyrics by the use of the modern setting. Since the precise character of student music has not come down to us, Orff's new setting of these lyrics is a fine beginning for learning about the musicality of this popular poetry from the medieval university.

Poems of this sort are products of the highly mobile university population of the period. The community was mobile since there were few permanent structures; when students and masters moved, the *universitas* moved. One of the most powerful weapons the *universitas* possessed was the *cessatio*. If things went bad between the host city and the *universitas,* a *cessatio* (closing) could be called and the *universitas* could threaten to move. The *cessatio* was a potent economic tool. When the university closed down in Paris in 1228–1229 (after a quarrel between the civil authorities and the *universitas* as a result of student riots during Lent), the English king, Henry III, was quick to seize his chance to lure the whole *universitas* from Paris to his more benevolent shores:

> Greetings to the masters and the whole body of scholars at Paris. Humbly sympathizing with the exceeding tribulations and distresses which you have suffered at Paris under an unjust law, we wish by our pious aid, with reverence to God and His Holy Church, to restore your status to its proper condition of liberty. Wherefore we have concluded to make known to your entire body that if it shall be your pleasure to transfer yourselves to our kingdom of England and to remain there to study we will for this purpose assign to you cities, towns, boroughs, whatsoever you may wish to select, and in every fitting way cause you to rejoice in a state of liberty and tranquility which should please God and fully meet your needs.

Although the entire *universitas* did not accept the king's invitation, many scholars did go to England, where they settled at Cambridge and Oxford. Ironically enough, a migration of students from Oxford to Cambridge in 1209 gave Cambridge greater prestige and a student body large enough to form its own *universitas.*

The reputation of intellectual centers like Oxford, Paris, and Bologna invited imitation in the 13th century. Other universities started up in this period in France, the Low Countries, and the Iberian peninsula, often modeled on the Paris *universitas.* (The Bologna model of having a corporation of students as opposed to a corporation of masters did not gain wide acceptance.) In Italy, universities developed at Siena, Pavia, and Vercelli as offshoots of the University of Bologna. In the 14th century many other European cities founded universities based on the Paris model. Some of these still exist: Prague (1348), Vienna (1365), Cracow (1364), Pecs in Hungary (1367).

Thomas Aquinas

The Golden Age of the University of Paris was the 13th century, since in that period Paris could lay fair claim to being the intellectual center of the Western world. It is a mark of the international character of medieval university life that some of its most distinguished professors were from outside France: Albert the Great was German; Alexander of Hales was English; Bonaventure and Thomas Aquinas were Italian.

Thomas Aquinas (1225?–1274) was the most famous and influential of the Parisian masters of the 13th century [176]. His intellectual influence went far beyond the lecture halls of Paris and is felt to the present. Born of noble parentage in southern Italy, Thomas joined the Preaching Friars of Saint Dominic (the Dominicans) in 1243. From 1245 to 1248 he studied with Albert the Great at both Paris and Cologne. He was made a *magister* of theology in 1258 after completing his doctoral studies. During this same period (from roughly 1256 to 1259) he lectured on theology in Paris. From 1259 to 1268 he was back in Italy, where he lectured and wrote at Orvieto (the papal court for a time), Rome, and Naples. From 1268 to 1272 he held a chair of theology again, when he returned to Naples to teach there. He died two years later on his way to a church council at Lyons in France.

Thomas Aquinas' life ended before he was fifty, but in that span he produced a vast corpus of writings (they fill forty folio volumes) on theology, philosophy, and biblical studies. It is a mark of his mobility that his masterpiece—the *Summa Theologica*—was composed at Rome, Viterbo, Paris, and Naples, although it was unfinished at his death. While his writings touched on a wide variety of subjects, at root Thomas Aquinas was interested in and made a lifetime study of a very basic problem: How does one harmonize those things that are part of human learning (reason) with those supernatural truths revealed by God in the Bible and through the teaching of the church (revelation)? Aquinas' approach was to steer a middle path through two diametrically opposed opinions, both of which had avid supporters in the Middle Ages: the position of *fideism,* which held that religious faith as an absolute is indifferent to the efforts of human reason (*credo quia absurdum est*—I believe because it is absurd) and *rationalism,* which insists that everything, revelation included, must meet the test of rational human scrutiny. Aquinas wanted to demonstrate what the Gothic cathedral illustrated:

176 Andrea da Firenze. *The Triumph of Saint Thomas Aquinas.* c. 1365. Fresco. Spanish Chapel, Santa Maria Novella, Florence. The saint is enthroned between Doctors of the Old and New Testaments, with personifications of the Virtues, Sciences, and Liberal Arts below.

that the liberal arts, the things and seasons of the world, and the mysteries revealed by God could be brought into some kind of intellectual harmony based on a single criterion of truth.

For Aquinas, reason finds truth when it sees evidence of truth. The mind judges something true when it has observed a sufficient number of facts to compel it to make that judgment. The mind gives assent to truth on the basis of evidence. Aquinas was convinced that there was a sufficient amount of observable evidence in the world to conclude the existence of God. He proposed five arguments in support of such a position. Still he recognized that such argumentation only yields a very limited understanding of God. Aquinas did not believe that the naked use of reason could ever discover or prove the mysteries about God revealed in the Bible: that God became a man in Jesus Christ or that there was a Trinity of persons in God. God had to tell us that. Our assent to it is not based on evidence, but on the authority of God who reveals it to us. If we could prove the mysteries of faith, there would have been no need of a revelation and no need of faith.

Thus for Aquinas there is an organic relationship between reason and revelation. Philosophy perfects the human capacity to know and revelation perfects one beyond self by offering salvation and eternal life. Aquinas stated this relationship between reason and revelation at the very beginning of his great work of theology, the *Summa Theologica*.

When we read Aquinas today we get some sense of his stark and rigorous attempt to think things through. For one thing, he offers no stylistic adornment to relieve his philosophical and rational discourse. For another, he makes clear that philosophical reasoning is difficult; it is not a pastime for the incompetent or the intellectually lazy. Yet Aquinas was not a mere machine for logic. He had the temperament of a mystic. Some months before he died he simply put down his pen; when his secretary asked him why he had stopped writing, Aquinas simply said that in prayer and quiet he had had a vision and that what he had written "seemed as straw." Aquinas was a rare combination of intellectual and mystic.

The philosophical tradition Aquinas used in his writing was that of the Greek philosopher Aristotle. He first knew Aristotle's work in Latin translations based on Arabic texts done by Moslem scholars in the south of Spain and North Africa. Later Aquinas was able to use texts translated directly out of Greek by a Flemish friar and sometime companion, William of Moerbeke. Aquinas' use of Aristotle was certainly not a novelty in the Middle Ages. Such Arabic scholars as Avicenna (980–1036) and Averröes of Córdova (1126–1198) commented on Aristotle's philosophy and its relationship to the faith of Islam. Jewish thinkers like the famous Moses Maimonides (born in Córdova in 1135, died in Egypt in 1204) made similar attempts to bridge Greek thought and their religious faith. Maimonides wrote his famous *Guide for the Per-*

plexed to demonstrate the essential compatibility of the Hebrew scriptures with the thought of Aristotle. Maimonides was determined that essentials of the biblical message not be compromised, but he likewise felt that in nonessentials there was room for human reflection. In this task of distinguishing the place of intellect and faith Maimonides anticipated the work of Thomas Aquinas by two generations.

Two other characteristics of the thought of Aquinas should be noted. First, his world view was strongly hierarchical. Everything has its place in the universe, and that place is determined in relationship to God. A rock is good because it *is* (to Aquinas existence was a gift), but an animal is more perfect because it has life and thus shares more of divine attributes. In turn, men and women are better still because they possess mind and will. Angels are closer yet to God because they, like God, are pure spirit.

This hierarchical world view explains other characteristics of Aquinas' thought in particular and medieval thought in general: it is wide-ranging, it is encyclopedic, and in interrelating everything it is synthetic. Everything fits and has its place, meaning, and truth. That a person would speak on psychology, physics, politics, theology, and philosophy with equal authority would strike us as presumptuous, just as any building decorated with symbols from the classics, astrology, the Bible, and scenes from everyday life would now be considered a hodgepodge. Such was not the case in the 13th century, since it was assumed that everything ultimately pointed to God.

Dante's *Divine Comedy*

In any discussion of the culture of the High Middle Ages two descriptive adjectives come immediately to mind: hierarchical and synthetic. It is a commonplace, for example, to compare the Gothic cathedral and the systematic treatises on philosophy and theology like the *Summa Theologica* of Saint Thomas Aquinas. On close inspection such comparisons may be facile, but they point to the following truths about this period that are relatively secure. Both the Gothic cathedral and the theology of Aquinas, for example, started from the tangible and sensual ("Nothing comes to the mind except through the senses" is a basic axiom for Aquinas) in order to mount in a hierarchical manner to the light that is God. Again, both writer and architect felt it possible to be universal in their desire to synthesize all human knowledge as prelude and pointer to the full revelation of God. Finally, they both constructed their edifices by the juxtaposition of tensions and syntheses.

177 Sandro Botticelli. *Dante.* c. 1480–1485. Oil on canvas, 24¼ × 18½" (54 × 47 cm). Collection Dr. Martin Bodmer, Cologny/Geneva.

If the Gothic cathedral and the *Summa* represent two masterpieces of the hierarchical and synthetic religious humanism of the Middle Ages, the *Divine Comedy* of Dante Alighieri (1265–1321) represents the same masterly achievement in literature. Dante [177] was a Florentine. He was nonetheless deeply influenced by the intellectual currents that emanated from the Paris of his time. As a comfortably fixed young man he devoted himself to a rigorous program of philosophical and theological study in order to enhance his already burgeoning literary talent. His published work gives evidence of a profound culture and a deep love for study. He wrote on the origin and development of language (*De Vulgari Eloquentia*), political theory (*De Monarchia*), and generalized knowledge (*Convivio*) as well as his own poetic aspirations (*Vita Nuova*). His masterpiece is the *Divine Comedy*.

Dante was exiled from Florence for political reasons in 1300. In his bitter wanderings in the north of Italy he worked on—and finally brought to conclusion—a long poem to which he gave a bitingly ironical title: *The Comedy of Dante Alighieri, A Florentine by Birth but Not in Behavior*. Dante called his poem a comedy since, as he noted, it had a happy ending and it was written in the popular language of the people. The adjective *divine* was added later; some say by Boccaccio, who in the next generation lectured on the poem in Florence and wrote one of the first biographies of the great poet.

The *Divine Comedy* relates a symbolic journey that the poet begins on Good Friday, 1300, through the world of hell, purgatory, and heaven. In the first two parts of his journey, Dante is guided by the ancient Roman poet Vergil, whose *Aeneid* was such an inspiration to him and from which he borrowed (especially from Book VI, which tells of Aeneas' own journey to the Underworld). From the border at the top of the Mount of Purgatory to the pinnacle of heaven where Dante glimpses the "still point of light" that is God, Dante's guide is Beatrice, a young woman Dante had loved passionately if platonically in his youth [178].

Every significant commentator on the *Comedy* has noted its careful organization. The poem is made up of one hundred cantos. The first canto of the *Inferno* serves as an introduction to the whole poem. There are then 33 cantos for each of the three major sections

178 Domenico di Michelino. *Dante and His Poem,* 1465. Fresco. Florence Cathedral. Dante, holding his *Comedy,* points to Hell, where his journey begins. Behind him is the Mount of Purgatory. At right is Florence (note the recently finished Cathedral with its dome), here a symbol of the heavenly city of Paradise. This fresco is one of several monuments to Dante in Florence.

(*Inferno, Purgatorio,* and *Paradiso*). The entire poem is written in a rhyme scheme called *terza rima* (*aba, bcb, cdc,* and so on) that is almost impossible to duplicate in English because of the shortage of rhyming words in our language. The number three and its multiples, symbols of the Trinity, occur over and over. The *Inferno* is divided into nine regions plus a vestibule, and the same number is found in the *Purgatorio*. Dante's *Paradiso* is constituted by the nine heavens of the Ptolemaic system plus the Empyrean, the highest heaven. This scheme mirrors the whole poem of 99 cantos plus one. The sinners in the *Inferno* are arranged according to whether they sinned by incontinence, violence, or fraud (a division Dante derived from Aristotle's *Ethics*), while the yearning souls of purgatory are divided in three ways according to how they acted or failed to act in relation to love. The saved souls in the *Paradiso* are divided into the lay folk, the active, and the contemplative. Nearest the throne of God, but reflected in the circles of heaven, are the nine categories of angels.

Dante's interest in the symbolic goes beyond his elaborate manipulation of numbers. In the *Inferno* sinners suffer punishments that have symbolic value; their sufferings both punish and instruct. The gluttonous live on heaps of garbage under driving storms of cold rain, while the flatterers are immersed in pools of sewage and the sexually perverse walk burning stretches of sand in an environment as sterile as their attempts at love. Conversely, in the *Paradiso,* the blessed dwell in the circles most symbolic of their

virtue. The theologians are in the circle of the sun since they provided such enlightenment to the world, and the holy warriors dwell in the sphere of Mars.

We can better appreciate the density and complexity of Dante's symbolism by looking at a single example. Our common image of Satan is that of a sly tempter (in popular art he is often in formal dress whispering blandishments in a willing ear with just a whiff of sulphur about him) after the manner of Milton's proud, perversely tragic, heroic Satan in *Paradise Lost*. For Dante, Satan is a huge, stupid beast, frozen in a lake of ice in the pit of hell. He beats six batlike wings (a demonic leftover from his angelic existence; see Isaiah 6:1–5) in an ineffectual attempt to escape the frozen pond that is watered by the four rivers of hell. He is grotesquely three-headed (a parody of the Trinity) and his slavering mouths remorselessly chew the bodies of three infamous traitors from sacred and secular history (Judas, Cassius, and Brutus).

Why does Dante portray Satan so grotesquely? It is clear that Dante borrowed some of the picture of Satan from Byzantine mosaics with which he would have been familiar in the Baptistery of Florence [179]. Beyond that, the whole complex of Satan is heavily weighted with symbolic significance. Satan lies in frozen darkness at a point in the universe farthest from the warmth and light of God. He is the fallen angel of light (Lucifer means "light-bearer"), now encased in a pit in the center of the earth excavated by the force of his own fall from heaven. Satan is immo-

179 Hell, detail of mosaic in vault of the Baptistery, Florence Cathedral. 13th century.
The giant, who is a Satan figure, his throne, and the serpents are all swallowing up human beings.

bile in contrast to God who is the mover of all things in the universe. He is totally inarticulate and stupid because he represents, par excellence, all of the souls of hell who have lost what Dante calls "the good of intellect." Satan, and all of the souls in hell, will remain totally unfulfilled as created rational beings because they are cut off from the final source of rational understanding and fulfillment: God. Intellectual estrangement from God is for Dante, as it was for Thomas Aquinas, the essence of damnation. This estrangement is most evident in the case of Satan, who symbolizes in his very being the loss of rationality and all that derives from that fact.

Dante, following a line of thought already developed by Suger and Aquinas, conceived the human journey as a slow ascent to the purity of God by means of the created things of this world. To settle for less than God was, in essence, to fail to return to the natural source of life, God. This explains why light is such a crucial motif in the *Divine Comedy* as it had been in the theories of Abbot Suger. Neither light nor the sources of light (the sun) is ever mentioned in the *Inferno*. The overwhelming visual impression of the *Inferno* is darkness—a darkness that begins when Dante is lost in the "dark wood" of Canto I and continues until he climbs from hell and sees above his head the stars (the word *stars* ends each of the three major parts of the poem) of the Southern Hemisphere. In the ascent of the mountain of purgatory, daylight and sunset are controlling motifs to symbolize the reception and rejection of divine light. In the *Paradiso* the blessed are bathed in the reflected light that comes from God. At the climax of the *Paradiso* the poet has a momentary glimpse of God as a point of light and rather obscurely understands that God, the source of all intelligibility, is the power that also moves the "sun and the other stars."

Within the broad reaches of Dante's philosophical and theological preoccupations the poet still has the concentrated power to sketch unforgettable portraits: the doomed lovers Paolo and Francesca—each of the tercets that tell their story starts with the word *amore* (love)—the haughty political leader Farinata degli Umberti, the pitiable suicide Pier delle Vigne, or the caricatures of gluttons like Ciacco the Hog. Damned, penitent, or saved, the characters are by turns both symbols and persons. Saint Peter represents the church in the *Paradiso* but also explodes with ferociously human anger at its abuses. Brunetto Latini in the *Inferno* with "his brown-baked features" is a condemned sodomite but still anxious that posterity at least remember his literary accomplishments.

It has been said that a mastery of the *Divine Comedy* would be a mastery of all that was significant about the intellectual culture of the Middle Ages. It is certainly true that the poem, encyclopedic and complex as it is, would provide a primer for any reader interested in the science, political theory, philosophy, literary criticism, and theology of the 13th century as well as a detailed acquaintance with the burning questions of Dante's time. The very comprehensiveness of the poem has often been its major obstacle for the modern reader. Beyond that hurdle is the strangeness of the Dantean world, so at variance with our own: earth-centered, manageably small, sure of its ideas of right and wrong, orthodox in its theology, prescientific in its outlook, Aristotelean in its philosophy. For all that, Dante is not to be read only for his store of medieval lore; he is, as T. S. Eliot once wrote, the most universal of poets. He had a deeply sympathetic appreciation of human aspiration, love and hate, the destiny of humanity, and the meaning of nature and history.

Questions for Further Discussion

1. We have suggested that the Gothic cathedral had more than a religious significance for the population of a medieval town; it had a social, economic, technological, and cultural value as well. Think about such influences in terms of some contemporary architectural works. What, for example, might a future scholar say about the 20th-century suburban shopping mall?

2. One basic idea of medieval culture was the notion that the reality of this world pointed to or was a symbol of the reality of the world of God, an idea that is hardly part of the modern consciousness. What leading ideas, philosophies, and ideologies of today's intellectual world most strongly deny or undermine the medieval position?

3. Our description of the medieval university points out its continuity with the universities of the present day. The university is a sign of the conservative nature of culture—culture as a protector of certain institutions and ideas. What other civil, social, or religious institutions have been conserved for a long period in the history of Western culture?

4. We have all known pain, suffering, guilt, and the burden of striving. In that sense, at least, Dante could write from some sense of experience about hell and purgatory. What, however, are the special problems involved in the writing of a poem like the *Paradiso*?

5. Compare the symbolism of light as it is used by Suger with the symbolism of Dante in the *Paradiso*. As a dramatic contrast with medieval light symbolism read a bit about Albert Speer's use of light for the Nazi rallies at Nuremburg in the 1930s. What were his sources and intentions as he used massive spotlights to create what he called "cathedrals of light"?

	GENERAL EVENTS	LITERATURE & PHILOSOPHY	ART

1280

13th cent. Dependence on Byzantine models in Italian painting

c. 1280–1290 Cimabue, *Madonna Enthroned; Crucifix,* Arezzo

1300 Pope Boniface VIII proclaims first Jubilee Year ("Holy Year")

1303 Philip the Fair of France humiliates Pope Boniface VIII

c. 1303–1321 Dante, *Divine Comedy*

c. 1300 New naturalism in Italian painting appears with work of Giotto

1305–1306 Giotto, Arena Chapel frescoes

c. 1308–1311 Duccio, *Maestà* altarpiece, Siena

1309

"Babylonian Captivity" of the Papacy

1309 "Babylonian Captivity" of the papacy at Avignon begins

1326 Earliest known use of cannon

1337–1453 "Hundred Years' War" between France and England

1346–1378 Reign of Charles IV, Holy Roman emperor

1346 English defeat French at Crécy

1348 Bubonic plague depopulates Europe

1356 English defeat French at Poitiers

1358 Revolt of lower classes *(Jacquerie)* in France

1363–1404 Reign of Philip the Bold, duke of Burgundy

1376 Popes return to Rome from Avignon

c. 1310 G. Pisano completes Pisa Cathedral pulpit; Giotto, *Madonna Enthroned*

1333 Martini, *Annunciation*

1338–1339 A. Lorenzetti, *Good Government* fresco, Siena

c. 1347–1360 Prague, as residence of Charles IV, becomes major art center

c. 1350–1360 Unknown Bohemian Master, *Death of the Virgin*

1348–1352 Boccaccio, *Decameron,* collection of tales

after 1350 Petrarch compiles *Canzoniere,* collection of poems

c. 1370 Saint Catherine of Siena urges end of "Babylonian Captivity"

1373 Petrarch, *Letter to Posterity,* autobiography

c. 1363 Court of dukes of Burgundy at Dijon becomes important center of International Style

1377

The Great Schism

1377–1399 Reign of Richard II in England

1378 "Great Schism" begins

1381 Peasant Revolt ("Wat Tyler Rebellion") in England

1399–1413 Reign of Henry IV in England

1413 English defeat French at Agincourt

1417 Council of Constance ends "Great Schism" with election of Pope Martin V

c. 1377 Wycliff active in English church reform; translates Bible into English

c. 1385–1400 Chaucer, *The Canterbury Tales,* collection of tales

c. 1377–1413 *Wilton Diptych*

1395–1399 Broederlam, *Presentation in the Temple and Flight into Egypt*

1395–1406 Sluter, *Well of Moses*

1413–1416 Limbourg Brothers, illustrations for *Très Riches Heures du Duc de Berry*

1417

ARCHITECTURE	MUSIC

1288–1309 Palazzo
Pubblico, Siena

1295 Santa Croce, Florence,
begun

1296 Florence Cathedral
(Duomo) begun

1298 Palazzo Vecchio,
Florence, begun

1332–1357 Gloucester Cathedral choir
(Perpendicular style)

14th cent. Secular
music flourishes

1325 Vitry, *Ars Nova Musicae*,
treatise describing new
system of musical notation

after 1337 Machaut, *Messe de
Notre Dame*, polyphonic setting
of the Ordinary of the Mass

c. 1345–1438 Doge's Palace, Venice

c. 1350 Landini famous in
Florence as performer and
composer of madrigals
and ballads

1386 Duomo of Milan begun

9
The 14th Century: A Time of Transition

Calamity, Decay, and Violence

The 14th century (often called the *Trecento,* Italian for "thirteen hundred") is usually described by historians as the age that marks the end of the medieval period and the beginning of the Renaissance in Western Europe. If we accept this rather neat description of the period we should expect to see strong elements of the medieval sensibility as well as some stirrings of the "new birth" (*Renaissance*) of culture that was the hallmark of 15th-century European life. We must be cautious, however, about expecting the break between "medieval" and "Renaissance" to be clean and dramatic. History does not usually work with the precision employed by the historians. Nor should we expect to see cultural history moving upward in a straight line toward greater modernity or greater perfection. In fact, the 14th century was a period of unparalleled natural calamity, institutional decay, and cruel violence.

The Black Death

Midway through the century, in 1348, bubonic plague swept through Europe in a virulent epidemic that killed untold numbers of people and upset trade, culture, and daily life in ways hard for us to imagine. It has been estimated that some cities in Italy lost as much as two-thirds of their population in that year.

One prominent figure who lived through that devastation was the Italian writer Giovanni Boccaccio (1312–1353). His great collection of stories, the *Decameron,* has a plague setting. A group of young men and women flee Florence to avoid the plague; during their ten days' sojourn in the country (*Decameron* is Greek for "ten days") they amuse each other by the telling of stories. Each of the ten young people tells two stories on each of the ten days. The resulting two hundred stories constitute a brilliant collection of folk tales, *fabliaux* (ribald fables), *exempla* (moral stories), and romances Boccaccio culled from the oral and written traditions of Europe. Because of their romantic elements, earthiness, and somewhat shocking bawdiness the *Decameron* has often been called the "Human Comedy" to contrast it with the lofty moral tone of Dante's epic work of an earlier generation.

However delightful and pleasing those stories are to read, they stand in sharp contrast to the horrific picture Boccaccio draws of the plague in his introduction to the *Decameron.* Boccaccio's account has the ring of authenticity. He had been an eyewitness to the events he describes. His vivid prose gives some small sense of what the plague must have been like for a people who possessed only the most rudimentary knowledge of medicine and no knowledge at all about the source of illness and disease.

The Great Schism

Nature was not the only scourge to affect the stability of Europe. The medieval Christian church, that most powerful and permanent large institution in medieval life, underwent convulsive changes in the 14th century, changes that were distant warning signals of the Reformation at the beginning of the 16th century.

A quick look at some dates indicates clearly the nature of these changes. In 1300 Pope Boniface VIII celebrated the great jubilee year at Rome that brought pilgrims and visitors from all over the Christian West to pay homage to the papacy and the church it represented and headed. This event was one of the final symbolic moments of papal supremacy over European life and culture. Within the next three years Philip the Fair of France imprisoned and abused the same pope at the papal palace of Anagni. The pope died as a result of his humiliating encounters with royal power; even Dante's implacable hatred of Boniface could not restrain his outrage at the humiliation of the office of the pope. By 1309 the papacy, under severe pressure from the French, had been removed to Avignon in southern France, where it was to remain for nearly 70 years. In 1378 the papacy was further weakened by the Great Schism, which saw European Christianity divided into hostile camps, each of which pledged allegiance to a rival claimant to the papacy. Not until 1417 was this breach in church unity healed; a church council had to depose three papal pretenders to accomplish the reunification of the church.

The general disarray of the church in this period spawned ever more insistent demands for church reforms. Popular literature (as both Boccaccio and, in England, Geoffrey Chaucer, clearly demonstrate) unmercifully satirized the decadence of the church. Great saints like the mystic Catherine of Siena (1347–1380) wrote impassioned letters to the popes at Avignon in their "Babylonian Captivity" demanding that they return to Rome free from the political ties of the French monarchy. In England, John Wyclif's cries against the immorality of the higher clergy and the corruption of the church fueled indignation at all levels. The famous Peasant Revolt of 1381 was greatly aided by the activism of people aroused by the ideas of Wyclif and his followers.

The 1381 revolt in England was only the last in a series of lower-class revolutions that occurred in the 14th century. The frequency and magnitude of these revolts (like that of the French peasants beginning in

1356) highlight the profound dissatisfactions with the church and the nobility in the period. It is not accidental that the story of Robin Hood, with its theme of violence toward the wealthy and care for the poor, began in the 14th century.

The Hundred Years' War

The terrible violence of the 14th century was caused not only by the alienation of the peasants but also by the Hundred Years' War between France and England. While the famous battles of the period—Poitiers, Crécy, Agincourt—now seem romantic and distant, it is undeniable that they brought unrelieved misery to France for long periods. Between battles, roaming bands of mercenaries pillaged the landscape to make up for their lack of pay. The various battles were terrible in themselves. One example must suffice. According to Jean Froissart's *Chronicles,* the English King Edward III sent a group of his men to examine the battlefield after the battle of Crécy (1346)—in which the English longbowmen slaughtered the more traditionally armed French and mercenary armies: "They passed the whole day upon the field and made a careful report of all they saw. According to their report it appeared that 80 banners, the bodies of 11 princes, 1200 knights, and 30,000 common men were found dead on the field." It is no wonder that Barbara Tuchman's splendid history of life in 14th-century France, *A Distant Mirror* (1978), should have been subtitled "The Calamitous Fourteenth Century."

Literature in Italy and England

Amid the natural and institutional disasters of the 14th century there were signs of intense human creativity in all the arts, especially in literature. In Italy, Dante's literary eminence was secure at the time of his death (1321) and the reputation of Italian letters was further enhanced by two other outstanding Tuscan writers: Francesco Petrarch and Giovanni Boccaccio, famed for the *Decameron.* In England, one of the greatest authors in the history of English letters was active: Geoffrey Chaucer. His life spanned the second half of the 14th century; he died, almost symbolically, in 1400.

Petrarch

It is appropriate to begin a discussion of 14th-century culture with Petrarch. His life spanned the better part of the century (1304–1374) and in that life we can see the conflict between the medieval and early Renaissance ideals being played out.

Petrarch (Petrarca in Italian) was born in Arezzo, a small town in Tuscany south of Florence. As a young man, in obedience to parental wishes, he studied law for a year in France and for three years at the law faculty in Bologna. He abandoned his legal studies immediately after the death of his father to pursue a literary career. To support himself he accepted some minor church offices but was never ordained to the priesthood.

Petrarch made his home at Avignon (and later at a much more isolated spot near that papal city, Vaucluse), but for the greater part of his life he wandered from place to place. He never could settle down; his restlessness prevented him from accepting lucrative positions that would have made him a permanent resident of any one place. He received invitations to serve as secretary to various popes in Avignon and, through the intercession of his close friend Boccaccio, was offered a professorship in Florence. He took none of these positions.

Petrarch was insatiably curious. He fed his love for the ancient classics by searching out and copying ancient manuscripts that had remained hidden and unread in the various monasteries of Europe. It is said that at his death he had one of the finest private libraries in Europe. He wrote volumes of poetry and prose, carried on a vast correspondence, advised the rulers of the age, took a keen interest in horticulture, and kept a wide circle of literary and artistic friends. At his death we know that he possessed pictures by both Simone Martini and Giotto, two of the most influential artists of the time. In 1348 he was crowned poet laureate of Rome, the first artist so honored since the ancient days of Rome.

One true mark of the Renaissance sensibility was a keen interest in the self and an increased thirst for personal glory and fame. Petrarch surely is a 14th-century harbinger of that spirit. Dante's *Divine Comedy* was totally oriented to the next life; the apex of Dante's vision is that of the soul rapt in the vision of God in eternity. Petrarch, profoundly religious, never denied that such a vision was the ultimate goal of life. At the same time, his work exhibits a tension between that goal and his thirst for earthly success and fame. In his famous prose work *Secretum (My Secret),* written in 1343, the artist imagines himself in conversation with Saint Augustine. In a dialogue extraordinary for its sense of self-confession and self-scrutiny Petrarch discusses his moral and intellectual failings, his besetting sins, and his tendency to fall into fits of depression. He agrees with his great hero Augustine that he should be less concerned with his intellectual labors and the fame that derives from them and concern himself more with salvation and the spiritual perfection of his life. However, Petrarch's argument has a note of ambivalence: "I will be true to myself as far as it is possible. I will pull myself together and collect my scattered wits, and make a great endeavor to possess my soul in patience. But even while we speak, a crowd of important affairs, though only of this world, is waiting for my attention."

The inspiration for the *Secretum* was Augustine's *Confessions,* a book Petrarch loved so much that he carried it with him everywhere. It may well have been the model for Petrarch's *Letter to Posterity,* one of the few examples of autobiography we possess after the time of Augustine. That Petrarch would have written an autobiography is testimony to his strong interest in himself as a person. The *Letter* was probably composed in 1373, a year before his death. Petrarch reviews his life up until 1351, where the text abruptly breaks off. The unfinished work is clear testimony to Petrarch's thirst for learning, fame, and self-awareness. At the same time, it is noteworthy for omitting any mention of the Black Death of 1348, which carried off the woman he loved. The letter is an important primary document of the sensibility of the 14th-century "proto-Renaissance."

Petrarch regarded as his most important works the Latin writings over which he labored with devotion and in conscious imitation of his most admired classical masters: Ovid, Cicero, and Vergil. Today, however, only the literary specialist or the antiquarian is likely to read his long epic poem in Latin called *Africa* (written in imitation of Vergil's *Aeneid*), or his prose work in praise of the past masters of the world (*De Viris Illustris*), or his meditations on the benefits of contemplative life (*De Vita Solitaria*). What has assured the literary reputation of Petrarch is his incomparable vernacular poetry, which he considered somewhat trifling but collected carefully into his *Canzoniere (Songbook).* The *Canzoniere* contains more than three hundred sonnets and 49 *canzoni* (songs) written in Italian during the span of his adult career.

The subject of a great deal of Petrarch's poetry is his love for Laura, a woman with whom he fell immediately in love in 1327 after seeing her at church in Avignon. Laura died in the plague of 1348. The poems in her honor are divided into those written in her lifetime and those mourning her untimely death. Petrarch poured out his love for Laura in over three hundred *sonnets,* fourteen-line poems he typically broke into an octave and a sestet. Although they were never actually lovers (Petrarch says in the *Secretum* that this was due more to her honor than to his; Laura was a married woman), his Laura was no mere literary abstraction. She was a flesh-and-blood woman whom Petrarch genuinely loved. One of the characteristics of his poetry, in fact, is the palpable reality of Laura as a person; she never becomes (as Beatrice does for Dante) a symbol without earthly reality.

The interest in Petrarch's sonnets did not end with his death. Petrarchism, by which is meant the Petrarchan form of the sonnet and particularly the poet's attitude to his subject matter—praise of a woman as the perfection of human beauty and the object of the highest expression of love—was introduced into other parts of Europe before the century was over. In England, Petrarch's sonnets were first imitated in form and subject by Sir Thomas Wyatt in the early 16th century. Although the Elizabethan poets eventually developed their own English form of the sonnet, the Renaissance English tradition of poetry owes a particularly large debt to Petrarch, as the poetry of Sir Philip Sidney (1554–1586), Edmund Spenser (1552–1599), and William Shakespeare (1564–1616) shows. Their sonnet sequences follow the example of Petrarch in linking together a series of sonnets in such a way as to indicate a development in the relationship of the poet to his love.

Chaucer

While it is possible to see the beginning of the Renaissance spirit in Petrarch and other Italian writers of the 14th century, the greatest English writer of the century, Geoffrey Chaucer (1340–1400), still reflects the culture of his immediate past. The new spirit of individualism discernible in Petrarch is missing in Chaucer. He is still very much a medieval man. Only in the later part of the 15th century, largely under the influence of Italian models, can we speak of the Renaissance in England. This underscores the valuable lesson about history that movements do not necessarily happen immediately and everywhere.

Scholars have been able to reconstruct Chaucer's life with only partial success. We know that his family had been fairly prosperous wine merchants and vintners and that he entered royal service early in his life, eventually becoming a squire to King Edward III. After 1373 he undertook various diplomatic tasks for the king, including at least two trips to Italy to negotiate commercial contracts. During these Italian journeys Chaucer came into contact with the writings of Dante, Petrarch, and Boccaccio. There has been some speculation that he actually met Petrarch, but the evidence is tenuous. Toward the end of his life Chaucer served as the customs agent for the port

Plate 13 Giotto. *The Meeting of Joachim and Anna*. c. 1305. Fresco. Arena Chapel, Padua.

left: **Plate 14** Simone Martini. *Annunciation.* 1333.
Tempera on panel, 8'8" × 10' (2.64 × 3.05 m). Uffizi,
Florence. The courtly elegance of the figures is in
strong contrast to the massive realism of Giotto's
Madonna.

below: **Plate 15** Doge's Palace, Venice. 1345–1438.
Unlike the heavily fortified Palazzo Pubblico at Siena,
this palace of the rulers of Venice, with its light,
open arches, reflects the stability and security of the
Venetian Republic.

of London on the river Thames. He was thus never a leisured "man of letters"; his writing had to be done amid the hectic round of public affairs that engaged his attention as a highly placed civil servant.

Like many other successful writers of the late medieval period, Chaucer could claim a widespread acquaintance with the learning and culture of his time. This was still an age when it was possible to read most of the available books. Chaucer spoke and wrote French fluently, and his poems show the influence of many French allegories and "dream visions." That he also knew Italian literature is clear from his borrowings from Dante and Petrarch and from his use of stories and tales in Boccaccio's *Decameron* (although it is not clear that he knew that work directly). Chaucer also had a deep knowledge of Latin literature, both classical and ecclesiastical. Furthermore, his literary output was not limited to the composition of original works of poetry. He made a translation from Latin (with an eye on an earlier French version) of Boethius' *Consolation of Philosophy* as well as a translation from French of the 13th century allegorical erotic fantasy *The Romance of the Rose*. He also composed a short treatise on the astrolabe and its relationship to the study of astronomy and astrology (two disciplines not clearly distinguished at that time).

The impressive range of Chaucer's learning pales in comparison with his most memorable and noteworthy talents: his profound feeling for the role of the English language as a vehicle for literature; his efforts to extend the range of the language (the richness of Chaucer's vocabulary was not exceeded until Shakespeare); and his incomparable skill in the art of human observation. Chaucer's characters are so finely realized that they have become standard types in English literature: his pardoner is an unforgettable villain, his knight the essence of courtesy, his wife of Bath a paradigm of rollicking bawdiness.

These characters, and others, are from Chaucer's masterpiece, *The Canterbury Tales,* begun sometime after 1385. To unify this vast work, a collection of miscellaneous tales, Chaucer used a typical literary device: a narrative frame, in this case a journey during which people tell each other tales. As noted, Boccaccio had used a similar device in the *Decameron.*

Chaucer's plan was to have a group of thirty pilgrims travel from London to the shrine of Thomas à Becket at Canterbury and back. After a general introduction, each pilgrim would tell two tales on the way and two on the return trip in order to pass the long hours of travel more pleasantly. Between tales they might engage in perfunctory conversation or prologues of their own to cement the tales further into a unified whole.

Chaucer never finished this ambitious project; he died before half of it was complete. The version we possess has a General Prologue in which the narrator, Geoffrey Chaucer, describes the individual pilgrims, his meeting with them at the Tabard Inn in London, and the start of the journey. Only 23 of the 30 pilgrims tell their tales (none tells two tales) and the group has not yet reached Canterbury. There is even some internal evidence that the material we possess was not meant for publication in its present form.

Although *The Canterury Tales* is only a draft of what was intended to be Chaucer's masterwork, it is of incomparable literary and social value. A close reading of the General Prologue, for instance—with its representative, although limited, cross-section of medieval society (no person lower in rank than a plowman or higher in rank than a knight appears)—affords an effortless entry into the complex world of late-medieval England. With quick, deft strokes Chaucer not only creates verbal portraits of people who at the same time seem both typical and uniquely real but also introduces us to a world of slowly dying knightly values, a world filled with such contrasts as clerical foibles, the desire for knowledge, the ribald taste of the lower social classes, and an appetite for philosophical conversation.

After the General Prologue, the various members of the pilgrim company begin to introduce themselves and proceed to tell their tales. Between the tales, they engage in small talk or indulge in lengthy prologues of their own. In the tales that he completed, we see that Chaucer drew on the vast treasury of literature, both written and oral, that was the common patrimony of medieval culture. The Knight's Tale is a courtly romance; the miller and reeve tell stories that spring from the ribald *fabliaux* tradition of the time; the pardoner tells an *exemplum* such as any medieval preacher might employ; the prioress draws from the legends of the saints; the nun's priest uses an animal fable, while the parson characteristically enough provides a somewhat tedious example of a medieval prose sermon.

Art in Italy

Giorgio Vasari's *Lives of the Artists* (1550), the earliest account of the rebirth of Italian art in the Renaissance, treats first of all the great Florentine painter Giotto di Bondone (1266 or 1267–1337). In his *Life of Giotto* Vasari pays tribute to Giotto's work and also gives him credit for setting painting once again on to the right path, from which it had strayed.

Later generations have accepted Vasari's assessment and have seen Giotto as a revolutionary figure not for the 14th century alone but for the entire history of European art, marking a major break with the art of the Middle Ages. Like all revolutionary figures, Giotto was more intimately linked with his past than his contemporaries and immediate successors realized, and to understand the magnitude of his achievements we must first see something of their context.

The Italo-Byzantine Background

Throughout the later Middle Ages art in Italy showed little of the richness and inventiveness of the great centers of northern Europe. Not only in France, where the University of Paris formed the intellectual capital of the Western world, but also in England and Germany, construction of the great Gothic cathedrals provided opportunities for artists to refine and develop their techniques. Sculptured decorations like *The Death of the Virgin* from Strasbourg Cathedral [180] are stylistically far more advanced than contemporary work in Italy. One of the reasons for this is that northern Gothic artists were beginning to return for inspiration not to their immediate predecessors but to classical art, with its realistic portrayal of the body and drapery. In Italy, however, artists were still rooted in the Byzantine tradition. Italian churches were generally decorated not with lifelike sculptural groups like the one from Strasbourg but with solemn and stylized frescoes and mosaics, a style called Italo-Byzantine.

There are notable exceptions to the generally conservative character of Italian art in the 13th century. Nicola Pisano (1220/1225–1284?) and his son Giovanni (1245/1250–1314) have been described as the creators of modern sculpture. Nicola's first major work was a marble pulpit for the Baptistery in Pisa completed in 1260, clearly influenced by the Roman sarcophagi the sculptor could see around him in Pisa. By crowding in his figures and filling the scene with lively detail Nicola recaptured much of the vitality and realism of late Roman art while retaining the expressive qualities of Gothic sculpture. The work of his son Giovanni was less influenced by classical models than by his contemporaries in northern Europe—so much so that some scholars believe he must

180 *The Death of the Virgin,* tympanum of the south transept portal, Strasbourg Cathedral. c. 1220. The expressive faces and elaborate drapery show the influence of classical sculpture.

181 Nicola Pisano. *Annunciation and Nativity*, detail of pulpit. 1259–1260. Marble. Baptistery, Pisa. By crowding his figures together Nicola was able to combine the scene of the Nativity with the Annunciation and the shepherds in the fields.

182 Giovanni Pisano. *Nativity and Annunciation to the Shepherds*, detail of pulpit. 1302–1310. Marble. Cathedral, Pisa. The slender figures and sense of space create an effect very different from that of the work of the artist's father.

have spent some time in France. In his pulpit for the cathedral at Pisa, finished in 1310, the figures are more elegant and less crowded than those of his father, and show an intensity of feeling typical of northern late Gothic art [181, 182]. Both of these great sculptors foreshadowed major characteristics in the art of the Renaissance, Nicola by his emphasis on classical models and Giovanni by the naturalism and emotionalism of his figures and by his use of space.

While some Italian sculptors were responding to influences from outside, painting in Italy remained firmly grounded in the Byzantine tradition. It was precisely this strongly conservative dependence on Byzantine models that permitted Giotto to make his revolutionary break with the past. Byzantine art was, after all, originally derived from classical art. Although its static and solemn characteristics seem a long way away from Greek or Roman styles, Byzantine painters and mosaicists inherited the late Hellenistic and Roman artists' ability to give their figures a three-dimensional quality and to represent foreshortening. With these techniques available to him, Giotto was better able to break away from the stereotyped forms of Italo-Byzantine art and bring to painting the same naturalism and emotional power that appear in Giovanni Pisano's sculptures.

Giotto's predecessor as the leading painter in Florence, and perhaps also his teacher, was Cimabue (1240?–1302?). Not enough of his work has survived for us to have a clear impression of how much Giotto owed to Cimabue's influence, but the crucifix he painted for the church of San Domenico in Arezzo shows a remarkable realism and sophistication in the depiction of Christ's body [183]. Cimabue shows a

183 Cimabue. *Crucifixion*. c. 1268–1271. Painted and gilded wood, 10′11″ × 8′8⅛″ (3.36 × 2.67 m). San Domenico, Arezzo.

genuine if incomplete understanding of the anatomy of the figure and, more important, uses it to enhance the emotional impact of his painting by emphasizing the sense of strain and weight. At the same time the draped loincloth is not merely painted as a decorative design but as naturalistically soft folds through which the limbs beneath are visible. If in other works, like the immense Santa Trinità *Madonna* [184], Cimabue is more directly in the Italo-Byzantine tradition, here at least he seems directly to prefigure the impact of Giotto's art.

The works of Cimabue's contemporary Duccio di Buoninsegna (1255/1260–1318/1319) are more directly Byzantine in inspiration, but here too the new spirit of the times can be felt. His greatest achievement was the huge *Maestà,* painted between 1308 and 1311, for the high altar of the cathedral of Siena, his native city. The majestic Madonna who gives the work its name faced the congregation [185], while both the front and back of the altarpiece were covered with small compartments filled with scenes from the lives of Christ and the Virgin. As Giotto was to do a few years later, Duccio developed the art of storytelling. The episodes themselves are familiar from earlier painters, but the range of emotional expression is new and astonishing, as Duccio reveals to us not only the physical appearance of each of his subjects but their emotional states as well. In a num-

left: 184 Cimabue. *Madonna Enthroned.* 1270–1285. Tempera on panel, 12'6" × 7'4" (3.81 × 2.24 m). Uffizi, Florence. Although much of the detail is Byzantine in inspiration, the scale of this painting has no Byzantine counterpart.

below: 185 Duccio. *Madonna Enthroned,* detail of front panel of *Maestà* Altar. c. 1308–1311. Tempera on panel, height 6'10½" (2.1 m). Cathedral Museum, Siena. Notice the greater gentleness of the faces and the softer, flowing robe of the Virgin here than in Cimabue's painting.

above: **186** Duccio. *The Annunciation of the Death of the Virgin,* from the *Maestà* Altar. c. 1308–1311. Tempera on panel. Cathedral Museum, Siena. One of the episodes from the *Maestà* altarpiece, this scene demonstrates Duccio's ability to create a convincing architectural space around his figures.

right: **187** Giotto. *Madonna Enthroned.* c. 1310. Tempera on panel, 10′8″ × 6′8″ (3.25 × 2.03 m). Uffizi, Florence. Although contemporary with Duccio's Madonna from the *Maestà* altarpiece, Giotto's painting has a much greater sense of weight and volume.

ber of the scenes the action takes place within an architectural setting that conveys a greater sense of space than we find in any earlier paintings, including those from the ancient world [186].

Giotto's Break with the Past

Great as was Duccio's contribution to the development of painting, it was achieved without any decisive break with the tradition in which he worked. Giotto, in the eyes of his contemporaries, represented a new era in the history of art. Even if we can now see the roots of some of his achievements in the works of Cimabue, the boldness of Giotto's vision, and the certainty with which he communicates it to us, represent one of the supreme achievements of Western art.

Giotto's preeminent characteristic was his realism. The Byzantine style had aimed for a rich, glowing surface, with elaborate linear designs. Now for the first time figures were painted with a sense of depth, their volume represented by a careful use of light and dark, so that they took on the same strength and presence as works of sculpture. Instead of being confronted with an image, spectators saw the living and breathing figures before them. In his great altarpiece of the Madonna enthroned, painted in 1310, Giotto brings us into the presence of the Virgin herself [187]. We see the majestic solidity of her form, an impression enhanced by the realistic throne on which she sits. This is achieved not only by the three-dimensional modeling of the figures but also by the sense of space that surrounds the Virgin and Child and separates them from the worshiping angels.

But Giotto's greatness lay not so much in his ability to create realistic images—to "imitate Nature," as his contemporaries called it—as in using these images for dramatic effect. Rather than confining himself to single subjects in individual panel paintings, like that of the Madonna enthroned, he preferred to work on a more complex and monumental scale. His chief claim to fame is the great cycle of frescoes that fills the walls of the Arena Chapel in Padua. In these panels, which illustrate the lives of the Virgin and of Christ, Giotto used the new naturalistic style he had developed to express an almost inexhaustible range of emotions and dramatic situations. In the scene depicting the meeting of Joachim and Anna, the parents of the Virgin, the couple's deep affection is communicated to us with simplicity and humanity [Plate 13, page 205]. The quiet restraint of this episode is in strong contrast to the cosmic drama of the lamentation over the dead body of Christ [188]. Angels wheel overhead, screaming in grief, while below Mary supports her dead son and stares fiercely into his face. Around her are the other mourners, each a fully characterized individual. If the disciple John is the most passionate in the expression of his sorrow, as he flings his arms out, no less moving are the silent hunched figures in the foreground.

Painting in Siena

Giotto's appeal was direct and immediate, and at Florence his pupils and followers continued to work under his influence for most of the rest of the 14th century, content to explore the implications of the master's ideas rather than devise new styles. As a result, the scene of the most interesting new developments in the generation after Giotto was Siena, where Duccio's influence (although considerable) was much less overpowering. Among Duccio's pupils was Simone Martini (c. 1285–1344), a close friend of Petrarch, who worked for a time at Naples for the French king Robert of Anjou and spent the last years of his life at the papal court at Avignon. In Martini's work we find the first signs of the last great development of Gothic art, the so-called International Style. The elegant courts of France and the French kingdoms of Italy had developed a taste for magnificent colors, fashionable costumes, and rich designs. Although Simone's Sienese background preserved him from the more extreme effects, his *Annunciation* has an insubstantial grace and sophistication that are in strong contrast to the solid realism of Giotto [Plate 14, page 206]. The resplendent robe and mantle of the angel Gabriel and the deep blue dress of the Virgin, edged in gold, produce an impression of great splendor, while their willowy figures approach the ideal of courtly elegance.

If Simone Martini was willing to sacrifice naturalism to surface brilliance, two of his contemporaries

188 Giotto. *Pietà* (*Lamentation*). 1305–1306. Fresco, 7'7" × 7'9" (2.31 × 2.36 m). Arena Chapel, Padua.

in Siena were more interested in applying Giotto's discoveries to their own work. Pietro Lorenzetti was born around 1280, his brother Ambrogio around 1285; both probably died in 1348, the year of the Black Death. The younger brother's best-known work is a huge fresco that decorates an entire wall in Siena's city hall, the Palazzo Pubblico; it was painted between 1338 and 1339 and illustrates the effects of good government on the city of Siena and the surrounding countryside [189]. The streets and buildings, filled with scenes of daily life, are painted with elaborate perspective. The richly dressed merchants with their wives, the craftsmen at work, and the graceful girls who dance in the street preserve for us a vivid picture of a lifestyle that was to be abruptly ended by the Black Death. The scenes in the country, on the other hand, show a world that survives even today in rural Tuscany: peasants at work on farms and in orchards and vineyards [190].

Art in Northern Europe

By the middle of the 14th century the gulf between artists in Italy and those north of the Alps had been reduced considerably. Painters like Simone Martini carried the latest developments in Sienese art to France, were in turn influenced by styles they found there, and subsequently brought them back to Italy. The growing tendency toward a unity of artistic style

above: 189 Ambrogio Lorenzetti. *Effects of Good Government* (scenes in the city). 1337–1339. Fresco. Sala dei Nove, Palazzo Pubblico, Siena. Note the skillful use of perspective.

below: 190 Ambrogio Lorenzetti. *Effects of Good Government*, detail (scenes in the countryside). 1337–1339. Fresco. Sala dei Nove, Palazzo Pubblico, Siena.

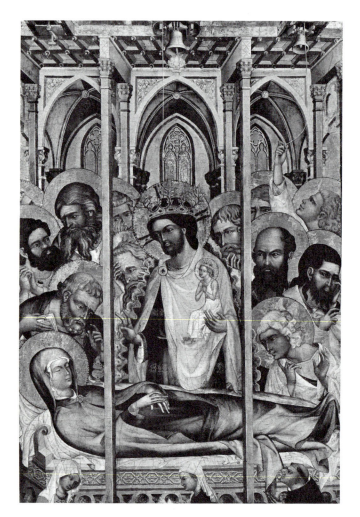

throughout Western Europe was further increased by political developments. When, for example, in 1347 the city of Prague became the residence of the Emperor Charles IV, it became a major art center rivaling even Paris in importance. Around 1360 an unknown Bohemian master working there painted a panel showing the death of the Virgin that combines the rich colors and careful architecture of Sienese painting with the strong emotional impact of northern Gothic art [191]. By the end of the century it was no longer possible to identify an artist's origins from the work. The *Wilton Diptych* was painted in England sometime after 1377 [192]. One of the two panels shows the young king Richard II accompanied by his patron saints, while on the other the Virgin and Child appear before the praying king, accompanied by eleven angels. They probably commemorate Richard's coronation in 1377, since he was eleven years old at the time. The wonderfully delicate yet rich colors and the careful use of shading have no parallel in English art of the period. The artist seems to have been familiar with the work of painters like Duccio and Simone Martini, but the elegance of style and technique are neither simply Italian nor French. The painter of the *Wilton Diptych* was working in a style that can only be called International.

One of the first great centers of the International Style was the court of the Duke of Burgundy at Dijon, where sculptors like the Dutchman Claus

left: 191 Unknown Bohemian Master. *Death of the Virgin*. 1350–1360. Tempera (?) on panel, 39 × 27¾″ (99 × 70 cm). Museum of Fine Arts, Boston (purchased, income of William Francis Warden Fund by exchange).

right: 192 French School. *Richard II Presented to the Virgin and Child by His Patron Saints* (*Wilton Diptych*). c. 1395. Oak panels, each 18 × 11½″ (46 × 29 cm). National Gallery, London (reproduced by courtesy of the Trustees).

193 Claus Sluter.
The Well of Moses. 1395–1406.
Marble, height of figures about 6′
(1.83 m). Chartreuse de
Champmol, Dijon. The horns represent rays of light (a usage based
on a Bible mistranslation).

Sluter and painters like the Flemish Melchior
Broederlam served Duke Philip the Bold, who ruled
there from 1364 to 1404, and his brother John, Duke
of Berry. Sluter (active about 1380–1406) was commissioned to provide sculpture for a monastery
founded near Dijon by Duke Philip, the Chartreuse
de Champmol. His most impressive work there is
the so-called *Well of Moses,* designed for the monastery's cloister [193]. Not really a well at all, it consists
of an elaborate base surrounded by statues of Moses
and five other Old Testament prophets on which
originally stood a crucifixion, now missing. At first
glance the style of the figures is reminiscent of earlier
Gothic statues, like those at Strasbourg, but a more
careful look shows a host of carefully depicted details. In the figure of Moses the textures of the heavy
drapery, the soft beard, and the wrinkled face are
skillfully differentiated, and the expression has the
vividness of a portrait. Equally realistic is the sense of
weight and mass of the body beneath the drapery.

But for the most attractive details in all of late
Gothic art we must turn to the *Très Riches Heures du
Duc de Berry,* an illustrated prayerbook commissioned by Philip the Bold's brother and completed in
1416. It was painted by the Limbourg brothers—Pol,
Hennequin, and Herman. They were Flemish in origin, may have spent some time in Italy, and finally
settled in France. Twelve illuminated pages are included in the book, which illustrate the twelve
months of the year. These pages are filled with an
almost inexhaustible range of details that combine to
depict the changing seasons of the year with poetry
and humanity. On the page representing February
the farm workers warming themselves inside the cot-
tage and the sheep huddling together outside attract
our attention immediately, but the whole painting is
filled with marvelously painted details, from the
steamy breath of the girl on the far right, stumbling

above left: 194 Limbourg Brothers. February page from the *Très Riches Heures du Duc de Berry*. 1416. Manuscript illumination, 8⅞ × 5⅜″ (22 × 14 cm), Musée Condé, Chantilly. The chart above the painting represents the signs of the zodiac for the month of February.

above right: 195 Limbourg Brothers. May page from the *Très Riches Heures du Duc de Berry*. 1416. Manuscript illumination, 8⅞ × 5⅜″ (22 × 14 cm), Musée Condé, Chantilly. The hunters blow their horns, but the courtiers are more interested in the ladies.

back through the snow toward a warm fireside, to the snow-laden roofs of the frozen village in the far distance [194]. In May we move from the world of peasants to that of the aristocracy as a gorgeously dressed procession of lords and ladies rides out in the midst of the fresh greenery of springtime with the roof and turrets of a great castle in the background [195]. The sense of idleness and the delightful conceits of chivalry seem to evoke the world of Chaucer, while stylistically the sense of perspective and elegance of the figures is still another reminder of the influence of Sienese art.

Late Gothic Architecture

As in the case of painting and sculpture, the generally unified style of northern Gothic architecture never really crossed the Alps into Italy. Although some of the most important Italian buildings of the 14th century are generally labeled Gothic, their style is very different from their northern counterparts. Two of the century's greatest churches illustrate this, both begun at Florence at the end of the 13th century—

ing feature does not even date to the 14th century: Its magnificent dome was built by the great early Renaissance architect Filippo Brunelleschi between 1420 and 1436 [196].

More self-consciously Gothic is the Duomo in Milan, begun in 1386, which perhaps makes one feel relieved that Italian architects in general avoided the chief features of northern Gothic style. The immensely elaborate facade, bristling with spires, and the crowded piers of the sides seem to be stuck on rather than integrated into the design. The presence of classical elements in the decorations is a reminder that by the time the Milan Duomo was completed the Renaissance had dawned [197].

Far more attractive are the secular public buildings of the age. The town halls of Florence and Siena, the Palazzo Vecchio (begun 1298) and the Palazzo Pubblico (begun 1288), convey the sense of strong government and civic pride that characterized life in these cities during the Trecento [198]. The towers served the double purpose of providing a lookout over the city and surrounding countryside while they ex-

196 Duomo, Florence. 1296–1436.

Santa Croce around 1295 and the cathedral (better known by the Italian word for cathedral, *duomo*) in 1296. Neither has buttresses and in both most of the wall surface is solid rather than pierced with the typical Gothic windows. The Duomo's most outstand-

198 Palazzo Pubblico, Siena. 1288–1309. The slits around the base of the gallery at the top of the tower were used for firing through on attackers below.

197 Duomo, Milan. Begun 1368. The classical moldings over the windows and doorways of the facade serve as a reminder that the Duomo was not completed until the Renaissance.

199 Choir, Gloucester Cathedral. 1332–1357.
The strong vertical lines show why the style of such buildings is called Perpendicular.

pressed the determination of the city rulers to resist attack. The most beautiful of all government centers is probably the Doge's Palace in Venice, a city where more than anywhere else Gothic architecture took on an almost magical quality of lightness and delicacy. The Doge's Palace (begun about 1345) is composed of a heavy upper story that seems to float on two arcades, the lower a short and sturdy colonnade and the upper composed of tall, slender columns. The effect is enhanced by the way in which the whole building seems suspended in space between sky and sea [Plate 15, page 206].

For a final look at the late Gothic architecture at its most typical we must turn to England, where the style of this period is generally known as Perpendicular. The choir of Gloucester Cathedral, built between 1332 and 1357, illustrates the reason for the label [199]. The vertical line is emphasized, and our eyes are carried up to the roof, where a complex web of ribs decorate the vault. Unlike the ribs in earlier buildings, these serve no structural purpose but have become purely decorative. Their delicacy seems an apt reflection in stone of the graceful precision of the *Wilton Diptych* and the *Très Riches Heures*.

200 A knight playing and singing to a lady,
manuscript illumination illustrating the *Romance of the Rose.*
Flemish, 14 × 10″ (36 × 25 cm). British Library, London.
The romantic interlude is enhanced by the idyllic surroundings;
a walled garden with a fountain playing.

Music: *Ars Nova*

While Giotto was laying the foundations of a new naturalistic style of painting and writers like Petrarch and Chaucer were breathing fresh life into literary forms, composers in France and Italy were changing the style of music. To some extent this was the result of social changes: musicians had begun to break away from their traditional role as servants of the church and to establish themselves as independent creative figures; most of the music that survives from the 14th century is secular. Much of it was written for singers and instrumentalists to perform at home for their own pleasure [200], or for the entertainment of aristocratic audiences like those depicted in the *Très Riches Heures.* The texts composers set to music were increasingly varied; ballads, love songs, even descriptions of contemporary events, in contrast to the religious settings of the preceding century.

As the number of people who enjoyed listening to music and performing it began to grow, so did the range of musical expression. The term generally used to describe the sophisticated musical style of the 14th century is *Ars Nova,* derived from the title of a treatise written by the French composer Philippe de Vitry (1291–1361) around 1325. The work was written in Latin and called *Ars Nova Musicae (The New Art of Music).* Although it is really concerned only with one aspect of composition and describes a new system of rhythmic notation, the term *ars nova* has taken on a wider use and is applied to the new musical style that began to develop in France in the early 14th century and soon spread to Italy.

Its chief characteristic is a much greater richness and complexity of sound than before. This was partly achieved by the use of richer harmonies; thirds and sixths were increasingly employed and the austere sound of parallel fifths, unisons, and octaves was generally avoided. Elaborate rhythmic devices were also introduced, including the method of construction called *isorhythm* (from the Greek word *isos,* which means equal). Isorhythm consisted of allotting to one of the voices in a polyphonic composition a repeated single melody. The voice was also assigned a repeating rhythmical pattern. Since the rhythmical pattern was of a different length from the melody, different notes would be stressed on each repetition. The purpose of this device was twofold: it both created a richness and variety of texture and imparted an element of unity to the piece.

The most famous French composer of this period was Guillaume de Machaut (1304?–1377), whose career spanned the worlds of traditional music and of the *Ars Nova.* He was trained as a priest and took holy orders, but much of his time was spent traveling throughout Europe in the service of the kings of Bohemia, Navarre, and France. Toward the end of his life he retired to Rheims, where he spent his last years as a canon. His most famous composition, and the most famous piece of music from the 14th century, is the *Messe de Notre Dame.* A four-part setting of the Ordinary of the Mass, it is remarkable chiefly for the way in which Machaut gives unity to the five sections that make up the work by creating a similarity of mood and even using a single musical motive that recurs throughout:

Machaut's *Messe de Notre Dame* is the first great example of the entire Ordinary of the Mass set to polyphonic music by a single composer. The Ordinary of the Mass refers to those parts of the Roman

Catholic liturgy that do not change from day to day in contrast to the Propers (the readings from the Gospel or Epistle), which change daily. The parts of the Ordinary are:

1. The *Kyrie Eleison:* the repeated Greek phrases that mean "Lord have mercy on us!" and "Christ have mercy on us!"
2. The *Gloria:* a hymn of praise sung at all masses except funerals and masses during Lent and Advent.
3. The *Credo:* the Profession of Faith sung after the Gospel.
4. The *Sanctus* and *Benedictus:* a short hymn based on the angelic praise found in Isaiah 6, sung at the beginning of the eucharistic prayer.
5. The *Agnus Dei:* the prayer that begins "Lamb of God," sung before Communion.

Machaut's *Messe de Notre Dame,* then, stands at the head of a long tradition of musical composition in which composers use the Ordinary of the Mass to express in their own cultural idiom the timeless truths of the liturgy. Machaut, in that sense, is the ancestor of the Renaissance compositions of Palestrina in the 16th century, the Baroque masses of Johann Sebastian Bach in the 18th century, and the frenetically eclectic contemporary *Mass* of Leonard Bernstein.

Machaut also contributed to another great musical tradition, that of secular song. With the increasing use of polyphony, composers began to turn their attentions to the old troubadour songs and write new settings that combined several different voices. Machaut's polyphonic secular songs took a number of forms. His *ballades* were written for two or three voices, the top voice carrying the melody while the others provided the accompaniment. These lower voices were probably sometimes played by instruments rather than sung. As in the ballades of earlier times the poems consisted of three stanzas, each of seven or eight lines, the last one or two lines being identical in all the stanzas to provide a refrain.

Many of these secular songs, both by Machaut and by other composers, deal with amorous topics, and often are addressed to the singer's beloved. The themes are predictable—the sorrow of parting, as in Machaut's *Au departir de vous*—reproaches for infidelity, protestations of love, and so on, but the freshness of the melodies and Machaut's constant inventiveness prevent them from seeming artificial.

The other important composer of the 14th century was the Italian Francesco Landini (1325–1397), who lived and worked in Florence. Blinded in his youth by smallpox, he was famous in his day as a virtuoso performer on the organ, lute, and flute. Among his surviving works are a number of *madrigals,* a form of word settings involving two or three verses set to the same music and separated by a refrain set to different music. In addition, he wrote a large number of *ballate* (ballads) including many for solo voice and two accompanying instruments. The vocal lines are often elaborate, and Landini makes use of rich, sonorous harmonies. But in the case of these and other works of the period, there is no specification of the instruments intended, or, indeed, of the general performance style Landini would have expected [201]. We know from contemporary accounts that in some cases performers would have changed the written notes by sharpening or flattening them, following the convention of the day. This practice of making

201 Music and musicians, manuscript illumination illustrating a treatise, *De Musica.* 14th century. Biblioteca Nazionale, Naples. Some of the instruments of the time are shown. The goddess Music is at center, playing a small organ. Grouped around her are musicians with stringed instruments, percussion, and wind instruments. The inset shows David, founder of church music, plucking a psaltery.

sounds other than those on the page was called *musica ficta* (fictitious music), but no systematic description of the rules followed has been handed down to us. As a result, modern editors and performers often have only their own historical research and instincts to guide them. Although the *Ars Nova* of the 14th century marks a major development in the history of music, our knowledge of it is far from complete.

The 14th century was a time of stark contrast between the horrors of natural and social disasters and the flowering of artistic and cultural movements that were the harbingers of the 15th-century Renaissance in Italy. Chaucer, as we have seen, died in 1400, the year that may be taken as the close of the medieval period. By that time, some of the prime figures of the Italian Renaissance—Donatello, Fra Angelico, and Ghiberti—were already in their teens. The great outburst of cultural activity that was to mark Florence in the 15th century was near, even though it would not make a definite impact on England until the end of the century. The calamitous 14th century was a costly seedbed for rebirth and human renewal.

Questions for Further Discussion

1. Boccaccio's *Decameron* was set in plague conditions. Can you think of settings for a contemporary *Decameron* after a great modern disaster? What kind of stories would be told and by whom?
2. Petrarch's sonnets were love poems in honor of Laura. They expressed a certain set of sentiments about love. What are the typical love sentiments and conventions, say, of contemporary love lyrics in music? Do they differ widely from the sentiments of Petrarch?
3. Chaucer's pilgrims were meant to be representative of medieval society. If Chaucer were writing today what representative types would he include so as to reflect a cross section of our society?
4. While there were some continuing links, Italian painting after Giotto begins to differ noticeably from painting in the north. What are the most apparent differences in style and technique?
5. Compare the architecture of Chartres Cathedral and a 14th-century public building like Siena's Palazzo Pubblico. What differences in function can you detect just by looking at them from the outside?

	GENERAL EVENTS	LITERATURE & PHILOSOPHY	ART

1400

FLORENTINE RENAISSANCE

The First Phase

General Events

15th cent. Florence center of European banking system

1417 Council of Constance ends "Great Schism"

1432 Florentines defeat Sienese at San Romano

Art

1401 Competition for North Doors of Florence Baptistery won by Ghiberti's *Sacrifice of Isaac*

1403 Ghiberti begins Baptistery doors; Brunelleschi, Donatello study Roman ruins

c. 1416-1417 Donatello, *Saint George*

1423 Fabriano, *The Adoration of the Magi,* International Style altarpiece

1425 Masaccio begins frescoes for Brancacci Chapel, Santa Maria del Carmine, Florence; *The Tribute Money* (1425), *Expulsion from the Garden* (c. 1425)

c. 1425-c. 1452 Ghiberti sculpts panels for East Doors of Florence Baptistery; *The Story of Jacob and Esau* (1435)

Use of linear perspective to create three-dimensional space; naturalistic rendering of figures; return to classical ideals of beauty and proportion: Masaccio, *The Trinity,* Santa Maria Novella, Florence (c. 1428)

c. 1430-1432 Donatello, *David,* first free-standing nude since antiquity

1434

The Medici Era

General Events

1434 Cosimo de' Medici becomes de facto ruler of Florence

1439-1442 Ecumenical Council of Florence deals with proposed union of Greek and Roman churches

1453 Fall of Constantinople to Turks; scholarly refugees bring Greek manuscripts to Italy

1464 Piero de' Medici takes power in Florence after death of Cosimo

1469 Lorenzo de' Medici rules city after death of Piero

1478 Pazzi conspiracy against the Medici fails

1489 Savonarola begins sermons against Florentine immorality

1492 Death of Lorenzo de' Medici

Literature & Philosophy

1446-1450 Gutenberg invents movable printing type

1456 *Gutenberg Bible* printed at Mainz

1462 Cosimo de' Medici founds Platonic Academy in Florence, headed by Marsilio Ficino

1465 First Italian printing press, at Subiaco

1470-1527 Height of humanist learning

1475 *Recuyell of the Historyes of Troye,* printed by William Caxton, first book published in English

c. 1476-1477 Lorenzo de' Medici begins *Comento ad Alcuni Sonetti*

1482 Ficino, *Theologia Platonica*

1486 Pico della Mirandola, *Oration on the Dignity of Man*

1490 Lorenzo de' Medici, *The Song of Bacchus*

1491 Lorenzo de' Medici, *Laudi*

Art

1434 Jan Van Eyck, *Giovanni Arnolfini and His Bride*

1445-1450 Fra Angelico, *Annunciation,* fresco for Convent of San Marco, Florence

c. 1455 Donatello, *Mary Magdalene;* Uccello, *Battle of San Romano*

1459-1463 Gozzoli, *The Journey of the Magi*

c. 1467-1483 Leonardo works in Florence

1475 The Medici commission Botticelli's *Adoration of the Magi* for Santa Maria Novella

1478-c. 1482 Botticelli, *La Primavera, The Birth of Venus, Pallas and the Centaur*

c. 1489 Michelangelo begins studies in Lorenzo's sculpture garden; *Madonna of the Stairs* (1489-1492)

1494

ROMAN RENAISSANCE

General Events

1494 Medici faction in exile; Savonarola becomes de facto ruler of Florence; Charles VIII of France invades Italy, beginning foreign invasions

1498 Savonarola burned at stake by order of Pope

Literature & Philosophy

c. 1494 Aldus Manutius establishes Aldine Press in Venice

1496 Burning of books inspired by Savonarola

1502 Erasmus, *Enchiridion Militis Christiani*

Art

1498-1499 Michelangelo, *Pietà*

late 15th-early 16th cent. Leonardo, *Notebooks*

c. 1495-1498 Leonardo, *Last Supper*

c. 1496 Botticelli burns some of his work in response to Savonarola's sermons

1501-1504 Michelangelo, *David*

1503

c. 1503-1505 Leonardo, *Mona Lisa*

1512 Medici power restored in Florence; Machiavelli exiled

1506 Erasmus travels to Italy

1509 Erasmus, *The Praise of Folly*

1513 Machiavelli, *The Prince*

1516 Erasmus, *Greek New Testament*

1506 Ancient *Laocoön* sculpture discovered

1520

10
The Early Renaissance

1417-1420 Brunelleschi designs and begins construction of Florence Cathedral dome (completed 1436)

1419-1426 Brunelleschi, Foundling Hospital

Use of classical order and proportion to achieve rational harmony of elements; Brunelleschi, Pazzi Chapel, Santa Croce, Florence (1430-1433)

1437-1452 Michelozzo, Convent of San Marco, Florence

1444-1459 Michelozzo, Palazzo Medici-Riccardi, Florence

c. 1450-1500 Johannes Ockeghem, motets, chansons, masses; *Missa pro Defunctis,* earliest known polyphonic requiem mass

1479-1492 Heinrich Isaac, court composer to Medici family and organist and choirmaster at Florence Cathedral, sets Lorenzo's poems to music

The Centrality of Florence

Except for January and February, when the surrounding hills are snow-flecked and the citizens sip *espressos* perhaps laced with brandy to ward off the winter chill, Florence is awash with tourists. After Easter, the crowd becomes a flood. Europeans, Asians, and Americans crowd the narrow streets, line up for museums, or sit amid a babble of languages on the steps of the Cathedral watching each other. From that Cathedral, the center of the city, one can walk in ten minutes to enough museums and churches to overwhelm even the most zealous lover of Renaissance painting, Donatello's sculpture, or the many monuments to Michelangelo's many-sided genius.

Why did this rather small city spread out on the banks of the Arno River inherit such a wealth of architecture, painting, and sculpture? The reason is that Florence is where the 15th-century *Renaissance* took place. It was this Renaissance that motivated much of the city's rich artistic activity. Renaissance means *rebirth;* it was in Florence that artists and intellectuals, inspired by their study of the Greek and Roman classics, began to make a new art modeled on the rich past of Rome and Athens.

It is true that classical culture had been known, at least in a disjointed form, throughout the Middle Ages. The medieval church and state themselves were deeply indebted to Roman law, literature, and artistic culture. What was peculiar about the rebirth of interest in classical culture in the 15th century was not that it utilized the ancient Roman and Greek past but that it set this past up as a model against which all artistic and literary work is judged. Long a source of culture, classical civilization now became a criterion for measuring human cultural activity. Humanists of the 15th century were convinced that by deep and careful study the classics of Greece and Rome could be used as revolutionary tools to restructure politics, reinterpret architecture, set new standards for art, increase both the intellectual and moral powers of the educated, and, in general, refurbish the older institutions that they had inherited from the near past.

The First Phase: Masaccio, Ghiberti, and Brunelleschi

At the beginning of the 15th century Florence had every reason for being a proud city. It stood on the main road connecting Rome with the north. Its language—known at the time as the Tuscan dialect or the Tuscan idiom—was the strongest and most developed of the Italian dialects; its linguistic power had been demonstrated more than a century earlier by Dante Alighieri and his literary successors, Petrarch and Boccaccio. The twelve great *Arti* or trade guilds of Florence were commercially important for the city; in addition, representatives of the seven senior guilds formed the body of magistrates that ruled the city from the fortress-like town hall, the Palazzo Vecchio. This "representative" government, limited though it was to the prosperous guilds, preserved Florence from the rise of the terrible city tyrants who plagued so many other Italian cities.

Florence had been one of the centers of the wool trade since the late Middle Ages. In the 15th century it was also the center of the European banking system. In fact, our modern banks (the word *bank* is from the Italian *banco*, which means a counter or table—the place where money is exchanged) and their systems of handling money are based largely on practices developed by the Florentines. They devised advanced accounting methods, letters of credit, and a system of checks; they were the first to emphasize the importance of a stable monetary system. The gold *florin* minted in Florence was the standard coin in European commerce for centuries.

Great Florentine banking families made and lost fortunes in trading and banking. These families—the Strozzi, Bardi, Tornabuoni, Pazzi, and Medici—were justly famous in their own time. They, in turn, were justly proud of their wealth and their city. The visitor to Florence today walks on streets named for these families and past palaces built for them. They combined a steady sense of business conservatism with an adventuresome pursuit of wealth and fame. No great Florentine banker would have thought it odd that one of this group began his will with the words "In the name of God and profit. Amen."

For all their renown and wealth, it was not the bankers who really gave Florence its lasting fame. By some mysterious stroke of good fortune Florence and its immediate surroundings produced, in the 15th century, a group of artists who revolutionized Western art to such an extent that later historians refer to the period as a time of rebirth in the arts.

The character of this revolutionary change in art is not easy to define, but we can evolve a partial definition by comparing two early 15th-century Florentine paintings. Sometime before 1423 a wealthy Florentine banker, Palla Strozzi, commissioned Gentile da Fabriano (c. 1385–1427) to paint an altarpiece for the Florentine church of Santa Trinità. The *Adoration of the Magi* [202], completed in 1423, is ornately framed in the style of Gothic art, with evidence of influences

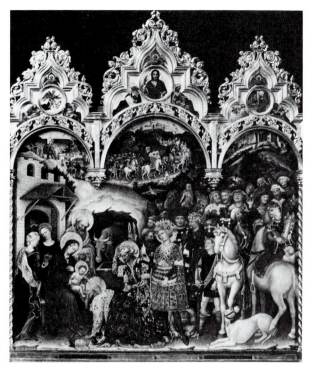

202 Gentile da Fabriano. *Adoration of the Magi*. 1423. Gold leaf and tempera on wood, 9'10" × 9'3" (3.02 × 2.81 m). Uffizi, Florence. This painting has the flat two-dimensional quality of most Byzantine and medieval painting.

the illusionistically painted architectural framing of the Trinity. The character of the architecture is Roman, its barrel vaulting and coffering sustained by Corinthian columns and pilasters. At the sides, and slightly lower, Mary looks out at the viewer, while Saint John looks at Mary. At the edge of the scene, members of the donor family kneel in profile. The entire scene has an intense geometrical clarity based on a pyramid, with God at the apex of the triangle formed with the line of donors and saints at the length of the base line.

In this single fresco appear many of the characteristics of Florentine Renaissance painting that mark it off from earlier painting styles: clarity of line, a concern for mathematically precise perspective, close observation of "real people," concern for psychological states, and an uncluttered arrangement that rejects the earlier tendency in painting to produce crowded scenes to fill up all the available space.

203 Masaccio. *The Holy Trinity*. 1428. Fresco, 21'10½" × 10'5" (6.66 × 3.19 m). Santa Maria Novella, Florence. The Holy Spirit is symbolized by the dove with outstretched wings between the heads of God and Christ.

from the miniature painting of Northern Europe and from the older painting tradition of Italy itself. The altarpiece is in the style called "International" because it spread far beyond the area of its origins in France. This style reflects the old-fashioned tendency to fill up the spaces of the canvas, to employ the brightest colors on the palette, to use gold lavishly for halos and in the framing, and to ignore any proportion between the characters and the space they occupy. Gentile's altarpiece is, in fact, a strikingly beautiful painting that testifies to the lush possibilities of the conservative International Gothic style.

Only about five years later Tommaso Guidi (1401–1428), known as Masaccio, who was the precocious genius of Florentine painting, painted a fresco, *The Holy Trinity* [203], for the Dominican Church of Santa Maria Novella in Florence that is strikingly different from the kind of painting that was done by Gentile. The most apparent difference is in the utilization of space. In *The Holy Trinity* the central figures of God the Father, the Holy Spirit, and the crucified Christ seem to stand in the foreground of deep three-dimensional space created by

204 Masaccio. *The Tribute Money*. c. 1425. Fresco, 8′4″ × 19′ (2.54 × 5.9 m).
Brancacci Chapel, Santa Maria del Carmine, Florence.

Masaccio's earlier frescoes in the Brancacci Chapel of the Church of the Carmine in Florence also show his revolutionizing style. His 1425 fresco called *The Tribute Money* [204] reflects his concern with realistic depiction of human beings. The central scene portrays Christ telling Peter that he can find the tax money for the temple in the mouth of a fish; at the left Peter recovers the coin of tribute; at the right he makes the tribute payment (Matthew 17:24–27). The clusters of figures surrounding Christ reflect a faithfulness to observed humanity that must have been startling to Masaccio's contemporaries, who had never seen anything quite like that in painting. The figures are in a space made believable by the receding lines of the buildings to the right. The fresco of the expulsion of Adam and Eve [205] in the same chapel shows not only realism in the figures but also a profound sense of human emotions: the shame and dismay of the first human beings as they are driven from the Garden of Paradise.

The revolutionary character of Masaccio's work was recognized in his own time. His influence on any number of Florentine painters who worked later in the century is clear. Two generations after Masaccio's death the young Michelangelo often crossed the Arno to sketch the frescoes in the Brancacci chapel. In the next century Giorgio Vasari (1511–1574) in his *Lives of the Artists* would judge Masaccio's influence as basic and crucial: "The superb Masaccio . . . adopted a new manner for his heads, his draperies, buildings, and nudes, his colours, and foreshorten-

ing. He thus brought into existence the modern style which, beginning during his period, has been employed by all of our artists down to the present day. . . ."

The innovative character of 15th-century art was not limited to painting. Significant changes were occurring in sculpture and architecture as well. A famous competition was announced in 1401 for the right to decorate the doors of the Florence Baptistery, dedicated to Saint John the Baptist and a focal point of Florentine life. The baptistery is an ancient octagonal Romanesque building, which in the 15th century had such a reputation for antiquity that some thought it had originally been a Roman temple. Vasari tells us that an eminent group of artists including Lorenzo Ghiberti (1378–1455) and Filippo Brunelleschi (1377–1466) were among the competitors. Ghiberti won.

A comparison of Brunelleschi's and Ghiberti's panels shows the differences between the two and allows us to infer the criteria used to judge the winner. The assigned subject for the competition was Abraham's sacrifice of Isaac (Genesis 22:1–14). Brunelleschi's version [206] has a certain vigor, but it is a busy and crowded composition. The figures of the servants spill out of the four-leaf or quatrefoil frame while the major figures (the ram, the angel, and the two principals) are in flattened two-dimensional profile with little background space.

By contrast, Ghiberti's panel on the same subject [207] is divided dramatically by a slashing diagonal

206 Filippo Brunelleschi. *The Sacrifice of Isaac.* 1401.
Gilt bronze, 21 × 17½" (53 × 44 cm).
Museo Nazionale del Bargello, Florence.

207 Lorenzo Ghiberti. *The Sacrifice of Isaac.* 1401.
Gilt bronze, 21 × 17½" (53 × 44 cm).
Museo Nazionale del Bargello, Florence. The winning panel.

205 Masaccio. *The Expulsion from the Garden.* c. 1427. Fresco,
6'6" × 2'9" (1.98 × .84 m). Brancacci Chapel, Santa Maria del
Carmine, Florence. Masaccio manages to convey not only deep
psychological distress but also a sense of movement; the man
and woman are actually walking out of the Garden of Paradise.

line separating the two sets of actors into clearly designated planes of action. The drastically foreshortened angel appears to be flying into the scene from deep space. Furthermore, as a close examination of the cast shows, Ghiberti's panel is a technical tour de force. Except for the figure of Isaac and Abraham's left foot (and part of the rock it rests on), the entire scene was cast as a single unit. Demonstrating his strong background as a goldsmith, Ghiberti finely modeled and skillfully finished his panel. It is a piece of fierce sentiment, mathematical perspective, and exquisite work.

Ghiberti worked for almost a quarter of a century on the North Doors, completing twenty panels. Just as he was finishing, the Cathedral authorities commissioned him in 1425 to execute another set of panels for the East Doors, those facing the Cathedral itself. This commission occupied the next quarter of a century (from roughly 1425 to 1452 or 1453), and the results of these labors were so striking that Michelan-

right: 208 Lorenzo Ghiberti. East Doors ("Gates of Paradise") of the Baptistery of Florence Cathedral. 1425–1452. Gilt bronze, height 17' (5.18 m).

below left: 209 Florence Cathedral in 1390. This is an artist's reconstruction of what the Cathedral looked like when Brunelleschi started work. *1* Façade and side wall; *2* gallery; *3* circular windows; *4, 5* first and second piers; *6* first major arch; *7* excavations for sacristy and tribune piers.

below right: 210 Florence Cathedral in 1418. *1* Buttressing; *2* completed tambour (drum); *3* side tribunes begun; *4* armature under construction; *5* vaulting under construction; *6* sacristy piers.

gelo later in the century said Ghiberti's East Doors were not unworthy to be called the "Gates of Paradise," and so they are often called today.

The panels of the East Doors [208] were radically different in style and composition from the North Door panels. The Gothic style quatrefoils were replaced by more classically severe rectangular frames. The complete set of panels was framed, in turn, by a series of portrait busts of prophets and sybils.

Although Filippo Brunelleschi lost to Ghiberti in the sculpture competition of 1401, he made a major contribution to this early developmental phase of Renaissance art in another area, architecture. During his stay in Rome, where he had gone with the sculptor Donatello after the competition, he made a study of Roman architectural monuments. In fact, Vasari records that Brunelleschi and Donatello were reputed to be treasure hunters because of their incessant prowlings amid the ruins of the Roman Forum. It was these intensive studies, together with his own intuitive genius, that gave Brunelleschi an idea for solving a problem then thought insoluble: how to construct the dome for the still unfinished Cathedral of Saint Mary of the Flower in Florence.

The Cathedral of Florence had been built by Arnolfo di Cambio in the previous century, over the remains of the older church of Santa Reparata. In the early 15th century, however, the church was still unfinished, although the nave was already complete [209]. No one had quite figured out how to span the great area without immense buttresses on the outside and supporting armatures on the inside. Brunelleschi worked on this problem between 1417 and 1420, trying, simultaneously, to solve the technical aspects of doming the building and convincing the skeptical cathedral overseers that it could be done. He eventually won the day, but work on the dome was not completed until 1436.

His solution, briefly, was to combine the buttressing methods of the Gothic cathedral and classical vaulting techniques that he had mastered by his careful study of the Roman Pantheon and other buildings from antiquity. By putting a smaller dome within the larger dome to support the greater weight of the outside dome, he could not only cover the great *tambour* or drum [210] but also free the inside of the dome from any need for elaborate armatures or supporting structures. This dome was strong enough to support the lantern that eventually crowned the whole construction. It was a breathtaking technical achievement, as well as an aesthetic success, as any person viewing Florence from the surrounding hills can testify. Years later, writing about his own work on the dome of Saint Peter's in the Vatican, Michelangelo

211 Filippo Brunelleschi. Foundling Hospital, Florence. 1419–1426. The glazed terra cotta medallions are from the Della Robbia workshop.

had Brunelleschi's dome in mind when he said: "I will create your sister; bigger but no more beautiful."

The technical brilliance of Brunelleschi's dome cannot be overpraised, but his real architectural achievement lies in his designs for buildings that make a break with older forms of architecture. His Foundling Hospital [211] with its open columned loggias and their graceful Corinthian pillars, arches, and entablature, is, despite its seeming simplicity, a highly intricate work, its proportions calculated with mathematical rigor. The building is an open departure from the heaviness of the Romanesque so common in the area of Tuscany as well as a rejection of the overly elaborate Gothic exteriors.

This same concern with classical order, proportion, and serenity can be seen in Brunelleschi's finest work, the chapel he designed for the Pazzi family next to the Franciscan Church of Santa Croce in Flor-

212 Filippo Brunelleschi. Pazzi Chapel, Florence. 1430–1433.

ence [212]. Its exterior evokes Roman austerity with its delicate columns, severe facade, and small dome reminiscent of the lines of Rome's Pantheon.

In this very brief look at three different art forms and artists in the early 15th century certain recurring words and themes give, as it were, a rough descriptive outline of what the Florentine Renaissance style reflects: a concern with, and the technical ability to handle, space and volume in a believable way; a studious approach to models of art from ancient Rome; a departure from the more ethereal mode of medieval otherworldliness to a greater concern for human realism. The Florentine artistic temperament leaped over its medieval heritage (although not completely) in order to reaffirm what it considered the classical ideal of ancient Rome and Greece.

The Medici Era

The Florentine Republic was governed by representatives of the major trade guilds. This control by a very select group of people who represented commercial power and wealth inevitably led to domination by the most wealthy of the group. From 1434 until 1492 Florence was under the control of one family: the Medici.

The Medici family had old, though up to then undistinguished, roots in the countryside around Florence. Their prosperity in the 15th century rested mainly on their immense banking fortune. By the middle of that century Medici branch banks existed in London, Naples, Cologne, Geneva, Lyons, Basle, Avignon, Bruges, Antwerp, Lübeck, Bologna, Rome, Pisa, and Venice. The great Flemish painting by Jan van Eyck, *Giovanni Arnolfini and His Bride* [213], in fact, commemorates van Eyck's witnessing of the marriage of this Florentine representative of the Medici bank in 1434 in Bruges. While it is more usual to look at the painting because of its exquisite technique, its rich symbolism, and its almost microscopic concern for detail, it is also profitable to view it sociologically as a testimony to how far the influence of the Medici extended.

Cosimo de' Medici

Cosimo de' Medici (de facto ruler of Florence from 1434 to 1464) was an astute banker and a highly cultivated man of letters. His closest friends were professional humanists, collectors of books, and patrons of the arts. Cosimo himself spent vast sums on the collecting and copying of ancient manuscripts. He had his copyists work in a neat cursive hand that would be the later model for the form of letters we call *italic*. His collection of books (together with those added by later members of his family) formed the core of the great humanist collection housed in the Laurentian library in Florence.

Although Cosimo never mastered Greek to any degree, he was intensely interested in Greek philosophy and literature. He financed the chair of Greek at the *Studium* of Florence. When Greek prelates visited Florence during the ecumenical council held in 1439 (the council sought a union between the Greek and Latin Churches), Cosimo took the opportunity to seek out scholars in the retinue of the prelates from Constantinople. He was particularly struck with the

brilliance of Genisthos Plethon (c. 1355–1452), who lectured on Plato. Cosimo persuaded Plethon to remain in the city to continue his lectures.

Cosimo's most significant contribution to the advancement of Greek studies was the foundation and endowment of an academy for the study of Plato. For years Cosimo and his heirs supported a priest, Marsilio Ficino, in order to allow him to translate and comment on the works of Plato. In the course of his long life (he died in 1499), Ficino translated into Latin all of Plato, Plotinus, and other platonic thinkers. He wrote his own compendium of platonism called the *Theologia Platonica*. These translations and commentaries had an immense influence on art and intellectual life in Italy and beyond the Alps.

Cosimo often joined his friends at a suburban villa to discuss Plato under the tutelage of Ficino. This elite group embraced Plato's ideas of striving for the ideal good and persistently searching for truth and beauty. This idealism became an important strain in Florentine culture. Ficino managed to combine his study of Plato with his own understanding of Christianity. It was Ficino who coined the term "Platonic love"—the spiritual bond between two persons who were joined together in the contemplative search for the true, the good, and the beautiful. Cosimo, a pious man in his own right, found great consolation in this Christian platonism of Ficino. "Come and join me as soon as you possibly can and be sure to bring with you Plato's treatise *On the Sovereign Good*," Cosimo once wrote his protégé; "there is no pursuit to which I would devote myself more zealously than the pursuit of truth. Come then and bring with you the lyre of Orpheus."

Cosimo, a fiercely patriotic Florentine, known to his contemporaries as *Pater Patriae* (Father of the Homeland), lavished his funds on art projects to enhance the beauty of the city, while, at the same time, glorifying his family name and atoning for his sins, especially usury, by acts of generous charity. He befriended and supported many artists. He was a very close friend and financial supporter of the greatest Florentine sculptor of the first half of the 15th century, Donato di Niccoló di Betto Bardi (1386–1466), known as Donatello. Donatello was an eccentric genius who cared for little besides his work; it was said that he left his fees in a basket in his studio for the free use of his apprentices or whoever else might be in need.

Even today a leisurely stroll around the historic center of Florence can in a short time give an idea of the tremendous range of Donatello's imaginative and artistic versatility. One need only compare his early

213 Jan van Eyck. *Giovanni Arnolfini and His Bride*. 1434. Oil on panel, 33 × 22½″ (83.82 × 57.15 cm). National Gallery, London (reproduced by courtesy of the Trustees). The artist painted himself standing in a doorway, reflected in the mirror. The words on the wall read "Jan van Eyck was here."

214 Donatello. *Saint George*. 1416–1417. Marble, height 6′5″ (1.96 m). Museo Nazionale
del Bargello, Florence. As the statue originally stood, the saint grasped a spear in his right hand.

right: 215 Donatello. *David*. c. 1430–1432. Bronze, height 5′2½″ (1.58 m). Museo Nazionale del
Bargello, Florence. The killing of Goliath is shown in this book at three different stages.
Michelangelo's *David* is calm as he prepares to attack (figure 227, page 242).
Bernini's *David* is determined, exerting all his strength during the attack. (figure 284, page 304).
Donatello's *David* is again calm as he seems to reflect on his victory, holding the sword
he has used to cut off the giant's head and resting one foot on the severed head itself.

Saint George [214], fiercely tense and classically severe, with the later bronze *David* [215]. The *Saint
George* is a niche sculpture originally executed for the
church of Orsanmichele, while the *David* is meant to
be seen from all sides. The *David,* a near lifesize figure, is the first freestanding statue of a nude figure
sculpted since Roman antiquity. It also marks a definite step in Renaissance taste: In spite of its subject, it

is more clearly "pagan" than biblical in spirit. The
sculptor obviously wanted to show the beauty of
form of this adolescent male clothed only in carefully
fashioned military leg armor and a Tuscan shepherd's
hat. The figure was most likely made for a garden.
Some scholars have speculated that the commission
was from Cosimo himself, although clear documentary proof is lacking.

Donatello's over-lifesize wooden figure of Mary Magdalene [216] seems light years away from the spirit of *David*. Carved around 1455, it shows the Magdalene as an ancient penitent, ravaged by time and her own life of penance. The viewer is asked, mentally, to compare this older woman with the younger sinner described in the Bible. The statue, then, is a profound meditation on the vanity of life, a theme lingering in Florentine culture from its medieval past, and, at the same time, a hymn to the penitential spirit that made the Magdalene a saint.

Cosimo de' Medici had a particular fondness for the Dominican Convent of San Marco in Florence. In 1437 he asked Michelozzo, the architect who designed the Medici palace in Florence, to rebuild the convent for the friars. One of the Dominicans who lived there was a painter of established reputation, Fra Angelico (1387–1455). When Michelozzo's renovations were done, Fra Angelico decorated many of the convent walls and most of the cells of the friars with paintings, executing many of these works under the watchful eye of Cosimo, who stayed regularly at the convent. Fra Angelico's famous *Annunciation* fresco [217] shows his indebtedness to the artistic tradition of Masaccio: the use of architecture to frame space; a sense of realism and drama; and a close observation of the actual world.

Another painter who enjoyed the Medici largesse was Paolo Uccello (1397–1475), who did a series of three paintings for the Medici palace commemorating the earlier battle of San Romano (1432) in which the Florentines defeated the Sienese. The paintings (now dispersed to museums in London, Florence,

above: 216 Donatello. *Saint Mary Magdalene*. 1455. Polychromed wood, height 6'2" (1.88 m). Museo dell' Opera del Duomo, Florence. Only traces of the original polychrome remain. This statue was damaged in the flood of 1966 but has been completely cleaned and restored.

left: 217 Fra Angelico. *Annunciation*. 1445–1450. Fresco, 7'6" × 10'5" (2.29 × 3.18 m). Monastery of San Marco, Florence. Botanists are able to identify the flowers in the garden.

and Paris) show Uccello's intense fascination with perspective [218]. The scenes are marked by slashing lines, foreshortened animals, receding backgrounds, and seemingly cluttered landscapes filled with figures of different proportions. When the three paintings were together as a unit they gave a panoramic sweep of the battle running across 34 feet (10.3 meters) of the wall space.

Cosimo's last years were racked with chronic illness and depression brought on by the premature deaths of his son Giovanni and a favorite grandson, as well as the physical weakness of his other son, Piero. Toward the end of his life Cosimo's wife once found him in his study with his eyes closed. She asked him why he sat in that fashion. "To get them accustomed to it," he replied. Cosimo de' Medici died on August 1, 1464. His position as head of the family and as first citizen of the city was taken by his son Piero, called "the Gouty" in reference to an affliction of gout from which he suffered all his life.

Piero de' Medici

Piero's control over the city lasted only five years. It was a time beset by much political turmoil as well as continued artistic activity. Piero continued to support his father's old friend Donatello and maintained

his patronage of Ficino's platonic labors and his generous support of both religious and civic art and architecture.

One new painter who came under the care of Piero was Alessandro di Mariano dei Filipepi (1444–1510), known more familiarly as Sandro Botticelli. Botticelli earlier had been an apprentice of the painter Fra Filippo Lippi (c. 1406–1469), but it was Piero and his aristocratic wife Lucrezia Tornabuoni (a highly cultivated woman who was a religious poet) who took Botticelli into their home and treated him as a member of the family. Botticelli stayed closely allied with the Medici for decades.

One tribute to the Medici was Botticelli's painting the *Adoration of the Magi* [219], a work commissioned for the Florentine church of Santa Maria Novella. The Magi are shown as three generations of the Medici family; there are also portraits of Lorenzo and Giuliano, the sons of Piero. The painting was paid for by a friend of the Medici family. Many scholars think it was a votive offering to the church in thanksgiving for the safety of the family during the political turmoil of 1466.

The theme of the Magi was a favorite of the Medici. They regularly took part in the pageants in the streets of Florence celebrating the Three Kings on the feast of the Epiphany (January 6). It is for that reason,

218 Paolo Uccello. *The Rout of San Romano: The Unhorsing of Bernardino della Carda.* 1455. Tempera on wood, 6′ × 10′7″ (1.83 × 3.22 m). Uffizi, Florence.

one presumes, that Piero commissioned a fresco of that scene for the chapel of his own palace. The painter was Benozzo Gozzoli (1420–1495), once an apprentice of Fra Angelico. Benozzo produced an opulent scene filled with personages of Oriental splendor modeled on the Greek scholars who had come to Florence during the ecumenical council and who stayed on to teach Greek. The fresco also included some contemporary portraits, including one of the artist himself [220].

Lorenzo the Magnificent

Piero de' Medici died in 1469. The mantle of power settled on the shoulders of his son Lorenzo, who accepted the responsibility with pragmatic resignation, since, as he said, "It bodes ill for any wealthy man in Florence who doesn't control political power." Lorenzo, a rather ugly man with a high raspy voice, became the most illustrious of the family; in his own day he was known as "the magnificent"—Lorenzo il Magnifico. His accomplishments were so many and varied that the last half of the 15th century in Florence is often called the "Laurentian Era."

Lorenzo continued the family tradition of art patronage by supporting various projects and by adding to the Medici collection of ancient gems, other

220 Benozzo Gozzoli. *The Journey of the Magi,* detail. 1459. Fresco, entire work, length 12′4½″ (3.77 m). Chapel, Medici Palace, Florence. The horseman, representing one of the Magi, is an idealized portrait of the Byzantine emperor John VII Paleologus, who visited Florence at the invitation of Cosimo de' Medici for the ecumenical council in 1439.

antiquities, and books. He was also more directly involved in the arts. Lorenzo was an accomplished poet, but his reputation as a political and social leader has made us forget that he was an important contrib-

219 Sandro Botticelli. *Adoration of the Magi.* 1475. Tempera on wood, 3′7½″ × 4′4¾″ (1.1 × 1.34 m). Uffizi, Florence. Cosimo de' Medici kneels at the Virgin's feet; Lorenzo is at left in the foreground; Giuliano is at the right against the wall. The figure in the right foreground is thought to be the artist.

utor to the development of vernacular Italian poetry. He continued the sonnet tradition begun by Petrarch. One of his most ambitious projects—done in conscious imitation of Dante's *Vita Nuova*—was a long work that alternated his own sonnets with extended prose commentaries; this was the *Comento ad alcuni sonetti* (*A Commentary on Some Sonnets,* begun around 1476–1477). In addition to this very ambitious work, Lorenzo wrote hunting songs, poems for the carnival season, religious poetry, and occasional pieces of burlesque poems with a cheerfully bawdy tone to them.

The poem for which Lorenzo is best known is "The Song of Bacchus." Written in 1490, its opening stanzas echo the old Roman dictum of living for the present because of the shortness of life and the uncertainty of the future.

Lorenzo de' Medici
THE SONG OF BACCHUS

How beautiful is youth,
That flees so fleetingly by.
Let him be who chases joy
For tomorrow there is no certainty.

Look at Bacchus and Ariadne
So beautiful and much in love.
Since deceitful time flees
They are always happy.

Joyful little satyrs
of the nymphs enamored,
In every cave and glade
Have set traps by the hundred;
Now, by Bacchus intoxicated,
Dance and leap without end.

Let him be who chases joy
For tomorrow there is no certainty.

Lorenzo's interests in learning were deep. He had been tutored as a youth by Ficino and as an adult he continued the habit of spending evenings with an elite group of friends and Ficino. He often took with him his friend Botticelli as well as a young sculptor who worked in a Medici-sponsored sculpture garden, Michelangelo Buonarroti.

The Laurentian patronage of learning was extensive. Lorenzo contributed the funds necessary to rebuild the university of Pisa and designated it the principal university of Tuscany (Galileo taught there in the next century). He continued to underwrite the study of Greek at the *Studium* of Florence.

The Greek faculty at Florence attracted students from all over Europe. Indeed, this center was a principal means by which Greek learning was exported to the rest of Europe, especially to countries beyond the Alps. English scholars like Thomas Linacre, John

Colet, and William Grocyn came to Florence to study Greek and other classic disciplines. Linacre was later to gain fame as a physician and founder of England's Royal College of Physicians. Grocyn returned to England to found the chair of Greek at Oxford. Colet used his training to become a biblical scholar and a founder of Saint Paul's School in London. The two greatest French humanists of the 16th century had, as young men, come under the influence of Greek learning from Italy. Guillaume Budé (died 1540) founded, under the patronage of the French kings, a library at Fontainebleau that was the beginning of the Bibliothèque Nationale of Paris. He also founded the Collège de France, still the most prestigious center of higher learning in France. Jacques Lefèvre d' Étaples had also studied in Florence and became the greatest intellectual church reformer of 16th-century France.

Lorenzo was less interested in painting than either his father Piero or his grandfather Cosimo. Nevertheless, some of the paintings done in his lifetime have come to epitomize the spirit of the age because of their close familial and philosophical links to Lorenzo's family. This is especially true of the work of Botticelli and, more specifically, his paintings the *Primavera* and the *Birth of Venus*.

Botticelli painted the *Primavera (Springtime)* [Plate 16, page 239] for a cousin of Lorenzo named Lorenzo di' Pierfrancesco. One of the most popular paintings in the history of Western art, the *Primavera* is an elaborate mythological allegory of the burgeoning fertility of the world. The allegory itself has never been fully explicated, but the main characters are clearly discernible: at the extreme right the wind god Zephyr pursues a nymph who is transmuted into the goddess Flora (next figure), who scatters her flowers; at the left are the god Mercury and three dancing Graces. Over the Graces and the central female figure (who represents Spring) is blind Cupid ready to launch an arrow that will bring love to the one he hits. The rich carpeting of springtime flowers and the background of the orange grove provide luxuriant surroundings.

In the 16th century Vasari saw the *Primavera* in Lorenzo di' Pierfrancesco's villa together with another painting by Botticelli, the *Birth of Venus* (1480). A gentle, almost fragile work of idealized beauty, the *Birth of Venus* [221] shows the wind gods gently stirring the sea breezes as Venus emerges from the sea and an attendant waits for her with a billowing cape. The Venus figure is inspired by the *Venus pudica* (the Modest Venus) figures of antiquity. The most significant aspect of this painting (and of the *Primavera*) is the impulse, motivated by platonism, to idealize the figures. Botticelli is not trying to depict a particular woman but the essential ideal of female beauty. The Venus of this painting reflects a complex synthesis of platonic idealism, Christian mysticism relating to the Virgin, and the classical ideal of the female figure of Venus.

Two other artists who lived in Laurentian Florence are of worldwide significance: Leonardo da Vinci (1452–1519) and Michelangelo Buonarroti. Leonardo came from a small Tuscan town near Florence called Vinci. He lived in Florence until the 1480s, when he left for Milan; from there he moved restlessly from place to place until his death in France. Leonardo has been called *the* genius of the Renaissance not so much for what he left in the way of art (although the *Last Supper* and the *Mona Lisa* are surely among the more famous set pieces of all time) as for the things that he dreamed of doing and the problems he set himself to solve and the phenomena he observed and set down in his *Notebooks.*

If we had nothing but the *Notebooks,* we would still say that Leonardo had one of humanity's most fertile minds. He left sketches for flying machines, submarines, turbines, elevators, ideal cities, and machines of almost every description [222]. His knowledge of anatomy was unsurpassed (he came very close to discovering the circulation path of blood), while his interest in the natural worlds of geology and botany was keen. The *Notebooks,* in short, reflect a restlessly searching mind that sought to understand the world and its constituent parts. Its chosen fields of inquiry are dominated by many of the characteris-

222 Leonardo da Vinci. *Helicopter or Aerial Screw.* c. 1485–1490. Bibliothèque de l'Institut de France, Paris.

221 Sandro Botticelli. *Birth of Venus.* 1480. Tempera on canvas, 6'7" × 9'2" (2.01 × 2.79 m). Uffizi, Florence.

above: 223 Leonardo da Vinci. *Last Supper*. 1495–1498.
Fresco. 14'5" × 28'1¼" (4.39 × 8.61 m). Refectory, Santa Maria
delle Grazie, Milan. The fresco was partially mutilated when a
doorway was cut through the wall in the Napoleonic era; it can
be seen below the figure of Christ.

right: 224 Leonardo da Vinci. *Madonna of the Rocks*. Begun
1483. Panel painting transferred to canvas. 78½ × 48". The
Louvre, Paris. Another painting on this theme also exists in the
National Gallery in London but the Louvre version is entirely
from the hand of Leonardo. The painting was to be part of a
large altarpiece for a chapel dedicated to the Virgin in Milan.

tics common to that period: a concern with mathematics, a deep respect for *seeing* the natural world,
and a love for beauty.

Leonardo's *Last Supper* [223] is a good example of
these characteristics. Leonardo chooses the moment
when Jesus announces that someone at the table will
betray him. The apostles are arranged in four distinct
groups. The central figure of Christ is highlighted by
the apostles who either look at him or gesture toward
him. Christ is halved by the central window space
behind him, with the lines of the room all converging
toward that point. The painting has great emotional
power even though it is one of the most carefully
mathematical paintings ever executed.

Leonardo's expressive power as a painter is ably
illustrated in his striking *Madonna of the Rocks* [224]
begun shortly after his arrival in Milan in 1483, a

above: **Plate 16** Sandro Botticelli. *La Primavera*. c. 1478. Tempera on canvas, 6'8" × 10'4" (2.03 × 3.14 m). Uffizi, Florence. This painting and the *Birth of Venus* (figure **221,** page 237) show what has been called the grace or the linear rhythm of Botticelli's most famous works. One can profitably compare the female faces in this painting with others in Botticelli's work to see the unique sensibility that the artist brought to his rendering of the feminine.

right: **Plate 17** Raphael. *Madonna of the Meadow*. 1506. Oil on panel, 44½ × 34¼" (113 × 87 cm). Kunsthistorisches Museum, Vienna. Saint John the Baptist is often shown with the Madonna and Child because of the close connection in the Bible between his birth and that of Jesus.

239

Plate 18 Jacopo Carucci da Pontormo. *Deposition.* c. 1528. Oil on panel, c. 11′ × 6′6″ (3.35 × 1.98 m). Capponi Chapel, Santa Felicità, Florence. The twisting serpentine figures seem suspended in an ethereal space of no definite location. The faces look blankly out with a sort of dumbstruck grief. Note the strange and eccentric colorations.

decade before he painted the *Last Supper*. The Virgin drapes her right arm over the figure of the infant Saint John the Baptist while her hand hovers in protective benediction over the Christ child. An exquisitely rendered angel points to the scene. The cavernlike space in the background would remind the perceptive viewer both of the cave at Bethlehem where Christ was born and the cave in which he would be buried. Leonardo's rendering of the jagged rocks stands in sharper relief because of the misty light in the extreme background. The particular beauty of the painting at least partially derives from the juxtaposition of the beautifully rendered persons in all their humanity with the wildly mysterious natural frame in which they are set.

The other great genius of the late 15th century is Michelangelo Buonarroti (1476–1564). After his early days in the sculpture garden of Lorenzo, he produced many of his greatest works in Rome; they are considered in the next chapter. However, even a few examples of his early works show both the great promise of Michelangelo's talent and some of the influences he absorbed in Florence under the Medici. The *Madonna of the Stairs* [225], an early marble relief, reflects his study of ancient reliefs or cameo carving (which he may well have seen in Lorenzo's collection). By 1498 his style had matured enough for him to carve, for a French cardinal in Rome, the universally admired *Pietà* [226], which combines his deep sensitivity with an idealism in the beauty of the Madonna's face that is reminiscent of Botticelli.

above: 225   Michelangelo. *Madonna of the Stairs.* 1489–1492. Marble, 21¾ × 15¾″ (55 × 40 cm). Casa Buonarroti, Florence.

left: 226   Michelangelo. *Pietà.* 1498–1499. Marble, height 5′9″ (1.75 m). Saint Peter's, Vatican, Rome.

Finally, this early period of Michelangelo's work includes a sculpture that has become almost synonymous with Florence: the *David* [227], carved in 1501–1504 from a massive piece of Carrara marble that had lain behind the cathedral in Florence since the middle of the previous century. The sculpture's great size and its almost photographically realistic musculature combine to make it one of Michelangelo's clearest statements of idealized beauty. The statue originally was intended to be seen from below with the left arm (the one touching the shoulder) facing the viewer and

the right side turned back toward the Cathedral. In fact, it was placed outside the Palazzo Vecchio as a symbol of the civic power of the city, where it remained until weathering and damage required its removal to a museum in the 19th century.

It has been said that Botticelli's paintings, the *Davids* of both Donatello and Michelangelo, and the general skepticism of a mind like Leonardo's are all symptoms of the general pagan tone of Laurentian Florence—that Athens and Rome, in short, seemed far more important to 15th-century Florence than

227 Michelangelo. *David.* 1501–1504. Marble, height 18′ (5.49 m). Academy, Florence. Unlike Donatello (figure 215, page 232) Michelangelo depicts David before his attack on Goliath. He is preparing to launch a stone from the sling. More than a century later, Bernini depicted a tense David during the attack.

Jerusalem did. There is no doubt that the classical revival was central to Florentine culture. Nor is there any doubt that the times had little patience with, or admiration for, medieval culture. However, the notion that the Renaissance spirit marked a clean break with medieval ideals must take into account the life and career of the Dominican preacher and reformer Fra Savonarola (1452–1498).

Savonarola lived at the Convent of San Marco in Florence from 1490 until his execution in 1498. His urgent preachings against the vanities of Florence in general and the degeneracy of its art and culture in particular had an electric effect on the populace. His influence was not limited to the credulous masses of the workers of the city. Lorenzo called him to his own deathbed in 1492 to receive the last sacraments even though Savonarola had been a bitter and open enemy of Medici control over the city. Savonarola, in fact, wanted a restored Republic with a strong ethical and theocratic base. Botticelli was so impressed by Savonarola that he burned some of his more worldly paintings, and scholars see in his last works a more profound religiosity derived from the contact with the reforming friar. Michelangelo, when an old man in Rome, told a friend that he could still hear the words of Savonarola ringing in his ears. Pico della Mirandola (1463–1494), one of the most brilliant humanists of the period, turned from his polyglot studies of Greek, Hebrew, Aramaic, and Latin to a devout life under the direction of the friar; only his early death prevented him from joining Savonarola as a friar at San Marco.

Savonarola's hold over the Florentine political order (for a brief time he was the de facto ruler of the city) came to an end in 1498 when he defied a papal excommunication and was then strangled in the public square before the Palazzo Vecchio. By that time, Lorenzo had been dead for six years and the Medici family had lost power in Florence. They were to return in the next century, but the Golden Age of Lorenzo had ended with a spasm of medieval piety. The influence of the city and its ideals, however, had already spread far beyond its boundaries.

The Character of Renaissance Humanism

Jules Michelet, a 19th-century French historian, first coined the word *Renaissance* specifically to describe the cultural period of 15th-century Florence. The broad outline of this rebirth is described by the Swiss historian Jakob Burckhardt in his massive work. *The Civilization of the Renaissance in Italy*, first published

in 1860, a book that is the beginning point for any discussion of the topic. Burckhardt's thesis is simple and persuasive. European culture, he argued, was reborn in the 15th century after a long dormant period that extended from the fall of the Roman Empire until the beginning of the 14th century.

The characteristics of this new birth, Burckhardt said, were first noticeable in Italy and were the foundation blocks of the modern world. It was in late 14th- and 15th-century Italy that new ideas about the nature of the political order developed of which the Republican government of Florence is an example, as well as the consciousness of the artist as an individual seeking personal fame. This pursuit of glory and fame was a sharp contrast to the self-effacing and world-denying attitude of the Middle Ages. Burckhardt also saw the thirst for classical learning, the desire to construct a humanism from that learning, and an emphasis on the good life as an intellectual repudiation of medieval religion and ethics.

Burckhardt's ideas have provoked strong reactions from historians and scholars, many of whom reject his theory as simplistic. Charles Homer Haskins, an American scholar, attacked Burckhardt's ideas in 1927 in a book whose title gives away his line of argument: *The Renaissance of the Twelfth Century*. Haskins pointed out that everything Burckhardt said about Florentine life in the 15th century could be said with equal justification about Paris in the 12th century. Furthermore (as noted in Chapter 7 of his textbook), scholars have also spoken of a Carolingian Renaissance identified with the court of the emperor Charlemagne.

What is the truth? Was there a genuine Renaissance in 15th-century Italy? Many scholars today try to mediate a position between Burckhardt and his detractors. They admit that something new was happening in the intellectual and cultural life of 15th-century Italy and that contemporaries were conscious of it. "May every thoughtful spirit thank God that it has been given to him to be born in this new age, so filled with hope and promise, which already enjoys a greater array of gifted persons than the world has seen in the past thousand years," wrote Matteo Palmieri, a Florentine businessman, in 1436. Yet this "new age" of which Palmieri spoke did not spring up overnight. The roots must be traced to Italy's long tradition of lay learning, the Franciscan movement of the 13th century, the relative absence of feudalism in Italy, and the long maintenance of Italian city life. In short, something new was happening precisely because Italy's long historical antecedents permitted it.

The question remains, however: What was new in the Renaissance? The Renaissance was surely more than a change in artistic taste or an advance in technological artistic skill. We need to go deeper. What motivated the shift in artistic taste? What fueled the personal energy that produced artistic innovation? What caused flocks of foreign scholars to cross the Alps to study in Florence and in other centers where they could absorb the "new learning"?

The answer to these questions, briefly, is this: there arose in Italy, as early as the time of Petrarch (1304–1372), but clearly in the 15th century, a strong conviction that humanist learning would not only ennoble and perfect the individual but could also serve as a powerful instrument for social and religious reform. Very few Renaissance humanists denied the need for God's grace, but all felt that human intellectual effort should be the first concern of anyone who wished truly to advance the good of self or society. The career of Pico della Mirandola, one of the most brilliant and gifted Florentine humanist scholars, illustrates this humanist belief.

Pico della Mirandola

Pico della Mirandola (1462–1494) was an intimate friend of Lorenzo de' Medici and a companion of the platonic scholar Marsilio Ficino. Precociously brilliant, Pico once bragged, not implausibly, that he had read every book in Italy. He was deeply involved with the intellectual life of his day.

Pico was convinced that all human learning could be synthesized in such a way as to yield basic and elementary truths. To demonstrate this, he set out to master all the systems of knowledge that then existed. He thoroughly mastered the Latin and Greek classics. He studied medieval Aristotleanism at the University of Paris and learned Arabic and the Islamic tradition. He was the first Christian in his day to take an active interest in Hebrew culture; he learned Hebrew and Aramaic and studied the *Talmud* with Jewish scholars.

At the age of twenty Pico proposed to defend at Rome his nine hundred *theses* (intellectual propositions) which he claimed summed up all current learning and speculation. Church leaders attacked some of his propositions as unorthodox, Pico left Rome, and the debate was never held.

The preface to these theses, called the *Oration on the Dignity of Man*, has often been cited as the first and most important document of Renaissance humanism. Its central thesis is that humanity stands at the apex of creation in such a way as to create the link between the world of God and that of the creation. Pico brings his wide learning to bear on this fundamental proposition: humanity is a great miracle. He not only calls on the traditional biblical and classical sources but cites, from his immense reading, the opinions of the great writers of the Jewish, Arabic, and Neoplatonic traditions. The enthusiasm of the youthful Pico for his subject is as apparent as his desire to display his learning.

Scholars disagree on Pico's originality as a thinker. Many argue that his writings are a hodgepodge of knowledge without any genuine synthesis. There is no disagreement, however, about Pico's immense ability as a student of languages and culture to open new fields of study and, in that way, contribute much to the enthusiasm for learning in his own day. His reputation attracted students to him. The most influential of these was a German named Johann Reuchlin (1455–1522), who came to Florence to study Hebrew with him. After mastering that language and Greek as well, Reuchlin went back to Germany to pursue his studies and to apply them to biblical scholarship. In the early 16th century he came under the influence of Martin Luther (see Chapter 12) but never joined the Reformation. Reuchlin passionately defended the legitimacy of biblical studies oriented to the original languages. When his approach was attacked in one of those periodic outbursts of anti-Semitism so characteristic of European culture of the time, Reuchlin, true to his humanist impulses, not only defended his studies as a true instrument of religious reform but also made an impassioned plea for toleration that was not characteristic of his time.

Printing Technology and the Spread of Humanism

The export of humanist learning was not restricted to the exchange of scholars between Italy and the countries to the north. Printing had been invented in the early 15th century, so books were becoming more accessible to the educated classes. The most famous humanist printer and publisher of the 15th century was Aldus Manutius (1449–1515), whose Aldine Press was in Venice, his native city (see map opposite). Aldus was a scholar in his own right; he learned Greek from refugee scholars who settled in Venice after the Fall of Constantinople in 1453. Recognizing the need for competent and reliable editions of the classical authors, he employed professional humanists to collate and correct manuscripts. Erasmus, the greatest of the northern humanists, was, for a time, in his employ.

Aldus was also a technical innovator. He designed Greek type faces, created italic type fonts (modeled after the scribal hand used for copying Florentine manuscripts), developed new inks, and obtained new

Renaissance Italy

Spain

Genoa

Venice

miles
0   100   200

0   100   200   300
kilometers

paper from the nearby town of Fabriano, still today a source of fine papers for artists and printmakers. His books were near pocketsize, easily portable, and inexpensive. The scope of the press's activities was huge: after 1494 Aldus (and, later, his son) published, in about twenty years, the complete works of Aristotle and the works of Plato, Pindar, Herodotus, Sophocles, Aristophanes, Xenophon, and Demosthenes. Aldus reissued the Latin classics in better editions and published vernacular writers like Dante and Petrarch as well as contemporary poets like Poliziano, the Florentine friend of Lorenzo.

The Aldine Press was not an isolated phenomenon. Germany, where printing really started, already had an active printing and publishing tradition. Johannes Gutenberg (c. 1395–1468) originated the method of printing from movable type that was then used with virtually no change until the late 19th cen-

tury. Gutenberg finished printing a Bible at Mainz in 1455. The first book printed in English, *The Recuyell* (collection) *of the Historyes of Troye*, was published by William Caxton in 1475. Historians have estimated that before 1500 European presses produced between six and nine million books in thirteen thousand different editions. Nearly fifty thousand of these books survive in libraries throughout the world.

This conjunction of pride in humanist learning and technology of printing had profound consequences for European culture. It permitted the wide diffusion of ideas to a large number of people in a relatively short time. There is no doubt that vigorous intellectual movements—one thinks immediately of the Protestant Reformation—benefited immensely from printing. This communications revolution was as important for the Renaissance period as radio, film, and television have been for our own.

Two Styles of Humanism

In the generation after the death of Lorenzo de' Medici the new learning made its way north, where it was most often put to use in attempts to reform the religious life of the area; in Italy, however, the learning remained tied to more worldly matters. The double usage of humanist learning for secular and spiritual reform can be better appreciated by a brief consideration of the work of the two most important writers of the period after the golden period of the Medicean Renaissance: Niccolò Machiavelli and Desiderius Erasmus.

Machiavelli

Niccolò Machiavelli (1469–1527), trained as a humanist and active as a diplomat in Florence, was exiled from the city when the Medici reassumed power in 1512. In his exile, a few miles from the city which he had served for many years, Machiavelli wrote a political treatise on politics called *The Prince*, which was published only after his death.

The Prince is often considered the first purely secular study of political theory in the West. Machiavelli's inspiration is the government of Republican Rome (509–31 B.C.). He sees Christianity's role in politics as a disaster that destroys the power of the state to govern. For that reason, Machiavelli asserts, the state needs to restrict the power of the church, allowing it to exercise its office only in the spiritual realm. The prince, as ruler of the state, must understand that the key to success in governing is in the exercise of power. Power is to be used with wisdom and ruthlessness. The prince, in a favorite illustration of Machiavelli, must be as sly as the fox and as brutal as the lion. Above all, the prince must not be deterred from his tasks by any consideration of morality beyond that of power and its ends. In this sense, cruelty or hypocrisy are permissible; judicious cruelty consolidates power and discourages revolution. Senseless cruelty is, however, counterproductive.

The basic theme of *The Prince* is the pragmatic use of power for state management. Previously the tradition of political theory had always invoked the transcendent authority of God to insure the stability and legitimacy of the state. For Machiavelli it was power, not the moral law of God, that provided the state with its ultimate sanction. The final test of the successful ruler was the willingness to exercise power judiciously and freedom from the constraints of moral suasion. "A prince must not keep faith when by doing so it would be against his self-interest," Machiavelli says in one of the most famous passages

228 Albrecht Dürer. *Erasmus of Rotterdam*. 1526. Engraving, 9¾ × 7½" (25 × 19 cm). Metropolitan Museum of Art, New York (Fletcher Fund, 1919). The Latin inscription says that Dürer made his drawing of Erasmus from life, while the Greek words below praise the power of the written word.

from his book. His justification is: " . . . If all men were good this precept would not be a good one but as they are bad and would not observe their faith with you, so you are not bound to keep faith with them." This bold pragmatism explains why the Catholic Church put *The Prince* on its *Index of Prohibited Books* and why the adjective "machiavellian" means, in English, devious or unscrupulous in political dealings. Machiavelli had such a bad reputation that many 16th-century English plays had a stock evil character—an Italian called "Old Nick." The English phrase "to be filled with the Old Nick," meaning to be devilish, derives from Machiavelli's reputation as an immoral man. But Machiavelli's realistic pragmatism also explains why Catherine the Great of Russia and Napoleon read him with great care.

Erasmus

Desiderius Erasmus (1466–1536) has been called the most important Christian humanist in Europe [228]. Educated in Holland and at the University of Paris,

Erasmus was a monk and priest who soon tired of his official church life. He became aware of humanist learning through his visits to England, where he met men like John Colet and Thomas More. Fired by their enthusiasm for the new learning, Erasmus traveled to Italy in 1506, with lengthy stays in both Rome and Venice. Thereafter, he led the life of a wandering scholar, gaining immense fame as both scholar and author.

Erasmus' many books were attempts to combine classical learning and a simple interiorized approach to Christian living. In the *Enchiridion Militis Christiani* (1502) he attempted to spell out this Christian humanism in practical terms. The title has a typical Erasmian pun; the word *enchiridion* can mean either "handbook" or "short sword"; thus the title can mean the handbook or the short sword of the Christian knight. His *Greek New Testament* (1516) was the first attempt to edit the Greek text of the New Testament by a comparison of extant manuscripts. Because Erasmus used only three manuscripts his version is not technically good, but it was a noteworthy attempt and a clear indication of how a humanist felt he could contribute to ecclesiastical work.

The most famous book Erasmus wrote, *The Praise of Folly* (1509), was dashed off almost as a joke while he was a house guest of Sir Thomas More in England. Again the title is a pun; *Encomium Moriae* can mean either "praise of folly" or "praise of More"—Thomas More, his host. *The Praise of Folly* is a humorous work, but beneath its seemingly lighthearted spoof of the foibles of the day there are strong denunciations of corruption, evil, ignorance, and prejudice in society. Erasmus flailed away at the makers of war (he had a strong pacifist streak), venal lawyers, and fraudulent doctors, but, above all, he bitterly attacked religious corruption: the sterility of religious scholarship and the superstitions in religious practice. Reading *The Praise of Folly* makes one wonder why Luther never won Erasmus over to the Reformation (Erasmus debated Luther, in fact). Erasmus remained in the old Church, but as a bitter critic of its follies and an indefatigable proponent of its reform.

This sweeping social criticism struck an obvious nerve. The book delighted not only the great Sir Thomas More (who was concerned enough about religious convictions to die for them later in the century) but also many sensitive people of the time. *The Praise of Folly* went through 27 editions in the lifetime of Erasmus and outsold every other book except the Bible in the 16th century.

Comparing Machiavelli and Erasmus is a bit like comparing apples and potatoes, but a few points of contact can be noted that help us to generalize about the meaning of the Renaissance. Both men were heavily indebted to the new learning coming out of 15th-century Italy. Both looked back to the great classical heritage of the past for their models of inspiration. Both were elegant Latinists who avoided the style and thought patterns of the medieval world. Machiavelli's devotion to the Roman past was total. He saw the historic development of Christianity as a threat and stumbling block to the fine working of the state. Erasmus, by contrast, felt that learning from the past could be wedded to the Christian tradition to create an instrument for social reform. His ideal was a Christian humanism based on this formula. It was a formula potent enough to influence thinking throughout the 16th century.

The tug and pull of classicism and Christianity may be one key to understanding the Renaissance. It may even help us understand something about the character of almost everything we have discussed in this chapter. The culture of the 15th century often was, in fact, a dialectical struggle: at times classical ideals clashed with biblical ideals; at other times, the two managed to live either in harmony or in a temporary marriage of convenience. The strains of classicism and Christianity interacted in complex and subtle ways. This important fact helps us to understand a culture that produced, in a generation, an elegant scholar like Ficino and a firebrand like Savonarola, a pious artist like Fra Angelico and a titanic genius like Michelangelo—and a Machiavelli and an Erasmus.

Questions for Further Discussion

1. One important aspect of Florentine culture was the patronage of the arts by wealthy families. In our own time, what are the greatest sources of art patronage? What does that tell us about the nature of our society?
2. To underscore the character of Pico's *Oration on the Dignity of Man*, compare it with some other more recent statements such as the Bill of Rights or William Faulkner's Nobel Prize acceptance speech.
3. In *The Praise of Folly* Erasmus attacks all manner of foibles in his culture. If you were to write a contemporary version of *The Praise of Folly*, what would rank high on your list of social follies? Which ones do you find the same when reading Erasmus?
4. How might modern techniques, inventions, and materials have helped Brunelleschi solve the engineering problem of the Florence Cathedral?
5. Both Donatello and Michelangelo (to name but two) did statues of David. Contrast the Donatello and Michelangelo figures in both style and intention.
6. Make a summary statement, based on your study of this chapter, of the meaning of the Florentine Renaissance.

	GENERAL EVENTS	LITERATURE & PHILOSOPHY	ART

1400

FLORENTINE RENAISSANCE

GENERAL EVENTS

1471-1484 Reign of Pope Sixtus IV (della Rovere)

1494 Foreign invasions of Italy begin

LITERATURE & PHILOSOPHY

c. 1494 Aldine Press established in Venice

ART

1471-1484 Perugino, Botticelli, and others decorate Sistine Chapel side walls

1493-1506 Ancient frescoes and statues uncovered in Rome; *Laocoön* found 1506

c. 1494 Decline of Medici power in Florence causes artists to migrate to Rome

1494-1495 Dürer's first trip to Venice

1503

HIGH RENAISSANCE IN ITALY

1503-1513 Reign of Pope Julius II (della Rovere)

c. 1510 Decline of Venetian trade as result of new geographic discoveries

1513-1521 Reign of Pope Leo X (de' Medici)

1517 Reformation begins in Germany with Luther's 95 Theses, challenging the practice of indulgences

c. 1500-1505 Giorgione, *Enthroned Madonna with Saint Liberalis and Saint Francis,* altarpiece

1505 Michelangelo called to Rome by Julius II to begin Pope's tomb; *Moses* (1513-1515), *Captives* (1527-1528)

1505-1508 Raphael works in Florence; *Madonna of the Meadows* (1505)

1508 Raphael begins frescoes for rooms in Vatican Palace; *The School of Athens,* Stanza della Segnatura (1510-1511)

1508-1511 Michelangelo, Sistine Chapel ceiling

c. 1510 Giorgione, *Fête Champêtre*

1511 Raphael, *Portrait of Julius II*

1515-1547 Francis I lures Leonardo and other Italian artists to France

Painting in Venice emphasizes brilliant color and light; less linear than in Rome and Florence; Titian, *The Assumption of the Virgin* (1518)

1519 Death of Leonardo

1519-1534 Michelangelo works on Medici Chapel sculptures

1520

MANNERISM AND LATE RENAISSANCE

1523-1534 Reign of Pope Clement VII (de' Medici)

1527 Sack of Rome by Emperor Charles V

1534 Churches of Rome and England separate

1545 Council to reform Catholic Church begins at Trent

c. 1524-1534 Strozzi, poem on Michelangelo's *Night*

1527 Luther translates Bible into German

1528 Castiglione, *The Courtier,* dialogue on ideal courtly life

1550 Vasari, *Lives of the Painters*

1558-1566 Cellini, *Autobiography of Benvenuto Cellini*

1561 *The Courtier* translated into English by Sir Thomas Hoby

1520 Death of Raphael

c. 1520 Mannerism emerges as artistic style

c. 1528 Pontormo, *Deposition,* Capponi Chapel, Santa Felicitá, Florence

c. 1534 Parmigianino, *Madonna of the Long Neck*

1534-1541 Michelangelo, *Last Judgment* fresco, Sistine Chapel

1538 Titian, *Venus of Urbino*

1554 Cellini casts bronze *Perseus* in Florence

1564 Death of Michelangelo

1576 Titian dies of plague

1603

ARCHITECTURE	MUSIC
1473–1480 Sistine Chapel built for Pope Sixtus IV	1473 Sistine Choir established by Sixtus IV
	1486–1494 Josquin des Préz intermittently in service of Sistine Choir as composer of masses and motets; *Tu Pauperum Refugium*
1504 Bramante, Tempietto, San Pietro in Montorio, Rome	
1506 Pope Julius II commissions Bramante to rebuild Saint Peter's Basilica	
1514 Death of Bramante; Raphael, Sangallo, and others continue work on Saint Peter's	1512 Julian Choir established by Julius II for Saint Peter's Basilica
1519–1534 Michelangelo, Medici Chapel, Church of San Lorenzo, Florence	
1524 Michelangelo, Laurentian Library, Florence, begun; entrance staircase finished 1559	1527 Adrian Willaert becomes choirmaster of Saint Mark's, Venice; multiple choirs and addition of instrumental music are Venetian innovations to liturgical music
1547 Michelangelo appointed architect of Saint Peter's; apse and dome begun 1547	1567 Palestrina, *Missa Papae Marcelli*
	1571–1594 Palestrina, choirmaster of Sistine Choir, in charge of musical reform for Vatican
1592 Michelangelo's dome for Saint Peter's finished by Giacomo della Porta	1603 Victoria, *Requiem Mass for the Empress Maria*

11
The High Renaissance in Italy

Popes and Patronage

Artists must work where their art is appreciated and their labors rewarded. Florence in the 15th century, shaped by the generous and refined patronage of the Medici and others, was an extremely congenial place for the talented artist. But when the political power of the Medici declined in the last decade of the century, many major artists inevitably migrated or were summoned to other centers of wealth and stability. The papal court at the Vatican in Rome was preeminently such a center.

In the 15th century (and even earlier) artists found rewarding work at the Vatican. Pope Sixtus IV (reigned 1471–1484) commissioned many artists famous in Florence—among them Ghirlandaio, Botticelli and Perugino—to fresco the side walls of the Sistine Chapel, named for himself, as well as work on other projects that caught his artistic fancy. Not the least of these projects was the enlargement and systematization of the Vatican library.

The period known as the High Renaissance really began, however, in 1503, when a nephew of Sixtus IV became Pope Julius II (died 1513); both were members of the Della Rovere family. Pope Julius was a fiery man who did not hesitate to don full military armor over his vestments and lead his papal troops into battle. Thanks to the influence of his papal uncle, he appreciated the fine arts, indulging his artistic tastes with the same singlemindedness that characterized his military campaigns. It was Pope Julius—called by his contemporaries *il papa terribile* (the awesome pope)—who summoned both Raphael Sanzio and Michelangelo Buonarotti to Rome.

Raphael

Raphael Sanzio (1483–1520) was born in Urbino, a center of humanist learning east of Florence dominated by the court of the Duke of Urbino. His precocious talent was first nurtured by his father, a painter, whose death in 1494 cut short the youth's education. The young Raphael then went to Perugia as an apprentice to the painter Perugino. Here his talents were quickly recognized. In 1505, at the age of 22, he moved on to Florence, where he worked for three years.

During his stay in Florence, Raphael painted a large number of madonnas in a style that has become almost synonymous with his name. The *Madonna of the Meadow* [Plate 17, page 239] is typical. In this painting Raphael arranged his figures in a pyramidal configuration in order to create a believable and balanced space. This geometrical device, which had already been popularized by Leonardo da Vinci, was congenial to the Renaissance preoccupation with rationally ordered composition. More important than the arrangement of shapes, however, is the beautiful modeling of the human forms, especially the figures of the two children, and the genuine sweetness and warmth conveyed by the faces of the figures. The head of the Madonna is peaceful and luminous, while the infant Christ and Saint John convey a somewhat more playful mood. The very human quality of the divine figure is, in fact, Raphael's trademark.

Raphael left Florence for Rome in 1508. By the following year, Pope Julius, whom Raphael later caught in an unforgettably fine portrait, had him working in the Vatican on a variety of projects. The pope, who genuinely loved Raphael, commissioned him to decorate various rooms of his palace. Raphael spent the rest of his brief life working on these projects, as well as filling assorted administrative posts for the papacy, including, at one time, the office of architect of Saint Peter's Basilica and at another time superintendent of the Vatican's collection of antiquities.

One of Raphael's most outstanding works and certainly one of the most important for defining the meaning of the 16th-century Renaissance in Rome is a large fresco executed in 1510–1511 on the wall of the Stanza della Segnatura, an office in the Vatican palace where documents requiring the pope's signature were prepared. Called now the *School of Athens* [229], the large fresco is a highly symbolic homage to philosophy that complements Raphael's similar frescoes in the same room that symbolize poetry, law, and theology.

The *School of Athens* sets the great philosophers of antiquity in an immense illusionistic architectural framework that must have been at least partially inspired by the impressive ruins of Roman baths and basilicas, and perhaps by the new Saint Peter's, then under construction. Raphael's fresco depicts Roman barrel vaulting, coffered ceilings, and broad expanses not unlike the still existing baths of ancient Rome. Occupying the center of the fresco, in places of honor framed by the receding lines of the architecture as a device to focus the viewer's eye, are the two greatest ancient Greek philosophers, Plato and Aristotle. Plato holds a copy of the *Timaeus* in one hand and with the other points to the heavens, the realm of ideal forms. Aristotle holds a copy of his *Ethics* and points to the earth, where his science of empirical observation must begin. Clustered about the two philosophers in varying poses and at various distances are other great figures of antiquity. Diogenes sprawls in front of the philosophers, while Pythagoras calculates on a slate and Ptolemy holds a globe. At the right, the idealized figure of Euclid with his compass is actually a portrait of Raphael's Roman protector, the architect Bramante. Raphael himself, in a self-portrait, looks out at the viewer at the extreme lower right corner of the fresco.

Raphael's *School of Athens* reflects a high degree of sensitivity to ordered space, a complete ease with classical thought, an obvious inspiration from the Roman architectural past, a brilliant sense of color and form, and a love for intellectual clarity—characteristics that could sum up the Renaissance ideal. That such a fresco should adorn a room in the Vatican, the center of Christian authority, is not difficult to explain. The papal court of Julius II shared the humanist conviction that philosophy is the servant of theology and that beauty, even if derived from a pagan civilization, is a gift of God and not to be despised. To underscore this point, Raphael's homage to theology across the room, his fresco called the *Disputà*, shows in a panoramic form similar to the *School of Athens* the efforts of theologians to penetrate divine mystery.

229 Raphael. *School of Athens.* 1510–1511.
Fresco, 26 × 18′ (7.92 × 5.48 m).
Stanza della Segnatura, Vatican Palace, Rome.

Michelangelo

In the lower center of Raphael's *School of Athens* is a lone figure leaning one elbow on a block of marble and scribbling, taking no notice of the exalted scene about him. Strangely isolated in his stonecutter's smock, the figure has recently been identified, at least tentatively, as Michelangelo. If the identification is correct, this is the younger artist's act of homage to the solitary genius who was working just a few yards away from him in the Sistine Chapel.

Michelangelo Buonarotti (1475–1564) was called to Rome in 1505 by Pope Julius II to create for him a monumental tomb. We have no clear sense of what the tomb was to look like, since over the years it went through at least five conceptual revisions. Certain features, however, at least in the initial stages, are definite. It was to have three levels; the bottom level was to have sculptured figures representing Victory and bound slaves. The second level was to have statues of Moses and Saint Paul, as well as symbolic figures of the active and contemplative life—representative of the human striving for, and reception of, knowledge. The third level, it is assumed, was to have an effigy of the deceased pope.

The tomb of Pope Julius II was never finished. Michelangelo was interrupted in his long labors by both Pope Julius himself and, after the pope's death, the popes of the Medici family, who were more concerned with projects glorifying their own family. What was finished of the tomb represents a twenty-year span of frustrating delays and revised schemes. Even those finished pieces provide no sense of the whole, but they do represent some of the highest achievements of world art.

One of the finished pieces is the *Moses* [230], begun after the death of Julius in 1513. We easily sense both the bulky physicality of Moses and the carefully modeled particulars of musculature, drapery, and hair. The fiercely inspired look on the face of Moses is appropriate for one who has just come down from Mount Sinai after seeing God. The face radiates both divine fury and divine light. It has often been said of Michelangelo that his works can overwhelm the viewer with a sense of awesomeness; Italians speak of his *terribilità*. If any single statue has this awesomeness, it is the *Moses*.

The highly finished quality of the *Moses* should be compared with the roughness of the *Captives* [231], which Michelangelo worked on for the tomb of Julius in Florence in 1527–1528. There is no evidence that Michelangelo intended to leave these figures in this crude state. Nevertheless, these magnificent works give a visual demonstration of the sculptor's methods. Michelangelo often said that a living figure was concealed in a block of marble and that only the

230 Michelangelo. *Moses*. 1513–1515.
Marble, height 8′4″ (2.54 m).
San Pietro in Vincoli, Rome.
The horns on Moses' head represent rays of light; the use of horns instead of rays is based on a mistranslation of the Vulgate Bible.

excess needed to be carved away to reveal it. The truth of the Neoplatonic notion that ideal form struggles to be freed from the confines of gross matter can almost be seen in these figures. A close examination reveals the bite marks of the sculptor's chisel as he worked to reveal each living figure by removing hard marble. Seldom do we have a chance, as we do here, to see the work of a great artist still unfolding.

It is not clear where the *Captives* fit into the overall plan of the tomb of Julius. It is most likely that they were meant to serve as corner supports for the bottom level of the tomb, writhing under the weight of the whole [232]. Whatever was the ultimate plan for these figures, they are a stunning testament to the monumentally creative impulse of Michelangelo the sculptor.

Michelangelo had hardly begun work on the pope's tomb when Julius commanded him to fresco the ceiling of the Sistine Chapel in order to complete the work done in the previous century under Sixtus IV. But Michelangelo resisted the project (he actually fled Rome and had to be ordered back by papal edict). He considered himself a sculptor, and there were technical problems presented by the shape of the ceiling. Nevertheless, he gave in and in three years (1508–1511) finished the ceiling. He signed it "Michelangelo, Sculptor" to remind Julius of his reluctance and his own true vocation.

left: 231 Michelangelo. Boboli *Captive*. 1527–1538. Marble, height 7'6½" (2.3 m). Accademia, Florence. These figures (four are extant) are often called the Boboli *Captives* because they were long kept in the Boboli Gardens in Florence before they were removed to the Accademia.

right: 232 Drawing of Tomb of Julius II. After Michelangelo, by his pupil Giacomo Rocchetti. Brown ink, 22½ × 15¼" (57 × 39 cm). Kupferstichkabinett, State Museums, Berlin. This drawing represents only one of many plans for the tomb of Julius. Note the slaves on the bottom level and Moses on the right of the second level. The semirecumbent figure of the deceased pope is supported by angelic figures in the top center, just under the allegorical figure of Victory.

right: 233 Michelangelo. Ceiling, Sistine Chapel. 1508–1512. Fresco, 44 × 128′ (13.41 × 39.01 m). Vatican Palace, Rome.

far right: 234 Schematic drawing of the iconographic plan of the Sistine ceiling.

The ceiling [233] is as difficult to describe as it is to observe when standing in the Sistine Chapel. The overall organization consists of four large triangles at the corners; a series of eight triangular spaces on the outer border; an intermediate series of figures; and nine central panels (four larger than the other five), all bound together with architectural motifs and nude male figures. The corner triangles depict heroic action in the Old Testament (Judith beheading Holofernes; David slaying Goliath; Haman punished for his crimes; the rod of Moses changing into a serpent), while the other eight triangles depict the biblical ancestors of Jesus Christ. The ten major intermediate figures are alternating portraits of pagan sibyls (prophetesses) and Old Testament prophets. The central panels are scenes from the Book of Genesis. The one closest to the altar shows God dividing darkness from light and the one at the other end shows the drunkenness of Noah (Genesis 9:20–27). This bare outline oversimplifies what is actually a complex, intricate design [234].

Michelangelo conceived and executed this huge work (128 by 44 feet, or 39 by 13.4 meters) as a single unit. Its overall meaning is a problem. The issue has engaged historians of art for generations but without satisfactory resolution. Any attempt to formulate an authoritative statement must include a number of elements:

1. Michelangelo's interest in the Neoplatonism that he had studied as a youth in Florence. Many writers have noted the Neoplatonic roots of his interest in the manipulation of darkness and light (the progression of darkness to light from the outer borders to the center panels; the panel of God creating light itself), the liberation of spirit from matter (the souls represented by nudes; the drunkenness of Noah, symbolic of humanity trapped by gross matter and thereby degraded), and the numerous geometrical allusions done in triads, a triple division being much loved in Neoplatonic number symbolism.
2. The Christian understanding of the Old Testament as a work pointing to the coming of Christ, combined with the notion that even pagan prophets were dimly prophetic figures of Christ.
3. The complex tree symbolism in seven of the nine central panels, which refer to the symbolism of the tree in the Bible (e.g., the tree of good and evil in the Genesis story, the tree of the Cross, etc.), as well as being allusions to the pope's family name, which happened to be Della Rovere (the oak tree).
4. The traditional theories of the relationship of the world of human wisdom (represented by the sibyls) and God's revelation (represented by the prophets).

In the panel depicting the *Creation of Adam* [235], to cite one specific example, many of these elements come together. A majestically muscular Adam rises, as if from sleep, from the bare earth as God stretches forth his creative finger to call him into being. God's left arm circles a woman and child who represent, simultaneously, Eve and her children and by extension the New Eve, who is the Blessed Virgin. Adam is a prefiguration of Christ. Below Adam a youth holding a cornucopia spilling forth leaves and acorns (symbols of the Della Rovere family) stands just above the Persian sibyl. Stylistically, the fresco demonstrates Michelangelo's intense involvement with masculine anatomy seen as muscular monumentality. His ability to combine great physical bulk with linear grace and a powerful display of emotion fairly well defines the adjective *michelangeloesque*, which was applied to many later artists who were influenced by his style.

Under the patronage of Popes Leo X and Clement VII—both from the Medici family—Michelangelo worked on another project, the Medici Chapel in the Florentine Church of San Lorenzo. This chapel is

235 Michelangelo. *Creation of Adam,* detail of the Sistine ceiling. 1508–1512.

236 Michelangelo.
Medici Chapel. 1519–1534.
Church of San Lorenzo,
Florence.

particularly interesting because Michelangelo designed and executed both the sculptures and the chapel in which they were to be placed. Although Michelangelo first conceived the project in 1519, he worked on it only in fits and starts from 1521 to 1534. He never completely finished the chapel. In 1545 some of his students put the statues into place.

The interior of the Medici Chapel [236] echoes Brunelleschi's Pazzi Chapel with its dome, its use of a light stone called *pietra serena*, its classical decoration, and its very chaste and severe style. The plan envisioned an altar at one end of the chapel and opposite it, at the other end, statues of the Madonna and Child with Saints Cosmas and Damian. The saints were the patrons of physicians, an allusion to the name *Medici*, which means "the doctor's family." At the base of these statues are buried in utter simplicity the bodies of Lorenzo the Magnificent and his brother Giuliano. On opposite walls are niches with idealized seated figures of relatives of Lorenzo the Magnificent, the Dukes Lorenzo and Giuliano de' Medici, in Roman armor. Beneath each are two symbolic figures resting on a sarcophagus, *Night* and *Day* and *Dawn* and *Dusk*.

This great complex, unfinished like many of Michelangelo's projects, is a brooding meditation on the shortness of life, the inevitability of death, and the Christian hope for resurrection. Both the stark decoration of the chapel and the positioning of the statues

237 Michelangelo. *Night,* detail of the tomb of Giuliano de' Medici. 1519–1534. Marble, length 6′4½″ (1.94 m). Medici Chapel, Church of San Lorenzo, Florence. Note the proportions of the body in relation to the sarcophagus lid. The owl and the mask are emblems of night and dreams.

(Duke Lorenzo seems always turned to the dark with his head in shadow while Duke Giuliano seems more readily to accept the light) form a mute testament to the rather pessimistic and brooding nature of their creator. When Michelangelo had finished the figure of *Night* [237], a Florentine poet name Strozzi wrote a poem in honor of the statue, with a pun on the name Michelangelo:

> The Night you see sleeping in sweet repose
> Was carved in stone by an angel.
> Because she sleeps, she has life.
> If you do not believe this, touch her and
> She will speak.

Michelangelo, an accomplished poet in his own right, answered Strozzi's lines with a pessimistic rejoiner:

> Sleep is precious; more precious to be stone
> When evil and shame are abroad;
> It is a blessing not to see, not to hear.
> Pray, do not disturb me. Speak softly!

The New Saint Peter's

In 1506 Pope Julius II, in a gesture typical of his imperious nature, commissioned the architect Donato Bramante (1444–1514) to rebuild Saint Peter's Basilica in the Vatican. Old Saint Peter's had stood on the Vatican hill since it was first constructed more than a thousand years earlier, during the time of the Roman emperor Constantine. By the early 16th century it had suffered repeatedly from roof fires, structural stresses, and the simple ravages of time. In the minds of the Renaissance "moderns" it was a shaky anachronism.

Bramante's design envisioned a central domed church with a floor plan in the shape of a Greek cross with four equal arms [238]. The dome would have been set on a columned arcade with an exterior columniated arcade, called a *peristyle*, on the outer perimeter of the building. Any of the four main doors was to be directly across from a *portal* or door on the opposite side. This central plan was not executed in Bramante's lifetime, but a small chapel he

Bramante, 1506   Sangallo, 1539

238 Floor plans for the new Saint Peter's Basilica, Rome. Maderna's final additions, especially the elongated nave, narthex, and facade, obscured Michelangelo's original design. *1* papal altar area under dome; *2* transept; *3* portal; *4* chapel (not all identified); *5* apse; *6* choir; *7* nave; *8* narthex; *a* Bernini's piazza (1656).

Michelangelo, 1546–1564   Maderna, 1606

239 Michelangelo. Saint Peter's, Rome, from the southwest. 1546–1564; completed 1590 by Giacomo della Porta.

built in 1502 next to the Church of San Pietro in Montorio, Rome, may give us a clue as to what Bramante had in mind. This *tempietto* (little temple) is believed to have been done in a style similar to what Bramante wanted later for Saint Peter's.

After Bramante's death a series of architects, including Raphael and Sangallo, worked on the massive project. Both these architects added a nave and aisles [see 238]. In 1546 Michelangelo was appointed architect, since the plans previously drawn up seemed unworkable. Michelangelo returned to Bramante's plan for a central domed Greek cross church but envisioned a ribbed arched dome somewhat after the manner of the cathedral in Florence but on a far larger scale.

The present Saint Peter's seen from the front gives us no clear sense of what Michelangelo had in mind when he drew up his plans. Michelangelo's church had a long nave and a facade added by Carlo Maderna in the early 17th century [see 238]. The colonnaded piazza was completed under the direction of Gian Lorenzo Bernini in 1663, almost a century after Michelangelo's death. Michelangelo lived to see the completion of the drum which was to support his dome. The dome itself was raised some thirty years after his death by Giacomo della Porta. The best way to understand what Michelangelo intended is to view

Saint Peter's from behind, from the Vatican Gardens, where one can see the great dome looming up over the arms of the Greek cross design [239].

The High Renaissance in Venice

The brilliant and dramatic outbreak of artistic activity in 16th-century Rome and Florence does not diminish the equally creative art being done in the Republic of Venice to the north. While Rome excelled in fresco, sculpture, and architecture, Venice was famous for its tradition of easel painting. Venice's impressive cosmopolitanism derived from its position as a maritime port and its trading tradition.

Because of the damp atmosphere of their watery city, Venetian painters quickly adopted oil painting, which had first been popularized in the north. Oil painting gave the artist unparalleled opportunities to enrich and deepen color by the application of many layers of paint. Oil painting in general, and Venetian painting in particular, put great emphasis on the brilliance of its color and the subtlety of its light. The sunny environment of Venice, with light reflecting off the ever-present waterways, further inspired the Venetian feel for color and light. Although it is a generalization subject to refinement, there is truth in the observation that Venetian painters emphasized color while painters in the south were preoccupied with line. Venetian painters, like their counterparts in northern Europe, had an eye for close detail and a love for landscape (an ironic interest, since Venice had so little of it).

Giorgione

The most celebrated and enigmatic painter in early 16th-century Venice was Giorgio di Castelfranco (c. 1477–1510), more commonly known as Giorgione. His large altarpiece, *Enthroned Madonna with Saint Liberalis and Saint Francis* [240], painted for the cathedral of his home town of Castelfranco, illustrates many of the characteristics of the Venetian Renaissance style. It is a highly geometric work (using the now conventional form of the triangle with the Madonna at the apex) typical of Renaissance aesthetics of form. At the same time it shows some idiosyncratic characteristics—the luminous quality of the armor of Saint Liberalis and the minutely rendered landscape. This landscape, with its two soldiers in the bend of the road and the receding horizon, echoes painters from the north like Jan van Eyck.

Far more typical of Giorgione's work are his paintings without religious content or recognizable

240 Giorgione. *Enthroned Madonna with Saint Liberalis and Saint Francis.* c. 1500–1505. Oil on panel, 6′6¾″ × 5′ (1.99 × 1.52 m). Cathedral, Castelfranco.

241 Giorgione. *Le Concert Champêtre.* c. 1510. Oil on canvas. 3′7¼″ × 4′6⅛″ (1.1 × 1.38 m). Louvre, Paris. The fleshy nudes would be much imitated by baroque artists like Rubens.

story line or narrative quality. Typical of these is *Le Concert Champêtre* [241], done in the last year of the painter's life. The two voluptuous nudes frame two young men who are shadowed but also glowing in their richly rendered costumes. The sky behind threatens a storm, but Giorgione counterposes the storm to a serene pastoral scene that includes a distant farmhouse and shepherds with their flock. What does the painting hope to convey? Why does one woman pour water into the well? Is the lute in the hand of one man or the recorder in the hand of the other woman a clue? We do not know. It may be an elaborate allegory on music or poetry. What is clear is that the painting is a frankly secular homage to the profane joy of life rendered with the richness and lushness of concept and color.

Titian

If Giorgione's life was short, that of his onetime apprentice Tiziano Vecelli (c. 1488–1576), known as Titian, was long. Titian brought the Venetian love for striking color to its most beautiful fulfillment. His work not only had an impact on his contemporaries but also on later Baroque painters in other countries, such as Peter Paul Rubens in Antwerp and Diego Velázquez in Spain.

Titian's artistic output during seventy years of activity was huge. His reputation was such that he was lionized by popes and princes. He was a particular favorite of the Holy Roman Emperor Charles V, who granted him noble rank after having summoned him on a number of occasions to work at the royal court. From this tremendous body of work two representative paintings, emblematic of the wide range of his abilities, provide a focus.

The huge panel painting in the Venetian Church of the Frari called the *Assumption of the Virgin* [242] shows Titian at his monumental best. The swirling color in subtly different shadings and the dramatic gestures of the principals, all of which converge on the person of the Madonna, give a feeling of vibrant upward movement; color and composition define the subject of the assumption of Mary into heaven. The energy in the panel, however, should not distract the viewer from its meticulous spatial relationships. The use of a triangular composition, the subtle shift from dark to light, the lines converging on the Madonna from both above and below are all part of carefully wrought ideas that give the work its final coherence.

Contrast the *Assumption* with Titian's work of twenty years later, the *Venus of Urbino* [243]. The religious intensity of the *Assumption* gives way to the sensual delight of the *Venus* done in homage to feminine beauty from a purely human perspective. The architectural background, evenly divided between light and dark coloration, replaces Giorgione's natural landscapes. The lushness of the nude figure is enhanced by the richness of the brocade, the small bouquet of flowers, the little pet dog, and the circumspect maids at their tasks around a rich clothes chest in the background. The *Venus of Urbino* reflects a frank love of the human body, which is presented in a lavish artistic vocabulary. It is obvious that Titian painted this work for an aristocratic and wealthy patron.

above: 242 Titian.
Assumption of the Virgin.
1516–1518. Oil on canvas,
22'6" × 11'8" (6.86 × 3.56 m).
Church of the Frari, Venice.

right: 243 Titian.
Venus of Urbino. 1538.
Oil on canvas,
3'11" × 5'5" (1.19 × 1.62 m).
Uffizi, Florence.

Mannerism

There is general agreement that at the end of the second decade of the 16th century High Renaissance, art in Italy, under severe intellectual, psychological, and cultural pressure, gave way to an art style that seemed to be an exaggeration of Renaissance form and a loosening of Renaissance intellectuality. It is not so much that a new school of artists arose but that a mood touched some artists at some point in their careers and captivated others totally. An earlier generation of art historians saw this tendency, called *Mannerism*, as a sign of decadence and decay. Scholarly opinion is less harsh today, viewing Mannerism as a distinct aesthetic to be judged on its own terms.

Mannerism is hard to define and the term is often used without any precise sense. The schema proposed by the art historian Frederick Hartt might serve in place of a strict definition:

High Renaissance

Content:	Normal, supernormal, or ideal; appeals to universal
Narrative:	Direct, compact, comprehensible
Space:	Controlled, measured, harmonious, ideal
Composition:	Harmonious, integrated, often centralized
Proportions:	Normative, idealized
Figure:	Easily posed, with possibility of motion to new position
Color:	Balanced, controlled, harmonious
Substance:	Natural

Mannerism

Content:	Abnormal or anormal; exploits strangeness of subject, uncontrolled emotion, or withdrawal
Narrative:	Elaborate, involved, abstruse
Space:	Disjointed, spasmodic, often limited to foreground plane
Composition:	Conflicting, acentral, seeks frame
Proportions:	Uncanonical, usually attenuated
Figure:	Tensely posed; confined or overextended
Color:	Contrasting, surprising
Substance:	Artificial

Using Hartt's schema we can detect Mannerist tendencies in some of Michelangelo's later work. The figures of *Night, Day, Dawn,* and *Dusk* seem to reflect the exaggerations of the Mannerist style Hartt describes. The entrance to the Laurentian Library [244]

244 Michelangelo. Vestibule of the Laurentian Library, Florence. Begun 1524, stairway completed 1559.

in Florence, begun by Michelangelo in 1524 to rehouse the Medici book collection, shows some of these characteristics. Its windows are not windows, its columns support nothing, its staircases with their rounded steps seem agitated and in motion, its dominant lines break up space in odd and seemingly unresolved ways.

Mannerist characteristics show up in only some of Michelangelo's works (the *Last Judgment* fresco in the Sistine Chapel might also be analyzed in this fashion), but some of his contemporaries quite clearly broke with the intellectual unity of the High Renaissance. Two in particular deserve some attention because they so clearly illustrate the Mannerist imagination.

Jacopo Carucci da Pontormo (1494–1557) was an eccentric and reclusive painter who had studied with Leonardo da Vinci in his youth. Pontormo's greatest painting is the *Deposition* [Plate 18, page 240], painted around 1528 for the church of Santa Felicità in Florence. The most striking feature of this work is its shocking colors: pinks, apple greens, washed-out blues. It is very hard to think of any other painting in the Renaissance to which this stunningly original and exotic work can be compared.

An even more dramatic example of the Mannerist aesthetic is by Francesco Mazzola (1503–1540), called Parmigianino. He painted the *Madonna of the Long Neck* [245] for a church in Bologna. The gigantic proportions in the picture space are made all the more exaggerated by forcing the eye to move from the tiny prophetic figure in the background to the single column and then to the overwhelmingly large Madonna. The infant almost looks dead; in fact, his hanging left arm is reminiscent of the dead Christ in

Michelangelo's *Pietà*. The Virgin's figure is rendered in a strangely elongated, almost serpentine, fashion. There is something oddly erotic and exotic about her due to the shape of her body, the long fingers, and the great curving "S" of her neck. The implied eroticism is reinforced by the partially clad figures clustered at her side.

How and under what circumstances Mannerism grew and matured is the subject of much debate. Some elements of that debate must include the intellectual and social upheavals of the time (everything from wars to the Protestant Reformation) and the human desire and need to innovate once the problems and potential of a given art style have been fully worked out. In a sense, Mannerism is a testament to the inventiveness and restlessness of the human spirit.

245 Parmigianino. *Madonna of the Long Neck.* c. 1534. Oil on panel, 7'1" × 4'4" (2.15 × 1.32 m). Uffizi, Florence.

Contrasting Renaissance Voices

Early 16th-century Renaissance culture was a study in contrasts. The period marked a time when some of the most refined artistic accomplishments were achieved, but it was also a period of great social upheaval. It must be remembered, for example, that the lives of both Raphael and Leonardo ended at precisely the time when Luther was struggling with the papacy. In 1527 Rome was sacked by the soldiers of the Emperor Charles V in an orgy of rape and violence the city had not seen since the days of the Vandals in the 5th century. It would be simplistic to reduce the period of the High Renaissance to a contrast between cool intellectual sophistication and intensely violent passion; nevertheless, it is true that two of the most interesting writers of the period in Italy do reflect rather precisely those opposing tendencies.

Castiglione

Baldassare Castiglione (1478–1529) served in the diplomatic corps of Milan, Mantua, and Urbino. He was a versatile man—a person of profound learning, equipped with physical and martial skills, and possessed of a noble and refined demeanor. Raphael's famous portrait of Castiglione [246] faithfully reflects both Castiglione's aristocratic and intellectual qualities.

While serving at the court of Urbino from 1504 to 1516 Castiglione decided to write *The Courtier,* a task that occupied him for the next dozen years. It was finally published by the Aldine Press in Venice in 1528, a year before the author's death. In *The Courtier,* cast in the form of an extended dialogue and borrowing heavily from the style and thought of ancient writers from Plato to Cicero, Castiglione has his learned friends discuss a range of topics—the ideals of chivalry, classical virtues, the character of the true courtier, the ideals of platonic love. Posterity remembers Castiglione's insistent plea that the true courtier should be a person of humanist learning, impeccable ethics, refined courtesy, physical and martial skills, and fascinating conversation. He should not possess any of these qualities to the detriment of any other.

The *uomo universale*—the well-rounded person—should do all things with what Castiglione calls *sprezzatura. Sprezzatura,* which is almost impossible to translate into a single English word, means something like effortless mastery. The courtier, unlike the pedant, wears learning lightly, while his mastery of sword and horse has none of the fierce clumsiness of the common soldier in the ranks. The courtier does

246 Raphael. *Baldassare Castiglione.* 1515–1516.
Oil on panel, transferred to canvas; 29½ × 25½" (75 × 65 cm).
Louvre, Paris.

everything equally well but with an air of unhurried and graceful effortlessness.

Castiglione's work was translated into English by Sir Thomas Hoby in 1561. It exercised an immense influence on what the English upper classes thought the educated gentleman should be. We can detect echoes of Castiglione in some of the plays of Ben Jonson as well as in the drama of William Shakespeare. When in *Hamlet* (III,i), for example, Ophelia cries out in horror at the lunatic behavior of Hamlet (at his loss of *sprezzatura?*) the influence of Castiglione is clear:

> Oh, what a noble mind is here o'erthrown!
> The courtier's, soldier's, scholar's eye, tongue, sword:
> The expectancy and rose of the fair state,
> The glass of fashion and the mould of form,
> The observed of all observers . . .

The most common criticism of Castiglione's courtier is that he reflects a world that is overly refined, too aesthetically sensitive, and excessively preoccupied with the niceties of decorum and decoration. The courtier's world, in short, is the world of the very wealthy, the very aristocratic, and the most select of the elite. If the reader shares that criticism when reading Castiglione, the *Autobiography of Benvenuto Cellini* should prove a bracing antidote to the niceties of Castiglione.

Cellini

Benvenuto Cellini (1500–1571) was a talented Florentine goldsmith and sculptor whose life, frankly chronicled, was a seemingly never-ending panorama of violence, intrigue, quarrel, sexual excess, egotism, and political machination. His *Autobiography,* much of it dictated to a young apprentice who wrote while Cellini worked, is a vast and rambling narrative of Cellini's life from his birth to the year 1562. We read vignettes about popes and commoners, artists and soldiers, cardinals and prostitutes, assassins and artists, as well as a gallery of other characters from the Renaissance demimonde of Medicean Florence and papal Rome.

Above all, we meet Benvenuto Cellini, who makes no bones about his talent, his life of love, or his taste for violence. Cellini is not one of Castiglione's courtiers. Cellini fathered eight legitimate and illegitimate children; he was banished from Florence for sodomy; imprisoned for assault; fled Rome after murdering a man; and fought on the walls of the

247 Benvenuto Cellini.
Perseus. 1545–1554.
Bronze, height 18' (5.48 m).
Loggia dei Lanzi, Florence.
Earlier models of this statue have been preserved in the museum of the Bargello in Florence, including the wax model Cellini first used.

Castel Sant' Angelo in Rome during the seige of 1527 in defense of the Medici pope Clement VII. Anyone who thinks of the Renaissance artist solely in terms of proportion, love of the classics, Neoplatonic philosophy, and genteel humanism is in for a rude shock when encountering Cellini's *Autobiography*.

One particular part of Cellini's book is interesting, not for its characteristic bravado or swagger, but for its insight into the working methods of an artist. In a somewhat melodramatic account Cellini describes the process of casting the bronze statue of Perseus that actually turned out to be his most famous work [247]. It now stands in the Loggia dei Lanzi just to the right of the Palazzo Vecchio in Florence.

Cellini does not belong to the first rank of sculptors, although nobody has denied his skill as a craftsman. The *Perseus,* finished in 1554 for Duke Cosimo I de' Medici, is a highly refined work made more interesting because of Cellini's record of its genesis.

Music in the 16th Century

Music at the Papal Court

The emphasis in this chapter on painting, sculpture, and architecture makes it easy to forget that many of these artistic creations were intended for the service of Roman Catholic worship. It should be no surprise that fine music was subsidized and nurtured in Rome at the papal court. In fact, the active patronage of the popes for both the creation and the performance of music dates back to the earliest centuries of the papacy. Gregorian chant, after all, is considered to be a product of the interest of Pope Gregory and the school of Roman chant. In 1473 Pope Sixtus IV established a permanent choir for his private chapel, which came to be the most important center of Roman music. Sixtus' nephew Julius II endowed the choir for Saint Peter's, the Julian Choir.

The Sistine Choir used only male voices. Preadolescent boys sang the soprano parts, while older men, chosen by competition, sang the alto, tenor, and bass parts. The number of voices varied then from 16 to 24 (the choir eventually became, and still is, much larger). The Sistine Choir sang *a cappella* (without accompaniment), although we know that the popes enjoyed instrumental music outside the confines of the church. Cellini, for example, mentions that he played instrumental motets for Pope Clement VII.

While Botticelli and Perugino were decorating the walls of the Sistine Chapel, the greatest composer of the age, Josquin des Prez (c. 1440–1521), was in the service of the Sistine Choir, composing and directing music for its members from 1486 to 1494. From his

music we can get some sense of the quality and style of the music of the time.

Josquin, who was Flemish, spent only those eight years in Rome, but his influence was widely felt in musical circles. He has been called the bridge figure between the music of the Middle Ages and the Renaissance. Although he wrote madrigals and many masses in his career, it was in the *motet* for four voices, a form not held to traditional usages in the way the masses were, that he showed his true genius for creative musical composition. Josquin has been most praised for homogeneous musical structure, a sense of balance and order, a feel for the quality of the word. These are all characteristics common to the aspirations of the 16th-century Italian humanists. In that sense, Josquin combined the considerable musical tradition of northern Europe with the new intellectual currents of the Italian south.

The Renaissance motet uses a sacred text sung by four voices in polyphony. Josquin divided his texts into clear divisions but disguised them by using overlapping voices so that one does not sense any break in his music. He also took considerable pains to marry his music to the obvious grammatical sense of the words while still expressing their emotional import by the use of the musical phrase. A portion of the motet *Tu Pauperum Refugium* ("Thou Refuge of the Poor") illustrates both points clearly. The text shows the principle of overlapping (look at the intervals at which the voices enter with, for example, the end of the phrase *obdormiat in morte*). Likewise, the descending voices underscore the sense of the words *ne unquam obdormiat in morte anima mea* ("lest my soul sleep in death") in a way that to one musicologist suggests death itself is entering.

The 16th-century composer most identified with Rome and the Vatican is Giovanni Pierluigi da Palestrina (1525–1594). He came from the Roman hill town of Palestrina as a youth and spent the rest of his life in the capital city. At various times in his career he was the choirmaster of the choir of Saint Peter's (the *cappella Giulia*), a singer in the Sistine Choir, choirmaster of two other Roman basilicas (Saint John Lateran and Saint Mary Major). Finally, from 1571 until his death he directed all music for the Vatican.

Palestrina flourished during the rather reactionary period in which the Catholic Church tried to reform itself in response to the Protestant Reformation by returning to the simpler ways of the past. It should not surprise us, then, that the more than one hundred masses he wrote were very conservative. His polyphony, while a model of order, proportion, and clarity, is nonetheless tied very closely to the musical tradition of the ecclesiastical past. Rarely does Palestrina move from the Gregorian roots of church music. For example, amid the polyphony of his *Mass in Honor of Pope Marcellus* one can detect the traditional melodies of the Gregorian *Kyrie, Agnus Dei,* and so on. Despite that conservatism, he was an extremely influential composer whose work is still regularly heard in the Roman basilicas. His music was consciously imitated by the Spanish composer Victoria (or Vittoria— c. 1548–1611), whose motet *O Vos Omnes* is almost traditional at Holy Week Services in Rome, and by William Byrd (c. 1543–1623), who brought Palestrina's style to England.

Venetian Music

The essentially conservative character of Palestrina's music can be contrasted with the much more adventuresome situation in Venice, a city less touched by the ecclesiastical powers of Rome. In 1527 a Dutchman, Adrian Willaert, became choirmaster of the Church of Saint Mark's. He in turn trained Andrea Gabrieli and his more famous nephew, Giovanni Gabrieli, who became the most renowned Venetian composer of the 16th century.

The Venetians pioneered the use of multiple choirs for their church services. Saint Mark's regularly used two choirs, called split choirs, which permitted greater variation of musical composition in that the choirs could sing to and against each other in increasingly complex patterns. The Venetians also were more inclined to add instrumental music to their liturgical repertoire. They pioneered in the use of the organ for liturgical music. The independent possibilities of the organ gave rise to innovative compositions that highlighted the organ itself. These innovations became, in time, standard organ pieces: the prelude, the music played before the services began (called in Italy the *intonazione*), and the virtuoso prelude called the *toccata* (from the Italian *toccare,* "to touch"). The *toccata* was designed to feature the range of the instrument and the dexterity of the performer.

Both Roman and Venetian music were deeply influenced by the musical tradition of the north. Josquin des Prez and Adrian Willaert were, after all, both from the Low Countries. In Italy their music came in contact with the intellectual tradition of Italian humanism. Without pushing the analogy too far it could be said that Rome gave the musician the same Renaissance sensibility that it gave the painter: a sense of proportion, classicism, and balance. The Venetian composers, much like Venetian painters of the time, were interested in color and emotion.

Questions for Further Discussion

1. It would be an excellent exercise in cultural analysis to compare the new Saint Peter's with some of the landmark churches of earlier times. What difference in religious and aesthetic sensibility does one find, for example, by looking at Chartres or Hagia Sophia after a study of Saint Peter's?
2. It has been suggested that Michelangelo's statues of the Dukes Lorenzo and Giuliano de' Medici inspired John Milton's two poems "L'Allegro" and "Il Penseroso." Read the poems. Does that suggestion merit serious consideration?
3. Raphael is famous for the beauty of his *madonnas,* a common subject in the history of art. Compare Raphael's madonnas with those of previous centuries. How different (or similar) are they? Contrast some specific madonnas, e.g., those of the Byzantine period, with those of Raphael, to sharpen your comparison.
4. If you were to create a modern "School of Athens," what modern thinkers would you place in your scene to illustrate the great minds that influence our culture? What would the architectural setting look like?
5. Castiglione's *The Courtier* was a model of what an educated person should be, how that person should act, what that person should know, and how that person should view the larger world. Are there such books today? What values, styles, achievements, and so on, do they emphasize?
6. A genius like Michelangelo is a rare phenomenon. Is there any person today who is famous in a number of fields who could be compared to Michelangelo? What factors make it difficult in our society for a single person to gain fame in areas as diverse as painting, sculpture, architecture, engineering, etc.?

	GENERAL EVENTS	LITERATURE & PHILOSOPHY	ART

1494

1500

| | | | 1494-1495 Dürer visits Italy |

GENESIS OF THE REFORMATION

	GENERAL EVENTS	LITERATURE & PHILOSOPHY	ART
	1515-1547 Reign of Francis I in France		1500 Dürer, *Self-Portrait*
	1517 Reformation begins in Germany with Luther's 95 Theses, challenging the practice of indulgences	1506-1532 Ariosto active in Italy	early 16th cent. Italian Renaissance art and thought spread northward
		1509 Erasmus, *The Praise of Folly*	c. 1505-1510 Bosch, *Garden of Earthly Delights,* triptych
	1519-1556 Reign of Charles V as Holy Roman Emperor	1516 More, *Utopia*	1508-1511 Dürer, *Adoration of the Trinity*
	1521 Excommunication of Luther by Pope Leo X	1521 Luther begins translation of Bible into German, published 1534	1513 Dürer, *Knight, Death and the Devil,* engraving
	1524-1525 Peasants' War in Germany	1524 Erasmus, *De Libero Arbitrio (On Free Will)*	1515 Grünewald, *Isenheim Altarpiece*

1525

SPREAD OF PROTESTANTISM

	GENERAL EVENTS	LITERATURE & PHILOSOPHY	ART
	1525 Francis I defeated by Charles V at Pavia	1525 Luther, *De Servo Arbitrio (On the Bondage of the Will)*	1525 Altdorfer, *Landscape,* early example of pure landscape painting
	1527 Sack of Rome by Charles V	1530 Budé persuades Francis I to found Collège de France as center for humanism	1528 Dürer, *Four Books on Human Proportions*
	1534 Henry VIII founds Anglican Church in England when Parliament passes Act of Supremacy		1529 Altdorfer, *Battle of Alexander and Darius*
			c. 1530 Clouet, *Portrait of Francis I*
	1539 Society of Jesus (Jesuits) founded by Saint Ignatius of Loyola	16th cent. Humanism spreads, along with interest in scientific inquiry; availability of books increases literacy	c. 1530-1550 Sacred art denounced as idolatry by reforming iconoclasts
			c. 1533-1540 Decorations by Rosso Fiorentino for Palace at Fontainebleau
			1539-1540 Holbein the Younger, *Portrait of Henry VIII*
		1543 Copernicus, *On the Revolution of Celestial Bodies;* Vesalius, *Seven Books on the Structure of the Human Body*	1540-1543 Cellini, *Saltcellar,* commissioned by Francis I
	1545-1564 Council of Trent initiates Counter-Reformation under Jesuit guidance		1548-1549 Goujon, *Fountain of the Innocents,* Louvre, Paris

1550

GROWTH OF COUNTER-REFORMATION

	GENERAL EVENTS	LITERATURE & PHILOSOPHY	ART
	1550-1555 Wars between Lutheran and Catholic princes in Germany; ended by Peace of Ausburg in 1555		c. 1562-1567 Breugel the Elder, *The Triumph of Death, Hunters in the Snow, Peasant Wedding*
	1556 Retirement of Charles V		
	1556-1598 Reign of Philip II in Spain and Netherlands		
	1558-1603 Reign of Elizabeth in England	1559 Pope Paul IV publishes first Index of Prohibited Books	
	1572 Saint Bartholomew's Day Massacre in France		

1575

RELIGIOUS AND NATIONALISTIC UNREST

	GENERAL EVENTS	LITERATURE & PHILOSOPHY	ART
	1581 United Provinces of Netherlands declare independence from Spain	1580 Montaigne's first *Essays*	
		c. 1587 Marlowe, *Tamburlaine,* tragedy	
	1585 England sends troops to support Netherlands against Spain	1590 Sidney, *Arcadia*	
		1590-1596 Spenser, *The Faerie Queene,* allegorical epic	
	1588 Philip's Spanish Armada defeated by English	1590-1610 Drama at height in Elizabethan England	c. 1590 Hilliard, *Portrait of a Youth,* miniature
	1598 Edict of Nantes establishes religious toleration in France	1593 Marlowe, *Dr. Faustus,* tragedy	c. 1600 Patronage for sacred art wanes in Reformation countries, flourishes in Counter-Reformation countries
	1607 English found colony of Virginia in New World	late 16th-early 17th cent. Cervantes active in Spain, Jonson in England, Tasso in Italy	
	1609 Independence of Netherlands recognized by Spain	c. 1600 Shakespeare, *Hamlet*	
		c. 1604-1605 Shakespeare, *Othello, King Lear, Macbeth*	
		1611 *Authorized Version* of Bible	
		1620 Francis Bacon, *Novum Organum*	

1620

12

The Renaissance in the North

1506 Rebuilding of Saint Peter's Basilica, Rome, begins

1519 Château of Chambord built by Francis I

Vernacular hymns stressed by Reformers; musical elements in Protestant services simplified by Luther to increase comprehension

Ein' Feste Burg ist Unser' Gott (A Mighty Fortress Is Our God), c. 1525–1530

1544 Gregorian chant is basis for first English-language litany in England

1549 Merbecke, *The Book of Common Praier Noted*

1546 Lescot and Goujon, Square Court of Louvre, begun

c. 1550 Reformation ends building of elaborate churches in Protestant countries

c. 1570 Tallis, English court organist, composes *Lamentations of Jeremiah*

1588 *Musica Transalpina* translated into English

1591 Byrd, *My Ladye Nevells Booke*

late 16th-early 17th cent. English madrigals by Byrd, Morley, and Weelkes follow Italian models; ayres by Dowland

The ideas and artistic styles that developed in Italy during the 15th and 16th centuries produced immense changes in the cultural life of England, France, Germany, and the Netherlands. As the Renaissance spread beyond the Alps, the new humanism it carried roused Northern Europe from its conservative intellectual patterns and offered an alternative to traditional religious doctrines. The infusion of Italian ideas produced a new breadth of vision that was responsible for some of the greatest northern painting and for important developments in music. By the end of the 16th century, under the influence of humanism a brilliant cultural life had developed in Elizabethan England, where Renaissance English drama achieved its greatest glory in the work of William Shakespeare.

This was not the first time northern Europe and Italy had come into contact. During the 14th century a style of late-Gothic painting reflecting the grace and elegance of courtly life on both sides of the Alps had developed. Known as the International Style, it was popular in both Italy and northern Europe. Furthermore, as early as the beginning of that century German scholars who had gone to study in Italy returned home with a new enthusiasm for classical antiquity. Nor was the northern Renaissance a purely imported phenomenon, the filling of a cultural void by the wholesale adoption of foreign ways and styles. Northern artists drew upon a rich native past and were able to incorporate exciting new ideas from Italy into their own vision of the world. One of the chief characteristics of northern Renaissance art, in fact, was its emphasis on individualism; painters like

Albrecht Dürer and Albrecht Altdorfer are as different from each other as they are from the Italian artists who initially influenced them.

The spread of Italian Renaissance ideas to the north was in many respects political rather than cultural. Throughout most of the 16th century the great monarchs of northern Europe vied with one another for political and military control over the states of Italy, and in the process were brought into contact with the latest developments in Italian artistic and intellectual life—and often based their own courts on Italian models. Francis I, who ruled France from 1515 to 1547, made a deliberate attempt to expose French culture to Italian influences by doing everything he could to attract Italian artists to the French court; among those who came were Leonardo da Vinci, Andrea del Sarto (1486–1530), and Benvenuto Cellini [248]. Francis and his successors also esteemed literature and scholarship highly. Francis' sister, Marguerite of Navarre, herself a writer of considerable gifts, became the center of an intellectual circle that included many of the finest minds of the age.

The history of Germany is intimately bound up with that of the Hapsburg family. In the first half of the 16th century the same Hapsburg who ruled Germany (under the old name of the Holy Roman Empire) as Charles V ruled Spain at the same time as Charles I. Charles was the principal competitor of Francis I for political domination of Italy, and although his interest in the arts was less cultivated than that of his rival his conquests brought Italian culture to both Spain and the north [249]. On his abdication in 1556 he divided his vast territories between his

248 Benvenuto Cellini.
The Saltcellar of Francis I. 1539–1543.
Gold, 10¼ × 13⅛″ (26 × 33 cm).
Kunsthistorisches Museum, Vienna.
The male figure is Sea; the female is Land.
"Both figures were seated with their legs interlaced, just as the arms of the sea run into the land," Cellini said.

249 Leone Leoni. *Bust of Emperor Charles V.*
1533–1555. Bronze, height 44″ (112 cm). Kunsthistorisches
Museum, Vienna. The sculptor deliberately portrayed the
German ruler as a Roman emperor, thus associating Charles
with both Italy and classical antiquity.

brother Ferdinand and his son Philip. The Austrian
and Spanish branches of the Hapsburg family remained the principal powers in Europe until the
1650s.

For most of the Renaissance, England remained
under the dominion of a single family, the Tudors,
whose last representative was Elizabeth I. Like her
fellow rulers, in the course of her long reign (1558–
1603) Elizabeth established her court as a center of art
and learning. Although the influence of Italian models on the visual arts was less marked in England than
elsewhere, revived interest in classical antiquity and
the new humanism it inspired is reflected in the
works of Shakespeare and other Elizabethan writers.

Although the art of the great northern centers
drew heavily on Italy for inspiration, another factor
was equally important. The 15th century was a period of almost unparalleled intellectual ferment, in
which traditional ideas on religion and the nature of
the universe were shaken and often permanently
changed. Many of the revolutionary movements of
the age were, in fact, northern in origin, and not surprisingly they had a profound effect on the art,
music, and literature being produced in the same

place and time. While northern artists were being influenced by the styles of their fellow artists south of
the Alps, their cultural world was being equally
shaped by theologians and scientists nearer home.
The intellectual developments of this world form a
necessary background to its artistic achievements.

The Reformation

On the eve of All Saint's Day in 1517, a German
Augustinian friar, Martin Luther (1483–1546),
tacked a parchment containing 95 academic propositions (*theses*) written in Latin on the door of the colle-
giate church of Wittenberg—the usual procedure for
advertising an academic debate [250]. Luther's theses
constituted an attack on the Roman Catholic doctrine

250 Lucas Cranach. *Portrait of Martin Luther.* c. 1526.
Oil on panel, 15 × 9″ (38 × 24 cm). Uffizi Gallery, Florence.

Religious Divisions in Europe c. 1600

- Catholicism
- Orthodox Christianity
- Anglicanism
- Calvinism
- Lutheranism

(Religious minorities are not represented)

of indulgences (forgiveness of punishment for sins, usually obtained either through good works or prayers along with the payment of an appropriate sum of money) [66]; a timely topic since an indulgence was currently being preached near Wittenberg to help raise funds for the rebuilding of Saint Peter's in Rome.

Luther's act touched off a controversy that went far beyond academic debate. For the next few years there were arguments among theologians, while Luther received emissaries and directives from the Vatican as well as official warnings from the pope.

Luther did not waver in his criticisms. On June 15, 1520, Pope Leo X (born Giovanni de' Medici, son of Lorenzo the Magnificent) condemned Luther's teaching as heretical and on January 3, 1521, excommunicated him from the Catholic Church. The Protestant Reformation had been born.

Luther's reformation principles began to be applied in churches throughout Germany and a rapid and widespread outbreak of other reforming movements was touched off by Luther's example. By 1523 radical reformers far more iconoclastic than Luther began to agitate for a purer Christianity free from any trace of "popery." These radical reformers are often called *anabaptists* because of their insistence on adult baptism even if there had been baptism in infancy (the word anabaptist means "baptized again"). Many of these anabaptist groups had radical social and political ideas, such as pacifism and the refusal to take oaths or participate in civil government, which appealed to the discontent of the lower classes. One outcome was the Peasants' War in Germany, put down with ferocious bloodshed in 1525.

The Reformation was not confined to Germany. In 1523, Zurich, Switzerland, accepted the reformation ideal for its churches. Under the leadership of Ulrich Zwingli (1484–1531), Zurich, and later Berne and Basel, adopted Luther's reforms, including the abolition of statues and images and the right of the clergy to marry. In addition, the system of sacraments was greatly modified and reduced to include only baptism and the Lord's Supper. In Geneva, John Calvin (1509–1564) preached a brand of Protestantism even more extreme than that of either Luther or Zwingli. Calvin's doctrines soon spread north to the British Isles, especially Scotland, under the Calvinist John Knox, and west to the Low Countries, especially Holland. In England, King Henry VIII (born 1491, reigned 1509–1547), formerly a stout opponent of Lutheranism, broke with Rome in 1534 after he failed to obtain a marital annulment from the pope [Plate 19, page 273]. In 1534 Henry issued the Act of Supremacy, declaring the English sovereign head of the church in England.

By the middle of the 16th century, therefore, Europe—for centuries solidly under the authority of the Church of Rome—was divided in a way that has remained essentially unaltered ever since. Spain and Portugal, Italy, most of France, southern Germany, Austria, parts of Eastern Europe (Poland, Hungary, and parts of the Balkans), and Ireland remained Catholic, while most of Switzerland, the British Isles, all of Scandinavia, northern and eastern Germany, and other parts of Eastern Europe gradually switched to Protestantism (see map, opposite).

Causes of the Reformation

What conditions permitted this rapid and revolutionary upheaval in Europe? The standard answer is that the medieval church was so riddled with corruption and incompetence that it was like a house of cards waiting to be toppled. This answer, while containing some truth, is not totally satisfactory since it does not explain why the Reformation did not happen a century earlier, when similar or worse conditions prevailed. Why had the Reformation not taken place during the 14th century, when there were such addi-

tional factors as plague, schisms, and wars as well as incipient reformers clamoring for change?

The exact conditions that permitted the Reformation to happen are hard to pinpoint, but any explanation must take into account a number of elements that were clearly emerging in the 16th century. First, there was a rising sense of nationalism in Europe combined with increasing resentment at the economic and political demands made by the papacy, many of which ignored the rights of individual countries. Thus Luther's insistence that the German rulers reform the Church because the Church itself was impotent to do so appealed to both economic and nationalistic self-interests.

Second, the idea of reform in the Church had actually been maturing for centuries, with outcries against abuses and pleas for change. Some of the great humanists who were contemporaries of Luther, including Erasmus of Rotterdam, Thomas More in England, and Jacques Lefèvre d'Étaples in France, had also pilloried the excesses of the church. These men, and many of their followers and devoted readers, yearned for a deeper, more interior piety, free from the excessive pomp and ceremony that characterized so much of popular medieval religion. Luther's emphasis on personal conversion and his rejection of much of the ecclesiastical superstructure of Catholicism appealed to the sensibilities of many people. That the reformers to the left of Luther demanded even more rejection of Catholic practices shows how widespread was the desire for change.

Third, there were a number of other factors clustered around the two already mentioned: the low moral and intellectual condition of much of the clergy was a scandal; the wealth and lands of the monastic and episcopal lords were envied. In short, a large number of related economic and political factors fed the impulses of the Reformation.

Renaissance Humanism and the Reformation

The relationship between Renaissance humanism and the Protestant Reformation is significant if complex. With the single exception of John Calvin, none of the major church reformers was a professional humanist, although all of them came into contact with the movement. Luther himself had no early contact with the "new learning," though he utilized its fruits. Nevertheless, humanism as far back as the time of Petrarch shared many intellectual and cultural sentiments with the Reformation. We should note these similarities before treating the wide differences between the two movements.

The reformers and the humanists shared a number of religious aversions. They were both fiercely critical of monasticism, the decadent character of most popular devotion to the saints, the low intellectual preparation of the clergy, and the general venality and corruption of the higher clergy, especially the papal *curia* (the body of tribunals and assemblies through which the pope governed the Church).

Both the humanists and the reformers felt that the scholastic theology of the universities had degenerated into quibbling arguments, meaningless discussions, and dry academic exercises bereft of any intellectual or spiritual significance. In a common reaction both rejected the scholastics of the medieval universities in favor of Christian writers of an earlier age. John Calvin's reverence in the 16th century for the writings of the early Christian church father and philosopher Augustine (354–430) echoed the equal devotion of Petrarch in the 14th.

Humanists and reformers alike spearheaded a move toward a better understanding of the Bible based not on the authority of theological interpretation but on close, critical scrutiny of the text, preferably in the original Hebrew and Greek. Indeed, the mastery of the three biblical languages (Latin, Greek, and Hebrew) was considered so important in the 16th century that schools were founded especially for the specific purpose of instruction in them. Some famous academic institutions, including Corpus Christi College, Oxford, the University of Alcalá, Spain, and the Collège de France in Paris, were founded for that purpose. Luther's own University of Wittenberg had three chairs for the study of biblical languages.

We can see the connection between humanist learning and the Reformation more clearly by noting some aspects of Luther's great translation of the Bible into German. Although there had been many earlier vernacular translations into German, Luther's, which he began in 1521, was the first produced entirely from the original languages, and the texts he used illuminate the contribution of humanist learning. For the New Testament he used the critical Greek edition prepared by Erasmus. For the book of Psalms he used a text published in Hebrew by the humanist printer Froben at Basel in 1516. The other Hebrew texts were rendered from a Hebrew version published by Italian Jewish scholars who worked in the Italian cities of Soncino and Brescia. His translations of the Apocrypha (books not found in the Hebrew canon) utilized the Greek edition of the Apocrypha printed in 1518 by Aldus Manutius at his press in Venice. As an aid for his labors Luther made abundant use of grammars and glossaries published by the humanist scholar Johannes Reuchlin.

In short, Luther's great achievement was possible only because much of the spadework had already been done by a generation of humanist philologists. This scholarly tradition endured: In 1611, when the translators of the famous English King James Version (see page 325) wrote their preface to the Bible, they noted that they had consulted commentaries and translations as well as translations or versions in Chaldee, Hebrew, Syriac, Greek, Latin, Spanish, French, Italian, and Dutch.

Although there were similarities and mutual influences between humanists and reformers, there were also vast differences. Two are of particular importance. The first relates to concepts of the nature of humanity. The humanist program was rooted in the notion of human perfectibility. This was as true of the Florentine humanists with their strong platonic bias as it was of northern humanists like Erasmus. The humanists put great emphasis on the profoundly Greek (or, more accurately, Socratic) notion that education can produce a moral person. Both humanist learning and humanist education had a strong ethical bias: learning improves and ennobles. The reformers, by contrast, felt that humanity was hopelessly mired in sin and could only be raised from that condition by the free grace of God. For the reformers, the humanists' position that education could perfect a person undercut the notion of a sinful humanity in need of redemption.

The contrast between these two points of view is most clearly evident in a polemical debate between Luther and Erasmus on the nature of the human will. In a 1524 treatise called *De Libero Arbitrio (On Free Will)*, Erasmus defended the notion that human effort cooperates in the process of sanctification and salvation. Luther answered in 1525 with a famous tract entitled *De Servo Arbitrio (On the Bondage of the Will)*. The titles of the two pamphlets provide a shorthand description of the severe tensions between the two points of view.

A second difference between the humanists and the reformers begins with the humanist notion that behind all religious systems lies a universal truth that can be detected by a careful study of religious texts. Pico della Mirandola, for example, thought that the essential truth of Christianity could be detected in talmudic, platonic, Greek, and Latin authors. He felt that a sort of universal religion could be constructed from a close application of humanist scholarship to all areas of religion. The reformers, on the other hand, held to a simple yet unshakable dictum: *Scriptura sola* (the Bible alone). While the reformers were quite ready to use humanist methods to investigate the sacred text they were adamant in their conviction that only the Bible held God's revelation to humanity.

right: Plate 19 Hans Holbein the Younger. *Henry VIII in Wedding Dress.* 1540. Oil on panel, 32½ × 29″ (83 × 74 cm). Galleria Barberini, Rome. Weddings were not uncommon events in Henry's life. This wedding, when he was in his 49th year, as the inscription says, was probably the ill-fated one to his fourth wife, Anne of Cleves (see figure **270,** page 288).

below: Plate 20 Matthias Grünewald. *Crucifixion* from the *Isenheim Altarpiece,* exterior. Completed 1515. Panel (with framing) c. 9′9½″ × 10′9″ (2.98 × 3.28 m). Musée d'Unterlinden, Colmar. Behind Mary Magdalene, who kneels in grief, stand Mary and John, while on the other side John the Baptist points to Christ's sacrifice. Beside him, in Latin, are inscribed the words "He must increase, but I must decrease." Above Christ are the initial letters of the Latin words meaning "Jesus of Nazareth, King of the Jews."

273

Plate 21   Pieter Bruegel the Elder. *Hunters in the Snow*. 1565. Oil on panel, 3′10″ × 5′3¾″ (1.17 × 1.62 m). Kunsthistorisches Museum, Vienna. Note Bruegel's careful use of color to suggest a cold, clear, sunless day. From his first crossing of the Alps in the 1530s Bruegel was inspired by mountain scenery, and it reappeared throughout his work. In this painting, the panoramic sweep from the foreground to the lofty peaks behind makes the scene appear a microcosm of human existence. Thus Bruegel's "world landscapes" or *Weltlandschaften* are both literal depictions of scenes from nature and symbolic representations of the relationship between human beings and the world around them.

We can see that there was an intense positive and negative interaction between humanism and the Reformation—a movement energized by books in general and the Bible in particular. The intensely literary preoccupations of 14th- and 15th-century humanism provided a background and impetus for the 16th-century Reformation. As a philosophical and cultural system, however, humanism was in general too optimistic and ecumenical for the more orthodox reformers. In the later 16th century humanism as a world view found a congenial outlook in the Christian humanism of Cervantes and the gentle skepticism of Montaigne, but in Reformation circles it was used only as an intellectual instrument for other ends.

Cultural Significance of the Reformation

Cultural historians have attributed a great deal of significance to the Reformation. Some have argued, for example, that with its strong emphasis on individuals and their religious rights, the Reformation was a harbinger of the modern political world. However, with equal plausibility one could make the case that with its strong emphasis on social discipline and its biblical authoritarianism, the Reformation was the last great spasm of the medieval world. Likewise, in a famous thesis developed in the early 20th century by the German sociologist Max Weber, Calvinism was seen as the seedbed and moving force of modern capitalism. Weber's proposition has lingered in our vocabulary in phrases like *the work ethic* or *the Puritan ethic*, although most scholars now see it as more provocative than provable. Regardless of the scholarly debates about these large questions, there are other, more clearly defined ways in which the Protestant Reformation changed the course of Western culture.

First, the Reformation gave a definite impetus to the already growing use of books in European life. The strong emphasis on the reading and study of the Bible produced inevitable concern for increased literacy. Luther, for example, wanted free education to be provided for all children of all classes in Germany.

The central place of the Bible in religious life made an immense impact on the literary culture of the time. Luther's Bible in Germany and the King James Version in England (to say nothing of the Anglican *Book of Common Prayer*) exercised an inestimable influence on the very shape of the language spoken by their readers. In other countries touched by the Reformation the literary influence of the Bible in translation was absolutely fundamental. In the Scandinavian countries, vernacular literature really begins with translations of the Bible. In Finland, a more extreme example, Finnish was used as a written language for the first time in translating the Bible.

251 Portion of a page from the Gutenberg Bible. 1455. Rare Books and Manuscripts Division, New York Public Library. The Latin text of the Lord's Prayer (Matthew 6:9–13) begins on the fourth line with "Pater noster." The first edition of this Bible, printed at Mainz, was probably of 150 copies.

The Bible was not the only book to see widespread diffusion in this period. Books, pamphlets, and treatises crisscrossed Europe as the often intricate theological battles were waged for one or another theological position. It is not accidental that the Council of Trent (1545–1564), a prime instrument of the Catholic counter-reform, stringently legislated the manner in which Bibles were to be translated and distributed. The fact that both a stern censorship and a list of forbidden books (the infamous *Index*) were instituted by the Catholic Church at this time is evidence that the clerical leadership recognized the immense power of books. The number of books circulating in this period is staggering: between 1517 and 1520 (even before his break with Rome) Luther's various writings sold about three hundred thousand copies in Europe.

None of this, of course, would have been possible before the Reformation for the simple reason that printing did not exist in Europe. The invention of the printing press (see page 245) and movable type revolutionized Renaissance culture north and south of the Alps in the same way that films, radio, and television have changed the 20th century [251]. There were two

252 Luther's German Psalter. Staatliche Lutherhalle, Wittenberg. The book is open at Luther's hymn "Ein' Feste Burg," which is taken from one of the Psalms. The Latin words above Luther's name mean "God our refuge and strength." The hymn itself is printed in German.

important side effects. The early availability of "book learning" undermined the dominance of universities, which had acted as the traditional guardians and spreaders of knowledge. Also, Latin began to lose its position as the only language for scholarship, since many of the new readers did not understand it. Luther fully grasped the implications of the spread of literacy, and his use of it to advance his cause was imitated countless times in the following centuries.

A second cultural fact about the Reformation, closely allied to the first, is also noteworthy. The reformers put a great emphasis on the *Word.* Besides reading and listening there was also singing, and the reformers—especially Luther—stressed the vernacular hymn. The hymn was seen as both a means of praise and an instrument of instruction. Luther himself was a hymn writer of note. His famous *"Ein' Feste Burg ist Unser' Gott"* ("A Mighty Fortress Is Our God") is one of the best-loved hymns in Christianity [252]. Indeed, the German musical tradition, which ultimately led to Johann Sebastian Bach in the 17th century, was very much the product of the Lutheran tradition of hymnody.

On the other hand, the 16th-century reformers had little need or sympathy for the plastic arts. They were in fact, militantly iconoclastic. One of the hallmarks of the first reformers was their denunciation of paintings, statues, and other visual representations as forms of papist idolatry. The net result of this iconoclastic spirit was that by the beginning of the 17th century patronage for the sacred visual arts had virtually died in countries where the Reformation was strong. With the single exception of Rembrandt (and the exception is a gigantic one) it is difficult to name any first-rate painter or sculptor who worked from a Reformation religious perspective after the 16th century, although much secular art was produced.

The attitude of the 16th-century reformers toward the older tradition of the visual arts may be best summed up by the church of Saint Peter's in Geneva, Switzerland. Formerly a Romanesque Catholic cathedral of the 12th century, Saint Peter's became Calvin's own church. The stained glass was removed, the walls whitewashed, the statues and crucifixes taken away, and a pulpit placed where the high altar once stood. The church of Saint Peter's is a thoroughly reformed church, a building whose entire function is for the hearing of the preached and read word. Gone is the older notion (represented, for example, by the Cathedral of Chartres) of the church reflecting the other-worldly vision of heaven in the richness of its art. Reformation culture was in short an *aural*, not a *visual*, culture.

Intellectual Developments: The Growth of Science

The 16th century was not merely a turning point in the history of religions; it was a decisive age in the history of science. In earlier times a scientist was likely enough to be an ingenious tinkerer with elaborate inventions who dabbled in alchemy, astrology, and magic [253]. The new Renaissance scientist, a

above: 253   Giulio Campagnola. *The Astrologer*. 1509. Engraving, 3¾ × 6″ (9.5 × 15 cm).
British Museum, London (reproduced by courtesy of the Trustees).
The old-fashioned astrologer is shown with all the paraphernalia of his craft,
immersed in mystical speculation and apparently accompanied by his pet monster.

below: 254   Hans Holbein the Younger. *Nikolaus Kratzer*. 1528. Tempera on panel,
32 × 26″ (83 × 67 cm.) Louvre, Paris. The new scientists are represented here by Kratzer,
official astronomer to the court of Henry VIII and a friend of Dürer.
The tools used in the calculation he is making are devised for maximum precision,
and the room where Kratzer is working is equipped as a laboratory.

person of wide learning with a special interest in mathematics and philosophy, would develop bold and revolutionary ideas but always subject them to the test of practical experience [254].

The age produced many advances in science. In England alone William Gilbert (1540–1603) discovered that the earth was a large magnet whose pole points approximately northward; Sir William Harvey (1578–1657) solved the problem of how the blood could "circulate"—get from the arteries to the veins and return to the heart—by postulating the existence of the then-undiscovered channels we now call capillaries; John Napier (1550–1615) discovered the very practical mathematical tool called the logarithm, which greatly reduced the time and effort needed to solve difficult equations. Elsewhere in Europe, the German Paracelsus (1493–1541) laid the foundations of modern medicine by his decisive rejection of traditional practices. Although his own theories were soon rejected, his insistence on observation and inquiry had important consequences, one of which can be seen in the work of Andreas Vesalius (1514–1564), who was born in Brussels and studied in Padua. Vesalius' *Seven Books on the Structure of the Human Body*, published in 1543, comprise a complete anatomical treatise, illustrating in minute detail and with impressive accuracy the human form [255].

The philosophical representative of the "new science" was Francis Bacon (1561–1626), who combined an active and somewhat disreputable political career with the writing of works intended to demolish traditional scientific views. The chief of these books was the *Novum Organum* (1620), which aimed to free science from the two-thousand-year-old grasp of Aristotle while at the same time warning against the unrestrained use of untested hypotheses.

Science and religion came into direct conflict in the work of the Polish astronomer Nicholas Copernicus (1473–1543), who studied at the universities of Cracow and Bologna. In 1543, the same year Vesalius' work appeared, he published *On the Revolutions of Celestial Bodies*, a treatise in which he denied that the sun and the planets revolve around the earth, and reverted instead to a long-dead Greek theory that the earth and planets orbit the sun. Catholic and Protestant theologians found themselves for once united in their refusal to accept an explanation of the universe that seemed to contradict the teaching of the Bible, but Copernicus' work, though not a complete break with the past, provided stimulus for Galileo's astronomical discoveries in the following century.

Furthermore, the general principle behind Copernicus' method had important repercussions for the entire history of science. Up to his time scientists had taken the position that, with certain exceptions, reality is as it appears to be. If the sun appears to revolve about the earth, that appearance is a "given" in nature, not to be questioned. Copernicus questioned the assumption, claiming that it was equally plausible to take the earth's mobility as a given, since everything that had been explainable in the old way was fully explainable in the new. He thus made a breach between "common sense" and scientific truth that every major scientist since has widened.

Painting in Germany

The conflict between Italian humanism, with its belief in human perfectibility, and the Reformation, which emphasized sin and the need for prayer, is reflected in the art of the greatest German painters of the early 16th century. It might even be said that the intellectual and religious battles of the times stimulated German art to its highest achievements, for both Albrecht Dürer (1471–1528) and Matthias Grünewald (about 1500–1528) are, in very different ways, towering figures in the development of European painting. In spite of his sympathy with Luther's beliefs, Dürer was strongly influenced by Italian ar-

255 Andreas Vesalius. *Third Musculature Table, from De humani corporis fabrica.* Brussels, 1543. National Library of Medicine, Bethesda, Maryland.

tistic styles and, through Italian models, by classical ideas. Grünewald, on the other hand, rejected almost all Renaissance innovations and turned instead to traditional northern religious themes, treating them with new passion and emotion. Other artists, meanwhile, chose not to wrestle with the problems of the times. Some, including Albrecht Altdorfer (1480–1538), preferred to stand back and create a world view of their own.

Dürer

Dürer was born in Nuremburg, the son of a goldsmith. Even as a child he showed remarkable skill in drawing. His father apprenticed him to a wood engraver, and in 1494–1495—after finishing his training—Dürer made the first of two visits to Italy. In Italy he saw for the first time the new technique of *linear perspective*, whereby all parallel lines converge at a single vanishing point, and came into contact with the growing interest in human anatomy. Quite as important as these technical discoveries, however, was his perception of a new function for the artist. The traditional German—indeed, medieval—view of the artist was as an artisan whose task was humbly, if expertly, to reproduce God's creations. Dürer adopted Renaissance humanism's conception of the artist as an inspired genius, creating a unique personal world. It is not by chance that a first glance at his *Self-Portrait* of 1500 [256] suggests a Christlike figure rather than a prosperous German painter of the turn of the century. The effect is intentional. The lofty gaze of the eyes underlines the solemn, almost religious nature of the artist's vision, while the prominent hand draws attention to his use of the pen and the brush to communicate it to us.

In his paintings Dürer shows a fondness for precise and complex line drawing rather than the softer use of mass and color typical of Italian art. In fact, much of his greatest work was created in the medium of graphic art. In 1498 he published a series of fifteen *woodcuts* illustrating the Revelation of Saint John, known as the *Apocalypse* series. Woodcut engravings are produced by drawing a design on a block of soft wood, then cutting away the surrounding wood to leave the lines of the drawing standing in relief. The blocks of wood can then be coated with ink and used to print an impression on paper. In the hands of Dürer this relatively simple technique was raised to new heights of expressiveness, as in his depiction of Saint Michael's fight against the dragon from the *Apocalypse* series [257]. In the upper part of the scene Michael and other angels, all of them with long hair curiously like Dürer's own, do battle with a gruesome horde of fiends, while the peaceful German landscape below seems untouched by the cosmic fight in progress. Dürer's vision of an apocalyptic struggle between good and evil reflected the spirit of the time, and copies of the *Apocalypse* series sold in large quantities. Growing discontent with the Church was, as we have seen, one of the causes of Luther's Reformation; the general sense of forthcoming trouble and upheaval gave Dürer's woodcuts a particular aptness.

The medium of *line engraving* was also one to which Dürer brought an unsurpassed subtlety and expressiveness. Unlike a woodblock, where the artist can complete the drawing before cutting away any

256 Albrecht Dürer. *Self-Portrait.* 1500. Panel, 25⅝ × 18⅞″ (64 × 48 cm). Alte Pinakothek, Munich. The frontal pose and solemn gaze are used to convey Dürer's belief in the seriousness of his calling.

257 Albrecht Dürer. *Saint Michael Fighting the Dragon,* from the *Apocalypse* series. 1498. Woodcut, 15½ × 11⅛″ (39 × 28 cm). British Museum, London (reproduced by courtesy of the Trustees). Note Dürer's characteristic signature in the center bottom.

material, the copper plate from which a line engraving is printed has to be directly incised with the lines of the design by means of a sharp-pointed steel instrument called a *burin*. The richness of effect Dürer achieved in this extremely difficult medium, as in his engraving of *Adam and Eve* [258], is almost incredible. The engraving furthermore demonstrates not only his technical brilliance but also the source of much of his artistic inspiration. The carefully shaded bodies of Adam and Eve reflect the influence of contemporary Italian ideals of beauty, while the proportions of the figures are derived from classical literary sources. Dürer made up for the lack of actual Greek and Roman sculpture in Germany by a careful reading of ancient authors, from which he derived a system of proportion for the human figure.

In 1505–1507 Dürer returned to Italy, where he spent most of his time in Venice, discussing theoretical and practical aspects of Renaissance art with Bellini and other Venetian artists. It was inevitable that the rich color characteristic of Venetian painting would make an impression on him, and many of his works of this period try to outdo even the Venetians in splendor.

His renewed interest in painting was, however, brief. For almost the rest of his life he devoted himself to engraving and to writing theoretical works on art. Between 1513 and 1515 he produced his three greatest engravings. The earliest of these, *Knight, Death, and the Devil* [259], again reflects contemporary religious preoccupations with its symbolic use of the Christian knight, accompanied by a dog who represents untiring devotion and beset by the temptations of the devil (in a particularly untempting guise, it must be admitted). Neither this fearsome creature nor the appearance of Death, armed with an hourglass, can shake the knight's steadfast gaze.

By the end of his life Dürer was acknowledged one of the great figures of his time. Like Luther, he made use of the new possibilities of the printing press to spread his ideas. At the time of his death he was working on *Four Books on Human Proportions*. This work, in Latin, aimed to accomplish for art what Vesalius' did for medicine. It was inspired by two of

258 Albrecht Dürer. *Adam and Eve*. 1504. Engraving, 9⅞ × 7⅝″ (25 × 19 cm). Metropolitan Museum of Art, New York (Fletcher Fund, 1919). The various animals represent the sins and diseases that resulted from Adam and Eve's eating of the tree of knowledge: the cat pride and cruelty, the ox gluttony and sloth, and so on.

259 Albrecht Dürer. *Knight, Death, and the Devil*. 1513. Engraving, 9¾ × 7½″ (25 × 19 cm). British Museum, London (reproduced by courtesy of the Trustees). The knight's calm determination reflects Dürer's confidence in the ability of the devout Christian to resist temptation. This engraving may have been inspired by Erasmus' book *Handbook of the Christian Knight* (see page 247).

the great intellectual concerns of the Renaissance: a return to classical ideals of beauty and proportion and a new quest for knowledge and scientific precision.

Grünewald

Although the work of Grünewald represents the other high point in German Renaissance art, very little is known about his life. Only in the 20th century did we discover his real name, Mathis Gothart Neithart; the date of his birth and early years of his career are still a mystery. Grünewald seems to have

260 Matthias Grünewald. Resurrection, from the *Isenheim Altarpiece,* first opening. Completed 1515. Panel, 8'2½" × 3'1½" (2.45 × .93 m). Musée d'Unterlinden, Colmar. Note the absence of any natural setting and the confused perspective, which give the scene an other-worldly quality.

worked for a while at the court of the Cardinal Archbishop of Mainz, but in the 1525 Peasants' War he sided with the German peasants in their revolt against the injustices of their rulers, after which his enthusiasm for Luther's new ideas kept him from returning to the Cardinal's service. He retired to Halle, where he died in 1528.

What we know about his political and religious sympathies—his support for the oppressed and for the ideals of the Reformation—is borne out by the characteristics of his paintings. Unlike Dürer, Grünewald never went to Italy, and he showed no interest in the new styles developed there. The Renaissance conception of ideal beauty and the humanist interest in classical antiquity left him unmoved. Instead, he turned again and again to the traditional religious themes of German medieval art, bringing to them a passionate, almost violent intensity that must at least in part reflect the religious heart-searchings of the times. Yet it would be a mistake to see Grünewald's unforgettable images as merely another product of the spirit of the age, for an artist capable of so unique and personal a vision is in the last analysis inspired by factors that cannot be explained in historical terms. All that can safely be said is that no artist, before or since, has depicted the Crucifixion as a more searing tragedy or Christ's Resurrection as more radiantly triumphant.

Both these scenes occur in Grünewald's greatest work, the *Isenheim Altarpiece*, finished in 1515, which was commissioned for the church of a hospital run by members of the Order of St. Anthony. The folding panels are painted with scenes and figures appropriate to its location, including saints associated with the curing of disease and events in the life of St. Anthony himself. In particular, the patients who contemplated the altarpiece were expected to meditate on Christ's Crucifixion and Resurrection and derive from them comfort for their own sufferings.

In his painting of Christ in the Crucifixion panel [Plate 20, page 273], Grünewald uses numerous details to depict the intensity of Christ's anguish—from his straining hands, frozen in the agony of death, to the thorns stuck in his festering body, to the huge iron spike that pins his feet to the cross. It is difficult to imagine anything further from the Italian Renaissance and its concepts of ideal beauty than this tortured image. Grünewald reveals an equal lack of interest in Renaissance or classical theories of proportion or perspective. The figure of Christ, for example, is not related in size to the other figures but dominates the panel, as a glance at the comparative size of the hands will show. Yet the sheer horror of this scene only throws into greater relief the triumph of the Resurrection [260]. Christ seems almost to

261 Albrecht Altdorfer. *Danube Landscape near Regensburg.* c. 1522–1525. Panel, 11 × 8⅝″ (28 × 22 cm). Alte Pinakothek, Munich. The only traces of human existence here are the road and the distant castle to which it leads.

have exploded out of the tomb, in a great burst of light that dazzles the viewers as well as the soldiers stumbling below. No greater contrast can be imagined than between the drooping body on the cross and this soaring weightless image that suggests a hope of similar resurrection to the sufferers in the hospital.

Altdorfer

The drama of Grünewald's spiritual images is in strong contrast to the quiet, poetic calm of the work of Albrecht Altdorfer. Although closer in style to Grünewald than to Dürer, Altdorfer found his favorite subject not in religious themes but in landscapes. *Danube Landscape near Regensburg* [261], probably dating from around 1525, is one of the first examples in the Western tradition of a painting without a single

human figure. From the time of the Greeks, art had served to tell a story, sacred or secular, or to illustrate some aspect of human behavior. Now for the first time the contemplation of the beauties of nature was in itself deemed a worthy subject for an artist. In this painting Altdorfer depicts a kind of ideal beauty very different from Dürer's *Fall of Man* but no less moving. Part of his inspiration may have come from the landscapes that can be seen in the background of paintings by Venetian artists like Giorgione, although there is no evidence that Altdorfer ever visited Italy. Even if he did, his sympathy with the forces of nature, its light and scale and sense of life, seems more directly inspired by actual contact.

In Altdorfer's most famous work, the *Battle of Alexander and Darius* [262], the thousands of soldiers under their mighty leaders wheel and turn in scenes of hectic activity. Their violence seems to express the

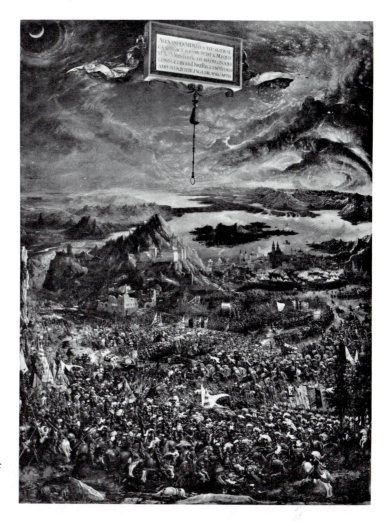

262 Albrecht Altdorfer. *Battle of Alexander and Darius.* 1529. Panel, 5'2" × 3'11" (1.58 × 1.2 m). Alte Pinakothek, Munich. The tassel hanging from the descriptive plaque floating above the scene leads the eye down to the center of the conflict, where Alexander pursues the Persian king Darius trying to escape in his chariot.

futility of human existence when set against the grandeur of the rivers and mountain peaks that provide their setting. The almost-mystical power of the natural world Altdorfer conveys was to be rediscovered later in the 19th century in the work of German romantic painters like Caspar David Friedrich (1774–1840; see page 000).

Painting in the Netherlands

The two greatest Netherlandish painters of the Renaissance, Hieronymus Bosch (c. 1450–1516) and Pieter Bruegel (1525–1569), are linked both by their pessimistic view of human nature and by their use of satire to express it. Bosch furthermore drew upon an apparently inexhaustible imagination to create a fantasy world that alternately fascinates and repels as the eye wanders from one bizarre scene to another. Although modern observers have interpreted Bosch's work in a variety of ways, it is generally agreed that, contrary to appearances, he was in fact a deeply religious painter. His chief subject is human folly in its innumerable forms, his theme that the inevitable punishment of sin is Hell. Salvation is possible through Christ, but few, according to Bosch, have the sense to look for it. His paintings show us the consequences.

Bosch

Almost nothing is known of Bosch's life, and his works must speak for themselves. The most elaborate in its fantasy is a *triptych* (a painting made up of three panels) known as the *Garden of Earthly Delights* [263], which was probably finished around 1510. Into it are crowded hundreds of nude figures engaged in activities that range from the unimaginable to the indescribable, all in pursuit of erotic pleasure. The movement from the apparently innocent scene of the creation of Eve on the left to the fires of Hell on the right illustrates Bosch's belief that the pleasures of the body lead to damnation along a road of increasing depravity. Even in the Garden of Eden we sense what is to come, as Adam sits up with excited enthusiasm on being presented with the naked Eve, while God seems to eye him nervously.

The bright world of the middle panel, in which the pallid, rubbery figures seem to arrange themselves (and one another) in every conceivable position and permutation, gives way on the right to a hallucinating vision of eternal damnation.

Bosch's symbolism is too complex and too private to permit a detailed understanding of the scene, yet his general message is clear enough: Hell is not terrifying so much as it is sordid and pathetic. The frantic scenes of activity are as senseless and futile as those of

worldly existence, but in Hell their monstrous nature becomes fully apparent.

The sources of Bosch's inspiration in this and other works are unknown. Many of his demons and fantastic animals seem related to similar manifestations of evil in medieval art, but no medieval artist ever devised a vision such as this or had the technique to execute it. To modern eyes some of his creations, like the human-headed monster on the right-hand panel turning both face and rear toward us, seem to prefigure the surrealist art of the 20th century. There is a danger, however, in applying labels from the art of later times to that of an earlier period. Bosch must simply be allowed to stand on his own as one of the great originals in the history of painting.

Bruegel

Pieter Bruegel, often called the Elder to distinguish him from his son of the same name, represents the culmination of Renaissance art in the Netherlands. Like that of Bosch, his work is often fantastic, and his crowded canvases are frequently filled with scenes of

263 Hieronymus Bosch. *Garden of Earthly Delights.* c. 1505–1510. Panel; center 7'2⅝″ × 6'4¾″ (2.2 × 1.95 m), each wing 7'2⅝″ × 3'2¼″ (2.2 × .97 m). Prado, Madrid. Perhaps surprisingly, this catalogue of the sins of the flesh was among the favorite works of the gloomy King Philip II of Spain.

grotesque activity. Some of his paintings suggest that he shared Bosch's view of the apparent futility of human existence and the prevalence of sin. In many of his pictures, however, the scenic backgrounds reveal a love and understanding of nature very different from Bosch's weird view of the world and represent one of the keys to understanding his work. For Bruegel, the full range of human activity formed part of a world in which there existed an underlying order. The beauty of nature forms the background not only to his pictures but actually to the lives of us all, he seems to say; by seeing ourselves as part of the natural cycle of existence we can avoid the folly of sin. If this interpretation of his work is correct, it places Bruegel with the humanists, who believed in the possibilities for human good, and there is some evidence to suggest that his friends did include members of a group of humanist philosophers active at Antwerp.

Although Bruegel's best-known paintings are scenes of peasant life, it is a mistake to think of him as unsophisticated. On the contrary, during the last years of his life, which he spent in Brussels, he was familiar with many of the leading scholars of the day

and seems to have been a man of considerable culture. He certainly traveled to Italy, where he was apparently unaffected by the art but deeply impressed by the beauty of the landscape. Back home, he may well have supported the move to free the Netherlands from Spanish rule; some of his paintings seem to contain allusions to Spanish cruelties.

Bruegel's vision is so rich and so understanding of the range of human experience that it almost rivals that of Shakespeare, who was born in 1564, five years before Bruegel's death. In his great painting *The Triumph of Death* [264], Bruegel looks with uncompromising honesty at the universal phenomenon of death—which comes eventually to all, rich and powerful or poor and hopeless. Unlike Bosch, who reminds us that the righteous (if there are any) will be saved, Bruegel seems to offer no hope. Yet the same artist painted the *Peasant Wedding Feast* [265], a scene of cheerful celebration. True, Bruegel's peasants find pleasure in simple rather than sophisticated delights, in this case chiefly food and drink, but he reminds us that some are luckier than others. The little boy in the foreground so completely engrossed in licking up

264 Pieter Bruegel the Elder. *The Triumph of Death*. c. 1562–1564. Oil on panel, 3'10" × 5'3¾" (1.17 × 1.62 m). Prado, Madrid. Note the huge coffin on the right, guarded by rows of skeleton-soldiers, into which the dead are being piled.

265 Pieter Bruegel the Elder. *Peasant Wedding Feast.* 1566–1567.
Oil on panel, 3'8⅞" × 5'4⅛" (1.14 × 1.63 m). Kunsthistorisches Museum, Vienna.
The composition of the painting is based on the diagonal line of the receding table
that leads the eye past the bride and the bagpiper to the back of the room.

every last delicious morsel of food is counterbalanced
by the bagpiper who looks wistfully and wanly over
his shoulder at the tray of pies going by. Nor should
we be too hasty to think of Bruegel's peasants as un-
thinking creatures, content with a brutish existence.
The bride certainly does not seem either bright or
beautiful, but she radiates happiness, and the general
air of merriment is very attractive.

Bruegel's most profound statements are perhaps
to be found in a cycle of paintings intended to illustrate the months of the year, rather like the *Très
Riches Heures* of the Limbourg Brothers a century
earlier. Bruegel finished only five of them, including
the magnificent *Hunters in the Snow* of 1565 [Plate 21,
page 274]. In the background tower lofty peaks,
which represent Bruegel's memory of the Alps, seen
on his trip to Italy. From the weary hunters in the
foreground a line of barren trees leads the eye to
fields of snow where peasants are hard at work. The
scene can hardly be called a happy one, but neither is
it unhappy. There is an inevitability in the way humans, animals, birds, and nature are all bound into a
unity, expressive of a sense of order and purpose.
The lesson of Italian humanism has been translated
into a very different language, spoken with a highly
individual accent, but Bruegel's northern scene seems
in its own way inspired by a similar regard for
human dignity.

266 Jean Clouet (?). *Francis I.* c. 1525–1530.
Tempera and oil on panel, 37¾ × 29⅛" (96 × 74 cm).
Louvre, Paris. This famous work is now thought to be by an
unknown artist rather than Clouet himself, but its style is very
similar to that of his many official portraits of the king.

267 Château of Chambord. Begun 1529. Although the turrets and pinnacles are reminiscent of French medieval architecture, the central block and much of the decorative detail suggest Italian Renaissance models.

Art and Architecture in France

France of the 16th century has little to compare with the artistic achievements of Germany and the Netherlands. The influence of Italian art on France was so strong, due in great part to the actual presence at the French court of Italian artists, that French painting was almost completely overwhelmed. The only native artist of note was Jean Clouet (c. 1485–1541), who was retained by Francis I chiefly to serve as his official portrait painter. Among the many portraits of the king attributed to Clouet is one of around 1530 [266] that does full justice to the sensual but calculating character of his master.

More interesting than French painting during the 16th century is French architecture. The series of luxurious châteaux that Francis I had built along the valley of the river Loire combined the airiness of the earlier French Gothic style with decorative motifs imported from Italian Renaissance architecture. The result was buildings like the beautiful Château of Chambord [267].

The love of decoration shown by the builders of Chambord emerges even more strongly as a feature of French architectural style in the design of the Square Court of the Louvre [268]. This structure was begun in 1546 by the architect Pierre Lescot (1510–1578) and the sculptor Jean Goujon (c. 1510–1568), working for once without Italian guidance. The facade of the court is a compendium of classical forms, from the window moldings to the Corinthian columns to the decorative motifs. The total effect, however, is very different from Italian buildings using the

268 Pierre Lescot and Jean Goujon. Facade of the Square Court of the Louvre, Paris. Begun 1546. The architectural and sculptural decoration is Italian in origin, but used here as typically French elaborate ornamentation.

same features. Instead of being grand or awe-inspiring the building seems graceful and harmonious, perhaps even a little fussy, and the emphasis on decoration became a prominent characteristic of French art in the following two centuries.

Elizabethan England

Throughout the 16th century English political and cultural life followed a path notably different from that of continental Europe, as it did so often in its previous history. The social unrest that had marked the later Middle Ages in England was finally brought to an end in 1485 by the accession of Henry VII, the first of the Tudor dynasty. For the entire 16th century, England enjoyed a new stability and commercial prosperity on the basis of which it began to play an increasingly active part in international politics.

Henry VIII's final break with the Catholic Church in 1534 led to the later development of ties between England and the other countries of the Reformation, particularly the Netherlands. When years of tension between the Netherlanders and their Spanish rulers finally broke into open rebellion, England—by now ruled by Queen Elizabeth I (born 1533, reigned 1558–1603)—supplied help secretly. Relations between Elizabeth and the Spanish king, Philip II, were already strained, and English interference in the Spanish Netherlands was unlikely to help. In 1585 a new Spanish campaign of repression in the Netherlands, coupled with the threat of a Spanish invasion of England, drove the queen to take more open action, and she sent six thousand troops to fight alongside the Netherlanders. Their presence proved decisive.

Philip's anger at his defeat and at the progress of the campaign for an independent Netherlands was turned in fury against England. The massive Spanish Armada, the largest fleet the world had ever seen, was ready early in 1588 and sailed majestically north,

below left: 269 Nicholas Hilliard(?). *Ermine Portrait of Queen Elizabeth I.* 1585. Oil on canvas, 41¾ × 35″ (106 × 89 cm). Hatfield House, England (collection of the Marquess of Salisbury). The ermine on the queen's sleeve is a symbol of virginity. The portrait as a whole is a symbol of her majesty, not intended to show her actual appearance.

below right: 270 Hans Holbein the Younger. *Anne of Cleves.* c. 1539–1540. Vellum applied to canvas, 25⅝ × 18⅞″ (65 × 48 cm). Louvre, Paris. Viewing this portrait, Henry VIII sent for Anne of Cleves and made her his fourth queen. Note the formal pose and the suitably modest downturned gaze.

271 Nicholas Hilliard. *Portrait of a Youth.* c. 1590. Parchment, 5⅜ × 2¾″ (14 × 7 cm). Victoria and Albert Museum, London. Crown copyright. The thorns of the wild rose that is growing in the foreground may represent friendship in adversity. (The miniature is shown here at almost exactly its actual size.)

In view of England's self-appointed position as bulwark of Protestantism against the Catholic Church in general and Spain in particular, it is hardly surprising that Renaissance ideas developed south of the Alps took some time to affect English culture. Few Italian artists were tempted to work at the English court or, for that matter, were likely to be invited there. Furthermore, England's geographic position inevitably cut it off from intellectual developments in continental Europe and produced a kind of psychological insularity that was bolstered in the late 16th century by a wave of national pride. The finest expression of this is probably to be found in the lines William Shakespeare put into the mouth of John of Gaunt in Act II scene i, of *Richard II,* a play written some six years after the defeat of the Spanish Armada:

This royal throne of kings, this sceptered isle,
This earth of majesty, this seat of Mars,
This other Eden, demi-Paradise,
This fortress built by Nature for herself
Against infection and the hand of war,
This happy breed of men, this little world,
This precious stone set in the silver sea,
Which serves it in the office of a wall
Or as a moat defensive to a house
Against the envy of less happier lands—
This blessed plot, this earth, this realm, this
England. . . .

On the other hand, the same spirit of nationalism was bound to produce a somewhat narrowminded rejection of new ideas from outside. English sculpture and painting suffered as a result.

The only foreign painter to work in England was himself a northerner, Hans Holbein the Younger (1497/8–1543), whose portrait of Henry VIII is reproduced on page 273. A magnificent portraitist, Holbein found himself sent by Henry to paint prospective brides so that the king could make his choice with at least some idea of their appearance—an effective if rather tedious method before photography. It must be added that the artist seems to have done his work rather too well, since his picture of Anne of Cleves [270] inspired Henry to marry the princess only to divorce her within six months, contemptuously dismissing her as his "Flanders Mare."

Apart from Holbein, English artists were virtually cut off from the new ideas current elsewhere. The only English painter of note during the 16th century was Nicholas Hiliard (1547–1619), best known for his *miniatures,* small portraits often painted in watercolor. The finest is of an unidentified young man who has something of the poetic melancholy of a Shakespearean lover [271]. When Hilliard turned to larger works, specifically to portraits of Queen Eliza-

only to be met by a fleet of much lighter, faster English ships commanded by Sir Francis Drake. The rest is part history, part legend. Even before the expedition sailed, Drake had "singed the beard of the King of Spain" by sailing into Cadiz harbor and setting fire to some of the Spanish galleons waiting there. The rest of the Armada reached the English Channel, where it was totally destroyed, partly by superior English tactics, partly by a huge storm promptly dubbed (by the victors, at least) the Protestant Wind. The subsequent tales told of English valor and daring brought a new luster to the closing years of the Elizabethan Age [269].

beth, he was inevitably inhibited by his monarch's demand for a painting that would look regal and imposing rather than realistic. The result [see figure 269] is a symbolic representation of majesty rather than a mere portrait.

Elizabethan Music

As in the visual arts, the Renaissance produced major stylistic changes in the development of music; nonetheless, in general, musical development in the Renaissance was marked by a less severe break with medieval custom than was the case with the visual arts. Although 16th-century European composers began to increase the complexity of their style, making frequent use of polyphony (several musical parts combined and sounding together), they continued to use forms developed in the High Middle Ages and the early Renaissance. In religious music the motet remained popular; this was a short choral piece for three or more voices, generally unaccompanied, set to a religious text. Composers also continued to compose *madrigals*, songs for three or more solo voices based generally on secular poems. For the most part these were intended for performance at home, and the skill of the singers was often tested by elaborate, interweaving polyphonic lines. The difficulty of the parts often made it necessary for the singers to use an instrumental accompaniment. This increasing complexity produced a significant change in the character of madrigals, which were especially popular in Elizabethan England. Nonetheless, 16th-century musicians were recognizably the heirs of their 13th- and 14th-century predecessors.

One of the results of this continuity was that English music suffered far less than the visual arts from the cultural isolationism of Elizabethan England; the Elizabethan Age, in fact, marks one of the high points in its history. Almost two hundred years earlier the English musician John Dunstable (c. 1385–1453) had been one of the leading composers in Europe. By bringing English music into the mainstream of continental developments he helped prepare the way for his Elizabethan successors.

A number of other factors were also responsible for the flourishing state of English music. To begin with, in England there had always been a greater interest in music than in the visual arts.

Also, the self-imposed ban on the importation of foreign art works and styles did not extend to printed music, with the result that by the early years of the reign of Elizabeth, Italian secular music began to circulate in English musical circles. A volume of Italian songs in translation was published in 1588 under the title *Musica Transalpina (Music from Across the Alps)*.

As for sacred music, when Henry VIII staged his break with the pope in 1534, he was not at all ready to convert wholeheartedly to Lutheranism or Calvinism and discard the sung parts of the liturgy. The services, psalms, and hymns the new Anglican Church had to devise generally (although by no means invariably) used English rather than Latin texts, echoing Luther's use of the vernacular, but continued for the most part to follow Catholic models.

Thus, when the first official version of the English litany was issued in 1544 by the Archbishop of Canterbury, Thomas Cranmer, it made use of the traditional Gregorian chant, simplified in such a way that only one note was allowed to each syllable of the text. This preserved the flavor of the original music, while making it easier for a listener to follow the meaning of the words and thereby participate more directly in the worship. The tendency to simplify is also visible, literally [272], in the first published musical setting of the words of the *Book of Common Prayer*, which had appeared in 1549. This first musical edition, *The Book of Common Praier Noted* (set to music) by John Merbecke (c. 1510–c. 1585), again used only one note to each syllable, and his settings followed the normal accentuation of the English words. This work is still used by the Episcopal Church.

In more elaborate music the effects of the Reformation were even less evident. Most of the professional composers of the day, after all, had been

272 John Merbecke. *Book of Common Praier Noted*. British Library, London (reproduced by courtesy of the Trustees). The Lord's Prayer is on the left page and part of the right page. The words are in English, but note the Latin title, *Agnus Dei (Lamb of God)*, retained on the right page.

And mu_____ sic dies, And_ mu_ sic dies.

brought up in a Catholic musical tradition, and while the split with Rome affected religious dogma (and of course permitted Henry to marry and divorce at will), it did not alter their freedom to compose as they wished. They continued to write pieces that alternated and combined the two chief styles of the day: blocks of chords in which every voice moved at the same time and the elaborate interweaving of voices known as *counterpoint.*

The musical forms also remained unchanged except in name. Among the most popular compositions throughout Europe were motets, short choral works, the words of which were often in Latin. English composers continued to write works of this kind but used English texts and called them *anthems.* A piece that used the full choir throughout was called a *full anthem* and one containing passages for solo voice or voices a *verse anthem.* English musicians nevertheless did not entirely abandon the use of Latin. A number of the greatest figures of the period continued to write settings of Latin texts as well as ones in the vernacular.

The dual nature of Elizabethan music is well illustrated by the career of Thomas Tallis (c. 1505–1585), who spent more than forty years of his life as organist of the Chapel Royal at the English Court. Although his official duties required him to compose works for formal Protestant occasions, he also wrote Latin motets and Catholic masses. Tallis was above all a master of counterpoint, bringing the technique of combining and interweaving a number of vocal lines to a new height of complexity in one of his motets, *Spem in Alium (Hope in Another),* written for no less than forty voices, each moving independently. In his anthems, however, he adopted a simpler style with a greater use of chord passages, so that the listener could follow at least part of the English text. His last works combine both techniques to achieve a highly expressive, even emotional effect, as in his setting of the *Lamentations of Jeremiah.*

Among Tallis' many pupils was William Byrd (c. 1543–1623), the most versatile of Elizabethan composers and one of the greatest in the history of English music. Like Tallis, he produced both Protestant and Catholic church music, writing three Latin masses and four English services, including the so-called Great Service for five voices. Byrd also composed secular vocal and instrumental music, including a particularly beautiful elegy for voice and strings, *Ye Sacred Muses,* inspired by the death of Tallis himself. The concluding bars, setting the words "Tallis is dead and music dies," demonstrate his ability to achieve considerable emotional pathos with simple means, in this case the rise of an octave in the next-to-last bar:

Much of Byrd's instrumental music was written for the *virginal,* an early keyboard instrument in the form of an oblong box small enough to be placed on a table or even held in the player's lap. It was once believed that the instrument was so called because of its popularity at the court of Elizabeth, the self-styled Virgin Queen, but references have been found to the name before her time, and its true origin is unknown. Forty-two pieces written for the virginal by Byrd were copied down in 1591 in an album known as *My Ladye Nevells Booke.* They include dances, variations, and fantasias and form a rich compendium of Byrd's range of style.

Byrd also wrote madrigals, songs performed by a small group of singers, often for their own entertainment at home. The madrigal had begun its life in Italy, where the words themselves were as important as the music, and Italian composers often chose poems that reflected the Renaissance interest in classical antiquity. The English madrigal was less concerned with Renaissance ideas of refinement than with the expression of emotional extremes. Many of the madrigals of Thomas Morley (1557–1602) are lighthearted in tone and fast moving, making use of refrains like "Fa-la-la." Among the best-known are *Sing we and chaunt it* and *Now is the month of Maying,* settings of popular verses rather than literary texts, intended not for an élite but for domestic performance by an increasingly prosperous middle class.

Other madrigals were more serious, even mournful. Both Morley and his younger contemporary Thomas Weelkes (c. 1575–1623) composed madrigals in memory of Henry Noel, an amateur musician who was a favorite at the court of Queen Elizabeth. Weelkes' piece *Noel, adieu* is striking for its use of extreme dissonances to express grief. In the following bars, the clash of C against C♯ seems strikingly modern in its harshness:

The most melancholy works of all Elizabethan music are the *ayres* of John Dowland (1562–1626), simple songs for one voice accompanied either by other voices or instruments. Dowland is the rare example of an Elizabethan musician who traveled widely. Irish by birth, he visited France, Germany, and Italy and even worked for a while at the court of

King Christian IV of Denmark; ultimately he settled in England.

Dowland was the greatest virtuoso of his day on the lute, a plucked string instrument that is a relative of the guitar, and used it to accompany his ayres. Dowland's gloomy temperament was given full expression both in the ayres and in his solo pieces for lute, most of which are as obsessively depressed and woeful as Morley's madrigals are determinedly cheerful. Popular in his own day, in more recent times Dowland's music has undergone something of a revival with the growth of interest in the guitar and other similar instruments.

English Literature: Shakespeare

English literature in the 16th century, unlike the visual arts and to a greater extent even than music, was strongly affected by new currents of Renaissance thought. One reason for this is purely practical. Soon after the invention of printing in Germany (see page 245), William Caxton (c. 1421–1491) introduced the printing press into England, and during the first half of the 16th century books became increasingly plentiful and cheap. With the spread of literature an increased literacy developed, and the new readers were anxious to keep in touch with all the latest ideas of their day.

The development of humanism in England undoubtedly influenced Erasmus of Rotterdam, who was brought into contact with humanist ideas during his visits there. In addition to teaching at Cambridge, Erasmus formed a warm personal friendship with the English statesman Sir Thomas More (1478–1535), who became Lord Chancellor in 1529.

More's *Utopia*, a philosophical romance in Latin describing an ideal world resembling that of Plato's *Republic*, was written under Erasmus' influence and was firmly based on humanistic ideals. Once introduced, these ideas caught on, and so did the use of classical or Italian models to express them. Sir Philip Sidney (1554–1586), the dashing youth who has been described as Castiglione's courtier come to life, wrote a series of sonnets in imitation of Petrarch and a romance, *Arcadia*, of the kind made popular in Italy by Lodovico Ariosto (1474–1533). Edmund Spenser (1552–1599), the greatest nondramatic poet of Elizabethan England, was also influenced by Ariosto and by Torquato Tasso (1544–1595), Ariosto's Italian successor in the production of massive epic poems. In *The Faerie Queene* Spenser combined the romance of Ariosto and the Christian allegory of Tasso to create an immensely complex epic. Its chivalrous hero, the Knight of the Red Cross, represents both Christianity and, through his resemblance to Saint George, England. At the same time the tests he undergoes make him a Renaissance version of the medieval figure of Everyman. The epic takes place in the imaginary land of Faerie, where the knight's path is frequently blocked by dragons, witches, wizards, and other magical creatures. All this mythological paraphernalia not only advances the plot but also pro-

273 The Globe Playhouse, London. 1599–1613. This conjectural reconstruction by C. Walter Hodges shows the playhouse during the years when Hamlet, King Lear, and other Shakespearean plays were first performed there.

THE GLOBE PLAYHOUSE
1599–1613
A Conjectural Reconstruction
by
C. Walter Hodges

KEY
A. The "Hut", with machinery for lowering the Heavenly throne to the stage.
B. The "Heavens".
C. Top stage, sometimes used as a music gallery.
D. Upper stage.
E. Window stages.
F. Inner stage, sometimes called the "Study".
G. "Traps" leading down to the "Hell" under the stage.
H. "Gentlemen's Rooms" or "Lords' Rooms".
J. Storage lofts, dressing rooms, etc.
K. Dressing rooms.
L. Backstage area.
M. Main entrances to auditorium.
N. Doorways connecting with gallery staircase.
O. Entrance to galleries and staircases.

Gallery Staircases

vides a series of allegorical observations on moral and political questions of the day. The result has, in general, been more admired than read.

The greatest of all English achievements in the Renaissance were in drama. The classical models of English drama were the Latin tragedies of Seneca and the comedies of Plautus and Terence, which, with the introduction of printing, became more frequently read and performed. These ancient Roman plays created a taste for the theater that English dramatists began to satisfy in increasing quantities.

At the same time the same prosperity and leisure that created a demand for new madrigals produced a growing audience for drama. To satisfy this audience, traveling groups of actors began to form, often attaching themselves to the household of a noble who acted as their patron. These companies gave performances in public places, especially the courtyards of inns. When the first permanent theater buildings were constructed, their architects imitated the form of the inn courtyards, with roofs open to the sky and galleries around the sides. The stage generally consisted of a large platform jutting out into the center of the open area known as the *pit* or *ground* [273].

The design of these theaters allowed—indeed, encouraged—people of all classes to attend performances regularly since the price of admission varied for different parts of the theater. The more prosperous spectators sat in the galleries, where they had a clear view of the stage, while the poorer spectators stood around the stage in the ground. Dramatists and actors soon learned to please these so-called *groundlings* by appealing to their taste for noise and spectacle.

Not all performances were given in public before so democratic an audience. The most successful companies were invited to entertain Queen Elizabeth and her court. The plays written for these state occasions were generally more sophisticated in both content and style than those for more general performance. The works written for the court of James I, Elizabeth's successor, are among the more elaborate of all.

In general, English drama developed from a relatively popular entertainment in the mid-16th century to a more formal artificial one in the early 17th century. It is probably no coincidence that the greatest of all Elizabethan dramatists, Shakespeare and Marlowe, wrote their best works at about the midpoint in this development, from about 1590 to 1610. Their plays reflect the increasing appreciation and demand for real poetry and high intellectual content without losing the "common touch" that has given their work its continual appeal.

Christopher Marlowe (1564–1593) was born two months before Shakespeare. Had he not been killed in a fight over a tavern bill at the age of 29, he might well have equaled Shakespeare's mighty achievements. It is certainly true that by the same age Shakespeare had written relatively little of importance, while Marlowe's works include the monumental two-part *Tamburlaine*, a vast tragic drama that explores the limits of human power; exuberant erotic verse like his *Hero and Leander*; and his greatest masterpiece, *Dr. Faustus*. Marlowe's use of *blank verse* for dramatic expression was imitated by virtually every other Elizabethan playwright, including Shakespeare. It consists of nonrhyming lines of iambic pentameter—lines of five metrical feet in which each foot has two syllables, the second one generally bearing the rhythmic stress. In style Marlowe's works reflect the passion and violence of his own life, their heroes striving to achieve the unachievable by overcoming all limits, only to be defeated by destiny.

Regret at the loss of what Marlowe might have written had he lived longer is balanced by gratitude for the many works William Shakespeare (1564–1616) left us. Shakespeare [274] is universally ac-

274 Title page of the First Folio, the first collected edition of Shakespeare's works, which was prepared by two of the playwright's fellow actors. London, 1623. Rare Books and Manuscripts Division, New York Public Library.

Mr. WILLIAM
SHAKESPEARES
COMEDIES,
HISTORIES, &
TRAGEDIES.

Published according to the True Originall Copies.

LONDON
Printed by Isaac Iaggard, and Ed. Blount. 1623.

knowledged the greatest writer in the English language, and one of the very greatest ever in any tongue. His position is best summarized in the words of his leading contemporary and rival playwright Ben Jonson (1572–1637): "He was not of an age, but for all time!"

Surprisingly little is known about Shakespeare's life. He was born at Stratford-upon-Avon; his early years and education seem to have been typical of provincial England, although no details are known. In 1582 he married Anne Hathaway; over the next three years they had three children. By 1592, he was established in London as an actor and playwright. Exactly how he became involved in the theater and what he did from 1585 to 1592 remain a mystery.

From the beginning of his time in London Shakespeare was associated with the leading theatrical company of the day, the Lord Chamberlain's Men, which changed its name to the King's Men at the accession of James I in 1603.

Shakespeare's earliest plays followed the example of classical models in being carefully constructed, although their plots seem sometimes unnecessarily overcomplicated. In the *Comedy of Errors* (1594–1594), for example, Shakespeare combined two plays by the Roman comic writer Plautus (c. 254–184 B.C.) to create a series of situations racked by mistaken identities and general confusion. The careful manipulation of plot in the early plays is achieved at the expense of characterization, and the poetry tends to use artificial literary devices. Even Shakespeare's first great tragedy, *Romeo and Juliet* (1595), is not altogether free from an excessive use of puns and plays on words, although the psychological depiction of the young lovers is convincing and the play contains some magnificent passages.

The comedies of the next few years, including both *The Merchant of Venice* (c. 1596) and *Twelfth Night* (c. 1600), are more lyrical. The brilliant wit of the earlier plays often is replaced by a kind of wistful melancholy. At the same time Shakespeare was attracted to historical subjects, generally drawn from English history, as in *Henry IV, Parts I and II* (1597–1598), but also from Roman history, as in *Julius Caesar*.

Julius Caesar (1599) is notable for a number of reasons. It shows that Shakespeare shared the renewed interest of his contemporaries in classical antiquity. It is, in fact, based directly on the *Lives* of Caesar, Brutus, and Mark Antony by the Greek historian Plutarch (c. 46–c. 127), which had appeared in a new translation by Sir Thomas North in 1579. *Julius Caesar* also illustrates Shakespeare's growing interest in psychological motivation rather than simply the sequence of events. The playwright tells us not so much what his characters do as why they do it, making use of the *soliloquy*, a kind of speech in which characters utter their thoughts out loud, without addressing them to anyone else, and thereby reveal to the audience the inner workings of their minds.

The use of this device becomes increasingly common in Shakespeare's supreme achievements, the series of tragedies he wrote between 1600 and 1605: *Hamlet* (c. 1600), *Othello* (c. 1604), *King Lear* (c. 1605), and *Macbeth* (c. 1605). In dramatic truth, poetic beauty, and profundity of meaning these four plays achieve an artistic perfection equaled only by the tragic dramas of Classical Greece. Through his protagonists, Shakespeare explores the great problems of human existence—the many forms of love, the possibilities and consequences of human error, the mystery of death—with a subtlety and yet a directness that remain miraculous through countless readings or performances and continue to provide inspiration to artists and writers [275].

275 Eugène Delacroix. *Hamlet and Horatio in the Graveyard.* 1839. Oil on canvas, 23 × 28″ (58 × 71 cm). Louvre, Paris. The great French Romantic painter (see page 376) here depicts Hamlet reflecting on mortality in Act V of *Hamlet*.

Shakespeare's later plays explore new directions. *Antony and Cleopatra* (c. 1607–1608) returns to Plutarch and to ancient Rome, but with a new richness and magnificence of language. The conciseness of his great tragedies is replaced by a delight in the sound of words, and the play contains some of the most musical of all Shakespearean verse. His very last works examine the borderline between tragedy and comedy with a sophistication that was perhaps intended to satisfy the new aristocratic audience of the court of King James I. *The Tempest* (1611), set on an enchanted island, blends high romance and low comedy to create a world of fantasy unlike that of any of the other plays.

In the year he wrote *The Tempest*, Shakespeare left London and retired to Stratford to live out the remaining years of his life in comparative prosperity. Although he continued to write, it is tempting to see in the lines he gave to Prospero toward the end of *The Tempest* (IV, i, 148–158) his own farewell to the theater, and to the world he created for it:

> Our revels now are ended. These our actors,
> As I foretold you, were all spirits, and
> Are melted into air, into thin air.
> And, like the baseless fabric of this vision,
> The cloud-capped towers, the gorgeous palaces,
> The solemn temples, the great globe itself—
> Yea, all which it inherit—shall dissolve
> And, like this insubstantial pageant faded,
> Leave not a rack behind. We are such stuff
> As dreams are made on, and our little life
> Is rounded with a sleep.

Questions for Further Discussion

1. How did the spread of printed matter affect life in the Renaissance? How does that compare with our times, in which some say that the age of communication by print is coming to an end, to be replaced by an age of instant electronic communication, chiefly radio and television? In your view, is this too extreme an opinion? If, however, it proves to be true, what is the effect likely to be?

2. The early leaders of the Reformation believed that the visual arts had little place in religion but encouraged the use of music in Protestant services. How justified do you think this decision is? What does the attitude tell you about the early reformers?

3. Shakespeare's plays were written for performance in a theatre very different from that of our time. What effects do modern production methods have on the way in which we experience the plays? How well do they adapt to films and TV?

4. During a time of crisis and violence, Montaigne chose to retire from the world and console himself with books and ideas. How practical in our own day would it be to attempt to do the same thing? How desirable or productive?

5. The great figures of the Renaissance—rulers and religious and philosophical leaders—were painted by the great artists of their day. Today images of the world's leaders are captured by the camera rather than by the paintbrush. What difference in perception is this likely to give when they are seen several hundred years from now?

6. Like many others, Hieronymus Bosch seems to have believed that physical pleasure corrupts and that sensuality leads to sin. How far back in the history of Western culture can this belief be traced, and how does it manifest itself in our own world?

	GENERAL EVENTS	LITERATURE & PHILOSOPHY	ART

1560

Left margin labels (top to bottom): DECLINE OF SPANISH POWER / THIRTY YEARS' WAR / PURITAN RULE / AGE OF LOUIS XIV AND XV

DECLINE OF SPANISH POWER

GENERAL EVENTS

1603-1625 Reign of James I in England

1609 Holland and Flanders given virtual independence in truce with Spain

1610-1643 Reign of Louis XIII in France; Marie de' Medici is regent during his minority

LITERATURE & PHILOSOPHY

1565 Teresa of Avila, *Autobiography*

1582-1584 John of the Cross, *The Dark Night*

1605-1615 Cervantes, *Don Quixote*

1611 Publication of *Authorized Version* of Bible, commissioned by King James I

ART

1595-1600 El Greco, *The Baptism of Christ*

1597-1604 Caravaggio and the Carracci at work in Rome

c. 1600-1602 Caravaggio, *The Doubting of Thomas, The Conversion of Saint Paul, The Martyrdom of Saint Matthew*

1604 A. Carracci, *The Flight into Egypt;* decorations for Palazzo Farnese Galleria completed

1616 Hals, *Banquet of the Officers of the Saint George Militia Company*

c. 1616-1617 Rubens, *The Rape of the Daughters of Leucippus*

1618

THIRTY YEARS' WAR

GENERAL EVENTS

1618 Thirty Years' War begins in Germany

1620 English Pilgrims land at Plymouth

1621-1665 Reign of Philip IV in Spain

1643 Five-year-old Louis XIV ascends throne of France under regency of his mother

1648 Peace of Westphalia

LITERATURE & PHILOSOPHY

1621 Donne appointed Dean of Saint Paul's, London

1632 Galileo, founder of modern physics, submits *Dialogue Concerning the Two Chief World Systems* to Pope Urban VIII; is tried and condemned in 1633

1637 Descartes, "Father of Modern Philsophy," publishes *The Discourse on Method*

1638 Galileo, *Dialogues Concerning Two New Sciences*

c. 1640 French Classical comedy and tragedy at height

1640-1643 Corneille, *Horace, Polyeucte,* tragedies

1641 Descartes, *Meditations*

1646 Crashaw, *Steps to the Temple*

ART

c. 1620 A. Gentileschi, *Judith and Holofernes*

1622-1625 Rubens paints cycle of 21 paintings glorifying Marie de Medici; Bernini, *The Rape of Proserpine*

1623 Bernini, *David;* Velázquez appointed court painter to Philip IV

c. 1625 Van Dyck, *Portrait of the Marchesa Cattaneo*

1627 Caravaggio's influence spreads northward when Louis XIII summons Vouet back from Rome to become court artist

1631 Claude Lorrain, *The Mill*

1632 Van Dyck court painter to Charles I

c. 1639 Ribera, *The Martyrdom of Saint Bartholomew*

1642 Rembrandt, *The Night Watch*

1645-1652 Bernini, *Saint Teresa in Ecstasy*

1649

PURITAN RULE

GENERAL EVENTS

1649 Execution of Charles I of England; Cromwell rules 1649-1658

LITERATURE & PHILOSOPHY

c. 1650 Locke active in England, Pascal in France, Spinoza in Holland

1651 Hobbes, *Leviathan*

c. 1659-1699 Poet and dramatist John Dryden active in England

ART

c. 1650 Poussin, *The Arcadian Shepherds;* Georges de La Tour, *Saint Sebastian Attended by Saint Irene*

1656 Velázquez, *Las Meninas*

1660

AGE OF LOUIS XIV AND XV

GENERAL EVENTS

1660 Restoration of monarchy in England under Charles II

1661 Louis XIV assumes full control of France

1682 Louis XIV moves court to newly remodeled Versailles

1688 Parliamentary enemies of James II invite William of Orange to invade England

1689 Declaration of Rights establishes English constitutional government; William and Mary rule

1715 Louis XIV dies after 72-year reign; Louis XV ascends throne

LITERATURE & PHILOSOPHY

1667 Milton, *Paradise Lost*, epic poem in tradition of Homer and Vergil

1670 Molière, *Le bourgeois gentilhomme*, comedy

1677 Racine, *Phèdre*, tragedy

1694 Voltaire born in Paris

ART

1662-1664 Vermeer, *Woman in Blue Reading a Letter*

1669 Death of Rembrandt; last *Self-Portrait*

1701 Rigaud, *Louis XIV*

1774

ARCHITECTURE	MUSIC
	late 16th cent. Birth of opera in Florence; development of *monody*
	1594–1595 Peri, *Dafne,* first play set to music, performed in Florence
	1600 Peri, *Euridice*
	Opera, concerto grosso, oratorio, cantata, and sonata established as musical forms; virtuoso tradition begins
	1607 Monteverdi, *L'Orfeo*

The Baroque World

Retention of classical vocabulary of Renaissance but on grandiose scale; civic planning and private-house construction also prevalent because of rise of middle classes

1629 Bernini appointed official architect of Saint Peter's, Rome

1631–1687 Longhena, Santa Maria della Salute, Venice

1638–1641 Borromini, Church of San Carlo alle Quattro Fontane, Rome; facade added 1665–1667

1652 Lully enters service of Louis XIV

1663 Bernini, piazza and colonnades for Saint Peter's, Rome; church proper completed by Carlo Maderno 1607–1615

1669–1685 Le Vau and Hardouin-Mansart, Garden facade Versailles

1678 Le Brun and Hardouin-Mansart begin Hall of Mirrors, Palace of Versailles

1674 Lully's *Alceste* first performed at Versailles

1685 Births of Bach, Handel, Scarlatti

c. 1720 Vivaldi, *The Four Seasons,* violin concertos

1721 J. S. Bach, *Brandenburg Concertos*

1723 Bach appointed Kantor of St. Thomas', Leipzig

1729 J. S. Bach, *St. Matthew Passion*

c. 1735 Rameau, *Les Indes Galantes*

1742 Handel's *Messiah* first performed

The Counter-Reformation Spirit

By about 1600 the intellectual and artistic movements of the Renaissance and Reformation had taken a new turn. Although the cultural activity of the next one hundred and fifty years was the natural outgrowth of earlier developments, the difference in spirit—already signaled by the middle of the 16th century—was striking.

The chief agent of the new spirit was the Roman Catholic Church. After initial shock at the success of Protestantism, the Catholic Church decided that the best defense was a well-planned attack. Switching to the offensive, the Church relied in great measure on new religious orders like the Jesuits, founded as early as 1534, to lead the movement known as the Counter-Reformation. Putting behind them the anxieties of the past, the chief representatives of the Counter-Reformation gave voice to a renewed spirit of confidence in the universality of the Church and the authority of its teachings. They reinforced this position by vigorous missionary work throughout Europe and in the Americas and the Far East.

At the same time, Catholics at home were reminded of the power and splendor of their religion by a massive quantity of works of art commissioned to enforce the chief principles of Counter-Reformation teachings. The official position of the Church had been newly stated at the Council of Trent, which met sporadically from 1545 to 1563. Now it was the task of religious leaders and, under their guidance, of the artists to make this position known to the faithful. New emphasis was placed on clarity and directness. The impression of the Church's triumphant resurgence was further reinforced by a new emphasis on material splendor and glory. In Rome itself the construction of a number of lavish churches was crowned by the completion at last of Saint Peter's and the addition of Bernini's spectacular *piazza,* or square, in front of it [276], while throughout Catholic Europe there developed a rich and ornate art that could do justice to the new demands for expressive power and spectacle.

The term used to describe the new style, at first in derision but since the 19th century simply as a convenient label, is *baroque.* The word's origins are obscure. It may be related to the Portuguese *barroco,* which means an irregularly shaped pearl, or perhaps to *baroco,* an Italian term used to describe a complicated problem in medieval logic. In any case, *baroque* came to be applied in general to anything elaborate and fanciful, in particular to the artistic style of the 17th and early 18th centuries.

276 Aerial view of Saint Peter's, Rome. Height of facade 147′ (44.81 m), width 374′ (114 m). The nave and facade were finished by Carlo Maderna (1556–1629) between 1606 and 1612, and the colonnades around the square were built between 1656 and 1663 to the design of Bernini (see page 306). The completion of Saint Peter's was one of the first great achievements of baroque architecture. (See also figure **239**, page 258.)

Although strictly speaking *baroque* is a term applied only to the visual arts, it is frequently used to describe the entire cultural achievement of the age. To extend its use to literature, music, and even intellectual developments of the same period inevitably implies that all the arts of the Baroque period had certain characteristics in common. In fact, a close comparison between the visual arts, music, and literature of the 17th and early 18th centuries does reveal a number of shared ideas and attitudes. It is important to remember from the outset, however, that this artistic unity is by no means obvious. A first glance at the cultural range of the period actually reveals a quite astonishing variety of styles, developing individually in widely separated places and subject to very different political and social pressures.

In this respect the Baroque period marks a significant break with the Renaissance, when Italy had been the center of virtually all artistic development. In spite of the impact of the Counter-Reformation, the Reformation itself had begun an irreversible process of decentralization. By the beginning of the 17th century, although Rome was still the artistic capital of Europe, important cultural changes were taking place elsewhere. The economic growth of countries like Holland and England, and the increasing power of France, produced a series of artistic styles that developed locally rather than being imported wholesale from south of the Alps. Throughout northern Europe the rise of the middle class continued to create a new public for the arts, which in turn affected the development of painting, architecture, and music. For the first time European culture began to spread across the Atlantic, carried to the Americas by Counter-Reformation missionaries [277].

The much greater geographic spread of artistic achievement was accompanied by the creation of new artistic forms in response to new religious and social pressures. In music, for instance, the 17th century saw the birth of opera and of new kinds of instrumental music, including works for orchestra like the *concerto grosso*. Painters continued to depict scenes from the Bible and from classical mythology but they turned increasingly to other subjects including portraits, landscapes, and scenes from everyday life. Architects constructed private town houses and started to take an interest in civic planning instead of devoting themselves exclusively to churches and palaces.

A similar richness and variety can be found in the philosophical and scientific thought of the period, which managed temporarily to reconcile its own pursuit of scientific truth with traditional theological and political attitudes. By the end of the 17th century, however, the practical discoveries of science had begun to undermine long-accepted ideas and to lay the basis for the new skepticism that came to dominate the 18th century.

It would be unwise to look for broad general principles operating in an age of such dynamic and varied change. Nonetheless, to understand and appreciate the baroque spirit as it appears in the individual arts it is helpful to bear in mind the chief assumptions and preoccupations shared by most baroque artists. Whatever the medium in which they worked, baroque artists were united in their commitment to strong emotional statements, to psychological exploration, and to the invention of new and daring techniques.

Perhaps the most striking of these is the expression of intense emotions. In the Renaissance artists had generally tried to achieve the calm balance and order they thought of as typically classical; in the Baroque period artists were attracted by extremes of feeling. Sometimes these strong emotions were personal. Painters and poets alike tried to look into their own souls and reveal by color or word the depths of their own psychic and spiritual experience. More often artists tried to convey intense religious emotions. In each case, far from avoiding painful or extremely emotional states as subjects, their works sought out and explored them.

277 Mexico City Cathedral. 1656–1671.

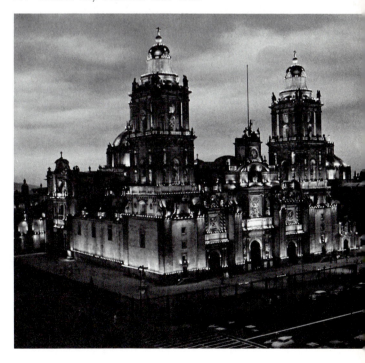

The concern with emotion produced in its turn an interest in what came to be called psychology. Baroque artists tried to explain how and why their subjects felt as strongly as they did by representing their emotional states as vividly and analytically as possible. This is particularly evident in 17th-century opera and drama, where music in the one case and words in the other were used to depict the precise state of mind of the characters.

The desire to express the inexpressible required the invention of new techniques. As a result, baroque art put great emphasis on virtuosity. Sculptors and painters achieved astonishing realism in the way in which they handled their media. Stone was carved in such a way as to give the effect of thin, flowing drapery, while 17th-century painters found ways to reproduce complex effects of light and shade. Baroque writers often used elaborate imagery and complicated grammatical structure to express intense emotional states. In music, both composers and performers began to develop new virtuoso skills; composers in their ability to write works of greater and greater complexity, and performers in their ability to sing or play music in the new style. In fact some pieces, like *toccatas*—free-form rhapsodies for keyboard—were principally intended to allow instrumentalists to demonstrate their technique, thus inaugurating the tradition of the virtuoso performer that reached a climax in the 19th century.

Baroque Art in Rome

The foundations of baroque style, which was to dominate much of European painting for 150 years, were laid in Rome around 1600 by two artists whose work at first glance seems to have little in common. Michelangelo Merisi (1573–1610), better known as Caravaggio—the name of his home town in northern Italy—explored the darker aspects of life and death in some of the most naturalistic and dramatic pictures ever painted. Annibale Carracci (1560–1609) preferred to paint light and elegant depictions of the loves of gods and goddesses and charming landscapes. That both artists exerted an immense influence on their successors says something for the extreme range of baroque painting.

Caravaggio and His Followers

Of the two painters, Caravaggio was certainly the more controversial in his day. His own life style did little to recommend him to the aristocratic and ecclesiastical patrons on whom he depended. From his first arrival in Rome around 1590 Caravaggio seems to have lived an unconventional and violent life, in continual trouble with the police and alienating potential friends by his savage temper.

Any chances Caravaggio had for establishing himself successfully in Rome were brought to an abrupt end in 1606 when he quarreled violently with an opponent in a tennis match and stabbed him to death. He avoided punishment only by fleeing to Naples and then to Malta, where he was thrown into prison for attacking a police officer. Escaping, he made his way to Sicily and then back to Naples, where yet again he got involved in a violent quarrel, this time in a sleazy inn. Seriously wounded, he heard of the pos-

below: 278 Caravaggio. *The Conversion of Saint Paul.* 1601–1602. Oil on canvas, 7'6½" × 5'9" (2.3 × 1.75 m). Cerasi Chapel, Santa Maria del Popolo, Rome. The artist produces a highly dramatic effect by letting the bright light of the divine vision strike the group head on, rather than from above. The future saint has fallen from his horse and lies in a trance as if trying literally to grasp what he has seen.

sibility of a pardon if he were to return to Rome, but on the journey back he died of a fever (brought on, it was said, by a final attack of rage at some sailors he mistakenly thought had robbed him). The pardon from the pope arrived a few days later.

The spirit of rebellion that governed Caravaggio's life can be seen in his art. In his depiction of religious scenes he refused to accept either the traditionally idealizing versions of earlier artists or the Counter-Reformation demands for magnificent display. Furthermore, instead of placing his figures in an elaborate setting in accordance with Counter-Reformation principles, Caravaggio surrounded them with shadows, a device that emphasizes the drama of the scene and the poverty of the participants.

Caravaggio's preference for extreme contrasts between light and dark, described by the Italian word *chiaroscuro,* was one of the aspects of his style most imitated by later painters. When not handled by a master, the use of heavy shadows surrounding brightly lit figures in the foreground tends to become artificial and overtheatrical, but in Caravaggio's works it always serves a true dramatic purpose. In his

painting *The Conversion of Saint Paul* [278], the future saint lies on the ground, paralyzed by shock and blinded by the divine light pouring down on him; his old servant stands in the background, in the darkness of bewilderment and ignorance. The repressed violence implicit in this scene becomes explicit in Caravaggio's painting *The Martyrdom of Saint Matthew* [279], one of three pictures painted between 1597 and 1603 for the Contarelli Chapel in the Church of San Luigi dei Francesi at Rome—Caravaggio's first important Roman commission. Caravaggio had seen and felt enough suffering to be able to portray it with painful realism, but the painting tells us as much about the reactions of the onlookers as about Matthew himself. They range from the sadistic violence of the executioner to the apparent indifference of the figures in shadow on the left; only the angel swooping down with the palm of martyrdom relieves the brutality and pessimism of the scene.

It would be a mistake to think of Caravaggio's work as without tenderness. In the *Madonna of Loreto* [280] he shows us not the remote grace of a Botticelli

below: 279 Caravaggio. *The Martyrdom of Saint Matthew*. c. 1602. Oil on canvas, 10′9″ × 11′6″ (3.3 × 3.5 m). Contarelli Chapel, San Luigi dei Francesi, Rome. The deeply moved onlooker at the very back of the scene is, according to one tradition, a self-portrait of the artist.

right: 280 Caravaggio. *Madonna of Loreto*. c. 1604. Oil on canvas, 8′6½″ × 4′10½″ (2.6 × 1.5 m). Cavaletti Chapel, San Agostino, Rome. The shabby clothes show the poverty of the two pilgrims.

281 Artemisia Gentileschi. *Judith and Holofernes.*
c. 1620. Oil on canvas.
Uffizi, Florence.

Virgin or the sweet, calm beauty of a Raphael Madonna but a simple Roman mother. As she stands gravely on the doorstep of her backstreet house where the plaster is falling away from the walls, two humble pilgrims fall to their knees in confident prayer. They raise their loving faces to the Virgin and Christ Child while turning toward us their muddy, travel-stained feet. It is perhaps not surprising that some of Caravaggio's contemporaries, brought up on the elegant and well-nourished Madonnas and worshipers of the Renaissance and surrounded by the splendor of Counter-Reformation art, should have found pictures like these disrespectful and lacking in devotion. It should be equally unsurprising that once

the initial shock wore off, the honesty and truth of Caravaggio's vision made a profound impact on both artists and the public.

Among the painters working at Rome who fell under the spell of Caravaggio's works was Orazio Gentileschi (1563–1639), who was born in Pisa and studied in Florence. Much impressed by Caravaggio's dramatic naturalism and concern for psychological truth, Gentileschi based his own style on that of his younger contemporary. Since he spent the last eighteen years of his life traveling and living in northern Europe, first in France and then in England, he played an important part in spreading a knowledge of Caravaggio's style outside Italy. At the same time,

above: 282 Annibale Carracci. *The Triumph of Bacchus and Ariadne*. 1597–1600. Fresco. Farnese Palace, Rome.
The god's chariot, drawn by tigers, is accompanied by a wild procession of cupids, nymphs, and satyrs.

moreover, he handed on his enthusiasm to a painter nearer home, his own daughter Artemisia (1592–1652/1653).

Artemisia Gentileschi has been described as the first woman in the history of the Western world to make a significant contribution to the art of her time. The question of why so few women achieved eminence in the visual arts before recent times is a complicated one, and the chief answers are principally social and economic rather than aesthetic. Certainly, Artemisia was typical of the few women painters of the Renaissance and Baroque periods who did become famous in that she was the daughter of a painter and therefore at home in the world of art and artists.

Gentileschi's most famous painting is *Judith and Holofernes* [281]. Done in *chiaroscuro* (the technique that strongly contrasts light and dark for dramatic purposes), the painting conveys a tremendous sense of violence as Judith and her maid loom over the drastically foreshortened body of Holofernes. There is a stark contrast between the realistic violence of the beheading and the sensual richness of the silken bed, the jewelery, and the cunning drapery. It is not inconceivable that the painter, herself a rape victim in her youth, poured her own passionate protest into

this painting of a woman taking retribution against a would-be defiler. This work depicts a scene from the biblical story of the Jewish heroine Judith, who used her feminine charms to save her people from an invading Assyrian army; she won the confidence of its general, Holofernes, and then beheaded him in the privacy of his tent.

The Carracci

It is a far cry from the dark, emotional world of Caravaggio and his followers to the brilliant, idealized world of Annibale Carracci, his brother Agostino, and his cousin Ludovico, all often spoken of collectively as the Carracci. The most gifted member of this Bolognese family was Annibale, whose earliest important work in Rome, the decoration of the *galleria* or formal reception hall of the Palazzo Farnese, was painted between 1597 and 1604, precisely the years when Caravaggio was working on the Contarelli Chapel. The many scenes in the galleria constitute a fresco cycle based on Greek and Roman mythology, depicting the loves of the Gods, including *The Triumph of Bacchus and Ariadne* [282]. The sense of exuberant life and movement and the mood of unrestrained sensual celebration seem at the furthest remove from Caravaggio's somber paintings, yet both artists share the baroque love of extreme emotion, and both show the same concern for realism of detail.

above: 283 Annibale Carracci. *The Flight into Egypt*. c. 1604. Oil on canvas, 3′ × 7′5⅝″ (.9 × 2.3 m). Doria-Pamphili Gallery, Rome. In spite of the Holy Family in the center foreground, the painting is not so much a religious one as a depiction of the landscape around Rome.

below: 284 Gian Lorenzo Bernini. *David*. 1623–1624. Marble, height 5′6¼″ (1.7 m). Borghese Gallery, Rome. It is said that Bernini carved the face while looking at his own in a mirror. The expression reinforces the tension of the pose.

The same blend of ideal proportion and realistic detail emerges in Annibale's landscape paintings, of which the best known is probably *The Flight into Egypt* [283]. The scene is the countryside around Rome, with the river Tiber in the foreground and the Alban Hills in the distance. The tiny human figures are carefully related in proportion to this natural setting, precisely balanced by the distant castle, and located just at the meeting point of the diagonal lines formed by the flock of sheep and the river. As a result, we perceive a sense of idyllic classical order while being convinced of the reality of the landscape.

Bernini and Borromini

The most influential of all Italian baroque artists of the Counter-Reformation was a sculptor and architect, not a painter. The sculptural achievement of Gian Lorenzo Bernini (1598–1680), of seemingly unlimited range of expression and unbelievable technical virtuosity, continued to influence sculptors until the 19th century; as the chief architect of Counter-Reformation Rome he permanently changed the face of that venerable city.

Born the son of a Florentine sculptor in Naples, Bernini showed signs of his extraordinary abilities from an early age. One of his first important works, a statue of *David* [284], seems to have been deliberately intended to evoke comparison with works by his illustrious predecessors. Unlike the *Davids* of Donatello [see figure 215, page 232] or Michelangelo [see figure 227, page 242], which are seen in repose, Bernini's figure is very definitely in the midst of action. From the bitten lips to the muscular tension of the arms to the final detail of the clenched toes of the right foot, this *David* seems to personify energy, almost exploding through space. Bernini gives the figure additional expressive power by his deep cuts in the stone, producing a strong contrast between light and dark. In its expression of violent emotion, its communication of the psychological state of its subject, and its virtuoso technique, the *David* is a truly baroque figure.

Many of Bernini's sculptures have religious themes like the *David*. Other works depict his aristocratic patrons with the same mastery he applied to less obviously spectacular subjects. The bust of Cardinal Scipione Borghese [285], with its quizzical expression and almost uncanny sense of movement, conveys the personality of the sitter with sympathy and subtlety. He also illustrates scenes from classical mythology. In *The Rape of Proserpine* [286] Pluto, the god of the underworld, seems to be striving toward the spectator as he catches up Proserpine in his arms. The sense of movement is underlined by the contrary

287 Francesco Borromini. Facade, San Carlo alle Quattro Fontane, Rome. Begun 1638, facade finished 1667. Length 52′ (15.86 m), width 34′ (10.36 m), width of facade 38′ (11.58 m). The curves and countercurves of the facade, together with the rich, almost cluttered, decoration, mark a deliberate rejection of the classical style.

Bernini's expansive personality and his success in obtaining important commissions brought him tragically if inevitably into conflict with the other great architect of baroque Rome, Francesco Borromini (1599–1667). Brooding and melancholy much of the time, Borromini spent most of his career in constant competition with his brilliant rival and finally committed suicide. Whereas Bernini was concerned with the broad sweep of a design and grandiose effects, Borromini concentrated on elaborate details and highly complex structures.

Borromini's greatest and most influential achievement was the church of San Carlo alle Quattro Fontane. The inside, designed between 1638 and 1641, was his first important work; the facade, which he added in 1665–1667, was his last [287]. On a relatively small exterior wall space Borromini has placed a wide range of decorative elements—columns, niches, arches, statues—while the facade itself flows in sinuous curves. The almost obsessive elaboration of design is in strong contrast with the clarity of many of Bernini's buildings, but its ornateness represents another baroque approach to architecture, one that was to have a continual appeal.

Baroque Art in France and Spain

In general, however, the more extravagant aspects of Italian baroque art never appealed greatly to French taste, which preferred elegance to display and restraint to emotion. Indeed, the conservative nature of French art found expression before the end of the century in the foundation of the Académie des Beaux-Arts, or Academy of the Fine Arts. The first of the special exhibitions organized by the Academy took place in 1667, under the patronage of Louis XIV. Both then and through the succeeding centuries Academy members saw their function as the defense of traditional standards and values rather than the encouragement of revolutionary new developments. Their innate conservatism affected both the works selected for exhibition and those awarded prizes. The tension between these self-appointed guardians of tradition and those artists who revolted against established ideas lasted well into the 19th century.

The closest parallel in French baroque painting to the intensity of Caravaggio is to be found in the strangely moving paintings of Georges de la Tour (1590–1652), whose candlelit scenes and humbly dressed figures are reminiscent of some aspects of the Italian's work. Yet the mood of such paintings as *The*

thrust of the girl as she tries vainly to escape. Here, too, the deep cutting of Pluto's face and beard produces a strong contrast to Proserpine's youthful appearance.

Works such as these would have been more than sufficient to guarantee Bernini's immortality, but his architectural achievements are equally impressive. The physical appearance of baroque Rome was enriched by numerous Bernini fountains, Bernini palaces, and Bernini churches. Most important of all was his work on Saint Peter's, where he created in front of the basilica a vast piazza with its oval colonnade, central obelisk, and fountains, an ensemble [see figure 276, page 298] that rivals in grandeur even the fora of Imperial Rome.

Plate 22 Diego Velázquez. *Las Meninas (The Maids of Honor).* 1651. Oil on canvas, 10'5" × 9' (3.18 × 2.74 m). Prado, Madrid. The red cross on the artist's breast, symbol of the noble Order of Santiago, was painted there after his death by the king's command. Velázquez regarded his nomination to the order in 1658 as recognition both of his own nobility and that of his art. He thus became one of the first victors in the war that artists had waged ever since the Renaissance for a social status equal to that of their patrons. Throughout the 16th and 17th centuries their aristocratic and ecclesiastical employers regarded them as little better than servants; only by the end of the 18th century were artists and musicians able to assert their social and political independence.

above: **Plate 23** Peter Paul Rubens. *The Rape of the Daughters of Leucippus*. c. 1618. Oil on canvas, 7'3" × 6'10" (2.21 × 2.08 m). Alte Pinakothek, Munich. According to the Greek legend, Castor and Pollux, twin sons of Zeus, carried off the two daughters of King Leucippus, who had been betrothed to their cousins. The myth here becomes symbolic of physical passion.

right: **Plate 24** Jan Vermeer. *Woman Reading a Letter*. 1662–1664. Oil on canvas, 18⅛ × 15¼" (46 × 39 cm). Rijksmuseum, Amsterdam. Much of the sense of balance and repose that Vermeer conveys is achieved by his careful color contrasts between blue and yellow and the repetition of rectangular surfaces such as the table, chair backs, and the map of the Netherlands on the wall.

Lamentation over Saint Sebastian [288] is much more restrained and poetic—the emotions are not stressed.

The greatest French painter of the 17th century, Nicolas Poussin (c. 1593–1665), echoed this French preference for restraint when he decisively rejected the innovations of Caravaggio, whose works he claimed to detest. He saw his own work as a kind of protest against the excesses of the baroque; a strong dislike of his Roman contemporaries nevertheless did not prevent his spending most of his life in Rome. It may seem strange that so French an artist should have chosen to live in Italy, but what drew him there was the art of ancient, not baroque, Rome. Poussin's only real and enduring enthusiasm was for the world of classical antiquity. His friends at Rome included the leading antiquarians of the day, and his paintings often express a nostalgic yearning for a long-vanished past.

Among Poussin's most poignant early works is *Et in Arcadia Ego* [289], in which four country dwellers gather at a large stone tomb amid an idyllic landscape. The inscription they struggle intently to decipher says *Et in Arcadia Ego* (I am also in Arcadia), a reminder that death exists even in the midst of such beauty and apparently simple charm. (Arcadia, although an actual region in Greece, was also used to refer to an imaginary land of perfect peace and beauty.) That charm is not altogether so simple, however. Poussin's rustic shepherds and casually dressed shepherdess seem to have stepped straight from some actual antique scene, such as Poussin often incorporated into his paintings, while the rich landscape is reminiscent of Venetian painting. The whole work therefore represents not so much the authentic representation of an actual past as the imaginative creation of a world that never really existed.

As his career developed, Poussin's style changed. The poetry of the earlier works was replaced by a

288 Georges de la Tour. *The Lamentation over Saint Sebastian.* 1645. Oil on canvas, c. 5′3″ × 4′3″ (1.6 × 1.3 m). State Museums, Berlin. The influence of Caravaggio is obvious. Nevertheless, the simplification of details and the distaste for violence (there is no blood around the arrow) are typical of the restraint of De la Tour's paintings.

289 Nicolas Poussin. *Et in Arcadia Ego.* c. 1630. Oil on canvas, c. 40 × 32″ (102 × 81 cm). Devonshire Collection, Chatsworth Settlement. Although influenced by classical sources, this early version of the subject has a poetic character that owes much to the art of Titian.

grandeur that sometimes verges on stiffness. The *Rape of the Sabine Women* [290] is conceived on a massive scale and deals with a highly dramatic subject, yet the desperate women and violent Roman soldiers seem almost frozen in motion. Every figure is depicted clearly and precisely, as in Carracci's *Triumph of Bacchus and Ariadne* [see figure 282, page 303], yet with none of the exuberance of the earlier artist. The artificial, contrived air is deliberate.

By the end of his life, Poussin had returned to the simplicity of his earlier style, but it was drained of any trace of emotion. Another version of the subject of *Et in Arcadia Ego* [291], painted some ten years after the earlier one, makes a revealing contrast. The same four figures study the same tomb, but in a mood of deep stillness. Gone is the urgency of the earlier painting—and much of the poetry. In its place Poussin creates a mood of philosophical calm and tries to recapture the lofty spirit of antiquity, most notably in the noble brow and solemn stance of the shepherdess. Compensating for the loss of warmth is the transcendent beauty of the image.

Even had Poussin been prepared to leave Rome and return to the French court, the austere nature of his art would hardly have served to glorify that most autocratic and magnificent of monarchs, Louis XIV (born 1638, reigned 1643–1715). For the most part the king had only second-rate artists available to him

above: 290   Nicolas Poussin. *Rape of the Sabine Women*. c. 1636–1637. Oil on canvas, 5'1" × 6'10½" (1.55 × 2.1 m). Metropolitan Museum of Art, New York (Harris Brisbane Dick Fund, 1946). By the time of this painting, Poussin was strongly influenced by the ancient sculptures he had studied in Rome, most notably in the careful depiction of the muscular structure of his figures.

below: 291   Nicolas Poussin. *Et in Arcadia Ego*. 1638–1639. Oil on canvas. 33½ × 47⅝" (85 × 121 cm). Louvre, Paris. In comparison with figure **289**, an earlier version, this treatment is calmer and less dramatic. The group is seen from the front, rather than diagonally, and both faces and poses are deliberately unemotional.

292 Claude Lorrain. *The Mill.* 1631 or 1637. Oil on canvas, 24¼ × 33¼" (61.5 × 85.5 cm). Museum of Fine Arts, Boston (Seth K. Sweetser Fund). Although this is one of Lorrain's early paintings, it already shows his ability to create a sense of infinite space and depth, in part by calculated contrasts between light and dark.

right: 293 Hyacinthe Rigaud. *Louis XIV.* 1701. Oil on canvas, 9'1½" × 6'2⅝" (2.78 × 1.9 m). Louvre, Paris. Louis was 63 when this portrait was painted. The swirling ermine-lined robes are a mark of the king's swagger. The ballet pose of the feet is a reminder of the popularity of dancing at the French court.

at court: like Poussin, the other great French painter of the day, Claude Lorrain (1600–1682) spent most of his life in Rome, and in any case was only really interested in painting landscapes [292].

Although most official court painters achieved only mediocre respectability, an exception must be made for Hyacinthe Rigaud (1659–1743), whose stunning portrait of Louis XIV [293] epitomizes baroque grandeur. It would be difficult to claim the intellectual vigor of Poussin or the emotional honesty of Caravaggio for this frankly flattering image of majesty. The stilted pose and the gorgeous robes might even suggest an element of exaggeration, almost of parody; yet a glance at the king's sagging face and stony gaze immediately puts such an idea to flight. Rigaud has captured his patron's outward splendor while not hiding his increasing weakness, due in great part to his decadent life style. The signs of physical collapse are visible—*Et in Versailles Ego.*

Louis XIV's most lasting artistic achievement was the Palace of Versailles, built a few miles outside

294 Aerial view, Palace of Versailles. 1661–1688. Width of palace 1935′ (589.79 m). The chief architects for the last stage of construction at Versailles were Louis le Vau (1612–1670) and Jules Hardouin-Mansart (1646–1708). Although the external decoration of the palace is classical in style, the massive scale is characteristic of baroque architecture.

Paris as a new center for the court [294]. The history of its construction is long and complicated, and the final result betrays some of the uncertainties that went into its planning.

Louis XIV, an acute politician and astute judge of human psychology, was well aware of the fact that the aristocratic courtiers who surrounded him were likely to turn on him at the faintest sign of weakness or hesitation on his part. By constructing at Versailles an elaborate setting in which he could consciously act out the role of Grand Monarch, Louis conveyed the image of himself as supreme ruler and thereby retained his mastery over the aristocracy.

The Palace of Versailles was therefore conceived of by the king in political terms. The architects' task, both inside and out, was to create a building that would illustrate Louis XIV's symbolic concept of himself as the Sun King. Thus each morning the king would rise from his bed, make his way past the assembled court through the Hall of Mirrors [295] where the seventeen huge mirrors reflected both the daylight and his own splendor, and enter the gardens along the main wing of the palace—which was laid out in an east–west axis to follow the path of the sun. At the same time both the palace and its gardens, which extend behind it for some two miles, were required to provide an appropriate setting for the balls, feasts, and fireworks displays organized there.

Given the grandiose symbolism of the ground plan and interior decorations, the actual appearance of the outside of the Palace of Versailles, with its rows of Ionic columns, is surprisingly modest. The simplicity of design and decoration is another demonstration of the French ability to combine the extremes of baroque art with a more classical spirit.

The Spanish reaction to the baroque was very different. Strong religious emotion had always been a characteristic of Spanish Catholicism, and the new possibilities presented by baroque painting were eagerly seized upon by artists like Jusepe de Ribera

295 Jules Hardouin-Mansart and Charles Lebrun. Hall of Mirrors, Palace of Versailles. Begun 1676. Length 240′ (73.15 m), width 34′ (10.36 m), height 43′ (13.11 m). The interior decoration was by Charles Lebrun (1619–1690), who borrowed the idea of a ceiling frescoed with mythological scenes from Carracci's painted ceiling in the Farnese Palace (see figure 282, page 303).

296 Jusepe de Ribera. *The Martyrdom of Saint Bartholomew*. c. 1638. Oil on canvas, 7'7¼" (2.34 m) square. Prado, Madrid. Unlike De la Tour (see figure **279**), Ribera refuses to soften the subject by idealizing his figures.

(1591–1652). Like Caravaggio, Ribera used peasants in his religious scenes, which were painted with strong contrasts of light and dark. In his *The Martyrdom of Saint Bartholomew* [296] Ribera spares us nothing in the way of realism as the saint is hauled into position to be flayed. The muscular brutality of his executioners and the sense of impending physical agony are almost masochistic in their vividness. Only in the compassionate faces of some onlookers do we find any relief from the torment of the scene.

Although paintings like Ribera's are representative of much of Spanish baroque art, the work of Diego Velázquez (1599–1660), the greatest Spanish painter of the Baroque period, is very different in spirit. Velázquez used his superlative technique to depict scenes brimming with life, preferring the court of Phillip IV (where he spent much of his career) and the lives of ordinary people to religious or mythological subjects.

The finest and most complex work of Velázquez is *Las Meninas*, or *The Maids of Honor* [Plate 22, page 307]. Unlike Louis XIV, the Spanish king was fortunate enough to have one of the greatest painters in history to preserve the memory of his court. It is to Philip IV's credit that he treated Velázquez with respect and honor. In return Velázquez produced a number of superb portraits of the monarch and his family.

Las Meninas is an evocation of life in the royal palace. The scene is Velázquez' own studio there; the five-year-old Princess Margarita has come, with her two maids, to visit the painter at work on a huge painting that must surely be *Las Meninas* itself. Despite the size of the picture, the mood is quiet, even intimate: two figures in casual conversation, a sleepy dog, a passing court official, who raises a curtain at the back to peer into the room. Yet so subtle is Velázquez' use of color that we feel the very presence of the room as a three-dimensional space filled with light, now bright, now shadowy. The reality of details like the little princess' hair or dress never distracts from the overall unity of color and composition. That Velázquez was justifiably proud of his abilities is shown by the two distinguished visitors whose presence is felt rather than seen, reflected as they are in the mirror hanging on the back wall: the king and queen themselves, come to honor the artist by visiting him in his own studio.

Baroque Art in the North

Most baroque art produced in northern Europe was intended for a middle-class rather than an aristocratic audience as in Italy, France, and Spain. Before examining the effects of this, however, we must look at two very notable exceptions, Peter Paul Rubens (1577–1640) and his assistant and later rival, Anthony van Dyck (1599–1641), both Flemish by birth.

Rubens and Van Dyck

Rubens is often called the most universal of painters because he produced with apparent ease an almost inexhaustible stream of works of all kinds—religious subjects, portraits, landscapes, mythological scenes— all on the grandest of scales. Certainly he must have been among the most active artists in history: in addition to running the workshop used for the production of his commissions, he pursued a career in diplomacy, which involved considerable traveling throughout Europe, and still had time for academic study. He is said to have spoken and written six modern languages and to have read Latin fluently. He was also versed in theology. Further, in contrast to solitary and gloomy figures like Caravaggio and Borromini, Rubens seems to have been contented in his personal life. After the death of his first wife he remarried, at the age of fifty-three, a girl of sixteen, Hélène Fourment, with whom he spent an ecstatically happy ten years before his death. The paintings of his last decade are among the most intimate and tender of all artistic tributes to married love [297].

For the most part, however, intimacy is not the quality most characteristic of Rubens' art. Generally his pictures convey something of the restless energy of his life. In *The Rape of the Daughters of Leucippus* [Plate 23, page 308] every part of the painting is filled with movement as the mortal women, divine riders, and even the horses are drawn into a single pulsating spiral. The sense of action, so characteristic of Rubens' paintings, is in strong contrast to the frozen movement of Poussin's depiction of a similar episode [see figure 290, page 310]. Equally typical of the artist is his frank delight in the girls' sensuous nudity and ample proportions—the slender grace of other artists' nudes was not at all to Rubens' taste.

Perhaps the most extraordinary achievement of Rubens' remarkable career was his fulfillment of a commission from Marie de' Medici, widow of Henry IV and mother of Louis XIII, to decorate an entire gallery with paintings illustrating her life. In a mere three years, from 1622 to 1625, he created 21 enormous paintings commemorating the chief events

in which she played a part, with greater flattery than truth. The splendid *The Journey of Marie de' Medici* [298] shows the magnificently attired queen on horseback at the Battle of Ponts-de-Cé, accompanied by the spirit of Power, while Fame and Glory flutter around her head. It hardly matters that the queen's forces were ignominiously defeated in the battle, so convincingly triumphant does her image appear.

Paintings on this scale required the help of assistants, and there is no doubt that in Rubens' workshop much of the preliminary work was done by his staff. One of the many artists employed for this purpose eventually became as much in demand as his former master for portraits of the aristocracy. Anthony van Dyck spent two years, 1618 to 1620, with Rubens before beginning his career as an independent artist. Although from time to time he painted religious subjects, his fame rests on his formal portraits, many of them produced during the years he spent in Italy and England.

Van Dyck's refined taste equipped him for satisfying the demands of his noble patrons that they be shown as they thought they looked rather than as

left: 297   Peter Paul Rubens. *Hélène Fourment and Her Children.* 1636–1637. Oil on canvas. Louvre, Paris. In this affectionate portrait of his young wife and two of their children, Rubens achieves a sense of immediacy and freshness by his lightness of touch.

right: 298   Peter Paul Rubens. *The Journey of Marie de' Medici.* 1622–1625. Oil on canvas, 14'11" × 9'6" (3.94 × 2.95 m). Louvre, Paris. This painting focuses on the triumphant figure of the queen. As in many of his large works, Rubens probably painted the important sections and left other parts to his assistants.

299 Anthony van Dyck. *Marchesa Elena Grimaldi, Wife of Marchese Nicola Cataneo.* c. 1625. Oil on canvas, 8'1" × 5'8" (2.7 × 1.73 m). National Gallery of Art, Washington (Widener Collection, 1942). Painted fairly early in Van Dyck's career during a stay in Genoa, the portrait emphasizes the aristocratic bearing of its subject by somber colors and an artificial setting.

they actually were. It is certainly difficult to believe that any real-life figure could have had quite the haughty bearing and lofty dignity of the Marchesa Cataneo [299] in Van Dyck's portrait of her, although the Genoese nobility of which she was a member was known for its arrogance.

International celebrities like Rubens and Van Dyck, at home at the courts of all Europe, were far from typical of northern artists. Indeed, painters in the Netherlands in particular found themselves in a very different situation from their colleagues elsewhere. The two most lucrative sources of commissions, the Church and the aristocracy, were unavailable to them because the Dutch Calvinist Church followed post-Reformation practice in forbidding the use of images in church, and because Holland had never had its own powerful hereditary nobility. Painters therefore depended on the tastes and demands of the open market.

One highly profitable source of income for Dutch artists in the 17th century was the group portrait, in particular that of a militia, or civic guard company. These bands of soldiers had originally served a practical purpose in the defense of their country, but their regular reunions tended to be social gatherings, chiefly for the purpose of eating and drinking. A group of war veterans today would hire a photographer to commemorate their annual reunion; the militia companies engaged the services of a portrait painter. If they were lucky or rich enough they might even get Frans Hals (c. 1580–1666), whose group portraits capture the individuality of each of the participants while conveying the general convivial spirit of the occasion [300]. Hals was certainly not the most

300 Frans Hals. *Banquet of the Officers of the Civic Guard of Saint George at Haarlem.* 1616. Oil on canvas, 5'8¼" × 10'6⅜" (1.75 × 3.24 m). Frans Halsmuseum, Haarlem. The diagonal lines of the curtains, banner, and sashes help bind the painting together and make it at the same time both a series of individual portraits and a single unified composition.

imaginative or inventive of artists, but his sheer ability to paint, using broad dynamic brush strokes and cleverly organized compositions, makes his works some of the most attractive of that period.

Very different in spirit was Jan Vermeer (1632–1675), who worked almost unknown in the city of Delft and whose art was virtually forgotten after his death. Rediscovered in the 19th century, it is now regarded as second only to Rembrandt's for depth of feeling. At first sight this may seem surprising, since Vermeer's subjects are rather limited in scope. A woman reading a letter [Plate 24, page 308], girls sewing or playing music—through such intimate scenes Vermeer reveals qualities of inner contemplation and repose that are virtually unique in the entire history of art. Unlike Hals, Vermeer applied his colors with the most perfect precision in the form of tiny dots, rendering the details with exquisite care. Like Velázquez' *Las Meninas* [see Plate 22, page 307],

his paintings are dominated by light so palpable as to seem to surround the figures with its presence. However, where Velázquez' canvas is suffused with a warm, Mediterranean glow, Hals' paintings capture the coolness and clarity of northern light. The perfection of his compositions creates a mood of stillness so complete that mundane activities take on a totally unexpected concentration and become endowed with a timeless beauty.

Rembrandt

Rembrandt van Rijn (1606–1669) is one of the most deeply loved of all painters. No summary of his achievement can begin to do justice to it. Born in Leiden in the Netherlands, he spent a short time at the university there before beginning his studies as a painter. The early part of his career was spent in

below: 301 Rembrandt. *The Militia Company of Captain Frans Banning Cocq (The Night Watch).* 1642. Oil on canvas, 11'9½" × 14'2½" (3.63 × 4.37 m). Rijksmuseum, Amsterdam. Recent cleaning has revealed that the painting's popular name, though conveniently brief, is inaccurate. Far from being submerged in darkness, the principal figures were originally bathed in light and painted in glowing colors.

Amsterdam, where he moved in 1631 and soon became known as a fashionable portrait painter. His life was that of any successful man of the time, happily married, living in his own fine house.

Rembrandt's interest in spiritual matters and the eternal problems of existence, however, coupled with his researches into new artistic techniques, seem to have prevented his settling down for long to a bourgeois existence of this kind. The artistic turning point of his career came in 1642, the year of the death of his wife, when he finished the painting known as *The Night Watch* [301]. Although ostensibly the same kind of group portrait as Hals' *Banquet of the Officers of the Civic Guard* [see figure 300], it is composed with much greater complexity and subtlety. The arrangement of the figures and the sense of depth show how far Rembrandt was outdistancing his contemporaries.

The price Rembrandt paid for his genius was growing neglect, which by 1656 had brought bankruptcy. The less his work appealed to the public of his day, the more Rembrandt retreated into his own spiritual world. About 1645 he set up house with Hendrickje Stoffels, although he never married her, and his unconventional behavior succeeded in alien-

ating him still further from his contemporaries. It was the faithful Hendrickje, however, who together with Titus, Rembrandt's son by his first marriage, helped put his financial affairs in some sort of order. Her death in 1663 left him desolate, and its effect on him is visible in some of the last self-portraits [302].

Throughout his life Rembrandt had sought self-understanding by painting a series of portraits of himself, charting his inner journey through the increasingly tragic events of his life. Without self-pity or pretense he analyzed his own feelings and recorded them with a dispassion that might be called merely clinical if its principal achievement were not the revelation of a human soul. By the time of Hendrickje's death, which was followed in 1668 by that of Titus, Rembrandt was producing self-portraits that evoke not so much sympathy for his sufferings as awe at their truth. The inexorable physical decay, the universal fate, is accompanied by a growth in spiritual awareness that must at least in part have come from Rembrandt's lifelong meditation on the Scriptures.

In the last years of his life Rembrandt turned increasingly to biblical subjects, always using them to explore some aspect of human feelings. In *Jacob Blessing the Sons of Joseph* [303] all the tenderness of family

below left: 302 Rembrandt. *Old Self-Portrait*. 1669. Oil on canvas, 23¼ × 20¾" (59 × 53 cm). Mauritshuis, The Hague. In his last self-portrait, painted a few months before his death, the artist seems drained of all emotion, his expression resigned and gaze fixed.

below right: 303 Rembrandt. *Jacob Blessing the Sons of Joseph*. 1656. Oil on canvas, 5'8¼" × 6'9" (1.75 × 2.1 m). Staatliche Kunstsammlungen Kassel, Galerie Alte Meister, GK 249. In his very personal version of the biblical story, painted in the year of his financial collapse, Rembrandt includes Asenath, Joseph's wife. Although she is not mentioned in the text, her presence here emphasizes the family nature of the occasion.

affection is expressed in the juxtaposition of the heads of the old man and his son, whose expression of love is surpassed only by that of his wife as she gazes almost unseeingly at her sons. The depth of emotion and the dark shadows mark that school of baroque painting initiated by Caravaggio, yet it seems almost an impertinence to categorize so universal a statement. Through this painting Rembrandt seems to offer us a deep spiritual comfort for the tragic nature of human destiny revealed by the self-portraits.

Baroque Music

Although the history of music is as long as that of the other arts, the earliest music with which most modern music lovers are on familiar ground is that of the Baroque period. It is a safe bet that many thousands of listeners have tapped their feet to the rhythm of a baroque concerto without knowing or caring anything about its historical context, and with good reason: baroque music, with its strong emphasis on rhythmic vitality and attractive melody, is easy to respond to with pleasure. Furthermore, in the person of Johann Sebastian Bach, the Baroque period produced one of the greatest geniuses in the history of music, one who shared Rembrandt's ability to communicate profound experience on the broadest level.

304 Pieter de Hooch. *The Music Party*. 1663.
Oil on canvas, 39 × 47″ (99 × 119 cm). Cleveland Museum of Art (gift of Hanna Fund). Some prosperous Dutch citizens are relaxing by both performing and listening to music.

The qualities that make baroque music popular today were responsible for its original success: composers of the Baroque period were the first since classical antiquity to write large quantities of music intended for the pleasure of listeners rather than the glory of God. The polyphonic music of the Middle Ages and the Renaissance, with its interweaving of many musical lines, had enabled composers like Machaut or Palestrina to praise the Lord on the highest level of intellectual achievement, but the result was a musical style far above the heads of most of their contemporary listeners. The Council of Trent, in accordance with Counter-Reformation principles, had even considered prohibiting polyphony in religious works in order to make church music more accessible to the average congregation before finally deciding that this would be too extreme a measure. For once, the objectives of Reformation and Counter-Reformation coincided, for Luther had already simplified the musical elements in Protestant services for the same reason (see page 276).

The time was therefore ripe for a general move toward sacred music with a wider and more universal appeal. Since at the same time the demand for secular music was growing, it is not surprising that composers soon developed a style sufficiently attractive and sufficiently flexible not only for the creation of masses and other liturgical works, but also of instrumental and vocal music that could be played and listened to at home [304].

In the field of instrumental music one of the greatest composers of the late Baroque period was Domenico Scarlatti (1685–1757). Like his predecessor Arcangelo Corelli (1653–1713), he wrote nothing but instrumental music. The greatest virtuoso of his day on the *harpsichord* (the keyboard instrument that was a primary forerunner of the modern piano), he wrote hundreds of *sonatas* (short instrumental pieces) for it and laid down the foundations of modern keyboard technique.

Scarlatti's contemporary Georg Friedrich Handel (1685–1759) was born at Halle in Germany, christened with a name he later changed to George Frederick Handel when he settled in England and became a naturalized citizen. London was to prove the scene of his greatest successes, among them the *Messiah*, first performed in Dublin in 1742. This *oratorio*, or sacred text set to music, is among the most familiar of all baroque musical masterpieces.

Handel also wrote works in a new form of musical entertainment that had been formulated at the beginning of the baroque period—*opera*, which consisted of a play in which the text was sung rather than spoken. Throughout the 17th century the taste for opera and operatic music swept Europe, attracting aristocratic and middle-class listeners alike. In the process, the public appetite for music with which it could identify grew even greater. Small wonder that 20th-century listeners have found pleasure and delight in music written to provide our baroque predecessors with precisely those satisfactions.

The Birth of Opera

Like much else of beauty, opera was born in Florence. Ironically enough, an art form that was to become so popular in so short a time was originally conceived of in lofty intellectual terms. Toward the end of the 16th century a number of thinkers, poets, and musicians began to meet regularly at the house of a wealthy Florentine noble, Count Giovanni Bardi. This group, known as the Florentine *Camerata*, objected strongly to the way in which the polyphonic style in vocal music reduced the text to incomprehensible nonsense. They looked back nostalgically to the time of the Greeks, when almost every word of Greek tragedy was both sung and accompanied by instruments, yet remained perfectly understandable to the spectators. Greek music itself was, of course, lost forever; but at least the group could revive what they considered its essence.

The result was the introduction of a musical form known as *monody*, or *recitative*, which consisted of the free declamation of a single vocal line with a simple instrumental accompaniment for support. Thus listeners could follow the text with ease. The addition of music also gave an emotional intensity not present in simple spoken verse, thus satisfying the baroque interest in heightened emotion.

Although in theory monody could be used for either sacred or secular works, its dramatic potential was obvious. In the winter of 1594–1595 the first play set to music, Jacopo Peri's *Dafine*, was performed in Florence. Its subject was drawn from classical mythology and dealt with Apollo's pursuit of the mortal girl Daphne, who turned into a laurel tree to elude him. In the words of a spectator, "The pleasure and amazement of those present were beyond expression." *Dafine* is now lost, but another work of Peri, *Euridice*, has survived to become the earliest extant opera. It too was based on a Greek myth, that of Orpheus and Euridice. The first performance took place in 1600, again in Florence, at the wedding of Henry IV of France to the same Marie de' Medici whom Rubens was to portray a generation later [see figure 298, page 314].

It is, of course, no coincidence that both of Peri's works as well as many that followed were written on classical subjects, since the *Camerata* had taken its initial inspiration from Greek drama. The story of Orpheus and Euridice, furthermore, had a special appeal for composers, since it told how the musician Orpheus was able to soften the heart of the King of the Underworld by his music and thereby win back his wife Euridice from the dead. The theme was treated many times in the music of the next 400 years, yet no subsequent version is more moving or psychologically convincing than the one by Claudio Monteverdi (1567–1643), the first great genius in the history of opera.

Monteverdi's *Orfeo* was first performed in 1607. Its composer brought to the new form not only a complete understanding of the possibilities of monody but in addition an impressive mastery of traditional polyphonic forms such as the madrigal. Equally important for the success of his works was Monteverdi's remarkable dramatic instinct and his ability to transform emotion into musical terms. The contrast between the pastoral gaiety of the first act of *Orfeo*, depicting the happy couple's love, and the scene in the second act in which Orpheus is brought the news of his wife's death is achieved with marvelous expressive power.

In *Orfeo*, his first opera, Monteverdi was able to breathe real life into the academic principles of the Florentine *Camerata*, but the work was written for his noble employer, the Duke of Mantua, and intended for a limited aristocratic public. Monteverdi lived long enough to see the new dramatic form achieve widespread popularity at all levels of society throughout Europe. It did not take long for a taste for Italian opera to spread to Germany and Austria and then to England, where by the end of the century Italian singers dominated the London stage. The French showed their usual unwillingness to adopt a foreign invention wholesale; nonetheless, the leading composer at the court of Louis XIV was a Florentine who tactfully changed his name from Giovanni Battista Lulli to Jean Baptiste Lully (1632–1687). His stately tragedies, which were performed throughout Europe, incorporated long sections of ballet, a custom continued by his most illustrious successor, Jean Philippe Rameau (1683–1764).

It was in Italy itself that opera won its largest public. In Venice alone, where Monteverdi spent the last thirty years of his life, at least sixteen theaters were built between 1637—when the first public opera house was opened—and the end of the century. As in the Elizabethan theater [see figure 273, page 292], the design of these opera houses separated the upper ranks of society, who sat in the boxes, from the ordinary citizens, who stood or sat on the ground level.

There is a notable similarity, too, between Elizabethan drama and opera in the way they responded to growing popularity. Just as the groundlings of Shakespeare's day demanded ever more sensational and melodramatic entertainment, so the increasingly demanding and vociferous opera public required new ways of being satisfied. The two chief means by which these desires were met became a feature of most operas written during the following century. The first was the provision of lavish stage spectacles involving mechanical cloud machines that descended from above and disgorged singers and dancers, complex lighting effects that gave the illusion that the stage was being engulfed by fire, apparently magical transformations, and so on—baroque extravagance at its most extreme. The second was a move away from the declamatory recitative of the earliest operas to self-contained musical "numbers" known as *arias*. (In the case of both opera and many other musical forms, we continue to use technical terms like *aria* in their Italian form—a demonstration of the crucial role played by Italy, and in particular Florence, in the history of music.) The function of music as servant of the drama was beginning to change. Beauty of melody and the technical virtuosity of the singers became the glory of baroque opera, although at the expense of dramatic truth.

Johann Sebastian Bach

In the year that saw the births of both Scarlatti and Handel, Johann Sebastian Bach (1685–1750) was born at Eisenach, Germany, into a family that had already been producing musicians for well over a century. With the exception of opera, which as a devout Lutheran did not interest him, Bach mastered every musical form of the time, pouring forth some of the most intellectually rigorous and spiritually profound music ever created.

It is among the more remarkable achievements in the history of the arts that most of Bach's music was produced under conditions of grinding toil as organist and choir director in relatively provincial German towns. Even Leipzig—where he spent 27 years from 1723 to his death as *kantor* (music director) at the school attached to Saint Thomas' Church—was far removed from the glittering centers of European culture where most artistic developments were taking place. As a result, Bach was little known as a composer during his lifetime and virtually forgotten after his death; only in the 19th century did all his works become known and published. He has since taken his place at the head of the Western musical tradition as

the figure who raised the art of polyphony to its highest level.

If the sheer quantity of music Bach wrote is stupefying, so is the complexity of his musical thought. Among the styles he preferred was the *fugue*, a word derived from the Latin word for flight. In the course of a fugue a single theme is passed from voice to voice or instrument to instrument (generally four in number), each imitating the principal theme in turn. The theme thus becomes combined with itself, and in the process the composer creates a seamless web of sound in which each musical part is equally important; this technique is called *counterpoint*. Bach's ability to endow this highly intellectual technique with emotional power is little short of miraculous. The range of emotions Bach's fugues cover can best be appreciated by sampling his two books of 24 fugues each, all prefaced by a prelude, known collectively as *The Well-Tempered Klavier* (*well-tempered* in this context means equally tempered; *klavier* is any keyboard instrument). Each of the 48 preludes and fugues creates its own mood while remaining logically organized according to contrapuntal technique.

Many of Bach's important works are permeated by a single concern, the expression of his deep religious faith. Many of them were written in his capacity as director of music at Saint Thomas' for performance in the church throughout the year. Organ music, masses, oratorios, motets; in all of these he could use music to glorify God and to explore the deeper mysteries of Christianity. His chorale preludes consist of variations on *chorales* (hymn tunes) and use familiar and well-loved songs as the basis for a kind of musical improvisation. He wrote some two hundred *cantatas*, short oratorios made up of sections of declamatory recitative and lyrical arias, which contain an almost inexhaustible range of religious emotions, from joyful celebrations of life to profound meditations on death. Most overwhelming of all is his setting of the *Saint Matthew Passion*, the story of the trial and Crucifixion of Jesus as recorded in the Gospel of Matthew. In this immense work Bach asserted his Lutheranism by using the German rather than the Latin translation of the Gospel and by incorporating Lutheran chorales. The use of self-contained arias is Italian, though, and the spirit of deep religious commitment and dramatic fervor can only be described as universal.

It would be a mistake to think of Bach as somehow unworldly and touched only by religious emotions. Certainly his own life had its share of domestic happiness and tragedy. His parents died when he was ten, leaving him to be brought up by an elder brother who treated him with less than complete kindness.

At the age of fifteen he jumped at the chance to leave home and become a choirboy in the little town of Luneberg. He spent the next few years moving from place to place, perfecting his skills as organist, violinist, and composer.

In 1707 Bach married his cousin, Maria Barbara Bach, who bore him seven children, of whom four died in infancy. Bach was always devoted to his family, and the loss of these children, followed by the death of his wife in 1720, made a deep impression on him. It may have been to provide a mother for his three surviving sons that he remarried in 1721. At any event his new wife, Anna Magdalena, proved a loving companion, bearing him thirteen more children and helping him with the preparation and copying of his music. One of the shortest but most touching of Bach's works is the little song he composed for her, *Bist du bei mir*, which has survived copied out in her notebook. The words are: "As long as you are with me I could face my death and eternal rest with joy. How peaceful would my end be if your beautiful hands could close my faithful eyes."

The move to Leipzig in 1723 was dictated at least in part by the need to provide suitable schooling for his children, although it also offered the stability and security Bach seems to have required. The subsequent years of continual work took their toll, however. Bach's sight had never been good, and the incessant copying of manuscripts produced a continual deterioration. In 1749 he was persuaded to undergo two disastrous operations that left him totally blind. A few months later his sight was suddenly restored, but within ten days he died of apoplexy.

Although the vast majority of Bach's works are on religious themes, the best known of all, the six Brandenburg concertos, were written for the private entertainment of a minor prince, the Margrave of Brandenburg. Their form follows the Italian *concerto grosso*, an orchestral composition in three sections, or *movements*, fast–slow–fast. The form had been pioneered by the Venetian composer Antonio Vivaldi (c. 1676–1741), who delighted in strong contrasts between the orchestra, generally made up of string instruments and a solo instrument, often a violin (as in his well-known set of four concertos *The Four Seasons*) but sometimes a flute, bassoon, or other wind instrument. Four of Bach's six Brandenburg concertos use not one but a group of solo instruments, although the group differs from work to work. The whole set forms a kind of compendium of the possibilities of instrumental color, a true virtuoso achievement requiring equal virtuosity in performance. The musical mood is light, as befits works written primarily for entertainment, but Bach was incapable of

writing music without depth, and the slow movements in particular are strikingly beautiful.

The second Brandenburg concerto is written for solo trumpet, recorder, oboe, and violin accompanied by a string orchestra. The first movement combines all of these to produce a brilliant rhythmic effect as the solo instruments now emerge from the orchestra, now rejoin it. The melodic line avoids short themes. Instead, as in much baroque music, the melodies are long, elaborate patterns that seem to spread and evolve, having much of the ornateness of baroque art. It does not require an ability to read music to see as well as hear how the opening theme of the second Brandenburg concerto forms an unbroken line of sound, rising and falling and doubling back as it luxuriantly spreads itself out.

The slow second movement forms a tranquil and meditative interlude. The brilliant tone of the trumpet would be inappropriate here and Bach therefore omits it, leaving the recorder, oboe, and violin quietly to intertwine in a delicate web of sound. After its enforced silence, the trumpet seems to burst out irrepressibly at the beginning of the third movement, claiming the right to set the mood of limitless energy that carries the work to its conclusion.

Philosophy and Science

Throughout the 17th century philosophy, like the visual arts, continued to extend and intensify ideas first developed in the Renaissance by pushing them to new extremes. With the spread of humanism the 16th century had seen a growing spirit of philosophical and scientific inquiry. In the Baroque period that fresh approach to the world and its phenomena was expressed in clear and consistent terms for the first time since the Greeks. It might be said, in fact, that if the Renaissance marked the birth of modern philosophy, the 17th century signaled its coming of age.

Briefly put, the chief difference between the intellectual attitudes of the medieval period and those inaugurated by the Renaissance was a turning away from the contemplation of the absolute and eternal to a study of the particular and the perceivable. Philosophy ceased to be the preserve of the theologians and instead became an independent discipline, no longer prepared to accept a supernatural or divine explanation for the world and human existence.

For better or worse, we are still living with the consequences of this momentous change. The importance of objective truth, objectively demonstrated, lies at the heart of all scientific method, and most modern philosophy. Yet great thinkers before the Renaissance, such as Thomas Aquinas (1225–1274), had also asked questions in an attempt to understand the world and its workings. How did 17th-century scientists and philosophers differ from their predecessors in dealing with age-old problems?

The basic difference lay in their approach. When, for example, Aquinas was concerned with the theory of motion, he discussed it in abstract, metaphysical terms. Armed with his copy of Aristotle, he claimed that "motion exists because things which are in a state of potentiality seek to actualize themselves." When Galileo wanted to study motion and learn how bodies move in time and space, he climbed to the top of the Leaning Tower of Pisa and dropped weights to watch them fall. It would be difficult to imagine a more dramatic rejection of abstract generalization in favor of objective demonstration.

305 Galileo Galilei. Telescopes. 1609. Museum of Science, Florence. After his death near Florence in 1642, many of Galileo's instruments, including these telescopes, were collected and preserved. The Museum of Science in Florence, where they can now be seen, was one of the earliest museums to be devoted to scientific rather than artistic works.

Galileo

The life and work of Galileo Galilei (1564–1642) are typical both of the progress made by science in the 17th century and of the problems it encountered. Galileo changed the scientific world in two ways: first, as the stargazer who claimed that his observations through the telescope proved Copernicus right (see page 278), for which statement he was tried and condemned by the Inquisition; and second as the founder of modern physics. Although he is probably better known for his work in astronomy, from the scientific point of view his contribution to physics is more important.

Born in Pisa, Galileo inherited from his father Vincenzo, who had been one of the original members of the Florentine *Camerata*, a lively prose style and a fondness for music. As a student at the University of Padua from 1581 to 1592 he began to study medicine but soon changed to mathematics. After a few months back in Pisa, he took a position at the University of Padua as professor of mathematics, remaining there from 1592 to 1600.

In Padua he designed and built his own telescopes [305] and saw for the first time the craters of the moon, sunspots, the phases of Venus, and other phenomena which showed that the universe is in a constant state of change, as Copernicus had claimed. From the time of Aristotle, however, it had been a firm belief that the heavens were unalterable, representing perfection of form and movement. Galileo's discoveries thus disproved what had been a basic philosophical principle for 2000 years and so outraged a professor of philosophy at Padua that he refused to shake his own prejudices by having a look through a telescope for himself.

The more triumphantly Galileo proclaimed his findings, the more he found himself involved in something beyond mere scientific controversy. His real opponent was the Church, which had officially adopted the Ptolemaic view of the universe: that the earth formed the center of the universe around which the sun, moon, and planets circled. This theory accorded well with the Bible, which seemed to suggest that the sun moves rather than the earth; for the Church the Bible naturally took precedence over any reasoning or speculation independent of theology. Galileo, however, considered ecclesiastical officials incompetent to evaluate scientific matters and refused to give way. When he began to claim publicly that his discoveries had proved what Copernicus had theorized but could not validate, the Church initiated a case against him on the grounds of heresy.

Galileo had meanwhile returned to his beloved Pisa, where he found himself in considerable danger from the Inquisition. In 1615 he left for Rome to defend his position in the presence of Pope Paul V. He failed, and as a result was censured and prohibited from spreading the Copernican theory either by teaching or publication.

In 1632 Galileo returned to the attack when a former friend was elected Pope. He submitted to Pope Urban VIII a *Dialogue Concerning the Two Chief World Systems*, having carefully chosen the dialogue form so that he could put ideas into the mouths of other characters and thereby claim that they were not his own. Once more, under pressure from the Jesuits, he was summoned to Rome. In 1633 he was put on trial after spending several months in prison. His pleas of old age and poor health won no sympathy from the tribunal. He was made to recant and humiliate himself publicly and was sentenced to prison for the rest of his life. (It might well have appealed to Galileo's sense of bitter irony that 347 years later, in 1980, Pope John Paul II, a fellow countryman of the Polish Copernicus, ordered the case to be reopened so that belated justice might be done.)

Influential friends managed to secure Galileo a relatively comfortable house arrest in his villa just outside Florence, and he retired there to work on physics. His last and most important scientific work, *Dialogues Concerning Two New Sciences*, was published in 1638. In it he examined many long-standing problems, including that of motion, always basing his conclusions on practical experiment and observation. In the process he established the outlines of many areas of modern physics.

In all his work Galileo set forth a new way of approaching scientific problems. Instead of trying to understand the final cause or cosmic purpose of natural events and phenomena, he tried to explain their character and the manner in which they came about. He changed the question from *why?* to *what?* and *how?*

306 Frans Hals. *René Descartes*. Oil on panel.
Statens Museum for Kunst, Copenhagen.
The great French philosopher spent many years in Holland, where his ideas found a receptive audience, and where Hals painted this portrait.

Descartes

Scientific investigation could not solve every problem of human existence. While it *could* try to explain and interpret objective phenomena, there remained other more subjective areas of experience involving ethical and spiritual questions. The Counter-Reformation on the one hand and the Protestant churches on the other claimed to have discovered the answers. The debates nevertheless continued, most notably in the writings of the French philosopher René Descartes (1596–1650), often called the "Father of Modern Philosophy" [306].

In many ways Descartes' philosophical position was symptomatic of his age. He was educated at a Jesuit school but found traditional theological teaching unsatisfactory. Turning to science and mathematics, he began a lifelong search for reliable evidence in his quest to distinguish truth from falsehood. Attacking philosophical problems, his prime concern was to establish criteria for defining reality. His chief published works, *The Discourse on Method* (1637) and the *Meditations* (1641), contain a step-by-step account of how he arrived at his conclusions.

According to Descartes, the first essential in the search for truth was to make a fresh start by refusing to believe anything that could not be decisively proved to be true. This required that he doubt all his previously held beliefs, including the evidence of his own senses. By stripping away all uncertainties he reached a basis of indubitable certainty on which he could build: that he existed. The very act of doubting proved that he was a thinking being. As he put it in a famous phrase in his second *Meditation: Cogito, ergo sum* (I think, therefore I am).

From this foundation Descartes proceeded to reconstruct the world he had taken to pieces by considering the nature of material objects. He was guided by the principle that whatever is clearly and distinctly perceived must exist. He was aware at the same time that our perceptions of the exact nature of these objects are extremely likely to be incorrect and misleading. When, for example, we look at the sun we see it as a very small disk, although the sun is really an immense globe. We must be careful, therefore, not to assume that our perceptions are bound to be accurate. All that they demonstrate is the simple existence of the object in question.

If the idea of the sun comes from the perception, however inaccurate, of something that actually exists, what of God? Is the idea of a divine Being imagined or based on truth? Descartes concluded that the very fact that we who are imperfect and doubting can conceive of a perfect God proves that our conception is based on a reality. In other words, who could ever have imagined God unless God existed? At the center of the Cartesian philosophical system, therefore, lay the belief in a perfect Being, not necessarily to be identified with the God of the Old and New Testaments, who had created a world permeated by perfect (that is, mathematical) principles.

At first sight this may seem inconsistent with Descartes' position as the founder of modern rational thought. It may seem even stranger that, just at the time when scientific investigators like Galileo were explaining natural phenomena without recourse to divine intervention, Descartes succeeded in proving to his own satisfaction the undeniable existence of a divine Being. Yet a more careful look at Descartes' method reveals that both he and Galileo shared the same fundamental confidence in the rational powers of human beings.

Literature in the 17th Century

French Classical Comedy and Tragedy

It is hardly surprising that the Baroque age, which put so high a premium on the expression of dramatic emotion, should have been an important period in the development of the theater. In France in particular, three of the greatest names in the history of drama were active at the same time, all of them benefiting at one point or another from the patronage of Louis XIV.

Molière was the stage name of Jean-Baptiste Poquelin (1622–1673), who was the creator of a new theatrical form, French classical comedy. Having first made his reputation as an actor, he turned to the writing of drama as a means of deflating pretense and pomposity. In his best works, the deceptions or delusions of the principal characters are revealed for what they are with good humor and considerable understanding of human foibles, but dramatic truth is never sacrificed to mere comic effect. Unlike so many comic creations, Molière's characters remain believable. Jourdain, the good-natured social climber of *Le Bourgeois Gentilhomme,* and Harpagon, the absurd miser of *L'Avare,* are by no means mere symbols of their respective vices but victims of those vices, albeit willing ones.

Classical influences play a quite stronger part in the works of the two greatest tragic dramatists of the age, Pierre Corneille (1606–1684) and Jean Racine (1639–1699). It was Corneille who created, as counterpart to Molière's comedy, French classical tragedy. Most of his plays take as their theme an event in classical history or mythology, which is often used to express eternal truths about human behavior. The themes of patriotism, as in *Horace,* or martyrdom, as in *Polyeucte,* are certainly as relevant today as they were in 17th-century France or in ancient Greece or Rome. However, most people's response to Corneille's treatment of subjects such as these is probably conditioned by the degree to which they enjoy the cut and thrust of rhetorical debate.

Racine may well provide for many modern readers an easier entry into the world of French classical tragedy. Although for the most part he followed the dramatic form and framework established by Corneille, he used it to explore different areas of human experience. His recurrent theme is self-destruction: the inability to control one's own jealousy, passion, or ambition and the resulting inability, as tragic as it is inevitable, to survive its effects. Furthermore, in plays like *Phèdre* he explored the psychological state of mind of his principal characters, probing for the same kind of understanding of motivation that Monteverdi tried to achieve in music.

The English Metaphysical Poets

In England the pinnacle of dramatic expression had been reached by the turn of the century in the works of Shakespeare, and nothing remotely comparable was to follow. The literary form that proved most productive during the 17th century was that of lyric poetry, probably because of its ability to express personal emotions, although the single greatest English work of the age was John Milton's epic poem *Paradise Lost*.

It might well be argued that the most important of all literary achievements of the 17th century was not an original artistic creation but a translation. It is difficult to know precisely how to categorize the Authorized Version of the Bible, commissioned by King James I and first published in 1611, often called the only great work of literature ever produced by a committee. The 54 scholars and translators who worked on the task deliberately tried to create a "biblical" style that would transcend the tone of English as it was then generally used. Their success can be measured by the immense influence the King James Bible has had on speakers and writers of English ever since (see page 272). It remained the Authorized Version for English-speaking peoples until the late 19th century, when it was revised in the light of new developments in biblical studies.

Of all 17th-century literary figures, the group known as the metaphysical poets, with their concern to give intellectual expression to emotional experience, make a particular appeal to modern readers. As is often pointed out, the label *metaphysical* is highly misleading for two reasons. In the first place, it suggests an organized group of poets consciously following a common style. It is true that the earliest poet to write in the metaphysical style, John Donne, exerted a strong influence on a whole generation of younger poets, but there never existed any unified group or school. Secondly, *metaphysical* seems to imply that the principal subject of their poetry was philosophical speculation on abstruse questions. It is certainly true that the metaphysical poets were interested in ideas and that they used complex forms of expression and a rich vocabulary to express them. The chief subject of their poems was not philosophy, however, but themselves—particularly their own emotions.

Yet this concern with self-analysis should not suggest a limitation of vision. Indeed, some critics have ranked John Donne (1572–1631) as second only to the Shakespeare of the Sonnets in range and depth of expression. His intellectual brilliance and his love of paradox and ambiguity make his poetry sometimes difficult to follow. Donne always avoided the conventional, either in word or thought, while the swift changes of mood within a single short poem from light banter to the utmost seriousness can confuse the careless reader. Although it sometimes takes patience to unravel his full meaning, the effort is more than amply rewarded by contact with one of the most daring and honest of poets.

Donne's poems took on widely differing areas of human experience, ranging from some of the most passionate and frank discussions of sexual love ever penned to profound meditations on human mortality and the nature of the soul. Born a Catholic, he traveled widely as a young man and seems to have led a hectic and exciting life. He abandoned Catholicism, perhaps in part to improve his chances of success in Protestant England, and in 1601, on the threshold of a successful career in public life, entered Parliament. The same year, however, he secretly married his patron's sixteen-year-old niece, Anne More. Her father had him dismissed and even imprisoned for a few days, and Donne's career never recovered from the disgrace.

Although Donne's marriage proved a happy one, its early years were clouded by debt, ill health, and frustration. In 1615, at the urging of friends, he finally joined the Anglican church and entered the ministry. As a preacher he soon became known as among the greatest of his day. By 1621 he was appointed to one of the most prestigious positions in London, Dean of Saint Paul's. During his last years he became increasingly obsessed with death. After a serious illness in the spring of 1631 he preached his own funeral sermon and died within a few weeks.

Thus the successful worldliness of the early years gave way to the growing somberness of his later career. We might expect a similar progression from light to darkness in his works, yet throughout his life the two forces of physical passion and religious intensity seem to have been equally dominant, with the result that in much of his poetry each is sometimes used to express the other.

Milton's Heroic Vision: *Paradise Lost*

While the past hundred years have seen a growing appreciation for Donne and his followers, the reputation of John Milton has undergone some notable ups and downs. Revered in the centuries following his death, Milton's work came under fire in the early

307 Eugène Delacroix. *Milton Dictating "Paradise Lost" to His Daughters*. c. 1826. Oil on canvas, 31 × 25″ (79 × 64 cm). Private Collection. This highly imaginative vision of the blind poet dictating his work was inspired during several years spent in England by Delacroix (1798–1863), a great French painter of the early 19th century (see page 376).

years of the 20th century from major poets like T. S. Eliot and Ezra Pound, who claimed that his influence on his successors had been pernicious and had led much of subsequent English poetry astray. Now that the dust of these attacks has settled, Milton has resumed his place as one of the greatest of English poets. The power of his spiritual vision, coupled with his heroic attempt to wrestle with the great problems of human existence, seem in fact to speak directly to the uncertainties of our own time.

Milton's life was fraught with controversy. An outstanding student with astonishing abilities in languages, he spent his early years traveling widely in Europe and in the composition of relatively lightweight verse—lightweight, that is, in comparison with what was to come.

By 1640, however, he had become involved in the tricky issues raised by the English Civil War and the related problems of church government. He launched into the fray with a series of radical pamphlets that advocated, among other things, divorce on the grounds of incompatibility. (It is presumably no coincidence that his own wife had left him six weeks after their marriage.) His growing support for Oliver Cromwell and the Puritan cause won him an influential position at home but considerable enmity in continental Europe, where he was seen as the defender of those who had ordered the execution of King Charles I in 1649. The strain of his secretarial and diplomatic duties during the following years destroyed his eyesight, but although completely blind he continued to work with the help of assistants [307].

When Charles II was restored to power in 1660 Milton lost his position and was lucky not to lose his life or liberty. Retired to private life, he spent his remaining years in the composition of three massive works, *Paradise Lost* (1667), *Paradise Regained* (1671), and *Samson Agonistes* (1671).

By almost universal agreement Milton's most important, if not most accessible, work is *Paradise Lost,* composed in the early 1600s and published in 1667. It was intended as an account of the fall of Adam and Eve, and its avowed purpose was to "justify the ways of God to men." The epic is in twelve books (originally ten, but Milton later revised the divisions), written in blank verse.

Milton's language and imagery present an almost inexhaustible combination of biblical and classical reference. From the very first lines of Book I, where the poet calls on a classical Muse to help him tell the tale of The Fall, the two great Western cultural traditions are inextricably linked. Indeed, like Bach, Milton represents the summation of these traditions. In his works, Renaissance and Reformation meet and blend to create the most complete statement in English of Christian humanism, the philosophical reconciliation of humanist principles with Christian doctrine. To the Renaissance Milton owed his grounding in the classics. In composing *Paradise Lost,* an epic poem that touches on the whole range of human experience, he was deliberately inviting comparison with Homer and Vergil. His language is also classical in its inspiration, with its long, grammatically complex sentences and preference for abstract terms. Yet his deeply felt Christianity and his emphasis on human guilt and repentance mark him as a product of the Reformation. Furthermore, although he may have tried to transcend the limitations of his own age, he was as much a child of his time as any of the other artists discussed in this chapter. The dramatic fervor of Bernini, the spiritual certainty of Bach, the psychological insight of Monteverdi, the humanity of Rembrandt—all have their place in Milton's work and mark him, too, as an essentially baroque figure.

Questions for Further Discussion

1. Most art of the Baroque period, with the notable exception of Holland, was commissioned either by aristocratic patrons or by the church. What forms of artistic patronage exist in our own society, and what effect does their character have on the arts today?

2. Some critics have criticized John Donne's love poetry for being too concerned with physical satisfaction and not enough with human relationships. Is this criticism justified? Explain. Can it be applied to any other love poetry, before or after Donne?

3. Assess the validity of Descartes' demonstration of the existence of a Perfect Being.

4. The Baroque age was characterized by a love of the spectacular whether at the court of Louis XIV, in Bernini's Rome, at the theater, in the paintings of Rubens, or in countless other areas. Does our own age share any of the baroque taste for elaborate display? If so, in what ways is it satisfied in the modern world?

5. Although Bach is now revered as one of the greatest composers of all time, he was almost completely forgotten for 75 years after his death. Milton, on the other hand, was highly praised in the 17th, 18th, and 19th centuries, yet severely criticized in our own. What factors determine the long-term reputation of creative artists?

6. Religious ecstasy is not an emotion with which most of us are very familiar. In what ways, if any, does it manifest itself in our world? Are we better or worse off without it?

	GENERAL EVENTS	LITERATURE & PHILOSOPHY	ART
1700			

1710-c. 1795 Rise of Prussia and Russia

1715 Death of Louis XIV

1715-1774 Reign of Louis XV in France

1711 Pope, *Essay on Criticism*

1712 Pope, *The Rape of the Lock,* mock-heroic epic

18th cent. Translations of classical authors; Pope's *Iliad* (1713-1720), *Odyssey* (1725-1726)

1726 Swift, *Gulliver's Travels;* Voltaire exiled from France (returns 1729)

1729 Swift, *A Modest Proposal*

1733-1734 Pope, *Essay on Man*

1734 Voltaire, *Lettres philosophiques*

1739 Hume, *Treatise of Human Nature*

c. 1715 Rococo style emerges in France

1717 Watteau, *Pilgrimage to Cythera*

c. 1730 Carriera, *Portrait of a Lady*

| **1740** | | | |

1740-1786 Reign of Frederick the Great in Prussia

1773-1814 Jesuits disbanded

1774-1792 Reign of Louis XVI and Marie Antoinette in France

1776 American Declaration of Independence

1778-1783 American War of Independence

1788 Collapse of French economy; riots in Paris

1750-1753 Voltaire at court of Frederick the Great in Potsdam

1751-1772 Diderot's *Encyclopédie* includes writings by Montesquieu and J. J. Rousseau

1758-1778 Voltaire sets up own court in Ferney

1759 Voltaire, *Candide*

1762 J. J. Rousseau, *The Social Contract*

1772 Political writer Thomas Paine meets Benjamin Franklin in London

1776 In Philadelphia, Paine publishes *Common Sense,* series of pamphlets

1776-1788 Gibbon, *History of the Decline and Fall of the Roman Empire*

1743-1745 Hogarth paints satirical series, *Marriage à la Mode*

1748 Excavations begin at Pompeii and Herculaneum; interest in ancient classical styles increases

Sculpture more virtuosic than profound; Queirolo, *Deception Unmasked* (after 1750)

1754 Boucher, *Cupid a Captive*

c. 1765 Gainsborough, *Mary, Countess Howe*

1769 Tiepolo, *The Immaculate Conception,* rococo style applied to religious subject

1771 Houdon, *Diderot*

1773 Fragonard, *Love Letters*

1774 Reynolds, *Three Ladies Adorning a Term of Hymen,* influenced by classical and Renaissance models

c. 1776 Vanvitelli, *The Great Cascade,* fountains at castle of Caserta near Naples

1784-1785 David, *Oath of the Horatii,* establishes official style of revolutionary art

c. 1785 Gainsborough, *Haymaker and Sleeping Girl*

| **1789** | | | |

1789 French Revolution begins; new American Constitution

1793 Execution of Louis XVI

1793-1795 Reign of Terror in France

1799-1804 Napoleon rules France as consul

1804-1814 Napoleon rules France as emperor

1792 Paine, *The Rights of Man*

c. 1790 Houdon, *George Washington,* statue

1800 David, *Napoleon Crossing the Alps*

1808 Canova, *Pauline Bonaparte Borghese as Venus*

| **1815** | | | |

ARCHITECTURE	MUSIC

1732 Boffrand begins Hôtel de Soubise, Paris; rococo style applied to room decoration

c. 1700-1730 Couperin leading composer of *style galant* music at French court

1743 Henry Hoare begins to lay out classical-inspired park at Stourhead

1743-1772 Neumann, Vierzehnheiligen Pilgrim Church near Bamberg

1755-1792 Soufflot converts church of Saint Geneviève into the Panthéon, neoclassical memorial for dead of French Revolution

1785-1796 Jefferson's state capitol, Richmond, Virginia, modeled on ancient Roman Maison Carée at Nîmes

1750 Death of J. S. Bach

c. 1750 C. P. E. Bach chief representative of emotional *empfindsamer Stil* at court of Frederick the Great

1750-1800 Development of classical style and symphonic form

1752 J. J. Rousseau, *Le Devin du Village,* opera

1759 Death of Handel

1761 Haydn ("Father of the Symphony") begins 30-year service with Esterhazy

1786 First performance of Mozart's *The Marriage of Figaro,* opera based on Beaumarchais play

1788 Mozart, *Symphony No. 40 in G minor*

1791 Mozart, *Piano Concerto 27 in B flat Major;* opera *The Magic Flute*

1791-1795 Haydn composes 12 symphonies during visits to London; *Symphony No. 104 in D Major* (1795)

14

The 18th Century: From Reason to Revolution

329

Age of Contradictions

Even the most determined cultural historians, fully armed with neat labels for successive stages of Western cultural development, acknowledge serious difficulty in categorizing the 18th century. Although it has often been called the Age of Enlightenment or the Age of Reason, these labels—which do, in fact, describe some of its aspects—fail to encompass the full spirit of the age.

From one perspective, the 18th century was an age of optimism. It had trust in science and in the power of human reason, belief in a natural order, and an overriding faith in the theory of progress—that the world was better than it had ever been and was bound to get better still. Looked at from another perspective, however, the 18th century was marked by pervasive resentment and dissatisfaction with established society. By its end, criticism and the press for reform had actually grown into a desire for violent change, producing the American and then the French revolutions. Furthermore, even these two apparently contradictory views—of unqualified optimism and of extreme discontent—do not cover all aspects of 18th-century culture. For example, one of the most popular artistic styles of the period, the rococo, was characterized by frivolity and lightheartedness. Rococo artists deliberately aimed to create a fantasy world of pleasure into which their patrons could escape from the problems around them.

The 18th century, then, presents an immense variety of artistic and intellectual ideas, seemingly contradictory yet in fact coexistent. Each style or idea seems far easier to grasp and categorize by itself than as part of an overall pattern of cultural development. Nevertheless, it is possible to discern at least one characteristic that links together a number of the diverse artistic achievements of the century: a conscious engagement with social issues. An opera such as Wolfgang Amadeus Mozart's *The Marriage of Figaro,* a series of satiric paintings of daily life such as William Hogarth's *Marriage à la Mode,* a mock epic poem such as Alexander Pope's *The Rape of the Lock,* and revolutionary ideas such as those of Jean Jacques Rousseau are all examples of ways in which artists and thinkers joined with political leaders to effect social change.

Meanwhile, artists who supported the Establishment and were resistant to change were equally engaged in social issues. They too used their art to express and defend their position. François Boucher's portraits of his wealthy aristocratic patrons, for example, often show them in the guise of Greek gods and goddesses, thus imparting a sense of glamour and importance to an aristocracy that was shortly to be fighting for its survival.

The contrast between revolutionaries and conservatives lasted right to the eve of the French Revolution. Jacques Louis David's famous painting *Oath of the Horatii* of 1784–1785 [308], a clarion call to action and resolve, was painted in the same year as Thomas Gainsborough's idealized picture of a *Haymaker and Sleeping Girl* [309]. The former, in keeping with the spirit of the times, prefigures the mood of revolution. The latter turns its back on reality, evoking a nostalgic vision of love among the haystacks. In so doing it reinforces the aristocracy's refusal to see

308 Jacques Louis David. *Oath of the Horatii.* 1784–1785. Oil on canvas, 10′10″ × 14′ (3.3 × 4.27 m). Louvre, Paris. The story of the Horatii, three brothers who swore an oath to defend Rome even at the cost of their lives, is here used to extol patriotism. Painted only five years before the French Revolution, David's work established the official style of revolutionary art.

the working classes as real people with serious problems of their own.

The 18th century opened with Louis XIV still strutting down the Hall of Mirrors at Versailles, but his death in 1715 marked the beginning of the end of absolute monarchy. Although most of Europe continued to be ruled by hereditary kings, the former emphasis on splendor and privilege was leavened with a new concern for the welfare of the ordinary citizen. Rulers such as Frederick the Great of Prussia (ruled 1740–1786) were no less determined than their predecessors to retain all power in their own hands, but they no longer thought of their kingdoms as private possessions to be manipulated for personal pleasure. Instead they regarded them as trusts, which required them to show a sense of duty and responsibility. They built new roads, drained marshes, and reorganized legal and bureaucratic systems along rational lines.

309 Thomas Gainsborough. *Haymaker and Sleeping Girl.* c. 1785. Oil on canvas, 7'5" × 4'10½" (2.26 × 1.49 m). Museum of Fine Arts, Boston (Theresa B. Hopkins and Seth K. Sweetser Fund). These charming and elegant peasants, neither of whom looks exactly ravaged by hard work in the fields, represent the artificial world of rococo art.

Because of their greater concern for the welfare of their people these new more liberal kings, often known as "enlightened despots," undoubtedly postponed for a while the growing demand for change. Inevitably, however, by drawing attention to the injustices of the past they stimulated an appetite for reform that they themselves were in no position to satisfy. Furthermore, for all their claims—Frederick the Great, for example, described himself as "first servant of the state"—their regimes remained essentially autocratic.

In France, center of much of the intellectual pressure for change, the despots were not even enlightened. Louis XV, who ruled from 1715 to 1774, showed little interest in the affairs of his subjects or the details of government. The remark often attributed to him, *Après moi le déluge* (After me, the flood), suggests that he was fully aware of the consequences of his indifference. Subsequent events fully justified his prediction, yet throughout his long reign he remained either unwilling or unable to follow the example of his fellow European sovereigns and impose some order on government. By the time his grandson Louis XVI succeeded him in 1774 the damage was done. Furthermore, the new king's continued reliance on the traditional aristocratic class, into whose hands he put wealth and political power, offended both the rising middle class and the peasants. When in 1788 the collapse of the French economy was accompanied by a disastrous harvest and consequent steep rise in the cost of food in the first phase of the Revolution, riots broke out in Paris and in rural districts. In reaction to the ensuing violence the "Declaration of the Rights of Man and Citizen," which asserted the universal right to "liberty, property, security, and resistance to oppression," was passed on August 26, 1789.

Declarations alone hardly sufficed, however; after two and a half years of continual political bickering and unrest, the Revolution entered its second phase. On September 20, 1792, a National Convention was assembled. One of its first tasks was to try Louis XVI, by now deposed and imprisoned, for treason. After unanimously finding him guilty, the Convention was divided on whether to execute him or not. He was finally condemned to the guillotine by a vote of 361 to 360 and beheaded forthwith. The resulting Reign of Terror lasted until 1795. During it, utopian theories of a republic based on liberty, equality, and fraternity were ruthlessly put into practice. The revolutionary leaders cold-bloodedly eliminated all opponents, real or potential, and created massive upheaval throughout all levels of French society. Political stability returned to France only with the arrival in 1799 of Napoleon Bonaparte and a military dictatorship.

Although the French Revolution was an obvious consequence of extreme historical pressures, many of its leaders were additionally inspired by the successful outcome of another revolution, that of the Americans against their British rulers. More specifically, the Americans had rebelled against not the British king but the British parliament. In 18th-century England the king was given little chance to be enlightened or otherwise, since supreme power was concentrated in the legislative assembly, which ruled both England itself and, by its appointees, British territories abroad. A series of economic measures enacted by Parliament succeeded in thoroughly rousing American resentment. The story of what followed the Declaration of Independence of July 4, 1776, is too involved to be summarized here. Its result was the signing of a peace treaty in 1783 and the inauguration of the new American Constitution in 1789.

Although the Declaration of Independence was certainly not intended as a work of literature, its author, generally assumed to be Thomas Jefferson, was as successful as any of the literary figures of the 18th century in expressing the more optimistic views of the age. The principles enshrined in it assume that human beings are capable of achieving political and social freedom. Positive belief in equality and justice is expressed in universal terms like *man* and *nature*—universal for their day, that is—typical of 18th-century enlightened thought [310].

Rococo and Neoclassical Styles in the Visual Arts

In spite of the changing social climate of the time, the vast majority of 18th-century artists still depended on the aristocracy for commissions. The baroque style had been partially evolved to satisfy just these patrons, and throughout the early part of the 18th century many artists continued to produce works following baroque precedents. Yet, despite the continued fondness for the baroque characteristics of richness and elaboration, there was a significant change of emphasis. The new enlightened despots and their courts had less time for pomposity or excessive grandeur. They wanted to be not so much glorified as entertained. In France, too, the death of Louis XIV served as an excuse to escape the oppressive ceremony of life at Versailles; the French court moved back to Paris, to live in elegant comfort.

The artistic style that developed to meet these new, less grandiose needs first reached its maturity in France. It is generally called *rococo,* a word derived from the French word *rocaille,* which means a kind of elaborate decoration of rocks and shells that often adorned the grottoes of baroque gardens. Rococo art makes plentiful use of shell motifs, along with other decorative elements like scrolls and ribbons, to produce an overall impression of lightness and gaiety. The subject matter is rarely serious, often frivolous, with strong emphasis on romantic dalliance and the pursuit of pleasure. Critics have often said that the only purpose of rococo art was to provide pleasure, but this is a somewhat incomplete view of its social role. The rococo style was aimed for the most part at an aristocratic audience; its grace and charm served the important purpose of shielding this class from the growing problems of the real world. The elegant picnics, the graceful lovers, the Venuses triumphant represent an almost frighteningly unrealistic view of life. Yet even the sternest moralist can hardly fail to respond to the enticing fantasy existence that the best of rococo art presents. In a sense the knowledge that the whole rococo world was to be so completely swept away imparts an added (and, it must be admitted, unintentional) poignance to its art. The existence of all those fragile ladies and their refined suitors was to be cut short by the guillotine.

310 Jean Antoine Houdon. *George Washington.* 1788. Marble, height 6′8″ (2.03 m). Virginia State Capitol, Richmond (courtesy of the Virginia State Library). The sculptor has emphasized the dignity and lofty calm of the first president.

Painting

The first and probably the greatest French rococo painter, Jean Antoine Watteau (1684–1721), seems to have felt instinctively the transitoriness and impermanence of the world he depicted. Watteau is best known for his paintings of *fêtes galantes,* elegant outdoor festivals attended by courtly figures dressed in the height of fashion. Yet the charming scenes are always touched with a mood of nostalgia that often verges on melancholy. In *Pilgrimage to Cythera* [Plate 25, page 341], for instance, the handsome young couples are returning home (despite the traditional title of the painting) from a visit to Cythera, the island sacred to Venus and to love. As they leave, a few of them gaze wistfully over their shoulders at the idyllic life, symbolized by the statue of Venus herself, which they must leave behind. Watteau thus emphasizes the moment of renunciation, underscoring the sense of departure and farewell by the autumnal colors of the landscape.

Francois Boucher (1703–1770), the other leading French rococo painter, was also influenced by Rubens. Lacking the restraint or poetry of Watteau's, Boucher's paintings carry Rubens' theme of voluptuous beauty to an extreme. His canvases often seem to consist of little beyond mounds of pink flesh, as in *Cupid a Captive* [311]. It would certainly be difficult to find profundity of intellectual content in most of his work, the purpose of which is to depict only one aspect of human existence. His visions of erotic delights are frankly intended to arouse other than aesthetic feelings.

Among Boucher's pupils was Jean Honoré Fragonard (1732–1806), the last of the great French rococo painters, who lived long enough to see all demand for rococo art disappear with the coming of the French Revolution. Although his figures are generally more clothed than those of Boucher, they are no less erotic. Even more than his master, Fragonard was able to use landscape to accentuate the mood of romance. In *Love Letters* [312], for example, the couple flirting in the foreground is surrounded by a jungle of trees and bushes that seems to impart a heady, humid air to the apparently innocent confrontation. The end of Fragonard's career is a reminder of how much 18th-century artists were affected by contemporary historical developments. When his aristocratic patrons either died or fled France during the Revolution, he was reduced to complete poverty. It was perhaps because Fragonard supported the ideals of the Revolution, in spite of its disastrous effect on his personal life, that Jacques Louis David, one of the Revolution's chief artistic arbiters, found him a job in the

right: 312 Jean Honoré Fragonard. *Love Letters.* 1773. Oil on canvas, 10′5″ × 7′1″ (3.17 × 2.17 m). Frick Collection, New York. Fragonard's style is much more free and less precise than Boucher's: compare the hazy, atmospheric landscape of this painting with the background of *Cupid a Captive.*

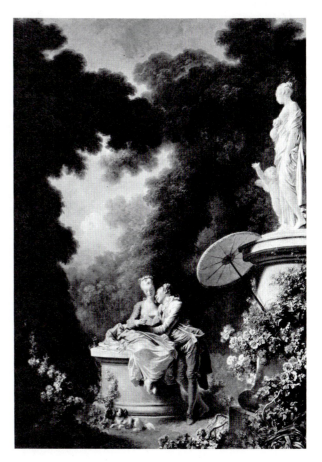

311 François Boucher. *Cupid a Captive.* 1754. Oil on canvas, 5′5″ × 2′9″ (1.64 × .83 m). Wallace Collection, London (reproduced by courtesy of the Trustees). Venus is seen in a relaxed and playful mood as she teases her little son by dangling his quiver of arrows above his head. Nonetheless, the presence of her seductive nymphs reminds us that she is not simply the goddess of motherly love.

Museums Service. The last representative of the rococo tradition died poor and in obscurity as a minor official in the new French Republic.

Taken together, the three leading representatives of rococo painting provide a picture of the fantasy life of 18th-century aristocratic society. The work of other rococo artists, however, gives us a clearer impression of what life was really like in that aristocratic world. The Venetian artist Rosalba Carriera (1675–1757) traveled widely throughout Europe producing large numbers of portraits in the rather unusual medium of *pastel,* dry sticks of color that disintegrate when rubbed on paper, leaving behind a fine powder. The medium is very delicate, but so, unfortunately, are the works executed in it, since the powder smudges easily and tends to fall off if the paper is shaken. It is unlikely that Carriera was concerned with conveying psychological depths. Her chief aim was to provide her subjects flattering likenesses that reinforced their own favorable visions of themselves. Works like her portrait of the Princess of Modena [313] emphasize the delicacy, charm, and sensuality of 18th-century society beauties.

English art in the 18th century was also notable for its aristocratic portraits. The more extreme elements of rococo eroticism had little appeal to the English nobility, but the artists who were commissioned to paint their portraits could hardly help being influenced by the style of their day. Thomas Gainsborough (1727–1788), who together with Sir Joshua Reynolds (1723–1792) dominated the English art of the time, even studied for a while with a pupil of Boucher. At a time when rococo art had already fallen into disfavor in France, Gainsborough was still producing paintings like *Haymaker and Sleeping Girl* [see figure 309], an idealizing rococo vision that recalls the world of Fragonard. Gainsborough's chief reputation, however, was made by his landscapes and portraits. Most of the portraits are themselves set against a landscape background, as in the case of *Mary, Countess Howe* [314]. In this painting, setting and costume are reminiscent of Watteau, but the dignified pose and cool gaze of the subject suggest that she had other than romantic thoughts in mind. There is no lack of poetry in the scene, though, and the resplendent shimmer of the countess' dress is perfectly set off by the more somber tones on the background.

Portraits and landscapes lend themselves naturally to rococo treatment, but what of religious art? One

below: 313 Rosalba Carriera. *Anna Sofia d'Este, Princess of Modena.* c. 1730. Pastel. Uffizi, Florence. The pale elegance of the subject is typical of most of Carriera's aristocratic sitters, as is the charming untidiness of her dress.

right: 314 Thomas Gainsborough. *Mary, Countess Howe.* c. 1765. Oil on canvas, 8 × 5′ (2.59 × 1.52 m). London County Council, Kenwood House (Iveagh Bequest). The wild background and threatening sky set off the subject, but their artificiality is shown by her shoes—hardly appropriate for a walk in the country.

of the very few painters who tried to apply rococo principles to religious subjects was the Venetian painter Giovanni Battista Tiepolo (1696–1770). Many of Tiepolo's most ambitious and best-known works are decorations for the ceilings of churches and palaces, for which projects he was helped by assistants. A more personal work is his painting *The Immaculate Conception* [315]. The light colors and chubby cherubs of Boucher and the haughty assurance of Gainsborough's society ladies are here applied to the life of the Virgin Mary.

For all its importance, however, the rococo style was not the only one to influence 18th-century painters. The other principal artistic movement of the age was *neoclassicism,* which increased in popularity as the appeal of the rococo declined.

There were good historical reasons for the rise of neoclassicism. The excavation of the buried cities of Herculaneum and Pompeii, beginning in 1711 and 1748 respectively, evoked immense interest in the art of classical antiquity in general and that of Rome in particular. The wall paintings from Pompeian villas of the 1st century A.D. were copied by countless visitors to the excavations, and reports of the finds were published throughout Europe. The German scholar Johannes Winckelmann (1717–1768), who is sometimes called the Father of Archaeology, played a major part in creating a new awareness of the importance of classical art; in many of his writings he encouraged his contemporaries not only to admire ancient masterpieces but to imitate them.

Furthermore, the aims and ideals of the Roman Republic—freedom, opposition to tyranny, valor—held a special appeal for 18th-century republican politicians, and the evocation of classical models became a characteristic of the art of the French Revolution. The painter who best represents the official revolutionary style is Jacques Louis David (1748–1825). His *Oath of the Horatii* [see figure 308] draws not only upon a story of ancient Roman civic virtue but also upon a knowledge of ancient dress and armor derived from excavations of Pompeii and elsewhere. The simplicity of its message—the importance of united opposition to tyranny—is expressed by the simple austerity of its style and composition, a far cry from the lush, effete world of Fragonard. David used the same lofty grandeur to depict Napoleon soon after his accession to power [316], although there is considerable if unintentional irony in the use of the revolutionary style to represent the military dictator.

below left: 315   Giovanni Battista Tiepolo. *The Immaculate Conception.* 1769. Oil on canvas, 9′2″ × 5′ (2.79 × 1.52 m). Prado, Madrid. The sense of weightlessness and the wonderful cloud effects are both typical of Tiepolo's style.

below right: 316   Jacques Louis David. *Napoleon Crossing the Alps.* 1800. Oil on canvas, 8′ × 7′7″ (2.44 × 2.31 m). Musée de Versailles. After he took his army across the Alps, Napoleon surprised and defeated an Austrian army. His calm, controlled figure guiding a wildly tearing horse is symbolic of his own vision of himself as bringing order to post-Revolution France.

317 Sir Joshua Reynolds. *Three Ladies Adorning a Term of Hymen*. 1773. Oil on canvas, 7'8" × 10'4½" (2.34 × 2.90 m). Tate Gallery, London (reproduced by courtesy of the Trustees). A term is a pillar topped with a bust, in this case of Hymen, god of marriage. Reynolds introduced a marriage theme because the fiancé of one of the ladies, who were the daughters of Sir William Montgomery, commissioned the painting. The neoclassical composition was deliberately chosen by the artist because it gave him "an opportunity of introducing a variety of graceful historical attitudes."

The austere poses and orderly decorations of ancient art came as a refreshing change for those artists who, regardless of politics, were tired of the excesses of the baroque and rococo styles. One of the most notable painters to introduce a neoclassical sense of statuesque calmness into his works was Sir Joshua Reynolds, Gainsborough's chief rival in England. *Three Ladies Adorning a Term of Hymen* [317] shows three fashionable ladies-about-town in the guise of figures from Greek mythology. Their static poses seem derived from actual ancient statues. The classical bust and antique vessel on the right are evidence of a careful attempt to imitate ancient models. Even the stool at center is based on examples found at Pompeii.

Although the rococo and neoclassical styles dominated most of 18th-century painting, a few important artists avoided both the escapism of the one and the idealism of the other to provide a more truthful picture of the age. The work of William Hogarth, for example, presents its own very individual view of aristocratic society in the 18th century.

As a master of line, color, and composition Hogarth was in no way inferior to such contemporaries as Fragonard or Gainsborough, but he used his skills to paint a series of "moral subjects" that satirized the same patrons his colleagues aimed to entertain and to flatter. In his series of paintings called *Marriage à la*

Mode he illustrated the consequences of a loveless marriage between an impoverished earl and the daughter of a wealthy city merchant who wants to improve his social position. By the second scene in the series, *Shortly After the Marriage* [318], matters have already started to deteriorate.

318 William Hogarth. *Shortly After the Marriage,* from the *Marriage à la Mode* series. 1743–1745. Oil on canvas, 27 × 35" (69 × 89 cm). National Gallery, London (reproduced by courtesy of the Trustees). Although he achieved his effects through laughter, Hogarth had the serious moral purpose of attacking the corruption and hypocrisy of his day.

Sculpture and Architecture

In general neither the rococo style nor neoclassicism inspired 18th-century sculptors to any great heights. Only the Italian sculptor Antonio Canova (1757–1822) and the Frenchman Jean Antoine Houdon (1741–1829) succeeded in using classical models with any real imagination or creativity [Houdon: figure 310, page 332, and figure 326, page 348]. Canova's portrait, *Pauline Bonaparte Borghese as Venus Victorious* [319], depicts Napoleon's sister with an idealized classical beauty as she reclines on a couch modeled on one found at Pompeii. The cool worldly elegance of the figure, however, is Canova's own contribution. Otherwise most sculpture of the period is relatively uninspired. For the most part sculptors were more concerned with displaying their virtuosity in works aimed at a brilliant effect than with exploring finer shades of meaning. For instance, the figure of *Deception Unmasked* [320] by the Genoese sculptor Francesco Queirolo (1704–1762) theoretically has serious religious significance; in practice its principal purpose is to dazzle us with the sculptor's skill at rendering such details as the elaborate net in which Deception hides.

Architects responded rather more successfully to the principal styles of the day. For serious projects such as major public buildings, architects tended to

320 Francesco Queirolo. *Deception Unmasked*. After 1752. Marble, height c. 5′8¼″ (1.75 m). Cappella Sansevero, Santa Maria della Pieta di Sangro, Naples. The figure is a Christian sinner freeing himself, with the help of an angel, from the net of deception.

319 Antonio Canova. *Pauline Bonaparte Borghese as Venus Victorious*. 1808. Marble, length 6′6″ (1.98 m). Borghese Gallery, Rome. Canova's blend of simplicity and grace was widely imitated by European and American sculptors throughout the 19th century. The apple is the apple of discord, inscribed "to the fairest." According to legend, the goddesses Aphrodite (Venus), Hera, and Athena each offered a tempting bribe to the Trojan Paris, who was to award the apple to one of them. Paris chose Venus, who had promised him the most beautiful of women. The result was the Trojan War, which started when Paris abducted his prize, Helen, wife of a Greek king.

337

follow classical models, as in the portico of the Pantheon in Paris [321], the design of which makes use of classical proportions. As might have been expected, the architects of the American Revolution also turned to classical precedents when they constructed their new public buildings. Thomas Jefferson's State Capitol at Richmond [322], for example, shows a conscious rejection of the rococo and all it stood for in favor of the austere world (as it seemed to him) of ancient Rome.

Rococo architecture, on the other hand, was principally concerned with delighting the eye rather than inspiring noble sentiments. It is most successful in decorative interiors like those of the Hôtel de Soubise in Paris [323], where the encrustation of ornament flows from the ceiling down on to the walls, concealing the break between them.

One region of Europe in which the rococo style did exert a powerful influence on religious architecture was southern Germany and Austria. Throughout the 17th century, a series of wars in that area had discouraged the construction of new churches or public buildings; with the return of relatively stable conditions in the German states new building became possible again. By one of those fortunate chances in the history of the arts, the fantasy and complexity of the rococo style provided a perfect complement to the new mood of exuberance. The result is a series of churches that is among the happiest of all rococo achievements.

The leading architect of the day was Balthazar Neumann (1687–1753), who had begun his career as an engineer and artillery officer. Among the many palaces and churches he designed, none is more spectacular than the Vierzehnheiligen (fourteen saints) near Bamberg. The relative simplicity of the exterior deliberately leaves the visitor unprepared for the spaciousness and elaborate decoration of the interior [Plate 26, page 342], with its rows of windows and irregularly placed columns. As in the Hôtel de Soubise, the joint between the ceiling and walls is hidden by a fresco which, together with its border, spills downward in a series of gracious curves. It is not difficult to imagine what John Calvin would have said of such an interior, but if a church can be allowed to be a place of light and joy, Neumann's design succeeds admirably.

Neoclassical Literature

The renewed interest in classical culture, visible in the portraits by Sir Joshua Reynolds and buildings like the Pantheon, also made a strong impression on literature. French writers like Racine (see page 324)

had already based works on classical models, and the *Fables* of Jean de la Fontaine. Fontaine (1621–1695) drew freely on Aesop and other Greek and Roman sources. Elsewhere in Europe, throughout the 18th century poets continued to produce works on classical themes, from the plays of Pietro Metastasio (1698–1782) in Italy to the lyric poetry of Friedrich von Schiller (1759–1805) in Germany.

The appeal of neoclassical literature was particularly strong in England, where major Greek and Roman works like Homer's *Iliad* and *Odyssey* or Vergil's *Aeneid* had long been widely read and admired. In the 17th century, Milton's *Paradise Lost* had represented a deliberate attempt to create an equally monumental epic poem in English. Before the 18th century, however, a number of important works, including the tragedies of Aeschylus, had never been translated into English.

The upsurge of enthusiasm for classical literature that characterized the 18th century English literary scene had two chief effects: poets and scholars began to translate or retranslate the most important classical authors, and creative writers began to produce original works on classical forms, dealt with classical themes, and included classical references. The general reading public was by now expected to understand and appreciate both the ancient masterpieces themselves and modern works inspired by them.

321 Germain Soufflot. Panthéon (Sainte Geneviève), Paris. 1755–1792. Originally built as the church of Sainte Geneviève, the building was converted into a memorial to the illustrious dead at the time of the French Revolution. The architect studied in Rome for a time; the columns and pediment were inspired by ancient Roman temples.

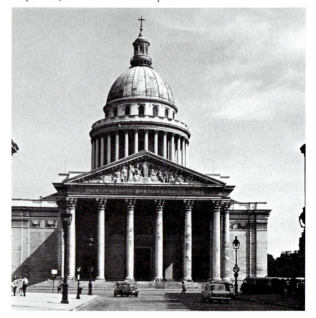

Pope

Alexander Pope (1688–1744), the greatest English poet of the 18th century, was one of a group of writers who called themselves Augustans. The name reveals the degree to which these writers admired and modeled themselves on the Augustan poets of ancient Rome. In 27 B.C. the victory of the first Roman emperor Augustus ended the chaos of civil war at Rome and brought peace and stability to the Roman world. The principal poets of Rome's Augustan age, writers like Vergil and Horace, had subsequently commemorated Augustus' achievement in works intended for a sophisticated public. In the same way in England the restoration to power of King Charles II in 1660 seemed to some of his contemporaries a return to order and civilization after the tumultuous English Civil War. The founders of the English Augustan movement, writers like John Dryden (1631–1700), explored not only the historical parallel by glorifying English achievement under the monarchy but also the literary one by imitating the highly polished style of the Roman Augustan poets in works intended for an aristocratic audience.

Neoclassic writers not only knew the ancient writers, but assumed their readers did as well. Such a literary philosophy in itself, however, was hardly likely to produce much in the way of original literature even though it might create a cultivated literary public. Pope's genius lay precisely in his awareness that the dry bones of classical learning needed to have life breathed into them. The spirit that would awaken art in his own time, as it had done for the ancient writers, was that of Nature—not in the sense of the natural world but in the sense of that which is universal and unchanging in human experience. Pope's conception of the vastness and truth of human experience given form and meaning by rules first devised in the ancient past represents neoclassicism at its best and most constructive.

Like Watteau, Pope suffered throughout his life from ill health. At the age of twelve an attack of spinal tuberculosis left him permanently crippled; perhaps in compensation he soon developed the passion for reading and for the beauty of the world around him that shines through his work. A Catholic in a Protestant country, he was unable to make a career for himself in public life or obtain public patronage for his literary work. As a result he was forced to support himself entirely by writing and translating. Pope's literary reputation was first made by the *Essay on Criticism,* but he won economic independence by producing highly successful translations of Homer's *Iliad* (1713–1720) and *Odyssey* (1721–1726) and an edition of the works of Shakespeare (1725). With the money he made from these he abandoned commercial publishing and confined himself, for the most part, to his house on the river Thames at Twicken-

322 Thomas Jefferson. State Capitol, Richmond, Virginia. 1785–1796. Like the Panthéon, Jefferson's building was modeled on a Roman temple, the Maison Carrée at Nîmes, but the austere spirit of the American Revolution prompted Jefferson to replace the elaborate Corinthian capitals of the original with simpler Ionic ones.

323 Germain Boffrand. *Salon de la Princesse, Hôtel de Soubise,* Paris. Begun 1732. Oval, 33 × 26′ (10.06 × 7.92 m). The decoration is typical of the rococo style. The shape of the room, the paintings that flow from ceiling to walls, and the reflections in the mirrors all create an impression of light and grace.

ham, where he spent the rest of his life writing, entertaining friends, and indulging his fondness for gardening.

Pope's range as a poet was considerable, but his greatest achievements were in satire. Like his fellow countryman Hogarth, his awareness of the heights to which humans can rise was coupled with an acute sense of the frequency of their failure to do so. In the long poem *Essay on Man* (1733–1734), for example, Pope combines Christian and humanist teaching in a characteristically 18th-century manner to express his philosophical position with regard to the preeminent place occupied by human beings in the divine scheme of life. He is at his best, however, when applying his principles to practical situations and uncovering human folly. His reverence for order and reason made him the implacable foe of those who in his eyes were responsible for the declining political morality and artistic standards of the day. It is sometimes said that Pope's satire is tinged with personal hostility. In fact, a series of literary and social squabbles marked his life, suggesting that he was not always motivated by the highest ideals; nonetheless, in his poetry he nearly always based his moral judgments on what he himself described as "the strong antipathy of good to bad," a standard he applied with courage and wit.

Classical Music

For the most part, music in the 18th century followed the example of literature in retaining a serious purpose, and was relatively untouched by the mood of the rococo style. At the French court, it is true, there was a demand for elegant, light-hearted music to serve as entertainment. The leading composer in this *style galant* was François Couperin (1668–1733), whose many compositions for keyboard emphasize grace and delicacy at the expense of the rhythmic drive and intellectual rigor of the best of baroque music. Elsewhere in Europe, however, listeners continued to prefer music that expressed emotion. At the court of Frederick the Great (himself an accomplished musician), for example, a musical style known as the *empfindsamer Stil,* or expressive style, developed.

The chief exponent of the expressive style was Carl Philipp Emanuel Bach (1714–1788), a son of Johann Sebastian Bach. His works have considerable emotional range and depth; their rich harmonies and contrasting moods opened up new musical possibilities. Like all his contemporaries, C. P. E. Bach was searching for a formal structure with which to organize them. A single piece or movement from a ba-

roque work had first established a single mood and then explored it fully, whether it be joyful, meditative, or tragic. Now composers were developing a musical organization that would allow them to put different emotions side by side, contrast them, and thereby achieve expressive variety.

By the middle of the 18th century a musical style developed that made possible this new range of expression. It is usually called *classical,* although the term is also used in a more general sense, which can be confusing. It would be as well to begin by carefully distinguishing between these two usages.

In its general sense, the term *classical* is frequently used to distinguish so-called "serious" music from "popular," so that all music likely to be met with in a concert hall or opera house, no matter what its age, is labeled classical. One reason this distinction is confusing is that for many composers before our own time, there was essentially no difference between serious and popular music. They used the same musical style and techniques for a formal composition to be listened to attentively by an audience of music-lovers, as for a religious work to be performed in church, or for dance music or background music for a party or festive occasion. Furthermore, used in this sense, *classical* tells us nothing significant about the music itself or its period or form. It does not even describe its mood, since many pieces of "classical" or "serious" music were in fact deliberately written to provide light entertainment.

The more precise and technical meaning of *classical* in relation to music denotes a musical style that was in use from the second half of the 18th century and reached its fulfillment in the works of Franz Joseph Haydn (1732–1809) and Wolfgang Amadeus Mozart (1756–1791). It evolved in answer to new musical needs the baroque style could not satisfy and lasted until the early years of the 19th century, when it in turn gave way to the romantic style. The figure chiefly responsible for the change from classical to romantic music was Ludwig van Beethoven (1770–1827). Although his musical roots were firmly in the classical style, he is more appropriately seen as a representative of the new romantic age and is discussed in Chapter 15.

It is no coincidence that the classical style in music developed at much the same time painters, architects, and poets were turning to Greek and Roman models, for the aims of classical music and neoclassical art and literature were very similar. After the almost obsessive exuberance and display of the baroque period, the characteristic qualities of ancient art—balance, clarity, intellectual weight—seemed especially appealing. The 18th-century composer, however, faced a different problem than did the artist or writer. Un-

Plate 25 Jean Antonie Watteau. *Pilgrimage to Cythera*. 1717. Oil on canvas, 4'3" × 6'4½" (1.3 × 1.94 m). Louvre, Paris. One ancient Greek tradition claimed the isle of Cythera as the birthplace of Venus, goddess of love; thus the island became symbolic of ideal, tender love. Note that the mood of nostalgia and farewell is conveyed not only by the autumnal colors but also by the late-afternoon light that washes over the scene.

Plate 26 Balthazar Neumann. The nave of Vierzehnheiligen Pilgrim Church, near Bamberg, West Germany. 1743–1772. This view of the interior shows the high altar at the back of the nave (center) and part of the oval altar in the middle of the church (left). The oval altar, the *Gnadenaltar* or "Mercy Altar," is a mark of the pilgrimage churches of southern Germany and Austria. Its shape is echoed in the oval ceiling paintings. The architect deliberately rejected the soaring straight lines of Gothic architecture and the balance and symmetry of the Renaissance style in favor of an intricate interweaving of surfaces, solid volumes, and empty spaces.

342

like literature or the visual arts, ancient music has disappeared almost without trace. As a result the classical style in music had to be newly invented to express ancient concepts of balance and order. In addition, it had to combine these intellectual principles with the no-less-important ability to express a wide range of emotion. Haydn and Mozart were the two supreme masters of the classical style because of their complete command of the possibilities of the new idiom within which they wrote.

The Classical Symphony

The most popular medium in the classical period was instrumental music. In extended orchestral works, *symphonies,* divided into a number of self-contained sections called *movements,* composers were most completely able to express classical principles.

One reason for this is the new standardization of instrumental combinations. In the baroque period, composers such as Bach had felt free to combine instruments into unusual groups that varied from composition to composition. Each of Bach's Brandenburg concertos was written for a different set of solo instruments. By about 1750, however, most instrumental music was written for a standard orchestra, the nucleus of which was formed by the string instruments: violins (generally divided into two groups known as first and second), violas, cellos, and double basses. To the strings were added wind instruments, almost always the oboe and bassoon and fairly frequently the flute; the clarinet began to be introduced gradually and by about 1780 had become a regular member of the orchestra. The only brass instrument commonly included was the French horn. Trumpets, along with the *timpani* or kettledrums, were reserved for reinforcing volume or rhythm. Trombones were never used in classical symphonies until Beethoven.

Orchestras made up of these instruments were capable of rich and varied sound combinations, ideally suited to the new classical form of the symphony. In general, the classical symphony has four movements (as opposed to the baroque concerto's three): a first, relatively fast one, usually the most complex in form; then a slow, lyrical movement, often songlike; a third movement in the form of a *minuet,* a stately dance; and a final one, which brings the entire work to a spirited and usually cheerful conclusion. As time went on, the length and complexity of the movements grew, and many of Haydn's later symphonies last for half an hour or more. In most cases, however, the most elaborate musical "argument" was always reserved for the first movement, presumably because during it the listeners were freshest and most able to concentrate.

The structure almost invariably chosen for the first movement of a classical symphony was that called *sonata form.* Since sonata form is not only one of the chief features of classical style but was also a principle of musical organization that remained popular throughout the 19th century, it merits our attention in some detail. The term itself is actually rather confusing, since the word *sonata* is used to describe a work in several movements, like a symphony, but written for one or two instruments rather than an orchestra. Thus a piano sonata is a piece for solo piano, a violin sonata is a piece for violin and an accompanying instrument, almost always a piano, and so on. A symphony is, in fact, a sonata for orchestra.

The term *sonata form,* however, does not, as might be reasonably expected, describe the form of a sonata but a particular kind of musical organization frequently found in the first movements of both symphonies *and* sonatas as well as other instrumental combinations like string quartets (two violins, viola, and cello). Since these movements are generally played at a fast *tempo* or speed, the term *sonata allegro form* is also sometimes used. (The Italian word *allegro* means "fast"; Italian terms are traditionally used in music, as we have seen.)

Unlike baroque music, with its unity based on the use of a single continually expanding theme (see page 318), sonata form is dominated by the idea of contrasts. The first of the three main sections of a sonata form movement is called the *exposition,* since it sets out, or "exposes," the musical material. This consists of at least two themes, or groups of themes, that differ from one another in melody, rhythm, and key. They represent, so to speak, the two principal characters in the drama. If the first theme is lively, the second may be thoughtful or melancholy; or a strong marchlike first theme may be followed by a gentle, romantic second one. During the exposition the first of these themes (or *subjects,* as they are often called) is stated, followed by a linking passage leading to the second subject and a conclusion that rounds off the exposition.

During the course of the movement it is of the utmost importance that listeners be able to remember these themes and identify them when they reappear. To help make this easier, classical composers replaced the long, flowing lines of baroque melodies with much shorter tunes, often consisting of only a few notes, comparatively easy to recognize when they recur. The difference between baroque and classical melody is clearly visible even on paper. Compare, for example, the continuous pattern of the melodic line on page 321, from Bach's Brandenburg Concerto No. 2, with the theme below from Mozart's *Symphony No. 40 in G minor.* The tune consists basically of a group of three notes *(a)* repeated three times to produce a melodic phrase *(b)*. This procedure is then repeated three more times to impress it firmly on our memory.

Just in case their listeners were still not perfectly familiar with the basic material of a movement, composers reinforced it by repeating the entire exposition note for note.

In the second section of a sonata-form movement, the *development,* the themes stated in the exposition are changed and varied in whatever way the composer's imagination suggests. One part of the first subject is often detached and treated on its own, passing up and down the orchestra, now loud, now soft, as happens in the first movement of Mozart's *Symphony No. 40* to the notes marked *a* above. Sometimes different themes will be combined and played simultaneously. In almost all cases the music passes through a wide variety of keys and moods. In the process the composer sheds new light on what have by now become familiar ideas.

At the end of the development the original themes return to their original form for the third section of the movement, the *recapitulation.* The first section is repeated, or recapitulated, with both first and second subjects now in the same key. In this way the conflict implicit in the development section is resolved. A final "tailpiece" or *coda* (from the Italian word for tail) is sometimes added to bring the movement to a suitably firm conclusion.

Sonata form embodies many of the classical principles of balance, order, and control. The recapitulation, which carefully balances the exposition, and the breaking down of the material in the development and its subsequent reassembling both emphasize the sense of structure behind a sonata-form movement.

Haydn

The long and immensely productive career of Franz Joseph Haydn (1732–1809) spanned a period of great change in both artistic and social terms. Born in Rohrau on the Austro-Hungarian border, he sang as a child in the choir of Saint Stephen's Cathedral in Vienna. After scraping together a living for a few pre-

carious years, in 1761 he entered the service of a wealthy nobleman, Prince Esterhazy.

Haydn began work for the prince on the same terms as any carpenter, cook, or artisan in his master's employ. That he was a creative artist was irrelevant, since social distinctions were made on grounds of wealth or birth, not talent. By the time he left the Esterhazy family, however, almost thirty years later, the aristocracy were competing for the privilege of entertaining him. The world was indeed changing; in the course of two visits to London he found himself feted and honored, and during his last years in Vienna he was among the most famous figures in Europe. Thus Haydn was one of the very first musicians to attain a high social position solely on the strength of his genius. His success signaled the new relationship between the artist and society that was to characterize the 19th century.

In personal terms Haydn seems to have been little affected by his fame. During the long years of service to Prince Esterhazy and his descendants he used the enforced isolation of the palace where he lived to experiment with all the musical forms available to him. In addition to operas, string quartets, piano sonatas, and hundreds of other pieces, he wrote some ninety symphonies that exploit almost every conceivable variation on sonata and other classical forms, winning him the nickname "Father of the Symphony." During his visits to London in 1791–1792 and 1794–1795 he wrote his last twelve symphonies, which are often known as the London Symphonies. Although less obviously experimental than his earlier works, they contain perhaps the finest of all his orchestral music; the slow movements in particular manage to express the greatest seriousness and profundity without tragedy or gloom.

Mozart

In 1781, in his fiftieth year and at the height of his powers, Haydn met a young man about whom he was to say a little while later to the young man's father: "Before God and as an honest man, I tell you that your son is the greatest composer known to me either in person or by name." Many of us, for whom the music of Wolfgang Amadeus Mozart (1756–1791) represents a continual source of inspiration and joy and a comforting reminder of the heights the human spirit can attain, would see no reason to revise Haydn's judgment [324].

Although Mozart's life, in contrast to Haydn's, was to prove one of growing disappointments and setbacks, his early years were comparatively happy. During his childhood he showed extraordinary musi-

324 Joseph Lange. *Mozart at the Pianoforte*. 1789. Oil. 13½ × 11½" (35 × 30 cm). Mozart Museum, Salzburg. This unfinished portrait shows the composer for once without the wig customary at the time. Mozart must have liked the painting because he had a copy made and sent to his father.

cal ability. By the age of six he could already play the violin and piano and had begun to compose. His father Leopold, himself a professional musician in the service of the Archbishop of Salzburg, where the family lived, took Wolfgang on a seemingly never-ending series of trips throughout Europe to exhibit his son's musical prowess. The effect of these trips on the boy's health and temperament can be imagined, but it was during them that he became exposed to the most sophisticated and varied musical ideas of the day; the universality of his own musical style must in part be due to the wide range of influences he was able to assimilate, from the *style galant* of the rococo to the Renaissance polyphonies he heard in Rome. From time to time father and son would return to Salzburg, where by this time they both held appointments at the court of the archbishop.

In 1772, however, the old archbishop died. His successor, Hieronymus Colloredo, was far less willing to allow his two leading musicians to come and go as they pleased. Artistic independence of the kind Haydn was to achieve was still in the future, and the next ten years were marked by continued quarreling between Mozart and his aristocratic employer. Fi-

nally, in 1781, when Mozart could take no more and asked the archbishop for his freedom, he was literally kicked out of the door of the palace. From 1781 to 1791 Mozart spent the last years of his life in Vienna, trying in vain to find a permanent position while writing some of the most sublime masterpieces in the history of music. When he died at the age of thirty-five, he was buried in a pauper's grave.

The relationship between an artist's life and work is always fascinating. In Mozart's case it raises particular problems. We might expect that continual frustration, poverty, and depression would have left its mark on his music, yet it is a grave mistake to look for autobiographical self-expression in the work of an artist who devoted his life to achieving perfection in his art. In general, Mozart's music reflects only the highest and most noble of human aspirations. Perhaps more than any other artist in any medium Mozart combines ease and grace with profound learning in his art to come as near to ideal beauty as anything can. Nevertheless, his music remains profoundly human. We are reminded many times not of Mozart's own suffering but of the tragic nature of life itself.

A year before his death Mozart wrote the last of his great series of concertos for solo piano and orchestra, the *Piano Concerto No. 27 in B♭*, K. 595 (Mozart's works are generally listed according to the catalogue first made by Köchel; hence the letter K that precedes their catalogue numbers). The wonderful slow movement of this work expresses, with a profundity no less moving for its utter simplicity, the resignation of one for whom the beauty of life is perpetually tinged with sadness. We can only marvel at so direct a statement of so universal a truth.

The need to earn a living, coupled with the inexhaustibility of his inspiration, drew from Mozart works in almost every conceivable category. Symphonies, concertos, masses, sonatas, string quartets are only some of the forms he enriched. It is his operas, however, that many admirers of Mozart would choose if faced with a decision as to what to save if all else were to be lost. Furthermore, his operas provide the clearest picture of his historical position.

Mozart's opera *The Marriage of Figaro* is based on a play of the same name by the French dramatist Pierre Augustin Beaumarchais (1732–1799). Although a comedy, the play, which was first performed in 1784, contains serious overtones. The plot is too complicated to permit even a brief summary, but among the characters are a lecherous and deceitful, though charming, Count; his deceived wife, the Countess; her maid Susanna, who puts up a determined resistance against the Count's advances; and

Susanna's husband-to-be, Figaro, who finally manages to outwit and embarrass the would-be seducer of his future wife, who is also his employer [325]. In other words, the heroes of the play are the servants and the villain their master. Written as it was on the eve of the French Revolution, Beaumarchais' play was interpreted rightly as an attack on the morals of the ruling classes and a warning that the lower classes would fight back. Beaumarchais himself was firmly associated with the moves toward social and political change; he was an early supporter of the American Revolution and helped organize French support for the insurgent colonists.

Mozart's opera was first performed in 1786. It retains the spirit of protest in the original but adds a sense of humanity and subtlety perhaps only music can bring. No one suffered more than Mozart from the highhandedness of the aristocracy, yet when *The Marriage of Figaro* gives voice to the growing mood of revolution, it does so as a protest against the abuse of human rights rather than in a spirit of personal resentment. In the first act, Figaro's aria *"Se vuol' ballare"* expresses the pent-up frustration of generations of men and women who had endured injustices and who could take no more. The musical form and expression is still restrained, indeed classical, but Mozart pours into it the feelings of the age.

Mozart's ability to create characters who seem real, with whose feelings we can identify, reaches its height in the Countess. Ignored and duped by her husband, the laughingstock of those around her, she expresses the conflicting emotions of a woman torn between resentment and deep attachment. Her aria in the third act, *"Dove sono,"* begins with a recitative in which she gives vent to her bitterness. Gradually it melts into a slow and meditative section where she asks herself what went wrong: "Where are those happy moments of sweetness and pleasure, where did they go, those vows of a deceiving tongue?" The poignant theme to which these words are set returns toward the end of the slow section to provide one of the most affecting moments in all opera. Mozart's gift for expressing human behavior at its most noble is conveyed in the aria's final section, where the Countess decides, in spite of everything, to try to win back her husband's love. Thus, in seven or eight minutes, we have been carried from despair to hope, and Mozart has combined his revelation of a human heart with music that by itself is of extraordinary beauty.

The opera as a whole is far richer than discussion of these two arias can suggest. For instance, among the other characters is one of the composer's most memorable creations, the pageboy Cherubino, whose aria *"Non so più"* epitomizes the breathless, agonizing joy of adolescent love. An accomplishment of another kind is exemplified by the *ensembles,* scenes in which a large number of characters are involved. Here Mozart combines clarity of musical and dramatic action while advancing the plot at a breakneck pace.

The Marriage of Figaro expresses at the same time

325 *The Marriage of Figaro.* Metropolitan Opera, New York, 1975. In this scene from Act II of Mozart's opera, the Count (second from left) is trying to assert his aristocratic authority against the combined arguments of his wife (left), Susanna (second from right), and Figaro (right). The singers are Evelyn Lear as the Countess, Wolfgang Brendel as the Count, Judith Blegen as Susanna, and Justino Diaz as Figaro.

the spirit of its age and the universality of human nature, a truly classical achievement. Equally impressively, it illuminates the personal emotions of individual people, and through them teaches us about our own reactions to life and its problems. As one distinguished writer has put it, in this work Mozart has added to the world's understanding of people—of human nature.

Intellectual Developments

While painters, poets, and musicians were reflecting the changing moods of the 18th century in their art, social and political philosophers were examining the problems of contemporary society in a more systematic way. Individual thinkers frequently alternated between optimism and despair, since awareness of the greatness of which human beings were capable was always qualified by the perception of the sorry state of the world. The broad range of diagnosis and of proposed solutions makes it difficult to generalize on the nature of 18th-century intellectual life, but two contrasting trends can be discerned. A few writers, notably Jonathan Swift, reacted to the problems of the age with deep pessimism, bitterly opposing the view that human nature is basically good. Others, convinced that progress was possible, sought to devise new systems of intellectual, social, or political organization. Rational humanists like Diderot and political philosophers like Rousseau based their arguments on an optimistic view of human nature. However, Voltaire, the best-known of all 18th-century thinkers, fitted into neither of these two categories—rather, he moved from one to the other. The answer he finally proposed to the problems of existence is as applicable to the world of today as it was to that of the 18th century, although perhaps no more welcome.

Swift's Savage Indignation

Perhaps the darkest of all visions of human nature in the 18th century was that of Jonathan Swift (1667–1745). In a letter to Alexander Pope he made it clear that, whatever his affection for individuals, he hated the human race as a whole. According to Swift, human beings were not to be defined automatically as rational animals, as so many 18th-century thinkers believed, but as animals *capable* of reason. It was precisely because so many of them failed to live up to their capabilities that Swift turned his "savage indignation" against them into bitter satire, never more so

than when the misuse of reason served "to aggravate man's natural corruptions" and provide him with new ones.

Swift was in a position to observe at close quarters the political and social struggles of the times. Born in Dublin, for much of his life he played an active part in supporting Irish resistance to English rule. After studying at Trinity College, Dublin, he went to England and in 1694 was ordained a priest in the Anglican church. For the next few years he moved back and forth between England and Ireland, taking a leading role in the political controversies of the day by publishing articles and pamphlets which, in general, were strongly conservative.

A fervent supporter of the monarchy and of the Anglican church, Swift had good reason to hope that his advocacy of their cause would win him a position of high rank. In 1713 these hopes were partially realized with his appointment as Dean of Saint Patrick's Cathedral in Dublin. Any chances he had of receiving an English bishopric were destroyed in 1714 by the death of Queen Anne and the subsequent dismissal of his political friends from power.

Swift spent the rest of his life in Ireland, cut off from the mainstream of political and cultural life. Here he increasingly emerged as a publicist for the Irish cause. During his last years his mind began to fail, but not before he had composed the epitaph under which he lies buried in Saint Patrick's Cathedral: *Ubi saeva indignatio ulterius cor lacerare nequit* (He has gone where savage indignation can tear his heart no more).

It was during his years in Ireland that Swift wrote his best-known work, *Gulliver's Travels,* first published in 1726. In a sense *Gulliver's Travels* has been a victim of its own popularity, since its surprising success as a work for young readers has distracted attention from the author's real purpose, to satirize human behavior. The first two of Gulliver's four voyages, to the miniature land of Lilliput and to Brobdingnag, the land of giants, are the best known. In these sections the harshness of Swift's satire is to some extent masked by the charm and wit of the narrative. In the voyage to the land of the Houyhnhnms, however, Swift draws a bitter contrast between the Houyhnhnms, a race of horses whose behavior is governed by reason, and their slaves the Yahoos, human in form but bestial in behavior. As expressed by the Yahoos, Swift's vision of the depths to which human beings can sink is profoundly pessimistic. His insistence on their deep moral and intellectual flaws is in strong contrast to the rational humanism of many of his contemporaries, who believed in the innate dignity and worth of human beings.

Rational Humanism:
The Encyclopedists

Belief in the essential goodness of human nature and the possibility of progress, which had first been expressed by the humanists of the Renaissance, continued to find supporters throughout the 18th century. Indeed, the enormous scientific and technical achievements of the two centuries since the time of Erasmus tended to confirm the opinions of those who took a positive view of human capabilities. It was in order to provide a rational basis for this positive humanism that the French thinker and writer Denis Diderot (1713–1784) [326] conceived the project of preparing a vast encyclopedia that would describe the state of contemporary science, technology, and thought and provide a system for the classification of knowledge.

Work on the *Encyclopédie,* as it is generally called, began in 1747; the last of its seventeen volumes appeared in 1765. By its conclusion, what had begun as a compendium of information had become the statement of a philosophical position: that the extent of human powers and achievements conclusively demonstrates that humans are rational beings. The implication of this position is that any political or religious system seeking to control the minds of individuals is to be condemned. It is hardly surprising, therefore, that some years before the conclusion of the project, the *Encyclopédie* had been banned by decree of Louis XV; the last volumes were published clandestinely.

In religious terms the *Encyclopédie* took a position of considerable skepticism, advocating freedom of conscience and belief. Politically, however, its position was less extreme and less consistent. One of the most distinguished philosophers to contribute political articles was Charles-Louis Montesquieu (1689–1755), whose own aristocratic origins may have helped mold his relatively conservative views. Both in the *Encyclopédie* and in his own writings Montesquieu advocated the retention of a monarchy, with powers divided between the king and a series of "intermediate bodies" that included parliament, aristocratic organizations, the middle class, and even the church. By distributing power in this way Montesquieu hoped to achieve a workable system of "checks and balances," thereby eliminating the possibility of a central dictatorial government. His ideas proved particularly interesting to the authors of the Constitution of the United States.

A very different point of view was espoused by another contributor to the *Encyclopédie,* Jean-Jacques Rousseau (1712–1778), whose own quarrelsome and neurotic character played a considerable part in influencing his political philosophy. Diderot had origi-

nally commissioned Rousseau to produce some articles on music, since the latter was an accomplished composer (his opera *Le Devin du Village* is still revived from time to time). After violently quarreling with Diderot and others, however, Rousseau spent much of an unhappy and restless life writing philosophical treatises and novels that expressed his political convictions. Briefly put, Rousseau believed that the natural goodness of the human race had been corrupted by the growth of civilization and that the freedom of the individual had been destroyed by the growth of society. For Rousseau humans were good and society was bad.

Rousseau's praise of the simple virtues like unselfishness and kindness and his high regard for natural human feelings have identified his philosophy with a belief in the "noble savage," but this is misleading. Far from advocating a return to primitive existence in some nonexistent Garden of Eden, Rousseau passionately strove to create a new social order. In *The Social Contract* of 1762 he tried to describe the basis of his ideal state in terms of the General Will of the people, which would delegate authority to individual

326 Jean Antoine Houdon. *Denis Diderot.* 1771. Terra cotta, height 16″ (41 cm). Louvre, Paris. Unlike most official portraiture of the 18th century, Houdon's works aim to reveal the character of his sitters. Here he vividly conveys Diderot's humanity and quizzical humor.

organs of government, although neither most of his readers nor Rousseau himself seemed very clear on how this General Will should operate.

Although Rousseau's writings express a complex political philosophy, most of his readers were more interested in his emphasis on spontaneous feeling than in his political theories. His contempt for the superficial and the artificial, and his praise for simple and direct relationships between individuals, did a great deal to help demolish the principles of aristocracy and continue to inspire believers in human equality.

Voltaire's Philosophical Cynicism: *Candide*

It may seem extravagant to claim that the life and work of François Marie Arouet (1694–1778), best known to us as Voltaire (one of his pen names), can summarize the events of a period as complex as the 18th century. That the claim can be not only advanced but also supported is some measure of the

327 Jean Baptiste Pigalle. *Voltaire*. 1770–1776. Marble, height 4′9⅜″ (1.47 m). Louvre, Paris. This most unusual statue of the great philosopher places a powerful head on the torso of an old man. The head was modeled from life when Voltaire was 76; the body is based on that of a Roman statue. The statue seems to represent the triumph of the spirit over the frailty of the body.

breadth of his genius. A writer of poems, plays, novels, and history; a student of science, philosophy, and politics; a man who spent time at the courts of Louis XV and Frederick the Great but also served a prison sentence; a defender of religious and political freedom who at the same time supported enlightened despotism, Voltaire was above all a man *engagé*—one committed to the concerns of his age [327].

After being educated by the Jesuits, he began to publish writings in the satirical style he was to use throughout his life. His belief that the aristocratic society of the times was unjust must have received strong confirmation when his critical position earned him first a year in jail and then, in 1726, exile from France. He chose to go to England, where he found a system of government that seemed to him far more liberal and just than the French one. On his return home in 1729 he discussed the advantages of English political life in his *Lettres philosophiques,* published in 1734, and escaped from the scandal and possibility of arrest his work created by spending the next ten years in the country.

In 1744 Voltaire was finally tempted back to the French court but found little in its formal and artificial life to stimulate him. He discovered a more congenial atmosphere at the court of Frederick the Great at Potsdam, where he spent the years from 1750 to 1753. Fredericks' warm welcome and considerable intellectual stature must have come as an agreeable change from the sterile ceremony of the French court, and the two men soon established a close friendship. It seems, however, that Potsdam was not big enough to contain two such powerful intellects and temperaments, for after a couple of years Voltaire quarreled with his patron and once again abandoned sophisticated life for that of the country.

In 1758 Voltaire finally settled in the village of Ferney, where he set up his own court. Here the greatest names in Europe—intellectuals, artists, politicians—made the pilgrimage to talk and, above all, listen to the sage of Ferney, while he published work after work, each of which was distributed throughout Europe. Only in 1778, the year of his death, did Voltaire return to Paris, where the excitement brought on by a hero's welcome proved too much for his failing strength.

It is difficult to summarize the philosophy of a man who touched on so many subjects. Nevertheless, one theme recurs continually in Voltaire's writings, the importance of freedom of thought. Voltaire's greatest hatred was reserved for intolerance and bigotry; in letter after letter he ended with the phrase he made famous, *Écrasez l'infâme* (Crush the infamous thing). The "infamous thing" is superstition, which breeds fanaticism and persecution. Those

328 *Candide*. New York. 1974. This is a scene from the Broadway musical adaptation of Voltaire's work, with music by Leonard Bernstein. Left to right: Paquette (Deborah St. Darr), Dr. Pangloss (Lewis J. Stadlen), Maximillian (Sam Freed), Candide (Mark Baker), Cunegonde (Maureen Brennan). Two of the songs in the musical are entitled "The Best of All Possible Worlds" and "What a Day for an Auto-da-Fé."

Voltaire judged chiefly responsible for superstition were the Christians, Catholic and Protestant alike.

Voltaire vehemently attacked the traditional view of the Bible as the inspired word of God. He claimed that it contained a mass of anecdotes and contradictions totally irrelevant to the modern world and that the disputes arising from it, which had divided Christians for centuries, were absurd and pointless. Yet Voltaire was far from being an atheist. He was a firm believer in a God who had created the world, but whose worship could not be tied down to one religion or another: "The only book that needs to be read is the great book of nature." Only natural religion and morality would end prejudice and ignorance.

Voltaire's negative criticisms of human absurdity are more convincing than his positive views on a universal natural morality. It is difficult not to feel at times that even Voltaire himself had only the vaguest ideas of what natural morality really meant. In fact, in *Candide* (1759), his best-known work, he reaches a much less optimistic conclusion [328]. *Candide* was written with the avowed purpose of ridiculing the optimism of the German philosopher Gottfried von Leibnitz (1646–1716), who believed that "everything is for the best in the best of all possible worlds." Since both intellect and experience teach that this is very far from the case, Voltaire chose to demonstrate the folly of unreasonable optimism, as well as the cruelty and stupidity of the human race, by subjecting his hero Candide to a barrage of disasters and suffering.

Throughout his journeys from Germany to Portugal to the New World and back to Europe, Candide has the opportunity to compare the theory of philosophical optimism with the evil, stupidity, and ignorance that he finds wherever he goes. The conclusion he reaches is expressed in the book's final words, "we must cultivate our gardens." The world is a cruel place where human life is of little account, but to give way to total pessimism is fruitless. Instead, we should try to find some limited activity we can perform well. By succeeding in this small task we can construct a little island of peace and sanity in a hostile world.

This message is, of course, hardly a comforting one. It is a measure of Voltaire's courage that his final advice to "cultivate our gardens" manages to extract something positive from the despair his humor and irony mask.

Questions for Further Discussion

1. Much of rococo art is deliberately escapist. Its purpose is to help us forget the problems of life rather than to solve them. Is this a legitimate function of art? What effect (if any) is such an approach likely to have on the quality of works of art?

2. One of the chief influences on the Fathers of the American Revolution was that of ancient Rome. How did this affect both the American Constitution and official American architecture?

3. Like many classical composers, Mozart used the same musical style for popular pieces like dance music and serenades and for more complex works like masses and symphonies. In our own time there is a wide gulf between so-called serious and popular music. Why did this split occur, and what effect has it had on the listening habits and musical tastes of the present generation?

4. How practicable is it in the modern world to follow Voltaire's advice to "cultivate our garden"? How desirable is it?

5. Throughout the 18th century, major developments in the visual arts were reflected on a small scale in domestic objects like crockery, furniture, tableware, and so on. To what extent today are trends in interior design and household goods related to larger artistic movements?

6. Many of the greatest writers of the 18th century chose to criticize their society by making fun of it. How powerful a weapon is satire, and how effective is it at producing social change?

	GENERAL EVENTS	LITERATURE & PHILOSOPHY	ART
1765			c. 1774 Copley leaves Boston to study in England
			1784-1785 David, *Oath of the Horatii*
1789			
REVOLUTIONARY AND NAPOLEONIC WARS	1789 French Revolution begins	1773 Goethe leads *Sturm und Drang* movement against neoclassicism	1799 David, *The Battle of the Romans and the Sabines*. Goya becomes court painter to Charles IV of Spain; *The Family of Charles IV* (1800)
	1793-1795 Reign of Terror in France	1774 Goethe, *The Sufferings of Young Werther*	19th cent. Romantic emphasis on emotion, nature, exotic images, faraway lands
	1799-1804 Napoleon rules France as consul	1790 Kant, *The Critique of Judgment,* expounding Transcendental Idealism	1808 Girodet, *The Entombment of Atala,* inspired by Chateaubriand's romantic novel *Atala*
	1804-1814 Napoleon rules France as emperor	1794 Blake, "London"	
	1812 Failure of Napoleon's Russian campaign	1798 Wordsworth, "Tintern Abbey"	1810 Friedrich, *Cloister Graveyard in the Snow*
	1814 Napoleon exiled to Elba Stephenson's first locomotive	1807-1830 Philosophy of Hegel published in Germany	1811 Ingres, *Jupiter and Thetis*
	1814-1815 Congress of Vienna	1808 Goethe's *Faust,* Part I	1814 Goya, *Executions of May 3, 1808,* a retreat from idealism in art
1815			
GROWTH OF INDUSTRIALIZATION	1815 Napoleon escapes Elba; defeated at Battle of Waterloo	1819 Schopenhauer, *The World as Will and Idea*	1818-1819 Géricault, *Raft of the Medusa,* first exhibited 1819
	1815-1850 Industrialization of England	c. 1820 English romantic peak	1820-1822 Goya paints nightmare scenes on walls of his house; *Saturn Devouring One of His Sons*
	1816 Wreck of French vessel *Medusa*	1820 Shelley, *Prometheus Unbound*	1824 Delacroix, *Massacre at Chios*
	1821 Death of Napoleon	1821 Byron, *Don Juan*	1827 Delacroix, *The Death of Sardanapalus*
	1821-1829 Greek War of Independence against Turks	1824 Byron dies in Greece	c. 1830 Social realism follows romanticism; Daumier, *The Legislative Belly* (1834)
	1830-1860 Industrialization of France and Belgium	1829-1847 Balzac, *The Human Comedy,* 90 realistic novels	
	1837-1901 Reign of Queen Victoria in England	1832 Goethe, *Faust,* Part II	
		1836-1860 Transcendentalist movement in New England	
		1837-1838 Dickens, *Oliver Twist*	
	1840-1870 Industrialization of Germany	1846 Sand, *Lucrezia Floriani*	1836 Constable, *Stoke-by-Nayland*
			1844 Turner, *Rain, Steam, and Speed*
		1847 E. Brontë, *Wuthering Heights*	c. 1847 Development of national styles. American artists influenced by Transcendentalism; Cole, *View of the Falls of Munda* (1847)
1848			
AGE OF NATIONALISM	1848 Revolutionary uprisings throughout Europe	1848 Marx, *Communist Manifesto*	1854-1855 Courbet, *The Painter's Studio*
	1859 Darwin publishes theory of evolution, *Origin of Species*	1851 Melville, *Moby-Dick*	c. 1860 American luminist painting develops; Heade, *Lake George* (1862)
	1860-1870 Unification of Italy	1853 Dickens, *Bleak House*	1866 Homer, *Prisoners from the Front,* chronicles Civil War
	1861-1865 American Civil War	1854 Thoreau, *Walden*	
	1866-1871 Unified Germany	1855 First edition of Whitman's *Leaves of Grass*	
	1867 Canada granted dominion status	1856-1857 Flaubert, *Madame Bovary*	
		1862 Hugo, *Les Misérables*	
	1869 First transcontinental railroad completed in America	1869 Tolstoy, *War and Peace*	
1870			
		1873-1877 Tolstoy, *Anna Karenina*	1870 Corot, *Ville d'Avray*
			c. 1880 Eakins uses photography and scientific techniques in search for realism; *The Swimming Hole* (1883)
1900			

The Romantic Era

1788 Mozart composes last three symphonies

1785–1796 Jefferson, State Capitol, Richmond, Virginia

1795 Debut of Beethoven as pianist

Development from classical to romantic music most evident in work of Beethoven; "Pathetique" *Sonata* (1799)

1804 First performance of Beethoven's "Eroica" *Symphony,* originally meant to honor Napoleon

1814 Beethoven's opera *Fidelio* performed

19th cent. Sequence of revival styles: neoclassical, neo-Gothic, neo-Renaissance; forms affected by growth of industry and technology

c. 1815–1828 Schubert creates genre of art song *(lied),* setting to music poetry of Goethe, Schiller, others

1822 Schubert, "Unfinished" *Symphony*

1824 First performance of Beethoven's *Symphony No. 9;* finale is choral version of Schiller's "Ode to Joy"

1836 Barry and Pugin begin neo-Gothic Houses of Parliament, London

1830 Berlioz, *Fantastic Symphony*

1831 Bellini's *bel canto* opera *Norma* performed

1835 Donizetti, *Lucia di Lammermoor*

c. 1835–c. 1845 Virtuoso performance at peak; brilliant composer-performers create works of immense technical difficulty: Chopin, *Piano Sonata in B flat Minor,* Op. 35 (1839)

1839 Chopin completes *Twenty-Four Preludes,* Op. 28

1842 Verdi's *Nabucco* performed; symbolic of Italians' suffering under Austrian rule

1846 Berlioz, *The Damnation of Faust*

1861–1874 Garnier, Opéra, Paris

1853 First performances of Verdi's *Il Trovatore* and *La Traviata,* the latter based on Dumas' novel *The Lady of the Camelias*

1853–1874 Wagner, *The Ring of the Nibelung;* first staged at new Bayreuth opera house 1876

1865 Wagner experiments with harmony in *Tristan and Isolde*

1874 First production of Mussorgsky's opera *Boris Godunov* in St. Petersburg

1876 Brahms, *Symphony No. 1 in C Minor*

1882 Wagner, *Parsifal*

1887 Verdi, *Otello;* Bruckner begins *Symphony No. 8 in C Minor*

353

The Concerns of Romanticism

The tide of revolution that swept away much of the old political order in Europe and America in the last quarter of the 18th century had momentous consequences for the arts. Both the American and the French revolutions had, in fact, used art as a means of expressing their spiritual rejection of the aristocratic society against which they were physically rebelling, and both had adopted the neoclassical style to do so. Jacques Louis David's images of stern Roman virtue [see figure 308, page 330] and Jefferson's evocation of the simple grandeur of classical architecture [see figure 322, page 339] represented, as it were, the revolutionaries' view of themselves and their accomplishments. Neoclassicism, however, barely survived into the beginning of the 19th century. The movement that replaced it, romanticism, eventually dominated virtually every aspect of 19th-century artistic achievement.

The essence of romanticism is particularly difficult to describe because romanticism is much more concerned with broad general attitudes than with specific stylistic features. Painters, writers, and musicians in the 19th century shared a number of concerns in their approach to their art. First was the important emphasis they placed on personal feelings and their expression. Ironically enough, the very revolutionary movements that had encouraged artists to rebel against the conventional styles of the early 18th century had themselves proved too restricting and conventional.

Second, emphasis on emotion rather than intellect led to the expression of subjective rather than objective visions; after all, the emotions known best are the ones we have experienced. The romantics used art to explore and dissect their own personal hopes and fears (more often the latter) rather than as a means to arrive at some general truth.

This in turn produced a third attitude of romanticism: its love of the fantastic and the exotic, which made it possible to probe more deeply into an individual's creative imagination. Dreams, for example, were a way of releasing the mind from the constraints of everyday experience and bringing to the surface those dark visions reason had submerged, as the Spanish artist Francisco Goya shows us unforgettably in a famous etching [329]. Artists felt free to invent their own dream worlds. Some chose to reconstruct such ages long past as the medieval period, which was particularly popular (Britain's Houses of Parliament [330] were begun in 1836 in the Gothic style of six centuries earlier). Others preferred to imagine remote and exotic lands and dreamed of life

in the mysterious Orient or on a primitive desert island. Still others simply trusted to the powers of their imagination and invented a fantasy world of their own.

A fourth characteristic of much romantic art is a mystical attachment to the world of nature that was also the result of the search for new sensations. Painters turned increasingly to landscape, composers sought to evoke the rustling of leaves in a forest or the noise of a storm, and poets tried to express their sense of union with the natural world. Most 18th-century artists had turned to nature in search of order and reason. In the 19th century the wild unpredictability of nature became emphasized, depicted neither objectively nor realistically but as a mirror of the artist's individual emotions. At the same time, the romantic communion with nature expressed a rejec-

329 Francisco Goya. *The Sleep of Reason Produces Monsters,* from *Los Caprichos.* 1796–1798. Etching, 8½ × 6″ (22 × 15 cm). Metropolitan Museum of Art, New York (gift of M. Knoedler & Company, 1918). The precise meaning of the work is not clear, but it evidently represents the inability of Reason to banish monstrous thoughts. Its title is written on the desk below the student, who sleeps with his head on his textbooks.

330 Charles Barry and A. W. N. Pugin. Houses of Parliament, London. 1836–1860. Length 940′ (286.51 m). The relative symmetry of the facade is broken only by the placing of the towers—Gothic in style, as is the decorative detail.

tion of the classical notion of a world centered on human activity.

These attitudes, and the new imaginative and creative power they unleashed, had two very different but equally important effects on the relationship between the artist and society. On one hand many creative artists became increasingly alienated from their public. Whereas they had once filled a precise role in providing entertainment or satisfying political and religious demands, now their self-expressive works met no particular needs except their own.

On the other hand, an increasing number of artists sought to express the national characteristics of their people by art. Abandoning the common artistic language of earlier periods and instead developing local styles that made use of traditional folk elements, artists were able to stimulate (and in some cases to initiate) the growth of national consciousness and the demand for national independence (see map, page 356). This was particularly effective in the Russian and Austrian empires (which incorporated many nationalities) and even in America, which had always been only on the fringe of the European cultural tradition, but it also became an increasingly strong tendency in the art of France and Italy, countries that

had hitherto shared the same general culture. Thus at the same time, some artists were retreating into a private world of their own creation, but others were in the forefront of the social and political movements of their own age.

The Intellectual Background

It might be expected that a movement like romanticism, which put a high value on the feelings of the moment at the expense of conscious reason, would remain relatively unaffected by intellectual principles. Nonetheless, a number of romantic artists did in fact draw inspiration from contemporary philosophy. A rapid survey of the chief intellectual developments of the 19th century therefore provides a background to the artistic ones.

The ideas that proved most attractive to the romantic imagination had developed in Germany at the end of the 18th century. Their chief spokesman was Immanuel Kant (1724–1804), whose *Critique of Judgment* (1790) defined the pleasure we derive from art as "disinterested satisfaction." Kant conceived of art as uniting opposite principles: it unites the general with the particular, for example, and reason with the imagination. For Kant, the only analogy for the way in which art is at the same time useless and yet useful was to be found in the world of nature.

Even more influential than Kant was Georg Wilhelm Friedrich Hegel (1770–1831), whose ideas continued to affect attitudes toward art and artistic criticism into the 20th century. Like Kant, Hegel stressed art's ability to reconcile and make sense of opposites, and to provide a *synthesis* of the two opposing components of human existence, called *thesis* (pure, infinite being) and *antithesis* (the world of nature).

Both Kant and Hegel developed their ideas in the relatively optimistic intellectual climate of the late 18th and early 19th centuries, and their approach both to art and to existence is basically positive. A very different position was that of Arthur Schopenhauer (1788–1860), whose major work, *The World as Will and Idea* (1819), expresses the belief that the dominating will, or power, in the world is evil. At the time of its appearance, Schopenhauer's work made little impression, due in large measure to the popularity of Kant's and Hegel's idealism. Schopenhauer himself did not help matters by launching a bitter personal attack on Hegel. But the failure of the nationalist uprisings of 1848 in many parts of Europe produced a growing mood of pessimism and gloom, against which background Schopenhauer's vision of a world condemned perpetually to be ravaged by strife and misery seemed more convincing. Thus his philosophy, if it did not mold the romantic movement, came to reflect its growing despondency.

It must be admitted, of course, that many of the major developments in 19th-century thought had little direct impact on the contemporary arts. The most influential of all 19th-century philosophers was probably Karl Marx (1818–1883), whose belief in the inherent evil of capitalism and in the historical inevitability of the proletarian revolution was powerfully expressed in the *Communist Manifesto* of 1848.

Marx's belief that revolution was both unavoidable and necessary was based at least in part on his own observation of working conditions in industrial England, where his friend and fellow Communist Friedrich Engels (1820–1895) had inherited a textile factory. Marx and Engels both believed that the factory workers, although creating wealth for the middle classes, received no benefit from it for themselves. Living in overcrowded, unsanitary conditions, the workers were deprived of any effective political power, and only kept quiet by the drug of religion, which offered them the false hope of rewards in a future life. The plight of the working classes seemed to Marx to transcend all national boundaries and create a universal proletariat that could only achieve freedom through revolution: "Workers of the world, unite! You have nothing to lose but your chains!"

The drive to political action was underpinned by Marx's economic philosophy, with its emphasis on the value of labor and, more generally, on the supreme importance of economic and social conditions as the true moving forces behind historical events. This so-called materialist concept of history was to have worldwide repercussions in the century that followed Marx's death. In our own time, writers such as Bertolt Brecht (1898–1956) have embraced Marxist principles, and Marxist critics have developed a school of aesthetic criticism that applies standards based on Marxist doctrines. For the 19th and early 20th centuries, however, Marx's influence was exclusively social and political.

Achievements in science and technology are reflected to a certain extent in romantic art, although chiefly from a negative point of view. The growing industrialization of life in the great cities, and the effect of inventions like the railway train on urban architecture served to stimulate a "back-to-nature" movement. Many artists contrasted the growing problems of urban life with an idyllic (and highly imaginative) picture of rustic bliss.

Scientific ideas had something of the same negative effect on 19th-century artists. The English Victorian writers (so called after Queen Victoria, who reigned from 1837 to 1901) responded to the growing scientific materialism of the age. Although few were, strictly speaking, romantics, much of their resistance to progress in science and industry and their portrayal of its evil effects has its roots in the romantic tradition. No scientific figure aroused more controversy than Charles Darwin (1809–1882), whose *Origin of Species* (1859) advanced the case for evolution. According to Darwin, living creatures had not been formed once and for all at the Creation, as described in the Book of Genesis, but had evolved over millennia according to a principle described by one of his supporters as "the survival of the fittest." The religious and social implications of Darwinism are still debated, but even in Darwin's own time evolutionary ideas were picked up, discussed, and developed.

The Birth of Romanticism

In each of the arts the birth of romanticism represents a clear and deliberate break with the past. The nature of that break differs in each case, and thus the music of Beethoven, the paintings of Goya, and the writings of Goethe at first seem to have little in common except their date. Yet a careful look at each of them shows that, for all their differences, they share a number of common concerns. The apparently limitless richness and variety of later romantic art is in fact unified by a specific series of preoccupations that are most clearly visible in its early stages.

Music: Beethoven

For many of the romantics, music was the supreme art. Free from the intellectual concepts involved in language and the physical limits inherent in the visual arts, it was capable of the most wholehearted and intuitive expression of emotion. Since Ludwig van Beethoven (1770–1827), widely regarded as the pioneer of musical romanticism, also manifested many characteristically romantic attitudes—such as love of nature, passionate belief in the freedom of the individual, and fiery temperament—it is not surprising that he has come to be regarded as the prototype of the romantic artist [331]. When he wrote proudly to one of his most loyal aristocratic supporters "There will always be thousands of princes, but there is only one Beethoven," he spoke for a new generation of creators. When he used the last movement of his *Symphony No. 9* to preach the doctrine of universal brotherhood he inspired countless ordinary listeners by his fervor. Even today familiarity with Beethoven's music has not dulled its ability to give dramatic expression to the noblest of human sentiments.

Beethoven was born in Bonn, Germany, where he received his musical training from his father. An alcoholic, Beethoven's father saw the possibility of producing a musical prodigy in his son. He forced him to practice hours at the keyboard, often locking him in his room and beating him on his return from drinking bouts. All possibilities of a happy family life were brought to an end in 1787 by the death of Beethoven's mother and his father's subsequent decline into advanced alcoholism. Beethoven sought compensation in the home of the von Breuning family, where he acted as private tutor. It was there that he met other musicians and artists and developed a love of literature that he kept throughout his life. He also struck up a friendship with a local minor aristocrat, Count Waldstein, who remained his devoted admirer until the composer's death.

In 1792 Waldstein was one of the aristocrats who helped Beethoven go to Vienna to study with Haydn, then regarded as the greatest composer of his day; but although Haydn agreed to give him lessons, the young Beethoven's impatience and suspicion, and Haydn's deficiencies as a teacher, did not make for a happy relationship. Nevertheless, many of the works Beethoven wrote during his first years in Vienna are essentially classical in both form and spirit; only by the end of the century had he begun to extend the emotional range of his music.

One of the first pieces to express the characteristically Beethovenian spirit of rebellion against Fate and the determination to struggle on is his *Piano Sonata No. 8 in C minor,* Op. 13, generally known as the "Pathétique." The first movement begins with a slow introduction, but unlike similar introductions in the classical music of Haydn, it sets the emotional tone of the entire piece rather than merely capturing the listener's attention. As is so often the case, the significance of Beethoven's music is as easy to grasp on hearing as it is difficult to express in words. The heavy, foreboding chords seem to try to pull themselves up, only to fall back again and again in defeat, until finally they culminate in a burst of defiant en-

ergy that sets the main *allegro* (fast) portion of this movement on its stormy way. Just before the very end of the movement the ghost of the slow introduction returns briefly, as if to emphasize the odds against which the struggle has been—and will be—waged.

It is important to understand precisely how Beethoven used music in a new and revolutionary way. Other composers had written music to express emotion long before Beethoven's time, from Bach's outpouring of religious fervor to Mozart's evocation of human joy and sorrow. What is different about Beethoven is that his emotion is autobiographical. His music tells us how he feels, what his succession of moods is, and what conclusion he reaches. It does other things at the same time, and at this early stage in his career for the most part it self-consciously fol-

331 Ferdinand Georg Waldmüller. *Ludwig van Beethoven.* 1823. 28 × 22¾" (72 × 58 cm). Painting now lost. Painted a year before the first performance of Beethoven's *Symphony No. 9 in D minor,* the portrait emphasizes the composer's stubborn independence by both the set of the mouth and the casual, even untidy, dress and hair. Beethoven, who had become irascible in his later years, allowed the artist only one sitting for this portrait commissioned by one of his music publishers.

Plate 27 Eugène Delacroix. *The Death of Sardanapalus*. 1826. Oil on canvas, c. 12′1″ × 16′3″ (3.68 × 4.95 m). Louvre, Paris. The painting makes no attempt to achieve archaeological accuracy but concentrates on exploiting the violence and cruelty of the story. Delocroix himself called this work "Massacre No. 2," a reference to his earlier painting, the *Massacre at Chios* (figure **348,** page 377). Although this suggests a certain detachment on the artist's part, there is no lack of energy or commitment in the free, almost violent, brush strokes.

Plate 28 Joseph Mallord William Turner. *The Slave Ship*. 1840. Oil on canvas, 3 × 4′ (91 × 1.22 m). Museum of Fine Arts, Boston (Henry Lillie Pierce Fund). The title of this painting is an abbreviation of a longer one: *Slavers Throwing Overboard the Dead and Dying; Typhoon Coming On*. Turner includes a horrifying detail at lower center: the chains still binding the slaves whose desperate hands show above the water. Note the extreme contrast between Turner's interpretation of color and light and that of the American luminists as shown in Heade's painting below.

Plate 29 Martin Johnson Heade. *Lake George*. 1862. Oil on canvas, 2′2″ × 4′2″ (.66 × 1.26 m). Museum of Fine Arts, Boston (bequest of Maxim Karolik). Note the smooth surface of the painting, which reveals no trace of the artist's brush strokes, and the extreme precision of the rendering of the rocks at right.

360

lows classical principles of construction, but the vivid communication of personal emotions is its prime concern. That Beethoven's range was not limited to anger and frustration is immediately demonstrated by the beautiful and consoling middle slow movement of the "Pathétique," with its lyrical main theme, but the final movement returns to turbulent passion.

Parallels for the turbulent style of the "Pathétique" can be found in other contemporary arts, especially literature, but although to some extent Beethoven was responding to the climate of the times, there can be no doubt that he was also expressing a personal reaction to the terrible tragedy that had begun to afflict him as early as 1796. In that year the first symptoms of his deafness began to appear; by 1798 his hearing had grown very weak, and by 1802 he was virtually totally deaf.

Nonetheless, although obviously affected by his condition, Beethoven's music was not exclusively concerned with his own fate. The same heroic attitude with which he faced his personal problems was also given universal expression, never more stupendously than in the *Symphony No. 3 in E♭*, Op. 55, subtitled the *Eroica,* the Heroic Symphony. As early as 1799 the French ambassador to Vienna had suggested that Beethoven write a symphony in honor of Napoleon Bonaparte. At the time Napoleon was widely regarded as a popular hero who had triumphed over his humble origins to rise to power as a champion of liberty and democracy. Beethoven's own democratic temperament made him one of Napoleon's many admirers. The symphony was duly begun, but in 1804, the year of its completion, Napoleon had himself crowned Emperor. When Beethoven heard the news, he angrily crossed out Napoleon's name on the title page. The first printed edition, which appeared in 1806, bore only the dedication "to celebrate the memory of a great man."

It would be a mistake to see the *Eroica* merely as a portrait of Napoleon. Rather, inspired by what he saw as the heroic stature of the Frenchman, Beethoven created his own heroic world in sound, in a work of vast dimensions. The first movement alone lasts for almost as long as many a classical symphony. Its complicated structure requires considerable concentration on the part of the listener. The form is basically the old classical sonata allegro form (see page 343), but on a much grander scale and with a wealth of musical ideas. Yet the principal theme of the movement, which the cellos announce at the very beginning, after two hammering, impatient chords demand our attention, is of a rocklike sturdiness and simplicity:

Beethoven's genius emerges as he uses this and other similarly straightforward ideas to build his mighty structure. Throughout the first movement his use of harmony and, in particular, discord, adds to the emotional impact, especially in the middle of the development section, where slashing dissonances seem to tear the orchestra apart. His classical grounding emerges in the recapitulation, where the infinite variety of the development section gives way to a restored sense of unity; the movement ends triumphantly with a long and thrilling coda. The formal structure is recognizably classical, but the intensity of expression, depth of personal commitment, and heroic defiance are all totally romantic.

The second movement of the *Eroica* is a worthy successor to the first. A funeral march on the same massive scale, it alternates a mood of epic tragedy, which has been compared with the impact of the works of the Greek playwright Aeschylus, with rays of consolation that at times achieve a transcendental exaltation. Although the many subtleties of construction deserve the closest attention, even a first hearing will reveal the grandeur of Beethoven's conception.

The third and fourth movements relax the tension. For the third, Beethoven replaces the stately minuet of the classical symphony with a *scherzo*—the word literally means joke and is used to describe a fast-moving, generally lighthearted piece of music. Beethoven's introduction of this kind of music, which in his hands often has something of the crude flavor of a peasant dance, is another illustration of his "democratization" of the symphony. The last movement is a brilliant and energetic series of variations on a theme Beethoven had composed a few years earlier for a ballet he had written on the subject (from classic mythology) of Prometheus, who defied the ancient gods by giving mortals the gift of fire, for which he was punished by Zeus—a final reference to the heroic mood of the entire work.

Many of the ideas and ideals that permeate the *Eroica* reappear throughout Beethoven's work. His love of liberty and hatred of oppression are expressed in his only opera, *Fidelio,* which describes how a faithful wife rescues her husband who has been unjustly imprisoned for his political views. A good performance of *Fidelio* is still one of the most uplifting and exalting experiences music has to offer. The concept of triumph over Fate recurs in his best-known symphony, the *Fifth,* Op. 67, while *Symphony No. 6,* Op. 68, the *Pastoral,* consists of a romantic evocation of nature and the emotions it arouses. *Symphony No. 9*, Op. 125, is perhaps the most complete statement of the human striving to conquer all obstacles and win through to universal peace and joy. In it Beethoven introduced a chorus and soloists to give voice to the "Ode to Joy" by his compatriot Friedrich Schiller (1759–1805). The symphony represents the most complete artistic vindication of Kant's Transcendental Idealism. It is also one of the most influential works of the entire romantic movement.

Painting: Goya

Just as Beethoven rejected the idealizing and universal qualities of classical music to achieve a more intense and personal communication, so painters began to abandon the lofty, remote world of neoclassical art for more vivid images. In the case of painting, however, the question of style was far more related to political developments. We have already seen in Chapter 14 that neoclassicism had become, as it were, the official artistic dress of the Revolution, so it was not easy for a painter working in France, still the center of artistic life, suddenly to abandon the revolutionary style. The problem is particularly visible in the works of Jacques Louis David (1748–1825), whose *Oath of the Horatii* [see figure 308, page 330] had been inspired by the prerevolutionary longing for austere Republican virtue. By the end of the Revolution, David had come to appreciate the advantages of peace; his painting *The Battle of the Romans and the Sabines* of 1799 [332] expresses his desire for an end to violence and bloodshed. The subject is drawn from Roman mythology and focuses on that moment when Hersilia, wife of the Roman leader Romulus, interrupts the battle between Romans and Sabines and begs for an end to war. Its significance is precisely the reverse of the *Oath of the Horatii*. In place of a masculine call to arms and sacrifice, David shows his heroine making an impassioned plea for peace. The style, however, remains firmly neoclassical, not only in the choice of subject but also in its execution. For all the weapons and armor, there is no sign of actual physical violence. The two opponents, with their heroic figures and noble brows, are idealized along typically neoclassical lines. The emotional

332 Jacques Louis David. *The Battle of the Romans and the Sabines*. 1799. Oil on canvas, 12′8″ × 17′3/4″ (3.86 × 5.2 m). Louvre, Paris. David may have intended his depiction of feminine virtue as a tribute to his wife, who had left him when he voted for the execution of Louis XVI but returned to him when he was imprisoned for a time.

gestures of Hersilia and others are also stylized and frozen. The painting is powerful, but it depicts a concept rather than individual human feelings.

The contrast between the neoclassical representation of the horrors of war and a romantic treatment of the same theme can be seen by comparing David's painting with *Execution of the Madrileños on May 3, 1808* [333] by Francisco Goya (1746–1828). In Goya's painting, nothing is idealized. The horror and the terror of the victims, their faceless executioners, the blood streaming in the dust all combine to create an almost unbearable image of protest against human cruelty. Goya's painting is romantic because it conveys to us his own personal emotions at the thought of the executions and because, great artist that he was, his emotions become our own.

As Beethoven convinces us of the necessity to struggle against the injustices of human beings and of Fate by his own passionate commitment, so Goya by his intensity urges us to condemn the atrocities of war. Furthermore, both Beethoven and Goya shared a common sympathy with the oppressed and a hatred of tyranny. The soldiers firing their bayoneted guns in Goya's painting were serving in the army of Napoleon; the event shown took place some four years after Beethoven had seen the danger Napoleon presented to the cause of liberty and had erased his name from the *Eroica*.

It was, of course, easier for an artist outside France to abandon the artistic language of neoclassicism for more direct ways of communication. Although from 1824 to his death Goya lived in France, he was born in Spain and spent most of his working life there. Removed from the mainstream of artistic life, he seems never to have been attracted by the neoclassical style. Some of his first paintings were influenced by the rococo style of Tiepolo [see figure 315, page 335], who was in Spain from 1762 until 1770, but his own introspective nature and the strength of his feelings seem to have driven him to find more direct means of expression. Personal suffering may have played a part also, since Goya, like Beethoven, became totally deaf.

In 1799 Goya became official painter to Charles IV, the king of Spain, and was commissioned to produce a series of formal court portraits. The most fa-

333 Francisco Goya. *Execution of the Madrileños on May 3, 1808*. 1814. Oil on canvas, 8'8¾" × 11'3¾" (2.66 × 3.45 m). Prado, Madrid. The painting shows the execution of a group of citizens of Madrid who had demonstrated against the French occupation by Napoleon's troops. The Spanish government commissioned the painting after the expulsion of the French army.

mous of these, *The Family of Charles IV* [334], was deliberately modeled on Velásquez' *Las Meninas* [see Plate 22, page 307]. Goya shows us the royal family—king, queen, children, and grandchildren—in the artist's studio, where they have come to visit. The comparison he intends us to make between his own painting and this of his distinguished predecessor is devastating. At first glance Goya's painting may seem just another official portrait, but it does not take a viewer very long to realize that something is very wrong at the court of Spain. Instead of grace and elegance, Goya's patrons radiate arrogance, vanity, and stupidity. The king and queen, in particular, are especially unappealing.

The effect of Goya's painting is not so much one of realism as of personal comment, although there is every reason to believe that the queen was in fact quite as ugly as she appears here. The artist is communicating his own feelings of disgust at the emptiness, indeed the evil, of court life. That he does so through the medium of an official court portrait that is itself a parody of one of the most famous of all court portraits is of course an intentional irony.

Even at the time of his official court paintings Goya was obsessed by the darker side of life. His engraving *The Sleep of Reason Produces Monsters* [see figure 329] foreshadowed the work of his last years. Between 1820 and 1822 he covered the walls of his own house with paintings that depict a nightmare world of horror and despair. *Saturn Devouring One of His Sons* [335] makes use of a classical myth to portray the god of Time in the act of destroying humanity, but the treatment owes nothing to neoclassicism. Indeed, no simple stylistic label seems adequate to describe so personal a vision. The intensity of expression, the fantastic nature of the subject, and the mood of introspection are all typically romantic, yet the totality transcends its components. No one but Goya has ever expressed a vision of human existence in quite these terms.

below left: 334 Francisco Goya. *The Family of Charles IV.* 1800. Oil on canvas, 9′2″ × 11′ (2.79 × 3.35 m). Prado, Madrid. In this scathing portrayal of the Spanish royal family the artist himself is working away quietly at the far left. The French writer Alphonse Daudet said the painting showed "the grocer and his family who have just won top prize in the Lottery."

below right: 335 Francisco Goya. *Saturn Devouring One of His Sons.* c. 1821. Fresco detached on canvas, 4′9½″ × 2′8⅛″ (1.46 × .83 m). Prado, Madrid. The painting originally decorated a wall in Goya's country house, La Quinta del Sordo (Deaf Man's Villa).

Literature: Goethe

The towering figure of Johann Wolfgang von Goethe (1749–1832) spans the transition from neoclassicism to romanticism in literature like a colossus. So great was the range of his genius that in the course of a long and immensely productive life he wrote works in a bewildering variety of styles. One of the first writers to rebel against the principles of neoclassicism, he used both poetry and prose to express the most turbulent emotions; yet he continued to produce works written according to neoclassical principles of clarity and balance until his last years, when he expressed in his writing a profound if abstruse symbolism.

Although the vein of romanticism is only one of many that runs through Goethe's work, it is an important one. As a young man Goethe studied law, first at Leipzig and then at Strassburg, where by 1770 he was already writing lyric poetry of astonishing directness and spontaneity. By 1773 he was acknowledged as the leader of the literary movement known as *Sturm und Drang* (Storm and Stress). This German manifestation of romanticism rebelled against the formal structure and order of neoclassicism, replacing it with an emphasis on originality, imagination, and feelings. Its chief subjects were nature, primitive emotions, and protest against established authority. Although the Storm and Stress movement was originally confined to literature, its precepts were felt elsewhere. For instance, it was partly under the inspiration of this movement that Beethoven developed his fiery style.

The climax of this period in Goethe's life is represented by his novel *The Sufferings of Young Werther* (1774), which describes how an idealistic young man comes to feel increasingly disillusioned and frustrated by life, develops a hopeless passion for a happily married woman, and ends his agony by putting a bullet through his head. All of these events but the last were autobiographical. Instead of committing suicide Goethe left town and turned his life experiences into the novel that won him international fame. Not surprisingly it became a key work of the romantic movement. Young men began to dress in the blue jacket and yellow trousers Werther is described as wearing, and some, disappointed in love, even committed suicide with copies of the book in their pocket—a dramatic if regrettable illustration of Goethe's ability to communicate his own emotions to others [336].

The years around the turn of the century found Goethe extending the range of his output. Along with such plays as the classical drama *Iphigeneia in Tauris,* which expressed his belief in purity and sin-

336 Tony Johannot. Illustration for a later edition of *The Sufferings of Young Werther.* 1852. By permission of Houghton Library, Harvard University. The hero has just declared his hopeless passion for Charlotte.

cere humanity, were stormy works like *Egmont,* inspired by the idea that human life is controlled by demonic forces. The work for which Goethe is probably best known, *Faust,* was begun about the turn of the century, although its composition took many years. Part One was published in 1808, and Part Two was only finished in 1832, shortly before his death.

The subject of Dr. Faustus and his pact with the devil had been treated before in literature, notably in the play by Christopher Marlowe (see page 293). The theme was guaranteed to appeal to the romantic sensibility with its elements of the mysterious and fantastic, and in Part One Goethe put additional stress on the human emotions involved. The chief victim of Faust's lust for experience and power is the pure and innocent Gretchen, whom he callously seduces and then abandons. She becomes deranged as a result. At the end of Part One of *Faust,* Gretchen is accused of the murder of her illegitimate child, condemned to death, and executed. Moving from irony to wit to profound compassion, the rich tapestry of Part One shows Goethe, like Beethoven and Goya, on the side of suffering humanity.

Part Two of *Faust* is very different. Its theme, expressed symbolically through Faust's pact with the devil, is nothing less than the destiny of Western culture. Our civilization's unceasing activity and thirst for new experience inevitably produces error and suffering; at the same time, it is the result of the divine spark within us and will, in the end, guarantee our salvation. In his choice of the agent of this salvation Goethe established one of the other great themes of romanticism, the Eternal Feminine. Faust is finally redeemed by the divine love of Gretchen, who leads him upward to salvation.

Music in the Romantic Era

Instrumental Music after Beethoven

After Beethoven, music could never again return to its former mood of classical objectivity. Although Beethoven's music may remain unsurpassed for its universalization of individual emotion, his successors tried—and in large measure succeeded—to find new ways to express their own feelings. Among the first to follow Beethoven was Hector Berlioz (1803–1869), the most distinguished French romantic composer who produced, among other typically romantic works, the *Fantastic Symphony,* which describes the hallucinations of an opium-induced dream, and *The Damnation of Faust,* a setting of Part One of Goethe's work. In both of these he used the full romantic apparatus of dreams, witches, demons, and the grotesque to lay bare the artist's innermost feelings—although, like Goethe, he never lost an innately classical streak.

A much more intimate and poetic form of romantic self-revelation is the music of Franz Schubert (1797–1828), who explored in the few years before his premature death the new possibilities opened up by Beethoven in a wide range of musical forms. In general he was happiest when working on a small scale, as evidenced by his more than six hundred *lieder* (songs), which are an inexhaustible store of musical and emotional expression.

On the whole, the more rhetorical nature of the symphonic form appealed to Schubert less, although the wonderful *Symphony No. 8 in B minor,* called the "Unfinished" because he only completed two movements, combines great poetic feeling with a genuine sense of drama. His finest instrumental music was written for small groups of instruments. The two *Trios for Piano, Violin, and Cello,* Op. 99 and 100, are rich in the heavenly melodies that seemed to come to him so easily; the second, slow movement of the *Trio in E♭,* Op. 100, touches profound depths of romantic expression. Like the slow movement of Mozart's *Piano Concerto No. 27 in B♭* (see page 345), its extreme beauty is tinged with an unutterable sorrow. But whereas Mozart seems to speak for humanity at large, Schubert moves us most deeply by communicating his own personal feelings.

Most 19th-century composers followed Beethoven in using the symphony as the vehicle for their most serious musical ideas. Robert Schumann (1810–1856) and Johannes Brahms (1833–1897) regarded the symphonic form as the most lofty means of musical expression, and each as a result wrote only four symphonies. Brahms did not even dare to write a symphony until he was 44, and is said to have felt the presence of Beethoven's works "like the tramp of a giant" behind him. When it finally appeared, Brahms' *Symphony No. 1 in C minor,* Op. 68, was inevitably compared with Beethoven. Although Brahms' strong sense of form and conservative style won him the hostility of the archromantics of the day, other critics hailed him as the true successor to Beethoven.

Both responses were, of course, extreme. Brahms' music certainly is romantic—with its emphasis on warm melody and a passion no less present for being held tightly in rein—but far from echoing the heaven-storming mood of his great predecessor, Brahms was really more at home in relaxed vein. Although the *Symphony No. 1* begins with a gesture of defiant grandeur akin to Beethoven's, the first movement ends by fading dreamily into a glowing tranquility. The lovely slow movement is followed not by a scherzo but by a quiet and graceful intermezzo or interlude, and only in the last movement do we return to the mood of the opening.

Closer to the more cosmic mood of the Beethoven symphonies are the nine symphonies of Anton Bruckner (1824–1896). A deeply religious man imbued with a romantic attachment to the beauties of nature, Bruckner combined his devout Catholicism and mystical vision in music of epic grandeur. It has often been remarked that Bruckner's music requires time and patience on the listener's part. His pace is leisurely and he creates huge structures in sound that demand our full concentration if we are to appreciate their "architecture." There is no lack of incidental beauty, however, and the rewards are immense. No other composer has been able to convey quite the tone of mystical exaltation that Bruckner achieves, above all in the slow movements of his last three symphonies. The *adagio* movement from the *Symphony No. 8 in C minor,* for instance, moves from the desolate romanticism of its opening theme to a mighty, blazing climax as thrilling and stirring as anything in 19th-century music.

The Age of the Virtuosos

Beethoven's emphasis on the primacy of the artist inspired another series of romantic composers to move in a very different direction from that of the symphony. Beethoven himself had first made his reputation as a brilliant pianist, and much of his

music, both for piano and for other instruments, was of considerable technical difficulty. As composers began to demand greater and greater feats of virtuosity from their performers, performing artists themselves came to attract more attention. Singers had already, in the 18th century, commanded high fees and attracted crowds of fanatical admirers, and continued to do so. Now, however, they were joined by instrumental virtuosos, some of whom were also highly successful composers.

The life of Frédéric Chopin (1810–1849) seems almost too romantic to be true [337]. Both in his piano performances and in the music he composed he united the aristocratic fire of his native Poland with the elegance and sophistication of Paris, where he spent much of his life. His concerts created a sensation throughout Europe, while his piano works exploited (if they did not always create) new musical forms like the *nocturne,* a short piano piece in which an expressive, if melancholy, melody floats over a murmuring, rustling accompaniment. Chopin is characteristically romantic in his use of music to express his own personal emotions. The structure of works like the twenty-four Preludes, Op. 28, is dictated not by formal considerations but by the feeling of the moment. Thus the first three take us from excited agitation to brooding melancholy to bubbling high spirits in just over three minutes.

In private, Chopin's life was dominated by a much-talked-about liaison with the leading French woman author of the day, George Sand (1804–1876). His early death from tuberculosis put the final romantic touch to the life of a composer who has been described as the soul of the piano.

Franz Liszt (1811–1886) shared Chopin's brilliant skill at the keyboard and joined to it his own more robust temperament. A natural romantic, he ran the gamut of romantic themes and experiences. After beginning his career as a handsome, impetuous young rebel, the idol of the salons of Paris, he conducted a number of well-publicized affairs and ended up by turning to the consolations of religion. His vast musical output includes some of the most difficult of all piano works (many of them inspired by the beauties of nature), two symphonies on the characteristically romantic subjects of Faust and Dante (with special emphasis, in the latter case, on the Inferno), and a host of pieces that made use of the folk tunes of his native Hungary.

Assessment of Liszt's true musical stature is difficult. He was probably a better composer than his present reputation suggests, although not so great a one as his contemporaries (and he) thought. As a virtuoso performer even he takes second place to Nic-

337 Eugène Delacroix. *Frédéric Chopin.* 1838. Oil on canvas, 18 × 15″ (46 × 38 cm). Louvre, Paris. Delacroix's portrait of his friend captures Chopin's romantic introspection. Delacroix himself was a great lover of music, though somewhat surprisingly the great romantic painter preferred Mozart to Beethoven.

338 Eugène Delacroix. *Paganini*. 1832. Oil on panel, 17¼ × 11½" (44 × 29 cm). Phillips Collection, Washington. The painting seems to convey all the intensity of the great virtuoso. It is less obviously realistic than the portrait of Chopin, but certainly as atmospheric.

colò Paganini (1782–1840), the greatest violinist of the age, if not of all time [338].

Like Chopin and Liszt, Paganini also composed, but it was his public performances that won him his amazing reputation. So apparently impossible were the technical feats he so casually executed that rumor spread that, like Faust, he had sold his soul to the devil. This typically romantic exaggeration was, of course, assiduously encouraged by Paganini himself, who cultivated a suitably ghoulish appearance to enhance his public image. Nothing more clearly illustrates the 19th century's obsession with music as emotional expression (in this case diabolical) than the fact that Paganini's concerts earned him both honors throughout Europe and a considerable fortune.

Musical Nationalism

Both Chopin and Liszt introduced the music of their native lands into their works, Chopin in his *mazurkas* and *polonaises* (traditional Polish dances) and Liszt in his *Hungarian Rhapsodies*. For the most part, however, they adapted their musical styles to the prevailing international fashions of the day.

Other composers placed greater emphasis on their native musical traditions. In Russia a group of five composers (Moussorgsky, Balakirev, Borodin, Cui, and Rimsky-Korsakov) consciously set out to exploit their rich musical heritage. The greatest of the five was Modest Moussorgsky (1839–1881), whose opera *Boris Godunov* (1874) is based on an episode in Russian history. It makes full use of Russian folk songs and religious music in telling the story of Tzar Boris Godunov, who rises to power by killing the true heir to the throne. Although Boris is the opera's single most important character, the work is really dominated by the chorus, which represents the Russian people. Moussorgsky powerfully depicts their changing emotions, from bewilderment to awe, to fear, to rage, and in doing so gives voice to the feelings of his nation.

Elsewhere in Eastern Europe composers were finding similar inspiration in national themes and folk music. The Czech composer Bedřich Smetana (1824–1884), who aligned himself with his native Bohemia in the uprising against Austrian rule in 1848, composed a set of seven pieces for orchestra that bear the collective title of *Má Vlast* (*My Fatherland*). The best known, *Vltava* (*The Moldau*), depicts the course of the river Vltava as it flows from its source through the countryside to the capital city of Prague. His fellow countryman Antonin Dvořák (1841–1904) also drew on the rich tradition of folk music in works like his *Slavonic Dances,* colorful settings of Czech folk tunes.

Opera in Italy: Verdi

Throughout the 19th century opera achieved new heights of popularity in Europe and "operamania" began to spread to America, where opera houses opened in New York in 1854 and Chicago in 1865. On both sides of the Atlantic opera houses are still dominated by the works of the two 19th-century giants in the history of opera—the Italian Giuseppe Verdi and the German Richard Wagner.

When Giuseppe Verdi (1813–1901) began his career, the Italian opera-going public was interested in beautiful and brilliant singing rather than realism of plot or action. This love of what is often called *bel canto* (beautiful song) should not be misunderstood. Composers like Gaetano Donizetti (1797–1848) and Vincenzo Bellini (1801–1835) used their music to express sincere and deep emotions and even drama, but the emotional expression was achieved primarily by means of song and not by a convincing dramatic situation. The plots of their operas serve only as an excuse for music; thus characters in *bel canto* operas are frequently given to fits of madness in order to give musical expression to deep emotion. Within the necessary framework provided by the plot a great singer, inspired by great music, could use the magic of the human voice to communicate a dramatic emotion that transcended the time and place of the action. Under the inspiration of Verdi and Wagner, however, opera began to move in a different direction. The subjects composers chose remained larger than life, but dramatic credibility became increasingly important.

Beginning in the 1950s, however, many music lovers began to discover a rich source of musical beauty and even drama in a work like Bellini's *Norma,* first performed in 1831. The revival and subsequent popularity of much early 19th-century opera is due in large measure to the performances and recordings of Maria Callas [339], whose enormous talent showed how a superb interpreter could bring such works to life. Following her example, other singers turned to *bel canto* opera, with the result that performances of *Norma* and of Donizetti's best-known opera, *Lucia di Lammermoor* (1835), have become a regular feature of modern operatic life, while lesser-known works are revived in increasing numbers.

The revival of *bel canto works* has certainly not been at the expense of Verdi, perhaps the best-loved of all opera composers. His works showed a new concern for dramatic and psychological truth. Even in his early operas like *Nabucco* (1842) or *Luisa Miller* (1849) Verdi was able to give convincing expression to human relationships. At the same time his music became associated with the growing nationalist movement in Italy. *Nabucco,* for example, deals ostensibly with the captivity of the Jews in Babylon and their oppression by Nebucadnezzar, but the plight of the Jews became symbolic of the Italians' suffering under Austrian rule. The chorus the captives sing as they think of happier days, *"Va, pensiero . . . "* ("Fly, thought, on golden wings, go settle on the slopes and hills where the soft breezes of our native land smell gentle and mild"), became a kind of theme song for the Italian nationalist movement, the Risorgimento, in large measure because of the inspiring yet nostalgic quality of Verdi's tune.

Verdi's musical and dramatic powers reached their first great climax in three major masterpieces, *Rigoletto* (1851), *Il Trovatore* (1853), and *La Traviata* (1853), which remain among the most popular of all operas. They are very different in subject and atmosphere. *Il Trovatore* is perhaps the most traditional in approach, with its gory and involved plot centering around the troubadour Manrico and its abundance of superb melodies. In *Rigoletto* Verdi achieved one of his most convincing character portrayals in the hunchback court jester Rigoletto, who is forced to suppress his human feelings and play the fool to his vicious and lecherous master, the Duke of Mantua. With *La Traviata* Verdi broke new ground in the history of opera by dealing with contemporary life rather than a historical or mythological subject.

The principal character of *La Traviata* is Violetta, a popular courtesan in Paris, who falls in love with Alfredo Germont, a young man from the provinces, and decides to give up her sophisticated life in the capital for country bliss. Her reputation follows her there, however, in the form of Alfredo's father. In a

339 Maria Callas as Norma in Bellini's opera. Covent Garden, London, 1957. The Greek-American Maria Callas (1923–1977), one of the great sopranos of this century, made her first professional debut in Verona in 1947. Her debuts at La Scala, Milan, Covent Garden, London, and the Metropolitan Opera, New York, followed in 1950, 1952, and 1956.

long and emotional encounter he persuades her to abandon his son and put an end to the disgrace she is bringing on his family [340]. Violetta, who is aware that she is suffering from a fatal illness, returns alone to the cruel glitter of her life in Paris. By the end of the opera, her money gone, she lies dying in poverty and solitude. At this tragic moment Verdi gives her one of his most moving arias, *"Addio del passato"* ("Goodbye to the past"), as she thinks back over her earlier life. Alfredo, who has finally learned of the sacrifice she has made for his sake, rushes to find her, only to arrive for a final farewell—Violetta dies in his arms.

Throughout the later part of his career Verdi's powers continued to develop and enrich, until in 1887 he produced in *Otello,* a version of Shakespeare's tragedy *Othello,* perhaps the supreme work in the entire Italian operatic tradition. From the first shattering chord that opens the first act to Otello's heartbreaking death at the end of the last, Verdi rose to the Shakespearean challenge with music of unsurpassed eloquence. In a work that is so consistently inspired it seems invidious to pick out highlights, but the ecstatic love duet of Act I between Otello and Desdemona deserves mention as one of the noblest and most moving of all depictions of romantic passion.

Opera in Germany: Wagner

The impact of Richard Wagner (1813–1883) on his times went far beyond the opera house. Not only did his works change the course of the history of music, but many of his ideas had a profound effect on writers and painters [341]. This truly revolutionary figure even became actively involved with the revolutionary uprisings of 1848 and spent a number of years in exile in Switzerland.

It is difficult to summarize the variety of Wagner's ideas, which ranged from art to politics to vegetarianism and in general are not noted for their tolerance. Behind many of his writings on opera and drama lay the concept that the most powerful form of artistic expression was one that united all the arts, music, painting, poetry, movement, in a single work of art, the *Gesamtkunstwerk* (all-art work). To illustrate this theory Wagner wrote both the words and music or what he called "music dramas" and even designed and built a special theater for their performance at Bayreuth, where they are still performed every year at the Bayreuth Festival.

A number of characteristics link all Wagner's mature works. First, he abolished the old separation between recitatives (in which the action was advanced) and arias, duets, or other individual musical numbers

340 *La Traviata.* Metropolitan Opera, New York, 1981. Alfredo's father begs Violetta to leave his son. This is the scene in Act II of Verdi's opera, set in the salon of Violetta's and Alfredo's country house. The singers are Cornell MacNeil as Giorgio Germont and Catherine Malfitano as Violetta. *La Traviata* was first performed in Venice in 1853 and in New York in 1856. Many noted sopranos have taken the role of Violetta, including Maria Callas (figure **339**).

(which held up the action). Wagner's music flowed continuously from the beginning to the end of each act with no pauses. Second, he eliminated the vocal display and virtuosity that had been traditional in opera. Wagner roles are certainly not easy to sing, but their difficulties are always for dramatic reasons and not to show off a singer's skill. Third, he put a new emphasis on the orchestra, which not only accompanied the singers but also provided a rich musical argument of its own. This was enhanced by his fourth contribution, the famous device of the *leitmotiv* (leading motif), which consisted of giving each of the principal characters, ideas, and even objects an individual theme of his, her, or its own. By recalling these themes and by combining them or changing them Wagner achieved highly complex dramatic and psychological effects.

Wagner generally drew his subjects from German mythology. By peopling his stage with heroes, gods, giants, magic swans, and the like, he aimed to create universal dramas that would express universal emotions. In his most monumental achievement, *The Ring of the Nibelung,* written between 1851 and 1874, he even represented the end of the world. *The Ring* consists of four separate music dramas, *The Rhinegold, The Valkyrie, Siegfried,* and *The Twilight of the Gods,* the plot of which defies summary. In music

of incredible richness Wagner depicted not only the actions and reactions of his characters but also the wonders of nature. In *Siegfried,* for example, we hear the rustling of the forest and the songs of woodbirds, while throughout *The Ring* and especially in the well-known "Rhine Journey" from *The Twilight of the Gods* the mighty river Rhine sounds through the music. At the same time *The Ring* has a number of philosophical and political messages, many of them derived from Schopenhauer (see page 356). One of its main themes is that power corrupts, while Wagner also adopted Goethe's idea of redemption by a woman in the final resolution of the drama.

No brief discussion can begin to do justice to so stupendous a work. It is probably easier to see Wagner's genius in operation by looking at a work on small scale, a single self-contained music drama—albeit one of some four hours' duration. *Tristan and Isolde* was first performed in 1865, and its very first notes opened a new musical era. Its subject is the overwhelming love of the English knight Tristan and the Irish princess Isolde, so great that the pair betray his dearest friend and lord and her husband, King Mark of Cornwall, and so overpowering that it can achieve its complete fulfillment only in death.

Wagner's typically romantic preoccupation with love and death may seem morbid and far-fetched, but

341 Wilhelm Beckmann. *Richard Wagner at His Home in Bayreuth.* 1880. Oil on canvas, 4′3¾″ × 5′1⅝″ (1.25 × 1.58 m). Richard Wagner Museum, Triebschen-Luzern, Switzerland. Characteristically, Wagner is holding forth to his wife and friends, in this case Liszt in his abbé's garb and the author Hans von Wolzogen. At lower left are some stage designs for Wagner's last work, *Parsifal.*

The music gives the sense of having no settled harmony or clear direction. This lack of *tonality,* used here for dramatic purpose, was to have a considerable influence on modern music.

The core of *Tristan and Isolde* is the long love scene at the heart of the second part, where the music reaches heights of erotic ecstasy too potent for some listeners. Whereas Verdi's love duet in *Otello* presents two noble spirits responding to one another with deep feeling but with dignity, Wagner's characters are racked by passions they cannot begin to control. If ever music expressed what neither words nor images could depict it is in the overwhelming physical emotion of this scene [342]. The pulsating orchestra and the surging voices of the lovers build up an almost unbearable tension that Wagner suddenly interrupts and breaks by the arrival of King Mark. Once again, as in the Prelude, fulfillment is denied both to the lovers and to us.

That fulfillment is reached only at the very end of the work in Isolde's *"Liebestod"* ("Love Death"). Tristan has died, and over his body Isolde begins to sing a kind of incantation. She imagines she sees the spirit of her beloved, and in obscure, broken words describes the bliss of union in death before sinking lifeless upon him. Although the *"Liebestod"* makes its full effect only when heard at the end of the entire work, even out of context the emotional power of the music as it rises to its climax can hardly fail to affect the sensitive listener.

19th-Century Literature

Romantic Poetry

English romantic poetry of the first half of the 19th century represents a peak in the history of English literature. Its chief writers, generally known as the romantic poets, touched on a number of themes characteristic of the age. William Wordsworth's deep love of the country led him to explore the relationship between human beings and the world of nature; Percy Bysshe Shelley and George Gordon, Lord Byron, probed the more passionate, even demonic aspects of existence; and John Keats expressed his own sensitive responses to the eternal problems of art, life, and death.

William Wordsworth (1770–1850), often called the founder of the romantic movement in English poetry, clearly described his aims and ideals in his critical writings. For Wordsworth, the poet was a person with special gifts, "endowed with more lively sensibility, more enthusiasm and tenderness, who

342 Scene from *Tristan and Isolde,* Act II. This is the Bayreuth staging designed and produced by Wagner's grandson, Wieland Wagner. First mounted in 1962, the production starred Wolfgang Windgassen and Birgit Nilsson as the lovers. The abstract sets and complex lighting have influenced much stage design since then.

under the sway of his intoxicating music it is difficult to resist. The sense of passion awakened but unfulfilled is expressed in the famous opening bars of the Prelude, with their theme that yearns upward and the discords that dissolve into one another only to hang unresolved in the air:

343 Thomas Phillips. *Lord Byron in Albanian Costume*. 1814. Oil on canvas, 29½ × 24½″ (75 × 62 cm). National Portrait Gallery, London. Byron is shown during his first visit to Greece, appropriately dressed for the role of romantic sympathizer with exotic lands and peoples.

has a greater knowledge of human nature, and a more comprehensive soul" than ordinary people. Rejecting artificiality and stylization, Wordsworth aimed to make his poetry communicate directly in easily comprehensible terms. His principal theme was the relation between human beings and nature, which he explored by thinking back calmly on experiences that had earlier produced a violent emotional reaction: his famous "emotion recollected in tranquility."

Wordsworth's emotion recollected in tranquility is in strong contrast to the poetry of George Gordon, Lord Byron (1788–1824), who filled both his life and work with the same moody, passionate frenzy of activity [343]. Much of his time was spent wandering throughout Europe, where he became a living symbol of the unconventional, homeless, tormented romantic hero who has come to be called Byronic after him. Much of his flamboyant behavior was no doubt calculated to produce the effect it did, but his personality must indeed have been striking for no less a figure than Goethe to describe him as "a personality of such eminence as has never been before and is not likely to come again." Byron's sincere commitment to struggles for liberty like the Greek war of independence against the Turks can be judged by the fact that he died while actually on military duty in Greece.

Percy Bysshe Shelley (1792–1822), who like Byron spent many of his most creative years in Italy, lived a life of continual turmoil. After being expelled from Oxford for publishing his atheist views, he espoused the cause of anarchy and eloped with the daughter of one of its chief philosophical advocates. The consequent public scandal, coupled with ill health and critical hostility to his works, gave him a sense of bitterness and pessimism that lasted until his death by drowning.

Shelley's brilliant mind and restless temperament produced poetry that united extremes of feeling, veering from the highest pitch of exultant joy to the most extreme despondency. His belief in the possibility of human perfection is expressed in his greatest work, *Prometheus Unbound* (1820), where the means of salvation is love, the love of human beings for one another expressed in the last movement of Beethoven's *Ninth Symphony*, rather than the redeeming female love of Goethe and Wagner. His most accessible works, however, are probably the short lyrics in which he seized a fleeting moment of human emotion and captured it by his poetic imagination.

Even Shelley's sensitivity to the poetic beauty of language was surpassed by that of John Keats (1795–1821), whose life, clouded by unhappy love and by the tuberculosis that killed him so tragically young, inspired poetry of rare poignance and sensitivity. In his *Odes* (lyric poems of strong feeling), in particular, he conveys both the glory and the tragedy of human existence and dwells almost longingly on the peace of death. In the wonderful "Ode to a Nightingale" the song of a bird comes to represent a permanent beauty beyond human grasp. The sensuous images, the intensity of emotion, and the flowing rhythm join to produce a magical effect.

The Novel

Although great novels have been written in our own time, the 19th century probably marked the high point in the creation of fiction. Increase in literacy and a rise in the general level of education resulted in a public eager for entertainment and instruction, and the success of such writers as Charles Dickens and Leo Tolstoy was due in large measure to their ability to combine the two. The best of 19th-century novels were those rare phenomena, great works of art that achieved popularity in their own day. Many of them are still able to enthrall the modern reader by their humanity and insight.

344 Auguste Charpentier. *George Sand*. Musée Carnavalet, Paris. This portrait shows the author at the time she first met Chopin, when she was 32. Note her large, lustrous eyes, which impressed even her detractors by their beauty.

Most of the leading novelists of the mid-19th century wrote within a tradition of realism that came gradually to replace the more self-centered vision of romanticism. Instead of describing an imaginary world of their own creation, they looked outward to find inspiration in the day-to-day events of real life. The increasing social problems produced by industrial and urban development produced not merely a lament for the spirit of the times but a passionate desire for the power to change them as well. In some cases writers were able to combine a romantic style with a social conscience, as in the case of the French novelist Victor Hugo (1802–1885), whose *Les Misérables* (1862) describes the plight of the miserable victims of society's injustices. The hero of the novel, Jean Valjean, is an exconvict who is rehabilitated through the agency of human sympathy and pity. Hugo provides graphic descriptions of the squalor and suffering of the poor, but his high-flown rhetorical style is essentially romantic.

Increasingly, however, writers found that they could best do justice to the problems of existence by adopting a more naturalistic style and describing their characters' lives in realistic terms. One of the most subtle attacks on contemporary values is *Madame Bovary* (1856–1857) by Gustave Flaubert (1821–1880). Flaubert's contempt for bourgeois society finds expression in his portrait of Emma Bovary, who tries to discover in her own provincial life the romantic love she reads about in novels. Her shoddy affairs and increasing debts lead to an inevitably dramatic conclusion. Flaubert is at his best in portraying the banality of her everyday existence.

Honoré de Balzac (1799–1850) was the most versatile of all French novelists. He created a series of some ninety novels and stories, under the general title of *The Human Comedy,* in which many of the same characters appear more than once. Above all a realist, Balzac depicted the social and political currents of his time while imposing on them a sense of artistic unity. His novels are immensely addictive. The reader who finds in one of them a reference to characters or events described in another novel hastens there to be led on to a third, and so on. Balzac thus succeeds in creating a fictional world that seems, by a characteristically romantic paradox, more real than historical reality.

Among the leading literary figures of Balzac's Paris, and a personal friend of Balzac himself, was the remarkable Aurore Dupin (1804–1876), better known by her pseudonym George Sand [344]. This redoubtable defender of women's rights and attacker of male privilege used her novels to wage war on many of the accepted conventions of society. In her very first novel, *Lélia* (1833) she attacked, among other institutions, the church, marriage, the laws of property, and the double standard of morality whereby women were condemned for doing what was condoned for men.

Unconventional in her own life, Sand became the lover of Chopin, with whom she lived from 1838 to 1847. Her autobiographical novel *Lucrezia Floriani* (1846) chronicles as thinly disguised fiction the remarkable course of this relationship albeit very much from its author's point of view.

If France was one of the great centers of 19th-century fiction, another was Russia, where Leo Tolstoy (1828–1910) produced, among other works, two huge novels of international stature, *War and Peace* (1863–1869) and *Anna Karenina* (1873–1877). The first is mainly set against the background of Napoleon's invasion of Russia in 1812. Among the vast array of characters is the Rostov family, aristocratic but far from wealthy, who, together with their acquaintances, have their lives permanently altered by the great historical events through which they live. Tolstoy even emphasizes the way in which the course of the war affects his characters by combining figures he created for the novel with real historical personages, including Napoleon himself, and allowing them to meet.

At the heart of the novel is the young and impressionable Natasha Rostov, whose own confused love life seems to reflect the confusion of the times. Yet its philosophy is profoundly optimistic, in spite of the tragedies of Natasha's own life and the horrors of war that surround her. Her final survival and triumph represent the glorification of the irrational forces of life, which she symbolizes as the "natural person," over sophisticated and rational civilization. Tolstoy's high regard for irrationality and contempt for reason link him with other 19th-century romantics, and his ability to analyze character through the presentation of emotionally significant detail and to sweep the reader up in the panorama of historical events make *War and Peace* the most important work of Russian realistic fiction.

Toward the end of his life Tolstoy gave up his successful career and happy family life to undertake a mystical search for the secret of universal love. Renouncing his property, he began to wear peasant dress and went to work in the fields, although at the time of his death he was still searching in vain for peace. Russia's other great novelist, Feodor Dostoyevsky (1821–1881), although he died before Tolstoy, had far more in common with the late 19th century than with the romantic movement, and he is accordingly discussed in Chapter 16.

The riches of the English 19th-century novel are almost unlimited. They range from the profoundly intellectual and absorbing works of George Eliot (1819–1880), the pen name of Mary Ann Evans, to *Wuthering Heights* (1847), the only novel by Emily Brontë (1818–1848) and one of the most dramatic and passionate pieces of fiction ever written. The book's brilliant evocation of atmosphere and violent emotion produces a shattering effect. Like the two already mentioned, many of the leading novelists of the time were women, and the variety of their works soon puts to flight any facile notions about the feminine approach to literature. Elizabeth Gaskell (1810–1865), for example, was one of the leading social critics of the day; her novels study the effects of industrialization on the poor.

If one figure stands out in the field of the English novel, it is Charles Dickens (1812–1870), immensely popular in his own lifetime and widely read ever since. It is regrettable that Dickens' best-known novel, *A Tale of Two Cities* (1859), is one of his least characteristic, since its melodramatic and not totally successful historical reconstruction of the French

345 George Cruikshank. *"Please sir, I want some more."* 1838. From *Oliver Twist, or The Parish Boy's Progress* by "Boz," published by Richard Bentley, London. New York Public Library. In the workhouse, young Oliver Twist dares to ask for a second bowl of gruel. George Cruikshank (1792–1878), a famed illustrator and caricaturist of the 19th century, illustrated more than 850 books; probably his best-known work is that for Oliver Twist.

Revolution may have deterred potential readers from exploring the wealth of humor, emotion, and imagination in his more successful books. Each of Dickens' novels creates its own world, peopled by an incredible array of characters individualized by their ticks and quirks of personality. His ability to move us from laughter to tears and back again gives his work a continual human appeal, although it has won him the censure of some of the severer critics.

Throughout his life Dickens was an active campaigner against social injustices and used his books to focus on individual institutions and their evil effects. *Oliver Twist* (1837–1838) attacked the treatment of the poor in workhouses and revealed Dickens' view of crime as the manifestation of a general failing in society [345]. In *Hard Times* (1854) he turned, like Mrs. Gaskell, to the evils of industrialization and pointed out some of the harm that misguided attempts at education can do.

Romantic Art

Painting and Architecture in France

Although the events of the French Revolution and Napoleon's subsequent dictatorship had an immediate impact on artists, writers, and musicians outside France, their effect on French artists was more complex. As we have seen earlier in this chapter, David was never able to throw off the influence of neoclassicism, and his immediate successors had a hard time finding a style that could do justice to romantic themes while remaining within neoclassical limits. One solution was offered by Anne-Louis Girodet-Trioson (1767–1824), whose painting *The Entombment of Atala* [346] depicts a highly romantic subject acted out, as it were, by classical figures.

The subject is from a popular novel by the French romantic novelist René de Chateaubriand (1768–1848) and depicts the burial of its heroine, Atala, in the American wilderness where the book is set. The other figures are her Indian lover, Choctas, and a priest from a nearby mission in the Florida swamps. The story of the painting therefore contains just about every conceivable element of romanticism: an exotic location, emphasis on personal emotion, the theme of unfulfilled love. Girodet provides for his characters a romantic setting, with its dramatic light and mysterious jungle background, but the figures themselves are idealized in a thoroughly classical way. Atala's wan beauty and elegant drapery and the muscular nudity of her lover are obviously reminiscent of classical models. Only the mysterious figure of the old priest provides a hint of romantic gloom.

It took a real-life disaster and a major national scandal to inspire the first genuinely romantic French painting. In 1816 a French government vessel, the *Medusa,* bound for Africa with an incompetent political appointee as captain, was wrecked in a storm. The 149 passengers and crew members were crowded onto a hastily improvised raft that drifted for days under the equatorial sun. Hunger, thirst, madness, and even, it was rumored, cannibalism had reduced the survivors to fifteen by the time the raft was finally sighted.

The young French painter Théodore Géricault (1791–1824), whose original enthusiasm for Napoleon had been replaced by adherence to the liberal cause, depicted the moment of the sighting of the raft in his painting *Raft of the Medusa* [347]. Horror at the suffering of the victims and anger at the corruption and incompetence of the ship's officers (and their political supporters) inspired a work that, from its first exhibition in 1819, created a sensation in artistic cir-

346 Anne-Louis Girodet-Trioson. *The Entombment of Atala.* 1808. Oil on canvas, 6′11¾″ × 8′9″ (2.13 × 2.67 m). Louvre, Paris. The anticlassical nature of the subject is emphasized by the Christian symbolism of the two crosses, one on Atala's breast and the other rather improbably placed high up in the jungle, outside the cave.

cles. Even the general public flocked to see a painting that so dramatically illustrated contemporary events. In the process they became exposed to the principles of romantic painting. Géricault's work deliberately rejects the ideal beauty of classical models. The agonizing torment of the survivors is powerfully rendered, and the dramatic use of lighting underlines the intense emotions of the scene.

When Géricault died following a fall from a horse, the cause of romanticism was taken up by his young friend and admirer, Eugène Delacroix (1798–1863), whose name has become synonymous with romantic painting. Although the subjects of many of his paintings involve violent emotions, Delacroix himself seems to have been aloof and reserved. He never married, or for that matter formed any lasting relationship. His *Journal* reveals him as a man constantly stimulated by ideas and experience but he preferred to live his life through his art, a true romantic. Among his few close friends was Chopin; his portrait of the composer [see figure 337, page 367] seems to symbolize the introspective creative vision of the romantic artist.

Like his mentor Géricault, Delacroix supported the liberal movements of the day. His painting *Massacre at Chios* [348] depicted a particularly brutal event in the Greek War of Independence. In 1824, the same year in which Lord Byron had died while supporting the Greek cause, the Turks massacred some 90 percent of the population of the Greek island of Chios, and Delacroix' painting on the subject was intended

347 Theodore Géricault. *Raft of the Medusa*. 1818. Oil on canvas, 16'1¼" × 23'6" (4.91 × 7.16 m). Louvre, Paris. Note the careful composition of this huge work, built around a line that leads from the bottom left corner to the top right, where a survivor desperately waves his shirt.

to rouse popular indignation. It certainly roused the indignation of the traditional artists of the day, one of whom dubbed it "the massacre of painting," principally because of its revolutionary use of color. Whereas David and other neoclassical painters had drawn their forms and then filled them in with color, Delacroix used color itself to create form. The result is a much more fluid use of paint.

Lord Byron figures again in another of Delacroix's best-known paintings, since it was on one of the poet's works that the artist based *The Death of Sardanapalus* [Plate 27, page 359]. The Assyrian king, faced with the destruction of his palace by the Medes, decided to prevent his enemies from enjoying his possessions after his death by ordering that his wives, horses, and dogs be killed and their bodies piled up, together with his treasures, at the foot of the funeral pyre he intended for himself. The opulent, violent theme is treated with appropriate drama; the savage brutality of the foreground contrasts with the lonely, brooding figure of the king reclining on his couch above. Over the whole scene, however, hovers an air of unreality, even of fantasy, as if Delacroix is trying to convey not so much the sufferings of the victims as the intensity of his own imagination.

Although with Delacroix's advocacy romanticism acquired a vast popular following, not all French artists joined the romantic cause. A fierce and bitter rear-guard action was fought by the leading neoclassical proponents, headed by Jean Auguste Dominque Ingres (1780–1867)—who was, in his own very dif-

below: 348 Eugène Delacroix. *Massacre at Chios*. 1824. Oil on canvas, 13'7" × 11'10" (4.19 × 3.64 m). Louvre, Paris. Rather than depict a single scene, the painter chose to combine several episodes, contrasting the static misery of the figures on the left with a swirl of activity on the right.

349 Jean Auguste Dominique Ingres. *Jupiter and Thetis*. 1811. Oil on canvas, 10'10" × 8'5" (3.3 × 2.57 m). Musée Granet, Aix-en-Provence. The figure of Jupiter, with his youthful face surrounded by a vast wreath of beard and hair, is highly unconventional. Thetis' arms and throat are purposely distorted to emphasize her supplication.

350 Jean Auguste Dominique Ingres. *La Comtesse d'Haussonville*. 1845. Oil on canvas, 4'5½" × 3'¼" (1.36 × .92 m). Frick Collection, New York. The artist seems to have been more interested in his subject's dress, which is marvelously painted, than in her personality. The reflection in the mirror reinforces the highly polished air of the painting.

351 Honoré Daumier. *Le Ventre législatif (The Legislative Belly)*. 1834. Lithograph, 11¹/₁₆ × 17¹/₁₆" (28.1 × 43.3 cm). Philadelphia Museum of Art (gift of Carl Zigrosser). Although obviously caricatures, the politicians ranged in tiers are recognizable as individual members of the legislative assembly of the time.

352 Gustave Courbet. *The Studio: A Real Allegory of the Last Seven Years of My Life*. 1855. Oil on canvas, 11'9¾" × 19'6⅝" (3.6 × 5.96 m). Louvre, Paris. Although most of the figures can be convincingly identified as symbols or real people, no one has ever satisfactorily explained the small boy admiring Courbet's work or the cat at his feet.

ferent way, as great a painter as Delacroix. The self-appointed defender of classicism, Ingres once said of Delacroix that "his art is the complete expression of an incomplete intelligence." Characteristically, his war against romantic painting was waged vindictively and on the most personal terms. Now that the dust has settled, however, it becomes clear that Ingres himself, far from religiously adhering to classical doctrines, was unable to suppress a romantic streak of his own. His extraordinary painting *Jupiter and Thetis* [349] deals with an event from Homer's *Iliad* and shows Thetis, the mother of Achilles, begging the father of gods and mortals to avenge an insult by the Greek commander Agamemnon to her son by allowing the Trojans to be victorious. The subject may be classical, but Ingres' treatment of it is strikingly personal, even bizarre. Sensuality blends with an almost hallucinatory sharpness of detail to create a memorable if curiously disturbing image. Even in his more conventional portraits [350] Ingres' stupendous technique endows subject and setting with an effect that is the very reverse of academic.

The style that in the end succeeded in replacing the

full-blown romanticism of Delacroix and his followers was not that of the neoclassical school, with its emphasis on idealism, but a style that stressed precisely the reverse qualities. The greatest French painters of the second half of the 19th century were realists, who used the everyday events of the world around them to express their views of life. One of the first realist artists was Honoré Daumier (1808–1879), who followed the example of Goya in using his work to criticize the evils of society in general and government in particular. In *The Legislative Body*—or, more accurately, *Belly* [351]—he produced a powerful image of the greed and corruption of political opportunists that has lost neither its bitterness nor, unfortunately, its relevance.

Equally political was the realism of Gustave Courbet (1819–1877), a fervent champion of the working class, whose ability to identify with ordinary people won him the label of Socialist. Courbet tried to correct this political impression of his artistic and philosophical position in a vast and not entirely successful allegorical work, *The Studio* [352]. Like Goya's royal portrait [see figure 334], the painting deliberately

353 Charles Garnier. Opéra, Paris. 1861–1875.
The incredibly rich and complex ornamentation has earned this style of architecture the label neobaroque.

evokes memories of Velásquez' *Las Meninas* [see Plate 22, page 307], although the artist is now placed firmly in the center of the picture, hard at work on a landscape, inspired by a nude model who may represent Realism or Truth. The various other figures symbolize the forces that made up Courbet's world. There is some doubt as to the precise identification of many of them, and it is not even clear that Courbet himself had any single allegory in mind. The total effect of the confusion, unintentional though it may be, is to underline the essentially romantic origins of Courbet's egocentric vision.

Neither romanticism nor its realistic vision made much impression on architectural styles in 19th-century France. French architects retained a fondness for classical forms and abandoned them only to revive the styles of the Renaissance. In some of the public buildings designed to meet the needs of the age, however, the elaborate decoration makes use of classical elements to achieve an ornateness of effect that is not very far from the opulent splendor of Delacroix' *Death of Sardanapalus*.

The most ornate of all 19th-century French buildings was the Paris Opera [353] of Charles Garnier (1824–1898). The new opera house had to be sufficiently large to accommodate the growing public for opera and sufficiently ostentatious to satisfy its taste.

Garnier's building, designed in 1861 and finally opened in 1875, makes use of classical ornamentation like Corinthian columns and huge winged Victories, but the total effect is highly unclassical, a riot of confusion that would surely have appalled classical and Renaissance architects alike.

Painting in Germany and England

Unlike their French counterparts, romantic artists in both England and Germany were particularly attracted by the possibilities offered by landscape painting. The emotional range of their work illustrates once again the versatility of the romantic style. The German painter Caspar David Friedrich (1774–1840) seems to have drawn some of his Gothic gloom from a tradition that had been strong in Germany since the Middle Ages, although he uses it to romantic effect. His *Cloister Graveyard in the Snow* [354], in fact, illustrates a number of romantic preoccupations, with its ruined medieval architecture and melancholy dream-like atmosphere.

The English painter John Constable (1776–1837), on the other hand, shared the deep and warm love of nature expressed by Wordsworth. His paintings convey not only the physical beauties of the landscape but also a sense of the less tangible aspects of the natural world. In *Stoke-by-Nayland* [355], for example, we not only see the peaceful rustic scene, with its squat, comforting church in the background, but we can even sense the light and quality of atmosphere, prompted by the billowing clouds that, responsible for the fertility of the countryside, seem about to release their moisture.

Constable's use of color pales besides that of his contemporary, Joseph Mallord William Turner (1775–1851). In a sense, the precise subjects of Turner's paintings are irrelevant. All his mature works use light, color, and movement to represent a cosmic union of the elements in which earth, sky, fire, and water dissolve into one another and every trace of the material world disappears. His technique is seen at its most characteristic in *The Slave Ship* [Plate 28, page 360].

Like Géricault's *Raft of the Medusa* [see figure 347], Turner's *Slave Ship* deals with a social disgrace of the time; in this case the horrifyingly common habit of the captains of ships loaded with slaves to jettison their entire cargo if an epidemic broke out. Turner only incidentally illustrates his specific subject—the detail of drowning figures in the lower right corner seems to have been added as an afterthought—and concentrates instead on conveying his vision of the grandeur and mystery of the universe.

right: 354 Caspar David Friedrich. *Cloister Graveyard in the Snow.* 1810. Oil on panel, 3'11⅝" × 5'10" (1.21 × 1.78 m). Formerly Nationalgalerie, Berlin (now lost). The vast bare trees in the foreground and the ruined Gothic abbey behind emphasize the insignificance of the human figures.

below: 355 John Constable. *Stoke-by-Nayland.* 1836. Oil on canvas, 4'1½" × 5'6¾" (1.26 × 1.69 m). Art Institute of Chicago (W. W. Kimball Collection). Note the contrast between the use of architecture here and in figure 354. Unlike Friedrich's gaunt ruin, Constable's church adds a final peaceful note to the quiet Suffolk scene.

The Romantic Era in America

The early history of the arts in America was intimately linked to developments in Europe. England, in particular, by virtue of its common tongue and political connections, exerted an influence on literature and painting that even the War of Independence did not end. American writers sought publishers and readers there, and modeled their style on that of English writers. American painters went to London to study, sometimes with less than happy results. John Singleton Copley (1738–1815), for example, produced a series of portraits in a simple, direct style of his own [356] before leaving Boston for England,

356 John Singleton Copley. *Portrait of Nathaniel Hurd.* c. 1765. Oil on canvas, 30 × 25½" (76 × 65 cm). Cleveland Museum of Art (gift of the John Huntington Art and Polytechnic Trust). In this portrait of a friend Copley avoids technical tricks. The result is an attractive simplicity of style that still lets him reveal something of the subject's personality.

357 Nathaniel Currier. *First Appearance of Jenny Lind in America: At Castle Garden, September 11, 1850,* detail. 1850. Lithograph. J. Clarence Davies Collection, Museum of the City of New York. The great soprano, inevitably known as the Swedish Nightingale, made a very successful tour of America under the management of P. T. Barnum in 1850–1851, during which she earned the staggering sum of $120,000 (multiply by ten for present value). At this first appearance in New York, the total receipts were $26,238. Nathaniel Currier (1813–1888) and James Merritt Ives (1824–1895), who became his partner in 1857, were lithographers who sold thousands of hand-colored prints that show many aspects of 19th-century American life.

where he fell victim to Sir Joshua Reynolds' Grand Manner [see figure 317, page 336]. Of American music we cannot say much, since the earliest American composers confined their attention to settings of hymns and patriotic songs. A recognizably American musical tradition of composition did not develop before the very end of the 19th century, although much earlier European performers found a vast and enthusiastic musical public in the course of their American tours [357].

In the case of literature and the visual arts, the French Revolution provided a change of direction, for revolutionary ties inevitably resulted in the importation of neoclassicism into America. With the dawning of the Romantic Era, however, American artists began to develop for the first time an authentic voice of their own. In many cases they still owed much to European examples. Indeed, the tradition of the expatriate American artist who left home to study in Europe and remained there had been firmly established by the 18th century. Throughout the 19th century writers like Washington Irving (1783–1859) and painters like Thomas Eakins (1844–1916) continued to bring back to America themes and styles they had acquired during their European travels. Something

about the very nature of romanticism, however, with its emphasis on the individual, seemed to fire the American imagination, and so for the first time American artists began to produce work that was both a genuine product of their native land and at the same time of international stature.

American Literature

In a land where daily existence was lived so close to the wildness and beauty of nature, the romantic attachment to the natural world was bound to make a special appeal. The romantic concept of the transcendental unity of humans and nature was quickly taken up in the early 19th century by a whole group of American writers who even called themselves the Transcendentalists. Borrowing ideas from Kant and from his English followers such as Coleridge and Wordsworth, they developed notions of an order of truth that transcends what we can perceive by our physical senses and which unites the entire world. One of their leading representatives, Ralph Waldo Emerson (1803–1882), underlined the particular importance of the natural world for American writers in his essay *The American Scholar,* first published in 1837. In calling for the development of a national literature, Emerson laid down as a necessary condition for its success that his compatriots should draw their inspiration from the wonders of their own country. A few years later he was to write: "America is a poem in our eyes; its ample geography dazzles the imagination, and it will not wait long for metres."

Emerson always tried to make his own work "smell of pines and resound with the hum of insects," but although his ideas have exerted a profound effect on the development of American culture, Emerson himself was a better thinker than creative artist. Far more successful as a literary practitioner of Transcendentalist principles was Henry David Thoreau (1817–1862), whose masterpiece *Walden* (1854) uses his day-to-day experiences as he lived in solitude on the shore of Walden Pond to draw general conclusions about the nature of existence. Thoreau's passionate support of the freedom of the individual led him to be active in the antislavery movement, and by the end of his life he had moved from belief in passive resistance to open advocacy of violence against slavery.

Ideas of freedom, tolerance, and spiritual unity reached their most complete poetic expression in the works of America's first great poet, Walt Whitman (1819–1892). His first important collection of poems was published in 1855 under the title *Leaves of Grass.* From then until his death he produced edition after edition, retaining the same title but gradually adding many new poems and revising the old ones.

Whitman was defiantly, even aggressively, an American poet, yet the central theme of most of his work was the importance of the individual. The contradiction this involves serves as a reminder of the essentially romantic character of Whitman's mission, since by describing the details of his own feelings and reactions he hoped to communicate a sense of the essential oneness of the human condition. Much of the time the sheer vitality and flow of his language helps to make his experiences our own, although many of his earlier readers were horrified at the explicit sexual descriptions in some of his poems. Above all, Whitman was a fiery defender of freedom and democracy. His vision of the human race united with itself and with the universe has a special significance for the late 20th century.

The essential optimism of the Transcendentalists, especially as interpreted by Whitman, is absent from the work of the two great American novelists of the 19th century, Nathaniel Hawthorne (1804–1864) and Herman Melville (1819–1891). Hawthorne in particular was deeply concerned with the apparently ineradicable evil in a society dedicated to progress. In *The Scarlet Letter* (1850), his first major success, and in many of his short stories he explored the conflicts between traditional values and the drive for change.

Melville imitated Hawthorne's example in combining realism with allegory and in dealing with profound moral issues. His subjects and style are both very different, however. *Moby-Dick* (1851), his masterpiece, is often hailed as the greatest of all American works of fiction. It shares with Goethe's *Faust* the theme of the search for truth and self-discovery, which Melville works out by using the metaphor of the New England whaling industry. Both Melville and Hawthorne were at their greatest when using uniquely American settings and characters to shed light on universal human experience.

American Painting

Under the influence of the Transcendentalists, landscape painting in America took on a new significance. Emerson reminded the artist who set out to paint a natural scene that "landscape has a beauty for his eye because it expresses a thought which to him is good, and this because the same power which sees through his eyes is seen in that spectacle." Natural beauty, in other words, is moral beauty, and both of them demonstrate the transcendental unity of the universe.

The earliest painters of landscapes intended to glorify the wonders of nature are known collectively as the Hudson River School. The foundations of their style were laid by Thomas Cole (1801–1848), himself born in England, whose later paintings combine grandeur of effect with accurate observation of details. His *Genesee Scenery* [358] is particularly successful in capturing a sense of atmosphere and presence.

By mid-century a new approach to landscape painting had developed. Generally called luminism, it aimed to provide the sense of artistic anonymity Emerson and other Transcendentalists demanded. In a way this is the exact antithesis of romanticism. Instead of sharing with the viewer their own reactions, the luminists tried by realism to eliminate their own presence and let nothing stand between the viewer and the scenes. Yet the results, far from achieving only a photographic realism, have an utterly characteristic and haunting beauty that has no real parallel in European art of the time. The painting *Lake George* [Plate 29, page 360] by Martin J. Heade (1819–1904), one of the leading luminists, seems almost to foreshadow the surrealist art of the 20th century.

358 Thomas Cole. *Genesee Scenery (Landscape with Waterfall)*. 1847. Oil on canvas, 4'3" × 3'3½" (1.3 × 1 m). Museum of Art, Rhode Island School of Design, Providence (Jesse Metcalf Fund). One of Cole's last works, this shows a meticulous care for detail that is never allowed to detract from the broad sweep of the view.

The two great American painters of the later 19th century, Winslow Homer (1836–1910) and Thomas Eakins (1844–1916), both used the luminist approach to realism as a basis for their own very individual styles. In the case of Homer, the realism of his early paintings was in large measure the result of his work as a documentary artist, recording the events of the Civil War. His style underwent a notable change as he became exposed to contemporary French impressionist painting (discussed in Chapter 16). His mysterious *Eagle Head* [359], is certainly far more than a naturalistic depiction of three women and a dog on a

361 Thomas Eakins. *Miss Van Buren.* c. 1889–1891.
Oil on canvas, 45 × 32″ (114 × 81 cm). Phillips Collection,
Washington. Note how, in contrast to the portraits by Ingres
(figure **350,** page 378) and Copley (figure **356,** page 381),
Eakins achieves deep feeling and sensitivity by the angle of
his subject's head and her position in the chair.

beach. By the way in which he has positioned the figures, Homer suggests rather than spells out greater emotional depths than initially meet the eye. The sense of restrained drama occurs elsewhere in his work, while the sea became a growing obsession with him and provided virtually the only subject of his last works.

Thomas Eakins used realism as a means of achieving objective truth. His pursuit of scientific accuracy led him to make a particular study of the possibilities of photography. Animals and, more particularly, humans in motion continually fascinated him. This trait can be observed in *The Swimming Hole* [360], where the variety of poses and actions produces a series of individual anatomical studies rather than a unified picture.

In his own day Eakins' blunt insistence on accuracy of perception did not endear him to a public that demanded more glamorous art. Yet if many of his works seem essentially antiromantic in spirit, foreshadowing as they do the age of mechanical precision, in his portraits he returns to the romantic tradition of expressing emotions by depicting them. The sitter in *Miss Van Buren* [361], as in most of his portraits, turns her eyes away from us, rapt in profound inner contemplation. The artist's own emotional response to the mood of his subject is made visible in his painting.

Painters such as Homer and Eakins, like Whitman and other writers discussed here, are important in the history of American culture not only for the value of their individual works. Their achievements demonstrated that American society could at last produce creative figures capable of absorbing the European cultural experience without losing their individuality. From this time on there could be no doubt that American artists and writers had their own distinctive contribution to make to the Western cultural tradition.

Questions for Further Discussion

1. The 19th century was marked by a notable change in the role and social position of the creative artist. What is the function of the artist in our present culture? What factors have gone to produce it? To what extent (if at all) do artists have any political influence today?
2. It is often said that one of the reasons for the popularity of music in the 19th century was the large number of people who played and sang at home for the entertainment of themselves and their friends. How much does actual involvement in an art for pleasure—playing an instrument, or painting, for example—help enjoyment?
3. The literature of the 19th century in general and the novels of Dickens in particular are often accused of being "too sentimental." What does this mean? Is it possible to distinguish between *sentiment* and *sentimentality*?
4. Many great artists, both in the 19th century and at other times, have suffered from physical disabilities (Beethoven, Goya) or chronic ill health (Chopin, Keats). How is physical suffering likely to affect the perceptions of a creative artist?
5. The 19th-century vision of romantic, ideal love is very different from the 19th and 20th century emphasis on physical passion and its gratification. What kind of psychological causes and effects does this suggest? Is one attitude more "normal" than the other?
6. The ease and speed of railway travel revolutionized life in Europe during the second half of the 19th century. What comparable effect has jet travel had on American life in the second half of the 20th? What are the principal gains and losses—if any?

GENERAL EVENTS	LITERATURE & PHILOSOPHY	ART

1860

GROWTH OF BIG BUSINESS

1876 Speech first transmitted through telephone by Alexander Graham Bell

1880-1914 Height of European colonialism

1886 Dedication of Statue of Liberty, presented by France to America

1866 Dostoyevsky, *Crime and Punishment*

1870-1914 New areas explored in writing: impact of subconscious on human behavior, the role of women

1863 Manet exhibits *Déjeuner sur l'Herbe* to public outrage

1874 Impressionism emerges when Monet and others exhibit at Café Guerbois, Paris; *Impression-Sunrise* (1873)

1875 Monet, *Red Boats at Argenteuil*

1876 Renoir, *Le Moulin de la Galette*

1879 First performance of Ibsen's realistic drama *A Doll's House*

c. 1880 Postimpressionists reject impressionism

1881-1882 Manet, *Bar at the Folies-Bergère*

1884-1886 Seurat, *A Sunday Afternoon on the Island of La Grande Jatte*

1881 Death of Dostoyevsky

1883-1892 Nietzsche, *Thus Spoke Zarathustra*

c. 1885 Protocubist experiments of Cézanne; *Still Life with Commode*

1886 Rodin, *The Kiss;* Degas, *The Tub*

1888 Van Gogh, *The Night Café*

1889 Van Gogh, *The Starry Night;* Cassatt, *Baby in Dark Blue Suit*

1890

HEIGHT OF EUROPEAN COLONIALISM

1890-1914 Industrialization of Russia

1899-1902 Boer War

1891 Shaw, drama critic for *Saturday Review,* champions Ibsen

1893 Wilde, *Salome*

1894 Kate Chopin, *The Story of an Hour*

1899 Kate Chopin, *The Awakening*

1891 Gauguin, *Ia Orana Maria*

1893 Munch, *The Scream;* Rodin begins *Balzac*

1894-1898 Kollwitz, *The Weavers,* etching based on Hauptmann play

c. 1902-1906 Cézanne paints last series of landscapes depicting *Mont Sainte-Victoire*

1900

RISE OF GERMAN MILITARY POWER

1901 Death of Queen Victoria of England; reign of Edward VII begins. First message sent over Marconi's transatlantic wireless telegraph

1903 Wright brothers make first airplane flight

1904 Russo-Japanese War

1905 First Revolution breaks out in Russia; Einstein formulates theory of relativity; first motion-picture theater opens in Pittsburgh

1908 Model T touring car introduced by Ford

1914 World War I begins

1900 Freud, *Interpretation of Dreams*

1913 Publication of *Swann's Way,* first volume of Proust's *Remembrance of Things Past;* final volume published posthumously (1927)

1903-1913 German expressionist movement *Die Brücke*

1905 First Fauve exhibition in Paris; Matisse, *The Joy of Living* (1905-1906)

1907-1914 Picasso and Braque develop cubism in Paris

1909 Nolde, *Pentecost;* Rodin, *Portrait of Mahler*

1911 Matisse, *The Red Studio.* German expressionist group *Der Blaue Reiter* formed

1912 Heckel, *Two Men at a Table (To Dostoyevsky)*

1914

16

Toward the Modern Era: 1870-1914

mid-19th cent. Liszt's symphonic poems precursors of *program music*

1886 R. Strauss begins tone poem *Don Juan*

1883 Birth of Gropius

1890-1891 Sullivan, Wainwright Building, St. Louis, first skyscraper

1893 Tchaikovsky, "Pathetique" *Symphony*, precedes composer's suicide. Mahler's *Symphony No. 1 in D*

1894 Debussy, musical impressionist, composes *Prélude à l'après-midi d'un faune*

1895 R. Strauss, *Till Eulenspiegel*

1896 Puccini champions *verisimo* in Italian opera; *La Boheme*

1899 R. Strauss, *A Hero's Life*

1905-1907 Gaudi, Casa Milá, Barcelona

1909 Robie House, Chicago, Frank Lloyd Wright's first big success

1900-1904 Puccini, *Tosca; Madama Butterfly*

1905 First performance of R. Strauss' opera *Salome*, based on Wilde's play; Debussy, *La Mer*

1908 Schoenberg, *Three Piano Pieces*, Op. 11, first major atonal work

1909-1910 Mahler, *Symphony No. 9*

1910-1913 Stravinsky composes *Firebird, Petrouchka, Rite of Spring* for Diaghilev's Ballet Russe in Paris

1911-1915 R. Strauss, *Alpine Symphony*

1912 Schoenberg, *Pierrot Lunaire*

1913 Ravel composes *Daphnis and Chloe* for Diaghilev

Distance lends perspective in human experience. The more intimately we are affected by events, the more difficult it is to evaluate them objectively. Looking back, we can see that the world in which we live, with its great hopes and even greater fears, began to take its present shape in the early years of the 20th century. The First World War of 1914 to 1918 marked an end to almost three thousand years of European political and cultural supremacy as well as the beginning of a world in which events in any corner of the globe could—and still do—have immense consequences for good or ill for the entire human race. The effects on the humanities of so vast a change in direction are the subject of Chapters 17 and 18. Here we will consider some of the causes and early symptoms of the change.

The period in which the modern world was formed is the historical era that directly affects our daily lives and, to repeat, this presents problems in evaluating it. Even though our cultural traditions go back to ancient Greece and Rome, and even though the cataclysmic events of the 20th century have not destroyed the value of centuries of accumulated experience, we naturally feel more intimately linked to the generation of our parents and grandparents than to more distant generations of ancestors of which we are also the product. Nevertheless, our parents and grandparents are the very people whose nearness to us in time and emotional impact makes them and their world more difficult to understand objectively.

Our own responses to the increasing complexity of historical forces during the formative stages of modern culture are still so confused that it is helpful to turn to the reactions of individual artists and thinkers who themselves lived through the times and can to some extent interpret them to us. Further, within the relatively limited sphere of artistic creativity we can observe at work forces that also operated on a much larger scale. As so often in the history of Western civilization, the arts provide a direct and powerful, if incomplete, expression of the spirit of an age—in this case an age that happens to be our own. It may even be that the enduring importance of the humanities as a reflection of human condition is one of the few aspects of Western civilization to survive a century of global turmoil and help us on our way into the 21st century.

362 Ludwig Meidner. *The Eve of the War*. 1914. Stadt. Kunsthalle, Recklinghausen. The distorted faces and violent, heaving composition reflect the spirit of a world on the point of collapse.

The Growing Unrest

By the last quarter of the 19th century there was a widespread if unfocused feeling in Europe that life could not continue as before. Social and political revolutions had replaced the old monarchies with more nearly equitable forms of government. Scientific and technological developments had affected millions of ordinary people, bringing them improved standards of living and a more congenial existence. As a result, a new mood of cheerfulness began to make itself felt in the great cities of Europe; in Paris, for example, the period became known as the *belle époque* (beautiful age).

But the apparent gaiety was only superficial. The price of the immense changes that made it possible had been unrest and violence, and the forces that had been built up to achieve them remained in existence. Thus, in a period of nominal peace, most of the leading countries in Europe were maintaining huge armies and introducing compulsory military service. Long before 1914 a growing mood of frustration led many people to assume that sooner or later war would break out—a belief that certainly did not help to avert it [362].

The many historical causes of this mood are beyond the scope of this book but some of the more important underlying factors are easy enough to perceive. In the first place, the growth of democratic systems of government had taught increasing numbers of people that they had a right to share in the material benefits made possible by the industrial revolution. Discontent grew on all sides. In the richest countries in Europe—France, England, and Germany—the poor compared their lot with that of the more affluent. At the same time, in the poorer European countries, including Ireland, Spain, Portugal, and all of Eastern Europe, everyone looked with envy at their wealthier neighbors. Even more significantly, those vast continents that the empire-building European powers were introducing to European civilization for the first time, including parts of Africa, Asia, and South America, began increasingly to resent European domination.

In the second place, the scientific progress that made possible improvements in people's lives created problems of its own. New medical advances reduced the rate of infant mortality, cured hitherto fatal diseases, and prolonged life expectancy. As a result the population of most of Europe soared to a record level, creating food and housing shortages. New forms of transport and new industrial processes

brought vast numbers of workers to the cities. In consequence, the lives of many people were uprooted and their daily existence became anonymous and impersonal.

Third, the growth of a world financial market, dependent primarily on the value of gold, gave new power to the forces of big business. In turn, the rise of capitalism, fiercely opposed by the growing forces of socialism [363], provoked the development of trade unions to protect the interests of the workers.

Finally, at a time when so many political and social forces were pitted against one another there seemed to be no certainty on which to fall back. Religion had lost its hold over intellectual circles by the 18th century, and by the end of the 19th century strong religious faith and its manifestation in churchgoing had begun to fall off drastically at all levels of society. The newly developing fields of anthropology and psychology, far from replacing religion, provided fresh controversy with their radically different explanations of human life and behavior.

In a state of such potential explosiveness it is hardly surprising that a major collapse of the fabric of European civilization seemed inevitable. Only in

363 Käthe Kollwitz. *March of the Weavers,* from *The Weavers Cycle.* 1897. Etching, 8⅜ × 11⅝″ (21 × 29 cm). University of Michigan Museum of Art, Ann Arbor. This print is based on a play, *The Weavers,* by the German playwright Gerhart Hauptmann (1862–1946) dealing with the misery and helplessness of both workers and owners in the industrial age. The axes and mattocks in the workers' hands point to the coming violence.

America, where hundreds of thousands of Europeans emigrated in the hope of making a new start, did optimism seem possible [364]. Events were moving at so fast a pace that few thinkers were able to detach themselves from their times and develop a philosophical basis for dealing with them. One of the few who did was Friedrich Nietzsche (1844–1900), whose ominous diagnosis of the state of Western civilization in *Thus Spake Zarathustra* (1883–1892) and other works led him to propose drastic remedies.

For Nietzsche religion, morality, science, and the arts represented merely the fantasies of feeble cowards unable to face reality. The only valid life force, according to Nietzsche, is the "will to power," the energy that casts off all moral restraints in its pursuit of independence. The being who would develop as the outcome of a highly Nietzschean process of evolution is the person who can survive the loss of illusions and, by the free assertion of the will, establish new values of nobility and goodness. Nietzsche called this superior individual an *Übermensch* (literally "overperson"). Like Schopenhauer in the early 19th century (see page 356), Nietzsche is valuable principally for the way in which he anticipated future ideas rather than because he was the leader of a movement. Unfortunately, his concepts were later taken up in a distorted form by many of the would-be world rulers of the 20th century, most notoriously the leaders of Nazi Germany.

Cut adrift from the security of religion or philosophy, the arts responded to the restless mood of the times by searching for new subjects and styles. Often these subjects and styles challenged principles that had been accepted for centuries. In music traditional concepts of harmony and rhythm were first radically extended and then, by some composers at least, completely discarded. In literature new areas of experience were explored, including the impact of the subconscious on human behavior, and traditional attitudes like the role of women were examined afresh. In the visual arts, the impressionists found a totally new way of looking at the world, which in turn opened up other exciting new fields of artistic expression. Whatever their defects, the formative years of the modern world were certainly not dull with respect to the arts.

New Movements in Art

Something of the feverish activity in the visual arts during this period can be gauged by the sheer number of movements and styles that followed one another in rapid succession: impressionism, post-impressionism, fauvism, expressionism, culminating in the birth of cubism around the time of World War I. Cubism is discussed in Chapter 17 because of its effects on the whole of 20th-century art, but all the other movements form important stages in the transition from traditional artistic styles to the art of our own time, much of which rejects any attempt at realism in favor of abstract values of line, shape, and color. An understanding of their significance is thus a necessary prerequisite for a full appreciation of modern abstract art. Quite apart from their historical interest, however, the artistic movements of the late 19th and 20th centuries have much visual pleasure to offer.

As so often in the past, the center of artistic activity was Paris, where Édouard Manet (1832–1883)

364 Frédéric Auguste Bartholdi. Statue of Liberty *(Liberty Enlightening the World)*. Constructed and erected in Paris, 1876–1884; disassembled, shipped to New York, re-erected, dedicated 1886. Hammered copper sheets over iron trusswork and armature; height of figure 151' (46 m), total height, including pedestal, above sea level 306' (93 m). This famous monument, which still dominates New York's harbor, became the symbol to European immigrants in the late 19th century of the welcome they would find in the New World. The colossal statue (the head alone is 13'6", or 4.4 m, high) was a gift from France to the United States. It was designed by the French sculptor Frédéric Auguste Bartholdi (1834–1904); its supporting framework was designed by the French engineer Gustave Eiffel (1832–1923), known mainly for his Eiffel Tower in Paris, France's national monument, completed in 1889.

365 Édouard Manet. *Le Déjeuner sur L'Herbe.* 1863. Oil on canvas, 7'3¾" × 8'10⅜" (2.15 × 2.7 m). Louvre, Paris. Manet probably based the landscape on sketches made out-of-doors but painted the figures from models in his studio, something a careful look at the painting seems to confirm.

had created a sensation in 1863 with his painting *Le Déjeuner sur l'Herbe (Luncheon on the Grass)* [365]. Public outcry had been directed against the subject of the painting, which shows a female nude among two fully clothed young men and another clothed female

366 Édouard Manet. *A Bar at the Folies-Bergère.* 1881–1882. Oil on canvas, 3'1½" × 4'3" (.95 × 1.3 m). Courtauld Institute Galleries, London (Courtauld Collection). Note the very impressionistic way in which Manet painted the girl's top-hatted customer, reflected in the mirror at right.

figure. Other artists had combined nude females and clothed males before in a single picture, but Manet's scene has a particular air of reality; the way the unclad young woman stares out from the canvas and the two smartly dressed young men appear nonchalantly indifferent to her condition can still take the spectator by surprise. The true break with tradition, however, lay not in the picture's subject but its style. The artist is much less interested in telling us what his characters are doing than in showing us how he sees them and their surroundings. Instead of representing them as rounded, three-dimensional forms, he has painted them as a series of broad, flat areas in which the brilliance of color is unmuted.

The massive, almost monumental human form reappears in one of Manet's last paintings, *A Bar at the Folies-Bergère* of 1881 [366], where the barmaid amid her bottles and dishes presents the same solid appearance as the nude in *Déjeuner*. If we glance over her shoulder, however, and look into the mirror as it reflects her back and the crowded scene of which we have temporarily become a part, the style changes. The sharp outlines and fully defined forms of the foreground are replaced by a blur of shapes and colors that conveys the general impression of a crowded theater without reproducing specific details. A comparison between the background of the two pictures makes it clear that between 1863 and 1881 something drastic had occurred in the way painters looked at scenes and then reproduced them.

367 Claude Monet. *Impression: Sunrise.* 1872. Oil on canvas,
19½ × 24½″ (50 × 62 cm). Musée Marmottan, Paris.
Although this was the painting after which the impressionist
movement was named, its use of impressionist techniques is
relatively undeveloped compared with **368** and **369**.

Impressionism

In 1874 a group of young artists organized an exhibition of their work during conversations at the Café Guerbois in Paris. Their unconventional approach to art and their contempt for traditional methods meant that normal avenues of publicity were closed to them; they hoped that the exhibition would succeed in bringing their work to public attention. It certainly did. One of the paintings, *Impression: Sunrise* [367] by Claude Monet (1840–1926), particularly scandalized the more conventional critics, some of whom derisively borrowed its title and nicknamed the whole group impressionists. Within a few years the impressionists had revolutionized European painting.

Although impressionism seemed at the time to represent a radical break with the past, it first developed out of yet another attempt to achieve greater realism, a tradition that had begun at the dawn of the Renaissance with Giotto. The impressionists concentrated, however, on realism of light and color rather than realism of form and sought to reproduce with the utmost fidelity the literal impression an object made on their eyes. If, for example, we look at a house or a human face from a distance, we automatically interpret it on the basis of our mental knowledge, and "see" details that are not really visible. Impressionist painters tried to banish all such interpretations from their art and to paint with an "innocent eye." In *Red Boats at Argenteuil* [368], Monet has recorded all the colors he saw in the water and the reflections of the boats without trying to blend them together conventionally (or intellectually). The result is not a painting of boats at anchor but a representation of the instantaneous impact on the eye of the lights and colors of those boats—that is, what the artist saw rather than what he knew.

368 Claude Monet. *Red Boats
at Argenteuil.* 1875. Oil on canvas,
23⅝ × 31⅞″ (60 × 81 cm).
Fogg Art Museum, Harvard University
(Maurice Wertheim bequest). Painted
the year after the first impressionist
exhibition in Paris, this shows Monet's
characteristic way of combining separate
colors to reproduce the effect of light.

Plate 30 Claude Monet. *Nymphéas (Water Lilies)*. 1920–1921.
Oil on canvas, 6'6″ × 19'7″ (1.98 × 5.97 m). Museum of Art,
Carnegie Institute, Pittsburgh (acquired through the generosity
of Mrs. Alan M. Scaife, 1962). This is one of a number of huge
paintings (in this case almost 20 feet long) that Monet produced
in the garden of his house in Giverny. Note the contrast with his
Red Boats at Argenteuil of 45 years earlier (figure **368,** page 392); in
Water Lilies there is a very different attitude to realism of form. The
greatly enlarged detail at right gives an idea of Monet's technique—
one that looks simple at first glance but actually results from many
separate, complex decisions. In every case the artist was guided by
purely visual factors rather than formal or intellectual ones.

Plate 31 Vincent van
Gogh. *The Night Café*. 1888.
Oil on canvas, 28½ × 36¼″
(72 × 92 cm). Yale
University Art Gallery, New
Haven (bequest of Stephen C.
Clark). Compare the lack
of perspective in Cézanne's
Mont Sainte-Victoire (figure
379, page 400) with the
highly exaggerated
perspective used by Van
Gogh here to achieve a sense
of violent intensity.

393

Plate 32 Henri Matisse. *The Red Studio.*
1911. Oil on canvas, 5′11¼″ × 7′2¼″
(1.81 × 2.19 m). Museum of Modern Art,
New York (Mrs. Simon Guggenheim
Fund). The paintings and small sculptures
in the studio are actual works by Matisse
himself; they show the brilliant colors
typical of fauve art.

Plate 33 Pablo Picasso. *Les
Demoiselles d'Avignon.* 1907. Oil on
canvas, 8′ × 7′8″ (2.43 × 2.33 m).
Museum of Modern Art, New York
(acquired through the Lillie P. Bliss
bequest).

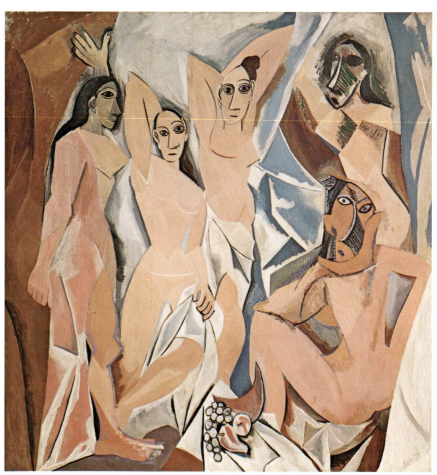

Throughout his long career Monet retained a total fidelity to visual perception. His fellow painter Paul Cézanne is said to have called him "only an eye, but my God what an eye!" His preoccupation with the effects of light and color reached its most complete expression in his numerous paintings of water lilies in his garden. In version after version he tried to capture in paint the effect of the shimmering, ever-changing appearance of water, leaves, and blossoms. The result, as in the *Water Lilies* of 1920 [Plate 30, page 393], reproduces not so much the actual appearance of Monet's lily pond as an abstract symphony of glowing colors and reflecting lights. Paradoxically, the most complete devotion to naturalism was to pave the way for abstraction and for what we know as modern art.

Monet's art represents impressionism in its purest form. Other painters, while preserving its general principles, devised variants on it. Pierre Auguste Renoir (1841–1919) shared Monet's interest in reproducing the effects of light in patches of color, but he brought to his subjects a human interest that derived from his own joy in life. It is a refreshing change, in fact, to find an artist whose work consistently explored the beauty of the world around him rather than the great problems of human existence. Nor was Renoir's interest limited, as was Monet's, to the wonders of nature. His most enduring love was for women as symbols of life itself; in his paintings they radiate an immense warmth and charm. His painting of the *Moulin de la Galette* [369], a popular Parisian restaurant and dance hall, captures the spirit of the crowd by means of the same fragmentary patches of color Monet had used in the background of *The Bar at the Folies-Bergère* [see figure 366], but Renoir adds his own sense of happy activity. The group in the foreground is particularly touching, with its sympathetic depiction of adolescent love. The boy leans impetuously forward, nervously fingering his chair, while the girl who has attracted his attention leans back and looks gravely yet seductively into his face, restrained by the protective arm of an older companion. Although the encounter may be commonplace, Renoir endows it with a significance and a humanity far different from Monet's more austere, if more literal, vision of the world by setting it against the warmth and movement of the background.

Unlike many other impressionists, Renoir traveled widely throughout Europe in order to see the paintings of the great Renaissance and Baroque masters. The influence of artists like Raphael, Velázquez, and Rubens is visible in his work. This combination of an impressionist approach to color with a more traditional attitude to form and composition emerges

369 Auguste Renoir. *Le Moulin de la Galette*. 1876. Oil on canvas, 4'3½" × 5'9" (1.31 × 1.75 m). Louvre, Paris. By using small patches of color Renoir achieves the impression of dappled sunlight filtering through the trees.

in *Two Girls at the Piano* [370], where the girls' arms have a genuine sense of roundness and weight. This painting is not a mere visual exercise, for Renoir endows his figures with a sense of self-assurance that only emphasizes their vulnerability.

The artist Edgar Degas (1834–1917) shared Renoir's interest in people, but unlike Renoir (who emphasized the positive side of life) he simply reported what he saw, stressing neither the good nor the bad. By showing us intimate moments in other people's lives, revealed by a momentary gesture or expression, his frankness, far from being heartless, as some of his critics have claimed, conveys the universality of human experience. Although Degas exhibited with the impressionists and, like them, chose to paint scenes from the everyday events of life, his psychological penetration distinguishes his art from their more literal approach to painting. Even the impressionist principle of capturing a scene spontaneously, in action, becomes in Degas' hands a powerful means of expression. One of the themes he turned to again and again was ballet, perhaps because of the range of movement it involved, although he also often underlined the gulf between the romantic façade of ballet

and its down-to-earth reality. In *The Rehearsal* [371] we are left in no doubt that neither ballet nor ballet dancers are entirely glamorous. Degas' point of view is emphasized by the unusual vantage point from which the stage is shown: close to and from a position high up on the side. Far from coldly observing and reproducing the scene, Degas creates an instant bond between us and the hard-worked dancers, based on our perception of them as human beings.

Degas' honesty won him the reputation of being a woman-hater, since many of his representations of female nudes lack the idealizing qualities of Renoir's and other painters' work. In a series of pastels he shows women caught unawares in simple natural poses. *The Tub* [372], with its unusual angle of vision, shows why these were sometimes called "keyhole visions." Far from posing, his subjects seem to be spied on while they are engrossed in the most intimate and natural activities.

One of Degas' closest friends was the American artist Mary Cassatt (1844–1926), who, after overcoming strong opposition from her father, settled in Europe to pursue an artistic career. Like Degas she painted spontaneous scenes from daily life, particu-

left: 370 Auguste Renoir. *Two Girls at the Piano*. 1892. Oil on canvas, 45½ × 34½″ (116 × 88 cm). Louvre, Paris. The position of the two girls, one leaning forward and resting her arm on the shoulder of the other, is almost exactly the same as that of the woman and the girl in the center of figure **369;** this position seems to have appealed to Renoir as a gesture of affection.

below: 371 Edgar Degas. *The Rehearsal*. 1874. Oil on canvas, 26 × 32¼″ (66 × 82 cm). Louvre, Paris. Degas' careful observation extends even to the director of the ballet troupe at the right-hand edge of the stage, hat almost over his eyes, holding the back of his chair.

372 Edgar Degas. *The Tub*. c. 1886. Pastel, 26.5″ (70 cm) square. Hill-Stead Museum, Farmington, Connecticut. The beautiful simplicity of Degas' drawing gives an impression of action glimpsed momentarily, as if by one passing by.

larly situations involving mothers and children. *Mother and Child* [373] shows a typical Cassatt composition, with the mother turned away from us and a child who is saved from sentimentality by his complete unawareness of our presence. Cassatt herself never married, but there is no reason to think that her paintings of children were created out of frustration. She seems to have had a rich and happy life, and her championship of the impressionist cause among her American friends led to many of them buying impressionist works and taking them home with them. Cassatt's artist friends had much to thank her for, and so do the curators of many American museums and galleries, which have inherited collections of impressionist paintings.

The impact of impressionism on sculptors was inevitably limited, since many of its principles were dependent on color and light and could only be applied in paint. Nevertheless, the greatest sculptor of the age (according to many, the greatest since Bernini), Auguste Rodin (1840–1918), reproduced in bronze something of the impressionist love of shifting forms and light and shadow. His remarkable figure of Balzac [374] demonstrates the irregularity of

373 Mary Cassatt. *Mother and Child*. c. 1889. Oil on canvas, 29 × 23½″ (74 × 60 cm). Cincinnati Art Museum (John J. Emery Endowment, 1928). By turning the mother's face away the artist concentrates attention on the child, an effect enhanced by the vague background.

374 Auguste Rodin. *Monument to Balzac*. 1897–1898. Bronze, height 8′10″ (2.7 m). Museum of Modern Art, New York (presented in memory of Curt Valentin by his friends). Unlike most sculptors who worked in bronze, Rodin avoided a smooth surface by roughening and gouging the metal.

surface by which Rodin converted two-dimensional impressionist effects to a three-dimensional format. It also reveals one of the ways in which he differed from his impressionist contemporaries, since his themes are generally massive and dramatic rather than drawn from everyday life. The portrait of Balzac shows the great novelist possessed by creative inspiration, rather than his actual physical appearance. The subject of this sculpture is really the violent force of genius (a concept also illustrated in his portrait of the composer Gustav Mahler [see figure 388, page 406], and Rodin conveys it with almost elemental power.

It should perhaps not be surprising that critics of the day were unprepared for such burning intensity. One of them dubbed the statue a "toad in a sack."

375 Auguste Rodin. *The Kiss*. 1886. Marble, height 6′2″ (1.9 m). Musée Rodin, Paris. As in his Balzac, the artist used the texture of his material to enhance the appearance of his work. But the smooth, slightly blurred surface of the marble here, in contrast to the rough surface of the portrait, produces a glowing effect.

But in retrospect Rodin breathed new life into sculpture. The "primitive" grandeur of his images formed a powerful attraction for 20th-century sculptors.

In general Rodin's works in marble are less impressionistic than those in bronze, but his famous *The Kiss* [375] achieves something of Renoir's blurred sensuality by the soft texture of the stone and the smooth transitions between the forms of the figures. Yet even though Rodin at times seems to strive for an impressionistic surface effect, the drama and full-blooded commitment of many of his works show the inadequacy of stylistic labels. We can only describe Rodin as a great romantic who used the impressionist style in works that foreshadow modern developments—that is, as a great original.

Post-Impressionism

As a stylistic category *post-impressionism* is one of the least helpful or descriptive terms in art history. The artists who are generally grouped together under it have as their only real common characteristic a rejection of impressionism for new approaches to painting. All of them arrived at their own individual styles. Their grouping together is therefore more a matter of historical convenience than critical judgment. The scientific precision of Georges Seurat (1859–1891), for example—whose paintings, based on simple geometric forms, are made up of thousands of tiny dots of paint applied according to strict theories of color [376]—has little in common with the flamboyant and exotic art of Paul Gauguin (1848–1903). Particularly in his last paintings, based on his experiences in Tahiti, Gauguin attacked primitive subjects in a highly sophisticated manner, producing results like *Ia Orana Maria* [377], which may attract or repel viewers but rarely leave them indifferent.

The greatest post-impressionist painter was Paul Cézanne (1839–1906). It would be difficult to overestimate the revolutionary quality of Cézanne's art, which has been compared to that of the proto-Renaissance Florentine painter Giotto as an influence on Western art. Cézanne's innovations brought to an end the six-hundred-year attempt since Giotto's time to reproduce nature in painting. In place of nature Cézanne looked for order; or rather he tried to impose order on nature, without worrying if the results were realistic. It is not easy to comprehend or express in intellectual terms the character of Cézanne's vision, although, as so often in the arts, the works speak for themselves. His paintings convey the essence, in terms of both shape and color, of his subject matter rather than its literal physical appearance. His *Still Life with Commode* [378] does not try to show

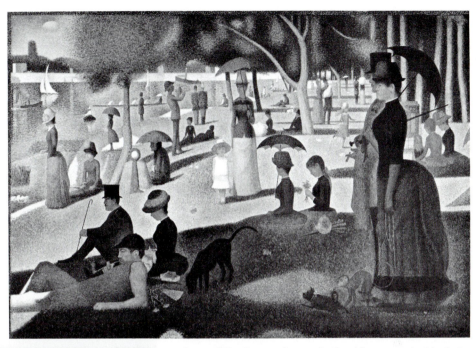

above: 376 Georges Seurat. *Sunday Afternoon on the Island of La Grande Jatte.* 1884–1886. Oil on canvas, 6′9″ × 10′3⅜″ (2.06 × 3.06 m). Art Institute of Chicago (Helen Birch Bartlett Memorial Collection). For all the casual activity in this scene of strollers in a park on an island in the River Seine, Seurat's remarkable sense of form endows it with an air of formality. Both shape and color (applied in minute dots) are rigorously ordered.

below: 378 Paul Cézanne. *Still Life with Commode.* c. 1885. Oil on canvas, 25⅜ × 31½″ (65 × 81 cm). Fogg Art Museum, Harvard University (Maurice Wertheim bequest).
So painstakingly did the artist work on the precise arrangement of the objects in his still lifes and on their depiction that the fruit usually rotted long before a painting was complete.

377 Paul Gauguin. *Ia Orana Maria.* 1891. Oil on canvas, 44¾ × 34½″ (114 × 88 cm). Metropolitan Museum of Art, New York (bequest of Samuel A. Lewisohn, 1951). The title means "We hail thee, Mary"; the painting shows a Tahitian Madonna and Child being worshiped by two women with an angel standing behind them. The whole scene presents a fusion of Western spiritual values and the simple beauty of primitive Polynesian life.

379 Paul Cézanne. *Mont Sainte-Victoire*. 1904–1906. Oil on canvas, 28⅞ × 36¼″ (73 × 92 cm). Philadelphia Museum of Art (George W. Elkins Collection). The reduction of the elements in the landscape to flat planes and the avoidance of the effect of perspective give the painting a sense of concentrated intensity.

how the fruit, vase, and cloth really look or reproduce their actual relationship to one another. On the contrary, the painter has deliberately distorted the surface of the table and the shape of the objects to achieve a totally satisfying design. Abstract considerations, in other words, take precedence over fidelity to nature. In the process a simple plate of fruit takes on a quality that can only be called monumental.

The miracle of Cézanne's paintings is that for all their concern with ideal order they are still vibrantly alive. *Mont Sainte-Victoire* [379] is one of a number of versions Cézanne painted of the same scene, visible from his studio window. Perhaps the contrast between the peaceful countryside and the grandeur of the mountain beyond partially explains the scene's appeal to him. He produced the transition from foreground to background and up to the sky by the wonderful manipulation of planes of pure color. It illustrates his famous advice to painters to "treat nature in terms of its geometrical shapes, of the sphere, the cylinder, and the cone," advice interpreted literally by the cubists in a somewhat later period. Yet equally the painting conveys the vivid colors of a Mediterranean landscape, with particular details refined away so as to leave behind the pure essence in all its beauty.

Nothing could be in greater contrast to Cézanne's ordered world than the tormented vision of Vincent van Gogh (1853–1890), the tragedy of whose life

found its expression in his work. The autobiographical nature of Van Gogh's painting, together with its passionate feelings, has a special appeal to modern sensibilities. In fairness to Van Gogh, however, we should remember that by giving expression to his desperate emotions the artist was, however briefly, triumphing over them. Further, in a way that only the arts make possible, the suffering of a grim, even bizarre life became transformed into a profound if admittedly partial statement on the human condition. Desperate ecstasy and passionate frenzy are not emotions common to most people, yet *The Starry Night* [380] communicates them immediately and unforgettably.

The momentum of swirling, flickering forms in *The Starry Night* is intoxicating, but for the most part Van Gogh's vision of the world was profoundly pessimistic. *The Night Café* [Plate 31, page 393] was described by the artist himself as "one of the ugliest I have done," but the ugliness is deliberate. Van Gogh's subject was "the terrible passions of humanity," expressed by the harsh contrasts between red, green, and yellow, which were intended to convey the idea that "the café is a place where one can ruin oneself, go mad, or commit a crime."

Much of Van Gogh's pessimism was undoubtedly the result of the unhappy circumstances of his own life, but it is tempting to place it in the wider context

380 Vincent van Gogh. *The Starry Night*. 1889. Oil on canvas, 29 × 36¼" (74 × 92 cm). Museum of Modern Art, New York (Lillie P. Bliss bequest). The impression of irresistible movement is the result of the artist's careful use of line and shape. The scene is dominated by spirals, vertical ones formed by the cypress trees and horizontal ones in the sky, which create a sense of rushing speed.

381 Vincent van Gogh. *Portrait of Dr. Gachet*. 1890. Oil on canvas, 26¼ × 22½" (67 × 57 cm). Private collection, U.S.A. Gachet was an amateur artist and friend of Van Gogh who often provided medical treatment for his painter acquaintances without taking any fee. Mentally ill and in despair, Van Gogh committed suicide while staying with Gachet.

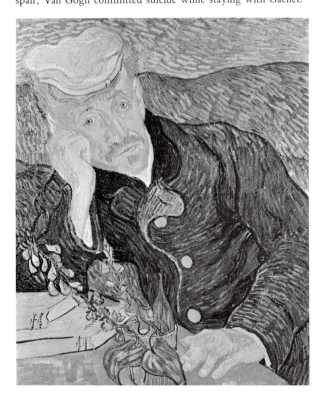

of his times and see it also as a terrifying manifestation of the growing social and spiritual alienation of society in the late 19th century. That Van Gogh was actually aware of this is shown by a remark he made about his *Portrait of Dr. Gachet* [381], the physician who treated him in his last illness. He had painted the doctor, he said, with the "heartbroken expression of our times."

Fauvism and Expressionism

By the early years of the 20th century the violent mood of the times had intensified still further, and artists continued to express this in their art. The impact of post-impressionists like Cézanne and Van Gogh inspired several new movements of which the most important was fauvism, which developed in France, and expressionism, which reached its high point in Germany.

The origin of the term *fauvism* reveals much of its character. In 1905 a group of artists exhibited paintings that broke with tradition so violently in their use of color and form that a critic described the painters as *les fauves* (the wild beasts). These painters had little in common apart from their desire to discard all traditional values; not surprisingly, the group broke up after a short while. But one of their number, Henri

Matisse (1869–1954), became a major force in 20th-century art.

Henri Matisse was the leading spirit of the fauves. His works are filled with the bold accents and brilliant color typical of fauvist art. Yet the flowing images of Matisse's paintings strike an individual note, expressing a mood of optimism and festivity curiously at odds with the times. One of his first important paintings, *The Joy of Life* [382], shows fields and trees in bright sunlight, where men and women are sleeping, dancing, and making music and love. It is difficult to think of any work of art further removed from the anguish of the years immediately preceding World War I than this image of innocent joy painted in 1905 and 1906.

Matisse was saved from the gloom of his contemporaries by his sheer pleasure in seeing and painting; his work eloquently communicates the delight of visual sensation. His still-life paintings, like those of Cézanne, sacrifice realism in effective and satisfying design, but his use of color and the distortion of the natural relationships of the objects he paints are even greater than Cézanne's. In *The Red Studio* [Plate 32, page 394], every form is clearly recognizable but touched by the painter's unique vision. It is as if Matisse compels us to look through his eyes and see familiar objects suddenly take on new, vibrant life.

Matisse's sunny view of the world was very unusual, however. In northern Europe, particularly, increasing social and political tensions inspired a group of artists who are generally known as the expressionists to produce works that are at best gloomy and foreboding, sometimes chilling.

The forerunner of expressionist art was the Norwegian painter Edvard Munch (1863–1944), whose influence on German painting was comparable to that of Cézanne on French. The morbid insecurity that characterized Munch's own temperament emerges with horrifying force in his best-known work, *The Scream* [383], from which the lonely figure's cry seems to reverberate visibly through space. This painting is more than autobiographical, how-

382 Henri Matisse. *The Joy of Life.* 1905–1906. Oil on canvas, 5′8½″ × 7′9¾″ (1.74 × 2.38 m). Barnes Foundation, Merion Station, Pennsylvania. By varying the sizes of the figures without regard to the relationship of one group to another the artist accentuates the sense of dreamlike unreality. Note Matisse's characteristically simple, flowing lines.

ever, since it reflects a tendency on the part of Norwegian and other Scandinavian artists and writers to explore social and psychological problems. Elsewhere in Europe the Spanish architect Antonio Gaudí (1852–1926) applied the same artistic principles to his buildings, with often startling results. His Casa Milá [384], an apartment house in Barcelona, like *The Scream,* makes use of restless, waving lines that seem to undulate as we look. The sense of disturbance is continued by the spiraling chimneys—although Gaudí's intention was neither to upset nor necessarily to protest.

By 1905 expressionist artists in Germany were using the bold, undisguised brushstrokes and vivid colors of fauvism to paint subjects with more than a touch of Munch's torment. The German expressionists, many of them grouped in "schools" with such names as *Die Brücke* (The Bridge) and *Der Blaue Reiter* (The Blue Rider), were relatively untouched by the intellectual and technical explorations of their contemporaries elsewhere. Instead, they were concerned with the emotional impact that a work could produce on the viewer. They were fascinated by the power of color to express mood, ideas, and emotion. They wanted their art to affect not only the eye but the viewer's inner sense. When they succeeded, as they often did, their works arouse strong emotions.

One of their principal themes was alienation and loneliness, so it is not surprising that they often turned to the writings of Dostoyevsky (see page 411)

383 Edvard Munch. *The Scream.* 1893. Oil on cardboard, 35½ × 28¾" (91 × 74 cm). Nasjonalgalleriet, Oslo. Munch himself once said, "I hear the scream in nature," and in this painting the anguish of the human figure seems to be echoed by the entire world around.

384 Antonio Gaudí. Casa Milá, Barcelona. 1907. Note the rough surface of the stone and the absence of any straight lines.

385 Erich Heckel. *Two Men at a Table (To Dostoyevsky).* 1912. Kunsthalle, Hamburg. The two figures seem separated from one another by doubt and distrust, each wrapped up in his own isolation. Behind them is a distorted image of the crucified Christ.

386 Emil Nolde. *Pentecost.* 1909. Oil on canvas, 2'8" × 3'6" (87 × 107 cm). Staatliche Museen Preussischer Kulturbesitz, Nationalgalerie, West Berlin. The broad, simplified faces and the powerful gestures of Christ in the center and of the two apostles clasping hands impart to the scene a concentration of emotional intensity.

for inspiration. *Two Men at a Table* [385], by Erich Heckel (1883–1970), is in fact subtitled *To Dostoyevsky.*

Emil Nolde (1867–1956), who identified himself with Die Brucke after 1906, was one of the few expressionists to paint biblical scenes. To these he brought his own ecstatic, barbaric intensity. *Pentecost* [386] shows the apostles seated around the table literally burning with inspiration; the tongues of flame of the biblical account are visible above their heads. Their faces have a masklike simplicity, but the huge eyes and heavy eyebrows convey frighteningly intense emotion. The image is far more disturbing than inspiring. Even in a religious context, expressionist art touches chords of alarm, even hysteria, unhappily appropriate to the times.

New Styles in Music

The impressionists had forced both artists and public to think afresh about painting and about seeing; by the early years of the 20th century musicians and music lovers, too, were to have many of their preconceptions challenged. Not only were traditional forms like the symphony either discarded or handled in a radically new way, but even the basic ingredients of musical expression, *melody, harmony,* and *rhythm,* were subject to startling new developments. Few

periods in the history of music are more packed with change, in fact, than those between 1870 and 1914, which saw a fresh approach to symphonic form, the rise of a musical version of impressionism, and the revolutionary innovations of the two giants of modern music, Schoenberg and Stravinsky.

Orchestral Music at the Turn of the Century

Although many extended orchestral works written in the last years of the 19th and the early 20th centuries were called symphonies by their composers, they would hardly have been recognizable as such to Haydn or Beethoven. The custom of varying the traditional number and content of symphonic movements had already begun during the romantic period; Berlioz had written his *Fantastic Symphony* as early as 1829 (see page 366). Nonetheless, by the turn of the century, so-called symphonies were being written that had little in common with one another, much less the classical symphonic tradition.

The driving force behind many of these works was the urge to communicate something beyond purely musical values. From the time of the ancient Greeks, many composers have tried to write instrumental music that tells a story or describes some event, including Vivaldi and his *Four Seasons* and Beethoven in his curious work known as the *Battle Symphony.* By the mid-19th century, however, composers had begun to devise elaborate *programs,* or plots, which their music would then describe. Music of this kind is generally known as *program music,* the first great exponent of which was Liszt (see page 367), who wrote works with titles like *Hamlet, Orpheus,* and *The Battle of the Huns,* for which he invented the generic description "symphonic poem."

The principle behind program music is no better or worse than many another. The success of any individual piece naturally depends on the degree to which narrative and musical interest can be combined. There are, to be sure, some cases where a composer has been carried away by eagerness for realism. Ottorino Respighi (1879–1936), for example, incorporated the sound of a nightingale by including a record player and a recording of live birdsong in a score.

No one was more successful at writing convincing program symphonies and symphonic poems (*tone poems,* as he called them) than the German composer Richard Strauss (1864–1949). One of his first successful tone poems, *Don Juan,* begun in 1886, deals with the familiar story of the compulsive Spanish lover from a characteristically late-19th century point of view. Instead of the unrepentant Don Giovanni of Mozart or Byron's amused (and amusing) Don Juan, Strauss presents a man striving to overcome the bonds of human nature, only to be driven by failure and despair to suicide. The music, gorgeously orchestrated for a vast array of instruments, moves in bursts of passion, from the surging splendor of its opening to a bleak and shuddering conclusion.

Strauss was not limited to grand and tragic subjects. *Till Eulenspiegel* is one of the most successful examples of humor in music. It tells the story of a notorious practical joker and swindler. Even when Till goes too far in his pranks and ends up on the gallows (vividly depicted by Strauss' orchestration), the music returns to a cheerful conclusion.

One of Strauss' most remarkable works, and one that clearly demonstrates the new attitude toward symphonic form, is his *Alpine Symphony,* written between 1911 and 1915. In one huge movement lasting some fifty minutes it describes a mountain-climbing expedition, detailing the adventures on the way (with waterfalls, cowbells, glaciers all in the music) and, at its climax, the arrival on the summit. The final section depicts the descent, during which a violent storm breaks out, and the music finally sinks to rest in the peace with which it opened. All this may sound more like the sound track to a movie than a serious piece of music, but skeptical listeners should try the *Alpine Symphony* for themselves. It is as far from conventional notions of a symphony as Cézanne's painting of *Mont Sainte-Victoire* [see figure 379] is from a conventional landscape, but genius

387 Lovis Corinth. *Salome.* 1899. Oil on canvas, 30 × 32″ (76 × 83 cm). Busch-Reisinger Museum, Harvard University (gift of Hans H. A. Meyn). Note the strikingly modern look of Salome, here representing the degeneracy of the artist's own times.

makes its own rules. Strauss' work should be taken on its own terms.

Not surprisingly, a composer capable of such exuberant imagination was also fully at home in the opera house. Several of Strauss' operas are among the greatest of all 20th-century contributions to the operatic repertoire. In some of them he was clearly influenced by the prevailingly gloomy and morbid mood of German expressionist art. His first big success, for example, was a setting of the English writer Oscar Wilde's play *Salome,* based on the biblical story, first performed to a horrified audience in 1905. After one performance in 1907 at the Metropolitan Opera House in New York, it was banned in the United States for almost thirty years. The final scene provides a frightening yet curiously moving depiction of erotic depravity, as Salome kisses the lips of the severed head of John the Baptist. This subject had been gruesomely represented by the German expressionist painter Lovis Corinth (1858–1925) in 1899 [387].

Works like *Don Juan* and the *Alpine Symphony* deal with stories we know or describe events with which we are familiar. In other cases, however, Strauss took as his subject his own life, and a number of his pieces, including the *Domestic Symphony* and the somewhat immodestly entitled *Hero's Life,* are frankly autobiographical. In this he was following a custom that had become increasingly popular in the late 19th century—the composition of music concerned with the de-

388 Auguste Rodin. *Gustav Mahler*. 1909. Bronze, height 13″ (34 cm). Musée Rodin, Paris. As in his Monument to Balzac (figure **374,** page 397), Rodin deliberately roughened the surface of the bronze for dramatic effect. In this case Mahler's hollow cheeks and intense gaze are powerfully suggested.

kovsky had become involved. In the light of this information the "Pathétique" Symphony takes on new poignance. Its last movement sinks mournfully into silence after a series of climaxes that seem to protest bitterly if vainly against the injustices of life.

The revelation of a composer's life and emotions through his music reached its most complete expression in the works of Gustav Mahler (1860–1911). Until around 1960, the centenary of his birth in Bohemia, Mahler's music was almost unknown and he was generally derided as unoriginal and overambitious. Now that he has become one of the most frequently performed and recorded of composers, we can begin to appreciate his true worth and learn the danger of hasty judgments.

The world of Mahler's symphonies is filled with his own anxieties, triumphs, hopes, and fears, but it also illuminates our own problem-ridden age. It may well be that Mahler speaks so convincingly and so movingly to a growing number of ordinary music lovers because his music touches on areas of human experience unexplored before his time and increasingly significant to ours. In purely musical terms, however, Mahler can now be seen as a profoundly original genius. Like Rodin, who produced a marvelous portrait of him [388], he stands as both the last major upholder of the romantic tradition and a pioneer in the modern world. Indeed, it was precisely his innovations that won him the scorn of earlier listeners: his deliberate use of popular, banal tunes, for example, and the abrupt changes of mood in his music. A symphony, he once said, should be like the world; it should contain everything. His own nine symphonies and *The Song of the Earth,* a symphony for two singers and orchestra, certainly contain just about every human emotion.

As early as the *Symphony No. 1 in D,* we can hear the highly individual characteristics of Mahler's music. The third movement of the symphony is a funeral march, but its wry, ironic tone is totally unlike any other in the history of music. The movement opens with the mournful sound of a solo double bass playing the old round "Frère Jacques," which is then taken up by the rest of the orchestra. There are sudden bursts of trite nostalgia and violent aggression until the mood gradually changes to one of genuine tenderness. After a gentle middle section the movement returns to the bizarre and unsettling spirit of the opening.

By the end of his life Mahler was writing much less optimistic music than *Symphony No. 1,* which—despite its third-movement funeral march—concludes with a long finale ending in a blaze of triumphant glory. Mahler's last completed works, *The*

tailed revelation of its composer's inner emotional life.

One of the first musicians to make his personal emotions the basis for a symphony was the late-romantic composer Peter Ilych Tchaikovsky (1840–1893), whose *Symphony No. 6 in B minor,* known as the "Pathétique," was written in the year of his death. An early draft outline of its "story" was found among his papers, describing its "impulsive passion, confidence, eagerness for activity," followed by love and disappointments, and finally collapse and death. It is now believed that the Russian composer's death from cholera was not, as used to be thought, accidental, but deliberate suicide. The reasons are still not clear, but they perhaps related to a potentially scandalous love affair in high places with which Tchai-

Song of the Earth and the *Symphony No. 9,* composed under the shadow of fatal heart disease and impending death, express all the beauty of the world together with the sorrow and ultimate resignation of one who has to leave it. The final movement of the *Symphony No. 9,* in particular, is a uniquely eloquent statement of courage in the face of human dissolution. Opening with a long, slow theme of great passion and nobility, the movement gradually fades away as the music dissolves into fragments and finally sinks into silence. Like all Mahler's music, and like the paintings of Van Gogh or Munch, the *Symphony No. 9* does not turn its back on the ugliness and tragedy of life; but Mahler, unlike many of his contemporaries, was able to see beyond them and express something of the painful joy of human existence. Perhaps that is why his music has become so revered in our own times.

Impressionism in Music

At about the same time painters in France were developing the style we call impressionist, Claude Debussy (1862–1918), a young French composer, began to break new musical ground. Abandoning the concept of the development to themes in a systematic musical argument, which lies behind classical sonata form and romantic symphonic structure, he aimed for a constantly changing flow of sound. Instead of dealing with human emotions, his music evoked the atmosphere of nature, the wind and rain and the sea. The emphasis on shifting tone colors led inevitably to comparisons with impressionist painting. Like Monet or Renoir, he avoided grand, dramatic subjects in favor of ephemeral, intangible sensations and replaced romantic opulence with refinement.

These comparisons should nevertheless not be exaggerated. Debussy and the impressionists shared a strong reaction against tradition in general and the romantic tradition in particular, in response to which they created a radically new approach to their respective arts, but impressionism permanently changed the history of painting, while the only really successful impressionist composer was Debussy himself. Later musicians have borrowed some of Debussy's musical devices, including his very fluid harmony and frequent dissonances, but Debussy never really founded a school. The chief developments in 20th-century music after Debussy took a very different direction, summed up rather unsympathetically by the French writer Jean Cocteau (1891–1963): "After music with the silk brush, music with the axe." These developments represent a more determined break with tradition than the refined style of Debussy. Indeed, with the passing of time Debussy's music appears increasingly to represent the last gasp of romanticism rather than the dawn of a new era.

Whatever his historical position, Debussy was without doubt one of the great creative musical figures in the last hundred years. He is at his best and most impressionist in orchestral works like *La Mer (The Sea),* which Debussy himself called symphonic sketches—a rather curious term that shows the composer for once willing to accept a traditional label. This marine counterpart of Strauss' *Alpine Symphony* is in three movements, the titles of which ("From Dawn to Noon on the Sea," "Play of the Waves," and "Dialogue of the Wind and the Sea") describe the general atmosphere that concerned Debussy rather than literal sounds. There are no birdcalls or thunderclaps in the music; instead the continual ebb and flow of the music suggest the mood of a seascape. The second movement, for example, depicts the sparkling sunlight on the waves by means of delicate, flashing violin scales punctuated by bright flecks of sound color from the wind instruments. It is scarcely possible to resist a comparison with the shimmering colors of Monet's *Water Lilies* [see Plate 30, page 393].

Elsewhere Debussy's music is less explicitly descriptive. His piano music, among his finest, shows an incredible sensitivity for the range of sound effects that instruments can achieve. Many of his pieces have descriptive titles—"Footsteps in the Snow," "The Girl with the Flaxen Hair," and so on—but often these were added after their composition as the obligatory touch of musical impressionism. Sometimes they were even suggested by Debussy's friends as their own personal reactions to his music.

The only composer to make wholehearted use of Debussy's impressionistic style was his fellow countryman Maurice Ravel (1875–1937), who, however, added a highly individual quality of his own. Ravel was far more concerned with classical form and balance than Debussy. His musical god was Mozart, and something of the limpid clarity of Mozart's music can be heard in many of his pieces—although certainly not in the all-too-familiar *Bolero.* His lovely *Piano Concerto in G* alternates a Mozartian delicacy and grace with an exuberance born of Ravel's encounters with jazz. Even in his most overtly impressionistic moments, like the scene in his ballet *Daphnis and Chloe* that describes dawn rising, he retains an elegance and verve distinctly different from the veiled and muted tones of Debussy.

Curiously enough, a composer who owed much to Debussy's musical innovations was the Italian opera composer Giacomo Puccini (1858–1924). A first hearing might suggest that nothing could be further from the delicate tone poems of Debussy than the violent and emotional mood of operas like *Tosca* and *Madama Butterfly*. Puccini was one of the leading composers in the Italian operatic school known as *verismo,* which aimed to bring to the opera house the realistic, true-to-life subjects with which writers like Flaubert dealt. *Madama Butterfly,* for example, concerns an American naval officer's heartless seduction of a young and innocent Japanese woman and the tragic consequences. Plots such as these were given drama and pathos by Puccini's remarkable sense of theater and his gift for memorable arias. Yet his musical style is far more sophisticated than is often realized. In descriptive passages like the dawn scene at the beginning of Act III in *Tosca,* or the bleak picture of Paris in the snow in *La Bohème* [389], we can clearly hear the influence of Debussy even if the language of impressionism has an Italian accent.

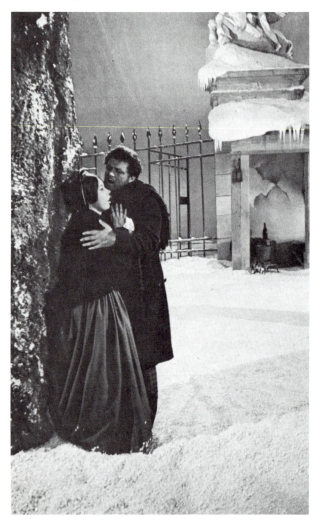

389 *La Bohème.* This is a scene from Act III of Puccini's opera as filmed at La Scala, Milan. The Unitel/Munich production was staged by Franco Zeffirelli. The central figures, Mimi and Rodolfo, are lovers, but Rodolfo's jealousy has been torturing them both, and they have agreed to part. Here, at the end of the act, they sing a regretful farewell to each other. Later, as the opera ends, the two are reunited in the joy of their revived love, but it is too late. Mimi, like Violetta in *La Traviata* (page 369), dies of consumption before her grief-stricken lover. The singers are Mirella Freni as Mimi and Gianni Raimondi as Rodolfo. *La Bohème,* first performed in 1896, is one of the most popular of all operas; one reason is that, though it is a tragedy, Puccini gave the struggling young artists who are its chief characters several scenes of delightfully antic comedy.

The Search for a New Musical Language

In 1908 the Austrian composer Arnold Schoenberg (1874–1951) wrote his *Three Piano Pieces,* Op. 11, in which he was "conscious of having broken all restrictions" of past musical traditions. After their first performance one critic described them as "pointless ugliness" and "perversion." In 1913 the first performance of *The Rite of Spring,* a ballet by the Russian-born composer Igor Stravinsky (1882–1971), was given in Paris, where he was then living. It was greeted with hissing, stamping, and yelling, and Stravinsky was accused of the "destruction of music as an art." Stravinsky and Schoenberg are now justly hailed as the founders of modern music, but we can agree with their opponents in at least one respect: their revolutionary innovations permanently changed the course of musical development.

It is a measure of their achievement that today listeners find *The Rite of Spring* exciting, even explosive, but perfectly approachable. If Stravinsky's ballet score has lost its power to shock and horrify, it is principally because we have become accustomed to music written in its shadow. *The Rite of Spring* has created its own musical tradition, one without which the music of the 20th century at all levels of popularity would be unthinkable. Schoenberg's effect has been less widespread and more subtle; nonetheless, no serious composer writing since his time has been able to ignore his music. It is significant that Stravinsky himself, who originally seemed to be taking music down a radically different "path to destruction," eventually adopted principles of composition based on Schoenberg's methods.

As is true of all apparently revolutionary breaks with the past, Stravinsky and Schoenberg were really only pushing to extreme conclusions developments that had been underway for some time. Traditional harmony had been collapsing since the time of Wagner, and Schoenberg only dealt it a death blow by his innovations. Wagner's *Tristan and Isolde* had opened with a series of chords that were not firmly rooted in any key and had no particular sense of direction (see page 371), a device Wagner used to express the poetic concept of restless yearning. Other composers followed him in rejecting the concept of a fixed harmonic center from which the music might stray as long as it returned there, replacing it with a much more fluid use of harmony. (Debussy, in his attempts to go beyond the bounds of conventional harmony, often combined chords and constructed themes in such a way as to avoid the sense of a tonal center; the result can be heard in the wandering, unsettled quality of much of his music.)

Schoenberg believed that the time had come to abandon a harmonic (or tonal) system that had served music well for over three hundred years but had simply become worn out. He therefore began to write *atonal* music—music that deliberately avoided traditional chords and harmonies. Thus Schoenberg's atonality was a natural consequence of earlier musical developments. At the same time, it was fully in accordance with the spirit of the times. The sense of a growing rejection of traditional values, culminating in a decisive and violent break with the past, can be felt not only in the arts but also in the political and social life of Europe; Schoenberg's drastic abandonment of centuries of musical tradition prefigured by only a few years the far more drastic abandonment of centuries of tradition brought by World War I.

There is another sense of which Schoenberg's innovations correspond to contemporary developments. One of the principal effects of atonality is a mood of instability, even disturbance, which lends itself to the same kind of morbid themes that attracted expressionist painters—in fact, many of Schoenberg's early atonal works deal with such themes. Schoenberg himself was a painter of some ability and generally worked in an expressionist style.

One of Schoenberg's most extraordinary pieces is *Pierrot Lunaire,* finished in 1912, a setting of twenty-one poems for women's voice and small instrumental group. The poems describe the bizarre experiences of their hero, Pierrot, who is an expressionist version of the eternal clown, and their mood is grotesque and at times demonic. The eighth poem, for example, describes a crowd of gigantic black moths flying down to block out the sunlight, while in the eleventh, entitled "Red Mass," Pierrot holds his own heart in his

blood-stained fingers to use as a "horrible red sacrificial wafer." Schoenberg's music clothes these verses in appropriately fantastic and macabre music. The effect is enhanced by the fact that the singer is instructed to *speak* the words at specific pitches. This device of *Sprechstimme* (speech melody), invented by Schoenberg for *Pierrot Lunaire,* is difficult to execute, but when it is done properly by a skilled performer, it imparts a wistfully dreamlike quality to the music.

The freedom atonality permitted the composer became something of a liability, and by the 1920s Schoenberg replaced it with a system of composition as rigid as any earlier method in the history of music. His famous *twelve-tone technique* makes use of the twelve notes of the chromatic scale (on the piano, all the black and white notes in an octave), which are arranged arbitrarily in a *row* or *series,* the latter term having given rise to the name *serialism* to describe the technique. The basic row, together with variant forms, then serves as the basis for a movement or even an entire work, with the order of the notes remaining always the same. The following example presents the row used in the first movement of Schoenberg's *Piano Suite,* Op. 25, together with three of its variant forms. No. 1 is the row itself, No. 2 its inversion (that is, the notes are separated by the same distance but in the opposite direction, down instead of up, and up instead of down), No. 3 is the row retrograde or backward, and No. 4 the inversion of this backward form, known as retrograde inversion.

Just as with program music, the only fair way to judge the twelve-tone technique is by its results. Not all works written in it are masterpieces, but we can hardly expect them to be. It is not a system that appeals to all composers or brings out the best in them, but few systems ever have universal application. A number of Schoenberg's own twelve-tone works, including his unfinished opera *Moses and Aaron* and the *Violin Concerto* of 1934, demonstrate that serial mensely complex, and frequently violent, his rhythmic patterns convey a sense of barbaric frenzy that is enhanced by the weight of sound obtained from the use of a vast orchestra. There are some more peaceful moments, notably the nostalgic opening section, but in general the impression is of intense exhilaration. Something of the rhythmic vitality of *The Rite of Spring* can be seen in this brief extract from the final orgiastic dance. The same melodic fragment is repeated over and over again, but in a constantly fluctuating rhythm that changes almost from bar to bar.

The Rite of Spring was the last of three ballets (the others were *The Firebird* and *Petrouchka*) that Stravinsky based on Russian folk subjects [390]. In the years following World War I he wrote music in a wide variety of styles, absorbing influences as varied as Bach, Tchaikovsky, and jazz. Yet a characteristically Stravinskian flavor pervades all his best works, with the result that his music is almost always instantly recognizable. Short, expressive melodies and unceasing rhythmic vitality, both evident in *The Rite of Spring,* recur in works like the *Symphony in Three Movements* of 1945. Even when, in the 1950s, he finally adopted the technique of serialism he retained his own unique musical personality. Indeed, Stravinsky is a peculiarly 20th-century cultural phenomenon, an artist uprooted from his homeland, cut off (by choice) from his cultural heritage, and exposed to a barrage of influences and counterinfluences. That he never lost his sense of personal identity or his belief in the enduring value of art makes him a 20th-century hero.

390 Vaslav Nijinsky as the Puppet Petrouchka in Igor Stravinsky's ballet of that name, as choreographed by Michel Fokine and performed by the Ballet Russe (see page 426). Paris, 1911. New York Public Library at Lincoln Center (Roger Pryor Dodge Collection). Nijinsky (1890–1950), a Russian, was one of the greatest dancers of all time. Fokine (1880–1942), also a Russian, was a choreographer who broke new ground in the ballet, just as the impressionists did in art and music.

New Subjects for Literature

Psychological Insights in the Novel

At the end of the 19th century many writers were still as concerned with exploring the nature of their own individual existences as they had been when the century began. In fact, the first years of the 20th century saw an increasing interest in the effect of the subconscious on human behavior, a result in large measure of the work of the Austrian psychoanalyst Sigmund

music can be both beautiful and moving. The 21st century will decide whether the system has permanent and enduring value.

Like *Pierrot Lunaire,* Stravinsky's *The Rite of Spring* deals with a violent theme. It is subtitled "Pictures from Pagan Russia" and describes a springtime ritual culminating in the sacrifice of a chosen human victim. Whereas Schoenberg had jettisoned traditional harmony, Stravinsky used a new approach to rhythm as the basis of his piece. Constantly changing, im-

Freud (1856–1939); the general conclusions Freud reached are discussed in Chapter 17. In many ways his interest in the part played by individual frustrations, repressions, and neuroses (particularly sexual) in creating personality was prefigured in the writing of two of the greatest novelists of the late 19th century, Fyodor Dostoyevsky (1821–1881) and Marcel Proust (1871–1922).

Self-knowledge played a major part in Dostoyevsky's work, and his concern for psychological truth led him into a profound study of his characters' subconscious motives. His sympathy with human suffering derived in part from his identification with Russian Orthodox Christianity, with its emphasis on suffering as a means to salvation. Although well aware of social injustices, he was more concerned with their effect on the individual soul than on society as a whole. His books present, to be sure, a vivid picture of the Russia of his day, with characters at all levels of society brought brilliantly to life. Nevertheless, he was able to combine realism of perception with a deep psychological understanding of the workings of the human heart. Few artists have presented so convincing a picture of individuals struggling between good and evil.

The temptation to evil forms a principal theme of one of his most powerful works, *Crime and Punishment*. In it he tells the story of a poor student, Raskolnikov, whose growing feeling of alienation from his fellow human beings leads to a belief that he is superior to society and above conventional morality. To prove this to himself Raskolnikov decides to commit an act of defiance: the murder of a defenseless old woman, not for gain but as a demonstration of his own power.

He murders the old woman and also her younger sister, who catches him in the act. Crime is followed immediately, however, not by the punishment of the law but by the punishment of his own conscience. Guilt and remorse cut him off even further from human contact until finally, in utter despair and on the verge of madness, he goes to the police and confesses to the murder. Here and in his other works Dostoyevsky underlines the terrible dangers of intellectual arrogance. The world he portrays is essentially cruel, one in which simplicity and self-awareness are the only weapons against human evil and suffering is a necessary price for victory.

Self-awareness is also the prime concern of one of the most influential of all modern writers, the French novelist Marcel Proust, although with very different results. Proust's youth was spent in the fashionable world of Parisian high society, where he entertained lavishly and mixed with the leading figures of the day

while writing elegant if superficial poems and stories. The death of his father in 1903 and of his mother in 1905 brought a complete change. He retired to his house in Paris and rarely left his sound-proofed bedroom, where he wrote the vast work for which he is famous, *Remembrance of Things Past*. The first volume appeared in 1913; the eighth and last volume was not published until 1927, five years after his death.

It is difficult to do justice to this amazing work. The lengthy story is told in the first person by a narrator who, though never named, obviously has much in common with Proust himself. Its entire concern is to recall the narrator's past life, from earliest childhood to middle age, by bringing to mind the people, places, things, and events that have affected him. In the course of the narrator's journey back into his past he realizes that all of it lies hidden inside him and that the tiniest circumstance—a scent, a taste, the appearance of someone's hair—can trigger a whole chain of memory associations. By the end of the final volume the narrator has decided to preserve the recollection of his past life by making it permanent in the form of a book—the book the reader has just finished.

Proust's awareness of the importance of the subconscious and his illustration of the way in which it can be unlocked have had a great appeal to modern writers, as has his *stream-of-consciousness* style, which appears to reproduce his thought processes as they actually occur rather than as edited by a writer for logical connections and development. Further, as we follow Proust's (or the narrator's) careful and painstaking resurrection of his past, it is important to remember that his purpose is far more than a mere intellectual exercise. By recalling the past we bring it back to life in a literal sense. Memory is our most powerful weapon against death.

Responses to a Changing Society: The Role of Women

Not all writers in the late 19th and early 20th centuries devoted themselves to the kind of psychological investigation found in the works of Dostoyevsky and Proust. The larger question of the nature of society continued to attract the attention of more socially conscious writers who explored the widening range of problems created by industrial life as well as a whole new series of social issues.

One of the most significant aspects of the development of the modern world has been the changing role of women in family life and in society at large. The issue of women's right to vote was bitterly fought out in the early years of the 20th century, and not until 1918 in Great Britain and 1920 in the United

States were women permitted to participate in the electoral process. On a more personal basis, the growing availability and frequency of divorce began to cause many women (and men) to rethink the nature of the marriage tie. The pace of women's emancipation from the stock role assigned to them over centuries was, of course, extremely slow, and the process is far from complete. A beginning had to be made somewhere, however, and it is only fitting that a period characterized by cultural and political change should also be marked by social change in this most fundamental of areas.

In the same way Dickens had led the drive against industrial oppression and exploitation in the mid-19th century, writers of the late 19th and early 20th centuries not only reflected feminist concerns but actively promoted them as well. They tackled a range of problems so vast that we can do no more than look at just one area, marriage, through the eyes of two writers of the late 19th century. One of them, Henrik Ibsen (1828–1906), was the most famous playwright of his day and a figure of international renown. The other, Kate Chopin (1851–1904), was ignored in her own lifetime even in her native America.

Ibsen was born in Norway, although he spent much of his time abroad. Most of his mature plays deal with the conventions of society and their consequences, generally tragic. Although many of them are technically set in Norway their significance was intended to be a general one. The problems Ibsen explored were frequently ones regarded as taboo, including venereal disease, incest, and insanity. The realistic format of the plays brought issues like these home to his audience with shocking force. At first derided, Ibsen eventually became a key figure in the development of drama, particularly in the English-speaking world, where his work was championed by George Bernard Shaw (1856–1950), himself later to inherit Ibsen's mantle as a progressive social critic.

In one of his first important plays, *A Doll's House* (1879), Ibsen dealt with the issue of women's rights. The principal characters, Torvald Helmer and his wife Nora, have been married for eight years, apparently happily enough. Early in their marriage, however, before Helmer had become a prosperous lawyer, Nora had secretly borrowed some money from Krogstad, a friend, to pay for her husband's medical treatment; she had told Torvald that the money came from her father, for Helmer himself was too proud to borrow. As the play opens Krogstad, to whom Nora is still in debt, threatens to blackmail her if she does not persuade Helmer to find him a job. When she refuses to do so Krogstad duly writes a letter to

Helmer revealing the truth. Helmer recoils in horror at his wife's deception. The matter of the money is eventually settled by other means and Helmer eventually forgives Nora, but not before the experience has given her a new and unforgettable insight into her relationship with her husband. In the final scene, she walks out the door, slams it, and leaves him forever.

Nora decides to abandon her husband on two grounds. In the first place she realizes how small a part she plays in her husband's real life. As she says, "Ever since the first day we met, we have never exchanged so much as one serious word about serious things." The superficiality of their relationship horrifies her. In the second place, Helmer's inability to rise to the challenge presented by the discovery of his wife's deception and prove his love for her by claiming that it was he who had borrowed and failed to repay the debt diminishes him in Nora's eyes. Ibsen tries to express what he sees as an essential difference between men and women when, in reply to Helmer's statement "One doesn't sacrifice one's honor for love's sake," Nora replies, "Millions of women have done so." Nora's decision not to be her husband's childish plaything—to leave the doll's house in which she was the doll—was so contrary to accepted social behavior that one noted critic remarked: "That slammed door reverberated across the roof of the world."

In comparison with the towering figure of Ibsen, the American writer Kate Chopin found few readers in her own lifetime; even today she is not widely known. Only recently have critics begun to do justice to the fine construction and rich psychological insight of her novel *The Awakening,* denounced as immoral and banned when first published in 1899. Its principal theme is the oppressive role women are forced to play in family life. Edna, its heroine, like Nora in *A Doll's House,* resents the meaninglessness of her relationship with her husband and the tedium of her daily existence. Her only escape is to yield to her sexual drives and find freedom not in slamming the door behind her but by throwing herself into a passionate if unloving affair.

In her short stories Kate Chopin dealt with the same kind of problem, but with greater delicacy and often with a wry humor. Frequently on the smallest of scales, these stories examine the prison that marriage seems so often to represent. In the course of a couple of pages Chopin exposes an all-too-common area of human experience and, like Ibsen, touches a chord that rings as true now as it did at the turn of the century.

Questions for Further Discussion

1. In what ways has the institution of marriage most significantly changed since the time of Ibsen's *A Doll's House*? What forces are principally responsible for the changes?
2. Artistic events like the impressionist and fauvist exhibitions or the first performance of Stravinsky's *The Rite of Spring* stimulated widespread public interest and massive publicity. Is it true that, in comparison, today there is a general public indifference to the arts? If so, why?
3. Mahler philosophically accepted the harsh criticism of his music during his lifetime by saying that it would only be appreciated fifty years after his death, a prediction fulfilled with uncanny precision. Why, in the history of the arts, is there so often a time lag between artistic achievement and general critical acceptance?
4. Much of the painting, music, and literature of the years preceding World War I is often described as decadent. What does *decadent* mean? Is it fair to use it as a descriptive term for the arts? Could it be applied to any artistic developments today?
5. The disasters that befell European society in the period from the end of the 19th century to the middle of the 20th drove large numbers of Europeans to emigrate to America. What effects did this have on American culture? How lasting was the European influence?
6. A parallel is often drawn between impressionism in painting and in music, and we commonly use terms like *line, color,* or *glow* about music, and *tone* or *rhythm* about the visual arts. How helpful is it to describe one art in terms of another? How interchangeable are their descriptive terms?

	GENERAL EVENTS	LITERATURE & PHILOSOPHY	ART

1901

1900-1905 Einstein researches the theory of relativity

1900-1905 Freud formulates basic ideas of psychoanalysis; *The Interpretation of Dreams* (1900)

1908-1915 Marinetti publishes futurist manifestos

1907 African sculpture fascinates artists in Paris: Picasso, *Les Demoiselles d'Avignon*. Retrospective of Cézanne's work in Paris. Picasso and Braque begin cubist experiments: Braque, *Violin and Palette* (1909-1910); Picasso, *Daniel-Henry Kahnweiler* (1910)

1909-1915 Italian futurists glorify technological progress

1910

1910 Death of Edward VII of England

1914 World War I begins; European colonialism wanes

1917 Bolshevik Revolution ends tsarist rule in Russia

1910 Death of Tolstoy

1910-1941 British Bloomsbury Group around Virginia and Leonard Woolf rejects Edwardian mentality

1913 Carl Jung breaks with Freud

1915-1916 Dada movement founded Café Voltaire in Zurich; Dada manifesto by Tristan Tzara (1918)

1917 Cocteau, scenario for ballet *Parade;* Wilfred Owen, "Dulce et Decorum Est." Leonard Woolf begins Hogarth Press

1910 Roger Fry's First Post-Impressionist Exhibition scandalizes London

c. 1911 German expressionism flourishes

1912 Kandinsky, *Concerning the Spiritual in Art*

1912-1914 Mondrian in Paris influenced by cubists; *Color Squares in Oval* (1914-1915)

1913 New York Armory Show brings avant-garde art to attention of American public

1915 End of futurist movement; Severini, *Armoured Train*

1915-1916 Dada artists begin assault on traditional concepts of art; Duchamp *L.H.O.O.Q.* (1919)

1916 Arp, *Fleur Marteau*

1917 Picasso designs *Parade* set

1918

1918 World War I ends; women granted right to vote in Great Britain

1920 Women granted right to vote in United States

1922 Fascists come to power in Italy after Mussolini's march on Rome

1927 Lindbergh's solo flight across Atlantic

1928 First sound movie produced

1929 Great Depression begins in Europe and America

1933 Nazis come to power in Germany under Hitler; first refugees leave country

1936-1939 Spanish Civil War; Guernica bombed 1937

1919 Yeats, "The Second Coming"

1922 Alienation and cultural despair themes in postwar literature: T. S. Eliot, *The Waste Land;* Joyce, *Ulysses.* Sinclair Lewis satirizes American middle class in *Babbitt*

1924 Freudian theory and dadaism foster surrealism; Breton, *First Surrealist Manifesto.* Freudian themes appear in American drama; O'Neill, *Desire Under the Elms* (1924)

c. 1925 Black cultural regeneration, "Harlem Renaissance," in Northern U.S. cities

1925 Eliot, *The Hollow Men;* Kafka, *The Trial*

1926 Kafka, *The Castle*

1929 V. Woolf, *A Room of One's Own*

1930 Freud, *Civilization and Its Discontents*

1932 Huxley warns against unrestrained growth of technology in *Brave New World*

1918 Chagall, *The Green Violinist*

1921 Picasso, *Three Musicians*

1921-1931 Klee teaches at Bauhaus; Kandinsky appointed professor in 1922

1924 Surrealism begins; Buñuel and Dali collaborate on films *Un Chien Andalou* (1929), *L'Âge d'Or (1930)*

1925 Eisenstein completes influential film *Potemkin*

1926 Gris, *Guitar with Sheet of Music;* Kandinsky, *Several Circles, No. 323;* Klee, *Around the Fish*

1927 Rouault, *This will be the last time, little Father! (Miserere* series)

1928 Magritte, *Man with Newspaper*

1930 Cocteau film *Blood of a Poet*

1931 Dali, *The Persistence of Memory*

1935-1940 WPA photographers active

1936 Riefenstahl, *Triumph of the Will,* film glorifying Nazis

1937 Picasso paints *Guernica* in protest against war; Dali uses Freudian symbolism in *Inventions of the Monsters*

1938 Eisenstein film *Alexander Nevskÿ,* score by Prokofiev; Riefenstahl, *Olympia*

1939

1939 Germany invades Poland; World War II begins

1939 First commercial TV

1941 United States enters War

1939 Death of Freud; Auden, *In Memory of Sigmund Freud*

1945 Orwell, *Animal Farm*

1942-1943 Mondrian, *Broadway Boogie-Woogie*

1944-1946 Eisenstein, *Ivan the Terrible,* parts I and II

1945

1945 World War II ends

1949 Orwell, *1984*

Between the World Wars

c. 1900 Jazz originates among black musicians of New Orleans

1909 Wright, Robie House, Chicago

c. 1910 Peak and decline of ragtime music; jazz becomes fully developed

1911 Piano rag composer Scott Joplin completes opera *Treemonisha*

1913 Stravinsky's *Rite of Spring* first performed in Paris

1917 Satie composes score for ballet *Parade*

1916 Death of futurist architect Antonio Sant' Elia in World War I

1919 Bauhaus design school founded at Weimar; Bauhaus ideas find wide acclaim in architecture and many industrial fields

Avant-garde composers come under influence of jazz and ragtime: Stravinsky, *L'Histoire du Soldat* (1918), Hindemith, *Klaviersuite* (1922)

1919-1920 Russian constructivist sculptor and visionary architect Tatlin builds model for *Monument to the Third International*

c. 1920 Chicago becomes jazz center; in New York's Harlem, Cotton Club provides showcase for jazz performers

1920s Josephine Baker and other American performers bring jazz and blues to Paris

1923 Schoenberg perfects twelve-tone technique (serialism)

1924 Gerswin, *Rhapsody in Blue*

1926 Gershwin, *Concerto in F Major* for piano

1930 Weill, *The Threepenny Opera,* text by Bertolt Brecht

1935 Gershwin's *Porgy and Bess,* first widely successful American opera

late 1930s Bauhaus architects Gropius and Van der Rohe flee Nazi Germany for U.S.

1943 Duke Ellington's symphonic suite *Black, Brown, and Beige* premieres at Carnegie Hall

1945 Stravinsky, *Symphony in Three Movements*

415

The "Great War" and Its Significance

The armed conflict that raged in Europe from 1914 to 1918 put to rest forever the notion that war was a heroic rite of passage conferring nobility and glory. The use of technology—especially poison gas, tanks, and planes—made possible slaughter on a scale hitherto only imagined by storytellers. The sheer numbers of soldiers killed in the major battles of World War I continue to stagger the imagination. By the end of the war the Germans had lost three and a half million men and the Allies five million.

The sociopolitical consequences of the "Great War" were monumental. The geopolitical face of Europe was considerably altered. The October Revolution of 1917 led by V. I. Lenin toppled the tzarist regime and produced a Communist government in Russia; it was a direct result of Russia's humiliation in the war. The punitive attitude of the Allies and the stricken state of Germany's economy after the war provided the seedbed from which Hitler's National Socialist movement (Nazism) sprang. Postwar turmoil led to Mussolini's ascendancy in Italy. England had lost many of its best young men in the war. Those who survived leaned toward either frivolity or pacifism.

Europe after World War I

Territory lost by

Germany   Bulgaria   Russia   Austria-Hungary

Culturally, World War I sounded the death knell for the world of settled values. The battle carnage and the senseless destruction, in no small part the result of callous and incompetent military leadership, made a mockery of patriotic slogans, appeals to class, and the metaphysical unity of nations. One result of this disillusionment was a spirit of frivolity but another was bitterness and cynicism about anything connected with military glory. A whole school of poets, many of whom did not survive the war, gave vent to their hatred and disgust with this first modern war.

The political upheavals and cultural tremors of the immediate postwar period coincided with a technological revolution in transportation and communications. After World War I radio came into its own. It is hard for us to comprehend what this information linkup meant for people previously isolated by lack of access to the larger world of information and culture. Similarly, the mass production of the automobile, made possible by the assembly-line techniques of Henry Ford in the United States, provided mobility to many who a generation before were confined to an urban neighborhood or a rural village. The widespread popularity of the cinema gave new forms of entertainment and instruction to those who already were accustomed to the voices of the radio coming into their homes each evening.

Literary Modernism

At the end of World War I the Irish poet William Butler Yeats (1865–1939), profoundly moved by unrest in his own country (particularly the Easter Rebellion of 1916) and the rising militarism on the Continent, wrote one of the most extraordinarily beautiful and prophetic poems of modern times, "The Second Coming." The title of the poem is deeply ironic because the title refers not to the glorious promised return of the Savior but an event the poet only hints at in an ominous manner. A line from that poem with its prescient look into the future, is as strikingly relevant for our times as it was for Yeats:

> Things fall apart; the centre cannot hold;
> Mere anarchy is loosed upon the world,
> The blood-dimmed tide is loosed, and
>   everywhere
> The ceremony of innocence is drowned;
> The best lack all conviction, while the worst
> Are full of passionate intensity.

T. S. Eliot

The year 1922 was a turning point for literary modernism. In that year T. S. Eliot (1888–1965), an expatriate American living in England, published his poem *The Waste Land* and James Joyce (1882–1941), an expatriate Irish writer living on the Continent, published his novel *Ulysses*. In their respective works Eliot and Joyce reflect some of the primary characteristics of what is called the modernist temper in literature. There is fragmentation of line and image, the abandonment of traditional forms, and overwhelming sense of alienation and human homelessness (both authors were self-imposed exiles), an ambivalence about the traditional culture, an intense desire to find some anchor in a past that seems to be escaping, a blurring of the distinction between reality "out there" and the world of subjective experience, and, finally, a straining and pushing of language to provide new meanings for a world they see as exhausted.

Both Eliot and Joyce reflect the conviction that, in Yeats' phrase, "the centre cannot hold." For Joyce, only art would give people a new world view that would provide meaning. Eliot felt that if culture was to survive one had to recover a sense of cultural continuity through a linkage of the artistic and religious tradition of the past. That perceived need for past cultural links helps explain why Eliot's poems are filled with allusions to works of art and literature as well as fragments from Christian rituals.

The gradual shift from cultural despair in *The Waste Land* can be traced in Eliot's later poems beginning with *The Hollow Men* (1925) and *Ash Wednesday* (1930) and culminating in *Four Quartets*, which were finished in the early Forties. The *Quartets* were Eliot's mature affirmation of his Christian faith as a bulwark against the ravages of modernist culture. To read *The Waste Land* and the *Four Quartets* in tandem is to see one way in which a sensitive mind moved from chaos to stability in the period between the wars.

Franz Kafka

Perhaps the quintessential modernist in literature is the Czech writer Franz Kafka (1883–1924). A German-speaking Jew born and raised in Prague, Kafka was by heritage alienated both from the majority language of his city and its predominant religion. An obscure clerk for a major insurance company in Prague, he published virtually nothing during his lifetime. He ordered that his works be destroyed after his death, but a friend did not accede to his wish. What we have from Kafka's pen is so unique that it has contributed the adjective *kafkaesque* to our language. A kafkaesque experience is one in which a person feels trapped by forces that seem simultaneously ridiculous, threatening, incomprehensible, and dangerous.

This is precisely the tone of Kafka's fiction. In Kafka's *The Trial* (1925) Joseph K. (note the near-anonymity of the name) is arrested for a crime that is never named by a court authority that is not part of the usual system of justice. At the end of the novel the hero (if he can be called that) is executed in a vacant lot by two seedy functionaries of the court. In *The Castle* (1926) a land surveyor known merely as K., hired by the lord of a castle overlooking a remote village, attempts in vain to approach the castle, to communicate with its lord, to learn of his duties. In time, he would be satisfied just to know if there actually is a lord who has hired him.

No critic has successfully uncovered the meaning of these novels—if in fact they should be called novels. Kafka's works might better be called extended parables that suggest, but do not explicate, a terrible sense of human guilt, a feeling of loss, and an air of oppression and muted violence.

Virginia Woolf

Virginia Woolf (1882–1941) is one of the most important writers in the period of literary modernism. Novels like *Mrs. Dalloway* (1925), *To the Lighthouse* (1927), and *The Waves* (1931) have been justly praised for their keen sense of narrative, sophisticated sense of time shifts, and profound feeling for the textures of modern life.

Woolf's reputation would be secure if she had only been known for her novels but she was also an accomplished critic, a founder (with her husband Leonard Woolf) of the esteemed Hogarth Press, and a member of an intellectual circle in London known as the Bloomsbury Group. That informal circle of friends was at the cutting edge of some of the most important cultural activities of the period. Lytton Strachey, the biographer, was a member, as was John Maynard Keynes, the influential economist. The group also included the art critics Roger Fry and Clive Bell, who championed the new art coming from France. The Bloomsbury Group also had close contacts with the mathematician-philosopher Bertrand Russell and the poet T. S. Eliot.

Two small books, written by Woolf as polemical pieces, are of special contemporary interest. *A Room of One's Own* (1929) and *Three Guineas* (1938) were passionate but keenly argued polemics against the discrimination of women in public intellectual life.

Woolf argued that English Letters had failed to provide the world with a tradition of great women writers not because women lacked talent but because social structures never provided them with a room of their own, that is, the social and economic aid to be free to write and think or the encouragement to find outlets for their work. Woolf, a brilliant and intellectually restless woman, passionately resented the kind of society that had barred her from full access to English university life and entry to the professions. Her books were early salvos in the coming battle for women's rights.

The Revolution in Art: Cubism

Between 1908 and 1914 two young artists, the Frenchman Georges Braque (1882–1963) and the expatriate Spaniard, Pablo Ruiz Picasso (1881–1973), began a series of artistic experiments in Paris that revolutionized the direction of Western painting. For nearly five hundred years painting in the West had attempted a reconstruction on canvas of a real or ideal world "out there" by the use of three-dimensional perspective and the rules of geometry. This artistic tradition, rooted in the ideas of the Italian Renaissance, created the expectation that when one looked at a painting one would see the immediate figures more clearly and proportionately larger while the background figures and the background in general would be smaller and less clearly defined. After all, it was reasoned, that is how the eye sees the real world. Braque and Picasso challenged that view as radically as Einstein, a decade before, had challenged all of the classical assumptions we had made about the physical world around us.

To Braque and Picasso paint on an essentially two-dimensional and flat canvas represented a challenge: how could one be faithful to a medium that by its very nature was not three-dimensional while still portraying objects which by their very nature *are* three-dimensional? Part of their answer came from a study of Paul Cézanne's many paintings of Mont Sainte-Victoire executed in the preceding century. Cézanne saw and emphasized the geometric characteristics of nature; his representations of the mountain broke it down as a series of geometrical planes. With the example of Cézanne and their own native genius, Braque and Picasso began a series of paintings to put this new way of "seeing" into practice. These experiments in painting began an era called "analytical cubism" since the artists were most concerned with exploring the geometric qualities of objects seen without reference to linear perspective.

Picasso's *Les Demoiselles D'Avignon* [Plate 33, page 394], painted in 1907, is regarded as a landmark of 20th-century painting. Using the traditional motif of a group of bathers (the title of the painting is a joke; it alludes to a brothel on Avignon Street in Barcelona), Picasso moves from poses that echo classical sculpture on the left to increasingly fragmented and distorted figures on the right. His acquaintance with African art prompted him to repaint the faces the same year to reflect his delight with the highly angular and "primitive" African masks he had seen in a Paris exhibition. The importance of this work rests in its violently defiant move away from both the classical perspective of Renaissance art and the experiments of Cézanne (compare page 398) in the previous century. It heralds the Cubism with which both Picasso and Braque became identified the following year.

A look at representative paintings by Braque and Picasso will help to clarify the aim of the cubists. In *Violin and Palette* [391] Braque depicts a violin so that the viewer sees, simultaneously, the front, the sides, and the back of the instrument while at the same time they appear on a single flat plane. The ordinary depth of the violin has disappeared. The violin is recognizable but the older notion of the violin as appearing "real" has been replaced by the artist's vision of the violin as a problem to be solved according to his vision and through his analysis.

In Picasso's portrait of *Daniel-Henry Kahnweiler* [392] the entire picture plane has become a geometric grid in which the traditional portrait form has been

left: 391   Georges Braque. *Violin and Palette*. 1909–1910. Oil on canvas, 36⅛ × 16⅞″ (92 × 43 cm). Solomon R. Guggenheim Museum, New York.

right: 392   Pablo Picasso. *Daniel-Henry Kahnweiler*. 1910. Oil on canvas, 39⅝ × 28⅝″ (101 × 73 cm). Art Institute of Chicago (gift of Mrs. Gilbert W. Chapman).

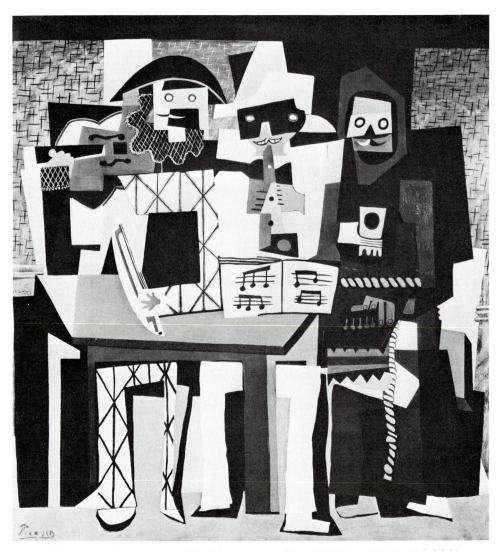

393 Pablo Picasso. *Three Musicians*. 1921. Oil on canvas, 6'8" × 6'2" (2.03 × 1.82 m). Philadelphia Museum of Art (A. E. Gallatin Collection). Another version of this painting, done in the same year, is much more severe, simplified, and painted with a simpler palette; it is in the Museum of Modern Art in New York.

broken into separate cubelike shapes and scattered without reference to traditional proportion. The viewer must reconstruct the portrait from the various positions on the cubist grid. Within the picture one detects here a face, there a clasped hand, and a table with a bottle on it. The intense preoccupation in this work with line and form can be noted by a close examination of the tilted surface facets that provide the painting with its artistic unity.

In the postwar period the impact of cubism on the artistic imagination was profound and widespread. Picasso himself moved away from the technically refined yet somewhat abstractly intellectual style of analytic cubism to what has been called synthetic cubism. In *Three Musicians* [393] he still employs the flat planes and two-dimensional linearity of cubism, as the geometric masks of the three figures and the way they are lined up clearly show, but their color, vivacity, playfulness, and expressiveness somehow make us forget that they are worked out in terms of geometry. These postwar paintings seem more humane, alive, and less intellectually abstract.

The visual revolution of cubism stimulated other artists to use the cubist insight in a variety of ways. Only a close historical analysis could chart the many ways in which cubism made its mark on subsequent above: **394** Juan Gris. *Guitar and Music Paper*. 1926. Oil on canvas, 25⅝ × 31⅞″ (65 × 81 cm). Collection of Mr. and Mrs. Daniel Saidenberg. It is interesting to compare this work with Braque's to get a sense of the diversity in cubist handling of a similar subject.

right: **395** Piet Mondrian. *Color Planes in Oval*. 1914–1915. Oil on canvas, 42⅜ × 31″ (108 × 79 cm). Museum of Modern Art, New York.

art, but a sampling shows both the richness and the diversity of art in the West after the Great War.

Some painters, like Juan Gris (1887–1927), continued to experiment rather faithfully with the problems Picasso and Braque explored before the war. His *Guitar and Music Paper* [394] demonstrates that such experimentation was not merely an exercise in copying. Other artists followed along the lines of Gris. The Dutch painter Piet Mondrian (1872–1944), after visits to Paris, where he saw cubist work, abandoned his earlier naturalistic works for paintings like *Color Planes in Oval* [395], a work whose main focus is on line and square highlighted by color.

The influence of cubism was not confined to a desire for simplified line and color even though such a trend has continued to our day in minimalist and hard edge art. The *Green Violinist* [396] by Marc Chagall (1889–   ) combines cubist touches (in the figure of the violinist) with the artist's penchant for dreamy scenes evoking memories of Jewish village life in Eastern Europe.

Although cubism was the most radical departure in modern art, it was not the only major art trend that overarched the period of the Great War. German painters continued to paint works in the expressionist style of the early years of the century. Perhaps the most accomplished exponent of expressionism was Wassily Kandinsky (1866–1944), who was also one of the few painters of his time who attempted to state his theories of art in writing. Kandinsky's *Concerning the Spiritual in Art* (1910) argued his conviction that the inner, mystical core of a human being is the truest source of great art. That attitude, together with Kandinsky's conviction that the physical sciences were undermining confidence in the solidity of the world as we see it, led him closer to color abstraction and further away from any form of representation. By 1926 he was attempting to express the infinity and formlessness of the world (indeed, the cosmos) in paintings like *Several Circles* [397] without appeal to any representative figures or sense of narration.

left: 396 Marc Chagall. *Green Violinist*. 1923–1924. Oil on canvas, 6'8" × 3'6¾" (1.98 × 1.09 m). Solomon R. Guggenheim Museum, New York. Note the complex stylistic character of this work with its elements of cubism, primitivism, and dreams. Chagall's work blends Parisian formalism with Russian nostalgia and Jewish mysticism.

below: 397 Wassily Kandinsky. *Several Circles*. 1926. Oil on canvas, 4'7⅛" (1.4 m) square. Solomon R. Guggenheim Museum, New York.

398 Salvador Dali. *The Persistence of Memory*. 1931. Oil on canvas, 9½ × 13″ (24 × 33 cm). Museum of Modern Art, New York (anonymous gift).

399 Salvador Dali. *Inventions of the Monsters*. 1937. Oil on canvas, 20⅛ × 30⅞″ (51 × 78 cm). Art Institute of Chicago (Joseph Winterbotham Collection).

Freud, Surrealism, and the Unconscious

In 1900, on the very threshold of the century, a Viennese physician, Sigmund Freud (1856–1939), published *The Interpretation of Dreams*—one of the most influential works of modern times. Freud argued that deep in the unconscious, which Freud called the *Id*, were chaotic emotional forces of life and love (called *Libido* or *Eros*) and death and violence (called *Thanatos*). These unconscious forces, often at war with each other, are kept in check by the *Ego*, which is the more conscious self, and the *Super Ego*, which is the formally received training of parental control and social reinforcements. Human life is shaped largely by the struggle of the Ego and Super Ego to prevent the deeply submerged drives of the *Unconscious* from emerging. One way to penetrate the murky realm of the human unconscious, according to Freud, was the dream. In the life of sleep and dreams the Ego and Super Ego are more vulnerable in their repressive activities. "The dream," Freud wrote, "is the royal road to the Unconscious." To put it simply, Freud turned the modern mind inward to explore those hidden depths of the human personality where the most primitive and dynamic forces of life dwell. Freudian psychoanalysis is not only a therapeutic technique to help anxious patients but also a descriptive philosophy that proposes to account both for human behavior and for culture in general.

After the Great War Freud's ideas were readily accessible to large numbers of European intellectuals. His emphasis on nonrational elements in human behavior exercised a wide influence on those who had been horrified by the carnage of the war. One group in particular was anxious to use Freud's theories about the dream world of the Unconscious as a basis for a new aesthetics. The result was the movement known as *surrealism*.

Surrealism was both a literary and artistic movement, gathered around the journal *Littérature,* edited in Paris by the French critic André Breton. In 1924 Breton published his first *Manifesto of Surrealism,* which paid explicit homage to Freud's ideas on the subjective world of the dream and the unconscious. "Surrealism," Breton declared, "is based on the belief in the superior reality of certain forms of association hitherto neglected, in the omnipotence of the dream, and in the disinterested play of thought."

The painters first associated with surrealism are familiar to every museumgoer: Jean Arp, Giorgio de Chirico, Max Ernst, Paul Klee, Joan Miró, Pablo Picasso. The Spanish artist Salvador Dali (1904–   ), who joined the movement in its later period, however, was to become almost synonymous with surrealism. His *The Persistence of Memory* [398] is perhaps the most famous surrealist painting. Its dreamlike quality comes from the juxtaposition of almost photographic realism with a sense of infinite quiet space and objects that seem unwilling to obey the laws of physics. The soft watches seem to melt in their plasticity. It is the very juxtaposition of solidity and lack of solidity that contributes to the "surreal" tone of the painting. In other paintings like *Inventions of the Monsters* [399], Dali's surreal world has more conscious allusions to the Freudian unconscious. There are open references to terror, violence, and sexuality. The double portrait is an allusion to the male/female principles that constitute each person, and Dali frequently alludes to this bisexual dynamic in his work.

Dali utilized strong realist draftmanship to set out his dream world. The iconography of his work, at least in the 1930s, was orthodox in its Freudianism. Another surrealist, René Magritte (1898–1967), was no less a draftsman but was less concerned with the dark side of the unconscious. His work, done with scrupulous attention to realistic detail, calls into question our assumptions about the reality of our world. In his *Man with a Newspaper* [400], even the title of the painting misleads us since the man, like a figure in the frame of a moving-picture film, has disappeared after the first frame.

Film was a major influence on Magritte's development—as it was on other surrealists. The motion-picture camera could be used to make images that corresponded closely with surreal intentions. Figures could dissolve, blend into other figures, be elongated, or slowly disappear. Some of the first artists associated with surrealism like the American Man Ray experimented with both still photography and moving pictures. Dali collaborated with his compatriot film director Luis Buñuel to produce two famous surrealistic films: *Un Chien Andalou* (1929) and *L'Âge d'Or* (1930). The French poet Jean Cocteau also produced a famous surrealistic film in 1931, *Blood of a Poet*.

One artist deserves a separate mention; although his association with the surrealist movement was important it does not adequately define his originality. The Swiss painter Paul Klee (1879–1940) had touched most of the major art movements of his day. He knew the work of Picasso in Paris; he exhibited for a time with the *Blaue Reiter* in Germany; after the war he taught at the famous design school in Germany called the *Bauhaus*. Finally, he showed his work at the first surrealist exhibition of art in Paris. It was characteristic of Klee's talent that he could absorb elements of cubist formalism, expressionist colorism, and the fantasy of the surrealists without being merely a derivative painter. He was, in fact, one of the most original and imaginative artists of the first half of the century. A painting like his 1926 *Around the Fish* [401] is typical. The cylindrical forms hint at cubism but the floating shapes, some enigmatic, and the brilliant coloring evoke the dreamlike world of the surreal.

We have already noted that Freud's pioneering researches into the nature of the unconscious profoundly impressed those writers associated with

400 René Magritte. *Man with a Newspaper.* 1928. 45½ × 32″ (116 × 81 cm). Tate Gallery, London.

401 Paul Klee. *Around the Fish.* 1926. Oil on canvas, 18⅜ × 25⅛″ (47 × 64 cm). Museum of Modern Art, New York (Abby Aldrich Rockefeller Fund).

André Breton. Other writers more fully explored the implication of Freud and his followers throughout this century in fiction, poetry, drama, and criticism. The great American dramatist Eugene O'Neill (1888–1953) restated basic Freudian themes of love and hate between children and parents (the so-called Oedipus and Electra complexes) in plays like *Desire Under the Elms* and *Mourning Becomes Electra*. Other writers of world repute like Franz Kafka and the American novelist William Faulkner (1897–1962) may not have been directly dependent on Freud's writings but their works are more approachable when we understand that they are dealing with similar issues and problems.

The Age of Jazz

Jazz is a peculiarly American contribution to Western culture. It was born out of the unique experience of American blacks. The matrix out of which jazz was born is an imperfectly documented history of a process that includes, among other elements: (1) certain intonations, rhythmic patterns (such as love of repetition), and melodic lines that come ultimately from the African ancestors of American blacks; (2) the tradition of the spirituals, Christian hymns sung both in the slave culture of the South and in the free churches of blacks after the Civil War; (3) the ineffable music of the blues, developed in the Deep South with its characteristic *blue note,* the flattening by a semitone of a note of the melodic line, which produces a sound hard to describe but instantly recognized; and (4) adaptations of certain European songs, especially French quadrilles and polkas, into a slightly different style of music that became known as ragtime.

Jazz made its first organized appearance in New Orleans around the turn of the century. The musicians, who were all black, performed without written music and were self-taught. They formed bands and played in the streets and in the cabarets of the city. By the end of World War I many of these musicians had migrated north to Chicago—which, in the early 1920s, was the center of jazz music. From there jazz spread to Harlem in New York City and to other urban centers of both coasts.

The influence of black jazz (and its white counterpart) on American culture is hard to overestimate. In fact, that period directly after World War I has been called "The Jazz Age," borrowing from an F. Scott Fitzgerald title. Some of the musicians of that era have permanent niches in American culture: the great blues singer Bessie Smith (1895–1937) and the trumpeter Louis Armstrong (1900–1975), along with such

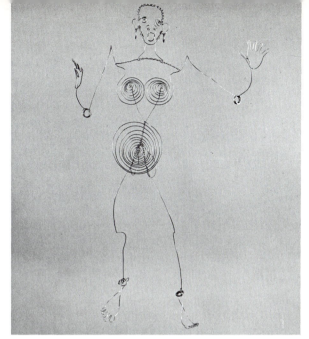

402 Alexander Calder. *Josephine Baker.* 1927–1929. Iron-wire construction, 39 × 23⅜ × 9¾" (99 × 57 × 25 cm). Museum of Modern Art, New York (gift of the artist). This is one of many such works Calder made during a stay in Europe in the late 1920s.

rediscovered masters as Eubie Blake (1883–1983) and Alberta Hunter. Jazz figures who reach down into contemporary culture would include such classic masters as Duke Ellington (1899–1974), Count Basie (1906–1984), and Lionel Hampton (1909–   ).

The popularity of jazz, a peculiarly black musical idiom, was soon appropriated by the predominant white culture in America so that often white jazz bands and the mass media (the first talking motion picture in this country starred a white actor, Al Jolson, portraying a black man in the *The Jazz Singer*) overshadowed the unheralded black musicians of the time. Only more recently have serious and systematic attempts been made to recover early jazz recordings (since written music is, by and large, nonexistent) and to bring out of retirement or obscurity the now-old blues singers who are the most authentic exponents of this art form.

Jazz as a musical and cultural phenomenon was not limited to the United States in the period after World War I. Jazz had a tremendous following in Paris in the 1920s, where one of the genuine celebrities was the black American singer Josephine Baker [402].

Just as Pablo Picasso had assimilated African sculptural styles in his painting so serious musicians on the Continent began to understand the possibilities of this American black music for their own ex-plorations in modern music. As early as 1913 Igor Stravinsky (1882–1971) utilized the syncopated rhythms of jazz in his pathbreaking ballet *The Rite of Spring*. His *L'Histoire du soldat* (1918) incorporates a "ragtime" piece Stravinsky composed based only on sheet-music copies he had seen of such music. Other avant-garde composers in Europe also came under the influence of jazz. Paul Hindemith's 1922 *Klaviersuite* shows the clear influence of jazz. Kurt Weill's 1928 *Dreigroschenoper (The Threepenny Opera),* with a libretto by Bertolt Brecht, shows a deep acquaintance with jazz—demonstrated notably in the song "Mack the Knife."

George Gershwin

The most persistent effort to transpose jazz into the idiom of symphonic and operatic music was that made by the American composer George Gershwin (1898–1937). In large symphonic works like *Rhapsody in Blue* (1924) and *Concerto in F Major* (1926), Gershwin utilized such jazz characteristics as blue notes, syncopation, and seemingly improvised variations on a basic theme (riffs) along with the more classically disciplined form of large orchestral music.

It is certainly appropriate, perhaps inevitable, that the first widely successful American opera should have a jazz background. George Gershwin's *Porgy and Bess* (1935) incorporated jazz and other black musical material such as the "shouting" spirituals of the Carolina coastal black churches to a libretto written by the Southern novelist Dubose Heyward. *Porgy and Bess* was not an immediate success in New York, but later revivals of it in the 1940s and after World War II established its reputation. In 1952 it had a full week's run at the famous La Scala opera house in Milan and in 1976 the Houston Opera mounted a full production with earlier cuts reintroduced into the text. It now ranks as a classic. Some of its most famous songs (such as "Summertime" and "It Ain't Necessarily So") have also become popular favorites.

Gershwin was white and thus had easier access to the world stage than many of the black musicians in the first half of this century. It has only been in the last decade or so that a fine composer like Scott Joplin (1868–1917), for example, has achieved any wide recognition in this country. The great blues singer Bessie Smith died after an automobile accident in the South because of delays in finding a hospital that would treat blacks. Many other singers and instrumentalists have remained in obscurity all their lives, although some—artists like the late Louis Armstrong—were so extraordinarily gifted that not even the hostile and segregated culture of the times could repress their talent.

Duke Ellington

One black American who managed to emerge decisively from the confines of black nightclubs into international fame was Edward Kennedy "Duke" Ellington (1899–1974). Ellington gained fame at the Cotton Club in Harlem in the 1920s both for his virtuoso orchestral skills and his prolific output as a composer. He was not only a successful writer of such popular musical pieces as "Take the A Train" and "Mood Indigo" but also a true original in his attempt to extend the musical idiom of jazz into a larger arena. Beginning after World War II, he produced any number of works for symphonic settings. His symphonic suite *Black, Brown, and Beige* had its first hearing at Carnegie Hall in 1943. This work was to be followed by others whose titles alone indicate the ambition of his musical interests: *Shakespearean Suite* (1957), *Nutcracker Suite* (1960), *Peer Gynt Suite* (1962), and his ballet *The River* (1970), which he wrote for the dance company of Alvin Ailey, a notable black choreographer.

Ballet: Collaboration in Art

In the period between the world wars one form of culture where the genius of the various arts most easily fused was the ballet. The most creative experiments took place in Paris through the collaboration of a cosmopolitan and talented group of artists.

The driving force behind ballet in this period in Paris was Serge Diaghilev (1872–1929), a Russian-born impresario who founded a dance company called the Ballet Russe, which opened its first artistic season in 1909. Diaghilev brought from Russia two of the most famous dancers of the first half of the century: Vaslav Nijinsky (1890–1950) and Anna Pavlova (1881–1931).

Diaghilev had a particular genius for recruiting artists to produce works for his ballet. Over the years the Ballet Russe danced to the commissioned music of Igor Stravinsky, Maurice Ravel, Serge Prokofiev, Claude Debussy, Erik Satie, and Darius Milhaud. In that same period sets, costumes, and stage curtains were commissioned from artists like Pablo Picasso, Georges Rouault, Naum Gabo, Giorgio de Chirico, and Jean Cocteau.

In 1917 Diaghilev produced a one-act dance called *Parade* in Paris. This short piece (revived in 1981 at

403 Pablo Picasso. Curtain for the ballet *Parade*. Paris, 1917. Tempera, 34'9" × 56'¾" (10.6 × 17.3 m). Musée National d'Art Moderne, Paris. Many critics agree that both the music and the text of the ballet served mainly to highlight Picasso's brilliant stage designs, which dominated the production.

the Metropolitan Opera with sets by the young English painter David Hockney) is an excellent example of the level of artistic collaboration Diaghilev could obtain. The story of the interaction of street performers and men going off to war was by the poet Jean Cocteau (1891–1963); the avant-garde composer Erik Satie contributed a score replete with street sounds, whistles, horns, and other accouterments of urban life. Pablo Picasso designed the curtain drop, the sets, and the costumes [403]. *Parade* had much to say about musicians, players, and street performers, so the production was readymade for Picasso's well-known interest in these kinds of people.

The collaborative effort of these important figures was a fertile source of artistic inspiration. Picasso had a great love for such work and returned to it on a number of other occasions. He designed the sets for *Pulcinella* (1920), which had music by Igor Stravinsky. He designed sets for a balletic interpretation of the Euripidean Greek tragedy *Antigone* done from a translation of the play into French by Jean Cocteau. In 1924 he also did designs for a ballet, which had original music written by Erik Satie, called *Mercury*.

Ballet, like opera, is an art form that lends itself to artistic integration. To enjoy ballet one must see the disciplined dancers in an appropriate setting, hear the musical score that at once interprets and guides the movements of the dancers, and follow the narrative or "book" of the action. It is no wonder that an organizational genius like Diaghilev would seek out and nurture the efforts of the most creative artists of his era.

Social Distress and Cultural Response

Perhaps the most salient feature of Western history between the two world wars was the rise of new forms of social governance that gave absolute authority to the state. Between 1918 and 1939 Italy and Spain fell under the rule of authoritarian forms of fascism, Germany became a Nazi state, the Soviet Union was established as a Marxist-Leninist Communist state, and the other Western states underwent economic and social distresses serious enough to threaten their democratic forms of government.

These new political systems were looked on by some as long-needed revolutionary structures of reform, by others as the inevitable and sad result of social and economic chaos, and by still others as a demonic force unleashed on the world.

The world of art and culture is never free of influence from the larger social and political realities of the world. Artists can either act as catalysts in a time of change or be agents of protest. They either serve new ideologies as apologists or they can provide alternative visions as escape from the world of sociopolitical reality. In the period between the wars all of these strategies were in evidence.

Art as Escape: Dada

A group of artists, writers, and musicians who gathered around the tables of the Café Voltaire in Zurich in 1915 founded a movement to protest what they considered the madness of the war and its senseless slaughter. They decided to fight the "scientific" and "rational" warmakers and politicians with nonsense language, ugly dissonant music, and a totally irreverent and iconoclastic attitude toward the great masterpieces of past culture. It was called *dada,* a nonsense word of disputed origin that could be a diminutive of "father" or the word for "yes" or a slang word for a hobbyhorse. One of its poets, Tristan Tzara, wrote a dada manifesto in 1918 that called for, among other things, a destruction of good manners, the abolition of logic, the destruction of memory, forgetfulness with respect to the future, and the elevation of the spontaneous as the highest good.

One of the most representative and creative of the dada artists was Marcel Duchamp (1887–1968), who after 1915 was associated with an avant-garde art gallery in New York founded by the American photographers Alfred Stieglitz (1864–1946) and Edward Steichen (1879–1973). Duchamp was a restless innovator who originated two ideas in sculpture that became part of the common vocabulary of modern art: sculptures with moving parts *(mobiles)* and sculptures constructed from preexisting fabricated material originally intended for other purposes *(readymades)*. Besides these important innovations Duchamp also has gained notoriety for his whimsically irreverent attitude toward art, illustrated by his gesture of exhibiting a urinal at an art show as well as his humorous but lacerating spoofs of high culture, the most "dada" of which is his famous defacement of the *Mona Lisa* [404].

The dadaists could not maintain the constant energy of their anarchy, so it was inevitable that they would move individually into other directions. Dada was a movement symptomatic of the crisis of the times, a reaction to chaos but no adequate answer to it. It is no small irony that while the dada theater

404 Marcel Duchamp. L.H.O.O.Q. 1919. Rectified readymade, pencil on colored reproduction of Leonardo's *Mona Lisa*; 7¾ × 4⅞″ (20 × 12 cm). Collection of Mrs. Mary Sisler, New York.

L.H.O.O.Q.

group performed in Zurich's Voltaire cabaret in 1916, there lived across the street an obscure Russian political activist in exile from his native land. He also would respond to the chaos of the time but in a far different way. His name was V. I. Lenin.

Art as Protest: *Guernica*

The late Protestant theologian Paul Tillich once called Picasso's *Guernica* [405] *the* great Protestant painting. He said this not because Picasso was religious (which he was not) but because of the quality and depth of Picasso's protest against inhumanity. The title of the painting comes from the name of a small Basque town that was saturation-bombed by Germany's Condor Legion in the service of Franco's Fascist rebel forces during the Spanish Civil War. Picasso completed the huge canvas in two months—May and June 1937—so that he could exhibit it at the Paris World's Fair for that year.

There have been intense studies of the genesis and development of *Guernica* in order to "unlock" its symbolism, but it would be safe to begin with Picasso's particular images. Many of these images recur over and over again in his work to convey Picasso's sense of horror at the destruction of war together with his muted affirmation of hope in the face of the horror. His iconography is reinforced by its somber palette—gradations of black, brown, and white.

The very complexity of images in *Guernica* at first glance seems chaotic, but prolonged looking reveals a dense and ordered rhythm. Starting at the left with the bull—Picasso's symbol of brute force, of Spain, and at times of the artist himself—we see beneath the animal a woman with a broken body of a child. The echo of the *Pietà* theme is obvious. In the lower center and to the right is a dismembered figure, in the cubist style, over whom rears up a "screaming" horse. At the top right of the work are Picasso's only hints of hope in the face of such evil: a small open window above a supplicant figure and an emerging figure holding a lamp. Over the center is an *oculus* (eye) in which a lamp burns and casts off light.

As a social document the importance of *Guernica* cannot be overestimated. The German bombing of the little town was an experiment in a new style of warfare, a style that would be refined into a deadly technique in World War II. In *Guernica* Picasso innovatively combines various stylistic techniques that were employed on the eve of World War I—expressionistic distortion and cubist abstraction—to protest a technological development that became a commonplace in the next war. In this sense *Guernica* is a pivotal document—it straddles two cataclysmic struggles in the century. *Guernica's* cry of outrage

405 Pablo Picasso. *Guernica*. 1937. Oil on canvas, 11′5½″ × 25′5¾″ (3.49 × 7.77 m).
On extended loan to the Museum of Modern Art, New York, for many years,
this famous painting was "returned" in the fall of 1981 to Spain, where it is hanging
in a Picasso wing of the Prado museum in Madrid.

provides an important observation about human culture. The painting reminds us that at its best the human imagination calls up the most primordial symbols of our collective experience (the woman and child, the horse and bull, the symbol of light) and invests them with new power and expressiveness fit for the demands of the age.

Art as Propaganda: Film

Propaganda is the diffusion of a point of view with the intention to persuade and convince. We usually think of it in political terms. Throughout history propagandists have used books, art, and music to spread their ideas. Inventions in the early part of the 20th century, however, added immeasurably to the propagandist's weapons.

Besides the radio the other medium that most successfully blended propaganda with attempts at some artistic vision in the first half of this century was film. Two acknowledged masters of the use of film for propaganda need be singled out since they set such a standard of excellence that, at least through their finest work, propaganda became high art.

Sergei Eisenstein (1898–1948) remains not only the greatest filmmaker the Soviet Union has produced but one of the most influential artists in the history of the cinema as well.

A dedicated supporter of the Russian Revolution, Eisenstein fully appreciated Lenin's observation that the cinema would become the foremost cultural weapon in winning the proletariat to the Revolution. From his early film *Strike!* (1925) to his last works, *Ivan the Terrible, Parts I and II* (1944/1946), Eisenstein was conscious of the class struggle, the needs of the working class, and the inevitable advance of socialism in history—themes dear to the official line of Stalin's U.S.S.R. Despite this orthodox line, Eisenstein was never an ideological hack. His films were meticulously thought out and he brought to bear his own considerable culture and learning to make films of high art. His *Alexander Nevskÿ* (1938) had an impressive musical score by Serge Prokofiev, and the two men worked closely to integrate musical and visual concepts. His vast *Ivan the Terrible* was deeply indebted to a study of El Greco's paintings; Eisenstein was struck by the cinematic possibilities in that Spaniard's striking canvases.

Eisenstein's most influential film was *Potemkin* (finished at the end of 1925), the story of the 1905 naval mutiny on the battleship *Potemkin* and the subsequent riot in Odessa that was put down by the tsarist police. The Communists saw in that historical incident a major foreshadowing of the October Revolution of 1917, which brought the Bolsheviks to power.

406 Sergei Eisenstein. Still from "Odessa steps sequence" from *Potemkin*. 1925. Museum of Modern Art Film Stills Archive, New York. This close-up is a classic shot in the history of film. It captures in a single image the horror of the entire scene.

407 Leni Riefenstahl. Still from "diving sequence" from *Olympia*. 1938. Note the original camera angle and the crisp image in this still. Riefenstahl's ingenious camera angles have been a model for documentary filmmakers.

The scene in *Potemkin* of the crowd cheering the mutineers on a broad flight of stairs in Odessa and the subsequent charge of the police is a classic sequence in film history. In that sequence Eisenstein used the device of *montage,* the sharp juxtaposition of shots by film cutting and editing, with such power that the scene would become a benchmark for subsequent filmmakers. His close-ups were meant to convey a whole scene quickly: a shot of a wounded woman cuts to a close-up of a clenched hand that slowly opens, telling the story of death in a moment. A crazily moving baby carriage is a macabre metaphor for the entire crowd in panic and flight. Shattered eyeglasses and blood pouring from an eye [406] become a terrible shorthand statement of police violence.

For sheer explicit propaganda one must turn to two documentary films made in Nazi Germany in the 1930s by the popular film actress and director Leni Riefenstahl (1902–   ). Her first great film was a documentary of the 1934 Nazi Congress in Nuremburg called *Triumph of the Will* (1936). Designed to glorify the Nazi Party and to impress the rest of the world, the film made ample use of the great masses of party stalwarts who gathered for their rally. That documentary allowed the young filmmaker to show the party congress as a highly stylized and ritualistic celebration of the Nazi virtues of discipline, order, congregated might, and the racial superiority of the Teutonic elite of the party members.

Riefenstahl's other great film, and arguably her masterwork, was a long documentary made at the Berlin Olympics of 1936 and issued in 1938 under the title *Olympia*. Riefenstahl used five camera technicians and 38 assistants as well as footage shot by news-agency photographers to make her film. The completed documentary, divided in two parts, pays tribute to the Olympic spirit of ancient Greece, develops a long section on the carrying of the Olympic torch to Berlin, records the homage to Hitler and the Nazi Party, and shows most of the major athletic competitions.

As a film *Olympia* is matchless in its imaginative use of the camera to catch the beauty of sport [407]. The vexing question is to what degree the film is political beyond the obvious homage paid to the German Reich, which sponsored the Olympics in 1936. Many critics note its elitist attitude to justify their contention that it is propaganda, albeit of a very high and subtle quality. Athletes are depicted as superior beings who act beyond the range of the ordinary mortal. They give all and seem almost demigods. The film praises the heroic, the conquest, the struggle. It praises the ritualized discipline of the crowds and lovingly seeks out examples of the adoring Berlin masses surrounding the party leaders.

Art as Propaganda: Photography

Photography is a 19th-century invention. During the 19th century photography had a complex technological evolution as photographers sought ways to make cameras and photographic equipment more mobile. As this mobility increased, photography developed a number of specialties: portraiture, landscapes, documentation, and reportage. More importantly and more basically, photography gave to the world what no other visual medium could: immediacy. Before the advent of photography it was the job of the field artist to transcribe an event in sketches and then transfer those drawings onto etching plates for reproduction in newspapers and magazines. With the photograph people could "see" events as they were actually happening. The idea that "a picture is worth a thousand words" has become a tired cliché, but it is difficult for us today to comprehend the impact the first photographs of war must have made when traveling photographers sent back to England pictures of dying soldiers in the Crimean War of the 1850s or when the American public first saw the pictures of death and devastation made by Mathew Brady (1823–1896) and his assistants during the Civil War in the 1860s.

Further technical advances, like the small, portable Kodak camera invented by the American George Eastman in the late 19th century, and 35mm cameras (including the famous Leica) invented in the early 20th century in Germany, contributed to the advance of photography in our century. In the period after World War I there was an intense interest in photography as a new instrument for art. Man Ray (1890–1976), an American artist living in Paris, experimented with darkroom manipulations to produce what he called *rayograms*. Laszlo Moholy-Nagy (1895–1946) taught a wide range of techniques in photography while he was an instructor at the influential Bauhaus school of design in Germany. When the school was closed by the Nazis, Moholy-Nagy came to the United States in 1933, where he continued to be a great influence on the development of American photography. A group of American photographers loosely connected with what was called the "f/64 Group" included pioneer photographers who are now recognized as authentic geniuses of the medium: Edward Weston (1886–1958), Ansel Adams (1902–1984), and Imogen Cunningham (1883–1975). We have already noted the influence of Alfred Stieg-

408 Walker Evans. *The Bud Fields Family at Home, Alabama.* 1935. Evans and James Agee often visited this family, and Agee wrote about them (as the "Woods" family) in *Let Us Now Praise Famous Men.* With Bud Fields, a one-mule tenant farmer, aged 59, are his second wife, Ivy, mid-20s, their daughter, 20 months, Ivy's daughter by an earlier common-law marriage, 8, Bud's and Ivy's son, 3, and Ivy's mother, early 50s.

litz on the avant-garde art of New York. These photographers, and others like them, emphasized direct, crisp, and nonmanipulative pictures that set the standard for much of modern photography.

In the United States the most powerful pictures between the world wars that were produced for social purposes were those photographs made to show the terrible economic deprivations of the Great Depression of the 1930s. In the mid-1930s the Farm Security Administration of the United States Department of Agriculture commissioned a number of photographers to record the life of America's rural poor. The resulting portfolios of these pictures taken by such photographers as Dorothea Lange, Arthur Rothstein, and Walker Evans have become classics of their kind. In 1941 the Pulitzer Prize-winning writer James Agee wrote a prose commentary on some of the photographs of Walker Evans. The photos of Evans and the text of James Agee were published together under the title *Let Us Now Praise Famous Men* [408]. Along with John Steinbeck's novel *The Grapes of Wrath* (itself turned into an Academy Award-winning film), Agee's book is one of the most moving documents of the Great Depression as well as a model of how word and picture can be brought together into an artistic whole for both social and aesthetic purposes.

409 Gino Severini. *Armored Train*. 1915. Oil on canvas, 46 × 34½″ (177 × 88 cm). Collection of Richard S. Zeisler, New York. The influence of cubism is obvious in this painting.

Art as Prophecy: From Futurism to *Brave New World*

Great art always has a thrust to the future. This chapter began with the observation of William Butler Yeats that "the centre cannot hold"—a prescient observation, as the aftermath of World War I was to show.

Not all artists were either so pessimistic or so prophetic as Yeats. A small group of painters, sculptors, architects, and intellectuals in Italy looked to the future with hope and to the past with contempt. Known as the *futurists,* they exalted the values of industrial civilization, the power of urban accomplishment, and (with equal intensity) despised the artistic culture of the past. The theorist of the movement was a Milanese poet and writer, Filippo Tommaso Marinetti (1876–1944), who issued a long series of futurist manifestos between 1908 and 1915.

In the few years during which futurism flourished its followers produced some significant painting,

sculpture, and ideas about city planning and urban architecture. World War I was to end their posturings; the sculptor Umberto Boccioni and the futurist architect Antonio Sant'Elia were both to die in 1916, victims of the war. Some of the futurists, including Marinetti, true to their fascination with power, war, destruction, and the exaltation of might, would be increasingly used as apologists for the emerging Fascist movement in Italy. Thus a painting like Gino Severini's *Armored Train* [409] proved prophetic in ways not quite appreciated in 1915.

The futurist romance with industrial culture and the idea of technological "progress" was not shared by all artists of the 20th century. We have already noted that T. S. Eliot pronounced his world a waste land. The American novelist Sinclair Lewis (1885–1951) viciously satirized American complacency in the postwar period. His novel *Babbitt* (1922) was a scathing indictment of the middle-class love of the concept of "a chicken in every pot and two cars in every garage." His philistine hero, George Babbitt, became synonymous with a mindless materialism in love with gadgets, comfort, and simplistic Midwestern values.

By contrast, the English novelist Aldous Huxley (1894–1963) saw the unrestrained growth of technology as an inevitable tool of totalitarian control over individuals and society. His 1932 novel *Brave New World* was a harbinger of a whole literature of prophetic warning about the dangers in our future. The two most famous prophetic works of the post-World War II era are *Animal Farm* (1945) and *1984* (1949), both by the English writer George Orwell, the pen name used by Eric Arthur Blair (1903–1950).

Huxley's *Brave New World* is set in the far distant future—600 A.F. (After [Henry] Ford, who had been deified as the founder of industrial society because he developed the assembly line). In this society babies are raised in state hatcheries according to the needs of the state. They are produced in five classes (from Alpha to Epsilon) so that the exact numbers of needed intellectuals (Alphas) and menials (Epsilons) are produced. The goal of society is expressed in three words: Community/Identity/Stability. All sensory experience is supplied either by machines or a pleasure-drug called *soma*. Individuality, family relationships, creativity, and a host of other "unmanageable" human qualities have been eradicated from society either by coercion or programming.

Toward the end of the novel there is a climactic conversation between John Savage, a boy from the wilds of New Mexico raised outside the control of society, and Mustapha Mond, one of the controllers of the "brave new world" of the future. Patiently,

Mustapha Mond explains to the uncivilized young man the reasons why certain repressions are inevitable and necessary in the society of the future. The reader sees rather clearly how aware Huxley is that the great humanistic achievements of the past—literature, art, religion—are threatening forces to any totalitarian society and as such are logical targets for a "scientifically" constructed society. His explanations now have a prescient and somber reality to us in the light of what we know about the real totalitarian societies of our own time.

Questions for Further Discussion

1. Compare Cézanne's various studies of *Mont Sainte-Victoire* with the cubist paintings of Picasso and Braque. In what ways did the cubists go beyond Cézanne? Discuss what Cézanne "saw" and what the cubists "saw."

2. Some people have called Franz Kafka a surrealistic writer. Do the surrealists and Kafka have anything in common that you can detect? Could you discuss Kafka and the surrealists in terms of *tone*?

3. Jazz has spawned a whole variety of styles. Could you report on the precise significance of New Orleans jazz, Bebop, progressive jazz, the Delta blues? What persistent themes appear in all these kinds of jazz? Which of these elements do you think most attracted European musicians earlier in this century?

4. Why do you suppose an authoritarian or totalitarian culture might find expressionist art enough of a threat to suppress it?

5. Are there contemporary analogues to such art movements as dada? futurism? surrealism?

6. Are we free from propaganda manipulation in the films we see?

	GENERAL EVENTS	LITERATURE & PHILOSOPHY	ART

THE ATOMIC ERA

1939

World War II and Aftermath

GENERAL EVENTS

1939 World War II begins; start of commercial television

1941 Japanese attack Pearl Harbor

1945 First atomic bombs used in warfare against Japan; World War II ends; Nazi extermination of Jews becomes widely known

1946 First meeting of UN General Assembly in London

1948 Israel becomes independent state; Berlin airlift marks beginning of "cold war"

1949 China becomes communist under leadership of Mao Zedung

LITERATURE & PHILOSOPHY

1945 Salinger, *The Catcher in the Rye*

1946 Orwell, *1984*; Sartre, *Existentialism as a Humanism*

Existentialist philosophy influences writers and dramatists: Camus, *The Stranger* (1946); Beckett, *Waiting for Godot* (1953)

1949 Miller's *Death of a Salesman* given Pulitzer Prize for Drama; Faulkner awarded Nobel Prize for Literature

ART

late 1930s Refugee artists Hoffman, Albers, Grosz bring ideas to America

1942 Cornell, *Medici Slot Machine*. Peggy Guggenheim exhibits European art at New York Gallery

1943 Pollock's first exhibition

c. 1945 New York becomes international art center; New York School includes abstract expressionism, color-field painting

1948 Pollock, *Number 1*

1949 Shahn, *Death of a Miner*

1950

The Beat Generation

1950 Korean War begins; FCC approves first commercial transmission of color TV

1952 U.S. explodes first hydrogen bomb

1954 School segregation outlawed by Supreme Court

1955 Civil Rights Movement starts in South

1957 First earth satellite launched by USSR

1950 Sociologist David Riesman writes *The Lonely Crowd*

1951 Langston Hughes, "Harlem," "Theme for English B"

1950s Alienation and anxiety become major themes of "Beat" writers Kerouac and Ginsberg

1951 Frankenthaler begins stained canvases: *The Bay* (1963); Moore, *Reclining Figure*

1950s Rauschenberg experiments with "combine" paintings and, with Cage, "happenings"

1953-1954 Motherwell, *Elegy to the Spanish Republic XXXIV*

c. 1955 Reaction to abstract expressionism results in "pop" art; Johns, *Flag* (1954-1955); Warhol *Soupcans*

1956 Hopper, *Office in a Small City*; Bergman film *Wild Strawberries*

1957-1960 Nevelson, *Sky Cathedral — Moon Garden + One*

1959 Rauschenberg, *Monogram*; Gottlieb, *Thrust*; Calder, *Big Red*

1960

The Youth Movement

1961 East Germans erect Berlin Wall; Soviets put first person in space

1962 First American orbits earth in space; transatlantic transmission of television signal via earth satellite

1963 President John F. Kennedy assassinated

1964 Massive buildup of American troops in Vietnam; Cultural Revolution in Communist China

1966 Founding of National Organization for Women in U.S.

1968 Assassination of Martin Luther King, Jr., and Robert F. Kennedy; youth movement at apex

1969 First walk on moon

1960 Wiesel, *Night*, memoir of Nazi concentration camps

1961 Heller, *Catch-22*, satire on absurdity of war

1963 Flannery O'Connor, "Revelation"

1964 Stoppard, *Rosenkrantz and Guildenstern Are Dead*

1970 Solzhenitsyn awarded Nobel Prize for Literature; Toffler, *Future Shock*; Nikki Giovanni, "Ego Tripping"

1971 Plath, *The Bell Jar*, published posthumously

1973 Pynchon, *Gravity's Rainbow*

1960 Johns, beer cans *Painted Bronze*

1960s Rothko panels for Houston Chapel, opened 1971

1962 Chamberlain, *Velvet White*, sculpture of crushed auto parts

1963 Smith, *Cubi I*: Manzu, Doors of Saint Peter's

1964 Kubrick, film *Dr. Strangelove*

1964-1966 Segal, *The Diner*; Kienholz, *The State Hospital*

1966 Oldenburg, *Soft Toilet*

1970s Resurgence of realism; incorporation of technology in art: videotapes, computers, lasers

1974 Kelly, *Grey Panels 2*; Pearlstein, *Two Female Nudes with Regency Sofa*

1975

1975 American withdrawal from Vietnam

1977 New Chinese government allows art previously banned

1981 First space shuttle flight

1976 Leslie, *The 7 A.M. News*

1981 Picasso's *Guernica* "returned" to Spain

1982

| ARCHITECTURE | MUSIC |

The Contemporary Contour

ARCHITECTURE

late 1930s Bauhaus architects Gropius and Van der Rohe flee Nazi Germany for U.S.

1943 Wright designs Guggenheim Museum, New York

c. 1947 Buckminster Fuller develops geodesic dome

1952 Le Corbusier, *L'Unité d'Habitation,* Marseille

Reinforced concrete technology results in building as sculpture: Nervi and Vitellozzi, *Palazzo dello Sport,* Rome (1956–1957)

1958 Van der Rohe and Johnson, Seagram Building, New York

1959 Guggenheim Museum completed

1959–1972 Utzon, Opera House, Sydney

1960 Niemeyer completes government buildings at Brasilia

1962 Saarinen, TWA Flight Center, New York

1970 Soleri begins utopian city Arconsanti in Arizona

1977 Piano and Rogers, Pompidou Center, Paris

1978 Pei, East Wing of National Gallery of Art, Washington, D.C.

MUSIC

1945 Britten composes opera *Peter Grimes*

1948 Structuralist Boulez composes *Second Piano Sonata;* LP recordings become commercially available

1950s Beginnings of electronic music; first use of synthesizer

1952 Boulez, *Structures;* Cage experiments with aleatoric music: *4' 3"*

1955–1956 Stockhausen, *Song of the Boys*

1958 Cage, *Concert for Piano and Orchestra*

1960 Penderecki, *Threnody for the Victims of Hiroshima*

1962 Britten, *War Requiem;* Shostakovich, *Symphony No. 13,* text from poems by Yevtushenko

1965 Stockhausen, *Mixtur*

c. 1965 Baez, Seeger, Dylan entertain with protest songs; height of rock music and Beatles; Lennon, *Yesterday;* eclectic music of Zappa and Mothers of Invention

1971 Shostakovich, *Symphony No. 15*

1973 Stockhausen, *Stop;* Britten, opera *Death in Venice*

1978 Penderecki, opera *Paradise Lost*

Toward a Global Culture

As we approach the end of the 20th century the period after 1945 seems to recede into history. It is difficult for us to remember what has happened to us as a culture in the two generations since the end of World War II. Events that have happened in the past decade or two are perhaps too close for us to know whether or not they have permanently changed us as a people. Was the moon landing of 1969 really a watershed in our consciousness as humans? Is the "American Century" so proudly forecast by commentators at the end of World War II slowly coming to an end? Has the revolution in communications already radically changed the way we learn things? Is the age of microtechnology and computers going to bring in a new, wonderful era or an antiutopia?

The postwar period is rightly called *The Atomic Era.* Developed largely by refugee scientists during World War II, atomic weaponry looms like an ominous shadow over all international tensions and all potentially belligerent situations. It is not simply a question of atomic bombs being bigger or more deadly weapons, although they are surely that. Atomic weapons can have long-term and little-understood consequences both for nature and for individuals who happen to survive their first devastation.

Because modern war is so far beyond the power of the human imagination to depict, contemporary artists have turned to satire as a way of expressing their fear and hatred of it. Novels like Joseph Heller's *Catch-22* and Thomas Pynchon's *Gravity's Rainbow* sketch out war in terms of insanity, irrationality, and the blackest of humor while Stanley Kubrick's brilliant movie *Doctor Strangelove* mounts a scathing attack on those who speak cooly about "megadeaths" and "mutual assured destruction" (MAD in military lingo). Any attempt at mere realism, these artists seem to say, pales into triviality.

Second, at the end of World War II the United States emerged both as a leading economic power in the world and as the leader of the "Free World" in its struggle against communism. This preeminence explains both the high standard of living in the West and the resentment of those who do not share it. Only lately have we understood that economic supremacy does not permit a nation to live free from outside forces. The energy crisis, the need for raw materials, the quest for labor, and the search for new markets bind many nations together in a delicate economic and social network of political relationships. The United States depends on other countries; the shifting patterns of economic relationships between North America, Europe, the Third World, Japan, and the oil producers are all reminders of how fragile that network really is.

The material satisfactions of Western life have spawned other kinds of dissatisfaction. While we may be the best-fed, best-housed, and best-clothed people in history, the hunger for individual and social meaning remains a constant in our lives. For instance, the many movements in this country—for civil rights, the rights of women, for minority recognition—are signs of that human restlessness that will not be satisfied by bread alone.

The incredible achievements of modern society have exacted their price. Sigmund Freud shrewdly pointed out in *Civilization and Its Discontents* (1929) that the price of advanced culture is a certain repression of the individual together with the need of that individual to conform to the larger will of the community. North Americans have always been sensitive to the constraints of the state, since their history began as a revolt against statist domination.

The Western world tends to see repression in terms that are more social than political. The very complexity of the technological management of modern life has led many to complain that we are becoming mere numbers or ciphers under the indifferent control of data banks and computers. Such warnings began as early as George Orwell's political novel *1984,* written right after the war (1946), and progress through David Riesman's sociological tract of the 1950s, *The Lonely Crowd,* to the futurist predictions of Alvin Toffler's *Future Shock* in the 1970s.

Art, of course, reflects not only the materials of its age but also its hopes and anxieties. The art, literature, and music of our times attempt to diagnose our ills, protest our injustices, and offer alternative visions of what life might be. On very exceptional occasions the voice of the artist can sum up a cultural condition in such a way that change can come. Who would have thought that an obscure convict, buried in the vast prison complex of the Siberian wasteland, would raise his voice against injustice and repression in such a way as radically to change the way a whole society is understood? That is surely what Alexsandr Solzhenitsyn has done in our own time with respect to the ominous character of Soviet communism.

Finally, the true artist can articulate a vision of what humanity can trust. In the midst of alienation, the artist can bring community and in the midst of ugliness, beauty. The artist, in short, acts not only as a voice of protest but as a voice of hope. The American novelist William Faulkner (1897–1962) spent a lifetime chronicling the violence, decay, injustice, poverty, and lost dreams of the American South. His novels are difficult to read, for they reflect the modernist sense of dislocated place and fragmented time. His most famous novel, *The Sound and the Fury* (1929), was notorious for its depiction of defective children, incestuous relationships, loutish drunkenness, and violence. In that sense it reflects the bleak landscape of the modern literary imagination. Yet Faulkner insisted that beneath the horror of modern life was a strong residue of human hope and goodness. Faulkner reaffirmed it ringingly in his acceptance speech when awarded the Nobel Prize for Literature in 1949: "I believe that man will not merely endure; he will prevail."

Existentialism

The philosophy that most persistently gripped the intellectual imagination of the Western world in the postwar period was existentialism. Existentialism is more an attitude than a single philosophical system. Its direct ancestry can be traced to the 19th-century Danish theologian and religious thinker Sören Kierkegaard (1813–1855), who set out its main emphases. Kierkegaard strongly reacted against the great abstract philosophical systems developed by such philosophers as Georg Hegel (1770–1831) in favor of an intense study of the individual person in his or her actual existing situation in the world. Kierkegaard emphasized the single individual ("the crowd is untruth") who exists in a specific set of circumstances at a particular time in history with a specific consciousness. Philosophers like Hegel, Kierkegaard once noted ironically, answer every question about the universe except "Who am I?," "What am I doing here?," and "Where am I going?"

This radically subjective self-examination was carried on all through the last century by philosophers like Friedrich Nietzsche and novelists like Fyodor Dostoyevsky, who are regarded as forerunners of modern existentialist philosophy. In our own century writers like Franz Kafka, the German poet Rainer Maria Rilke, the Spanish critic Miguel de Unamuno, and, above all, the German philosopher Martin Heidegger gave sharper focus to the existentialist creed. The writer who best articulated existentialism both as a philosophy and a style of life, however, was the French writer and philosopher Jean-Paul Sartre (1905–1980).

Sartre believed it the task of the modern thinker to take seriously the implications of atheism. If there is not God, Sartre insisted, then there is no blueprint of what a person should be and there is no ultimate significance to the universe. People are thrown into life and their very aloneness forces them to make decisions about who they are and what they shall be. "People are condemned to be free," Sartre wrote. Existentialism was an attempt to help people understand their place in an absurd world, their obligation to face up to their freedom, and the kinds of ethics available to people in a world bereft of any absolutes.

Sartre began his mature career just as Germany was beginning its hostilities in the late 1930s. After being a prisoner of war in Germany Sartre lived in occupied France, where he was active in the French Resistance, especially as a writer for the newspaper *Combat*. With the novelist Albert Camus (1913–1960) and the writer Simone de Beauvoir (1908–   ) his was the major voice demanding integrity in the face of the absurdities and horrors of wartorn Europe. Such an attitude might be considered a posture if it were not for the circumstances in which these existentialist writers worked.

The appeal of existentialism was its marriage of thought and action, its analysis of modern anxiety, and its willingness to express its ideas through the media of plays, novels, films, and newspaper polemics. After the close of the war in 1945 there was a veritable explosion of existentialist theater (Samuel Beckett, Harold Pinter, Jean Gênet, Eugène Ionesco) and existentialist fiction (Camus, Sartre, Beauvoir) in Europe. In the United States existentialist themes were eagerly taken up by intellectuals and writers who were attracted to its emphasis on anxiety and alienation.

The so-called Beat writers of the 1950s embraced a rather vulgarized style of existentialism filtered through the mesh of jazz and the black experience. Such beat writers as the late Jack Kerouac, Gregory Corso, and Allan Ginsberg embraced the existentialist idea of alienation even though they rejected the austere tone of their European counterparts. Their sense of alienation was united with the idea of experience heightened by ecstasy either of a musical, sexual, or chemical origin. The Beats, at least in that sense, were the progenitors of the Hippies of the 1960s.

The existentialist ethic has remained alive mainly through the novels of Albert Camus. In works like *The Stranger* (1942), *The Plague* (1947), and *The Fall* (1956), Camus, who disliked being called an existentialist, continues to impress his readers with heroes who fight the ultimate absurdity of the world with lucidity and dedication and without illusion.

Painting Since 1945

Art critic Barbara Rose has written that the history of world art in the second half of the 20th century bears an unmistakable American stamp. It is hard to quarrel with that judgment since in the 1940s the United States, and more specifically New York, became the center of new impulses in art, much the way Paris had been in the first half of the century.

Part of this geographic shift from Paris to New York can be explained by the pressures of World War II. Numerous artists and intellectuals fled the totalitarian regimes of Europe to settle in America. Refugee artist teachers like Hans Hofmann (1880–1966), Josef Albers (1888–1976), and George Grosz (1893–1959) brought European ideas to a new generation of American painters. The American patron and art collector Peggy Guggenheim, then married to the surrealist painter Max Ernst, fled her European home when war broke out to return to New York City, where at her Art of This Century gallery she exhibited such European painters as Braque, Léger, Arp, Brancusi, Picasso, Severini, and Miró. She quickly became patron to American painters who eventually led the American avant-garde. Peggy Guggenheim's support of this group in New York was crucial to the "Americanization" of modern art.

History nevertheless rarely records total and immediate shifts in artistic style. Thus, while a revolution was taking place in American art and, for that matter, in world art, some excellent artists continued to work in an older tradition relatively untouched by this revolution. Edward Hopper (1882–1967), for instance, continued to produce paintings that explored his interest in light and his sensitivity to the problems of human isolation and loneliness. His *Office in a Small City* [410] is a late example of Hopper's twin concerns. Ben Shahn (1898–1969) never lost the social passion that had motivated his work all through the 1930s. His *Death of a Miner* [411] is both a tribute to and an outcry against the death of a workingman in a senseless accident.

Another painter who remained untouched by the American revolution in painting is Georgia O'Keeffe (1887–   ), who had her first show in New York in 1916 at the galleries of Alfred Stieglitz, the photographer she married in 1924. Her early paintings, like *Calla Lily with Red Roses* [412], show both a masterful sense of color and a precise sense of line. She belonged to the early strain of American modernism but continued in her own style. O'Keeffe has not only been recognized as a major artist in her own right but as the focus for serious discussion about a feminist aesthetic in art for our time.

Abstract Expressionism

The artists mentioned above have a secure reputation in the history of art, but it was the abstract expressionists who gave art in the period after 1945 its "unmistakable American stamp." The term *abstract expressionism* is a useful one because it alludes to two characteristics fundamental to the work of these artists: it was devoid of recognizable content (and thus abstract) and it used color, line, and shape to express interior states of subjective aesthetic experience. *Action painting* and *New York School* are two other terms used to classify these painters.

The acknowledged leader of the abstract expressionists was the Wyoming-born painter Jackson Pollock (1912–1956), who had his first one-man show at Peggy Guggenheim's Art of This Century gallery in 1943. Pollock's early work was characterized by an interest in primitive symbolism, deriving from the artist's long encounter with the psychology of Carl Jung. By the early 1940s, under the influence of the surrealists and their technique of automatic creation—in which the artist allows the unconscious rather than the conscious will to stimulate the act of creation—he had begun to depart radically from traditional ways of painting.

At first Pollock discarded brush and palette for sticks, small mops, and sponges to apply paint in coarse, heavy gestures. Then he set aside instruments altogether and poured, dripped, and spattered paint

410 Edward Hopper. *Office in a Small City.* 1953. Oil on canvas, 28 × 40″ (71 × 102 cm). Metropolitan Museum of Art, New York (George A. Hearn Fund, 1953). Hopper had established this style in the late 1920s. Note the way he uses light here to set the emotional scene of this painting.

right: 411 Ben Shahn. *Death of a Miner*. 1949. Tempera on muslin treated with gesso, on panel, 2'3" × 4' (.69 × 1.22m). Metropolitan Museum of Art, New York (Arthur H. Hearn Fund, 1950).

below: 412 Georgia O'Keeffe. *Calla Lily with Red Roses*. 1927. Oil on canvas, 30 × 48" (76 × 122 cm). Private collection. O'Keeffe combined the traditional subject matter of flowers with a simplicity of line and a bold sense of color to create a unique style. Clearly neither a "realistic" nor an "abstract" painter, she uses elements of both.

directly on the canvas in nervous gestural lines rather than enclosed shapes. For his colors he mixed the expensive oils of the artists with the utilitarian enamels used by house painters. Perhaps most radically, instead of using an easel he rolled out large expanses of canvas on the floor of his studio and applied paint in his unusual manner as he walked around and on them. The dimensions of the finished painting were fixed when Pollock decided to cut out from this canvas a particular area and then attach it to the traditional wooden support or stretcher.

The result of these unorthodox procedures was huge paintings composed of intricate patterns of dribbles, drops, and lines—webs of color vibrant in their complexity [413]. The energy-filled nets of

right: 413 Jackson Pollock. *Number 1, 1948*. 1948. Oil on canvas, 5'8" × 8'8" (1.73 × 2.64 m). Museum of Modern Art, New York (purchase). The theoretical basis for such random painting can be traced to the Freudian practice of free association and the surrealist adaptation of that technique for art called *psychic automatism*.

paint extended to the limits of the stretched canvas and by implication beyond, seeming to have no beginning or end and hence attracting the stylistic label *over-all painting.* Neither did these colors and lines suggest the illusion of space receding in planes behind the surface of the picture, although they did create a sense of continuous rhythmic movement.

Other painters of the New York School in the 1940s and 1950s were more interested in the potentialities of large fields of color and abstract symbol systems, often with obvious psychological meanings. Adolph Gottlieb (1903–1974) painted a series of "bursts" in the 1950s in which a luminous sunlike color field hung over a primordial exploding mass [414]. Robert Motherwell (1915–   ) did hundreds of paintings in which huge primitive black shapes are in the foreground of subtle, broken color fields [415]. Mark Rothko (1903–1970) experimented restlessly with floating color forms of the most subtle variation and hue. In the 1960s Rothko painted a series of panels for a chapel in Houston [Plate 34, page 443] in which he attempted with some success to use color variations alone to evoke a sensibility of mystical awareness of transcendence.

What did these artists have in common? Their energy and originality make it difficult to be categorical although some generalizations are possible. They all continued the modernist tendency to break with the older conventions of art. As the cubists turned away from traditional perspective so the abstract expressionists turned away from recognizable content to focus on the implications of color and line. Second, they were *expressionists,* which is to say that they were concerned with the ability of their paintings to express not what they saw but what they felt and what they hoped to communicate to others. As one critic has put it, in an age when organized religion could no longer compel people with the notion of revelation, these artists wished to express their sense of ultimate meaning and their thirst for the infinite. "Instead of making cathedrals out of Christ, Man, or 'Life,'" painter Barnett Newman wrote, "we are making them out of ourselves, out of our own feeling."

The desire to expand the possibilities of pure color detached from any recognizable imagery has been carried on and extended by a second generation of color-field painters, the most notable of whom is Helen Frankenthaler (1928–   ). Around 1951 Frankenthaler began to saturate unprimed canvases with poured paint so that the figure (the paint) merged into the ground (the canvas) of the work. By staining the canvas she carried Pollock's action painting one step further, emphasizing the pure liquidity of paint and the color that derives from it. Frankenthaler uses the thinnest of paints to take advantage of the light contrast between the paint and the unstained canvas (unlike Pollock she does not paint "all over" her ground). The result has been paintings with the subtlety of watercolors but distinctively and inescapably different [Plate 35, page 443].

The Return to Representation

It was inevitable that some artists would break with abstract expressionism and return to a consideration of the object. This reaction began in the middle 1950s with painters like Jasper Johns (1930–   ), whose "Flag" series [416] heralded a new appreciation of objects. Further, Johns' art focused on objects taken from the mundane world. Johns went on to paint and sculpt targets, toothbrushes, beer cans, and even his own artist's brushes. This shift signaled a whimsical and ironic rejection of highly emotive, content-free, and intellectualized abstract art.

Robert Rauschenberg (1925–   ) was another artist who helped define the sensibility emerging as a counterforce to abstract expressionism in the 1950s. Rauschenberg had studied at Black Mountain College, an experimental school in North Carolina, under the tutelage of the refugee Bauhaus painter Josef Albers. A more important influence from his Black Mountain days was the avant-garde musician and composer John Cage (1912–   ), who encouraged experiments combining music, drama, dance, art, and other media into coherent artistic wholes which were called *happenings.* Rauschenberg began to experiment with what he called "combine" paintings that utilized painting combined with any number of assembled objects in a manner that had deep roots in the avant-garde. By 1959 he was doing large-scale works like his *Monogram* [417], which combined an

416 Jasper Johns. *Flag.* 1954. Encaustic, oil, and collage on fabric mounted on plywood, 3'6¼" × 5'⅝" (1.07 × 1.54 m). Museum of Modern Art, New York (gift of Philip Johnson in honor of Alfred Barr, Jr.). The rather banal subjects Johns uses can easily distract us from his excellent technique. This work makes dramatic use of encaustic—painting with molten colored wax.

417 Robert Rauschenberg. *Monogram.* 1955–1959. Freestanding combine, 5'4½" × 3'6" × 5'3¼" (1.64 × 1.07 × 1.61 m). Moderna Museet, Stockholm. Although Rauschenberg's work was originally considered a spoof and putdown of the abstract expressionists—a sort of modernist dada—he is now regarded as one of the foremost American painters.

assortment of elements (including a stuffed goat!) in an outrageous yet delightful collage.

The third artist who emerged in the late 1950s is Andy Warhol (1930–   ). Warhol has become notorious for his paintings of soup cans, soap boxes, Cola bottles, and the other throwaway detritus of our society, which has made his name synonymous with *pop art,* a term first used in England to describe the art of popular culture. The long-range judgment on Warhol as a serious artist may be harsh, but he understands one thing very well: taste today is largely shaped by the incessant pressure of advertising, the mass media, pulp writing, and the transient culture of fads. Warhol, who started his career as a commercial illustrator, has exploited that fact relentlessly.

Over the years Warhol has increasingly turned his attention away from painting and toward printmaking, videotapes, movies, and Polaroid photography. His subjects tend to be the celebrities of the film and social world. Whether his art is a prophetic judgment on our culture or a subtle manipulation of it is difficult to answer since Warhol can be bafflingly indirect. His lightly retouched silkscreen prints of entertainment celebrities [418] seem banal and of little permanent value, but that may be exactly what he wishes to express.

Painting from the 1970s is difficult to categorize. Some artists continue to explore color-field painting with great verve. Others, such as Ellsworth Kelly, Kenneth Noland, and Frank Stella, explore more for-

mal elements with carefully drawn "hard edges," primary colors, and geometrically precise compositions. They are almost ascetic in their use of line and color, as recent "minimalist" works of an artist like Ellsworth Kelly show [419].

above right: 418   Andy Warhol. *Mick Jagger.* 1975. Acrylic paint and silkscreen enamel on canvas, 40″ (102 cm) square. Private collection. Warhol, more than any other artist, has turned the tables on the "alienated artist" image by his love of the commercial, the sensational, and the celebrities called "beautiful people." In short, Warhol has attempted to create an amalgam of Madison Avenue and high culture.

right: 419   Ellsworth Kelly. *Gray Panels 2.* 1974. Oil on canvas, 7′8″ × 8′6″ (2.34 × 2.59 m). Leo Castelli Gallery, New York. Compare Frankenthaler's emphasis on color (see Plate 35, page 443)with Kelly's geometric, almost colorless style here. The contrasting approaches strikingly exhibit the divergence of painters after abstract expressionism.

Plate 34   The Rothko Chapel, Rice University, Houston. Consecrated 1971. Chapel designed by Philip Johnson. Murals by Mark Rothko. This ecumenical chapel was named in memory of the artist, who completed its fourteen monochromatic panels several years before his suicide. Shown here is a dance performed during an interfaith service for world hunger. Rothko intended that the paintings would enable each viewer to receive a personal message—of devotion or of peace. One critic has said that the artist wished to elevate modernist doubt to a mythic level. But one of the founders of the chapel said at its consecration: "We are cluttered with images, and only abstract art can bring us to the threshold of the divine."

Plate 35   Helen Frankenthaler. *The Bay*. 1963. Acrylic resin on canvas, 6'8¾" × 6'9¾" (2.02 × 2.08 m). Detroit Institute of Arts (gift of Dr. and Mrs. Hilbert d. DeLawter). Frankenthaler's work attains the luminosity of watercolor by her practice of thinning her pigments to the consistency of washes.

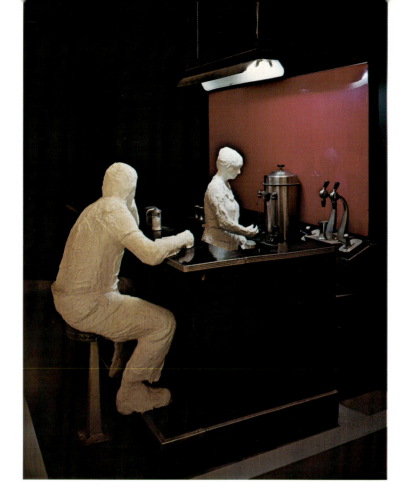

Plate 36 George Segal. *The Diner*. 1964–1966. Plaster, wood, chrome, formica, masonite, fluorescent lamp; 8′6″ × 9′ × 7′3″ (2.59 × 2.75 × 2.14 m) Walker Art Center, Minneapolis (gift of the T. B. Walker Foundation). During the past ten or so years Segal has been coloring his plaster casts in primary colors (usually red or blue), giving them an eerily garish air. He has also been producing some large commissioned pieces for outdoor display.

Plate 37 Renzo Piano and Richard Rogers. Georges Pompidou National Center for Art and Culture, Paris. 1977. In the last few years this center has taken on a lively bohemian air—nearby streets are lined with galleries and adjoining plazas are dotted with street performers and musicians.

Another group of painters has gone back totally to the recognizable object painted in a manner so realistic that critics have called them "photorealists." Less glossy than the photorealists but almost classical in their fine draftsmanship are the erotically charged nudes of Philip Pearlstein, who takes a position somewhere between the fragmented world of cubism and the slick glossiness of popular magazines. His *Two Female Models on Regency Sofa* [420] is a serious and unsentimental study of the female figure.

For Alfred Leslie (1927–) the past can still be a teacher for the modern painter. In a work like *7 A.M. News* [421] Leslie combines an eye for contemporary reality and the use of *chiaroscuro,* a technique he consciously borrows directly from the 17th-century painter Caravaggio. With Alfred Leslie we have come, as it were, full circle from the abstract expressionist break with tradition to a contemporary painter who consciously looks back to the 17th-century masters for formal inspiration.

One can say that two intellectual trends seem to have emerged in American painting in this period.

421   Alfred Leslie. *7 A.M. News.* 1976–1978. Oil on canvas, 7 × 5' (2.13 × 1.52 m). Allan Frumkin Gallery, New York. Note the sharp juxtaposition of light and dark (*chiaroscuro*). It is interesting to compare Leslie's use of this technique with that of the great masters of *chiaroscuro,* Caravaggio and Rembrandt.

420   Philip Pearlstein. *Two Female Models on Regency Sofa.* 1974. Oil on canvas, 5' × 5'10" (1.52 × 1.78 m). Private collection, New York. It is interesting to compare Pearlstein's nudes with those of an artist like Titian (for example, see figure **243**, page 260). Pearlstein makes no effort to hide the "painterly" quality of his work; he does not wish to produce a photographic image.

One strain, abstract expressionism and its various offspring, is heavily indebted to the modernist intellectual tradition, with its many roots in psychological theories of Jung and Freud and the existentialist vocabulary of anxiety and alienation. By contrast, the work of painters like Johns, Warhol, Rauschenberg, and others is far more closely linked to the vast world of popular culture in post-industrial America. Its material, its symbols, and its intentions reflect the values of consumer culture more than the work of the New York School of the 1940s. Pop art, largely free from the brooding metaphysics of the abstract expressionists, can be seen—perhaps simultaneously—as a celebration and a challenge to middle-class values.

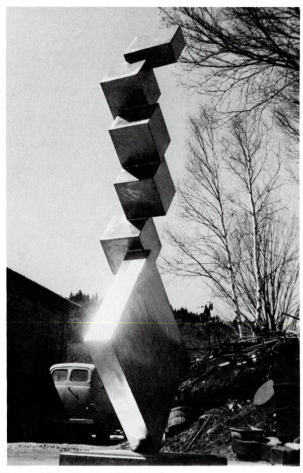

above left: 422 Giacomo Manzù. Doors of Saint Peter's. 1963. Cast bronze, 24′3″ × 11′9″ (7.4 × 3.6 m). Vatican City, Rome. Manzù's doors are at the extreme left of the portico, opposite the entrance that is used only every 25 years, during Holy Year.

above right: 423 David Smith, *Cubi I.* 1963. Stainless steel, height 10′4″ (3.15 m). Detroit Institute of Arts (Founders Society Purchase, Special Purchase Fund). Critics have called Smith one of the most important American sculptors of this century. His work is derived from European modernism but is seen as an original progression beyond it. Smith himself took this photograph at Bolton Landing, New York.

424 Alexander Calder. *Big Red.* 1959. Painted sheet metal and steel wire, 6′2″ × 9′6″ (1.88 × 2.9 m). Whitney Museum of American Art, New York (gift of the Friends of the Whitney Museum of American Art). The name *mobiles* was first given to Calder's moving sculptures by Marcel Duchamp; Calder's large stationary abstract sculptures are called, not surprisingly, *stabiles.* Calder was capable of doing portraits in wire; see the one of Josephine Baker (figure **402,** page 425).

425 Louise Nevelson. *Sky Cathedral—Moon Garden + One,* detail. 1957–1960. Painted wood, 9'1" × 10'10" × 19" (2.77 × 3.3 × .48m). Milly and Arnold Glimcher Collection. This detail shows how Nevelson meticulously assembled the large structure. She once fought prejudices about women sculptors and is now acknowledged as a major artist.

Contemporary Sculpture

Sculpture since 1945 shows both continuities and radical experimentation. The Italian sculptor Giacomo Manzù (1908–   ) still works with traditional forms of bronze-casting to produce works like the Doors of Saint Peter's [422], commissioned by the Vatican in the 1950s and cast in the 1960s. While his style is modern, the overall concept and the nature of the commission hark back to the Italian Renaissance and earlier.

Much of contemporary sculpture has utilized newer metals (stainless steel or rolled steel, for instance) and welding techniques to allow some freedom from the inherent density of cast bronze, the traditional metal of the sculptor. David Smith (1906–1965) used his skills as a onetime auto-body assembler to produce simple and elegant metal sculptures that reflected his not inconsiderable technical skills with metal as well as his refined sense of aesthetic balance. In works like *Cubi I* [423] he utilized stainless steel to produce a geometrically balanced work of solidity that conveys a sense of airy lightness.

Alexander Calder (1898–1976) used his early training as a mechanical engineer to combine the weightiness of metal with the grace of movement. Mobiles like *Big Red* [424] are made of painted sheet metal and wire; these constructions move because they are so delicately balanced that they respond to even the slightest currents of air. Calder once said that people think monuments "come out of the ground, never out of the ceiling"; his mobiles were meant to demonstrate just the opposite.

Other contemporary sculptors have expanded the notion of assembling disparate materials into a coherent artistic whole. Employing far from traditional materials, these artists utilize a variety of found and manufactured articles of the most amazing variety to create organic artistic wholes. Louise Nevelson (1900–   ), for example, uses pieces of wood, many of which had been lathed or turned for commercial uses, to assemble large-scale structures that seem at the same time to function as walls closing off space and as containers to hold the items that make up her compositions [425]. Joseph Cornell (1903–1972), early influenced by both surrealism and dada, constructed small boxes that he filled with dime-store trinkets, maps, bottles, tops, stones, and other trivia. In contrast to the larger brooding, almost totemic spirit of Nevelson, Cornell's painstakingly

426 Joseph Cornell. *Medici Slot Machine*. 1942. Construction, 15½ × 12 × 4¼″ (39 × 30 × 11 cm). Location unknown. Though links with dada and surrealism show in Cornell's work, his sense of nostalgia and lost innocence marks his art in a distinctive fashion.

427 Edward Kienholz. *The State Hospital*, detail. 1966. Mixed media, 8 × 12 × 10′ (2.44 × 3.66 × 3.05 m). Moderna Museet, Stockholm (© Edward Kienholz). Kienholz' work provokes violent feelings at times. In 1966 public officials tried to remove certain works from a one-man show of his in Los Angeles.

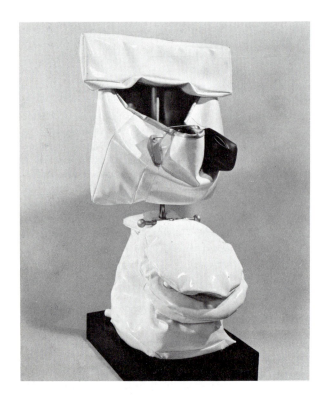

organized boxes [426] allude to a private world of fantasy.

The sculptural interest in *assemblage* has been carried a step further by such artists as George Segal (1924–   ) and Edward Kienholz (1927–   ). Their works re-create entire tableaux into which realistically sculptured figures are placed. Segal, once a painting student of Hans Hofmann in New York, likes to cast human figures in plaster of Paris and then set them in particular but familiar settings [Plate 36, page 444]. The starkness of the lone white figures evokes a mood of isolation and loneliness not unlike that of the paintings of Edward Hopper. Kienholz, a

428 Claes Oldenburg. *Soft Toilet*. 1966. Vinyl filled with kapok, painted with liquitex, and wood; height 4′4″ (1.27 m). Whitney Museum of American Art, New York (50th Anniversary Gift of Mr. and Mrs. Victor W. Ganz). Oldenburg's art works through parody; its humor is based on the well-known principle that humor derives from the expected becoming the unexpected.

California-based artist, is far more prepared to invest his works with strong social comment. His *State Hospital* [427] is a strong, critical indictment of the institutional neglect of the mentally ill. The chained figure at the bottom of the tableau "dreams" of his own self-image (note the cartoonlike bubble) on the top bunk. In the original version of this powerful piece goldfish were swimming in the plastic-enclosed faces of the two figures.

Both Segal and Kienholz have certain ties to pop art but neither works within its whimsical or humorous vein. Claes Oldenburg (1929–   ), however, is one of the more humorously outrageous and inventively intelligent artists working today. He has proposed (and, in some cases, executed) monumental outdoor sculptures depicting teddy bears, ice-cream bars, lipsticks, and baseball bats. From the 1960s on he has experimented with sculptures that turn normally rigid objects into "soft" or "collapsing" versions made from vinyl or canvas and stuffed with kapok. A piece like his *Soft Toilet* [428] is at the same time humorous and mocking. It echoes pop art and recalls the oozing edges so characteristic of surrealism.

Overarching these decades of sculptural development is the work of the British sculptor Henry Moore (1898–   ). Moore's work, which extends back into the 1920s, is a powerful amalgam of the monumental tradition of Western sculpture deriving from the Renaissance masters like Michelangelo and his love for the forms coming from the early cultures of Africa, Mexico, and pre-Columbian Latin America. From these two sources Moore has worked out hauntingly beautiful works—some on a massive scale—which speak of the most primordial realities of art.

Moore's *Reclining Figure* [429] is a complex work that illustrates many of the sculptor's mature interests. The outline is obviously that of a woman in a rather abstract form. There is also the hint of bonelike structures, a favorite motif in Moore's abstract sculpture, and holes pierce the figure. The holes, Moore once said, reminded him of caves and openings in hillsides with their hint of mystery, and critics have also noted their obvious sexual connotations. The figure reclines after the fashion of Etruscan and Mexican burial figures. In a single work Moore hints at three primordial forces in the universal human experience: life (the female figure), death (the bonelike configurations), and sexuality (the holes). It is a sculpture contemporary in style but timeless in its message.

Most of the sculpture just discussed was made for a gallery or a collector. Thanks to increased government and corporate patronage in recent decades it is possible for the average citizen to see outdoor sculpture as part of the urban environment. A walk in the downtown area of Chicago, for example, provides a chance to see monumental works of Picasso, Chagall, Bertoia, Calder, and Oldenburg. The fact that the federal government had set aside a certain percentage of its building budget for works of art to enhance public buildings has been an impetus for wider diffusion of modern art and sculpture. In one sense, the government, the large foundations, and the corporation have supplanted the church and the aristocracy as the patrons for monumental art in our time.

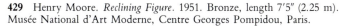

429 Henry Moore. *Reclining Figure*. 1951. Bronze, length 7′5″ (2.25 m). Musée National d'Art Moderne, Centre Georges Pompidou, Paris.

Architecture

The most influential American architect of this century was Frank Lloyd Wright (1869–1959). Wright was a disciple of Louis Sullivan (1856–1924), who had built the first skyscrapers in the United States in the last decade of the 19th century. Like Sullivan, Wright championed an architecture that produced buildings designed for their specific function with an eye to the natural environment in which the building was to be placed and with a sensitivity to what the building should "say." "Form follows function" was Sullivan's famous aphorism for this belief. For Wright and his disciples there was something ludicrous about making a post office look like a Greek temple and then building it in the center of a Midwestern American city. Wright wanted an *organic* architecture—an architecture that grows out of its location rather than being superimposed on it.

For decades Wright designed private homes, college campuses, industrial buildings, and churches that reflected this basic philosophy. In the postwar period Wright finished his celebrated Solomon R. Guggenheim Museum [430] in New York City from plans he had made in 1943. This building, one of Wright's true masterpieces, is a capsule summary of his architectural ideals. Wright was interested in the flow of space rather than its obstruction ("Democracy needs something basically better than a box"), so the Guggenheim Museum interior tries hard to eliminate corners and angles. The interior is essentially one very large room with an immensely airy central space. Rising from the floor in a continuous flow for six stories is a long simple spiraling ramp cantilevered off the supporting walls. A museumgoer can start walking down the ramp to view an exhibition without ever encountering a wall or partition. The viewing of the art is a continuous unfolding experience. Thus the *function* of the museum (to show art) is accomplished by the *form* of the building.

The exterior of the Guggenheim Museum vividly demonstrates the possibilities inherent in the new building materials becoming available in this century. By the use of reinforced or ferroconcrete one can model or sculpt a building easily. The Guggenheim Museum, with its soft curves and cylindrical forms, seems to rise up from its base. The undulating lines stand in sharp contrast to the boxy angles and corners of most of the buildings found in New York City. By using such a design, made to fit a rather restricted urban space, the Guggenheim almost takes on the quality of sculpture.

The sculptural possibilities of reinforced and prestressed concrete have given other architects the means to "model" buildings in dramatically attractive ways. The Italian engineer and architect Pier Luigi Nervi (1891–1979) demonstrated the creative use of concrete in a series of buildings he designed for the 1960 Olympic Games in Rome [431]. Eero Saarinen (1910–1961) showed in the TWA Flight Center at John F. Kennedy Airport in New York City [432] that a building can become almost pure sculpture; Saarinen's wing motif is peculiarly appropriate for an airport terminal. That architects have not exhausted the potentialities of this modeled architecture seems clear from the recently opened Opera House complex in Sydney, Australia [433]. Here the

430 Frank Lloyd Wright. Solomon R. Guggenheim Museum, New York. 1957–1959. Reinforced concrete; diameter at ground level c. 100′ (30.48 m), at roof level 128′ (39 m), height of dome 92′ (28 m). This building has been called the most discussed architectural monument of the century. A generation after its completion, it is still startling to remember that it is in the heart of New York City.

431 Pier Luigi Nervi and Annibale Vitellozzi. Palazzetto dello Sport, Rome. 1956–1957. Even the exterior of this building gives an impression of the spacious and uncluttered space inside where large athletic contests can be viewed. The walls beneath the concrete dome are of glass. The Y-shaped ferroconcrete columns are reminiscent of caryatids: their outstretched "arms" support the dome.

Danish architect Jörn Utzon utilized Saarinen's wing motif, but it is not a slavish copy since Utzon gives it a new and dramatic emphasis.

The influential French architect Le Corbusier (1887–1965; born Charles Édouard Jeanneret-Gris) did not share Wright's enthusiasm for "organic" architecture. Le Corbusier saw architecture as a human achievement that should stand in counterpoint to the world of nature. During his long career Le Corbusier designed and oversaw the construction of both individual buildings and more ambitious habitations ranging from apartment complexes to an entire city. One of his most important contributions to architecture is his series of Unités d'Habitation in Marseille (1952) and Nantes (1957). These complexes were attempts to make large housing units into livable modules that would not only provide a living space but would also be sufficiently self-contained to incorporate shopping, recreation, and walking areas [434]. Le Corbusier used basic forms (simple squares, rectangles) for the complexes and set them on pylons both to give more space beneath the buildings and to

434 Le Corbusier. L'Unité d'Habitation, Marseille. 1947–1952. Length 550′ (167.64 m), height 184′ (56.08 m), width 79′ (24.08 m). The individual balconies have colored panels that interrupt the starkness of the white concrete construction. Note the unfinished look of the rough concrete stairwell, a touch typical of Le Corbusier.

below left: 432 Eero Saarinen. Trans World Flight Center, Kennedy Airport, New York. 1962. Perhaps no other modern building shows more clearly the sculptural quality of concrete. Note the hint of a bird in flight in the roof that flares out on two sides, with a projecting canopy between them.

below right: 433 Jörn Utzon. Opera House, Sydney, Australia. 1959–1972. Reinforced concrete, height of highest shell 200′ (60.96 m). This building is all the more dramatic because of its location on a point jutting out into Sydney's harbor. Structural technology was pushed almost to its limits in this building, one of the most difficult construction jobs ever undertaken. The shells, which form both roof and walls of the space they enclose, are covered with cream and white ceramic tiles; their openings are closed with two layers of thick amber-tinted glass to keep out noise and provide views for people in the lobbies.

break up their rather blocky look. Many of these buildings would be set in green park areas situated to capture something of the natural world and the sun. The basic building material was concrete and steel (often the concrete was not finished or polished since Le Corbusier liked the texture of the material). Less inspired architects have utilized these same concepts for public housing with indifferent success—as visits to the peripheries of most urban centers will attest.

Le Corbusier's influence in North America has mainly been derivative. Two other European architects, however, have had an immense impact on American architecture. Walter Gropius (1883–1969) and Ludwig Miës van der Rohe (1896–1969) came to

this country in the late 1930s, refugees from Nazi Germany. Both men had long been associated with the German school of design, the Bauhaus.

Miës van der Rohe's Seagram Building [435] in New York City, designed with Philip Johnson (1906–   ), beautifully illustrates the intent of Bauhaus design. It is a severely chaste building of glass and anodized bronze set on stainless steel pylons placed on a wide granite platform. The uncluttered plaza (broken only by pools) contrasts nicely with the essentially monolithic glass building that rises up from it. The lines of the building are austere in their simplicity while the materials are few and well chosen, with a resultant integration of the whole. It illustrates the "modern" principle of the Bauhaus that simplicity of design results in an aesthetically harmonic whole—"less is more" according to the slogan of this art.

The Seagram Building now seems rather ordinary to us, given the unending procession of glass-and-steel buildings found in most of our large city centers. That many of these buildings are derivative cannot be denied; that they may result in sterile jungles of glass and metal is likewise a fact. Imitation does not always flatter the vision of the artist but excesses do not invalidate the original goal of the Bauhaus designers. They were committed to crispness of design and the imaginative use of material. In the hands of a master architect that idea is still valid, as the stunning new East Wing of the National Gallery of Art in Washington, D. C., clearly demonstrates [436]. This building, designed by I. M. Pei (1917–   ), utilizes pink granite and glass within the limits of a rather rigid geometric design to create a building monumental in scale without loss of lightness or crispness of design.

One can profitably contrast the chaste exterior East Wing of Washington's National Gallery with the Georges Pompidou National Center for Arts and Culture in Paris [Plate 37, page 444], designed by Renzo Piano and Richard Rogers. The Pompidou Center was opened in 1977 as a complex of art, musical research, industrial design, and public archives. The architects eschewed the clean lines of classical sculpture, covering the exterior with brightly colored heating ducts, elevators, escalators, and building supports. It has been an extremely controversial building since its inception but Parisians (and visitors) have found it a beautiful and intriguing place. Whether its industrial style will endure is, of course, open to question, but for now its garishness and nervous energy have made it a cultural mecca. It may even in time rival that other monument once despised by Parisians and now practically a symbol for the city, the Eiffel Tower.

435 Ludwig Miës van der Rohe and Philip Johnson. Seagram Building, New York. 1958. Height 512′ (156.2 m). Compare the severe, clean lines of the Seagram Building with the more ornate, broken-up lines of the older buildings in the background.

436 I. M. Pei. East Wing, National Gallery of Art, Washington. 1978. Pei managed to combine a stunningly "modernist" look with a "classical" one that prevents his building from clashing with the older buildings on the Mall leading to the Capitol.

Some Trends in Contemporary Literature

By the end of World War II literary figures who had defined the modernist temper—writers like T. S. Eliot, James Joyce, Thomas Mann, Ezra Pound—were either dead or had already done their best work. Their passionate search for meaning in an alienated world, however, still inspired the work of others. The great modernist themes received attention by other voices in other media. The Swedish filmmaker Ingmar Bergman (1918–   ) began a series of classic films starting with *Wild Strawberries* in 1956, done in black and white, which explored the loss of religious faith and the demands of modern despair. The enigmatic Irish playwright (who lives in France and writes in French and English) Samuel Beckett (1906–   ) has produced plays like *Waiting for Godot* (1952) that explore an absurdist world beyond logic, decency, and the certainty of language itself.

Waiting for Godot, for all its apparent simplicity, is maddeningly difficult to interpret. Two characters, Vladimir and Estragon, wait at an unnamed and barren crossroads for Godot. Their patient wait is interrupted by antic encounters with two other characters. In the two acts, each representing one day, a young boy announces that Godot will arrive the next day. At the end of the play Vladimir and Estragon decide to wait for Godot although they toy momentarily with the idea of splitting up or committing suicide if Godot does not come to save them.

The language of *Godot* is laced with biblical allusions and religious puns. Is Godot God and does the play illuminate the nature of an absurd world without final significance? Beckett does not say and critics do not agree, although they are in accord with the judgment that *Waiting for Godot* is a classic—if cryptic—statement about language, human relations, and the ultimate significance of the world.

Gradually, as the war receded in time other voices that told us of the horrors of the war experience began to be heard. The most compelling atrocity of the war period, the extermination of six million Jews and countless other dissidents or enemies in the Nazi concentration camps, has resulted in many attempts to tell the world that story. The most significant voice of the survivors of the event is the European-born Elie Wiesel (1928–   ), himself a survivor of the camps. Wiesel describes himself as a "teller of tales." He feels a duty, beyond the normal duty of art, to keep alive the memory of the near-extermination of his people. Wiesel's autobiographical memoir *Night* (1960) recounts his own years in the camps. It is a terribly moving book with its juxtaposition of a young boy's fervent faith as it comes in contact with the demonic powers of the camp.

In the United States an entirely new generation of

writers has defined the nature of the American experience. Arthur Miller's play *Death of a Salesman* (1949) explores the failure of the American dream in the person of its tragic hero, Willie Loman, an ordinary man defeated by life. J. D. Salinger's *Catcher in the Rye* (1951) documented the bewildering coming of age of an American adolescent in so compelling a manner that it was, for a time, a cult book for the young. Southern writers like Eudora Welty, William Styron, Walker Percy, and Flannery O'Connor have continued the meditations of William Faulkner about an area of the United States that has tasted defeat in a way no other region has. Poets like Wallace Stevens, Theodore Roethke, William Carlos Williams, and Marianne Moore have continued to celebrate the beauties and terrors of both nature and people.

We have already noted that existentialism was well suited to the postwar mood. One aspect of existentialism's ethos was its insistence on protest and human dissatisfaction. That element of existential protest has been very much a part of the postwar scene. The civil rights movement of the late 1950s and early 1960s became a paradigm for other more recent protests such as those against the Vietnam war; in favor of the rights of women; for the rights of the dispossessed, underprivileged, or the victims of discrimination. The literature of protest has been very much a part of this cry for human rights.

First, and foremost, one can trace the Afro-Americans' struggle for dignity and full equality through the literature they produced, especially in the period after the First World War. The great pioneers were those writers who are grouped loosely under the name of the "Harlem Renaissance." Writers like Claude McKay, Jean Toomer, Countee Cullen, and, above all, Langston Hughes refused the stereotype of the Negro to craft an eloquent literature demanding humanity and unqualified justice. The work of these writers presaged the powerful torrent of black fiction chronicling racial injustice in America. Two novels in particular, Richard Wright's *Native Son* (1940) and Ralph Ellison's *Invisible Man* (1952), have taken on the character of American classics. Younger writers followed, most notably James Baldwin, whose *Go Tell It On the Mountain* (1953) fused vivid memories of black Harlem, jazz, and the intense religion of the black church into a searing portrait of growing up black in America.

For many of the younger black writers in America the theme of black pride has been linked with the consciousness of being a woman. Nikki Giovanni (1936–   ) has produced a whole body of poetry celebrating both her sense of "blackness" and her pride in her femininity. Her poetry has been a poetic blend of black history and female consciousness done in an American mode.

The rightful claims of women have been advanced in our day by an activist spirit that seeks equality of all people, free from any sexual discrimination. The battle for women's rights began in the last century. It was fought again in the drive for women's suffrage in the first part of this century and continues today in the feminist movement. The cultural oppression of women has been a major concern of the great women writers of our time. Writers like Doris Lessing, Margaret Atwood, Adrienne Rich, Maxine Kumin, and others are exploring feminine consciousness in great depth and from different angles of vision.

Two contemporary poets deserve particular mention, since both of them dealt so clearly with the dissatisfaction of women. Sylvia Plath (1932–1963) and Anne Sexton (1928–1974) used the imagery of traditional sexual roles to complain about the restraints of their position. Ironically enough, the precociously talented Sylvia Plath and Anne Sexton briefly knew each other when they studied poetry together. Sylvia Plath not only produced an important body of poetry but a largely autobiographical novel *The Bell Jar* (1962), describing most of her short and unhappy life. Anne Sexton, by contrast, wrote only poetry.

A Note on the Postmodern

For the past decade or so some literary critics have been insisting, with varying degrees of acceptance, that much of contemporary literature has moved beyond the modernist preoccupation with alienation, myth, fragmentation of time, and the interior states of the self. The most debated question now is: What exactly has followed modernism (by definition it is postmodern) and does it have a shaping spirit? Further, who are its most significant practitioners? The latter question seems to be the easier of the two. Many critics would mention the following among those who are setting and defining the postmodernist literary agenda: Italo Calvino in Italy; Jorge Luis Borges in Argentina; Gabriel García Márquez in Colombia; and a strong group of American writers that includes Donald Barthelme, Robert Coover, John Barth, Stanley Elkin, Thomas Pynchon, Renata Adler, Susan Sontag, and Kurt Vonnegut, Jr.

That list of writers represents far-ranging and diverse sensibilities. What do they hold in common that permits them to be considered representative postmodernists? Some critics see the postmodernists as those who push the modernist world view to its extreme limit. Postmodernist writing, these critics would say, is less concerned with traditional plot lines, more antirational, more private in its vision, more concerned to make the work a private world of meanings and significations. This is hardly a satisfactory definition since it merely defines the postmodern as more of the same. It does not define, it merely extends the definition. Postmodernism is a form of literary art in the process of birth. It must build on what modernism has accomplished but it must find its own voice.

It is impossible to make art today as if cubism or abstract expressionism had never existed, just as it is impossible to compose music as if Stravinsky had never lived. Further, we cannot live life (or even look at it) as if relativity, atomic weapons, and Freudian explorations of the unconscious were not part of our intellectual and social climate. If art is to be part of the human enterprise it must surely reflect its past without being a prisoner of it. In fact, most of the great achievements in the arts have done precisely that; they have mastered the tradition and then extended it. The terrain of modernism has been fairly well mapped; it is time to move on. But in what direction?

Music Since 1945

Avant-Garde Developments

Since World War II many avant-garde composers have been moving toward greater and greater complexity of musical organization, coupled with an increasing use of new kinds of sound. At the same time other musicians, disturbed by their colleagues' obsessive concern for order, have tried to introduce an element of chance, even chaos, into the creation of a work of music. Both the "structuralists" and the advocates of random music have attracted followers, and only time will tell which approach will prove more fruitful.

Before considering the nature of these two schools in detail, some general observations are in order. It must be admitted that advanced contemporary music presents a tough challenge to the patience and sympathy of many sincere music-lovers. Unlike the visual arts and literature, modern music seems, superficially at least, to have made a virtually complete break with past traditions. Furthermore, much of it seems remote from our actual experience. Developments in painting or architecture are visible around us in one

form or another on a daily basis, and modern writers deal with problems that affect us in our own lives. Many creative musicians, however, have withdrawn to the scientific laboratory, where they construct their pieces with the aid of machines and in accordance with mathematical principles. It is hardly surprising that the results may seem sterile at first.

Yet it is well worth making an effort to understand and enjoy the latest developments in music. Concentration and open-mindedness will remove many of the barriers. So will persistence. Music lovers who listen twenty times to a recording of a Chopin waltz or a Mahler symphony for every one time they listen to a work by Boulez or Stockhausen can hardly expect to make much progress in understanding a new and admittedly difficult idiom. Much of today's music may well not survive the test of time, but it is equally probable that some pieces will become the classics of the 21st century. By discriminating listening we can play our own part in judging which music is worthless and which will be of permanent value.

The principle of precise musical organization had already become important in 20th-century music with the serialism of Arnold Schoenberg. Schoenberg's ordering of pitch (the melodic and harmonic element of music) in rigidly maintained twelve-note rows has been extended by recent composers to other elements. Pierre Boulez (1925–   ), for example, constructed rows of twelve note-durations (the length of time each note sounds), twelve levels of volume, and twelve ways of striking the keys for works like his *Second Piano Sonata* (1948) and *Structures* for two pianos (1952). In this music every element (pitch, length of notes, volume, and attack) is totally ordered and controlled by the composer in accordance with his predetermined rows, since none of the twelve components of each row can be repeated until after the other eleven.

The effect of this "total control" is to eliminate any sense of traditional melody, harmony, or counterpoint along with the emotions they evoke. Instead the composer aims to create a pure and abstract "structure" that deliberately avoids any kind of subjective emotional expression.

There remains, however, one element in these piano works that even Boulez cannot totally control—the human one. All the composer's instructions, however precise, have to be interpreted and executed by a performer, and as long as composers are dependent on performers to interpret their works they cannot avoid a measure of subjectivity. Different pianists will inevitably produce different results, and even the same pianist will not produce an identical performance on every occasion.

437 From Karlheinz Stockhausen. *Nr. 11 Refrain.* Copyright 1961 by Universal Edition (London), Ltd., London. Used by permission. This portion of the score was reproduced in the composer's own work, *Test on Electronic and Instrumental Music.* The system of musical notation that Stockhausen devised for this piece is as revolutionary as the music itself; it is explained in a preface to the score.

It was to solve this problem that in the 1950s some composers began to turn to *electronic music,* the sounds of which are produced not by conventional musical instruments but by an electronic oscillator, a machine that produces pure sound waves. A composer can order the sounds by means of a computer and then transfer them to recording tape for playback. In the last few years the process of manipulating electronic sound has been much simplified by the invention of the *synthesizer,* a piece of equipment that can produce just about any kind of sound effect. In combination with a computer, machines like the Moog synthesizer can be used either for original electronic works or for creating electronic versions of traditional music, as in the popular "Switched-on Bach" recordings.

From its earliest days, electronic music has alarmed many listeners by its apparent lack of humanity. The whistles, clicks, and hisses that characterize it may be eerily appropriate to the mysteries of the space age, but they have little to do with traditional musical expression. Indeed, composers of electronic music have had considerable difficulty in inventing formal structures for organizing the vast range of sounds available to them. In addition, there still exists no universally agreed-on system of writing down electronic compositions; most of them exist only on tape. It is probably significant that even Karlheinz Stockhausen (1928–   ), one of the leading figures in electronic music, has tended to combine electronic sounds with conventional musical instruments (437). His *Mixtur* (1965), for example, is written for five orchestras, electronic equipment, and loudspeakers. During performance the sounds produced by the orchestral instruments are electronically altered and simultaneously mixed with the instrumental sound and with a prerecorded tape. In this way an element of live participation has been reintroduced.

For all its radical innovations, however, *Mixtur* at least maintains the basic premise of music in the Western tradition: that composers can communicate with their listeners by predetermining ("composing") their works according to an intellectual series of rules. The laws of baroque counterpoint, classical sonata form, or Stockhausen's ordering and altering of sound patterns all represent systems that have enabled composers to plan and create musical works. One of the most revolutionary of all recent developments, however, has been the invention of *aleatoric* music. The name is derived from the Latin word *alea* (a dice game) and is applied to music in which an important role is played by the element of chance.

One of the leading exponents of this kind of music is the American composer John Cage (1912–   ), who has been much influenced by Zen philosophy. Adopting the Zen attitude that one must go beyond logic in life, Cage has argued that music should reflect the random chaos of the world around us and so does not seek to impose order on it. His *Concert for Piano and Orchestra* of 1958 has a piano part consisting of 84 different "sound events," some, all, or none of which are to be played in any random order. The orchestral accompaniment consists of separate pages of music, some, all, or none of which can be played by any (or no) instrument, in any order and combination. Clearly every performance of the *Concert* is going to be a unique event, largely dependent on pure chance for its actual sound. In other pieces Cage has instructed the performers to determine the sequence of events by even more random methods, including the tossing of coins.

Works like these are, of course, more interesting for the questions they ask about the nature of music than for any intrinsic value of their own. Cage has partly reacted against what he regards as the excessive organization and rigidity of composers like Boulez and Stockhausen, but at the same time he has also raised some important considerations. What is the function of the artist in the modern world? What is the relationship between creator and performer? And what part, if any, should the listeners themselves play in the creation of a piece of music? Need it always be a passive one? If Cage's own answers to questions like these may not satisfy everyone, he has at least posed the problems in an intriguing form.

Traditional Approaches to Modern Music

Not all composers have abandoned the traditional means of musical expression. Musicians like Benjamin Britten (1913–1976) and Dmitri Shostakovich (1906–1975) demonstrated that an innovative approach to the traditional elements of melody, harmony, and rhythm can still produce exciting and moving results. Nor can either of them be accused of losing touch with the modern world. Britten's *War Requiem* (1962) is an eloquent plea for an end to the violence of contemporary life, while Shostakovich's entire musical output reflects his uneasy relationship with Soviet authority. His *Symphony No. 13* (1962) includes settings of poems by the Russian poet Yevtushenko on antisemitism in Russia and earned him unpopularity in Soviet artistic and political circles.

Both Britten and Shostakovich did not hesitate to write recognizable "tunes" in their music. In his last symphony, *No. 15* (1971), Shostakovich even quoted themes from Rossini's *William Tell Overture* (the familiar "Lone Ranger" theme) and from Wagner. The work is at the same time easy to listen to and deeply serious. Like much of Shostakovich's music, it is concerned with the nature of death (a subject also explored in his *Symphony No. 14*). Throughout its four movements, Shostakovich's sense of rhythm is much in evidence, as is his feeling for orchestral color, in which he demonstrates that the resources of a traditional symphony orchestra are far from exhausted. The final mysterious dying close of *Symphony No. 15* is especially striking in its use of familiar ingredients—repeating rhythmic patterns, simple melodic phrases—to achieve an unusual effect.

If Shostakovich demonstrated that a musical form as old-fashioned as the symphony can still be used to create masterpieces, Britten did the same for opera. His first great success, *Peter Grimes* (1945), employed traditional operatic devices like arias, trios, and choruses to depict the tragic fate of its hero, a man whose alienation from society leads to his persecution at the hands of his fellow citizens. In other works Britten followed the example of many of his illustrious predecessors in turning to earlier literary masterpieces for inspiration. *A Midsummer Night's Dream* (1960) is a setting of Shakespeare's play, while *Death in Venice* (1973) is based on the story by Thomas Mann. In all of his operas Britten writes music that is easy to listen to (and, equally important, not impossible to sing), but he never condescends to his audience. Each work deals with a recognizable area of human experience and presents it in a valid musical and dramatic form. It is always dangerous to make predictions about the verdict of posterity, but from today's vantage point the music of Britten seems to have as good a chance as any of surviving into the next century.

Popular Music

No discussion of music since 1945 would be complete without mention of pop music, the worldwide appeal of which is a social fact of our times. Much of pop music is American in origin, although its ancestry is deeply rooted in the larger Western musical tradition. Its development both in this country and abroad is so complex as to be outside the scope of this book. One cannot adequately describe in a few pages the character of folk music, rhythm and blues, country and western, and the various shades of rock, much less sketch out their tangled interrelationships.

A single example demonstrates this complexity. During the 1960s, protest singers like Joan Baez, Pete Seeger, and Bob Dylan had in their standard repertoire a song called "This Land Is Your Land." The song had been written by Woody Guthrie as an American leftist reaction to the sentiments expressed in Irving Berlin's "God Bless America." Guthrie had adapted an old mountain ballad sung by the Carter Family, who had been a formative part of country and western music at the Grand Ol' Opry since the late 1920s. The Carters played and sang mountain music that was a complex blending of Old English balladry, Scottish drills, some black music, and the hymn tradition of the mountain churches.

The worldwide appeal of pop music must be recognized. The numbers in themselves are staggering. Between 1965 and 1973 nearly twelve hundred different recorded versions of the Beatles' song "Yesterday" (written by Paul McCartney and John Lennon) were available. By 1977 the Beatles had sold over one hundred million record albums and the same number of singles. Elvis Presley had sold more than eighty million singles at the time of his death in 1977; today, some years after his death, all his major albums remain in stock in record stores. Behind the Iron Curtain records and tapes are among the more prized objects in the underground or black-market economy.

The very best of popular music, both folk and rock, is sophisticated and elegant music. Classic rock albums of the Beatles like *Revolver* reflect influences from the blues, ballads, the music of India, jazz harmonies, and some baroque orchestrations. The talented (and outrageous) Frank Zappa and the Mothers of Invention dedicated their 1960s album *Freak Out* to "Charles Mingus, Pierre Boulez, Anton Webern, Igor Stravinsky, Willie Dixon, Guitar Slim, Edgar Varèse, and Muddy Waters." Zappa's experiments with mixing rock and classical music are deemed serious enough for Zubin Mehta and the Los Angeles Philharmonic to attempt some joint concerts. The popular folk singer Judy Collins' most successful album of the 1960s—*Wildflowers*—was orchestrated and arranged by Joshua Rifkin, a classical composer once on the music faculty of Princeton University. The crossbreeding of folk, rock, and classical modes of music continues with increasing interest in the use of electronic music and advanced amplification systems.

The folk and rock music of the 1960s saw itself as in the vanguard of social change and turmoil. Rock music was inextricably entwined with the youth culture. In fact, popular music provided one of the most patent examples of the so-called generation gap. If the Beatles upset the older generation with their sunny irreverence, their coded language about drugs, and their open sexuality, groups like the Rolling Stones were regarded by many as a clear menace to society. With their hard-driving music, their aggressive style of life, their sensuality, and their barely concealed flirtation with violence and nihilism, the Stones were seen by many as a living metaphor for the anarchy of the turbulent 1960s. It was hardly reassuring for parents to see their young bring home a Stones album entitled *Their Satanic Majesties Request* inside the cover of which is an apocalyptic collage of Hieronymus Bosch, Ingres, Mughal Indian miniatures, and pop photography. Nor were many consoled when the violence of the music was translated into actual violence as rock stars like Jimi Hendrix, Janis Joplin, Phil Ochs, and Jim Morrison destroyed themselves with alcohol or drugs.

Whatever the long-range judgment of history may be, pop music in its variegated forms is as much an indicator of our present culture as the novels of Dickens were of the 19th century. It partakes of both brash commercial hype and genuine social statement. The record album of a major rock group today represents the complex interaction of advanced technology, big business, and high-powered marketing techniques as well as the music itself. Likewise, a rock concert is not merely the live presentation of music to an audience but a multimedia "happening" in which the plastic arts, dramatic staging, sophisticated lighting and amplification, and a medley of other visual and aural aids are blended to create an artistic whole with the music. Beyond (or under) this glitter, notoriety, and hype, however, is a music arising from real issues and expressing real feelings. New wave and punk rock, for instance, reflect the alienation of the working-class youth of Great Britain today.

Finally, pop music is not a phenomenon of the moment alone. Its roots are in the tribulations of urban blacks, the traditionalism of rural whites, the protest of activists, and the hopes and aspirations of the common people, causes with a lengthy history in the United States yet still alive today. Pop music, then, is both a social document of our era and a record of our past.

The very best pop music hymns the joy of love, the anxiety of modern life, the yearning for ecstasy, and the damnation of institutionalized corruption. Rock music in particular creates and offers the possibility of ecstasy. For those who dwell in the urban wastelands of posttechnological America or the stultifying structures of post-Stalinist Eastern Europe the vibrant beat and incessant sound of rock music must be a welcome, if temporary, refuge from the bleakness of life.

Questions for Further Discussion

1. Walk around your college campus and look at the newer buildings. How many of them reflect the ideas and notions of the great modern architects? In how many does "form follow function"? How many exemplify the maxim that "less is more"? How do they relate to their environment?

2. Examine some examples of slick high-quality commercial art such as record-album covers or high-fashion advertising. How much of modern or contemporary art has commercial illustration absorbed?

3. Reflect a bit on the contemporary rock concert as a multimedia event. To what degree does the music depend on visuals (such as lighting), costumes, staging, and so on? Can you make any aesthetic correlations between a rock concert and, say, an opera or a mass celebrated in a medieval cathedral?

4. Sartre argued that existentialism is a philosophy that is rooted in its serious commitment to the consequences of atheism. If you are a nonbeliever, do you draw the same conclusions as Sartre? If you are a believer, how do you react to Sartre's program for life?

5. Look at a large open space in your town and try to visualize or conceptualize a monumental sculpture for it. What material, form, and plan would best express your ideas for that space?

6. In the last two chapters we talked a good deal about modernism and postmodernism. To what degree do you consider yourself a modern or postmodern person? To what characteristics of the modernist temperament do you most passionately react, either in a positive or negative way?

Suggestions for Listening

Chapter 1: The Beginnings of Civilization

There is little doubt that music played a role in the lives of all the peoples discussed in this chapter, but what instruments were used in the earliest periods, or what they actually sounded like, can now only be conjectured. We do know that a musical culture existed in Egypt as early as the 4th millennium B.C. and that chiefly small harps and flutes were used to produce quiet and reserved music in the Old Kingdom (before the 18th century B.C.). The introduction of Asiatic instruments and music at the beginning of the New Kingdom (16th century B.C.) brought a complete change and an orchestra that included large harps, lutes, oboes, and assorted percussion instruments such as drum and sistrum. The musical pendulum swung back around 600 B.C. with the reinstitution of ancient sacred rites—with the result that Plato, Herodotus, and other Greek writers reported the highly restrained character of Egyptian music. Egyptian music, in any event, doubtless influenced the development of Greek music (see Chapters 3 and 4). And in the early Christian era, Alexandria was an important center of psalm-singing as part of Christian worship.

Ancient Mesopotamia and Egypt nevertheless served as subject matter for later composers, as two examples show. The 20th-century Czech composer Bohuslăv Martinŭ wrote his *The Epic of Gilgamesh* (1955) for orchestra, chorus, and soloists; this is a dignified and sometimes moving setting of extracts from the epic, including the death of Enkidu (available on Supraphon 1121808).

Much more familiar is Giuseppe Verdi's late–19th-century version of ancient Egypt in his opera *Aida,* commissioned by the Khedive of Egypt for the new Opera House in Cairo and produced there in 1871 (many recordings available). Verdi did inspect some old Egyptian musical instruments in the Archaeological Museum in Florence and said that he used a few Egyptian musical themes. The splendid result is scarcely the Egypt of any of the pharaohs but is surely romantic Italian opera at its grandest.

Chapter 2: Jerusalem and the Biblical Tradition

Nothing has survived of the actual music performed in biblical times, but we can gain some idea of its character from Jewish liturgical music of later periods. A disc in Philips' *International Series* (PH 6856001) entitled "Jewish Music" offers a good selection of religious chants and hymns from the Hebrew tradition. The same disc also includes music played on the *shofar* (ram's horn), which is the only musical instrument used by Orthodox Jews in divine services after the destruction of the Second Temple in A.D. 70 and the only biblical instrument to survive to the present.

The words of the psalms have provided a source of inspiration for composers of all ages. The music of the later composers does not reflect the music of the biblical period, but it does reflect the power of the poetry of these great writings. Two 20th-century works, in particular, mentioned in the text of this chapter, are worthy of note: Leonard Bernstein's *Chichester Psalms* (1965) and Igor Stravinsky's *Symphony of Psalms* (1930). Both compositions conducted by their composers are available: Bernstein on Columbia MS 6792 and, more recently, on Deutsche Grammofon (DG 2709077); Stravinsky on Columbia MS 6548. Also of particular musical interest is the Hungarian composer Zoltán Kodály's *Psalmus Hungaricus* (1923), available on Hungariton SLPX 11392.

Chapter 3: Early Greece

Because evidence for the actual sound of Greek music is very scanty, the few recorded examples of modern reconstructions are discussed in the Suggestions for Listening following Chapter 4.

The number of composers in more recent times who have chosen Greek poems or subjects for their works is legion. The *Iliad* and the *Odyssey* have provided the theme for a great number of operas, from Claudio Monteverdi's *Il Ritorno d' Ulisse in Patria (The Return of Odysseus to his Native Land)* of 1641, available on Telefunken 4635024, to Michael Tippett's *King Priam* of 1962 (London LDR 73006). Sappho's poems have been set to music by several composers, including the 20th-century Italian Luigi Dallapiccola; the only opera of any note devoted to her is Charles Gounod's *Sapho* (1851).

Chapter 4: Classical Greece and its Aftermath

Apart from two fragments from the 5th century B.C., one of doubtful authenticity, the earliest Greek music to have survived dates to the late 2nd century B.C. Two hymns to Apollo were found on the walls of the Treasury at Delphi and a *skolion* (drinking song) was found carved on the tombstone of Seikilos, who died in Asia Minor around 100 B.C. All three pieces have been reconstructed and performed, and a number of recordings are available. Probably the most reliable one is that in Volume 1 of the *History of Music in Sound,* produced jointly by the Oxford University Press and RCA.

But beyond these tantalizing fragments is silence. One of the great creative achievements in our humanistic tradition is lost, probably forever. At various times in the history of music, composers have tried to imagine the effects produced by a Greek drama performed with music in order to imitate it. The earliest surviving opera, Jacopo Peri's *Euridice* of 1600 (available on Telefunken 2635014), is the result of Renaissance curiosity about the Greeks, while Carl Orff's versions of *Antigone* and *Oedipus the King* represent 20th-century interpretations. Other composers have handled Greek dramatic subjects with greater freedom, retaining the stories but interpreting them in their own style. Perhaps the most powerful of all works based on a Greek play is Richard Strauss' *Elektra*, first performed in 1908 and available in a superb recording on London 1269. Although Strauss and his librettist Hugo von Hoffmansthal approached their subject from a modern point of view, incorporating ideas from the works of Freud and others, the shattering emotional impact of *Elektra* perhaps goes some way toward reproducing the original effect of the tragedies when first performed.

Another 20th-century composer, Igor Stravinsky, set a Latin version of *Oedipus the King* to music in his *Oedipus Rex* (1927), available on London 1168. Although very different in spirit from Strauss' opera, Stravinsky's score is in its own way equally impressive, if more austere. Elsewhere he tried to recapture a different aspect of the Greek world, the sense of the balance and clarity that are so closely identified with the Classical period. Two of his ballet scores, *Orpheus* (1948) and the beautiful *Apollon Musagète*, or *Apollo Leader of the Muses* (1928), are available on Columbia MS 6646 in versions conducted by the composer.

Martha Graham's ballet *Clytemnestra*, inspired by the *Oresteia*, is one of the great classics of modern dance as well as a reminder of the expressive power dance can bring to the reenactment of ancient myths.

Chapter 5: The Roman Legacy

Apart from occasional literary references and the discovery at Pompeii and elsewhere of some musical instruments, we know very little about Roman music or how it was made. Cultured Romans would in any event have turned to Greek music for intellectual pleasure, and so distinguished a non-professional lyre-player and singer as Nero would doubtless have performed only Greek works. The local composers' output would have been encountered in more popular form on such public occasions as theatrical performances, games, and processions.

Roman history and literature, however, provided as rich and frequent an inspiration for later composers as for writers and artists. Nero himself figured prominently in at least one early opera, Claudio Monteverdi's *L'incoronazione di Poppea* (*The Coronation of Poppea*), which was first produced in 1642 in Venice and concerns the emperor's mistress Poppea who replaces the empress and assumes her place on the throne. Cleopatra has appeared frequently on the operatic stage both alone and with her eminent lovers—in Handel's *Julius Caesar* (1724), Domenico Cimarosa's *Cleopatra* of 1791, in the 1914 *Cléopâtre* of Jules Massenet (who also wrote an opera titled *Roma* two years earlier), and Samuel Barber's *Antony and Cleopatra* (1966), among others.

Robert Schumann wrote a *Julius Caesar Overture*, and both Marc Blitzstein and Darius Milhaud wrote incidental music for Shakespeare's *Julius Caesar*. The distinguished American composer Virgil Thomson, among others, has written incidental music for Shakespeare's *Antony and Cleopatra*.

One further work illustrates the impact of Roman literature—in this case Vergil's *Aeneid*—on the Western artistic tradition. Between 1856 and 1858 the French composer Hector Berlioz created a mammoth operatic work, *The Trojans*, that has come to be appreciated as one of the magnificent peaks of 19th-century musical drama. It is available in a superb recorded performance on Philips 6709002.

Chapter 6: The World of Byzantium

Byzantine music is much less well known in the West than the great tradition of medieval religious music, Gregorian Chant. Byzantine music is nevertheless a living tradition of the Orthodox Church. Modern versions of Byzantine chant show the influences of the centuries but allow us to catch the peculiarities of the music, which is in spirit somewhat closer to Jewish and Oriental music than to the religious chants of the West. One of the most interesting and atmospheric recordings of Byzantine music was actually made on Mount Athos in Greece, a recording of the Easter Liturgy sung by the monastic community of Athos (DG ARC 2533413). Another record, Philips 6830194, is a setting of the Liturgy of Saint John Chrysostom.

The words of the Liturgy of Saint John Chrysostom have also been set to music by modern composers, particularly those with a personal attachment to the Orthodox Church. Tchaikovsky, normally associated with intensely dramatic and romantic music, wrote a setting of the Byzantine Liturgy (Angel SZ 3876). Sergei Rachmaninoff's version of the Liturgy is available on Angel S 3864.

Chapter 7: The Age of Charlemagne

Intense studies over the past hundred years have given scholars and musicians very precise notions about early medieval chant, and many recordings are available for the serious listener. One older collection is the two-record *A Treasury of Gregorian Chants* (SDBR 3159), an anthology of church music sung by a variety of monastic choirs. More useful for study is the Schola Antiqua recording (directed by R. John Blackley) called *A Guide to Gregorian Chant* (VSD 71217). This set has very fine liner notes and a discussion of the origin and development of Gregorian music. The Cappella Musicale of the Milan Cathedral in Italy has recorded representative examples of Ambrosian music in a recording called simply *Ambrosian Chant* (DG ARC 2533158). For a musical setting of a medieval play one might begin with the New York Pro Musica rendering of the *Play of Daniel* (MCA 2504).

Chapter 8: The High Middle Ages: The Search for Synthesis

The Musical Heritage Society has made available a rich historical anthology of music for study and enjoyment in its *History of Western Music*. Volume I, "The Music of the Early Middle Ages" (two discs: OR 349, OR 350), provides a fine and wide-ranging selection of medieval music from chants and simple organum to conductus and motet. For a sense of the strong devotion to the Virgin prevalent in the Middle Ages the student might sample some music and verse dedicated to the Virgin from 11th- and 12th-century Spain. The music, derived from the court of Alfonso X, is available on the following recording: *Las Cantigas de Santa Maria* (VSD 71175). For secular music the Vanguard recording (VCS 10049) called "The Jolly Minstrels" is worthwhile, especially for its attention to the musical instruments of the High Middle Ages. One of the finest recordings of the Carl Orff *Carmina Burana* is the Deutsche Grammophon (139362) version performed by the Berlin Opera Company (the Latin and German text comes with translations).

Chapter 9: The 14th Century: A Time of Transition

Machaut's music has been recorded many times. The Seraphim label (S–6092) has a collection of his ballads and other shorter pieces. Deutsche Grammaphon (D. KG. ARC 2533054) has recorded the *Messe de Notre Dame,* which should be the focus for listening in this chapter. The Haydn Society's useful *Masterpieces of Music before 1750* has selections from Machaut and Landini on their recording subtitled "Gregorian Music to the Sixteenth Century" (HS 9038). The records in the *Masterpieces of Music* series generally are most useful.

Chapter 10: The Early Renaissance

While music was very much a part of Florentine life, the composition of music did not undergo the great rebirth that one associates with 15th-century art in that city. Lorenzo de' Medici was keenly interested in music; many of his poems and songs were set to music by the German (or, perhaps, Flemish) composer and organist Heinrich Isaac, who was in his employ from 1479 until Lorenzo's death in 1492. The Pro Musica group of New York has recorded some of Isaac's compositions for Lorenzo's poetry under the title *Music for the Court of Lorenzo the Magnificent* (MCA 2508). The same group has also recorded a more general disc of *Florentine Music* (MCA 2515), which is representative of the period.

One of the most influential and representative composers in the north was Johannes Ockeghem (1420–1496). The style of his secular music can be seen in a Nonesuch recording of his *Motets:Chansons* (Nonesuch 71336). Ockeghem

also composed the earliest Requiem Mass (Funeral Mass) we possess. The London-based Pro Cantione Antiqua has recorded it as *Missa Pro Defunctis* (D. G. Arc. 2533145).

Chapter 11: The High Renaissance in Italy

Palestrina has been relatively well served by the recording companies, and a number of his works are currently available. The *Missa Papae Marcelli* and a *Missa Brevis* are coupled on Angel Seraphim S 60187, in fine performances by the choir of King's College, Cambridge. The listener in search of complete authenticity, however, should turn to Everest 3193, on which three motets are performed by the Sistine Choir, recorded live in a concert at the Vatican. Music by Victoria, Palestrina's great contemporary, can be found on two Argo discs. On ZRG 570 his *Requiem Mass for the Empress Maria* is coupled with four motets, and Argo 5149 is devoted to his *Responsories for Tenebrae,* a work that gives a good impression of the somber splendor of his style.

Giovanni Gabrieli is best represented by two magnificent recordings of his music, Columbia MS 7142 and Columbia M 30937, which were actually made in Venice, in the Basilica of Saint Mark's. The sense of space, with the brass choirs answering one another from opposite sides of the church, has been brilliantly captured by the engineers, and the extremely reverberant acoustics make it possible to hear the music as it was originally conceived. Quite apart from the documentary value of the discs, the sumptuous grandeur of the sound—and of course of the music itself—should appeal to the most unhistorically minded of listeners. Played at full volume on good equipment, it seems to summon up all the pomp and display of a Venetian festive occasion.

Chapter 12: The Renaissance in the North

Northern Renaissance music is well represented on disc, with a number of interesting anthology albums available, as well as recordings of individual composers' works. Music from the court of Henry VIII can be found on Argo ZRG 566, an album entitled *To Entertain a King*. A two-record set of Elizabethan music is available on Nonesuch 73010, *Music of Shakespeare's Time*. Those preferring to cross the Channel can turn to *Love and Dalliance in Renaissance France* on Turnabout 34380, while listeners of a quieter disposition might prefer *Music of the English Home, 1570–1670* on Turnabout 34709.

Tallis' *Lamentations of Jeremiah* is available in a fine performance on Archive 2533113, very conveniently coupled with Byrd's *Latin Mass in Three Parts*. The whole of Byrd's keyboard collection, *My Ladye Nevells Booke,* is available in a four-record set, L'Oiseau-Lyre D29D–4. A judicious selection in listening is advised; more than a side at a time can daunt even the most devoted Byrd lover. For the madrigals of Morley and his contemporaries, a useful anthology is available on Turnabout 34202. Julian Bream has recorded several collections of Dowland's lute music, including one on RCA LSC 2819 that also contains some pieces by Byrd. There are a number of recordings of Dowland ayres, among them Turnabout 34510 and Nonesuch 71167. Individual choices will vary, but both provide a good selection.

Finally, there are two notable 20th-century reactions to the Renaissance in northern Europe. The English composer Ralph Vaughan Williams entitled one of his best works *Fantasia on a Theme by Thomas Tallis* (1910). Written for strings, it consists of a series of variations on an especially beautiful theme by his distinguished predecessor. Angel S 36101 contains a sensitive performance of the *Fantasia* as well as Vaughan Williams' other *Fantasia*, this one on "Greensleeves," a tune often attributed to no less a composer than Henry VIII.

Matthias Grünewald, about whom we know virtually nothing, may seem a rather unlikely hero for a 20th-century opera, but *Mathis der Maler* (1938) by Paul Hindemith takes as its subject the last years of the artist's life and his painting of the *Isenheim Altarpiece*. The work's real subject is an eternally relevant one, the relationship of the artist to society and, in more general terms, the purpose of art itself. It is not an easy opera since both text and music are complex and packed with meaning, but it well repays the effort. Its message is a profound one, and the experience of hearing a great 20th-century artist turn to the past in order to come to terms with the future is very impressive. A dedicated and moving performance is available on Angel SZCX 3869 (3 discs).

Chapter 13: The Baroque World

The first opera now extant, Peri's *Euridice* (1600), is available on Telefunken 2635014 in a serviceable performance. Monteverdi's *L'Orfeo* (1609) can be found on Telefunken 3635020 in a rather more lively version; his work is by far the more interesting of the two, and the performances tend to underline the fact. A touching and beautiful demonstration of the emotional power of Monteverdi's style can be found on CBS M35138, where Frederica von Stade sings Penelope's long lament to the absent Ulysses, "Torna, torna," from one of Monteverdi's last operas, *Il Ritorno d' Ulisse in Patria (The Return of Ulysses to His Native Land)* (1641). Later 17th-century opera is well represented by *La Calisto* by Pier Francesco Cavalli (1602–1676), sung by an all-star cast on Argo ZNF 11/12. The purist should beware, however, since the edition used is modern, with considerable touching up. French opera of the same period has been relatively neglected, although Lully's *Alceste* (1674) and Rameau's *Les Indes Galantes* are both available, the former on CBS M3–34580 and the latter on CBS M3–32973.

The number of discs of baroque instrumental music is stupefying. Vivaldi's popular set of violin concertos, *The Four Seasons,* is available in more than thirty different recorded versions. Other Vivaldi concertos can be found in profusion, ranging from his Concertos for Piccolo (a good version is on Nonesuch 71022) to the interesting Concerto for Two Cellos on Nonesuch 71104, a particularly useful record, since it also includes a Concerto for Bassoon and two Double Concertos, one for oboe and violin and the other for guitar and viola d'amore. The baroque enthusiast who wants to explore the comparatively unknown world of Vivaldi's opera (and has plenty of time to spare) can turn to *Tito Manlio,* available in a five-record set, Philips 6769004.

Other Italian baroque composers are also well represented, including Corelli, whose popular *Christmas Concerto* can be found on DGG 2530070, along with works by three other baroque masters, Locatelli, Manfredini, and Torelli. Albinoni's popular *Adagio for Strings* (most of which is a modern "reconstruction" of a fragment of dubious authenticity) has been recorded a number of times, including a version on London 7102, which conveniently couples it with works by Bach and Handel.

The listener wishing to explore Handel's music is faced with an astonishing number of riches. The best introduction to his operas is probably *Alcina,* stunningly recorded on London 1361 by a cast that includes Joan Sutherland. His popular *Water Music* and *Royal Fireworks Music* are available in a large number of versions. Argo ZRG 697 conveniently couples the latter with excerpts from the former in stylish performances. It would be daring to recommend a single version of *Messiah,* a work that can be performed in so many different styles. Those in search of authenticity can turn to Angel S–3705, where the scale of the original forces is preserved, while CBS M25603 and Angel Seraphim S6056 give a better idea of how *Messiah* generally sounds in the Anglo-Saxon world. A final curiosity is the performance conducted by Sir Thomas Beecham on RCA AGL3–2444, utterly unauthentic but immensely enjoyable.

As for Bach, the quantity of his output is fully mirrored in the number of discs available of his music. There are some thirty versions of the Brandenburg Concertos to choose from. The performances directed by Yehudi Menuhin on Angel 54787 manage to combine authenticity with verve and affection, and the version on London 2225 has a special interest in that the conductor is Benjamin Britten, one of the 20th century's greatest composers. Many of the other recordings, though, are equally satisfactory. Telefunken is at present in the process of releasing recordings of the entire series of cantatas, a massive project made particularly worthwhile by the inclusion of the scores of the works in the albums. Telefunken 2635362 includes Cantata 78 and is one of the finest of the series. A good middle-of-the-road performance of the *Saint Matthew Passion* can be found on London 1431.

No lover of Bach should miss his violin concertos—the Double Concerto for two violins in particular—available in fine performances on Philips 9500226. As for his keyboard music, the classic performance of the *Goldberg Variations* by Rosalyn Tureck on CBS M2 35900 will appeal to those who like Bach on the piano, while harpsichord devotees can turn to Angel S3796. There are so many different recitals of Bach organ music, with such a variety of programs, that recommendation seems fruitless. Finally, two personal favorites: Otto Klemperer's recording of the *Mass in B*

Minor, perhaps the most lofty of all Bach's religious works, on Angel S3720, is perhaps not totally authentic in all musicological respects but it conveys the strength and vision of the music with incomparable grandeur. At the other end of the scale a recital of Bach arias by Janet Baker on Angel S37229 includes a restrained but infinitely touching version of *Bist du bei mir,* the song Bach wrote for his wife Anna Magdalena.

Chapter 14: The 18th Century: From Reason to Revolution

Chief interest in the 18th century will inevitably concentrate on the music of Haydn and Mozart, but that of C.P.E. Bach should by no means be ignored, although it is not of the same quality. Six of his flue sonatas, played by the great French flutist Jean-Pierre Rampal, are available on Nonesuch 71034, while Philips 6500830 couples two of his oboe concertos in stylish performances. With these two discs and perhaps CMX Oryx 23, which includes a flute concerto and a cello concerto, the imaginative listener can re-create the atmosphere of the court of Frederick the Great, where Frederick played the flute and Voltaire talked.

Haydn's 104 symphonies are all available, in the performances of Antal Dorati conducting the Philharmonica Hungarica, on 48 discs in London's Stereo Treasury Series. Dorati's interpretations combine musical sensitivity and vitality with the latest in musicological research—the albums are worth buying for the accompanying notes alone, written by the great Haydn scholar H. C. Robbins Landon. The number of symphonies may seem daunting, but virtually every one has interest or beauty or both; London Records has put us all in its debt by making them available on its bargain label. The six-record album London STS 15319/24 contains the last twelve "London" symphonies (named after the city, not the record company); they provide a good starting point, but the middle-period symphonies should not be neglected. STS 15127–30 contains Nos. 49–56, which include some marvelous works.

Haydn's string quartets, 82 in all, also offer rich rewards and are available in a wide number of different combinations. RCA ARL 1–1409, which contains Op. 64, No. 5, and Op. 76, No. 2, in excellent performances by the Cleveland Quartet, will provide appropriate temptation to explore further. And anyone who thinks of Haydn as a composer only of lighthearted, cheerful music should listen to one of his wonderful, inspired masses. Two of the best are both available in eloquent performances under the direction of Leonard Bernstein; No. 7 *(Mass in Time of War)* on Columbia M 32196 and No. 9 *(Lord Nelson Mass)* on Columbia M 35100.

Mozart is, deservedly, the most recorded of all composers, and any selection of works and performances can only dimly reflect the richness of choice. For little more than the price of a movie, you can buy a two-record Columbia bargain label album, MC 30368, with *Symphonies No. 35, 39, 40,* and *41* in splendid performances conducted by George

Szell. Another similar pair of discs (Columbia MC 30841), also directed by Szell, couples the *Symphony No. 41* with *Piano Concerto 21,* K. 467, and *Violin Concerto 5,* K. 219, and throws in the popular serenade *Eine Kleine Nachtmusik.* Either set will provide deep satisfaction. The wonderful *Piano Concerto 27,* K. 595, can be found on a number of discs, including Philips 6500948, which couples a restrained but poetic performance by Alfred Brendel with an equally fine version of another beauty, *Piano Concerto 18,* K. 456.

A number of discs collect together some of Mozart's lighter music, including London STS 15088, with two serenades and some incidental music for the theater, or another inexpensive Columbia set, MG 34586, which contains excellent performances of *Serenade 4,* K. 203, and *Serenade 5,* K. 204. One of his most attractive chamber works is the *Clarinet Quintet,* K. 581, which is coupled with the less well-known *Clarinet Trio,* K. 498, on Angel S 36241. Some of his finest religious music can be found in the *Mass in C minor,* K. 427, well performed on an inexpensive Seraphim disc, S–60257.

As for Mozart's opera, it is difficult to imagine any better way of spending money (or time) than on one of his last four great works—or, better still, on all of them. The following suggestions are, of course, based on personal taste, a particularly crucial factor when it comes to the sound of the human voice. Probably none of us will ever hear a perfect performance (or one, at any rate, that perfectly satisfies us) and different listeners will prefer different compromises. To take *The Marriage of Figaro,* for example, Angel S 3608 provides authoritative conducting (Carlo Maria Giulini), an unsurpassed Countess (Elisabeth Schwarzkopf), and a cast that, with the exception of a roughly sung Count, is almost on the same level. DG 2711007, on the other hand, offers the insightful (perhaps even too insightful) Count of Dietrich Fischer-Dieskau and a more balanced cast, with equally fine conducting by Karl Böhm—but how one misses Schwarzkopf! Either set, though, will provide years of pleasure.

Mozart's other two Italian operas, *Don Giovanni* and *Cosi Fan Tutte,* offer similar dilemmas. Otto Klemperer's *Don Giovanni* on Angel S 3700 is massive yet surprisingly flexible, while Böhm's on DG 2709085 has a particularly fine performance of the title role by Sherrill Milnes and suffers from the advantages and disadvantages of having been recorded at a live performance.

The Magic Flute, Mozart's last opera, is given a loving interpretation by George Solti on London 1397, but for some of the most beautiful tenor singing on record we must turn to DG 2709017 and Fritz Wunderlich's performance of the part of Tamino. Finally, there are a number of worthwhile collections of individual arias extracted from the operas, including a superb recital by Margaret Price on RCA AGL1–2124.

No record collection would be complete without Mozart's *Requiem Mass,* on which he was working at the time of his death. Commissioned by a mysterious stranger (who really wanted to pass the work off as his own), its composition was approached with foreboding on Mozart's part, who felt it to be prophetic of his own approaching end. A pupil of his, Süssmayer, produced the final version that is now performed. Yet if parts of the *Requiem* betray the circumstances of its composition, its great moments reach heights lofty even for Mozart. The performance on Philips 802862 does justice to most of them.

Chapter 15: The Romantic Era

Music of the Romantic Era more than that of any other period continues to appeal to performers as well as to listeners. The number of recorded versions of, say, the Beethoven symphonies or Chopin's piano music is so vast, and covers so wide a price range, that recommendation is nearly impossible. The few suggestions that follow are therefore intended for a hypothetical newcomer to romantic music who wants a representative sample of some of the great names, at a reasonable cost, to build a basic record collection.

Two editions of the nine Beethoven symphonies that are highly recommendable are those of George Szell on Columbia M7X–30281 and of Bruno Walter on Odyssey Y730051 (in each case on seven discs.) Szell's versions are taut and dramatic, Walter's more warm and lyrical. Neither is exactly a model of the latest in high-fidelity sound, but both provide great performances of great music at an astonishingly low price. A four-record Columbia set (M4X821) includes performances by Rudolf Serkin of the "Pathétique" sonata and two other popular Beethoven piano sonatas, the "Moonlight" and the "Appassionata," his *Piano Concerto No. 5 in E♭*, Op. 73, the *"Emperor,"* and Szell's versions of the *Fifth* and *Ninth symphonies*—again excellent value.

Schubert's two marvelous trios can be found on Philips Fest. 6770001. The English soprano Janet Baker provides a two-disc collection of his songs on Seraphim S–6083, and Dietrich Fischer-Dieskau, the greatest of all Schubert interpreters, has recorded all of his songs for male voice at least once. Any Fischer-Dieskau Schubert record is worthwhile; a personal favorite is DG 2530229, with songs to words by Goethe. London STS–15061 couples the "Unfinished" *Symphony No. 8 in B minor* with the early *Symphony No. 2 in B♭*.

Berlioz' popular *Symphonie Fantastique*, Op. 14, is available in good versions by Pierre Monteux (London STS–15423) and Seiji Ozawa (Odyssey Y–31923), and a splendid but rather fuzzy-sounding one of Sir Thomas Beecham (Seraphim S–60165). One of the most enjoyable examples of musical nationalism is Smetana's *Ma Vlast,* seven short orchestral pieces. An excellent version directed by the Czech conductor Rafael Kubelik can be found on DG 2707054. As for romantic piano music, differing tastes make recommendation particularly dangerous, but no one, surely, would quarrel with Artur Rubinstein's blend of fire and poetry in Chopin on RCA LSC–4000 or RCA LSC–4016. Liszt's *Hungarian Rhapsody No. 3, Spanish Rhapsody,* and *Transcendental Études* are available on two Columbia discs, Col./Mel. MX–33928, in performances by the Russian pianist Lazar Berman that will either inspire or depress any aspiring virtuoso, depending on degree of self-confidence and competitive spirit.

Like Beethoven's, Brahms' symphonies present a perpetual challenge to conductors. Both Szell and Walter recorded editions, but listeners in search of variety might prefer Rafael Kubelik's interpretation on London STS–1 5001/4. A good bargain version of *Symphony No. 1 in C minor,* Op. 68, is Herbert von Karajan's on London STS 15194.

Anton Bruckner has been less well served by the record companies, but Walter's versions of *Symphony No. 7 in E* and *Symphony No. 9 in D minor* are available in inexpensive Odyssey discs Y2–35238 and Y 35220. The *Symphony No. 8 in C minor* can be found in fine performances by Eugen Jochum (Angel S 3893) and George Solti (London 2219), the former interpretation mystical and lingering, the latter strong and dramatic.

Bel canto opera is increasingly well represented on disc. There are several different recordings of Maria Callas as Norma in Bellini's work, some live and some made in the recording studio. Angel S–3615 is a safe choice, although by no means the only one. A stunning *Lucia di Lammermoor,* with Callas and Giuseppe di Stefano, conducted by Karajan, from a live performance at Berlin in 1955 is available from time to time and should absolutely not be missed. A more recent Bellini recording is also highly recommended: *I Puritani,* with Monserrat Caballe and Alfredo Kraus, conducted by Riccardo Muti on Angel SCZX3881.

With Verdi the embarrassment of riches becomes even greater. Choice of an edition of *La Traviata* depends above all on the Violetta. Caballe on RCA LSC–6180 and Victoria de los Angeles on Angel S–3623 are both splendid, although accompanied by eccentric conducting in the case of the former and an inferior supporting cast in the case of the latter. A two-record set of Verdi arias sung by Leontyne Price, VCS–7063, contains warm and loving performances of some wonderful music, including arias from *La Traviata.* There are several impressive recordings of *Otello,* including a fine one on RCA CRL3–2951 with Placido Domingo, and a bargain-label recording on RCA AGL3–1969 presents Jon Vickers at an early stage in his career as interpreter of the opera's central role, not so subtle as he was to become, but already intense and moving.

The sheer length of Wagner's works creates special problems, although they are well worth overcoming. The complete recording of *The Ring* on nineteen discs, London RING–S, is one of the great monuments in the history of sound recording. Solti's conducting is almost always inspired, and the cast includes the greatest Wagnerians of the age. Obviously, the set represents a major investment of money and time, but for once really will provide (in the well-worn phrase) a lifetime of pleasure.

For listeners who want to sample Wagner's music before embarking on a complete Rhine journey, Seraphim S–60167 couples the wonderful final scene from *The Valkyrie* with a duet from the much earlier *Flying Dutchman* (not part of *The Ring*). An immensely satisfying performance of *Tristan and Isolde* recorded live at Bayreuth is available on DG 2713001 with the incomparable Swedish soprano Birgit Nilsson. Extracts from this five-record set, including the Prelude, most of the Love Duet, and the Love Death, can be found on DG 136433. Nilsson's singing and

Karl Bohm's conducting should definitely not be missed. The true impact of Wagner's music can only come through an exposure to either whole works or extended scenes from them, but purely orchestral extracts have become deservedly popular, although no substitute for the real thing. Ormandy's two-disc Columbia album, MC 30300, provides a good collection.

Chapter 16: Toward the Modern Era: 1870–1914

The music of Richard Strauss is well represented on disc, with a large number of versions available of his most popular tone poems. *Don Juan* and *Till Eulenspiegel* are conveniently coupled with the "Dance of the Seven Veils" from the opera *Salome* on Columbia MS 68–2. The whole of *Salome* can be found in a stunning performance on London 1218. The recording of the *Alpine Symphony* on London 6981 is excitingly played and vividly recorded. For listeners who might prefer Strauss in a quieter, more mellow vein, Kiri Te-Kanawa's performances of six of his songs and the *Four Last Songs,* all for soprano and orchestra, on Columbia MS 35140, are gorgeously sung and movingly interpreted.

Performances of Mahler tend to arouse strong feelings. The old performances by Bruno Walter, a disciple and later close personal friend of the composer, are certainly authentic, but they do not necessarily represent the last word on Mahler's music. In the *Symphony No. 1,* for example, Walter's easygoing, lyrical approach on Odyssey Y–30047 is very different from the tension of James Levine's on RCA ARL–0894, and both are equally valid. For the *Symphony No. 9,* George Solti's version on London 2220 provides a noble and sincere version of this great work. Economy-minded listeners will be tempted by Leonard Bernstein's four-disc set on Columbia M4X 31427, which includes both *Symphony No. 1* and *Symphony No. 9* and throws in the brooding and dramatic *Symphony No. 6* (sometimes known as the "Tragic") for good measure. The album provides an excellent introduction to Mahler's music.

The popularity of Debussy is attested to by the wide selection of recordings available. Choice is especially difficult for *La Mer.* A handy Columbia recordings MS 6754, couples it with the same composer's popular *Prélude à l'après-midi d'un faune (Prelude for the Afternoon of a Faun)* and Ravel's second suite from *Daphnis and Chloe.* A two-disc album of Debussy's orchestral music can be found on Columbia MG 30950, which includes *La Mer* and several other works. Seraphim S–60253 provides a good selection of the piano music, including the well-known "*Clair de Lune.*" Not to be missed are the beautiful string quartets by Debussy and Ravel. Each composer wrote only one, and they are usefully coupled on a number of records, including Philips 835361.

Magnificently sensitive and poetic performances by Maurizio Pollini of Schoenberg's piano works, available on DG 2530531, make this often-difficult music attractive and moving to hear. *Pierrot Lunaire* is never an easy work to appreciate or to perform. Its sinister beauty takes getting used to, but the excellent version on Nonesuch 71251 will certainly help. Listeners interested in exploring Schoenberg's later music will find a fine performance of the *Variation for Orchestra* of 1928 on London 6984, coupled with another very different set of variations, Elgar's *Enigma Variations.* Perhaps the greatest of all Schoenberg's achievements is the opera *Moses and Aaron*—which, somewhat surprisingly for so complex a work, is among his most immediately accessible compositions. Even listeners without a special interest in contemporary music will find the barbaric splendor of the "Dance around the Golden Calf" and the drama of the final scene easy to appreciate. An impressive performance is available on Columbia M2–33594, conducted by Pierre Boulez, himself a leading figure in contemporary music.

As for Stravinsky, choice of a performance of *The Rite of Spring* is particularly difficult. Stravinsky's own performance on Columbia MS–6319 obviously has a special interest, but those who prefer a more modern reading may well want to turn to Claudio Abbado's recording on DG 2530635. The three ballets, *The Firebird, Petrouchka,* and *The Rite of Spring,* all conducted by the composer, are available in a three-disc album, Columbia D3–705. Of his later works, *The Symphony in Three Movements* and a suite from the ballet *Pulcinella* are coupled on Seraphim S–60188, while Columbia MS–6272 provides a useful selection of some of his last works, coupled with extracts from the earlier *Soldier's Tale* and the beautiful *Octet.* Almost all these works have been used by choreographers (notably George Balanchine) as the basis of ballets, and some listeners may well find that ballet provides an easy way of becoming familiar with Stravinsky's music.

Chapter 17: Between the World Wars

The discography of jazz is huge, although recordings of some of the early jazz artists are hard to come by on a regular basis. The Houston Grand Opera has been in the vanguard of performing American operas coming from the jazz tradition. Their performance of ragtime composer Scott Joplin's opera *Treemonisha* is available (DG 270–7083), as is their completely uncut version of George Gershwin's *Porgy and Bess* (ARL 3–2109). Stravinsky's *Histoire du soldat* is available in a full performance by the Boston Symphony (DG 2530609) and in many recordings in partial or excerpted versions. There are innumerable recordings of Duke Ellington's popular music. His more classically oriented music is less recorded but *Black, Brown, and Beige* (JCS 8015) and an anthology of his *Suites* (Pablo 2310762) are currently available.

Chapter 18: The Contemporary Contour

In recent years Pierre Boulez has become better represented on disc as a conductor than as a composer, and his interpretations of 19th- and 20th-century music have a special interest. Among the outstanding recordings of his own works is a version of the *Second Piano Sonata* performed by Maurizio Pollini on DG 2530803, which brings a welcome note of poetry to this angular music. A more recent work for voice and orchestra, *Pli selon Pli (Fold upon Fold)* of 1960, is conducted by Boulez himself on Columbia M–30296.

Two of Stockhausen's more recent pieces for instruments, *Stop* (1973) and *Ylem* (1973), are coupled on DG 2530442, directed by the composer. Another DG disc, 138811, contains one of his earliest and best electronic pieces, *Gesang der Junglinge (Song of the Boys)* of 1955–1956, which superimposes the sound of the human voice, electronically distorted, on a purely electronic background. The listener inspired by this to explore the subject of electronic music further may well find that a two-record set from Nonesuch offers considerable assistance. Entitled *The Nonesuch Guide to Electronic Music* (Nonesuch HC 73018), the set includes a handy and informative book.

The music of Shostakovich is well represented on disc. All his fifteen symphonies and fifteen string quartets are available, including an excellent version of *Symphony No. 15* on London 7130. His last work, a *Sonata for Viola and Piano* completed just before his death in 1975, can be found on Columbia/Melodic M–35109. A somber, brooding piece, it confirms the composer's ability to stir deep human emotions by relatively simple musical means. The music is far from consoling, representing as it does Shostakovich's deeply pessimistic attitude to his own approaching death, but it offers a profound musical experience and one that requires no special effort on the part of a sensitive listener.

Britten's *Peter Grimes* is available in a thrilling recording conducted by Colin Davis on Philips 6769014, featuring Jon Vickers' interpretation of the title role, one of the most eloquent operatic performances of our time. It is difficult to imagine that any listener could remain unmoved by the opera's final scenes, in which the anguish of Grimes' madness and desperation finally cuts him off from all human contact and drives him to suicide. The action of the opera takes place in a small English fishing village; the atmosphere of the sea pervades the whole score. The orchestral interludes between the scenes, known as the "Sea Interludes," are sometimes played in a concert version and convey much of the spirit of the whole work. A fine version can be found on Columbia M–34529, coupled with Britten's *Suite on English Folktunes*. A very different work is *Death in Venice* (1973), available on London 13109. This operatic version of Thomas Mann's story consists of a poetic and deeply felt meditation on life, love, art, sex, and death. Its dreamlike air will perhaps not appeal to all, but it contains many musical beauties, not least Britten's delicate use of a small orchestra. Although originally intended for performance in a small theater, it made a great impression on the audience even when given in the vast space of the Metropolitan Opera House in New York.

Further Reading

Chapter 1: The Beginnings of Civilization

Aldred, C. *The Egyptians*. New York: Praeger, 1961. A short but comprehensive account of Egyptian culture by one of the leading Egyptologists of the century.

Childe, V. Gordon. *What happened in History*. Baltimore: Penguin, 1942. One of the most important of all books on the early development of civilization. The author's account is strongly influenced by his political views but is fundamental to an understanding of modern research on early Mesopotamia.

Daniel, G. *The First Civilizations*. New York: Crowell, 1968. An excellent account, both of early civilization and of modern scholarship, which succeeds in making difficult material easy to read.

Frankfort, H. *The Art and Architecture of the Ancient Orient*. Baltimore: Penguin, 1970. The best single-volume guide to its subject. Technical in places but written with immense breadth of knowledge and fully illustrated.

————, et al. *Before Philosophy*. Baltimore: Penguin, 1949. Subtitled "The Intellectual Adventure of Ancient Man," this book discusses Egyptian and Mesopotamian views on life, death, the function of the state, and the nature of the world. Not easy to read, but well worth the effort.

Hood, S. *The Arts in Prehistoric Greece*. Baltimore: Penguin, 1978. An up-to-date introduction to Minoan and Mycenaean art. The author, who has himself dug both in Crete and at Mycenae, includes evidence from the most recent excavations.

Lange, K., and M. Hirmer. *Egypt*. London: Phaidon, 1956. A superb collection of photographs of Egypt and Egyptian art, with a good introduction.

Marinatos, S., and M. Hirmer. *Crete and Mycenae*. New York: Abrams, 1960. Chiefly valuable for its pictures, although Marinatos' commentary is authoritative and informative.

Renault, Mary. *The King Must Die*. New York: Pantheon, 1958. An engrossing novel that retells the Theseus legend, with particularly interesting emphasis on the civilization of ancient Greece.

————. *The Bull from the Sea*. New York: Pantheon, 1962. A companion novel to *The King Must Die,* this describes the parts of the Theseus legend set in Athens and gives a vivid, if hypothetical, picture of Bronze Age religious customs.

Strommenger, E., and M. Hirmer. *The Art of Mesopotamia*. New York: Abrams, 1964. Highly recommended.

Warren, P. *The Aegean Civilizations*. Oxford: Elsevier-Phaidon, 1975. A good general account of Bronze Age Aegean culture, especially well illustrated. The author includes an interesting account of his own excavations in Crete.

Woolley, Charles L. *Ur of the Chaldees*. Baltimore: Penguin, 1954. An engrossing account of the excavations at Ur by one of the greatest of modern archaeologists.

Chapter 2: Jerusalem and the Biblical Tradition

Alter, Robert. *The Art of Biblical Narrative*. New York: Basic Books, 1981. An excellent work by a distinguished literary critic.

Anchor Bible. Garden City, NY: Doubleday. A continuing series of volumes on each of the books of the Bible by eminent scholars. Excellent.

Anderson, Bernhard W. *Understanding the Old Testament*. 3rd ed. Englewood Cliffs, NJ: Prentice-Hall, 1975. The standard college text for biblical study. First-rate scholarship; readable.

Bright, John. *A History of Israel*. Philadelphia: Westminster, 1972. The standard work by an American scholar.

Buttrick, George, et al. *The Interpreter's Dictionary of the Bible*. 4 vols. New York: Abingdon, 1962. Excellent and comprehensive dictionary of the Bible.

DeVaux, Roland. *Ancient Israel: Its Life and Institutions*. New York: McGraw-Hill, 1965. A basic work by an eminent French scholar and archaeologist.

Frye, Northrop. *The Great Code: The Bible and Literature*. New York: Harcourt Brace Jovanovich, 1981. Reliable and extremely readable work.

Henn, T. R. *The Bible as Literature*. New York: Oxford, 1970. Good work on literary value of the Bible.

Heschel, Abraham. *The Prophets*. New York: Harper, 1963. A classic study by an outstanding Jewish scholar.

The Interpreter's Bible. New York: Abingdon, 1957. Informative multivolume commentary on the entire Bible.

May, Herbert. *Oxford Bible Atlas*. New York: Oxford, 1974. Basic for maps of the biblical period.

Pritchard, J. B. *Ancient Near Eastern Texts Relating to the Old Testament*. Princeton, NJ: Princeton University Press, 1969. Anthology of important texts from Egypt, Babylonia, and other areas that shed light on the Bible; indispensable.

Schneidau, Herbert. *Sacred Discontent: The Bible and Western Tradition*. Baton Rouge: Louisiana State University, 1976. A brilliant study of the cultural impact of the Bible on subsequent Western culture.

Chapter 3: Early Greece

Boardman, J. *The Greek Overseas*. Baltimore: Penguin, 1973. A vivid and informative account of the development and effects of Greek colonization.

Burn, A. R. *The Lyric Age of Greece*. London: Arnold, 1960. Historical, cultural, and literary events in 7th-

and 6th-century B.C. Greece discussed in a major study.

Bury, J. B., and R. Meiggs. *A History of Greece to the Death of Alexander the Great*. 4th ed. New York: St. Martin's, 1975. The best single-volume history of ancient Greece.

Charbonneaux, M., and V. Charbonneaux. *Archaic Greek Art*. New York: Braziller, 1971. A lavishly illustrated survey of all forms of Archaic art.

Coldstream, J. N. *Geometric Greece*. London: Methuen, 1977. A technical but readable account of all aspects of life in Geometric Greece.

Johnston, A. *The Emergence of Greece*. Oxford: Elsevier-Phaidon, 1976. Primarily an up-to-date account of the archaeology of early Greece, the book also gives an excellent synthesis of history and art.

Luce, J. V. *Homer and the Heroic Age*. New York: Harper, 1975. A masterly account of the historical background of the Homeric epics, although the author's view that Homer's world chiefly reflects that of the Mycenaeans is by no means universally shared.

Page, D. L. *Sappho and Alcaeus*. Oxford: Oxford University Press, 1955. A study of the poets that includes translations of most of the surviving fragments of their works.

Renault, Mary. *The Praise Singer*. New York: Pantheon, 1978. A novel of the life of a Greek bard and of Athens and other cities in the 6th century B.C., with the poet Simonides as narrator.

Wace, J. B., and F. H. Stubbings. *A Companion to Homer*. New York: St. Martin's, 1962. A collection of essays discussing many aspects of the Homeric epics; historical, literary, and archeological.

Chapter 4: Classical Greece and Its Aftermath

Burn, A. R. *Alexander the Great and the Hellenistic Empire*. London: Macmillan, 1947. A clearly written introduction to the period that is both brief and entertaining.

Cornford, F. M. *Before and After Socrates*. Cambridge: Cambridge University Press, 1960. Reprint of an earlier work written in 1932 by the

great Plato scholar; not always easy, but rewarding.

Flaceliere, R. *Daily Life in Greece at the Time of Pericles*. New York: Macmillan, 1965. A fascinating account filled with information and intelligently illustrated.

Kitto, H. D. F. *The Greeks*. Rev. ed. Baltimore: Penguin, 1957. This book, often unconventional and even controversial in its views, remains the best and most stimulating single-volume introduction to Greek culture in all its aspects.

Lattimore, R. *The Poetry of Greek Tragedy*. Baltimore: Johns Hopkins, 1958. A sensitive study of Greek tragedy from a literary point of view.

Ling, R. *The Greek World*. Oxford: Elsevier-Phaidon, 1976. Handsomely illustrated, a good introduction to the art and archaeology of Classical Greece.

Pickard-Cambridge, A. W. *The Dramatic Festivals of Athens*. 2nd ed. Oxford: Oxford University Press, 1968. One of the standard works on Greek drama. Perhaps more for the specialist than the general reader but contains much valuable information.

Renault, Mary. *The Nature of Alexander*. New York: Pantheon Books, 1975. A beautifully illustrated biography by the noted author of a number of novels about the ancient world, including two about Alexander, *Fire From Heaven* and *The Persian Boy*.

Schefold, K. *The Art of Classical Greece*. New York: Crown, 1967. Closely argued and not always easy to read; its detailed study and analysis of the art of the period provides far more than a simple survey.

Taplin, O. *The Stagecraft of Aeschylus*. Oxford: Oxford University Press, 1977. Discusses the work of all three of the Greek tragedians as plays rather than as poetry and is an up-to-date examination of problems in the staging of Greek drama. Often highly technical but very illuminating.

Tarn, W. W. *Alexander the Great*. Boston: Beacon, 1956. In two volumes, the first containing the narrative and the second sources and special studies. Even the reader who does not want the details of the second

part should read the narrative, a classic account.

Taylor. A. E. *Plato: The Man and His Work*. London: Methuen, 1948. A masterly examination of Plato and his philosophy, still enlightening even if it does not reflect the most recent scholarship.

Chapter 5: The Roman Legacy

Brendel, O. J. *Etruscan Art*. Baltimore: Penguin, 1978. The most up-to-date survey of Etruscan painting and sculpture, with numerous illustrations.

Brion, M. *Pompeii and Herculaneum: The Glory and the Grief*. London: Elek, 1960. A popular but scholarly account of the excavations of the buried cities and of life there in Roman times. Entertaining and informative.

Commager, S., ed. *Virgil, a Collection of Critical Essays*. Englewood Cliffs, NJ: Prentice-Hall, 1966. The literature on Vergil is immense and wideranging, but this volume of essays provides a useful survey of modern critical approaches and suggests some further directions for the interested reader to explore.

Dudley, D. R. *The Civilization of Rome*. New York: Mentor, 1962. A handy one-volume survey of Roman culture, more useful for history than for art or literature.

Graves, Robert. *I, Claudius* and *Claudius the God*. Baltimore: Penguin, 1977. These two historical novels, originally published in 1934, are re-creations of the Roman world that are both scholarly and thoroughly absorbing. Highly recommended.

Hanfmann, G. M. A. *Roman Art*. New York: Norton, 1975. The best introduction to the subject, with a very full selection of illustrations, sensitive comments, and up-to-date bibliographical notes.

Kahler, H. *Rome and Her Empire*. London: Methuen, 1963. A more technical survey of Roman art of the imperial period with a fine selection of color plates.

Luck, G. *The Latin Love-Elegy*. London: Methuen, 1959. A detailed study of Catullus and his successors that is easier to follow if the reader has some knowledge of Latin.

Otis, B. *Virgil: A Study in Civilized Poetry.* Oxford: Oxford University Press, 1964. Perhaps the single most important book on Vergil to appear in recent years. Sensitive and perceptive, it merits careful reading.

Pallottino, M. *The Etruscans.* Baltimore: Penguin, 1975. A revised version of the standard work by the most eminent Etruscologist of our time, covering all aspects of Etruscan culture. Especially good on the language.

Rose, H. J. *A Handbook of Latin Literature.* 3rd ed. New York: Dutton, 1961. A good single-volume account.

Scullard, H. H. *From the Gracchi to Nero.* 3rd ed. London: Methuen, 1970. A useful survey of the history of the late Republic and the early empire, reflecting the state of modern scholarly opinion.

Vickers, M. *The Roman World.* Oxford: Elsevier-Phaidon, 1977. A fully illustrated account of Roman art and archaeology, also valuable for its discussion of the rediscovery of classical antiquity in the Renaissance.

Wilder, Thornton. *Ides of March.* New York: Grosset & Dunlap, 1956. A brilliant and engrossing fictional narration of the last days of Julius Caesar.

Yourcenar, Marguerite. *Memoirs of Hadrian.* New York: Farrar, Straus, 1963. A superb evocation of the personality of one of the truly extraordinary Romans.

Chapter 6: The World of Byzantium

Beckwith, John. *The Art of Constantinople.* New York: Phaidon, 1961. A brief survey of Byzantine art from A.D. 330 to 1453 with good illustrations.

Gibbon, Edward. *The Decline and Fall of the Roman Empire.* Many editions; the standard version is in 9 vols., edited by J. Bury in 1914. This monumental work, first published in 1776, is still the single best work on the period of Rome's decline. For a panoramic view of the period in this chapter and an example of

how English should be written, it is unparalleled.

Grabar, André. *Byzantium: Byzantine Art in the Middle Ages.* London: Methuen, 1966. A sensitive and original study of Byzantine art and culture by an acknowledged expert in the field.

———. *The Golden Age of Justinian.* New York: Odyssey, 1967. A splendid work by one of the best scholars in the field.

MacDonald, William. *Early Christian and Byzantine Architecture.* New York: Braziller, 1967. A handy survey with good photographs and schematics of important buildings.

Sherrard, P. *Constantinople.* Oxford: Oxford University Press, 1965. An important study for its historical learning.

Simson, Otto von. *The Sacred Fortress.* Chicago: University of Chicago Press, 1948. The best book on the artistic heritage of Ravenna.

Talbot Rice, David, and Tamara Talbot Rice. *Icons and Their History.* London: Thames and Hudson, 1974. Fine scholarship with good bibliographies and beautiful plates.

Vidal, Gore. *Julian.* New York: Vintage, 1977. This novel, originally published in 1964, is a brilliant evocation of Christianity and Classicism in conflict toward the end of the Roman Empire.

Ware, Timothy. *The Orthodox Church.* Baltimore: Penguin Paperback, 1969. A reliable, nontechnical survey.

Chapter 7: The Age of Charlemagne

Almedingen, E. M. *Charlemagne: A Study.* London: Bodley Head, 1968. A readable and thorough biography of the man in relation to his times.

Boussard, Jacques. *The Civilization of Charlemagne.* Translated by Frances Partridge. New York: McGraw-Hill, 1968. A well-illustrated survey with a detailed bibliography of more specialized sources.

Brault, Gerard. *The Song of Roland.* 2nd vol. University Park: University of Pennsylvania Press, 1978. A critical edition of the work with exhaustive notes. Essential.

Brondsted, Johannes. *The Vikings.* Translated by Kalle Skov. New York: Penguin Books, 1960. A

basic survey of the Northmen; with some illustrations in black and white.

Bullough, Donald. *The Age of Charlemagne.* New York: Putnam, 1966. Well-written and lavishly illustrated.

Folz, Robert. *The Coronation of Charlemagne: 25th December 800.* Translated by J.E. Anderson. London: Routledge & Kegan Paul, 1974. A detailed but readable study of Charlemagne's imperial ideals.

Henderson, George. *Early Medieval.* New York: Penguin Books, 1972. Part of the "style and civilization" series; an extremely readable and thorough study of artistic styles in the early medieval period with 150 illustrations and a thorough bibliography.

Knowles, David. *Christian Monasticism.* New York: McGraw-Hill, 1969. A readable survey of the history of Christian monasticism by a distinguished monastic historian.

Riche, Pierre. *Daily Life in the World of Charlemagne.* Translated by JoAnn MacNamara. Philadelphia: University of Pennsylvania Press, 1978. A fascinating and indispensable study of all facets of Carolingian life.

Thorpe, Lewis (trans.). *Einhard and Notker the Stammerer: Two Lives of Charlemagne.* New York: Penguin Books, 1969. Basic sources from the period with a good introduction.

Chapter 8: The High Middle Ages: The Search for Synthesis

Adams, Henry. *Mont-Saint-Michel and Chartres.* Garden City, NY: Doubleday Anchor, 1959. A brilliant, albeit eccentric, work on the culture of the Gothic world. While its scholarship has been superseded in this century, it is still an aesthetic classic.

Aubert, Marcel. *Gothic Cathedrals of France and Their Treasures.* London: Nicholas Kaye, 1959. A handy encyclopedia of Gothic architecture by a noted French scholar of the era.

Cobban, A. B. *The Medieval University: Their Development and Organization.* London: Methuen, 1975. A work of solid scholarship that summarizes and adds to the ongoing research of the last hundred years. Excellent bibliographies.

Daly, Lowrie. *The Medieval University: 1200–1400*. New York: Sheed & Ward, 1961. Less scholarly than Cobban's work but a handy and readable introduction.

Gilson, Etienne. *Reason and Revelation in the Middle Ages*. New York: Scribner, 1966. A brief but excellent survey of the intellectual milieu of the period by one of the foremost authorities of our century.

Gimpel, Jean. *The Medieval Machine: The Industrial Revolution of the Middle Ages*. New York: Penguin, 1977. A wonderful introduction to technology in medieval times.

Golding, William. *The Spire*. New York: Harcourt, 1964. A brilliant fictional evocation of medieval cathedral building.

Holmes, Urban T. *Daily Living in the Twelfth Century*. Madison: University of Wisconsin, 1966. An extremely readable account of ordinary life in medieval London and Paris drawn from documentary evidence.

Knowles, David. *The Evolution of Medieval Thought*. New York: Vintage, 1962. A classic study of medieval thought from Augustine to the eve of the Reformation.

Macauley, David. *Cathedral: The Story of Its Construction*. Boston: Houghton Mifflin, 1973. A book for young and old readers on the construction of a cathedral, with pen-and-ink drawings by the author. A fascinating and lovely work that is simple but richly informative.

Panofsky, Erwin. *Abbot Suger*. Princeton, NJ: Princeton University Press, 1946. A translation of Suger's booklets on Saint Denis with an important introduction and full notes. Indispensable for the period.

Simson, Otto von. *The Gothic Cathedral*. New York: Harper, 1964. A classic work on the aesthetics of the Gothic era in the Ile-de-France. The work is quite valuable for its study of Saint Denis and Chartres.

Singleton, Charles. *The Divine Comedy of Dante Alighieri*. 6 vols. Princeton, NJ: Princeton University Press, 1972. The commentary in English by the foremost authority on Dante in America. There are separate volumes of the poem in English with

companion volumes of commentary. Excellent and indispensable.

Weisheipl, James. *Friar Thomas D'Aquino: His Life, Thought, and Work*. Garden City, NY: Doubleday, 1974. Reflects the current state of Thomistic studies; scholarly, with good notes and bibliography.

Chapter 9: The 14th Century: A Time of Transition

Gardner, John. *The Life and Times of Chaucer*. New York: Knopf, 1976. A readable biography by a contemporary American novelist, critic, and literary scholar.

Lerner, Robert. *The Age of Adversity: The Fourteenth Century*. Ithaca, NY: Cornell, 1968. A brief but readable survey of the period covering both historical and cultural events of the century.

Martindale, Andrew. *The Complete Paintings of Giotto*. New York: Abrams, 1966. After a brief introduction the book consists of a fully illustrated catalogue of Giotto's paintings with some excellent detailed photographs.

Meiss, Millard. *Painting in Florence and Siena after the Black Death*. New York: Harper Torchbooks, 1964. A brilliant work of scholarship that treats "The arts, religion and society in the mid-Fourteenth Century."

Pope-Hennessy, John. *Italian Gothic Sculpture*. London: Phaidon, 1972. An excellent illustrated survey. The comprehensive bibliography is especially valuable.

Stubblebine, James (ed.). *The Arena Chapel Frescoes*. New York: Norton, 1969. A collection of essays on Giotto's frescoes, illustrated.

Tuchman, Barbara. *A Distant Mirror: The Calamitous Fourteenth Century*. New York: Knopf, 1978. A brilliant work by one of our best popular writers on history. The book focuses almost exclusively on France and as a result lacks some balance. A joy to read and very revealing nevertheless.

White, John. *Art and Architecture in Italy 1250–1400*. Baltimore: Pelican, 1966. A useful single-volume survey, comprehensive yet detailed. Highly recommended.

Wilkins, Ernest H. *Life of Petrarch*. Chicago: University of Chicago,

1961. An exemplary biography valuable for its discussion of Italy in the 14th century and Petrarch's relationship with such figures as Boccacio, Giotto, Simone Martini, and Chaucer.

Chapter 10: The Early Renaissance

Brucker, Gene. *Renaissance Florence*. New York: Wiley, 1969. A fine study of the city of Florence in the 15th century.

Burckhardt, Jakob. *The Civilization of the Renaissance in Italy*. 2 vols. New York: Harper Torchbooks, 1958. The classic work on the Renaissance; the point of departure for all subsequent studies.

Ergang, Robert. *The Renaissance*. Princeton: Van Nostrand, 1967. A quite competent, if uneven, textbook on the Renaissance, which includes Italy and other countries.

Hartt, Frederick. *A History of Italian Renaissance Art*. London: Thames and Hudson, 1970. The standard survey text, with good bibliographies on individual artists.

Hay, Denys, ed. *The Renaissance Debate*. New York: Holt, Rinehart and Winston, 1965. An anthology of texts, ancient and modern, on the meaning of the term *renaissance* with respect to Italy.

Kristeller, Paul, and P. Wiener. *Renaissance Essays*. New York: Harper Torchbooks, 1968. Essays on various aspects of the Italian Renaissance by the best scholars of the period.

Trinkaus, Charles. *In Our Image and Likeness*. 2 vols. Chicago: University of Chicago Press, 1970. A profound study of Italian Humanism. Very important.

Chapter 11: The High Renaissance in Italy

Logan, Oliver. *Culture and Society in Venice 1470–1790: The Renaissance and Its Heritage*. New York: Scribner's, 1972. A readable and well-illustrated survey.

Mazzeo, Joseph. *Renaissance and Revolution: The Remaking of European Thought*. New York: Pantheon, 1966. Intellectual history of the highest order; valuable for the entire period of the Renaissance.

Morris, James. *The World of Venice*. New York: Harcourt Brace Jovanovich, 1974. A wonderful impression of Venice by one of the finest travel essayists writing in English (now Jan Morris).

Murray, Linda. *The High Renaissance*. New York: Praeger, 1967. A readable and lavishly illustrated art history available in paperback.

Partner, Peter. *Renaissance Rome 1500–1559: A Portrait of a Society*. Berkeley: University of California Press, 1976. An excellent social portrait of the city during the High Renaissance; also available in paperback.

Setton, Kenneth, et al. *The Renaissance: Maker of Modern Man*. Washington: National Geographic Society, 1970. Illustrated with many color photographs.

Stone, Irving. *The Agony and the Ecstasy*. New York: Doubleday, 1961. An overwrought but highly readable novel about Michelangelo and his times.

Wohl, Alice, and Hellmut Wohl, ed. and trans. *Ascanio Condivi's Life of Michelangelo*. Baton Rouge: Louisiana State University Press, 1976. A translation of and commentary on an early life of Michelangelo. Illustrated, with excellent notes.

Chapter 12: The Renaissance in the North

Benesch, O. *The Art of the Renaissance in Northern Europe*. London: Phaidon, 1965. The most authoritative single-volume survey, with abundant illustrations.

Bradley, A. C. *Shakespearean Tragedy*. Greenwich, CT: Fawcett, 1965. Although this book, which contains a series of lectures on *Hamlet, Othello, King Lear* and *Macbeth,* was first published in 1904, it remains one of the most influential of all works of Shakespearean criticism.

Cambell, O. J., and E. G. Quinn, eds. *A Shakespearean Encyclopedia*. New York: Crowell, 1966. A valuable source of information on a wide variety of Shakespearean topics.

Cuttler, C. D. *Northern Painting from Pucelle to Bruegel*. New York: Holt, Rinehart and Winston, 1968. A good up-to-date survey that incorporates much important scholarly research in a concise but compre-

hensive account. Very well illustrated, with particularly good color plates.

Dickens, A. G. *Reformation and Society in Sixteenth-Century Europe*. New York: Harcourt Brace Jovanovich, 1966. A very readable survey, with profuse illustrations.

Fellowes, E. H. *William Byrd*. Oxford: Oxford University Press, 1948. The standard work on Byrd, authoritative but technical in places.

Harbage, A., ed. *Shakespeare, The Tragedies: A Collection of Critical Essays*. Englewood Cliffs, NJ: Prentice-Hall, 1965. This collection of recent essays provides a good impression of the present state of Shakespearean criticism.

Panofsky, E. *The Life and Art of Albrecht Dürer,* 4th ed. Princeton, NJ: Princeton University Press, 1955. A magisterial account by one of the greatest of all art historians. Difficult at times, but immensely rewarding.

Reese, G. *Music in the Renaissance*. New York: Norton, 1959. A thorough and painstaking account of European music in the Renaissance, especially useful for reference.

Smart, A. *The Renaissance and Mannerism in Northern Europe and Spain*. New York: Harcourt Brace Jovanovich, 1972. A very handy guide to Northern Renaissance art, surprisingly well-illustrated for the size and price.

Weinstein, D., ed. *The Renaissance and the Reformation: Sources in Western Civilization*. New York: Free Press, 1965. An anthology of original writings by Luther, Calvin, Montaigne, and others.

Chapter 13: The Baroque World

Bennett, John. *Four Metaphysical Poets*. New York: Vintage Books, 1953. This handy little book contains perceptive essays on Donne, Crashaw, and two other metaphysical poets along with a selection of their poetry.

Blunt, Anthony. *Nicolas Poussin*. Princeton, NJ: Princeton University Press, 1966. A massive and authoritative work that discusses the artist from every conceivable point of view. Fully illustrated.

Bukofzer, Manfred E. *Music in the Baroque Era*. New York: Norton, 1947. Although beginning to show signs of age, still the best single-volume treatment of its subject.

David, H. T., and A. Mendel. *The Bach Reader*. London: Dent, 1966. This unusual and fascinating book traces the life of Bach in contemporary letters and documents.

Kahr, Madlyn M. *Dutch Painting in the Seventeenth Century*. New York: Harper, 1978. A concise and readable survey, with full discussions of Rembrandt, Vermeer, and Hals. The plentiful black-and-white illustrations include some useful details.

Keast, William R. (ed.). *Seventeenth Century English Poetry*. New York: Oxford, 1962. A very useful collection of essays on the metaphysical poets in general and Donne in particular.

Martin, John Rupert. *Baroque*. New York: Harper, 1977. A good recent survey of baroque art that examines some of its concepts as well as its developments. Fully illustrated in black-and-white.

Orrey, Leslie. *A Concise History of Opera*. London: Thames & Hudson, 1972. The first five chapters give a very readable account of the early development of opera with some fascinating illustrations.

Schweitzer, A. *J. S. Bach*. London: Black, 1962. In spite of its obvious deficiencies—it is out of date in places and its author was not a professional musicologist—this is a book to be read by all lovers of Bach's music. Its devotion and insight remain unsurpassed.

Sewter, A. C. *Baroque and Rococo*. New York: Harcourt, 1972. A conveniently brief and readable survey of 17th- and early 18th-century art with a good proportion of color plates.

Willey, B. *The Seventeenth Century Background*. New York: Doubleday, 1953. An excellent introduction to 17th-century intellectual developments, including discussions of Galileo, Descartes, Hobbes, and Milton.

Wittkower, R. *Art and Architecture in Italy: 1600–1750*. New York: Penguin, 1973. A survey of Italian art that combines superb scholarship with clarity of expression.

Chapter 14: The 18th Century: From Reason to Revolution

Church, W. F. (ed.). *The Influence of the Enlightenment on the French Revolution.* Lexington, MA: Heath, 1964. This handy little book, one of the Heath Problems in European Civilization Series, contains a number of essays on the intellectual origins of the French Revolution.

Einstein, A. *Mozart.* London: Bassell, 1946. A marvelous book, packed with insight into Mozart's life and works.

Hazard, P. *European Thought in the 18th Century.* London: Hollis & Carter, 1954. First published in French in 1946, this remains one of the most complete and authoritative accounts of the development of ideas in the 18th century.

Honour, H. *Neo-Classicism.* New York: Penguin, 1968. A brilliant and entertaining discussion of one of the chief artistic consequences of the Age of Enlightenment, with a varied selection of illustrations.

Kalnein, W., and M. Levey. *Art and Architecture of the 18th Century in France.* New York: Penguin, 1972. A thorough survey of painting, sculpture, and architecture of the period with good discussions of the leading artists. Plentifully illustrated in black-and-white.

Levey, M. *Rococo to Revolution.* New York: Praeger, 1966. A survey of 18th-century painting, eminently readable and well illustrated.

Mellers, W. *The Sonata Principle.* New York: Schocken, 1969. Rather broader than its title suggests, this book discusses both the life and the works of all the leading composers from the birth of classical style to the early 19th century. Stimulating and full of ideas.

Palmer, R. R. *The Age of the Democratic Revolution: Europe and America 1760–1800.* 2 vols. Princeton, NJ: Princeton University Press, 1959–1964. These thorough and scholarly volumes examine the French and American revolutions as part of a worldwide movement in favor of change. By no means light reading but thoroughly rewarding.

Schoneberger, A., and H. Soehner. *The Age of Rococo.* New York: McGraw-Hill, 1960. A sumptuous and fully illustrated survey of rococo art.

Waterhouse, E. *Painting in Britain 1530–1790,* 4th ed. New York: Penguin, 1978. Although the first two-fifths of this book cover material strictly outside the range of the 18th century, the accounts of Gainsborough, Reynolds, and Hogarth in the remaining sections are excellent and should not be missed.

Chapter 15: The Romantic Era

Canaday, J. *Mainstreams of Modern Art,* 2nd ed. New York: Holt, Rinehart and Winston 1981. A survey of the development of painting in the period discussed in this and the following two chapters that combines scholarship, deep feeling, and unusually enjoyable prose. Highly recommended, not least for the large number of illustrations.

Einstein, A. *Music in the Romantic Era.* New York: Norton, 1947. Not an easy book, but a very worthwhile one, this discusses the philosophical and social issues behind romanticism in music rather than providing detailed musical analyses. Very good on nationalism and problems of musical aesthetics.

Friedlaender, W. *David to Delacroix.* Cambridge, MA: Harvard University Press, 1952. Although this inevitably does not reflect more recent research, it remains a magisterial (and mercifully brief) summary of the history of French romantic painting.

Holt, E. G. (ed.). *From the Classicists to the Impressionists.* New York: Doubleday Anchor, 1966. A useful and absorbing anthology of writings on art and architecture by 19th-century artists and literary figures.

Johnson, E. *Charles Dickens: His Tragedy and Triumph.* New York: Viking Press, 1977. An updated and abridged edition of an earlier two-volume work, this fine biography, particularly good on Dickens' visits to America, is clearly inspired by its author's deep love and knowledge of his subject.

Kolodin, I. *The Interior Beethoven.* New York: Knopf, 1975. Subtitled "A Biography of the Music," this book discusses the creative process behind Beethoven's greatest works and relates them to his life. Technical in places, but rewarding.

Matthiessen, F. O. *American Renaissance.* New York: Oxford University Press, 1968. First published in 1941, this is an authoritative account of American 19th-century literature built around extended critical discussion of Emerson, Thoreau, Hawthorne, Melville, and Whitman.

Mellers, W. *Romanticism and the Twentieth Century.* New York: Schocken, 1969. A very handy survey of the styles and chief works of many of the principal composers of the 19th century and some of those of the 20th. Brief but full of ideas.

Metraux, G. S., and F. Crouzet. *The Nineteenth Century World.* New York: Mentor, 1963. Originally a UNESCO publication, this contains essays on a wide range of aspects of 19th-century life and thought, including political and social developments, science and technology, religion, the arts, and philosophy.

Novak, B. *American Painting of the Nineteenth Century.* New York: Praeger, 1969. A very useful discussion of the chief trends in American 19th-century painting, with handy biographical notes on the leading artists. Good illustrations.

Osborne, C. *The Complete Operas of Verdi.* New York: Knopf, 1970. A fascinating book that combines synopses and analyses of all of Verdi's operas with the story of his life and extended extracts from his letters.

Rosenblum, R. *Transformations in Late Eighteenth Century Art.* Princeton, NJ: Princeton University Press, 1969. A description of the last stages of neoclassicism that has itself become something of a classic. Particularly valuable on architecture. Profusely illustrated.

Chapter 16: Toward the Modern Era: 1870–1914

Goldwater, R. *Symbolism.* New York: Harper, 1979. A thoughtful and absorbing account of the ideas and principles behind much of early

20th-century art. Among the artists discussed are Van Gogh, Gauguin, and Rodin. Well illustrated.

Grossman, L. *Dostoevsky: His Life and Work.* Indianapolis: Bobbs-Merrill, 1975. As the title suggests, this book combines biography with a critical discussion of Dostoyevsky's works. Authoritative and understanding, it incorporates important information its author gained from conversations with Dostoyevsky's widow.

Holbrook, D. *Gustav Mahler and the Courage To Be.* New York: Vision, 1975. A difficult but fascinating book that uses an analysis of Mahler's *Symphony No. 9* as the basis for an extended psychoanalytical study of the composer. A rare attempt to study the many levels of meaning of a major work of art.

Meyer, M. *Ibsen.* Garden City, NY: Doubleday, 1971. This massive book provides a highly readable account of the great dramatist's life and work and at the same time conveys much of the intellectual atmosphere of the age.

Muller, J. E. *Fauvism.* New York: Praeger, 1967. A brief, well-illustrated survey of fauvism, with special attention to the work of Matisse. Useful biographical notes on the principal artists.

Myers, B. S. *The German Expressionists: A Generation in Revolt.* New York: Praeger, 1966. A concise edition of an earlier, longer work by the same author, this is a detailed evaluation of expressionist art, including a valuable section on its origins. Among the numerous illustrations are some fine color plates.

Painter, G. D. *Marcel Proust.* New York: Penguin, 1977. A marvelous two-volume account of the life of Proust; indispensable reading for anyone who seeks to understand one of the major creative figures of the century.

Reich, W. *Schoenberg: A Critical Biography.* New York: Praeger, 1971. This thorough study of Schoenberg's life and music is especially valuable; includes extensive quotations from the composer's own writings.

Rewald, J. *History of Impressionism,* 4th ed. New York: New York Graphic Society, 1973. An authoritative and informative guide to the origins and chief developments of the Impressionist movement. Highly recommended.

Schapiro, M. *Paul Cézanne.* New York: Abrams, 1965. This magisterial account consists of a short introduction followed by detailed discussions of many of Cézanne's most important works, accompanied in each case on the facing page by a magnificent color plate of the work.

Stuckenschmidt, H. *Twentieth-Century Music.* New York: McGraw-Hill, 1970. A handy little volume that begins with Wagner, Strauss, and Mahler and takes the story of modern music up to the present. Very useful diagrams and some fascinating illustrations.

Tuchman, B. W. *The Proud Tower.* New York: Random House, 1966. An engrossing study of the intellectual and political climate of the years preceding World War I; both scholarly and highly readable.

Chapter 17: Between the World Wars

Arnason, H. H. *History of Modern Art,* 2nd ed. Englewood Cliffs, NJ: Prentice-Hall, 1977. A standard survey of modern art. Profusely illustrated and very readable.

Ellmann, Richard, and Charles Feidelson. *The Modern Tradition: Backgrounds of Modern Literature.* New York: Oxford University Press, 1965. An invaluable anthology of aesthetic, philosophical, literary, and belletristic texts illuminating the modernist temper. Basic.

Fussell, Paul. *The Great War and Modern Memory.* New York: Oxford University Press, 1976. A classic study of World War I and the literary imagination. Brilliant and readable.

Hughes, Robert. *The Shock of the New.* New York: Knopf, 1981. A profusely illustrated, readable, and highly opinionated study of artistic modernism.

Hull, David S. *Film in the Third Reich.* Berkeley: University of California, 1969. A brilliant study of German film and its relationship to totalitarian ideology.

Lippard, Lucy (ed.). *Surrealists on Art.* Englewood Cliffs, NJ: Prentice-Hall, 1970. An anthology of texts behind the surrealist movement and as such a valuable source for the study of culture between the wars.

Lyons, Len. *The 101 Best Jazz Albums.* New York: Morrow, 1980. A combination discography and history of jazz through recorded music. Readable and very useful.

Newhall, Beaumont. *The History of Photography from 1839 to the Present Day,* rev. ed. New York: New York Graphic Society, 1978.

Wilson, Edmund. *Axel's Castle.* New York: Scribner, 1936. Reprinted many times, this is the classic statement about modernism in literature by one of the foremost American literary critics of the period.

Chapter 18: The Contemporary Contour

Armstrong, Tom, et al., *200 Years of American Sculpture.* New York: Whitney Museum, 1976. A very valuable catalogue of the Whitney Bicentennial show with copious biographies and bibliographies of individual artists.

Cage, John. *Silence.* Cambridge, MA: M.I.T. Press, 1969. The paperback edition of Cage's writing; a wonderful resource for a study of the avant-garde.

Kaufmann, Walter (ed.). *Existentialism from Dostoevsky to Sartre.* New York: New American Library, 1975. A handy anthology of texts, even if some scholars would quarrel with the editor's notion of seeing all existentialism under the rubric of revolt.

Klein, Marcus (ed.). *The American Novel Since World War II.* New York: Fawcett, 1969. A useful anthology by eminent American novelists on the state of fiction into the 1970s.

Sandler, Irving. *The Triumph of American Painting.* New York: Praeger, 1970. A readable and thorough study of art since abstract expressionism. Highly recommended.

Yates, Gayle Graham. *What Women Want: The Idea of the Movement.* Cambridge, MA: Harvard, 1975. A readable history of the women's movement. Fine social history.

Glossary

Terms *italicized* within the definitions are themselves defined in the Glossary.

abacus (1) The slab that forms the upper part of a *capital*. (2) A computing device using movable counters.

a cappella Italian for "in chapel style." Describes music sung without instrumental accompaniment.

acropolis Literally, the high point of a Greek city, frequently serving as a refuge in time of war. The best known is the acropolis in Athens.

aleatory music Music made in a random way after the composer sets out the elements of the musical piece.

allegory A dramatic or artistic device in which the superficial sense parallels or represents a deeper, more profound sense.

allegro Italian for "fast" or "lively"; a musical direction.

ambulatory Covered walkway around the *apse* of a church.

amphora Greek jar or vase.

apse Eastern end of a church, generally semicircular, that frames the area of the altar.

architrave The lowest division of the *entablature*. See figure 58.

archivolt The molding that frames an arch.

aria Song for a solo voice in an opera, an oratorio, or a cantata.

armature In architecture, a means of supporting or bracing a structurally weak part of a building.

Ars Nova Latin for "new art." Term used for the more complex music of the fourteenth century, marked by richer harmonies and elaborate rhythmic devices.

assemblage The making of a sculpture or other three-dimensional artwork from a variety of materials. Compare *montage*.

atelier A workshop, usually that of an artist or craftsperson.

atonality The absence of a key or tonal center to a piece of music.

atrium An open court in front of a church or in a Roman home.

aulos Greek wind instrument, similar to an oboe, but consisting of two pipes.

ballad A narrative poem or song with simple stanzas and a refrain that is usually repeated at the end of each stanza.

baritone Male singing voice of medium *register* between a *bass* and a *tenor*.

barrel vault A semicircular *vault* unbroken by ribs or groins.

basilica Originally a large hall used in Roman times for public meetings, law courts, etc. Later applied as a term for a specific type of Christian church.

bass The lowest male singing voice; the lowest voice in *polyphonic* music.

beat The unit for measuring time and *meter* in music.

black figure A technique used in greek vase painting that involved painting figures in black paint in silhoutte and incising details with a sharp instrument. It was used throughout the archaic period. Compare *red figure*.

blank verse Unrhymed verse often used in English epic and dramatic poetry. Its *meter* is *iambic pentameter*. Compare *heroic couplet*.

blue note A flatted third or seventh note in a chord, characteristic of jazz and blues music.

Bronze Age The period in which bronze (an alloy of tin and copper) was the chief material for tools and weapons. It began in Europe c. 3000 B.C. and ended around 1000 B.C. with the gradual introduction of iron.

burin Steel gouging tool to make copper *engravings*.

buttress An exterior architectural support.

caliph An Arabic word for a leader or ruler.

canon From the Greek meaning a "rule" or "standard." In architecture it is the standard of proportion. In literature, it is the authentic list of an author's works. In music, it is the melodic line sung by overlapping voices. In Western religious language it means either the list of accepted books in the Bible or the authoritative eucharistic

prayer of the mass or an officially promulgated church law.

cantata A short musical composition, usually religious, for solo voices, chorus, and orchestra. In contrast to opera, it is not staged.

canzoniere The Italian word for "songbook."

capital The head or crowning part of a column, taking the weight of the *entablature*. Compare figure 58.

catharsis Literally, "cleansing" or "purgation." Term used by Aristotle to describe the effect of tragic drama on a spectator.

cathedra The bishop's throne. From this comes the word *cathedral*—the place where the bishop presides.

cella The inner shrine of a Greek or Roman temple.

chancel The part of a church that is east of the *nave*, including the *choir* and *sanctuary*.

chansons de geste "Songs of deeds": epic poems and tales disseminated by poets and *jongleurs* in the early Middle Ages.

chapter The body of clergy who advise a bishop and conduct services at a cathedral.

chevet The eastern or altar end of a church.

chiaroscuro In painting, the use of strong contrasts of light and dark.

choir The part of the church between the *nave* and *sanctuary* where monks or members of the cathedral chapter sang the church offices.

chorale A simple hymn tune sung either in unison or in harmony.

clerestory A row of windows in the upper part of a wall just below the roof and above an adjoining roof.

cloister The enclosed garden of a monastery surrounded by a covered walkway; by extension, the monastery itself or any covered walkway.

codex A manuscript volume.

coffer Indented panels in a roof or ceiling.

concerto A piece of music for one or more solo instruments and orchestra usually with three contrasting movements.

concerto grosso A piece of music similar to a concerto but meant to feature the entire orchestra.

consul One of two Roman officials elected annually to serve as the highest authorities of the republic.

contralto The lowest female singing voice.

contraposto In sculpture, placing a human figure so that one part (for example, the shoulder) is turned in a direction opposite to that of another part (in this case, the hip and leg).

cori spezzati Italian for "split choirs." The use of two or more choirs for a musical performance.

Corinthian An order of architecture, very popular in Rome, which featured highly decorated *capitals*. Compare *Doric; Ionic*.

cornice The upper part of the *entablature*. See figure **58**.

counterpoint Two or more distinct melodic lines sung or played simultaneously in a single unified composition. See *figure*.

cruciform Shaped or arranged like a cross.

cuneiform A system of writing, common in the ancient Near and Middle East, using characters of wedged shapes. Compare *hieroglyphics*.

cupola In architecture, a dome.

dialectics A logical process of arriving at the truth by juxtaposing contrary opinions; a common technique in medieval philosophy and theology.

dithyramb Choral hymn to the Greek god Dionysus, often wild and violent in character. Later any violent song, speech, or writing. Compare *paean*.

Doric One of the Greek orders of architecture; severe and simple in style. Compare *Corinthian; Ionic*.

echinus The lower part of a *capital*.

encaustic A painting technique using molten wax colored by pigments.

engraving (1) The art of producing a depressed design on a wood or metal block by cutting it with a tool. (2) The impression made from such a block of wood or metal by ink that fills the design. See *burin; etching; woodcut*.

entablature The upper part of a

greek or Roman temple above the columns consisting of an *architrave, frieze,* and *cornice.*

entasis The characteristic swelling of a Greek column at a point about a third from its base.

epic A long narrative poem celebrating the deeds of a noble character.

Epicureanism School of philosophy led by the Greek philosopher Epicurus, who held that pleasure was the chief aim of life.

epithet Adjective, noun, or phrase used to describe the special characteristics of a person or object.

essay A short literary composition, usually in prose, dealing with a single subject.

etching (1) The art of producing a depressed design on a metal plate by cutting lines through a wax coating and then applying corrosive acid that removes the metal under the lines. (2) The impression or image made from such a plate by ink that fills the design. Compare *engraving; woodcut.*

facade The front of a building.

ferroconcrete A modern building material consisting of poured concrete and reinforced steel meshing or steel rods.

foot In poetry, the unit for measuring meter.

foreshortening The artistic technique by which a sense of depth and three-dimensionality is obtained by the use of receding lines.

forum The central area of a Roman city or town containing the principal civic and religious buildings.

fresco A painting technique that employs the use of paint on wet plaster.

friar A member of any of the religious orders of begging brothers founded in the Middle Ages.

frieze The middle section of an *entablature,* between the *architrave* and *cornice.* A band of painted or carved decorations often found running around the outside of a Greek or Roman temple.

fugue A polyphonic composition, generally for two to four voices (vocal or instrumental) in which the same themes are passed from voice to voice and combined in *counterpoint.*

Gesamtkunstwerk German for "total work of art." A term coined by Rich-

ard Wagner referring to an artistic ensemble in which elements from literature, music, art, and dance are combined into a single artistic unity.

gouache An opaque watercolor medium.

Greek cross A cross in which all the arms are of equal length.

Gregorian chant Monophonic music usually sung without any instrumental accompaniment. Also called plainsong. Compare *melisma; neum; trope.*

hamartia Literally "failure" or "error." Term used by Aristotle to describe the character flaw that would cause the tragic end of an otherwise noble hero.

happening In art, a multimedia event performed with audience participation so as to create a single artistic expression.

heroic couplet The meter generally employed in epic poetry, consisting of pairs of rhyming *iambic pentameter* lines. Compare *blank verse.*

hieroglyphics A system of writing in which characters consist of stylized pictures of actual objects, animals, or humans (part or whole). The Egyptian hieroglyphic script is the best known but by no means the only one. Compare *cuneiform.*

high relief See *relief.*

hippodrome A race course for horses and chariots. Compare *spina.*

homophony Music in which a single melody is supported by a harmonious accompaniment. Compare *monophonic.*

Homo sapiens The scientific term for the human species.

hubris The Greek term for "insolence" or "excessive pride."

humanist In the Renaissance, one trained in the ancient classics and employed to use those skills or dedicated to their pursuit. More generally, one who studies the humanities as opposed to the sciences.

iambic pentameter The meter of poetry written in lines consisting of five groups (pentameter) of two syllables each, the second syllable stressed more than the first (iambic foot).

icon Greek word for "image." Panel paintings used in the Orthodox Christian church as representations of divine realities.

iconography   The set of symbols and allusions that give meaning to a complex work of art.

interval   Musical term for the difference in pitch between two musical notes.

Ionic   One of the Greek orders of architecture, elaborate and graceful in style. Compare *Doric; Corinthian.*

italic   The typeface *like this* developed during the Renaissance and based on a kind of handwriting used in manuscript copying. It first appeared in Venice.

jamb   Upright piece of a window or door, often highly decorated in medieval buildings.

jongleur   Wandering minstrel. A professional musician, actor, or mime who went from place to place in order to entertain.

key   In music, a series of notes related to one another on which a piece of tonal music is based.

keystone   The central stone of an arch.

kithara   An elaborate seven-stringed *lyre* used in Greek and Latin music.

kore   Type of standing female figure produced in the Archaic period in Greece.

kouros   Type of standing male statue, generally of a nude, produced in Greece in the Archaic period.

lancet   A narrow; pointed window or arch in a Gothic cathedral.

lekythos   Small Greek vase for oil or perfume, used most often in funeral ceremonies.

line engraving   A kind of engraving in which the image is made by scored lines of varying width.

lintel   A piece that spans two upright posts.

liturgy   The rites used in public and official worship.

low relief   See *relief.*

lunette   Semicircular space in a wall for window or decoration.

lyre   Small stringed instrument used in Greece and Rome. Compare *kithara.*

Madonna   Italian for "my lady." Used generically for the Blessed Virgin Mary.

madrigal   *Polyphonic* song for three

or more voices, with verses set to the same music and a refrain set to different music.

mandorla   Almond-shaped area of light surrounding a religious figure in a work of art.

meander   Decorative pattern of Greek geometric art in the form of a maze.

melisma   In Gregorian chant, singing an intricate chain of notes on one syllable. Compare *trope.*

meter   A systematically arranged and measured rhythm in poetry and music.

metopes   Square slabs often decorated with sculptures that alternate with *triglyphs* to form the *frieze* of a *Doric* temple.

Minnesingers   German medieval musicians of the aristocratic class who composed songs of love and chivalry. See *troubadours.*

mobile   A sculpture so constructed that its parts move either by mechanical or natural means.

mode   (1) In ancient and medieval music an arrangement of notes forming a scale which, by the character of the intervals, determines the nature of the composition. Compare *tetrachord.* (2) In modern music one of the two classes, major or minor, into which musical scales are divided.

monophonic   From the Greek meaning "one voice." Describes music consisting of a single melodic line. Compare *polyphonic.*

montage   (1) In film, the art or process of conveying an idea and/or mood by the rapid juxtaposition of different images and camera angles. (2) In art, the kind of work produced from pictures or parts of pictures already produced and now forming a new composition. Compare *assemblage.*

motet   A short choral composition based on a religious text. Compare *madrigal.*

movement   In music, an individual section of a *symphony, concerto,* or other extended musical composition.

mullions   The lines dividing windows into separate units.

mural   Wall paintings or paintings or mosaics attached to a wall.

narthex   The porch or vestibule of a church.

nave   From Latin meaning "ship." The central space of a church.

Neanderthal   Early stage in the development of the human species, lasting from about 100,000 B.C. to around 35,000 B.C.

Neolithic   Last part of the Stone Age when agriculture had been developed but weapons and tools were still made from stone. It began in the Near East in 8000 B.C. and in Europe in 6000 B.C.

neum   The basic symbol used in the notation of *Gregorian chant.*

occulus   From the Latin for "eye." The circular opening in the top of a dome.

octave   From the Latin word for "eight." The series of notes that comprise the modern musical scale.

ode   A lyric poem, usually exalted and emotional in character.

Opus Dei   Latin for "work of God." Used to describe the choral offices sung by monks during the course of the day.

oral composition   The composition and transmission of literary works by word of mouth as in the case of the Homeric epics.

oratorio   An extended musical composition for solo singers, chorus, and orchestra on a religious subject; unlike opera, it is not staged.

orchestra   In music, a group of instrumentalists, including string players, organized to perform music.

organum   An early form of *polyphonic* music in which one or more melodic lines were sung along with the song line of plainsong. See *Gregorian chant.*

overture   An instrumental composition played as an introduction to an opera, ballet, or oratorio.

Orientalizing   Name used to describe the period and style of Greek art (late 8th century to 600 B.C.) that shows the influence of Eastern styles of art.

paean   A Greek hymn to Apollo and other gods either asking for help or giving thanks for help received. Later generally applied to any song of praise or triumph.

Paleolithic   The Old Stone Age, during which human beings first appeared and manufactured tools. It began about two and a half million years ago.

Pantocrator From the Greek meaning "one who rules over all." Used for those figures of Christ found in the *apses* of Byzantine churches.

parable A story told to point out a philosophical or religious truth.

parallelism A literary device, common in the Psalms, of either repeating or imaging one line of poetry with another that used different words but expresses the same thought.

pastel A drawing made by using colored chalks on paper.

pediment The triangular space formed by the roof *cornices* on a Greek or Roman temple.

pendentives Triangular architectural devices used to support the dome of a structure; the dome may rest directly on the pendentives.

Peripatetic Greek for "walking around." Specifically applied to the followers of the philosopher Aristotle.

peristyle An arcade, usually of columns, around the outside of a building. The term is often used of temple architecture.

piazza Italian term for a large open public square.

pietra serena Italian for "serene stone." A characteristic building stone used in Italy so called because of its pale color.

pilaster A vertical rectangular wall decoration in the form of a projecting pillar.

plainsong See *Gregorian chant.*

polis The Greek word for "city" used to designate the independent city-states of ancient Greece.

polyphonic From the Greek meaning "many voices." Describes a musical composition built from the simultaneous interweaving of different melodic lines into a single whole. Compare *monophonic.*

portal A doorway, usually of a church, cathedral, or large public building.

Presocratic Collective name for all Greek philosophers before the time of Socrates.

prophet From the Greek meaning "one who speaks for another." In the Hebrew and Christian tradition, one who speaks with the authority of God. In a secondary sense, one who speaks of the future with authority.

Psalter A collection of some or all of the Psalms for use in worship.

recitative A style of musical declamation halfway between speech and song. Sometimes the term is used in its Italian form: *recitativo.*

red figure A technique used in Greek vase painting that involved painting red figures on a black background and adding details with a brush. Compare *black figure.*

register In music, the range of notes within the capacity of a human voice or an instrument.

relief Sculptural technique whereby figures are carved out of a block of stone, part of which is left behind to form a background. Depending on the degree to which the figures project, the relief is described as either high or low.

sanctuary In religion, a sacred place. In a church, the part where the altar is found.

sarcophagus From the Greek meaning "flesh-eater." A stone (usually limestone) coffin.

satyr Greek mythological figure usually shown with a man's head and body and an animal's ears and tail.

scherzo A lighthearted and fast-moving piece of music.

score In music, the written form of a musical composition.

skolion A Greek drinking song, usually sung during banquets.

soliloquy A speech delivered by an actor or actress either while alone on the stage or unheard by other characters, generally constructed so as to indicate the inner feelings of the character.

sonata An extended instrumental musical composition generally in three or four movements.

sonata form A structural form for instrumental music that employs exposition, development, and recapitulation as its major divisions.

sonnet A fourteen-line poem either of eight lines (octave) and six lines (sextet) or three quatrains and a final couplet. Often attributed to Petrarch, the form was modified by poets like Spenser, Milton, Shakespeare, and Keats.

soprano The highest female voice in singing (or the male voice before puberty).

spandrel A triangular space above a window in a *barrel vault* ceiling or the space between two arches in an arcade.

spina A monument at the end of a stadium or *hippodrome.* The obelisk in St. Peter's square was originally the *spina* for the race course of Nero's circus.

squinches Either columns or *lintels* used in the corners of a room to carry the weight of a superimposed mass. Their use is not unlike that of *pendentives.*

stele Upright stone slab decorated with relief carving frequently used as a grave marker.

still life In art, the depiction of a group or cluster of inanimate objects.

Stoicism School of Greek philosophy, later popular at Rome, which taught that the universe is governed by Reason and that Virtue is the only good in life.

suite In music, a collection of various movements performed as a whole sometimes with a linkage in key or theme between the movements.

symphonic poems A one-movement orchestral work meant to illustrate a nonmusical object such as a poem or view of nature. Also called a tone poem.

symphony An extended orchestral composition generally in three or four movements in sonata form.

synthesizer An electronic device used to produce and control sounds that is used for making music.

tambour The drum that supports the *cupola* of a church; also spelled *tambur.*

tempera A painting technique using pigment diluted with egg white or some other water soluble gelatinous substance.

tenor The highest range of the masculine voice. In medieval *organum* it is the voice that holds (Latin "tenere" to hold) the melody of the plainsong. Compare *Gregorian chant.*

terra cotta Italian for "baked earth." The glazed or unglazed fired clay employed for ceramics and for sculptural reliefs often used in architectural decoration.

tesserae Small pieces of colored stone used in making a mosaic.

tetrachord Musical term for a series of four notes; two tetrachords make a *mode.*

tholos Term in Greek architecture for a round building.

toccata In music, a virtuoso composition for a keyboard instrument characterized by a rather free style with long, technically difficult passages.

toga Flowing woolen garment worn by Roman citizens.

tonality In music, the organization of all tones and chords of a piece in relation to the first tone of a key.

tone poem See *symphonic poem*.

transept In a *cruciform* church, the entire part of the church that is set at right angles to the *nave*.

triglyphs Rectangular slabs divided by two vertical grooves into three vertical bands; these alternate with *metopes* to form the *frieze* of a *Doric* temple.

triptych A painting made up of three panels; one of two panels is called a diptych; more than three panels is a polyptych.

trompe l'oeil French phrase meaning "trick of the eye." An artwork, usually a painting, in which the viewer seems to see real objects rather than their artistic representation. The most famous example in antiquity was the painting of a fly on a bowl of fruit so cunningly done that people tried to brush the fly away.

trope In *Gregorian chant,* words added to long *melismas*.

troubadours Musicians of southern France during the Middle Ages who composed songs of love and chivalry; called trouvères in northern France and *Minnesingers* in Germany.

trumeau A supporting pillar for a church *portal,* common in medieval churches.

tympanum The space, usually decorated, above a *portal,* between the *lintel* and arch.

value (1) In music, the length of a note. (2) In painting, the quality of a color that makes it seem dark or light.

vanishing point In perspective, the point at which receding lines seem to converge and disappear.

vault A roof composed of arches of masonry construction.

virginal A stringed keyboard instrument, sometimes called a spinet, which was a predecessor of the harpsichord.

virtuoso A person who exhibits great technical ability, especially in musical performance.

volutes Spirals that form an *Ionic capital*.

voussoir Wedge-shaped block in an arch.

woodcut A wood block with a raised design produced by gouging out unwanted areas, or the impression or image made from such a block by inking the raised surfaces.

ziggurat An Assyrian or Babylonian stepped pyramid.

Index

Ficino, Marsilio, 154, 231, 234, 236, 244, 247: *Theologia Platonica,* 231
fiction, *see* novels
fideism, 194
film, 417, 425, 436, 452–453: propagandistic, 429–431, **430;** surrealistic, 424
Firenze, Andrea da, *The Triumph of Saint Thomas Aquinas,* **195**
Fitzgerald, F. Scott, 425
Flaubert, Gustave, 408: *Madame Bovary,* 374
Florence: banking and commerce in, 224, 230; Baptistery, 226–229, **227, 228;** Brancacci Chapel, Santa Maria del Carmine, 226, **226, 227;** Cathedral (Duomo), **197, 198,** 217, **217, 228,** 229; Dominican Convent of San Marco, 233, **233,** 243; Foundling Hospital, 229, **229;** government of, 224, 230, 243; guilds in, 224, 230; Laurentian Library, 261, **261;** Medici Chapel, 255–257, **256;** Medici era in, 230–243; Palazzo Vecchio, 217, 224; Pazzi Chapel, 229–230, **230,** 256; Platonic Academy, 154; Renaissance origins in, 224–230; Renaissance style in, summarized, 225, 230; Santa Croce, 216–217; Spanish Chapel, Santa Maria Novella, **195;** *Studium,* 231, 236
Florentine *Camerata,* 319, 322
Fokine, Michel, *Petrouchka,* **410**
fora: imperial, 124, **125;** Republican, 110, **111,** 113
Ford, Henry, 2, 417
Four Evangelists and Their Symbols, The, 163–164, **163**
Fourment, Hélène, 313
14th century, *see* Trecento
fourth (music), 96
Fragonard, Honoré, 333–334, 335, 336: *Love Letters,* 333, **333**
France: art and architecture in (1500s), **286,** 287–288, **287;** Baroque art in, 306–312, **309, 310, 311, 312;** classical comedy and tragedy in, 324–325; Italian influence on court of, 268, 287; romantic art and architecture in, **359,** 376–380, **376, 377, 378, 379, 380**
Francis I, King of France, 268, 287
Francis of Assisi, Saint, 47
Frankenthaler, Helen, 440–441: *The Boy,* **443**
Frederick Barbarossa, Holy Roman Emperor, 174–175
Frederick the Great, King of Prussia, 331, 340, 349
French Revolution, 331–332: arts and literature affected by, 330, **330,** 333–334, 335, 346, 354, 362, **362,** 376, 382
Freud, Sigmund, 82, 410–411, 423, 445, 455: *Civilization and Its Discontents,* 436; *The Interpretation of Dreams,* 423; surrealism and, 423–425
Friedrich, Caspar David, 283, 380:

Friedrich, Caspar David, (*cont.*) *Cloister Graveyard in the Snow,* **381**
friezes, 68
Froben, Johann, 272
Froissart, Jean, *Chronicles,* 203
Fry, Roger, 418
f/64 Group, 431
fugues, 320
full anthems, 291
funeral rituals, 7: Egyptian, 9–10, **9, 10**
futurism, 432, **432**

Gabo, Naum, 426
Gabrieli, Andrea, 265
Gabrieli, Giovanni, 265
Gainsborough, Thomas, 334, 335, 336: *Haymaker and Sleeping Girl,* 330–331, **331,** 334; *Mary, Countess Howe,* 334, **334**
Galilei, Vincenzio, 322
Galileo Galilei, 236, 278, 322–323, 324: *Dialogue Concerning the Two Chief World Systems,* 323; *Dialogues Concerning Two New Sciences,* 323; telescopes designed by, 322, **322**
Gandharan, 100
García Márquez, Gabriel, 454
gargoyles, 186, **186**
Garnier, Charles, Paris Opera, 380, **380**
Gaskell, Elizabeth, 375
Gaudi, Antonio, Casa Milá, 403, **403**
Gauguin, Paul, 398: *Ia Orana Maria,* 398, **399**
Gemistos Plethon, Georgius, 154, 231
Gênet, Jean, 437
Geneva, Saint Peter's, 276
Gentile da Fabriano, *Adoration of the Magi,* 224–225, **225**
Gentileschi, Artemisia, 303: *Judith and Holofernes,* **302,** 303
Gentileschi, Orazio, 302–303
Geometric pottery, 59, 60–61, **60, 61,** 62, 72, **72**
geranos, 72
Géricault, Théodore, *Raft of the Medusa,* 376, **377,** 380
Germany: expressionism in, 402–404, **404,** 405, 422, **422;** Hapsburg rule in, 268–269; painting and engraving in (1500s), **273,** 278–283, **279, 280, 281, 282, 283;** Reformation in, 269–271; romantic painting in, 380, **381**
Germany, Nazi, 390, 416, 427
Gershwin, George, 426: *Porgy and Bess,* 426
Gesamtkunstwerk (all-art work), 79, 370
Ghiberti, Lorenzo, 221: Doors of Florence Baptistery, 226–229, **227, 228;** *The Sacrifice of Isaac,* 226–227, **227**
Ghirlandaio (Domenico di Tommaso Bigordi), 250
Gibbon, Edward, 135, 136
Gilbert, William, 277
Gilgamesh, 16–17
Ginsberg, Allan, 437
Giorgione (Giorgio di Castelfranco), 258–259, 260: *Le*

Giorgione, (*cont.*) *Concert Champêtre,* 259, **259;** *Enthroned Madonna with Saint Liberalis and Saint Francis,* 258, **259**
Giotti di Bondone, 153, 203, 207–208, 209, 210, 211–212, 219, 398: Arena Chapel frescoes, **205,** 212, **212;** *Madonna Enthroned,* 211, **211;** *The Meeting of Joachim and Anna,* **205**
Giovanni, Nikki, 454
Girodet-Trioson, Anne-Louis, *The Entombment of Atala,* 376, **376**
Giza: Pyramids, 10; Sphinx, 10, **10**
gladiatorial contests, 107, **107,** 138
Gloucester Cathedral, 218, **218**
Glueck, Nelson, 34
God: Biblical notion of, 42–43, 45; Christian notions of, 135, 142–143, 195; Descartes's views on, 324; light mysticism and, 183–184, 185, 186
Goethe, Johann Wolfgang von, 122, 357, 365–366, 371, 373: *Faust,* 365–366, 383; *Iphigeneia in Tauris,* 365; *The Sufferings of Young Werther,* 365, **365**
Golias, Saint, 193
Good Shepherd, The, 144, **144**
Gospel Book of Charlemagne, 163–164, **163**
Gothic, International, *see* International Style
Gothic, use of term, 182
Gothic architecture, 180–190, **181, 182, 183, 184, 187,** 191: late, **206,** 216–218, **217, 218;** light mysticism and, 183–186; romanticism and revival of, 354, **355;** sculptural programs in, 185–186, **185, 186, 190,** 208–209, **208;** stained-glass windows in, **140,** 183–185, **184,** 188, **188;** technological virtuosity of, 189; verticality in, 182–183
Gothic cathedrals: Aquinas's treatises compared to, 194–195, 196; as artifacts of humanist enterprise, 189–190; economic impact of, 187–188; master craftsmen of, 188–189; schools associated with, 191; social functions of, 186–187
Gothic period, *see* Middle Ages, High
Gothic type, 165
Goths, *see* Ostrogoths
Gottlieb, Adolph, 440: *Thrust,* **440**
Goujon, Jean, Square Court of the Louvre, 287–288, **287**
Goya, Francisco, 357, 363–364, 366: *Execution of the Madrileños on May 3, 1808,* 363, **363;** *The Family of Charles IV,* 364, **364,** 379–380; *Saturn Devouring One of His Sons,* 364, **364;** *The Sleep of Reason Produces Monsters,* 354, **354,** 364
Gozzoli, Benozzo, *The Journey of the Magi,* 235, **235**
Grabar, André, 154
Grave Stele of Crito and Timarista, **84**

Great Schism, 202
Greece, ancient, 8, 10, 14, 30, 52–103; in Age of Colonization, 53, 61–64: Archaic, 53, 64–73; architecture in, **55,** 59, 68, **68, 76, 79,** 85–93, **85, 86, 87, 88, 91, 92, 93,** 98–99, **99, 101, 101, 102, 102,** 123; in Bronze Age (Mycenaean culture), 7, 23, 28–30, 52–53, 60; Byzantine culture and, 154; city-states of (poleis), 20, 53, 61, 110; Classical, 53, 64, 66–67, 68, 72, 73, 76–93, 101, 103; dance in, 72; drama in, 72, 76, 79–83, 96; Etruscan culture compared to, 108–109; fresco painting in, 97, **97;** Hellenistic, 76, 93, 99, 100–103; Heroic, 53–61; historical periods in, summarized, 53, 76; history of, 53, 61, 64, 72–73, 76–78, 93, 99, 100; Late Classical, 76, 93–99; morality tradition in, 53, 59; music in, 70–72, 96–97, **96, 97,** 107, 319; mythology of, 25, 28, 53–54, 59, 70; Orientalizing in, 61–62, 63–64; patronage in, 101; philosophy in, 69–70, 76, 93–96, 113–114; poetry in, 53, 54–59, 68–69, 107; realism tradition in, 60, 64, 67, 83, 91, 101; reason, balance, and order as concerns in, 60, 77, 83–86, 91, 101, 102; religion in, 30, 53–54, 59, 70; Renaissance and renewed interest in, 154, 224, 230, 231, 236, 242–243, 280; Roman conquest of, 76, 100, 103; Roman Empire and culture of, 106, 107, 112, 113–114, 119; sculpture in, **52, 55,** 59, 63–67, **63, 65, 66, 67, 78,** 83–86, **83, 84, 86,** 88–91, **88, 91,** 92–93, **93,** 97–98, **97, 98, 99, 101, 101,** 102–103, **102, 103,** 119; sports in, 138; standard of human beauty in, 84–85; transition to Iron Age in, 52–53; vase painting in, **54, 57,** 59–63, **59, 60, 61, 62,** 67–68, **67, 80,** 85, **89;** Western cultural tradition and, 6, 30
Greek War of Independence (1821–1830), 373, 376–377
Gregorian chant, 162, 172–173, **172, 173,** 190, 191, 264, 265, 290
Gregory the Great, Pope, 162, 172, 264
Gris, Juan, 420: *Guitar and Music Paper,* 420, **421**
Grocyn, William, 236
Gropius, Walter, 451–452
Grosz, George, 438
grotesques, **186**
ground (theater), 293
groundlings, 293
Grünewald, Matthias (Mathis Grothart Niehart), 278, 281–282: *Crucifixion,* **273,** 281; *Isenheim Altarpiece,* **273,** 281–282, **281;** *Resurrection,* 281–282, **281**
Gudea, 18, **19**
Guggenheim, Peggy, 438
guilds, 188, 224, 230
Gutenberg, Johannes, 245

Photograph credits (continued from copyright page)

Ltd., London/Lord Chamberlain's Office, St. James Palace. **103:** A/AR. **104:** FU. **105:** A/AR. **106:** FU. **107, 108, 109:** A/AR. **110:** FU. **111:** Servizio Editoriale Fotografico/AR. **115, 116, 117, 118:** FU. **119, 120, 121:** A/AR.

Chapter 6   122: AH. **125:** From Kenneth John Conant, *Early Medieval Church Architecture,* The Johns Hopkins Press, Baltimore, 1942, Plate VIb/NYPL. **127:** Ara Güler, Istanbul. **128:** H. **129:** WS. **130:** H. **131:** LVM. **132:** A/AR. **133:** LVM. **134:**A/AR. **136, 137:** LVM. **138:** LVM. **139, 140:** A/AR. **141, 142:** Fotocielo, Rome. **143, 144:** A/AR. **145:** S/AR. **146:** H. **147, 148:** MPA.

Chapter 7   151: Am. **152:** (Karol, Evangeliar, fol. 14v) AM. **153:** (Ms. 32, fol. 83r). **154:** AM. **155:** (Cod. 1861, fol. 25). **156:** G/AR. **157:** After Walter Horn and Ernest Born, *The Plan of Saint Gall,* University of California Press, 1979, Vol. II, p. xii/Univ. of Cal. Press. **158:** After Kenneth J. Conant, *Carolingian and Romanesque Architecture* (The Pelican History of Art, Second integrated editions, revised 1978), p. 159, fig. 113/4, copyright © Kenneth John Conant, 1978/NYPL. **159:** HRV. **160:** M. **162:** CAISSE. **163:** Bulloz, Paris. **164:** AM.

Chapter 8   165: Top: After Prof. Sumner Mck. Crosby, Yale University; bottom, M. **166:** MA/EA. **167:** From: Banister Fletcher, *A History of Architecture,* 18th edition, pg. 584; Copyright Royal Institute of British Architects, University of London, permission granted by the Athlone Press, London. **168:** AFK. **169:** CAISSE. **170:** A/AR. **171** left: JR. **172:** G/AR. **173:** (Ms. Fr. 19093, fols. 5, 22v,20). **174:** James Austin, Cambridge, England. **175:** BPK. **176:** A/AR. **177:** HH. **178:** S/AR. **179:** A/AR.

Chapter 9   180: CAISSE. **182, 183:** A/AR. **184:** SG. **185, 186:** A/AR. **187:** SG. **188, 189, 190:** A/AR. **193:** CAISSE. **194, 195:** G/AR. **196, 197, 198:** A/AR. **199:** AFK. **200:** (Ms. Harl. 4425 fol. 12v), S/AR. **201:** (Ms. V.A.14, C.47), S/AR.

Chapter 10   202, 203, 204: A/AR. **205:** S/AR. **206, 207, 208:** A/AR. **209, 210:** Reprinted from *Brunelleschi: Studies of His Technology and Inventions* by Frank D. Prager and Gustina Scaglia, drawings by George Rich, by permission of the M.I.T. Press, Cambridge, Massachusetts. © 1970 by The Massachusetts Institute of Technology. **211:** Albert Renger-Patzsch/Galerie Wilde, West Germany. **212, 214:** A/AR. **215:** Archivio Fotografico Soprintendenza, Firenze. **216, 217:** A/AR. **218, 219:** SG. **220:** A/AR. **221:** SG. **223:** A/AR. **224, 225:** Lauros/G/AR. **226:** Sansaini/AR. **227:** A/AR.

Chapter 11   229, 230, 233, 235, 236, 237: A/AR. **238:** Bramante, Sangallo and Michelangelo floor plans from Paul Le Tarouilly *Vatican,* Vol. I, "The Basilica of St. Peter", Academy Editions, London, 1953; Maderna floor plan: A/AR. **239, 240, 241, 242, 243, 244, 245:** A/AR. **246:** CAISSE. **247:** A/AR.

Chapter 12   250: A/AR. **254:** RMN. **260:** F. Bruckmann KG/ARB. **263:** MAS. **264:** A/AR. **266:** RMN. **267:** CAISSE. **268:** RMN. **269:** Courtauld Institute photograph used by permission of the Marquess of Salisbury. **273:** Reprinted by permission of Coward-McCann, Inc. from *Shakespeare And The Players* by C. Walter Hodges. Copyright 1948 by C. Walter Hodges, NYPL. **274:** Rare Books and Manuscripts Division, NYPL. **275:** RMN.

Chapter 13   276: A/AR. **277:** Pan American World Airways. **276, 277, 278, 279, 280, 281, 282, 283, 284, 285, 286, 287:** A/AR. **288:** Jorg P. Anders, West Berlin. **291:** RMN. **293:** A/AR. **294:** Courtesy of The French Government Tourist Office, New York. **295:** CAISSE. **296:** A/AR. **297, 298:** RMN. **300:** Foto A. Dingjan. **305:** S/AR. **306:** Hans Petersen. **307:** Paul Jensen.

Chapter 14   308: CAISSE. **310:** Dementi Foster Studios. **313:** A/AR. **315:** MAS. **316:** A/AR. **318, 319, 320:** A/AR. **321:** Pierre Berger/PR. **322:** Ward Allan Howe/Ewing Galloway, New York. **323:** Wayne Andrews, Grosse Point, Michigan. **324:** Austrian State Library, Vienna. **325:** Copyright © Beth Bergman 1981, New York. **326:** CAISSE. **327:** G/AR. **328:** Martha Swope, New York.

Chapter 15   330: Noel Hobgood/PR. **331:** Die Piperdrucke Verlags-GMBH. **332, 333, 334, 335:** A/AR. **337:** RMN. **339:** Collection of Henry Wisneski. **340:** Copyright © Beth Bergman 1981, New York. **342:** German Information Center, New York. **344:** © Françoise Foliot, Paris. **345:** General Research Division, NYPL. **346:** RMN. **347, 348, 349:** G/AR. **352:** Agraci/ARB. **353:** AFK. **354:** PBK.

Chapter 16   362: Paul Wiemann, Recklinghausen. **364:** Jack Boucher—National Park Service. **365:** G/AR. **367:** M. Routhier, Paris. **369, 370, 371:** RMN. **381:** Werner H. Kramarsky, New York. **383:** O. Vaering. **384:** MAS. **388:** © Bruno Jarret, Paris. **389:** Unitcl, Munich.

Chapter 17   398: Soichi Sunami. **403:** RMN. **404:** Alain Tarica Ltd., London. **407:** Phoenix Films, New York. **408:** The Library of Congress, Washington, D.C.

Chapter 18   411 © Estate of Ben Shahn 1985. **412:** Hirschl & Adler Galleries, Inc., New York. **417:** © Robert Rauschenberg 1985; photo courtesy Leo Castelli, Inc., New York. **418:** © Andy Warhol 1985; photo © 1985 by Harry Shunk, New York. **419:** Photo by Eric Pollitzer/Leo Castelli Inc., New York. **420, 421:** Courtesy Allan Frumkin Gallery, New York. **423:** David Smith/David Smith Papers, on deposit from the Smith Estate at the Archives of American Art, Smithsonian Institution. © Estate of David Smith, 1981. **425:** Photo by Al Mozell, The Pace Gallery, New York. **426:** Robert Mates and Paul Katz, The Solomon R. Guggenheim Museum, New York. **429:** RMN. **431:** A/AR. **432:** Ezra Stoller © ESTO, Mamaroneck, New York. **433:** Australian Information Service Photo by John Tanner. **435:** Ezra Stoller © ESTO, Mamaroneck, New York. **436:** Norman McGrath, New York.

Works by Arp, Braque, Calder, Cassat, Chagall, Duchamp, Kandinsky, Magritte, Severini: © ADAGP, Paris, 1985. Work by Klee: © ADAGP, Paris/COSMOPRESS, Geneva, 1985. Works by Degas, Gris, Le Corbusier, Matisse, Monet, Picasso, Renoir, Rodin, Rouault, Warhol: © SPADEM/ Paris/VAGA, New York, 1985. Works by Dali: © Salvador Dali SPADEM, Paris/VAGA, New York, 1985. Work by De Chirico: © SIAE, Italy/VAGA. New York, 1985. Work by Mondrian: © BEELDRECHT, Amsterdam/VAGA, New York, 1985.